W9-AQO-716

Henry F. Salerno has been a member of the English Department of Purdue University since 1957. He holds a Ph.D. from the University of Illinois and is the editor, with Mordecai Marcus, of CROSS SECTION: ESSAYS ON CONTEMPORARY AMERICA (1963). He translated and edited SCENARIOS OF THE COMMEDIA DELL'ARTE (1967), is the editor and founder of *First Stage,* A Quarterly of New Drama, and has published articles and reviews in numerous journals.

English Drama

IN TRANSITION

1880-1920

Edited by

HENRY F. SALERNO

PEGASUS

New York

Contents

TO MY FATHER AND MOTHER

English Drama in Transition

1880 - 1920

Introduction

AFTER THE lively dramatic activity of the Restoration and eighteenth century, the English drama of the nineteenth century suffered a decline in the number and quality of new plays offered in the theatres, though the variety of theatrical entertainment increased. This decline continued until the last two decades of the century, when a transition to modern drama took place and there was a resurgence of serious drama. The new forms of popular theatre that developed during the century include the pantomime, vaudeville, extravaganzas, burletta and burlesque—the last two being mostly travesty or broad farce with music. Many theatrical stars and personalities emerged and gained popular approval, often on the basis of a very slight theatrical offering. The great stars—Edmund Kean (1787–1833), William C. Macready (1793–1873), and Charles Kemble (1775–1854)—made their reputations doing cut versions of Shakespeare and revivals of the work of other English dramatists. Texts were sacrificed to the demands of these stars, and new plays offered by these actors were fashioned to highlight their particular talents. Besides the introduction of the star system, a number of other factors contributed to the process of driving serious new plays and playwrights from the theatre and welcoming the work of hacks.

One of these factors was the patent system. Until 1843 when the patent law was repealed, only two theatres were licensed to do legitimate drama—Drury Lane and Covent Garden. All other theatres, called "minor" houses, were forbidden to do plays with dialogue. That, of course, included practically all of English drama from the beginning up to the nineteenth century. However, these "minor" houses might ask for special license to do legitimate drama and a few were occasionally granted such license; or they might do a legitimate drama and risk paying a fine. But the common practice was to present plays without dialogue, such as the pantomime, which became famous, and plays with music, which were allowable. As a result, the burletta, usually a farce with music, came into great popularity; eventually the burletta came to mean any kind of drama with music—farce, melodrama, pantomime, or burlesque. The prevailing fashion was to present varied theatrical entertainment—a melodrama, pantomime, and animal acts on the same program. Thus theatre became a kind of variety show.

The larger and rowdier audiences of the nineteenth century not only demanded more and more of this variety, but the bulk of them came from the lower classes and thus were less literate than the audiences of the previous century. The power of this audience, especially those who frequented the gallery and the pit, was demonstrated by their ability to force down the price of admission during the famous "O.P." (Old Prices) riots and by their ability to make or kill a show, regardless of the reputation of a drama. For instance, *The Count of Monte Cristo,* a play that was done so successfully in America that Eugene O'Neill's father built a career playing it, was killed when it was acted by the much admired Charles Fechter (1824–1879) at the Adelphi. During a rather long scene in which the dying old prisoner tells the hero, Edmund Dantes, the secret hiding place of the gold, a man in the pit called out: "If you please, sir, shall you be much longer a-dying?" After that, the play was laughed off the stage. It was to this audience that the managers had to direct their theatrical entertainment, and it was this audience that determined the offerings of the theatres—the kind of entertainment Tennyson referred to in his sonnet to Macready:

> . . . *brainless pantomime*
> *And those gilt gauds men-children swarm to see.*

To maintain a steady stream of entertainment, the theatres hired hacks, called "stock authors." These writers often had to produce a script within two or three days. To keep up the pace, they often resorted to adaptations of popular novels, stories, mythological material, and plays from the French. Dickens and Scott were among the most frequently plundered authors. The copyright laws were so lax at the time that most of these adaptations were open acts of piracy. One of the "stock authors," James Robinson Planche (1796–1880) who wrote burlesques, extravaganzas, and melodramas for the Adelphi, Lyceum, and The Olympic, was responsible for reform of the dramatic copyright as a result of litigation over the piracy of his own work. The Dramatic Copyright Act of 1833 protected dramatic works, and the Literary Copyright of 1842 consolidated the law but still left non-dramatic works open to piracy. In 1861 the law was extended to include non-dramatic works, but the author himself had to "adapt" the work before publication in order to protect it. However, the law was so ambiguous that the copyright performance came into being because the general assumption seemed to be that a play published before being performed was free of the copyright law. Thus the author hired actors to give a public reading or "performance" of the work in order to ensure its copyright. Even Shaw had to resort to copyright performances to protect his plays. Not until the Copyright Act of 1911 was full protection given an author's work. Meanwhile, novels, stories, and plays in other languages, particularly in French, were freely translated and adapted for the English stage.

Dickens' serialized novels were often pirated as they came off the press. Though his work made money for other writers and for the theatres, he himself never profited from the commercial success of these adaptations. Of the dozen novels of Dickens adapted successfully for the stage by various stock authors, the most memorable and popular were versions of *Oliver Twist, David Copperfield, A Tale of Two Cities,* and *Martin Chuzzlewit.* At many of the theatres, like the Strand, adaptations of Dickens were more popular than Shakespeare.

Although Dickens' novels made popular plays, he himself never made a career in the theatre. He in fact did write four plays for the stage, but after the last, *The Lamplighter,* was withdrawn after a first reading, he gave up the stage and devoted himself to his more successful career as novelist. It seems strange that the man who could write such vivid and often very funny scenes in his novels could not make a career of the stage, whereas the hacks who adapted his novels for the stage invariably produced successful shows.

Those seasoned professionals who wrote for the theatres knew their business and their audience very well. They worked for all the emotional and sensational effects possible. In *London's Lost Theatres of the Nineteenth Century,* Erroll Sherson quotes John Hollingshead's description of the scene of Nancy's murder in a version of *Oliver Twist:*

> Nancy was always dragged round the stage by her hair, and after this effort, Sykes always looked up defiantly at the gallery, as he was doubtless told to do in the marked prompt-book. He was always answered by one loud and fearful curse, yelled by the whole mass like a Handel Festival Chorus. The curse was answered by Sykes dragging Nancy, twice round the stage, and then like Ajax, defying the lightning. The simultaneous yell then became louder and more blasphemous. Finally, when Sykes, working up to a well-rehearsed climax, smeared Nancy with red ochre, and taking her by the hair (a most powerful wig) seemed to dash her brains out on the stage, no explosion of dynamite invented by the modern anarchist, no language ever dreamed of in Bedlam, could equal the outburst.

All the emotional and visceral effects of the most popular theatre—the violence, the macabre, the absolute focusing of strong feeling on the monstrous villain, the complete involvement, the mixture of horror and theatrical thrill—are suggested by this performance and its response. It portrays the popular theatre and its audience, the taste of both performers and responders, and is a graphic illustration of what was commercial and thus successful during the nineteenth century.

Serious dramatists could not compete with this kind of theatrical spectacle. A Shakespeare could compete with the bear-baiting pits next door to the Globe or the slaughterhouse drama of his contemporaries, but not with an audience that could not stand to listen to long speeches or wanted a variety show of fast-moving entertainment that startled the eye and did not make great demands on the ear. Thus Shakespeare was revived by Kean and Macready and Kemble, but with sensational effects and often with interpolated scenes of eye-filling spectacle, scenes mentioned but never written into the Shakespearean texts. Coleridge's remark on seeing Kean's performance suggests both the sensational effect and the ruthless cutting of the text; he said it was like "reading Shakespeare by flashes of lightning."

The only serious literary men writing drama were the poets—Byron, Shelley, Keats, Wordsworth, and Browning. But they were not stage craftsmen, and the public theatre did not open its doors to their work; thus they could not develop any of the stage craftsmanship necessary to make them dramatists. They wrote verse drama which we now call closet drama because it is apparently meant to be read rather than staged. It is significant that a theatre hack could take Byron's poem *Mazeppa* and adapt it for the stage, using a real horse and a nearly naked man or woman and bring off a popular success—successful both for the theatre and the performer. One attractive woman, Ada Isaacs Menken, played the role in flesh tights and built a career on it. The theatre wanted Byron's adapted *Mazeppa* played by an attractive woman in flesh tights but not Byron's *Manfred*.

The craving for sensational variety was so great that even the patented theatres, Drury Lane and Covent Garden, were compelled to offer not simply Shakespearean and other English revivals, but animal acts and tight-rope spectacles as well in an effort to draw crowds as large as those frequenting the other theatres.

To accommodate the growing audiences, the theatres were made larger, some seating as many as two or three thousand people. The stage itself shrank back behind the proscenium, and thus away from the audience. These developments and the fact of the larger and often lower-class audiences who filled the gallery and the pit made spectacle more commercial than literary drama and comedy with music more attractive than serious drama. The enlargement of the theatre, of course, created practical problems: it was more difficult for the actors to be heard; facial expression, subtle gesture, and the fine nuances of delivery were lost or missed by three-fourths of the audience; verbal rapport between actor and audience diminished and with that lost rapport, of course, went loss of interest in plays depending a great deal on language for their theatrical effect. Scenic interest and development, then, became more and more a matter of broad gesture, eye-catching stage action, and clever stage devices. Plays of broad comedy and the macabre were most sought after. At the popular Booth Theatres, for instance, which were set up during Bartholomew Fair, the typical offering was a Gothic melodrama, such as *Monk and Murderer: Or the Skeleton Spectre* and a pantomime, *Mirth and Magic: Or a Trip to Gibraltar,* with a Harlequin, Pantaloon, and Columbine. The melodrama had to have at least two appearances of a ghost; otherwise it was considered unsatisfactory.

What the drama required was a group of writers who could combine the seriousness of the verse dramatists with the theatrical craftsmanship of the popular dramatists. In the middle of the century, the actor-playwright Dion Boucicault (1822–1890), one of the most prolific writers and producers of the theatre, introduced some seriousness of theme in such plays as *The Octoroon* and *Colleen Bawn.* Boucicault was also responsible for introducing realistic touches in his action and decor, but these were used chiefly to heighten the effect of thrill and sensation. He depended more on stage tricks and spectacular action— cleverly staged fires, last-minute rescues in front of speeding trains, and so on—than upon dialogue and character, which were usually trivial and functional in the most mechanical sense. In a review of the revival of Boucicault's *Colleen Bawn* in 1896, Shaw comments that it was "far superior to the average modern melodrama." But Boucicault, despite some of his innovations, was for the most part typical of the theatre of sensation. He was simply more skillful at stage tricks than any of his contemporaries and gave his melodramas a veneer of seriousness.

Thomas W. Robertson (1829–1871) is one of the few serious dramatists whose work precedes the transition period. He wrote a more natural dialogue than his contemporaries, and he introduced some realistic scene and subject matter. His most impressive play, *Caste* (1867), is highly regarded by critics, including Shaw, who considered it an epoch-making play. One of Robertson's plays, *The Ladies' Battle* (1851), was adapted from Scribe, and another, *Progress* (1869), from Sardou. In *Caste* he attempted to depart from the stereotypes of melodrama and to present genuine character portraits—Eccles, the drunken father, Sam Gerridge, the good-natured plumber, and his wife Polly. Though they come off, as Shaw suggests, as Dickensian portraits, Robertson tried to draw real people and to catch the sound and flavor of their speech. And Robertson was moderately successful at humanizing his upper-class characters, Hawtrey and Marquise. All of these efforts are genuine departures from the contrived and stereotyped melodramas of the day.

Two French dramatists whose work became important to the English drama of the second half of the century—both to the serious and to the popular theatre—were Scribe and Sardou. They introduced the *pièce-bien-faite* or the so-called well-made play. Their technique is characterized by facile plotting, exploitation of sentimentality, use of theatrical devices at crucial moments (letters and suddenly discovered wills), type characters, surprise, coincidence, the pathetic scene, neatly worked out high points for the conclusion of scenes, and happy endings. Actually, most of these techniques and devices are to be found in the English drama of the eighteenth century, especially in sentimental comedy—but Scribe and Sardou put them all together, perfected them, and made them work like a well-machined clock. What the well-made play had was a kind of mechanical polish and efficiency that offered sure entertainment; what the well-made play lacked was a sense of character, a seriousness of theme, and living language. Plotting was all; in the working out of the plot, the dramatists used characters as technical constructs to be adjusted and readjusted to the demands of whatever neat twists and turns occurred in the plot.

The technique of the well-made play was first used successfully in serious social drama by Ibsen—the letters in *A Doll's House* being the most obvious example. Ibsen's work was made available to the English theatre and reader in William Archer's translations, and Ibsen's later contemporaries in England, Oscar Wilde, Henry A. Jones, A. W. Pinero, and even George Bernard Shaw, made the technique of the well-made play a part of their craftsmanship. Thus the well-made play came to be a part of the serious as well as of the popular theatre.

Jones and Pinero, the first innovators of serious contemporary social themes in the public theatre, each introduced something new in his use of the well-made play: some concern for character, and some approach to social and domestic problems, as evidenced by *The Liars* and *The Second Mrs. Tanqueray*. Their plays were and still are stage-worthy. Often their presentation of a social or domestic problem challenges the middle-class image of itself. But invariably, as in Pinero's *The Second Mrs. Tanqueray,* the challenge is lost in the denouement and the play lands safely back in the middle of respectable morality.

The transition period introduced not only new themes and subject matter—the questions of prostitution and poverty, of social equality and conformity, of justice before the law as practiced, of the problems created by class and caste differences— but also the courage to look at these from a new vantage point. Perhaps the most important single influence in the theatre at the time was Ibsen. From Ibsen and Shaw, and those who appeared during their time and after them, came innovations which sharply set off modern drama from traditional drama. The new dramatists perceived human life and suffering in such terms that a new image of man began to emerge: man so involved in a relativistic morality that he finds himself in irreconcilable conflict with his society; man not only as a destructive but as a self-destructive creature; man, in a contradictory image, as capable of improving himself and his lot on an immense scale; man in crisis, finding it necessary to sever himself from a dead and deadly past which endangers both his present and future; man sharply questioning all social phenomena—social institutions, conventions, ideals, mores, and the entire social structure; man exploring his personal and psychological maladjustment in the contemporary world.

Traditional genres also underwent some changes. The comedy of manners, in the work of Oscar Wilde and W. Somerset Maugham, amused and dazzled audiences with its brilliant wit, sexual and social intrigue, and the masking and unmasking of its characters in the Restoration manner. However, Wilde combines these with his well-learned techniques of the well-made play—the long-lost child and the conveniently discovered evidence make for a happy ending. Maugham introduces more realistic touches—the inevitable consequences, in the real world of society, of sexual intrigue and chicanery, the revelation in sharp, penetrating dialogue of the often shabby world of the leisure class and its intrigue. Shaw's synthesis of the comedy of manners and the play of ideas creates the unique and most successful serious drama. In Shaw, the brilliant wit of the comedy of manners serves to sharpen the edge of his satire on social conventions and attitudes and to dissect the anatomy of a moribund middle-class morality. In the new verse drama of Yeats, there is the exploration of the subjective: myth and symbol and poetic image are used to evoke and explore the inner world of his characters. The exploration of this inner world becomes the concern of the symbolist playwrights, not only of Yeats's time but of the later dramatists of the twentieth century. Also, experimentation with verse in modern drama and with dramatic styles from exotic theatres, such as the Noh of Japan, continues up through the latest of the modern dramatists.

The representative genres of the period, then, include the comedy of manners, the problem and thesis play, the domestic tragedy, and the symbolist plays of the new Irish theatre. Each playwright gave his proper genre his unique stamp. Oscar Wilde's *The Importance of Being Earnest* is one of the most amusing and purest of the new comedy of manners. Pinero's and Jones's plays also attempt some brilliance of language, but the dramatic life of their plays depends, finally, more on plot and idea than on language. Maugham's *Our Betters,* which falls within the transition period (1915), is close to Wycherley. His characterizations are satirically sharp and have a cynical edge, his wit is biting and brilliant, and his focus upon upper-class manners and mores is devastating—more immediate in impact than that of his Restoration ancestors. Though *The Circle* is considered Maugham's best play, Maugham himself found fault with the crucial motivation.

Shaw, in both *Mrs. Warren's Profession* and *Major Barbara,* makes effective use of the tone and devices of the well-made play and the comedy of manners. In Shaw, the devices serve as part and parcel of his wit, his paradoxes, and his amusing surprises. Both the wit and the devices have the same function in Shaw's theatrical strategy—to alienate the audience from its conventional assumptions about moral behavior and surprise them into a state of intellectual perception, while ridiculing their romantic sentiments and at the same time amusing them with romantic entertainment. In the hands of a lesser dramatist, like John Galsworthy, the devices of the well-made play help, as in Ibsen, in the workmanlike job of sorting out the plot, while the most serious business of the dramatist concerns itself with important social problems. Language in Galsworthy's play is more realistic and commonplace than that found in Wilde, Shaw, or Maugham. Shaw subordinates these devices to his proper and higher concerns; Galsworthy depends on them for more substantial purposes. His play is among the more realistic dramas—that is, the language and the characterizations approximate the ordinary. He deals with social forces in conflict, but he uses a more commonplace prose than such brilliant stylists as Wilde and Shaw. What Shaw once said of Pinero can be generally applied to these realistic dramatists—that they are adroit describers of people, much as "the ordinary man sees and judges them."

That area of dramatic tone and focus which stands between comedy and tragedy—the area identified as *drame* by the French—becomes more and more the work area of the transitional dramatists and their successors. The problem plays, realistic plays like Galsworthy's *The Silver Box*, the symbolist drama, and often drama identified as "comedy" or "tragedy" fall into this widening and unidentifiable no man's land between comedy and tragedy. The developing popularity of the problem play and thesis play—the play that deals with human suffering caused by imperfect social institutions and imperfect application of social ideas—begins to define the age of the *drame*. Hints of the deterministic nature of poverty, of class and class attitudes, of social conventions and social morality occur not only in the work of Ibsen, but in the work of Shaw, Galsworthy, and even Barrie in *The Admirable Crichton*. Both Barrie and Galsworthy see that social justice and equity are impossible within a class structure—that injustice and inequity are taken for granted, more or less, by both master and servant. Shaw's heroes and heroines rebel against the injustices of the class structure—though in *Mrs. Warren's Profession,* for example, clearly the class structure, that is, Mrs. Warren's choices within her class, determines the nature of her rebellion. Also, Shaw hoped to improve the effects of the system and to rectify the injustices of the system by the actions of his hero and heroine in *Major Barbara,* though not, as it appears, to reconstruct the class system. Shaw's revolutionaries are upper-class intellectuals and socialists who work *within* the class structure and apparently do not intend an upheaval from below. Shaw's plays subject the corruption and delusions of the unenlightened members of the upper class to critical scrutiny and ridicule.

The main force and thrust of the transition dramatists is, then, toward the social play—whether it be the problem plays of Galsworthy, the brilliant comedies and thesis plays of Shaw, or even the comedies of Maugham.

The plays of Synge and Yeats are a reaction to the social and realistic concerns of the problem plays. Synge and Yeats deplored the language, the prosaic vision, the drab characterizations of most of these dramatists. They wanted plays in which characters spoke a beautiful language, not the flat speeches of the realistic problem plays; they wanted characters who demonstrated an inner life of some beauty of feeling, not the commonplace types who peopled the social plays. Thus both looked to myth and legend, to strange and evocative stories of love, adventure, and death. The language of Yeats was poetry—poetry he revised again and again, seeking to achieve a perfection that often seemed elusive. The language of Synge was heightened prose—the music and rhythm of poetry he found in the speech of the Irish folk of the Aran Islands.

In experimentation, seriousness, brilliance of language, vision, and conception, the English and Irish drama, through the work of these dramatists, achieved a peak of artistic life and production comparable to that of the Restoration theatre. Shaw's career as critic and dramatist spans the entire period, and it is no coincidence that his work represents the major achievement of the period, because the work of Shaw synthesizes the best that the transition playwrights attempted: the use of traditional forms in the exploration of new dramatic material, the skill and crafts-manship of the most professional and most popular dramatists to project the art and thought of a vigorous genius, a keen and practical theatrical sense to challenge old truths. The culmination of Shaw's great career and, perhaps, of this period, is *Saint Joan,* certainly one of the great tragedies in the English language. The transition period, then, charted the bold and vigorous guide lines for the development of English drama in the twentieth century. The latest explorations in dramatic style and subject matter are no bolder and often no more penetrating or astonishing than those of Shaw and his contemporaries. The dissenters from the traditional stage image of the middle class and its self-complacent respectability are still in the minority, though the minority tends to be louder and more violent. Much of Shaw still has the ring of vigorous iconoclasm. The works of Shaw, Yeats, Maugham, and Synge ring with as much life today as the day they were created. The period stands as a high point in the history of English drama. And Yeats, that most mystical and elusive of verse dramatists, has still to find his proper reward in the modern theatre.

Henry Arthur Jones
[1851-1929]

Henry Arthur Jones, a passionate pioneer for the belief that plays should be printed and read as literature, was the most popular playwright of the 1890's. He tried to help the public see the difference between fine drama and good theatre. He was not a genius but a man whose achievements were attained entirely by his own efforts. He was born in Grandborough, Buckinghamshire, on September 20, 1851, the son of a tenant farmer. He had only six years of formal schooling and began to earn his own living at the age of twelve, working for his uncle, a draper at Ramsgate, where he spent six or seven miserable years before becoming a commercial traveler. During these years he read constantly to educate himself. When, at the age of eighteen, he saw his first play, he realized that more than anything he wanted to be a playwright, and he began writing—sketches, stories, and even novels, all of which were rejected. In 1875, he married Jane Eliza, with whom he had three sons and four daughters.

His early plays reflected his strong Puritanical background and his views on church and business. *Saints and Sinners* (1884), although a poor play, was a powerful attack on commercial philistinism and the discrepancies between religious protestations and practices. *The Triumph of the Philistines* (1895) and *The Middleman* (1889), two later plays, were written on the same theme. Jones's ninth play, *The Silver King* (1882), was an instant success and gave him such financial security that he was able to give

23

up his job and devote his time to playwriting. Altogether he wrote about ninety plays, all with a strong moral note which the middle class loved. As his material success increased, he became, except for his views on the church, more and more reactionary. However, he was the first English dramatist to move toward an honest and free treatment of social problems, a realistic treatment of character and motivation. It is unfortunate that the demands of producer, manager, and audience compelled him to compromise and give conventional endings to his plays that questioned social mores. *Michael and His Lost Angel* (1896) treated the daring subject of an illicit passion, but in the end the characters succumbed to conventional views, declared themselves repentant, and were punished. The notebooks that Jones kept indicated that he contemplated several plays much more ambitious in both scope and treatment than any he was ever able to write. He believed that drama would always remain a popular art because a fine dramatist would have no audience, that no playwright could stray from the taste and thought of the body of playgoers. However, he hoped that by giving the public the best it would accept, he could gradually elevate the public's taste. He wrote many impassioned statements on the necessity for plays to be printed and pass into literature. He said that outside literature a country could have no national drama—only successful plays. Also he spoke of the need for a national repertory group with sustained traditions of acting and authorship, and fought to abolish censorship.

In 1897 he wrote *The Liars,* an amusing, satirical picture of the smart set of the time. He was a good craftsman; Shaw said he had mastered dramatic construction with considerable technical skill. He knew how to arouse the audience's interest in his characters and maintain it. One of his most successful types was the middle-aged character who at the end of the play draws the threads together and brings the younger, more emotional characters back to reality.

His later years were plagued with ill health; he died of pneumonia at the age of seventy-seven, on January 7, 1929.

The Liars opened at the Criterion in 1897. This play is considered one of Jones's lighter pieces but was, nevertheless, one of his most brilliant. In his review, Shaw considered it a "very keen and accurate picture of smart society." The play attempts an objective and clinical look at high society. The detachment, as Shaw observed, suggests the point of view of an English traveler describing pygmies or Zulus. Jones handles the dialogue of his characters with wit and control. Its success on the stage was no doubt the result of the wit, the telling characterization, and the shock of exposing what lay beneath the glitter of this class. What has become apparent to the modern reader and audience is the neat plotting. It is overplotted, or, as Jones himself might put it, at moments the construction of the play "becomes so ingenious as to be noticeable," and at such moments "it passes its limits, and convicts the playwright of an attempt not to paint human nature, but to show his own cleverness." The play depends too much on coincidence, on exchange of letters and telegrams; as a result, the construction at these points becomes obtrusive. These faults were not apparent to Jones's contemporaries, who valued his ability to create character, write brilliant dialogue, and apply the scalpel to the society of his time.

WORKS

A Clerical Error, 1878
The Silver King, 1882
Saints and Sinners, 1884
Breaking a Butterfly, 1884 (Adaptation of Ibsen's *A Doll's House*)
The Middleman, 1889
The Dancing Girl, 1891
The Crusaders, 1891
The Case of Rebellious Susan, 1894
The Masqueraders, 1894
The Triumph of the Philistines, 1895

The Rogue's Comedy, 1896
Michael and His Lost Angel, 1896
The Physician, 1897
The Liars, 1897
The Maneuvers of Jane, 1898
Mrs. Dane's Defense, 1900
The Hypocrites, 1906
Dolly Reforming Herself, 1908
We Can't Be as Bad as All That, 1910
The Divine Gift, 1913

The Liars

AN ORIGINAL COMEDY IN FOUR ACTS

"The Liars" was produced at the Criterion Theatre, London, under the management of Sir Charles Wyndham, on Wednesday the 6th of October, 1897, and ran there (excepting the summer vacation) till the end of November, 1898.

CAST

COL. SIR CHRISTOPHER DEERING
EDWARD FALKNER
GILBERT NEPEAN
GEORGE NEPEAN
FREDDIE TATTON
ARCHIBALD COKE
WAITER
TAPLIN
GADSBY
FOOTMAN
MRS. CRESPIN
BEATRICE EBERNOE
DOLLY COKE
FERRIS
LADY ROSAMUND TATTON
LADY JESSICA NEPEAN

SYNOPSIS OF SCENERY

ACT I

SCENE—*Tent on the Lawn of Freddie Tatton's House
in the Thames Valley, after Dinner,
on a Summer Evening.*

ACT II

SCENE—*Private Sitting-Room Number Ten at "The Star
and Garter" at Shepperford on the following
Monday Evening.*

ACT III

SCENE—*Lady Rosamund's Drawing-Room, Cadogan
Gardens, Chelsea, on the Tuesday Morning.*

ACT IV

SCENE—*Sir Christopher Deering's Rooms in Victoria
Street on the Tuesday Evening.*

TIME—*The Present.*

ACT ONE

SCENE: *Interior of a large tent on the lawn of* FREDDIE TAT-TON'S *house in the Thames valley. The roof of the tent slopes up from the back of the stage. An opening at back discovers the lawn, a night scene of a secluded part of the Thames, and the opposite bank beyond. Small opening left. The tent is of Eastern material, splendidly embroidered in rich Eastern colours. The floor is planked and some rugs are laid down. The place is comfortably furnished for summer tea and smoking room. Several little tables, chairs, and lounges, most of them of basketwork. On the table spirit-decanters, soda-water bottles, cigars, cigarettes, empty coffee cups, match-box, etc. Some plants in the corners. Lamps and candles lighted.*

TIME: *After dinner on a summer evening.*

[*Discover* ARCHIBALD COKE *and* "FREDDIE" TATTON. COKE, *a tall, pompous, precise man, about fifty, is seated at side table, smoking.* FREDDIE, *a nervous, weedy little creature about thirty, with no whiskers and nearly bald, with a very squeaky voice, is walking about.*]

FREDDIE [*very excited, very voluble, very squeaky*]: It's all very well for folks to say, "Give a woman her head; don't ride her on the curb." But I tell you this, Coke, when a fellow has got a wife like mine, or Jess, it's confoundedly difficult to get her to go at all without a spill, eh?

COKE: It is perplexing to know precisely how to handle a wife [*drinks, sighs*]—very perplexing!

FREDDIE: Perplexing! It's a d—ee—d silly riddle without any answer! You know I didn't want to have this house-party for the Regatta—[COKE *looks at him.*]—I beg your pardon. Of course I wanted to have you and Dolly, and I didn't mind Gilbert and Jess. But I didn't want to have Falkner here. He's paying a great deal too much attention to Jess, and Jess doesn't choke him off as she should. Well, I thoroughly made up my mind if Jess came, Falkner shouldn't.

COKE: Yes?

FREDDIE: Well, Rosamund said he should. So I stuck out, and she stuck out, in fact we both stuck out for a week. I was determined he shouldn't come.

COKE: Then why did you give in?

FREDDIE: I didn't.

COKE: But he's here!

FREDDIE: Yes, but only for a few days. Rosamund invited him, unknown to me, and then—well—you see, I was obliged to be civil to the fellow. [*Very confidential.*] I say, Coke—we're tiled in, aren't we? Candidly, what would you do if you had a wife like Rosamund?

COKE [*sententiously*]: Ah! Just so! [*Drinks.*]

FREDDIE: You're the lucky man of us three, Coke.

COKE: I must own my wife has some good points—

FREDDIE: Dolly got good points! I should think she has!

COKE: But she's terribly thoughtless and frivolous.

FREDDIE: So much the better. Give me a woman that lets a man call his soul his own. That's all I want, Coke, to call my soul my own. And—[*resolutely*] some of these days—[*very resolutely*] I will, that's all!

[*Enter* MRS. CRESPIN, *a sharp, good-looking woman between thirty and thirty-five.*]

MRS. C.: Is Mr. Gilbert Nepean leaving for Devonshire tonight?

FREDDIE: Yes. He takes the eleven thirty-four slow and waits for the down fast at Reading.

MRS. C.: Tonight?

FREDDIE: Yes. His steward, Crampton, has been robbing him for years, and now the fellow has bolted with a heap of money and a farmer's wife.

MRS. C.: Mr. Nepean must go tonight?

FREDDIE: Yes. Why?

MRS. C.: Lady Jessica and Mr. Falkner have gone for a little moonlight row. I thought Mr. Nepean might like to stay and steer.

FREDDIE: Oh, Lady Jessica knows the river well.

MRS. C.: Ah, then Mr. Nepean can look after the steward. After all, no husband need emphasize the natural absurdity of his position by playing cox to another man's stroke, need he.

[*Enter* COLONEL SIR CHRISTOPHER DEERING, *a genial, handsome Englishman about thirty-eight, and* GEORGE NEPEAN, *a dark, rather heavy-looking man about the same age.*]

SIR C.: Oh, nonsense, Nepean; you're mistaken!

GEORGE: You'd better say a word to Falkner—

SIR C. [*with a warning look*]: Shush!

GEORGE: If you don't, I shall drop a very strong hint to my brother.

SIR C. [*more peremptorily*]: Shush, Shush!

FREDDIE: What's the matter?

SIR C.: Nothing, Freddie, nothing! Our friend here [*trying to link his arm in* GEORGE'S—GEORGE *stands off*] is a little old-fashioned. He doesn't understand that in all really innocent flirtations ladies allow themselves a very large latitude indeed. In fact, from my very modest experience with the sex—take it for what it's worth—I should say the more innocent the flirtation, the larger the latitude the lady allows herself, eh, Mrs. Crespin?

MRS. C.: Oh, we are all latitudinarians at heart.

SIR C.: Yes; but a lady who practises extensively as a latitudinarian rarely becomes a—a—a longitudinarian, eh?

MRS. C.: Oh, I wouldn't answer for her! It's a horrid, wicked world; and if once a woman allows one of you wretches to teach her the moral geography of it, it's ten to one she gets her latitude and longitude mixed before she has had time to look at the map.

FREDDIE [*to* SIR CHRISTOPHER]: I say, I'm awfully sorry about this. You know I told Rosamund how it would be if we had Falkner here—

SIR C. [*draws* FREDDIE *aside*]: Shush! Tell Lady Rosamund to caution Lady Jessica—

FREDDIE: I will. But Rosamund generally does just the opposite of what I tell her. Don't be surprised, old fellow, if you hear some of these days that I've—well, don't be surprised.

SIR C.: At what?

FREDDIE: Well, I shall—now, candidly, old fellow—we're tiled in, quite between ourselves—if you found yourself landed as I am, what would you do?

SIR C.: You mean if I found myself married?

FREDDIE: Yes.

SIR C.: I should make the best of it.

GEORGE [*to* SIR C.]: Then it's understood that you'll give Falkner a hint?

SIR C.: My dear fellow, surely your brother is the best judge—

GEORGE: Of what he doesn't see?

SIR C.: He's here.

GEORGE: He's leaving for Devonshire tonight—unless I stop him. Will that be necessary?

SIR C.: No. Falkner is my friend. I introduced him to Lady Jessica. If you insist, I'll speak to him. But I'm sure you're wrong. He's the very soul of honour. I didn't live with him out there those three awful years without knowing him.

GEORGE: I don't see what your living three years in Africa with him has got to do with it, eh, Mrs. Crespin?

MRS. C.: Let's see how it works out. Falkner behaves most gallantly in Africa. Falkner rescues Mrs. Ebernoe. Falkner splendidly avenges Colonel Ebernoe's death, and strikes terror into every slave-dealer's heart. Falkner returns to England covered with glory. A grateful nation goes into a panic of admiration, and makes itself slightly ridiculous over Falkner. Falkner is the lion of the season. Therefore we may be quite sure that Falkner won't make love to any pretty woman who comes in his way. It doesn't seem to work out right.

SIR C.: But Falkner is not an ordinary man, not even an ordinary hero.

MRS. C.: My dear Sir Christopher, the one cruel fact about heroes is that they are made of flesh and blood! Oh, if only they were made of waxwork, of Crown Derby ware, or Britannia metal; but, alas and alas! they're always made of flesh and blood.

COKE: Where did Falkner come from? What were his people?

SIR C.: His grandfather was what Nonconformists call an eminent divine; his father was a rich city merchant; his mother was a farmer's daughter. Falkner himself is a—well, he's a Puritan Don Quixote, mounted on Pegasus.

MRS. C.: Put a Puritan Don Quixote on horseback, and he'll ride to the—Lady Jessica, eh?

SIR C.: Hush! He'll love and he'll ride away.

MRS. C. [*significantly*]: I sincerely hope so.

COKE: I must say that Falkner is less objectionable than Dissenters generally are. I have an unconquerable aversion to Dissenters.

SIR C.: Oh, I hate 'em. But they saved England, hang 'em! And I'm not sure whether they're not the soundest part of the nation today.

MRS. C.: Oh, pray don't tell them so, just as they're getting harmless and sensible—and a little artistic.

[*A piano is played very softly and beautifully at a distance of some twenty yards. They all listen.*]

MRS. C.: Is that Mrs. Ebernoe?

SIR C.: Yes.

MRS. C.: What a beautiful touch she has!

SIR C.: She has a beautiful nature.

MRS. C.: Indeed! I thought she was a little stiff and unsociable. But perhaps we are too frivolous.

SIR C.: Perhaps. And she hasn't quite recovered from poor Ebernoe's death.

[*Enter* LADY ROSAMUND *and* DOLLY COKE *in evening dress.* DOLLY *is without any wrap on her shoulders.*]

MRS. C.: But that's nearly two years ago. Is it possible we still have women amongst us who can mourn two years for a man? It gives me hopes again for my sex.

FREDDIE [*his back to* LADY ROSAMUND]: I know jolly well Rosamund won't mourn two years for me.

LADY R. [*a clear-cut, bright, pretty woman*]: You're quite right, Freddie, I shan't. But if you behave very prettily meantime, I promise you a decent six weeks. So be satisfied, and don't make a disturbance down there [*with a little gesture pointing down*] and create the impression that I wasn't a model wife.

COKE [*in a very querulous, pedantic tone to* DOLLY]: No wrap again! Really, my dear, I do wish you would take more precautions against the night air. If you should take influenza again—

DOLLY [*pretty, empty-headed little woman*]: Oh, my dear Archie, if I do, it is I who will have to cough and sneeze!

COKE: Yes; but it is I who will be compelled to listen to you. I do wish you would remember how very inconvenient it is for me when you have influenza.

DOLLY: Oh, my dear, you don't expect me to remember *all* the things that are inconvenient to you. Besides, other people don't wrap up. Jessica is out on the river with absolutely nothing on her shoulders.

MRS. C.: Is it not a physiological fact that when our hearts reach a certain temperature our shoulders may be, and often are, safely left bare?

[GEORGE NEPEAN *has been listening. He comes some steps towards them as if about to speak, stops, then turns and exits with great determination.*]

SIR C.: Mrs. Crespin, you saw that?

MRS. C.: Yes. Where has he gone?

SIR C.: I suppose to tell his brother his suspicions. I'm sure you meant nothing just now, but— [*glancing round*]—we are all friends of Lady Jessica's, aren't we?

MRS. C.: Oh, certainly. But don't you think you ought to get Mr. Falkner away?

SIR C.: He'll be leaving England soon. These fresh outbreaks amongst the slave-traders will give us no end of trouble, and the Government will have to send Falkner out. Meantime—

MRS. C.: Meantime, doesn't Mrs. Ebernoe play divinely?

SIR C. [*politely intercepting her*]: Meantime it's understood that nothing more is to be said of this?

MRS. C.: Oh, my dear Sir Christopher, what more can be said? [*Exit.*]

SIR C. [*holds the tent curtains aside for her to pass out; looks after her, shakes his head, perplexed, then turns to* COKE]: Coke, what do you say, a hundred up?

COKE: I'm agreeable! Dolly! Dolly!

[LADY ROSAMUND, DOLLY, *and* FREDDIE *are chattering very vigorously together.*]

DOLLY [*doesn't turn round to him*]:

Well? [*Goes on chattering to* LADY ROSAMUND *and* FREDDIE.]

COKE: You had a tiresome hacking cough, dear, during the greater portion of last night.

DOLLY: Did I? [*Same business.*]

COKE: It would be wise to keep away from the river.

DOLLY: Oh, very well, dear. I'll try and remember. [*Same business.*]

COKE [*turns, annoyed, to* SIR CHRISTOPHER]: I'm a painfully light sleeper. The least thing disturbs me, and— [*Looks anxiously at* DOLLY, *who is still chattering, then turns to* SIR C.] Do you sleep well?

SIR C. [*links his arm in* COKE'S]: Like a top. Never missed a night's rest in my life.

[*Takes* COKE *off at opening.*]

FREDDIE [*has been talking angrily to* LADY ROSAMUND]: Very well then, what am I to do?

DOLLY: Oh, do go and get a whisky and soda, there's a dear Freddie!

FREDDIE: That's all very well, but if Jessica goes and makes a fool of herself in my house, people will say it was my fault.

LADY R.: What—example, or influence, or sheer desperate imitation?

FREDDIE [*pulls himself up, looks very satirical, evidently tries to think of some crushing reply without success*]: I must say, Rosamund, that your continued chaff of me and everything that I do is in execrable taste. For a woman to chaff her husband on all occasions is—well, it's in very bad taste, that's all I can say about it! [*Exit.*]

DOLLY: Freddie's getting a dreadful fidget. He's nearly as bad as Archie.

LADY R.: Oh, my dear, he's ten times worse. One can't help feeling some small respect for Archie.

DOLLY: Oh, do you think so? Well, yes, I suppose Archie is honourable and all that.

LADY R.: Oh, all men are honourable. They get kicked out if they aren't. My Freddie's honourable in his poor little way.

DOLLY: Oh, don't run Freddie down. I rather like Freddie.

LADY R.: Oh, if you had to live with him—

DOLLY: Well, he always lets you have your own way.

LADY R.: I wish he wouldn't. I really believe I should love and respect him a little more if he were to take me and give me a good shaking, or do something to make me feel that he's my master. But [*sighs*] he never will! He'll only go on asking everybody's advice how to manage me—and never find out. As if it weren't the easiest thing in the world to manage a woman —if men only knew.

DOLLY: Oh, do you think so? I wonder if poor old Archie knows how to manage me!

LADY R.: Archie's rather trying at times.

DOLLY: Oh, he is! He's so frumpish and particular, and he's getting worse.

LADY R.: Oh, my dear, they do as they grow older.

DOLLY: Still, after all, Freddie and Archie aren't quite so awful as Gilbert.

LADY R.: Oh, Gilbert's a terror.

I hope Jessica won't do anything foolish—

[*A very merry peal of laughter heard off, followed by* LADY JESSICA'S *voice.*]

LADY J. [*heard off*]: Oh, no, no, no, no, no! Please keep away from my dress! Oh, I'm so sorry! [*Laughing a little.*] But you are— so—so—

[*Another peal of laughter.*]

FALKNER [*heard off, a deep, rich, sincere, manly tone*]: So ridiculous! I don't mind that!

LADY J. [*heard off*]: But you'll take cold. Do go and change!

FALKNER [*heard off*]: Change? That's not possible!

[LADY JESSICA *appears at opening at back, looking off, smothering her laughter. She is a very bright, pretty woman, about twenty-seven, very dainty and charming. Piano ceases.*]

LADY J.: Oh, the poor dear, foolish fellow! Look!

LADY R.: What is it?

LADY J.: My ten-and-sixpenny brooch! He kept on begging for some little souvenir, so I took this off. That quite unhinged him. I saw he was going to be demonstrative, so I dropped the brooch in the river and made a terrible fuss. He jumped in, poor dear, and fished it up. It was so muddy at the bottom! He came up looking like a *fin-de-siècle* Neptune—or a forsaken merman—or the draggled figurehead of a penny Thames steamboat.

LADY R. [*very seriously*]: Jess, the men are talking about you.

LADY J. [*very carelessly*]: Ah, are they? Who is?

LADY R.: My Freddie says that you—

LADY J. [*interrupting on "says"*]: My dear Rosy, I don't mind what your Freddie says any more than you do.

LADY R.: But George has been fizzing up all the evening.

LADY J.: Oh, let him fizz down again.

LADY R.: But I believe he has gone to give Gilbert a hint—

LADY J. [*showing annoyance*]: Ah, that's mean of George! How vexing! Perhaps Gilbert will stay now.

LADY R.: Perhaps it's as well that Gilbert should stay.

LADY J.: What? My dear Rosy, you know I'm the very best of wives, but it does get a little monotonous to spend all one's time in the company of a man who doesn't understand a joke— not even when it's explained to him!

LADY R.: Jess, you really must pull up.

DOLLY: Yes, Jess. Mrs. Crespin was making some very cattish remarks about you and Mr. Falkner.

LADY J.: Was she? Rosy, why do you have that woman here?

LADY R.: I don't know. One must have somebody. I thought you and she were very good friends.

LADY J.: Oh, we're the best of friends, only we hate each other like poison.

LADY R.: I don't like her. But she says such stinging things about my Freddie, and makes him so wild.

LADY J.: Does she? I'll ask her down for the shooting. Oh! I've got a splendid idea!

LADY R.: What is it?

LADY J.: A new career for poor gentlewomen. You found a school and carefully train them in all the best traditions of the gentle art of husband-baiting. Then you invite one of them to your house, pay her, of course, a handsome salary, and she assists you in "the daily round, the common task" of making your husband's life a perfect misery to him. After a month or so she is played out and retires to another sphere, and you call in a new—lady-help!

LADY R.: Oh, I don't think I should care to have my Freddie systematically henpecked by another woman.

LADY J.: No; especially as you do it so well yourself. Besides, your Freddie is such a poor little pocket-edition of a man—I hope you don't mind my saying so—

LADY R.: Oh, not at all. He's your own brother-in-law.

LADY J.: Yes; and you may say what you like about Gilbert.

DOLLY: Oh, we do, don't we, Rosy?

LADY J.: Do you? Well, what do you say?

DOLLY: Oh, it wouldn't be fair to tell, would it, Rosy? But Mrs. Crespin said yesterday—

[LADY ROSAMUND *glances at* DOLLY *and stops her.*]

LADY J.: About Gilbert?

DOLLY: Yes.

LADY J.: Well, what did she say?

[DOLLY *glances at* LADY ROSAMUND *inquiringly.*]

LADY R.: No, Dolly, no!

LADY J.: Yes, Dolly! Do tell me.

LADY R.: No, no!

LADY J.: I don't care what she said, so long as she didn't say he could understand a joke. That would be shamefully untrue. I've lived with him for five years, and I'm sure he can't. But what did Mrs. Crespin say, Rosy?

LADY R.: No, it really was a little too bad.

DOLLY: Yes. I don't much mind what anybody says about Archie, but if Mrs. Crespin had said about him what she said about Gilbert—

LADY J.: But what did she say? Rosy, if you don't tell me, I won't tell you all the dreadful things I hear about your Freddie. Oh, do tell me! There's a dear!

LADY R.: Well, she said— [*Begins laughing.*]

[DOLLY *begins laughing.*]

LADY J.: Oh, go on! go on! go on!

LADY R.: She said—no, I'll whisper!

[LADY JESSICA *inclines her ear,* LADY ROSAMUND *whispers;* DOLLY *laughs.*]

LADY J.: About Gilbert! [*Beginning to laugh.*]

LADY R.: Yes. [*Laughing.*]

[*They all join in a burst of laughter which grows louder and louder. At its height enter* GILBERT NEPEAN. *He is a man rather over forty, much the same build as his brother* GEORGE; *rather stout, immobile, uninteresting features; large, coarse hands; a habit of biting his nails. He is dressed in tweeds, long light ulster and trav-*

elling cap, which he does not remove. As he enters, the laughter, which has been very boisterous, suddenly ceases. He goes up to table without taking any notice of the ladies; very deliberately takes out cigar from case, strikes a match which does not ignite, throws it down with an angry gesture and exclamation; strikes another which also does not ignite; throws it down with a still angrier gesture and exclamation. The third match ignites, and he deliberately lights his cigar. Meantime, as soon as he has reached table, LADY JESSICA, *who stands behind him, exchanges glances with* DOLLY *and* LADY ROSAMUND, *and makes a little face behind his back.* LADY R. *winks at* LADY JESSICA, *who responds by pulling a mock long face.* LADY R. *steals off.* DOLLY *shrugs her shoulders at* LADY JESSICA, *who pulls her face still longer.* DOLLY *and* ROSAMUND *steal quietly off after* LADY R. GILBERT *is still busy with his cigar.* LADY JESSICA *does a little expressive pantomime behind his back.*]

GILBERT: What's all this tomfoolery with Falkner?

LADY J.: Tomfoolery?

GILBERT: George says you are carrying on some tomfoolery with Falkner.

LADY J.: Ah! that's very sweet and elegant of George. But I never carry on any tomfoolery with anyone—because I'm not a tomfool, therefore I can't.

GILBERT: I wish for once in your life you'd give me a plain answer to a plain question.

LADY J.: Oh, I did once. You

shouldn't remind me of that. But I never bear malice. Ask me another, such as—if a herring and a half cost three ha'-pence, how long will it take one's husband to learn politeness enough to remove his cap in his wife's presence?

GILBERT [*instinctively takes off his cap, then glancing at her attitude, which is one of amused defiance, he puts the cap on again*]: There's a draught here.

LADY J.: The lamp doesn't show it. But perhaps you are right to guard a sensitive spot.

GILBERT: I say there's a confounded draught.

LADY J.: Oh, don't tell fibs, dear. Because if you do, you'll go—where you *may* meet me; and then we should have to spend such a very long time together.

GILBERT [*nonplussed, a moment or two; takes out his watch*]: I've no time to waste. I must be down in Devonshire tomorrow to go into this business of Crampton's. But before I go, I mean to know the truth of this nonsense between you and Falkner.

LADY J.: Ah!

GILBERT: Shall I get it from you—or from him?

LADY J.: Wouldn't it be better to get it from me? Because he mightn't tell you *all?*

GILBERT: *All?* Then there is something to know?

LADY J.: Heaps. And if you'll have the ordinary politeness to take off that very ugly cap, I'll be very sweet and obedient and tell you *all.*

GILBERT: Go on!

LADY J.: Not while the cap sits there!

GILBERT: I tell you I feel the draught.

[LADY JESSICA *rises, goes to the tent openings, carefully draws the curtains. He watches her, sulkily.*]

LADY J.: There! now you may safely venture to uncover the sensitive spot.

GILBERT [*firmly*]: No.

LADY J. [*serenely, seated*]: Very well, my dear. Then I shan't open my lips.

GILBERT: You won't?

LADY J.: No; and I'm sure it's far more important for you to know what is going on between Mr. Falkner and me than to have that horrid thing sticking on your head.

GILBERT [*takes a turn or two, bites his nails, at length sulkily flings the cap on the chair*]: Now!

LADY J.: Mr. Falkner is very deeply attached to me, I believe.

GILBERT: He has told you so?

LADY J.: No.

GILBERT: No?

LADY J.: No; but that's only because I keep on stopping him.

GILBERT: You keep on stopping him?

LADY J.: Yes; it's so much pleasanter to have him dangling for a little while, and *then*—

GILBERT: Then what?

LADY J.: Well, it is pleasant to be admired.

GILBERT: And you accept his admiration?

LADY J.: Of course I do. Why shouldn't I? If Mr. Falkner admires me, isn't that the greatest compliment he can pay to your taste? And if he spares you the drudgery of being polite to me, flattering me, complimenting me, and paying me the hundred delicate little attentions that win a woman's heart, I'm sure you ought to be very much obliged to him for taking all that trouble off your hands.

GILBERT [*looks furious*]: Now understand me. This nonsense has gone far enough. I forbid you to have anything further to say to the man.

LADY J.: Ah, you forbid me!

GILBERT: I forbid you. And, understand, if you do—

LADY J.: Ah, take care! Don't threaten me!

GILBERT: Do you mean to respect my wishes?

LADY J.: Of course I shall respect your wishes. I may not obey them, but I will respect them.

GILBERT [*enraged, comes up to her very angrily*]: Now, Jessica, once for all—

[*Enter* GEORGE, GILBERT *stops suddenly.*]

GEORGE: The dog-cart's ready, Gilbert. What's the matter?

GILBERT: Nothing. [*To* LADY JESSICA.] You'll please to come on to me at Teignwick tomorrow.

LADY J.: Can't. I've promised to go to Barbara, and I must keep my promise, even though it parts me from you.

[*Enter* SERVANT.]

SERV.: You've only just time to catch the train, sir.

GILBERT: I'm not going.

SERV.: Not going, sir?

GILBERT: No.

[*Exit* SERVANT.]

LADY J. [*appeals to* GEORGE]: Isn't it dear of him to stay here on my account when he knows he ought to be in Devon? Isn't it sweet to think that after five long years one has still that magnetic attraction for one's husband?

GILBERT: No. I'm hanged if I stay on your account. [*Goes up to opening, calls out.*] Hi! Gadsby! I'm coming! Understand, I expect you at Teignwick tomorrow.

LADY J.: Dearest, I shan't come.

GILBERT: I say you shall!

LADY J.: "Shall" is not a pretty word for a husband to use. [*Takes up the cap he has thrown down and stands twiddling the tassel.*]

GILBERT [*after a furious dig at his nails*]: George, I expect this business of Crampton's will keep me for a week, but I can't tell. Look after everything while I'm away. [*To* LADY JESSICA.] You won't come to Teignwick?

LADY J.: I've promised Barbara. Here's your cap.

GILBERT: Good-bye, George! [*Looks at* LADY JESSICA, *and is then going off at back.*]

LADY J.: Ta, ta, dearest!

GILBERT [*turns, comes a step or two to* LADY JESSICA, *livid with anger; speaks in her ear*]: You'll go just one step too far some day, madam, and if you do, look out for yourself, for, by God! I won't spare you!

[*Exit.* LADY JESSICA *stands a little frightened, goes up to opening at back, as if to call him back, comes down.* GEORGE *stands watching her, smoking.*]

LADY J. [*after a little pause*]: George, that was very silly of you to tell

Gilbert about Mr. Falkner and me.

GEORGE: I thought you had gone far enough.

LADY J.: Oh no, my dear friend. You must allow me to be the best judge of how far—

GEORGE: How far you can skate over thin ice?

LADY J.: The thinner the ice the more delicious the fun, don't you think? Ah, you're like Gilbert. You don't skate—or joke.

GEORGE: You heard what Gilbert said?

LADY J.: Yes; that was a hint to you. Won't it be rather a tiresome task for you?

GEORGE: What?

LADY J.: To keep an eye on me, watch that I don't go that one step too far. And not quite a nice thing to do, eh?

GEORGE: Oh, I've no intention of watching you—

[*Enter* FALKNER.]

[*Looking at the two*]. Not the least intention, I assure you. [*Exits.*]

LADY J.: So tomorrow will break up our pleasant party.

FALKNER [*about forty, strong, fine, clearly cut features, earnest expression, hair turning gray, complexion pale and almost gray with continued work, anxiety, and abstinence*]: And after tomorrow?

LADY J.: Ah, after tomorrow!

FALKNER: When shall we meet again?

LADY J.: Shall we meet again? Yes, I suppose. Extremes do meet, don't they?

FALKNER: Are we extremes?

LADY J.: Aren't we? I suppose I'm the vainest, emptiest, most irresponsible creature in the world—

FALKNER: You're not! you're not! You slander yourself! You can be sincere, you can be earnest, you can be serious—

LADY J.: Can I? Oh, do tell me what fun there is in being serious! I can't see the use of it. There you are, for instance, mounted on that high horse of seriousness, spending the best years of your life in fighting African slave-traders and other windmills of that sort. Oh do leave the windmills alone! They'll all tumble by themselves by-and-by.

FALKNER: I'm not going to spend the best years of my life in fighting slave-traders. I'm going to spend them—in loving you. [*Approaching her very closely.*]

LADY J.: Oh, that will be worse than the windmills—and quite as useless. [*He is very near to her.*] If you please—you remember we promised to discuss all love-matters at a distance of three feet, so as to allow for the personal equation. Your three feet, please.

FALKNER: When shall we meet again?

LADY J.: Ah, when? Where do you go tomorrow night, when you leave here?

FALKNER: I don't know. Where do you?

LADY J.: To my cousin Barbara's.

FALKNER: Where is that?

LADY J.: Oh, a little way along the river, towards town; not far from Staines.

FALKNER: In what direction?

LADY J.: About two miles to the

nor'-nor'-sou'-west. I never was good at geography.

FALKNER: Is there a good inn near?

LADY J.: There's a delightful little riverside hotel, the Star and Garter, at Shepperford. They make a specialty of French cooking.

FALKNER: I shall go there when I leave here tomorrow. May I call at your cousin's?

LADY J.: It wouldn't be wise. And I'm only staying till Monday.

FALKNER: And then?

LADY J.: On Monday evening I go back to town.

FALKNER: Alone?

LADY J.: No, with Ferris, my maid. Unless I send her on first.

FALKNER: And you will?

LADY J.: No, I don't think so. But a curious thing happened to me the last time I stayed at Barbara's. I sent Ferris on with the luggage in the early afternoon, and I walked to the station for the sake of the walk. Well, there are two turnings, and I must have taken the wrong one.

FALKNER: What happened?

LADY J.: I wandered about for miles, and at half-past seven I found myself, very hot, very tired, very hungry, and in a very bad temper, at the Star and Garter at Shepperford. That was on a Monday too.

FALKNER: That was on a Monday?

LADY J.: Yes—hark! [*Goes suddenly to back, looks off.*] Oh, it's you, Ferris! What are you doing there?

[FERRIS, *a perfectly trained lady's maid, about thirty, dark, quiet, reserved, a little sinister-looking, appears at opening at back with wrap in hand.*]

FERRIS: I beg pardon, my lady. But I thought you might be getting chilly, so I've brought you this.

LADY J.: Put it on the chair.

FERRIS: Yes, my lady. [*Exit.*]

LADY J. [*yawns*]: Heigho! Shall we go into the billiard room? [*Going.*]

FALKNER: No. How long do you mean to play with me?

LADY J.: Am I playing with you?

FALKNER: What else have you done the last three months? My heart is yours to its last beat. My life is yours to its last moment. What are you going to do with me?

LADY J.: Ah, that's it! I'm sure I don't know. [*Smiling at him.*] What shall I do with you?

FALKNER: Love me! love me! love me!

LADY J.: You are very foolish!

FALKNER: Foolish to love you?

LADY J.: No; not foolish to love me. I like you for that. But foolish to love me so foolishly. Foolish to be always wanting to play Romeo, when I only want to play Juliet sometimes.

FALKNER: Sometimes? When?

LADY J.: When I am foolish too—on a Monday evening.

FALKNER: Ah! will you drive me mad? Shall I tear you to pieces to find out if there is a heart somewhere within you?

LADY J. [*struggling*]: Hush! someone coming.

[FALKNER *releases her.* SIR CHRISTOPHER *saunters in at back, smoking. Exit* LADY JESSICA.]

SIR C.: Drop it, Ned! Drop it, my

dear old boy! You're going too far.

FALKNER: We won't discuss the matter, Kit.

SIR C.: Yes we will, Ned. George Nepean has been making a row, and I—well, I stroked him down. I said you were the soul of honour—

FALKNER: You were right. I am the soul of honour.

SIR C.: And that you didn't mean anything by your attentions to Lady Jessica.

FALKNER: You were wrong. I do mean something.

SIR C.: Well, what?

FALKNER: That's my business—and Lady Jessica's.

SIR C.: You forget—I introduced you here.

FALKNER: Thank you. You were very kind. [*Going off.*]

SIR C. [*stopping him*]: No, Ned; we'll have this out, here and now, please.

FALKNER [*angrily*]: Very well, let's have it out, here and now!

SIR C. [*with great friendship*]: Come, old boy, there's no need for us to take this tone. Let's talk it over calmly, as old friends and men of the world.

FALKNER: Men of the world! If there is one beast in all the loathsome fauna of civilization that I hate and despise, it is a man of the world! Good heaven, what men! what a world!

SIR C.: Quite so, old fellow. It is a beastly bad world—a lying, selfish, treacherous world! A rascally bad world every way. But bad as it is, this old world hasn't lived all these thousands of years without getting a little common sense into its wicked old noddle—especially with regard to its love affairs. And, speaking as an average bad citizen of this blackguardly old world, I want to ask you, Ned Falkner, what the devil you mean by making love to a married woman, and what good or happiness you expect to get for yourself or her? Where does it lead? What's to be the end of it?

FALKNER: I don't know—I don't care! I love her!

SIR C.: But, my good Ned, she's another man's wife.

FALKNER: She's married to a man who doesn't value her, doesn't understand her, is utterly unworthy of her.

SIR C.: All women are married to men who are utterly unworthy of them—bless 'em! All women are undervalued by their husbands—bless 'em! All women are misunderstood—bless 'em again!

FALKNER: Oh, don't laugh it off like that. Look at that thick clown of a husband. They haven't a single idea, or thought, or taste in common.

SIR C.: That's her lookout before she married him.

FALKNER: But suppose she didn't know, didn't understand. Suppose experience comes too late!

SIR C.: It generally does—in other things besides marriage!

FALKNER: But doesn't it make your blood boil to see a woman sacrificed for life?

SIR C.: It does—my blood boils a hundred times a day. But marriages are made in heaven, and if once we set to work to repair celestial mistakes and indiscretions, we shall have our hands full. Come down to brass tacks.

What's going to be the end of this?

FALKNER: I don't know—I don't care! I love her!

SIR C.: You don't know? I'll tell you. Let's go over all the possibilities of the case. [*Ticking them off on his fingers.*] Possibility number one—you leave off loving her—

FALKNER: That's impossible.

SIR C.: Possibility number two—you can, one or the other, or both of you, die by natural means; but you're both confoundedly healthy, so I'm afraid there's no chance of that. Possibility number three—you can die together by poison, or steel, or cold Thames water. I wouldn't trust *you* not to do a fool's trick of that sort; but, thank God, she's got too much sense. By the way, Ned, I don't think she cares very much for you—

FALKNER: She will.

SIR C.: Well, well, we shall see. Possibility number four—you can keep on dangling at her heels, and being made a fool of, without getting any—"forrarder."

FALKNER: Mine is not a physical passion.

SIR C. [*looks at him for two moments*]: Oh, that be hanged!

FALKNER: I tell you it is not.

SIR C.: Well then, it ought to be.

FALKNER [*very angrily*]: Well then, it is! And say no more about it. What business is it of yours?

SIR C. [*nonplussed*]: Possibility number five—a liaison with her husband's connivance. Gilbert Nepean won't make a mari complaisant. Dismiss that possibility.

FALKNER: Dismiss them all.

SIR C.: Don't you wish you could? But you'll have to face one of them, Ned. Possibility number six—a secret liaison. That's nearly impossible in society. And do you know what it means? It means in the end every inconvenience and disadvantage of marriage without any of its conveniences and advantages. It means endless discomfort, worry, and alarm. It means constant sneaking and subterfuges of the paltriest, pettiest kind. What do you say to that, my soul of honour?

FALKNER: I love her. I shall not try to hide my love.

SIR C.: Oh, then, you want a scandal! You'll get it! Have you thought what sort of a scandal it will be? Remember you've stuck yourself on a pedestal, and put a moral toga on. That's awkward. It wants such a lot of living up to. Gilbert Nepean is a nasty cuss and he'll make a nasty fuss. Possibility number seven, tableau one—Edward Falkner on his moral pedestal in a toga-esque attitude, honoured and idolized by the British public. [*Striking a heroic attitude.*] Tableau two—a horrible scandal, a field day for Mrs. Grundy; Edward Falkner is dragged from his pedestal, his toga is torn to pieces, his splendid reputation is blown to the winds, and he is rolled in the mud under the feet of the British public who, six months ago, crowned him with garlands and shouted themselves hoarse in his praise. Are you prepared for that, my soul of honour?

FALKNER: If it comes.

SIR C. [*shakes his head, makes a*

wry face, then proceeds]: Possibility number eight. Last remaining possibility, only possible possibility—pull yourself together, pack up your traps, start tomorrow morning for Africa or Kamtschatka, Jericho or Hong-Kong. I'll go with you. What do you say?

FALKNER: No.

SIR C.: No?

FALKNER: I wonder at you, Deering—I wonder at you coming to lecture me on love and morality.

SIR C.: Ah, why?

FALKNER [*with growing indignation*]: I love a woman with the deepest love of my heart, with the purest worship of my soul. If that isn't moral, if that isn't sacred, if that isn't righteous, tell me, in heaven's name, what is? And you come to lecture me with your cut and dried worldly-wise philosophy, your mean little maxims, you come to lecture me on love and morality—you!

SIR C.: Yes, I do! I may have had my attachments, I may have done this, that, and the other. I'm not a hero, I'm not on a pedestal, I never put on a moral toga. But I owe no woman a sigh or a sixpence. I've never wronged any man's sister, or daughter, or wife. And I tell you this, Ned Falkner, you're a fool if you think that anything can come of this passion of yours for Lady Jessica, except misery and ruin for her, embarrassment and disgrace for you, and kicking out of decent society for both of you.

FALKNER [*very firmly*]: Very well. And will you please be the first to cut me. Or shall I cut you?

SIR C.: You mean that, Ned?

FALKNER: Yes; if I'm a fool, leave me to my folly. [*Very strongly.*] Don't meddle with me.

SIR C.: You do mean that, Ned? Our friendship is to end?

FALKNER: Yes.

SIR C.: Very well. You'll understand some day, Ned, that I couldn't see an old comrade, a man who stood shoulder to shoulder with me all these years —you'll understand I couldn't see him fling away honour, happiness, reputation, future, everything, without saying one word and trying to pull him up. Goodbye, old chap. [*Going off.*]

[FALKNER *springs up generously, goes to him warmly, holding out both hands.*]

FALKNER [*cries out*]: Kit!
SIR C.: Ned!

[*The two men stand with hands clasped for some time, then* FALKNER *speaks in a soft, low, broken voice.*]

FALKNER: I love her, Kit—you don't know how much. When I see her, that turn of her head, that little toss of her curls, the little roguish face she makes— God couldn't make her like that and then blame a man for loving her! If He did—well, right or wrong, I'd rather miss heaven than one smile, one nod, one touch of her finger-tips!

SIR C.: Oh, my poor dear old fellow, if you're as far gone as that, what the deuce am I to do with you?

[*Enter* BEATRICE EBERNOE, *a tall,*

dark woman, about thirty, very beautiful and spirituelle.]

BEA.: Ned, here's a messenger from the Colonial Office with a very urgent letter for you.

FALKNER: For me?

[Enter SERVANT bringing letter to FALKNER.]

SERV.: Important, sir. The messenger is waiting in the hall for your answer.

FALKNER [taking letter]: Very well, I'll come to him.

[Exit SERVANT.]

FALKNER [reading letter]: More trouble out there. They want me to go out at once and negotiate. They think I could win over the chiefs and save a lot of bloodshed.

SIR C.: You'll go, Ned?

FALKNER: I don't know.

SIR C. [to BEATRICE]: Help me to persuade him.

BEA.: Can I? Have I any influence? Ned, for the sake of old days—

FALKNER: Ah, no—let me be—I must think this over. [Exit with distracted manner.]

BEA.: Have you spoken to him?

SIR C.: Yes; I gave him a thorough good slanging. Not a bit of use. When one of you holds us by a single hair, not all the king's horses and all the king's men can drag us back to that beggarly dusty old towpath of duty.

BEA.: I won't believe men are so weak.

SIR C.: Aren't we? There never was so sensible a man as I am in the management of other men's love affairs. You should have heard me lecture Ned. But once put me near you, and I'm every bit as bad as that poor fool I've been basting! [Indicating FALKNER by inclination of the head towards the direction he has gone.]

BEA.: Oh, no, Kit, I won't have you say that.

SIR C.: But I am. How beautifully you played just now.

BEA.: Did I?

SIR C.: Don't do it again.

BEA.: Why not?

SIR C.: It's taking an unfair advantage of me. You oughtn't to rouse those divine feelings in a man's heart. You oughtn't to make me feel like a martyr, or a king, or a saint in a cathedral window, with all heaven's sunlight streaming through me! You oughtn't to do it! Because devil a ha'porth of a king, or a martyr, or a saint is there in me—and after you've been playing to me and lifted me into that seventh heaven of yours, I feel so mean and shabby when I drop down to earth again, and find myself a hard, selfish man of the world.

BEA.: Oh, I think there's a great deal of the martyr and saint and king in you.

SIR C.: Do you? I believe there is! I know there would be if you'd only screw me up to it—and keep me screwed up. Beatrice, there's nothing I couldn't do if you would only—

BEA. [going away from him]: Kit, you mustn't speak of this again. I can't quite forget.

SIR C.: There's no need. While he was alive I never had one disloyal thought towards him. Now he's dead; who could be so fitted to take care of his dearest treasure as his oldest friend?

BEA. [*going away*]: I can't quite forget.

SIR C.: But you're young. What do you mean to do with your life?

BEA.: I'd some thoughts of entering a sisterhood.

SIR C.: Ah, no! Surely there are plenty of dear good ugly women in the world who can do that.

BEA.: But I must enjoy the luxury of self-sacrifice. Tell me how I can drink the deepest of that cup.

SIR C.: Marry me. I'll give you the most splendid opportunities. Now, if you and I were to join our forces, and take our poor Ned in hand, and—

BEA.: Hush!

[FALKNER *re-enters, evidently very much distracted.*]

SIR C. [*after a little pause, goes up to him*]: Well, Ned, what are you going to do?

FALKNER [*in an agony of indecision*]: I don't know! I don't know!

SIR C.: You'll go, Ned? I'll go with you!

[*Enter* LADY JESSICA *at back.*]

BEA.: You'll go, Ned?

LADY J.: Go? Where?

FALKNER: Nowhere. I shan't go, Kit. The man's waiting. I must give him my answer.

[*Exit* L. LADY JESSICA *looks after him.* SIR CHRISTOPHER *shrugs his shoulders at* BEATRICE.]

SIR C.: Not all the king's horses, nor all the King's men.

CURTAIN

ACT TWO

SCENE: *Private sitting-room in the Star and Garter, Shepperford-on-Thames, a room in a small high-class riverside hotel, furnished in the usual incongruous hotel fashion. Large French windows both right and left take up a good part of the back of the stage, and open upon a veranda which runs along outside. The pillars and roof of the veranda are smothered with trails of flowers and creeping plants. Beyond the veranda and very near to it is the Thames with opposite bank. Door down stage right. A sofa down stage right. A sideboard left. On the sideboard, plates, knives, forks, etc., dishes of fine peaches, grapes, and strawberries, and a bottle each of hock, claret, and champagne, as described in the text. A small table with writing materials at back between windows. A small table with white cloth laid, down stage, a little to the left of centre. A fireplace down stage left.*

[*Discover* FALKNER *in evening dress and French* WAITER.]

FALKNER: Crême à la Reine. We might have some trifle before the soup.

WAITER: Anchovy salad? Caviare?

FALKNER: Caviare.

WAITER: Bien, m'sieu. At what hour will m'sieu dine?

FALKNER: I don't know; I'm not sure that my friend will come at all. But tell the cook to have everything prepared, so that we can have dinner very soon after my friend arrives.

WAITER: Bien, m'sieu.

FALKNER [*reading menu*]: Caviare. Crême à la Reine. Rouget à l'Italienne. Whitebait. Petites Timbales à la Lucullus. Mousse de Foies Gras en Belle Vue. Is your cook equal to those entrées?

WAITER: Oh, sir, he is equal to anything. Trust to me, sir. The cook shall be magnifique. The dinner shall be magnifique.

FALKNER [*continuing*]: Poulardes poêlées, sauce Arcadienne. Selle de Mouton. Ortolans. Salade. Asperges en Branches. Pouding Mousseline, sauce Eglantine. Soufflé Glacé à l'Ananas. Dessert. [WAITER *points to the dessert on the sideboard.*] And the wines?

WAITER [*pointing to the wines on the sideboard*]: Ayala, seventy-five. Johannesburg, sixty-eight. Château Haut-Brion, seventy-five. I have brought them from London myself. We have not these vintages here.

FALKNER: Good.

WAITER: It is but one friend that m'sieu expect?

FALKNER: Only one friend.

WAITER: Bien, m'sieu. [*Exit.*]

[FALKNER *alone walks restlessly about the room for a few seconds, comes down; is arrested by something he hears outside the door, shows great delight. Re-enter* WAITER.]

WAITER: A lady; she say will Mr. Falkner please to see her? She have lost [*coughing*] her way.

FALKNER: Show her in.

[FALKNER *alone walks eagerly about room for a few seconds; his manner very eager and impatient and quite different from what it had been before. Re-enter* WAITER, *showing in* LADY JESSICA *most charmingly and coquettishly dressed in summer outdoor clothes. She comes in rather tempestuously, speaking as she enters, and going up to* FALKNER.]

LADY J. [*all in a breath*]: Oh, my dear Mr. Falkner, I've been staying with my cousin, and I was walking to the station, and by some unlucky chance I must have taken the wrong turning, for instead of finding myself at the station, I found myself here; and as I'm very hungry, would you think it very dreadful if I asked you to give me just a mere mouthful of dinner?

FALKNER [*intensely calm low voice*]: I'm delighted. [*To* WAITER.] Will you let us have dinner as soon as it is ready?

WAITER: In half an hour, sir. And the friend, sir?

FALKNER: The friend?

WAITER: The friend that m'sieu expect—the friend of the dinner?

FALKNER: Oh, yes—if he comes, show him in.

LADY J. [*alarmed*]: You don't expect—

FALKNER [*glancing at* WAITER]: Hush!

WAITER [*absolutely impassive face*]: Bien, m'sieu! [*Exit.*]

FALKNER: I'm so glad you've come. Look. [*Holding out his hand.*] I'm trembling with delight. I knew you would be here.

LADY J.: I'm sure you didn't, for I didn't know myself two hours ago. It was only by chance that I happened to take the wrong turning.

FALKNER: No; the right turning. And not by chance. It was not chance that brought you to me.

LADY J.: Oh, please, not that strain. I can't play up to it. Sit down and let us discuss something mundane—say dinner.

FALKNER [*giving her the menu*]: I hope you'll like what I've ordered. I sent the waiter up to London for some of the dishes and the wines.

LADY J. [*takes menu, looks at it, shows symptoms of great mock terror*]: What? You surely don't expect my poor little appetite to stand up to this dinner. Oh, let me be a warning to all, never to take the wrong turning when it may lead to a menu like this.

FALKNER: That's for your choice. You don't suppose I'd offer you anything but the very best.

LADY J.: Yes, but a little of the very best is all I want; not all of it.

FALKNER: Take all of it that I can set before you.

LADY J.: Oh, but think—there may be other deserving ladies in the world.

FALKNER: There is but you.

LADY J. [*looks at him very much amused*]: And I came here to cure you of this folly. Ah, me! [*Reading the menu.*] Mousse de Foies Gras. Poulardes poêlées, sauce Arcadienne—what is sauce Arcadienne?

FALKNER: I don't know. Love is the sauce of life. Perhaps it's that.

LADY J.: Yes, but don't dish it up too often or too strong. It's sure to be wasted.

FALKNER: My love for you is not wasted.

LADY J.: No?

FALKNER: You'll return it. You'll love me at last.

LADY J.: Shall I? Crême à la Reine. Roguet à l'Italienne. And if I did, what then?

FALKNER: Join your life to mine. Come to Africa with me.

LADY J. [*shakes her head*]: Impossible! We should only shock the British public. They wouldn't understand us. Ortolans. Salade. Asperges en Branches. Besides, what would everybody say?

FALKNER: We shouldn't hear them.

LADY J.: No; but they'd be talking all the same. Ha, ha! They'd called us the eloping philanthropists.

FALKNER: Would that matter?

LADY J.: Oh, yes. A philanthropist may not elope. A tenor may. Doesn't it show the terrible irony there is in the heart of things, that the best meaning philanthropist in the world may not elope with his neighbour's wife? Pouding Mousseline, sauce Eglantine. What makes you so eager to go hunting slave-traders in Africa?

FALKNER: My father spent half his fortune putting slavery down. My grandfather spent half his life and died a pauper for the same cause.

LADY J.: Well then, you should send a subscription to the Aborigines' Protection Society. That is how I keep up our family traditions.

FALKNER: How?

LADY J.: My father had a shocking reputation, and my grandfather, Beau Lillywhite— Oh! [*Shrug.*] So I follow in their footsteps—at a respectful distance. I flirt with you. Soufflé Glacé à l'Ananas. There's no flirting in Central Africa, I suppose?

FALKNER: No flirting. Only heat and hunger and thirst, and helpless misery prolonged to a horrible death.

LADY J. [*genuinely moved*]: Oh, I'm so sorry! Don't think me heartless about *that*. Perhaps if I had lived amongst it as you have—

FALKNER: Ah, if you had! you'd do as I ask you. You'd give all your heart to me, you'd give all your woman's care and tenderness to them, and you'd never hear one whisper of what people said of you.

LADY J. [*looking at him with real admiration*]: How earnest you are! How devoted!

[*Enter* WAITER *with knives and forks; he goes to table and begins laying it.*]

LADY J. [*to* WAITER]: What is sauce Arcadienne?

WAITER: Pardon! The cook is splendid. He is magnifique— but he has [*gesture*] renversée the sauce Arcadienne all over the shop.

FALKNER: It doesn't matter.

LADY J.: Oh, I had set my heart on sauce Arcadienne.

FALKNER: The cook must make some more sauce Arcadienne.

WAITER: Ah, that is impossible till the middle of the night.

LADY J.: Ah, what a pity! It is the one thing I long for, sauce Arcadienne.

FALKNER: Why?

LADY J.: Because I don't know what it is.

WAITER: He will give you some sauce Marguerite.

LADY J.: What is sauce Marguerite?

WAITER [*all the while laying table*]: Ah, it is delicieuse. It is the very best sauce that is in all the world.

LADY J.: Va pour la sauce Marguerite! Oh, this dinner!

WAITER: Ah, there is the beast of the organ man.

LADY J.: No, let him be. I like music—and monkeys. [*To* FALKNER.] Tell them to make haste.

FALKNER: Hurry the dinner.

WAITER: Bien! [*Exit.*]

LADY J. [*taking out watch*]: Half-past seven, I've not an hour to stay.

FALKNER: Yes, your life if you will.

LADY J.: Ah, no! You must be sensible. Think! what could come of it if I did love you? I should only break your heart or—what would be far worse—break my own.

FALKNER: Break it then—or let me break it. It's better to feel, it's better to suffer, than to be meanly happy. I love you, but I'd rather smother you in tears and blood than you should go on living this poor little heartless, withered life, choked up with all this dry society dust.

Oh, can't I make you feel? Can't I make you live? Can't I make you love me?

LADY J. [*after a moment's pause, looking at him with great admiration*]: Perhaps I do in my heart of hearts!

FALKNER: Ah! [*Springs to seize her; she struggles with him.*]

LADY J.: Mr. Falkner! Mr. Falkner! If you please. Do you hear? Mr. Falkner! [*Tears herself free.*] Will you please go and stop that horrid organ? Will you, please?

[FALKNER *bows, exit at door.* LADY JESSICA, *panting, flurried, out of breath, goes up to the window, fanning herself with handkerchief, passes on to veranda, stays there for a few moments fanning herself, suddenly starts back alarmed, comes into room, stands frightened, listening.* GEORGE NEPEAN *appears on veranda, comes up to window, looks in.*]

LADY J. [*trying to appear indifferent*]: Ah, George!

GEORGE: I thought I caught sight of you. May I come in?

LADY J.: Certainly.

GEORGE [*entering*]: I'm not intruding?

LADY J.: Intruding! Oh, no. Have you heard from Gilbert?

GEORGE: Yes, I had a letter this morning. He may be back in two or three days.

LADY J. [*embarrassed*]: Yes?

[*A pause. The organ outside stops in the middle of a bar.*]

GEORGE [*glancing at table*]: You're dining here?

LADY J.: Yes, just a small party. What brings you here?

GEORGE: I was going on to some friends at Hersham. I was waiting for the ferry when I caught sight of you. [*Glancing at table and sideboard.*] You're giving your friends rather a good dinner.

LADY J.: H'm, rather. I've heard the cooking's very good here. [*A little pause.*] There's a nest of cygnets outside. Have you seen them?

GEORGE: No.

LADY J. Do come and look at them; they are so pretty.

[*Going off at window followed by* GEORGE *when* FALKNER *enters at door. The two men look at each other.* LADY JESSICA *shows very great confusion and embarrassment. A long awkward pause.* GEORGE *looks very significantly at the sideboard and table.*]

GEORGE [*to* LADY JESSICA]: Gilbert must know of this. You understand? [*Bows. Exit by window and veranda.*]

LADY J. [*who has stood very frightened and confused*]: Did you hear? What can I do? What can I do?

FALKNER [*calm, almost triumphant*]: You must join your life to mine now.

LADY J.: No, no! If you wish me ever to have one kind thought of you, get me out of this! Do something, find somebody to dine with us. Understand me, I know myself, if this leads to a scandal, I shall hate you in a week. Oh, do something! do something!

FALKNER: Be calm. Be sure I'll do all I can to save you from a scandal. If that is impossible, be sure I'll do all I can to protect you from it.

LADY J.: Ah, no! Save me from it. I can't face it. I can't give up my world, my friends. Oh, what can I do? I'll go back to town—

FALKNER: What good will that do? You had far better stay now. Sit down, be calm. Trust to me.

LADY J.: Oh, you are good, and I'm such a coward.

FALKNER: Let us think what is the best thing to do.

LADY J.: Can't we get somebody to dine with us?

LADY R. [*heard outside*]: Oh, can't you wait, Freddie?

LADY J. [*looking off*]: Hark! Rosy! [*Goes up to window.*]

FREDDIE [*heard off*]: What! Row two more miles without a drink?

LADY J.: She's there in a boat with Freddie and another man. The men are landing. If we could only get them to stay and dine with us! We must! Go and find George Nepean and bring him back here. Make haste. When you come back, I'll have Rosy here.

FALKNER: In any case rely on me. I'm as firm as the earth beneath you. [*Exit.*]

LADY J. [*goes up to window*]: Rosy! Rosy! Come here! Yes, through there. Shush!

[LADY ROSAMUND *appears in the veranda.*]

LADY R.: Jess! What's the matter? [*Entering room.*]

LADY J.: Everything. You and Freddie must stay and dine here.

LADY R.: We can't, we're going on to dine with Mrs. Crespin at her new place, and we've got Jack Symons with us.

LADY J.: Va pour Jack Symons, whoever he may be! He must stay and dine too!

LADY R.: Impossible. Mrs. Crespin has asked some people to meet us. As her place is on the river Jack proposed we should row down and dress there. What are you doing here? I thought you were at Barbara's.

LADY J.: I was going back to town tonight. I thought I'd walk to the station—it's so delightful across the fields. Well, you know the path, I went on all right till I came to those two turnings, and then—I must have taken the wrong one, for, instead of finding myself at the station, I found myself here.

LADY R.: Well?

LADY J.: I'd been wandering about for over an hour, I was very hungry; I remembered Mr. Falkner was staying here; so I came in and asked him to give me some dinner.

LADY R.: It was very foolish of you!

LADY J.: Yes, especially as George Nepean was waiting for the ferry and caught sight of me on the veranda.

LADY R.: George Nepean!

LADY J.: He came in, saw Mr. Falkner, put a totally wrong construction on it all, and threatened to let Gilbert know.

LADY R.: How could you be so imprudent, Jess? You must have known that—

LADY J.: Oh, don't stand there rowing me. Help me out of this and I promise you I won't get into another.

LADY R.: Why didn't you explain to George how it happened?

LADY J.: So I would. Only when he came in I was alone. I felt sure he would put a wrong construction on it, so I told him I was dining here with a little party—then Mr. Falkner came in, and I was too confused to say anything. Besides, I couldn't very well tell him the truth, because—

LADY R.: Because what?

LADY J.: Well, it's very curious, but the last time I was staying with Barbara the very same thing happened.

LADY R.: What?

LADY J.: I was walking to the station, and I must have taken the wrong turning, for, instead of finding myself at the station, I found myself here.

LADY R.: What, twice?

LADY J.: Yes.

LADY R.: Oh, impossible!

LADY J.: No, it isn't; for it actually happened.

LADY R.: Do you mean to tell me that you—

LADY J. [*taking her up on the "tell"*]: Yes, I do. The sign-post is most deceptive.

LADY R.: It must be.

LADY J.: But the other time it was really a mistake, and I dined here all alone.

LADY R.: Honour?

LADY J.: Really, really honour!

LADY R.: I cannot imagine how you, a woman of the world—

LADY J.: Oh, do not nag me. Mr. Falkner has gone for George. You must stay here and tell George you are dining with me.

LADY R.: What about Freddie and Jack? See if they've come back to the boat.

LADY J. [*looking off at window*]: Not yet. Here's Mr. Falkner—alone.

[*Re-enter* FALKNER *at window.*]

Well, where is he?

FALKNER [*to* LADY ROSAMUND]: How d'ye do? [*To* LADY JESSICA.] He took a fly that was waiting outside and drove to the post-office. I went there and made inquiries. He stopped, sent off a telegram—

LADY J.: That must have been to Gilbert.

FALKNER: Then he drove off towards Staines. Shall I follow him?

LADY J.: Yes. No. What's the use? He may be anywhere by this.

LADY R.: Besides, we can't stay to dinner.

LADY J.: You must—you must! I must be able to tell Gilbert that somebody dined with me.

LADY R.: Jess, I'll write to George when I get back tonight, and tell him that I dined with you here.

LADY J.: Oh, you good creature! No! Write now, on the hotel paper. Then he'll see you were actually here.

LADY R.: Pens, ink, and paper.

FALKNER [*at table upstage*]: Here!

[LADY ROSAMUND *moves upstage.*]

LADY J.: Rosy, I've got a better plan than that.

LADY R.: What?

LADY J.: Could you be in town tomorrow morning?

LADY R.: Yes—why?

LADY J.: Write to George to call

on you there. I'll drop in a little before he comes. Then we can see what frame of mind he is in, and explain things accordingly. We can manage him so much better between us.

LADY R.: Very well, make haste. Mr. Falkner, will you go into the bar, run up against my husband and his friend, and keep them busy there till I get back into the boat?

FALKNER: Very well. [*Exit.*]

LADY R.: Now, what shall I say?

LADY J. [*dictating*]: "My dear George"—

LADY R. [*writing*]: "My dear George"— Oh, this pen! [*Throws away the pen, takes up another, tries it.*]

LADY J.: We must make it very short and casual as if you didn't attach much importance to it.

LADY R. [*throws away second pen*]: That's as bad!

LADY J. [*taking out a gold stylograph, giving it to* LADY ROSAMUND]: Here's my stylograph. Take care of it. It was a birthday present.

LADY R.: "Monday evening. My dear George"—

LADY J. [*dictating*]: "Jess has told me that you have just been here and that you were surprised at her presence. She fears you may have put a wrong construction on what you saw. She was too flurried at the moment to explain. But if you will call on me tomorrow morning, at Cadogan Gardens at"—what time will suit you?

LADY R.: Twelve?

LADY J.: Yes, and I'll be there a few minutes before.

LADY R. [*writing*]: "Twelve."

LADY J. [*dictating*]: "I will give you a full explanation. You will then see how very simple the whole affair was, and how little cause you had for your suspicions of her." That will do, won't it?

LADY R.: Yes, I think. "Yours sincerely"—no, "Yours affectionately, Rosy."

LADY J.: "P.S. You had perhaps better say nothing about this to Gilbert until after we have met. When you see how trifling the matter is, you can tell Gilbert or not, as you please."

LADY R. [*writing*]: "As you please. George Nepean, Esquire." What's his number?

LADY J.: Two-twenty.

LADY R. [*writing*]: "Two-twenty, Sloane Street."

LADY J.: What about Freddie? Shall we tell him?

LADY R.: Oh, no! I wouldn't trust my Freddie in a matter of this kind. He'd put a wrong construction on it—men always do. [*Puts letter in envelope, seals it.*]

LADY J.: But if George asks him?

LADY R.: Freddie won't come up to town tomorrow. We'll see how George takes it, and we'll keep Freddie out of it, if we can. [*She has risen, leaving stylograph on writing-table, where it remains. She seals letter.*] Stamp?

LADY J.: I've got one in my purse.

LADY R. [*has caught sight of the menu, has taken it up*]: Jess, you'll go straight to the station now?

LADY J.: Yes, I'm awfully hungry—

LADY R.: Yes, but I don't think this dinner would agree with you. [*Puts the menu down significantly.*]

LADY J.: Very well. But I am hungry.

LADY R.: And Jess, if I get you out of this—you won't take the wrong turning again?

LADY J.: No! no!

LADY R.: Honour?

LADY J.: Honour! Really honour! Rosy, you know this is only a silly freak—nothing more.

LADY R.: I may be sure of that, Jess? Honour?

LADY J.: Honour! Really, really honour!

LADY R. [kisses her]: I must be going. Tomorrow!

LADY J.: Tomorrow at Cadogan Gardens, ten minutes to twelve.

LADY R. [at window]: Those men are in the boat. My Freddie is looking for me. What shall I tell him? [Exit at window.]

[Enter WAITER.]

LADY J. [giving letter]: Please get that posted at once.

WAITER [taking letter]: Bien, madame. [Exit with letter.]

[Re-enter FALKNER at window.]

LADY J.: They've gone?

FALKNER: Yes. What have you done?

LADY J.: Rosy has written to George to come and see her tomorrow morning at Cadogan Gardens. You had better come too.

FALKNER: At what time?

LADY J.: Say a quarter to one. George will have gone by then and we can tell you if he accepts our explanation.

FALKNER: What is the explanation to be?

LADY J.: That Rosy and I were dining together here, that she hadn't arrived, that you happened to come into the room, and that George saw you and put a wrong construction on it. That will be all right, won't it?

FALKNER: Yes—I daresay. I wish it had been possible to tell the truth.

LADY J.: The truth? What truth? Rosy was actually here, and she might have stayed and dined with me—only she didn't—and—well, if it isn't the truth, it's only a little one.

FALKNER: I think those things are all the same size.

LADY J.: Oh, please don't be disagreeable, just at our last moment too.

FALKNER: Our last moment! Ah, no, no, no! [Approaching her.]

LADY J.: Ah, yes, yes, yes! I promised Rosy I'd go straight to the station—

FALKNER: There's no train till eight fifty. What harm can there be in your staying to dinner now?

LADY J.: I promised Rosy I wouldn't. I'm fearfully hungry—

[Enter WAITER with letter on salver.]

WAITER [advancing with letter on salver to LADY JESSICA]: Pardon, is this letter for madame?

LADY J. [takes letter, shows fright]: Yes. Excuse me. Who brought it? [Opens letter, takes out telegram.]

WAITER: She is here in the passage.

LADY J. [opens telegram; shows great alarm. Calls]: Ferris.

FERRIS [coming to door]: Yes, my lady.

LADY J.: Come in.

WAITER: Bien, madame. [Exit.]

LADY J.: When did this telegram come?

FERRIS: This afternoon, my lady.

The moment I got in, Mr. Rawlins said to me, "Mr. Nepean is coming back tonight; I've just had a telegram from him to get his room ready. And I expect this telegram is for her ladyship," he said, and he gave me that telegram, and I said, "I expect it is." "What time will her ladyship be back tonight?" he said. "I don't know," I said. "Where is her ladyship now?" he said. "I don't know," I said.

LADY J.: You didn't know?

FERRIS: No, my lady.

LADY J.: Then why did you come here?

FERRIS [*confused*]: The other night when I was bringing your ladyship's shawl to the tent, I happened to hear you mention this hotel. I didn't think anything of it, your ladyship, and I didn't in the least expect to find you here, I assure your ladyship. But I thought your ladyship would like to be apprised that Mr. Nepean was coming home tonight, and so I came, as I may say by pure chance, my lady; just as you might have come yourself, my lady.

LADY J.: Quite right, Ferris. [*To* FALKNER.] Mr. Nepean is coming home tonight. He reaches Paddington at ten.

FERRIS: I've got a cab outside, my lady, and I've looked out the trains. If we make haste, we can drive over to Walton and just catch a train there. But we haven't a moment to spare.

LADY J.: Come then.

FERRIS: I hope I've done right, my lady?

LADY J.: Quite right, Ferris. No. Please don't trouble to come

out, I'd rather you didn't. Rosy and I will dine with you some other night. [*Exit* FERRIS.] Goodnight.

FALKNER: And tomorrow?

LADY J.: Tomorrow? [*Grimace.*] Petits rows conjugals sauce tartare. [*Exit at door.*]

[*Enter* WAITER *with two little morsels of caviare.*]

FALKNER: What's that?

WAITER: Caviare on toast, sir.

FALKNER: Hang the caviare. Bring in the soup.

WAITER: Ah, it is not yet ready, two, three minutes. I am very sorry, but the cook say the sauce Marguerite—

FALKNER: What about it?

WAITER: It will not be made.

FALKNER: Very well.

WAITER: And the salade?

FALKNER: What about the salad?

WAITER: Will m'sieu mix it?

FALKNER: No, mix it yourself.

WAITER: Bien, m'sieu.

FALKNER: Waiter!

WAITER: Sir!

FALKNER [*pointing to the cover laid for* LADY JESSICA]: Take those confounded things away.

WAITER: Sir!

FALKNER: Take those confounded things away; I'm going to dine alone.

WAITER: Bien, m'sieu. [*Takes up the things, the second cover, and the one plate of caviare, leaving the other on the table in* FALKNER'S *place. Is going off with them.*]

FALKNER: Bring in the soup.

WAITER: Bien, m'sieu.

[*Exit with things.* SIR CHRISTOPHER'S *voice heard outside.*]

SIR C.: Mr. Falkner?

WAITER: Yes, sir. In number ten, sir.

SIR C.: Has he dined?

WAITER: Not yet, sir. What name, sir?

SIR C.: Oh never mind my name. Show me in.

WAITER [*at door, announcing*]: The friend of the dinner.

[*Enter* SIR CHRISTOPHER *in morning dress. Exit* WAITER.]

SIR C. [*very cordially*]: Ah, dear old boy, here you are. [*Shaking hands cordially.*] All alone?

FALKNER [*very sulky*]: Yes.

SIR C. [*looking at table*]: You haven't dined?

FALKNER: No.

SIR C.: That's all right. I'll join you. What's the matter?

FALKNER: Nothing.

SIR C.: Nothing?

FALKNER [*very sulky throughout*]: No. What should be?

SIR C.: You look upset.

FALKNER: Not at all.

SIR C.: That's all right. [*Going up to table very ravenously.*] I say, old chap, dinner won't be long, eh?

FALKNER: No, why?

SIR C.: I'm famished. I was over at Hounslow, I had no end of work to get through, so I stuck to it. I've had nothing but a biscuit and a glass of sherry since breakfast. I was going up to town for dinner, then I remembered you wrote to me from here; so I thought I'd run over on the chance of finding you. And here you are. [*Cordially.*] Well, how are you?

FALKNER: I'm very well.

SIR C.: That's all right. And, and—

old fellow—about the lady?

FALKNER: What about her?

SIR C.: You're going to behave like a good true fellow and give her up, eh?

FALKNER: Yes, I suppose.

SIR C.: That's all right. Love 'em, worship 'em, make the most of 'em! Go down on your knees every day and thank God for having sent them into this dreary world for our good and comfort. But, don't break your heart over 'em! Don't ruin your career for 'em! Don't lose a night's rest for 'em! They're not worth it—except one! [*Very softly.*]

FALKNER [*same sulky mood*]: You're full of good advice.

SIR C.: It's the only thing I am full of. I say, old fellow, could you hurry them up with the dinner?

[FALKNER *goes and rings bell.*]

SIR C. [*casually taking up the menu*]: No, Ned; they're not worth it, bless their hearts. And the man who— [*Suddenly stops, his face illuminated with delighted surprise.*] Ned!

FALKNER: What?

SIR C. [*pointing to menu*]: This isn't the menu for tonight?

FALKNER: Yes.

SIR C. [*incredulously*]: No! Dear old fellow! [*Looking at him with great admiration.*] Dear old fellow! I say, Ned, you do yourself very well when you're all alone.

FALKNER: Why shouldn't I?

SIR C.: Why shouldn't you? Why shouldn't you? [*Perusing menu.*]

FALKNER: Why shouldn't I? Excuse me a moment.

[*Exit at door.* SIR CHRISTOPHER,

left alone, reads over the menu, showing great satisfaction, then goes up to sideboard, takes up the bottles of wine, looks at them, shows great satisfaction, rubs his hands, brings down champagne, places it R. *of table, ditto hock, places it* L. *of table, brings down claret, looks at brand, hugs it delightedly; sits on table up* C., *puts claret down, picks up stylo. pen, reads inscription, coming down, then goes to window* L. C., *looks off, gives a sigh, comes down, puts pen in waistcoat pocket. Enter* WAITER.]

WAITER [*putting soup on table*]: Mr. Falkner says will you please excuse him? He has gone to London just now, this minute.

SIR C.: Gone to London!

WAITER: On very important business. He say will you please make yourself at home with the dinner?

SIR C. [*puzzled*]: Gone to London! What on earth— [*Resolutely and instantly takes seat at head of table.*] Serve up the dinner! Sharp!

WAITER: Caviare on toast?

SIR C.: Oh, damn the caviare! Open the champagne!

[*Takes the morsel of caviare and throws it down his throat; helps himself to soup, peppers it vigorously, meantime,* WAITER *opens champagne and pours out a glass.*]

SIR C.: The fish! Quick! and the entrées, bring them both up at the same time—bring up the whole bag of tricks!!

[SIR CHRISTOPHER *throws spoonful after spoonful of soup down his throat. The organ outside strikes up in the middle of the bar at which it left off, a very rowdy street tune.*]

CURTAIN

ACT THREE

SCENE: LADY ROSAMUND'S *drawing-room, Cadogan Gardens, a very elegant modern apartment, furnished in good taste. Door at back. Door right. Large bow window forming an alcove up stage right. Fireplace left.* LADY ROSAMUND *discovered in outdoor morning dress. Footman showing in* LADY JESSICA *at back.*

FOOTMAN [*announces*]: Lady Jessica Nepean. [*Exit* FOOTMAN.]

LADY R.: Well, dear?

LADY J. [*kisses* LADY ROSAMUND *very affectionately*]: Oh, Rosy—

LADY R: What's the matter?

LADY J.: Directly you had gone Ferris came in with a telegram from Gilbert, saying he was coming home last night. Of course I flew back to town. When I got there I found a later telegram saying he hadn't been able to finish his business, and that he would come back today.

LADY R. [*taking letter from pocket*]: He reaches Paddington at twelve.

LADY J.: How do you know?

LADY R. [*giving letter*]: Read that.

LADY J. [*looking at handwriting*]: From George Nepean.

LADY R.: Yes. He came here an hour ago to see me, and left that note. I'm afraid George means to be very horrid.

LADY J. [*reading*]: "Dear Lady Rosamund, I shall, of course, be quite ready to listen to any explanation you may have to offer. I will come back to Cadogan Gardens on my return from Paddington. I am now on my way there to meet Gilbert, who arrives from Devon at twelve. It is only fair to tell you that on leaving Lady Jessica last evening I telegraphed him I had a most serious communication to make to him, and that on his arrival I shall tell him exactly what I saw." George does mean to be horrid. [*Retaining letter.*]

LADY R.: I cannot imagine how you—

LADY J.: Oh, do not preach. I tell you it was the signpost. It is most deceptive.

LADY R.: It must be. The next time you come to that signpost—

LADY J.: I shall know which turning to take! You needn't fear.

LADY R.: My Freddie's in a small fever.

LADY J.: What about?

LADY R.: My coming up to town this morning.

LADY J.: You're sure he'll stay down there? He won't come up and—interfere?

LADY R.: Oh no, poor old dear! I snubbed him thoroughly and left him grizzling in his tent, like Achilles. He'll stay there all day, fuming and trying to screw up his courage to have a tremendous row with me when I get back to dinner this evening. I know my Freddie so well!

[FREDDIE *saunters in at back, half timid, half defiant.*]

[*looking at him with amused surprise*] Hillo, my friend! Hillo!

FREDDIE [*very severe and dignified, takes no notice of her*]: How do, Jess?

[LADY JESSICA *alternately reads* GEORGE'S *letter and looks at* FREDDIE.]

LADY R.: What has brought you to town?

FREDDIE: I came up with a purpose.

LADY R.: Oh, don't say that. People are always so horrid who do things with a purpose.

FREDDIE: I came up with Mrs. Crespin. She has lost the address of the cook that you gave her last evening. I told her you were in town. She will call here for it.

LADY R. [*sweetly*]: Very well.

FREDDIE: Do you intend to stay in, or go out this morning?

LADY R.: That depends. I may stay in—or I may go out. What are you going to do?

FREDDIE: That depends. I may stay in—or—I may go out.

LADY R.: Very well, dear, do as you please. I'll take the alternative. [*To* LADY JESSICA.] Come and take your things off in my room.

LADY J. [*glancing at* FREDDIE]: But don't you think—

FREDDIE [*with great dignity*]: I have come up to town this morning, because for the future I intend to place everything in this house on a new basis, an entirely opposite basis from that on which it now stands.

LADY R.: You're going to turn all the furniture upside down! Oh, I wouldn't!

FREDDIE: Hitherto I have been content to be a cipher in this establishment. I will be a cipher no longer.

LADY R.: No, I wouldn't. Come along, Jess!

LADY J.: But—

LADY R.: We'll talk it over upstairs. Run away to your club, Freddie, and think over what figure you would like to be. I daresay we can arrange it.

[*Exit* LADY ROSAMUND, R., *taking off* LADY JESSICA, *and closing the door rather sharply behind her.*]

FREDDIE [*left alone, marches up to the door, calls out in a forcible-feeble scream*]: I will not be a cipher! I will not be a cipher! [*Comes to centre of stage, gesticulates, his lips moving, sits down very resolutely, and then says in a tone of solemn conviction.*] I will *not* be a cipher!

[*Enter* FOOTMAN *announcing.*]

FOOTMAN: Sir Christopher Deering!

[*Enter* SIR CHRISTOPHER. *Exit* FOOTMAN.]

SIR C. [*shaking hands*]: I've just come on from Lady Jessica's. They told me I should find her here.

FREDDIE: She's upstairs with my wife.

SIR C.: Can I see her for a few minutes?

FREDDIE: I don't know. Deering, old fellow, we're tiled in, aren't we? If I ask your advice—

SIR C.: Certainly, Freddie. What is it?

FREDDIE: I've been married for seven years—

SIR C.: Seven years is it? It doesn't seem so long.

FREDDIE: Oh, doesn't it? Yes, it does. Rosy and I have never quite hit it off from the first.

SIR C.: No? How's that?

FREDDIE: I don't know. When I want to do anything, she doesn't. When I want to go anywhere, she won't. When I like anybody, she hates them. And when I hate anybody, she likes them. And—well—there it is in a nutshell.

SIR C.: Hum! I should humour her a little, Freddie—let her have her own way. Try kindness.

FREDDIE: Kindness? I tell you this, Deering, kindness is a grand mistake. And I made that grand mistake at starting. I began with riding her on the snaffle. I ought to have started on the curb, eh?

SIR C.: Well, there's something to be said for that method in some cases. Kindness won't do, you say? Why not try firmness?

FREDDIE: I have.

SIR C.: Well?

FREDDIE: Well, firmness is all very well, but there's one great objection to firmness.

SIR C.: What's that?

FREDDIE: It leads to such awful rows, and chronic rowing does upset me so. After about two days of it, I feel so seedy and shaky and nervous, I don't know what to do. [*Has a sudden wrathful outburst.*] And she comes up as smiling as ever!

SIR C.: Poor old fellow!

FREDDIE: I say, Deering, what would you advise me to do?

SIR C.: Well, it requires some consideration—

FREDDIE [*with deep conviction*]: You know, Deering, there must be some way of managing them!

SIR C.: One would think so. There must be some way of managing them!

FREDDIE [*has another wrathful outburst*]: And I used to go and wait outside her window, night after night, for hours! What do you think of that?

SIR C.: I should say it was time very badly laid out.

FREDDIE [*pursuing his reminiscences*]: Yes, and caught a chill on my liver and was laid up for six weeks.

SIR C.: Poor old fellow!

FREDDIE: I say, Deering, what would you do?

SIR C.: Well—well—it requires some consideration.

FREDDIE [*walking about*]: You know, Deering, I may be an ass—

SIR C.: Oh!

FREDDIE [*firmly*]: Yes. I may be an ass, but I'm not a *silly* ass. I may be a fool, but I'm not a *d—ee—d* fool! Now there's something going on this morning between Rosamund and Jess. They're hobnobbing and whispering, and when two of 'em get together—

SIR C.: Oh, my dear fellow, when two women get together, do you think it can ever be worth a man's while to ask what nonsense or mischief they're chattering? By the way, did you say that I could see Lady Jessica?

FREDDIE: She's upstairs with Rosy. I'll send her to you. Deering, if you were married, would you be a cipher in your own house?

SIR C.: Not if I could help it.

FREDDIE [*very determinedly*]: Neither will I. [*Exit.*]

[SIR CHRISTOPHER, *left alone, takes out the stylograph and looks at it carefully. In a few seconds enter* LADY JESSICA, R. *As she enters he drops left hand which holds the stylograph.*]

SIR C.: How d'ye do?

LADY J.: How d'ye do? You wish to see me?

[SIR CHRISTOPHER *presents the stylograph,* LADY JESSICA *shows alarm.*]

SIR C.: I see from the inscription that this belongs to you.

LADY J. [*taking stylograph*]: Where did you find it?

SIR C.: In a private sitting-room at the Star and Garter at Shepperford.

LADY J.: I must have left it there some time ago. I could not imagine where I had lost it. Thank you so much.

SIR C.: Pray don't mention it. [*An awkward pause.*] Good morning.

LADY J.: Good morning. [SIR CHRISTOPHER *has got to door at back.*] Sir Christopher—[SIR

CHRISTOPHER *stops.*] You were at Shepperford—?

SIR C.: Last evening.

LADY J.: Pretty little spot.

SIR C.: Charming.

LADY J.: And a very good hotel?

SIR C.: First class. Such splendid cooking!

LADY J.: The cooking's good, is it!—oh, yes, I dined there once, some time ago.

SIR C.: I dined there last night.

LADY J.: Did you? At the table d'hôte?

SIR C.: No, in a private sitting-room. Number ten.

LADY J.: With a friend, I suppose?

SIR C.: No. All alone.

LADY J.: All alone? In number ten?

SIR C.: All alone. In number ten.

LADY J.: I suppose you—I suppose—

SIR C.: Suppose nothing except that I had a remarkably good dinner, that I picked up that stylograph and brought it up to town with me last night. And there is an end of the whole matter, I assure you. Good morning.

LADY J.: Good morning. Sir Christopher—you— [SIR CHRISTOPHER *is again arrested at door.*] you—a— I may trust you?

SIR C.: If I can help you—yes.

LADY J.: Nothing—nothing is known about my being there?

SIR C.: Your being there?

LADY J. [*after a pause—embarrassed*]: I was to have dined in number ten.

SIR C.: All alone?

LADY J. [*same embarrassed manner*]: No—with Mr. Falkner. I was coming up to town from my cousin's. I started to walk to the station. I must have taken the wrong turning, for instead of finding myself at the station, I found myself at the Star and Garter. I was very hungry and I asked Mr. Falkner to give me a mere mouthful of dinner.

SIR C.: A mere mouthful.

LADY J.: And then George Nepean caught sight of me, came in, saw Mr. Falkner, and telegraphed my husband that I—of course Gilbert will believe the worst, and I—oh, I don't know what to do!

SIR C.: Can I be of any service?

LADY J.: How would you advise me to—to get out of it?

SIR C.: Let us go over the various possibilities of the case. There are only two.

LADY J.: What are they?

SIR C.: Possibility number one—get out of it by telling fibs. Possibility number two—get out of it by telling the truth. Why not possibility number two?

LADY J.: Oh, I couldn't!

SIR C.: Couldn't what?

LADY J.: Tell my husband that I was going to dine with Mr. Falkner.

SIR C.: But it was quite by accident?

LADY J.: Oh, quite!

SIR C.: Eh!

LADY J.: Quite!

SIR C.: Well—?

LADY J.: But if Gilbert made inquiries—

SIR C.: Well?

LADY J.: It was such a very good dinner that Mr. Falkner ordered.

SIR C.: It was! But, if he didn't expect you, why did he order that very excellent dinner?

LADY J.: I'm sure you ought to be the last person to ask that, for it seems you ate it.

SIR C.: I did.

LADY J.: It's an ill wind that blows nobody good!

SIR C.: I'm not grumbling at the wind, or at the dinner, but if I'm to help you out of this, you had better tell me all the truth. Especially as I'm not your husband. Now frankly, is this a mere indiscretion or—

LADY J.: A mere indiscretion, nothing more. Honour—really, really honour.

SIR C.: A mere indiscretion that will never be repeated.

LADY J.: A mere indiscretion that will never be repeated. You believe me?

SIR C. [*looking at her*]: Yes, I believe you, and I'll help you.

LADY J.: Thank you! Thank you!

SIR C.: Now, did Falkner expect you?

LADY J.: He ought not.

SIR C.: He ought not. But he did.

LADY J.: I told him I shouldn't come.

SIR C.: Which was exactly the same as telling him you would.

LADY J.: Have you seen Mr. Falkner?

SIR C.: Only for a minute just before dinner. He came up to town.

LADY J.: Without any dinner?

SIR C.: Without any dinner. To come back to these two possibilities.

LADY J.: Yes, Rosy and I have decided on—on—

SIR C.: On possibility number one, tell a fib. I put that possibility first out of natural defer-

ence and chivalry towards ladies. The only objection I have to telling fibs is that you get found out.

LADY J.: Oh, not always.

SIR C.: Eh!

LADY J.: I mean, if you arrange things not perhaps exactly as they were, but as they ought to have been.

SIR C.: I see. In that way a lie becomes a sort of idealized and essential truth—

LADY J.: Yes. Yes—

SIR C.: I'm not a good hand at—idealizing.

LADY J.: Ah, but then you're a man! No, I can't tell the truth. Gilbert would never believe me. Would you—after that dinner?

SIR C.: The dinner would be some tax on my digestion.

[LADY ROSAMUND *enters* R., *followed by* FREDDIE, *with a self-important and self-assertive air.*]

LADY R.: Good morning, Sir Christopher.

SIR C. [*shaking hands*]: Good morning, Lady Rosamund.

LADY R.: Jess, I've had to tell Freddie.

LADY J.: And I've had to tell Sir Christopher. He was at Shepperford last evening, and he has promised to help us.

FREDDIE: I must say, Jess, that I think you have behaved—well—in a—confounded silly way.

LADY J.: That is perfectly understood.

FREDDIE [*solemnly*]: When a woman once forgets what is due—

LADY J.: Oh, don't moralize! Rosy, Sir Christopher, do ask

him not to improve the occasion.

SIR C.: The question is, Freddie, whether you will help us in getting Lady Jessica out of this little difficulty.

FREDDIE: Well, I suppose I must join in.

LADY J.: Now, Rosy, do you fully understand—

SIR C.: I don't think I do. What is the exact shape which possibility number one has taken—or is going to take?

LADY R.: Jess and I had arranged to have a little *tête-à-tête* dinner at Shepperford. Jess got there first. I hadn't arrived. George saw Jess at the window, and came in. At that moment Mr. Falkner happened to come into the room, and Jess knowing that appearances were against her, was confused, and couldn't on the spur of the moment give the right explanation.

SIR C.: I suppose the waiter will confirm that right explanation?

LADY J.: The waiter? I hadn't thought of that. Waiters will confirm anything, won't they? Couldn't you settle with the waiter?

SIR C.: Well, I—

LADY J.: You did have the dinner, you know!

SIR C.: Very well. I'll settle with the waiter.

[*Enter* FOOTMAN.]

FOOTMAN [*announcing*]: Mrs. Crespin!

[*Enter* MRS. CRESPIN. *Exit* FOOTMAN.]

MRS. C. [*shows a little surprise at seeing them all, then goes very affectionately to* LADY ROSAMUND]: Good morning, dear. Good morning, Sir Christopher. [SIR CHRISTOPHER *bows. To* FREDDIE.] I've seen you. [*Goes to* LADY JESSICA.] Good morning, dearest. [*Kisses her.*]

LADY J.: Good morning, dearest. [*Kisses her.*]

MRS. C. [*to* LADY JESSICA. *Looking anxiously at her*]: You're looking pale and worried.

LADY J.: Me? Oh, no, I'm sure I don't, do I?

SIR C.: Not to masculine eyes.

MRS. C. [*to* LADY ROSAMUND]: Dear, I've lost the address of that cook. Would you mind writing it out again?

LADY R.: Certainly. [*Goes to writing table and writes.*]

MRS. C. [*to* LADY JESSICA]: What's the matter with our dear friend George Nepean?

LADY J.: Matter?

MRS. C.: I ran against him in a post-office on my way from Paddington just now.

LADY J.: Yes?

MRS. C.: Your husband is quite well, I hope?

LADY J.: My husband? Oh, quite! He always is quite well. Why?

MRS. C.: George Nepean seemed so strange.

LADY J.: How?

MRS. C.: He said he was going to Paddington to meet your husband—and he made so much of it.

LADY J.: Ah! You see, my husband is a big man, so naturally George would make much of it.

MRS. C.: I always used to go to the station to meet my husband—when I had one.

LADY J. [*a little triumphantly*]: Ah, Rosy and I know better than to kill our husbands with too much kindness.

MRS. C.: Still, I think husbands need a little pampering—

SIR C.: Not at all. The brutes are so easily spoilt. A little overdose of sweetness, a little extra attention from a wife to her husband, and life is never the same again!

FREDDIE [*who has been waiting eagerly to get a word in*]: I suppose you didn't mention anything to George Nepean about our dining with you last evening?

MRS. C. [*alert*]: Did I? Let me see! Yes! Yes! I did mention that you were over. Why?

[*They all look at each other.*]

FREDDIE: Oh, nothing, nothing!

MRS. C.: I'm so sorry. Does it matter much?

LADY J.: Not in the least.

LADY R.: Oh, not in the least.

FREDDIE: Not in the least.

SIR C.: Not at all.

MRS. C.: I'm afraid I made a mistake.

LADY R.: How?

MRS. C.: Your husband—

LADY R.: Oh, my dear, what does it matter what my Freddie says or does or thinks, eh, Freddie? [*Frowning angrily aside at* FREDDIE.] There's the address of the cook. [*Giving the paper on which she has been writing.*]

MRS. C.: Thank you so much. Good morning, dearest. [*Kiss.*]

LADY R.: Good morning, dearest. [*Kiss.*]

MRS. C. [*going to* LADY JESSICA]: Good-bye, dearest. [*Exit.*]

LADY J.: Good-bye, dearest. [*Kiss.*]

MRS. C. [*very sweetly, shaking hands*]: Good-bye, Sir Christopher.

SIR C.: Good-bye.

MRS. C.: You are quite sure that I didn't make a mistake in telling George Nepean that Lady Rosy and Mr. Tatton dined with me last evening?

SIR C.: It was the truth, wasn't it?

MRS. C.: Of course it was.

SIR C.: One never makes a mistake in speaking the truth.

MRS. C.: Really? That's a very sweeping assertion to make.

SIR C.: I base it on my constant experience—and practice.

MRS. C.: You find it always answers to tell the truth?

SIR C.: Invariably.

MRS. C.: I hope it will in this case. Good-bye! Good-bye! Good-bye!

[*Exit* MRS. CRESPIN. *They all stand looking at each other, nonplussed.* SIR CHRISTOPHER *slightly touching his head with perplexed gesture.*]

SIR C.: Our fib won't do.

LADY R.: Freddie, you incomparable nincompoop!

FREDDIE: I like that! If I hadn't asked her, what would have happened? George Nepean would have come in, you'd have plumped down on him with your lie, and what then? Don't you think it's jolly lucky I said what I did?

SIR C.: It's lucky in this instance. But if I am to embark any further in these imaginative enterprises, I must ask you, Freddie, to keep a silent tongue.

FREDDIE: What for?

SIR C.: Well, old fellow, it may

be an unpalatable truth to you, but you'll never make a good liar.

FREDDIE: Very likely not. But if this sort of thing is going on in my house, I think I ought to.

LADY R.: Oh, do subside, Freddie, do subside!

LADY J.: Yes, George—and perhaps Gilbert—will be here directly. Oh, will somebody tell me what to do?

SIR C.: We have tried possibility number one. It has signally failed. Why not possibility number two?

LADY J.: Tell the truth? My husband would never believe it! Besides, he threatened that he wouldn't spare me. And he won't. No! No! No! Somebody dined with me last night, or was going to dine with me, and that somebody was a woman.

[*Enter* FOOTMAN.]

FOOTMAN[*announcing*]: Mrs. Coke!

[*Enter* DOLLY.]

DOLLY [*going to* LADY R.]: Ah, my dear Lady Rosamund—

[*Exit* FOOTMAN.]

LADY J. [*goes affectionately and a little hysterically to her*]: Dolly! How good of you! [*Kissing her.*]

DOLLY: What's the matter?

LADY J.: Dolly, you dined with me, or were going to dine with me at the Star and Garter at Shepperford last evening. Don't say you can't, and didn't, for you must and did!

DOLLY: Of course I'll say anything that's—necessary.

LADY J.: Oh, you treasure!

DOLLY: But I don't understand—

[LADY JESSICA *takes her aside and whispers eagerly.*]

SIR C. [*glancing at* LADY JESSICA *and* DOLLY]: Possibility number one—with variations. I'm not required any further.

LADY R.: Oh, Sir Christopher, you won't desert us?

SIR C.: Certainly not, if I can be of any use. But if this is to be a going concern, don't you think the fewer partners the better?

LADY R.: Oh, don't go. You can help us so much.

SIR C.: How?

LADY R.: Your mere presence will be an immense moral support to us.

SIR C. [*uncomfortable*]: Thank you! Thank you!

LADY R.: You can come to our assistance whenever we are in the lurch, corroborate us whenever we need corroboration—and—

SIR C.: Bolster up generally.

LADY R.: Yes. Besides, everybody knows you are such an honourable man. I feel they won't suspect you.

SIR C. [*uncomfortable*]: Thank you! Thank you!

DOLLY [*to* LADY JESSICA]: Very well, dear. I quite understand. After George went away, you were so upset at his suspicions that you came back to town without any dinner. Did I stay and have the dinner?

SIR C.: No, no. I wouldn't go so far as that.

DOLLY: But what did I do? I must have dined somewhere didn't I? Not that I mind if I didn't dine anywhere. But won't it seem funny if I didn't dine somewhere?

LADY J.: I suppose it will.

DOLLY: Very well then, where did I dine? Do tell me. I know I shall get into an awful muddle if I don't know. Where did I dine?

[*Enter* FOOTMAN.]

FOOTMAN [*announcing*]: Mr. George Nepean.

[*Enter* GEORGE NEPEAN. *Exit* FOOTMAN.]

GEORGE [*enters very frigidly, bows very coldly. Very stiffly*]: Good morning, Lady Rosamund! [*To the others—bowing.*] Good morning.

LADY R. [*very cordially*]: My dear George, don't take that tragic tone. [*Insists on shaking hands.*] Anyone would suppose there was something dreadful the matter. I've just explained to Sir Christopher your mistake of last night.

GEORGE: My mistake?

LADY J.: You shouldn't have left so hurriedly, George. I sent Mr. Falkner after you to explain. Dolly, tell him.

DOLLY: Jess and I had arranged to have a little dinner all by our two selves—

GEORGE: Indeed!

DOLLY: There's nothing strange in that, Sir Christopher?

SIR C.: Not at all. I am sure any person of either sex would only be too delighted to dine *tête-à-tête* with you.

DOLLY: And when I got there, I found poor Jess in an awful state. She said you had come into the room and had made

the most horrid accusations against her, poor thing!

GEORGE: I made no accusation.

LADY J.: What did you mean by saying that Gilbert must know?

GEORGE: Merely that I should tell him what I saw.

LADY J.: And you have told him?

GEORGE: Yes, on his arrival an hour ago.

LADY J.: Where is he?

GEORGE: Round at Sloane Street waiting till I have heard Lady Rosamund's explanation.

LADY R.: Well, you have heard it. Or, rather, it's Dolly's explanation. The whole thing is so ridiculously simple. I think you ought to beg Jess's pardon.

GEORGE: I will when I am sure that I have wronged her.

FREDDIE: Oh, come, I say, George! you don't refuse to take a lady's word—

LADY R.: Freddie, subside!

DOLLY [*to* GEORGE]: Poor Jess was so much upset by what you said that she couldn't eat any dinner, she nearly had hysterics, and when she got a little better, she came straight up to town, poor thing!

GEORGE: What was Mr. Falkner doing there?

LADY J.: He was staying in the hotel and happened to come into the room at that moment. [*A little pause.*]

LADY R.: Is there anything else you would like to ask?

GEORGE: No.

LADY R.: And you're quite satisfied?

GEORGE: The question is not whether I'm satisfied, but whether Gilbert will be. I'll go and fetch him. Will you excuse me?

SIR C. [*stops him*]: Nepean, I'm sure you don't wish to embitter your brother and Lady Jessica's whole future life by sowing jealousy and suspicion between them. Come now, like a good fellow, you'll smooth things over as much as you can.

GEORGE: I shall not influence my brother one way or the other. He must judge for himself.

[*Exit.* SIR CHRISTOPHER *shrugs his shoulders.*]

DOLLY: I got through very well, didn't I? [*To* LADY JESSICA.]

LADY J.: Yes, dear. Thank you so much. But George didn't seem to believe it, eh?

FREDDIE: It's so jolly thin. A couple of women dining together! what should a couple of women want to dine together for? Oh, it's too thin, you know!

LADY J.: And you don't think Gilbert will believe it? He must! he must! Oh, I begin to wish that we had tried—

SIR C.: Possibility number two. I'm afraid it's too late now.

LADY J.: Oh, what shall I do? Do you think Gilbert will believe Dolly?

LADY R.: He must if Dolly only sticks to it.

DOLLY: Oh, I'll stick to it. Only I should like to know where I dined. Where did I dine?

[*Enter* FOOTMAN *to* DOLLY.]

FOOTMAN: If you please, ma'am, Mr. Coke is waiting for you below.

DOLLY [*with a scream*]: Oh, dear! Oh, dear! I'd quite forgotten!

LADY R.: What?

DOLLY: I arranged to meet Archie here and take him on to the dentist's. [*To* FOOTMAN.] Tell Mr. Coke I'll come in a moment.

[*Exit* FOOTMAN.]

DOLLY [*to* LADY JESSICA]: Dear, I must go—

LADY J.: You can't! You must stay now and tell Gilbert— mustn't she, Sir Christopher?

SIR C: I'm afraid you must, Mrs. Coke. You are our sheet-anchor.

DOLLY: But what can I tell Archie?

LADY R.: Can't you put him off, send him away?

DOLLY: What excuse can I make? He is so fidgety and inquisitive. He'll insist on knowing everything. No, I must go.

LADY J. [*desperate*]: You can't! You can't! You must stay! Couldn't we tell Archie and ask him to help us?

SIR C. [*impatiently to* LADY R.]: Oh!

DOLLY: Oh, I wouldn't tell Archie for the world. He wouldn't understand.

[*Enter, L.,* ARCHIBALD COKE, *in very correct frock coat very prim and starchy.*]

COKE: Good morning, Rosy! Freddie! Sir Christopher! [*Nodding all round.*] Now, Dolly, are you ready?

DOLLY: I—I—

LADY J.: She can't go, Archie.

COKE: Can't go?

LADY J.: She—she isn't well.

COKE: Not well? [*Alarmed.*] Not influenza again?

DOLLY: No, not influenza. But I'd rather not go.

COKE: Oh, nonsense, nonsense! I cannot take the gas alone. [*To* SIR CHRISTOPHER.] I've a terrible dread of the gas. I'm sure they'll give me too much some day. Now, Dolly.

LADY R. [*to* SIR CHRISTOPHER]: Gilbert will be here directly. Can't you get him away?

SIR C.: Coke, your wife isn't just the thing, as you can see. I'll go to the dentist's with you. Come along! I'll see they give you the right dose.

COKE [*resisting*]: No. My wife is the proper person to go to the dentist with me, and see that the gas is rightly administered. Come, Dolly!

LADY J. [*comes desperately to* COKE]: Dolly can't go!

COKE: Why not?

LADY J.: She must stay here and tell Gilbert that she dined with me last evening.

COKE: Tell Gilbert that she dined with you last evening! What for?

SIR C. [*aside to* LADY ROSAMUND]: We're taking too many partners into this concern.

COKE: She dined with me. Why should she tell Gilbert she dined with you?

LADY J.: If you must know, I was coming to the station from Barbara's, and I must have taken the wrong turning—

COKE [*very suspicious*]: The wrong turning—

LADY J.: Yes, for instead of finding myself at the station, I found myself at the Star and Garter.

COKE: The Star and Garter!

LADY J.: And as I was frightfully hungry I asked Mr. Falkner to give me a little dinner.

COKE: A little dinner.

LADY J.: George Nepean happened to come in, and seeing the dinner things laid, actually suspected me of dining with Mr. Falkner! And he has told Gilbert, and don't you see—if Dolly will only say that it was she who was dining with me —don't you see?

COKE: No, I don't. I cannot lend myself to anything of the sort. And I expressly forbid Dolly to say that she dined with you.

LADY J.: But she has said so. She has just told George Nepean.

COKE: That George Nepean!

DOLLY: I couldn't leave poor Jess in a scrape. And now I have said so, I must stick to it, mustn't I? You wouldn't have me tell another one now.

COKE: Well, I'm surprised! Really, I consider it quite disgraceful.

FREDDIE: Look here, Coke, we can't let Gilbert think that Jess was dining with Falkner, can we? He'd only make a howling scandal, and drag us all into it. We've got to say something. I know it's jolly thin, but can you think of a better one?

COKE: No, and I decline to have anything to do with this! I should have thought my character was too well known for me to be asked to a—a— It is too disgraceful! I will not lend my countenance to anything of the kind!

LADY R.: Very well then, will you please take yourself off and leave us to manage the affair ourselves?

COKE: No, I will not forfeit my self-respect, I will not permit my wife to forfeit her self-respect by taking part in these proceedings. Really, it is—it is— it is too disgraceful.

[LADY JESSICA *suddenly bursts into tears, sobs violently.*]

SIR C. [*comes up to him, very calm, touches him on the shoulder*]: Coke, I assure you that theoretically I have as great an objection to lying as you or any man living. But Lady Jessica has acted a little foolishly. No more. Of that I am sure. If you consent to hold your tongue, I think Gilbert Nepean will accept your wife's explanation and the affair will blow over. If, however, you insist on the truth coming out, what will happen? You will very likely bring about a rupture between them, you may possibly place Lady Jessica in a position where she will have no alternative but to take a fatal plunge, and you will drag yourself and your wife into a very unpleasant family scandal. That's the situation.

COKE: But it places me in a very awkward position. No, really, I cannot consent— I'm an honourable man.

SIR C.: So are we all, all honourable men. The curious thing is that ever since the days of the Garden of Eden, women have had a knack of impaling us honourable men on dilemmas of this kind, where the only alternative is to be false to the truth or false to them. In this instance I think we may very well keep our mouths shut without suffering any violent pangs of conscience about the matter. Come now!

COKE [*overwhelmed*]: Well, understand me, if I consent to keep my mouth shut, I must

not be supposed to countenance what is going on. That is quite understood?

SIR C.: Oh, quite! Quite! We'll consider you as strictly neutral.

COKE [*rising up, violently*]: No! On second thoughts, I really cannot. I cannot!

LADY R.: Very well! Then will you go away and leave us to manage it as we can?

COKE: And I had arranged to take the gas so comfortably this morning. It's most unfair to place me in a position of this kind. I must protest—I really—

[*Enter* FOOTMAN.]

FOOTMAN [*announcing*]: Mr. Gilbert Nepean. Mr. George Nepean.

COKE: Oh!

[*Enter* GILBERT *and* GEORGE NEPEAN. *Exit* FOOTMAN.]

LADY R. [*advances very cordially to* GILBERT, *who does not respond*]: Good morning, Gilbert.

GILBERT: Good morning. Good morning, Coke.

COKE [*very uncomfortable*]: Good morning.

GILBERT [*nodding*]: Freddie! Deering! [*Looks at* LADY JESSICA, *who looks at him. They do not speak. Pause, looking round.*] I thought I was coming here for a private explanation.

LADY R.: No, Sir Christopher. If Gilbert is determined to carry this any further we shall need the unbiassed testimony of an impartial friend, so that everybody may know exactly what did occur. Please stay.

SIR C. [*puts down hat*]: Whew! [*To himself.*]

LADY R.: Gilbert, don't be foolish. Everybody here knows all about the stupid affair of last evening.

GILBERT: Everybody here knows? Well, I don't. I shall be glad to be informed. [*Looks round.*]

[COKE *shows symptoms of great discomfort.*]

SIR C.: Nepean, I'm sure you don't wish to make any more than is necessary of Lady Jessica's trifling indiscretion—

GILBERT: I wish to make no more of it than the truth, and I'll take care that nobody makes less of it. Now—[*to* LADY JESSICA, *very furiously*]—you were dining with this fellow, Falkner, last evening?

LADY J.: No.

GILBERT: No? Then whom did you dine with?

LADY J.: If you speak like that I shan't answer you.

GILBERT: Will you tell me what I ask?

LADY J.: No!

GILBERT: No, you won't? Perhaps, as you all know, somebody else will oblige me. Coke—

COKE [*most uncomfortable*]: Really, I—I don't know all the particulars, and I would prefer not to be mixed up in your private affairs.

GILBERT: Deering—you?

SIR C.: My dear fellow, I only know what I've heard, and hearsay evidence is proverbially untrustworthy. Now, if I may offer you a little advice, if I were you I should gently take Lady Jessica by the hand, I should gently lead her home, I should gently use all those endearing little arts of persuasion and entreaty which a husband may legitimately use to his wife, and I should gently beguile her into telling me the whole truth. I should believe everything she told me, I shouldn't listen to what anybody else said, and I should never mention the matter again. Now, do as I tell you, and you'll be a happy man tomorrow, and for the rest of your life. [*Pause.*]

GILBERT [*looks at* LADY JESSICA]: No. [SIR CHRISTOPHER *shrugs his shoulders.*] I came here for an explanation, and I won't go till I've got it.

LADY R.: My dear Gilbert, we're patiently waiting to give you an explanation, if you'll only listen to it. Dolly, do tell him how it all happened, and let him see what a donkey he is making of himself.

DOLLY: Yes, Gilbert, I wish you wouldn't get in these awful tempers. You frighten us so that in a very little while we shan't know whether we're speaking the truth, or whether we're not.

GILBERT: Go on!

DOLLY: Jess and I had arranged to have a little *tête-à-tête* dinner at Shepperford and talk over old times, all by our two selves [COKE *gets very uncomfortable*]—hadn't we, Jess? Rosy, you heard us arranging it all?

LADY R.: Yes, on the last night you were at our place.

DOLLY: Yes. Well, Jess got there first and then Mr. Falkner happened to come into the room, and then George happened to come in and wouldn't wait to listen to Jess's explanation, would he, Jess? Well, when I got there, I found Jess in strong hysterics, poor old dear! I couldn't get her round for ever so long. And as soon as she was better she came straight up to town. And that's all. [*Pause.*]

GILBERT: And what did you do?

DOLLY [*very nervous*]: I came up to town too.

GILBERT: Without any dinner?

DOLLY: No—I—

GILBERT: Where did you dine?

DOLLY: I didn't really dine anywhere—not to say dine. I had some cold chicken and a little tongue when I got home. [*Pause.*] And a tomato salad.

COKE [*very much shocked at* DOLLY]: Oh, of all the—

[SIR CHRISTOPHER *nudges him to be quiet.*]

GILBERT: Coke, what do you know of this?

COKE: Well—I know what Dolly has just told you.

GILBERT: You allow your wife to dine out alone?

COKE: Yes—yes—on certain occasions.

GILBERT: And you knew of this arrangement?

COKE: Yes—at least, no—not before she told me of it. But after she told me, I did know.

GEORGE: But Jessica said that she expected a small party.

DOLLY: I was the small party.

GILBERT [*to* COKE]: What time did Dolly get home last evening?

COKE: Eh? Well, about—

DOLLY: A little before nine.

GEORGE: Impossible! I was at Shepperford after half-past seven. If Lady Jessica had hys-

terics, and you stayed with her, you could scarcely have reached Kensington before nine.

DOLLY: Well, perhaps it was ten. Yes, it was ten.

GILBERT: Coke, were you at home last evening when your wife got back?

COKE: I? No—yes, yes—no—not precisely.

GILBERT [*growing indignant*]: Surely you must know whether you were at home or not when you wife returned?

COKE: No, I don't. And I very much object to be cross-questioned in this manner. I've told you all I know, and—I—I withdraw from the whole business. Now, Dolly, are you ready?

GILBERT: No, stop! I want to get at the bottom of this and I will. [*Coming furiously to* LADY JESSICA.] Once more, will you give me your version of this cock-and-bull story?

[*Enter* FOOTMAN.]

FOOTMAN [*announcing*]: Mr. Falkner!

GILBERT: Ah!

SIR C.: Nepean! Nepean! Control yourself!

[*Enter* FALKNER. *Exit* FOOTMAN.]

GILBERT: Let me be, Deering. [*Going to* FALKNER.] You were at Shepperford last evening. My wife was there with you?

FALKNER: I was at Shepperford last evening. Lady Jessica was there. She was dining with Lady Rosamund—

LADY R.: No! No!

GILBERT: Lady Jessica was dining with Lady Rosamund?

FALKNER: I understood her to

say so, did I not, Lady Rosamund?

LADY R.: No! No! It was Mrs. Coke who was dining with Lady Jessica.

FALKNER: Then I misunderstood you. Does it matter?

GILBERT: Yes. I want to know what the devil you were doing there?

SIR C.: Nepean! Nepean!

GILBERT: Do you hear? What the devil were you doing there? Will you tell me, or—

[*Trying to get at* FALKNER, SIR CHRISTOPHER *holds him back.*]

LADY J. [*rises very quietly*]: Mr. Falkner, tell my husband the truth.

FALKNER: But, Lady Jessica—

LADY J.: Yes, if you please—the truth, the whole truth, and nothing but the truth. Tell him all. I wish it.

GILBERT: You hear what she says. Now then, the truth—and be damned to you!

FALKNER [*looks around, then after a pause, with great triumph*]: I love Lady Jessica with all my heart and soul! I asked her to come to me at Shepperford last evening. She came. Your brother saw us and left us. The next moment Lady Rosamund came, and she had scarcely gone when the maid came with your telegram and took Lady Jessica back to town. If you think there was anything more on your wife's side than a passing folly and amusement at my expense, you will wrong her. If you think there is anything less on my side than the deepest, deepest, deepest love and worship, you will wrong me. Understand this. She is guiltless. Be sure of that. And now you've got the truth, and be damned to *you*. [*Goes to door at back—turns.*] If you want me, you know where to find me. [*To* LADY JESSICA.] Lady Jessica, I am at your service—always! [*Exit at back. They all look at each other.*]

SIR C. [*very softly to himself*]: Possibility number two—with a vengeance!

CURTAIN

ACT FOUR

SCENE: *Drawing-room in* SIR CHRISTOPHER'S *flat in Victoria Street. Left at back a large recess, taking up half the stage. The right half is taken up by an inner room furnished as library and smoking-room. Curtains dividing library from drawing-room. Door up stage, left. A table down stage, right. The room is in great confusion, with portmanteau open, clothes, etc., scattered over the floor; articles which an officer going to Central Africa might want are lying about.*

[TIME: *night, about half-past nine o'clock.*]

[SIR CHRISTOPHER *and* TAPLIN *are busy packing. Ring at door.*]

SIR C.: See who it is, Taplin; and come back and finish packing the moment I am disengaged.

[*Exit* TAPLIN. *He re-enters in a few moments, showing in* BEA-TRICE *in evening dress.* SIR CHRISTOPHER *goes to her, and shakes hands cordially. Exit* TAPLIN.]

BEA.: I was out dining when you called. But I got your message and I came on at once.

SIR C.: I couldn't wait. I had to come back and pack. [*Going on with his packing.*] I haven't one half-moment to spare.

BEA.: When do you start?

SIR C.: Tomorrow morning. It's very urgent. I've been at the War Office all the afternoon. You'll excuse my going on with this. I've three most important duties to fulfil tonight.

BEA.: What are they?

SIR C. [*packing*]: I've got to pack. I've got to persuade Ned to come out there with me—if I can. And I've got [*looking straight at her*] to make you promise to be my wife when I come home again.

BEA.: Oh, Kit, you know what I've told you so often!

SIR C. [*packing always*]: Yes, and you're telling it me again, and wasting my time when every moment is gold. Ah, dear, forgive me, you know I think you're worth the wooing. And you know I'm the man to woo you. And you know I'm ready to spend three, five, seven, four-teen, or twenty-one years in winning you. But if you'd only say "Yes" this minute, and let me pack and see Ned, you'd save me such a lot of trouble. And I'll do all the lovemaking when I come back.

BEA.: Where is Ned?

SIR C.: Playing the fool for Lady Jessica. There never was but one woman in this world that was worth playing the fool for, and I'm playing the fool for her. I've sent for Ned to come here. That's a digression. Come back to brass-tacks. You'll be my wife when I come home?

BEA.: Let me think it over, Kit.

SIR C.: No. You've had plenty of time for that. I can't allow you to think it over any longer.

BEA.: But it means so much to me. Let me write to you out there.

SIR C. [*very determinedly*]: No. [*Leaves his packing, takes out his watch.*] It's a little too bad of you when I'm so pressed. Now, I can only give you five minutes, and it must absolutely be fixed up in that time. [*With great tenderness and passion.*] Come, my dear, dear chum, what makes you hesitate to give yourself to me? You want me to come well out of this, don't you?

BEA.: You know I do!

SIR C.: Then you don't love your country if you won't have me. Once give me your promise, and it will give me the pluck of fifty men! Don't you know if I'm sure of you I shall carry everything before me?

BEA.: Will you? Will you? But if you were to die—

SIR C.: I won't die if you're waiting to be my wife when I come home. And you will? You will? I won't hear anything but "Yes."

You shan't move one inch till you've said "Yes." Now! say it! Say "Yes!" Say "Yes"—do you hear?

BEA. [*throwing herself into his arms*]: Yes! Yes! Yes! Take me! Take me!

SIR C. [*kissing her very reverently*]: My wife when I come home again.

[*A pause.*]

BEA.: You know, Kit, I can love very deeply.

SIR C.: And so you shall, when I come home again. And so will I when I come home again. [*Looking at his watch.*] A minute and a quarter! I must get on with my packing.

BEA.: Kit, there will be some nursing and other woman's work out there?

SIR C.: Yes, I suppose—

BEA.: I'll come with you.

SIR C.: Very well. How long will it take you to pack?

BEA.: Half an hour.

SIR C.: All right! I must wait here for Ned. Come back and have some supper by-and-by.

BEA.: Yes—in half an hour.

SIR C.: We might be married at Cairo—on our way out?

BEA.: Just as you please.

SIR C.: Or before we start tomorrow morning?

BEA.: Will there be time?

SIR C.: Oh, I'll make time.

[*Enter* TAPLIN.]

TAPLIN: Mr. Gilbert Nepean is below, Sir Christopher.

SIR C. [*glancing at his packing*]: Show him up, Taplin.

[*Exit* TAPLIN.]

SIR C. [*holding* BEATRICE'S *hand*]: Tomorrow morning, then?

BEA.: Yes, I've given you some trouble to win me, Kit?

SIR C.: No more than you're worth.

BEA.: I'll give you none now you have won me.

[*Enter* TAPLIN.]

TAPLIN [*announcing*]: Mr. Gilbert Nepean.

[*Enter* GILBERT NEPEAN. *Exit* TAPLIN.]

BEA.: How d'ye do?

GILBERT: How d'ye do? [*Shaking hands.*]

BEA.: And good-bye. [*To* SIR CHRISTOPHER.] No, I won't have you come down all those stairs, indeed I won't. Au revoir. [*Exit.*]

GILBERT: Excuse my coming at this hour.

SIR C.: I'm rather pressed. What can I do for you?

GILBERT: I have been down to Shepperford this afternoon. It seems you dined there last evening.

SIR C.: I did.

GILBERT: I want to get all the evidence.

SIR C.: What for?

GILBERT: To guide me in my future action. Deering, I trust you. Can I take that fellow's word that my wife is guiltless?

SIR C.: I'm sure you can.

GILBERT: How do you know?

SIR C.: Because he'd give his head to tell you that she is not.

GILBERT: Why?

SIR C.: It would give him the chance he is waiting for—to take her off your hands.

GILBERT: Take her off my hands —he's waiting for that?

SIR C.: Don't you see he is? And don't you see that you're doing your best to make him successful?

GILBERT: How?

SIR C.: Don't think when you've married a woman that you can sit down and neglect her. You can't. You've married one of the most charming women in London, and when a man has married a charming woman, if he doesn't continue to make love to her some other man will. Such are the sad ways of humankind! How have you treated Lady Jessica?

GILBERT: But do you suppose I will allow my wife to go out dining with otheɪ men?

SIR C.: The best way to avoid that is to take her out to dinner yourself—and to give her a good one. Have you dined tonight?

GILBERT: Dined? No! I can't dine till I know what to believe.

SIR C.: The question is, what do you want to believe? If you want to believe her innocent, take the facts as they stand. If you want to believe her guilty, continue to treat her as you are doing, and you'll very soon have plenty of proof. And let me tell you, nobody will pity you. Do you want to believe her innocent?

GILBERT: Of course I do.

SIR C.: Where is she?

GILBERT.: I don't know—at home, I suppose.

SIR C.: Go home to her—don't say one word about what has happened, and invite her out to the very best dinner that London can provide.

GILBERT: But after she has acted as she has done?

SIR C.: My dear fellow, she's only a woman. I never met but one woman that was worth taking seriously. What are they? A kind of children, you know. Humour them, play with them, buy them the toys they cry for, but don't get angry with them. They're not worth it, except one! Now I must get on with my packing.

[SIR CHRISTOPHER *sets to work packing.* GILBERT *walks up and down the room, biting his nails, deliberating.* GILBERT, *after a moment or two, speaks.*]

GILBERT: Perhaps you're right, Deering.

SIR C.: Oh, I know I am!

GILBERT: I'll go to her.

SIR C. [*busy packing*]: Make haste, or you may be too late.

[GILBERT *goes to door. At that moment enter* TAPLIN.]

TAPLIN [*announcing*]: Mr. Falkner!

[*Enter* FALKNER. *Exit* TAPLIN. GILBERT *and* FALKNER *stand for a moment looking at each other. Exit* GILBERT; FALKNER *looks after him.*]

SIR C.: Well?

FALKNER [*very elated*]: You want to see me?

SIR C.: Yes. You seem excited.

FALKNER: I've had some good news.

SIR C.: What?

FALKNER: The best. She loves me.

SIR C.: You've seen her?

FALKNER: No.

SIR C.: Written to her?

FALKNER: Yes. I've just had this answer. [*Taking out letter.*]

SIR C.: Where is she?

FALKNER: Still at her sister's. [*Reading.*] "I shall never forget the words you spoke this morning. You were right in saying that your love would not be wasted. I have learned at last what it is worth. You said you would be at my service always. Do not write again. Wait till you hear from me, and the moment I send for you, come to me." I knew I should win her at last, and I shall!

SIR C.: Après?

FALKNER: What does it matter? If I can persuade her I shall take her out to Africa with me.

SIR C.: Africa! Nonsense! There's only one woman in the world that's any use in that part of the globe, and I'm taking her out myself.

FALKNER: Beatrice.

SIR C.: We are to be married to-morrow morning.

FALKNER: I congratulate you—with all my heart. [*Shaking hands warmly.*]

SIR C.: Thank you. [*Pause.*] You'll come with us, Ned?

FALKNER: If she will come too.

SIR C.: Oh, we can't have her.

FALKNER: Why not?

SIR C.: In the first place, she'd be very much in the way. In the second place—it's best to be frank—Lady Deering will not recognize Lady Jessica.

FALKNER: Very well. [*Turns on heel.*] Good-night, Kit! [*Very curtly.*]

SIR C.: No. Ned, you're still up that everlasting *cul-de-sac*—playing the lover to a married woman, and I've got to drag you out of it.

FALKNER: It's no use, Kit. My mind is made up. Let me go.

SIR C.: To the devil with Lady Jessica? No, I'm going to stop you.

FALKNER: Ah, you'll stop me! How?

SIR C.: There was a time when one whisper would have done it. [*Whispers.*] Duty. You know that you're the only man who can treat peaceably with the chiefs. You know that your going out may save hundreds, perhaps thousands of lives.

FALKNER: I'm not sure of that.

SIR C.: You're not sure? Well then, try it—put it to the test. But you know there's every chance. You know the whole country is waiting for you to declare yourself. You know that you have a splendid chance of putting the crown on your life's work, and you know that if you don't seize it, it will be because you stay here skulking after her!

FALKNER: Skulking!

SIR C.: What do you call it? What will everybody call it? Ned, you've faced the most horrible death day after day for months. You've done some of the bravest things out there that have been done by any Englishman in this generation; but if you turn tail now there's only one word will fit you to the end of your days, and that word is "Coward!"

FALKNER: Coward!

SIR C.: Coward! And there's only one epitaph to be written on you by-and-by—"Sold his honour, his fame, his country, his duty, his conscience, his all, for a petticoat!"

FALKNER: Very well, then, when I die, write that over me. I tell you this, Kit, if I can only win her—and I shall, I shall, I feel it—she'll leave that man and come to me; and then!—I don't care one snap of the fingers if Africa is swept bare of humanity from Cairo to Cape Town, and from Teneriffe to Zanzibar! Now argue with me after that!

SIR C.: Argue with you? Not I! But I wish there was some way of kidnapping fools into sense and reason and locking them up there for the rest of their lives.

[*Enter* TAPLIN.]

TAPLIN [*announcing*]: Lady Jessica Nepean, Lady Rosamund Tatton.

[*Enter* LADY JESSICA *and* LADY ROSAMUND. *Exit* TAPLIN. LADY JESSICA *shows delighted surprise at seeing* FALKNER, *goes to him cordially.* LADY ROSAMUND *tries to stop* LADY JESSICA *from going to* FALKNER.]

LADY J. [*to* FALKNER]: I didn't expect to find you here.

FALKNER: I am waiting for you.

LADY R. [*interposing*]: No, Jess, no. Sir Christopher! [*Aside to him.*] Help me to get her away from him.

[LADY JESSICA *and* FALKNER *are talking vigorously together.*]

SIR C.: One moment. Perhaps we may as well get this little matter fixed up here and now. [*Takes out watch, looking ruefully at his packing.*] Lady Jessica, may I ask what has happened since I left you this morning?

LADY J.: Nothing. My husband went away in a rage. I've stayed with Rosy all day.

LADY R.: We've been talking it all over.

LADY J.: Oh, we've been talking it all over—[*gesture*]—and over and over, till I'm thoroughly —seasick of it!

LADY R.: And so I persuaded her to come and talk it over with you.

SIR C. [*glancing at his packing, to* LADY JESSICA]: You can't arrive at a decision?

LADY J.: Oh, yes, I can; only Rosy won't let me act on it.

LADY R.: I should think not.

SIR C.: What is your decision?

LADY J.: I don't mind for myself. I feel that everything is in a glorious muddle, and I don't care how I get out of it, or whether I get out of it at all.

SIR C.: But on the whole the best way of getting out of it is to run away with Mr. Falkner?

LADY J.: Mr. Falkner has behaved splendidly to me.

SIR C.: He has! He's a brick! And I'm quite sure that in proposing to ruin your reputation, and make you miserable for life, he is actuated by the very best intentions.

LADY J.: I don't care whether I'm happy or miserable for the rest of my life.

SIR C.: You don't care now, but you will tomorrow and next week, and next year, and all the years after.

LADY J.: No, I shan't! I won't!

FALKNER: I'll take care, Lady

Jessica, that you never regret this step. Your mind is quite made up?

LADY J.: Yes, quite.

FALKNER: Then no more be said.

[*Offering arm. Gesture of despair from* LADY ROSAMUND. SIR CHRISTOPHER *soothes her.*]

SIR C.: One moment, Ned! [*Takes out his watch, looks ruefully at his packing, half aside.*] Good Lord! when shall I get on with my packing? [*Puts watch in pocket, faces* FALKNER *and* LADY JESSICA *very resolutely.*] Now! I've nothing to say in the abstract against running away with another man's wife! There may be planets where it is not only the highest ideal morality, but where it has the further advantage of being a practical way of carrying on society. But it has this one fatal defect in our country—it won't work! You know what we English are, Ned. We're not a bit better than our neighbours, but, thank God! we do pretend we are, and we do make it hot for anybody who disturbs that holy pretence. And take my word for it, my dear Lady Jessica, my dear Ned, it won't work. You know it's not an original experiment you're making. It has been tried before. Have you ever known it to be successful? Lady Jessica, think of the brave pioneers who have gone before you in this enterprise. They've all perished, and their bones whiten the antimatrimonial shore. Think of them! Charley Gray and Lady Rideout—flitting shabbily about the Continent at cheap *table d'hôtes* and gambling clubs, rubbing shoulders with all the blackguards and demimondaines of Europe. Poor old Fitz and his beauty—moping down at Farnhurst, cut by the county, with no single occupation except to nag and rag each other to pieces from morning to night. Billy Dover and Polly Atchison—

LADY J. [*indignant*]: Well!

SIR C.: —cut in for fresh partners in three weeks. That old idiot, Sir Bonham Dancer—paid five thousand pounds damages for being saddled with the professional strong man's wife. George Nuneham and Mrs. Sandys—George is conducting a tramcar in New York, and Mrs. Sandys—Lady Jessica, you knew Mrs. Sandys, a delicate, sweet little creature, I've met her at your house—she drank herself to death, and died in a hospital. Not encouraging, is it? Marriage may be disagreeable, it may be unprofitable, it may be ridiculous; but it isn't as bad as that! And do you think the experiment is going to be successful in *your case?* Not a bit of it! No. Ned, hear me out. [*Turns to* LADY JESSICA.] First of all, there will be the shabby scandal and dirty business of the divorce court. You won't like that. It isn't nice! You won't like it. After the divorce court, what is Ned to do with you? Take you to Africa? I do implore you, if you hope for any happiness in that state to which it is pleasing Falkner and Providence to call you, I do implore you, don't go out to Africa with him. You'd never stand the climate and the hardships, and you'd bore each other to death in a week. But if you don't go out to Africa, what are you to do? Stay in England, in society? Everybody will cut you. Take a place in the country? Think of poor old Fitz down at Farnhurst! Go abroad? Think of Charley Gray and Lady Rideout. Take any of the other dozen alternatives and find yourself stranded in some shady hole or corner, with the one solitary hope and ambition of somehow wriggling back into respectability. That's your side of it, Lady Jessica. As for Ned here, what is to become of him? [*Angry gesture from* FALKNER.] Yes, Ned, I know you don't want to hear, but I'm going to finish. Turn away your head. This is for Lady Jessica. He's at the height of his career, with a great and honourable task in front of him. If you turn him aside you'll not only wreck and ruin your own life and reputation, but you'll wreck and ruin his. You won't! You won't! His interests, his duty, his honour all lie out there. If you care for him, don't keep him shuffling and malingering here. Send him out with me to finish his work like the good, splendid fellow he is. Set him free, Lady Jessica, and go back to your home. Your husband has been here. He's sorry for what is past, and he has promised to treat you more kindly in the future. He's waiting at home to take you out. You missed a very good dinner last night. Don't miss another tonight. I never saw a man in a better temper than your husband. Go to him, and do, once for all, have done with this other folly. Do believe me, my dear Ned, my dear Lady Jessica, before it is too late, do believe me, it won't work, it won't work, it won't work! [*A little pause.*]

LADY J.: I think you're the most horrid man I ever met!

SIR C.: Because I've told you the truth.

LADY J.: Yes, that's the worst of it! It is the truth.

LADY R.: It's exactly what I've been telling her all the afternoon.

FALKNER: Lady Jessica, I want to speak to you alone.

LADY J.: What's the use? We've got to part.

FALKNER: No! No!

LADY J.: Yes, my friend. I won't ruin your career. We've got to part: and the fewer words the better.

FALKNER: I can't give you up.

LADY J.: You must! Perhaps it's best. You can always cherish your fancy portrait of me, and you'll never find out how very unlike me it is. And I shall read about you in the newspapers and be very proud—and—come along, Rosy!

[*Going off.* FALKNER *is going after her.*]

SIR C. [*stopping him*]: It can answer no purpose, Ned.

FALKNER: What the devil has it got to do with you? You've taken her from me. Leave her to me for a few minutes. Lady Jessica, I claim to speak to you alone.

LADY J.: It can only be to say "Good-bye."

FALKNER: I'll never say it.

LADY J.: Then I must. Good-bye!
FALKNER: No—say it to me alone.
LADY J.: It can only be that—no more—
FALKNER: Say it to me alone. [*Pointing to curtains.*]
LADY J.: Rosy, wait for me. I won't be a minute.

[*Going to* FALKNER. LADY ROSAMUND *makes a little movement to stop her.* SIR CHRISTOPHER *by a gesture silences* LADY ROSAMUND *and allows* LADY JESSICA *to pass through the curtains where* FALKNER *has preceded her.*]

SIR C. [*to* LADY JESSICA]. Remember his future is at stake as well as yours. Only the one word.
LADY J. [*as she passes through curtains*]: Only the one word.
SIR C. [*to* LADY ROSAMUND]: You'll excuse my packing. I've not a moment to waste.

[*Enter* TAPLIN.]

TAPLIN: Mr. Gilbert Nepean, Sir Christopher; he says he must see you.
SIR C.: You didn't say Lady Jessica was here?
TAPLIN: No, Sir Christopher.
SIR C.: I'll come to him.

[*Exit* TAPLIN. LADY ROSAMUND *passes between the curtains.* SIR CHRISTOPHER *is going to door, meets* GILBERT NEPEAN *who enters very excitedly.*]

GILBERT [*off left*]: Deering! Deering, she's not at home! She's not at her sister's. You don't think she has gone to that fellow?
SIR C.: Make yourself easy. She is coming back to you.
GILBERT: Where is she?

SIR C.: Will you let me take a message to her? May I tell her that for the future you will treat her with every kindness and consideration?
GILBERT: Yes—yes. Say—oh—tell her what you please. Say I know I've behaved like a bear. Tell her I'm sorry, and if she'll come home I'll do my best to make her happy in future.
SIR C.: And [*taking out watch*] it's rather too late for dinner, may I suggest an invitation to supper?
GILBERT: Yes—yes.
SIR C.: Lady Rosamund—[*Calls.*]

[LADY ROSAMUND *enters.*]

GILBERT: You—

[*Going towards curtains.* SIR CHRISTOPHER *intercepts him.*]

LADY R.: We stepped over to ask Sir Christopher's advice.
SIR C.: And, strange to say, they've taken it.
GILBERT [*trying to get to curtains*]: Where is Jessica?
SIR C. [*stopping him*]: No. I'm to take the message. Lady Jessica, your husband is waiting to take you to supper. You've only just time to go home and dress.

[LADY JESSICA *draws curtains aside, turns and throws a last agonized adieu to* FALKNER, *who stands speechless and helpless.* LADY JESSICA *then controls her features and comes out to* GILBERT. *The curtains close.*]

GILBERT: Will you come home and dress and go to the Savoy to supper? [*Offering arm.*]
LADY J.: Delighted. [*Taking his arm.*]

GILBERT: And you, Rosy?

LADY R.: I can't. [*Looking at watch.*] It's nearly ten o'clock! Good-night, Sir Christopher. Good-night, dearest. [*Kissing* LADY JESSICA.] Good-night, Gilbert. Take care of her, or you'll lose her. Excuse my running away, I must get back to my poor old Freddie.

[*Exit* LADY ROSAMUND. FALKNER'S *face appears through the curtains.* LADY JESSICA *sees it.*]

SIR C.: Good-night, Lady Jessica, and good-bye!

LADY J.: Good-night, Sir Christopher, and—[*at* FALKNER] one last "Good-bye."

[*She looks towards curtains as if about to break away from* GILBERT *and go to* FALKNER.]

SIR C.: Good-night, Nepean!

GILBERT: Good-night, Deering.

SIR C.: Try and keep her. She's worth the keeping.

GILBERT: I'll try.

[*Exeunt* LADY JESSICA *and* GILBERT. SIR CHRISTOPHER *goes towards door with them;* FALKNER *comes forward in great despair from curtains, throws himself into chair against table, buries his face in his hands.*]

SIR C. [*goes to him very affectionately*]: Come! Come! My dear old Ned! This will never do! And all for a woman! They're not worth it. [*Aside, softly.*] Except one! They're not worth it. Come, buckle on your courage! There's work in front of you, and fame, and honour! And I must take you out and bring you back with flying colours! Come! Come! My dear old fellow!

FALKNER: Let me be for a minute, Kit. Let me be!

[*Enter* BEATRICE. SIR CHRISTOPHER *goes to her.*]

BEA.: What's the matter?

SIR C.: Hush! Poor old chap! He's hard hit! Everybody else seems to be making a great mess of their love affairs. We won't make a mess of ours!

BEA.: No. You'll get over this, Ned! We'll help you. You'll get over it!

FALKNER [*rising with great determination*]: Yes, I shall pull round. I'll try! I'll try! Tomorrow, Kit! We start tomorrow?

SIR C. [*putting one arm round each affectionately*]: Tomorrow! My wife! My friend! My two comrades!

CURTAIN

Sir Arthur Wing Pinero
[1855-1934]

Arthur Pinero was born at Islington on May 24, 1855. His father was a solicitor and when his business fell off, Pinero was obliged to work in his father's office. As a result, his education was scanty and often interrupted; he did most of his reading by himself in the office and, chiefly because it was the usual course for a solicitor's son to follow, he bound himself to the law at the age of ten. However, he was interested in being an actor, and by the time he was nineteen, he had become the handyman for a stock company in Edinburgh. He remained with this company for five years, and eventually acted supporting roles, but he came to realize that he would never be a first-rate actor and in 1884 he ceased to act. His acting experience had taught him much about the mechanics of stagecraft and what was theatrically effective. He had, in 1877 at the age of twenty-two, begun to write and after he gave up acting, he wrote in earnest. In fifty-five years he wrote fifty-four plays, plays of every sort. His experience of the law had brought him to see society in terms of lust, greed, and revenge, and he always wrote of these human weaknesses from a somewhat cynical point of view. The turning point in his career came with the production of *The Money Spinner* (1881). It concerned gamblers, and not one character was without fault—even the heroine cheated. However, while Pinero was not sentimental in his treatment of theme, neither was he a reformer. His next success, *Imprudence*

(1881), concerned ill-natured, selfish people, and was written in the same cynical spirit.

Now that he was financially secure, he was able, in 1883 after four years of persistent wooing, to marry an actress, Myra Holme, who had been previously married and had one daughter. Although they had no children, Pinero was always very fond of his stepdaughter.

When Pinero was thirty, he suddenly realized that the temper of society was sentimental; and so he temporarily abandoned his cynicism and set himself to write comedies that emphasized the foibles of his characters. The action resulting from these foibles—rather than dialogue—created the humor. He wrote four such farces, all extremely successful, between 1885 and 1892. But Pinero was wise enough to perceive that the public would tire of this, and consequently wrote *The Profligate,* which dealt with the double standard, a topic heretofore avoided, and *Lady Bountiful* (1891), which concerned a love affair between a woman of wealth and a man who must earn his living—both imbued with his earlier cynicism. In 1893 he wrote *The Second Mrs. Tanqueray,* another of the domestic problem plays that Jones was also writing. But the then powerful actor-managers refused it, believing the public would not accept it. Finally, when Pat Campbell, a brilliant young actress, was persuaded to act the lead, it was produced, and to everyone's amazement was an overwhelming success. From then on Pinero used a formula involving three main characters: a luxury-loving woman, and two men, one who sympathizes with the woman, the other a liberal. These three he was to use over and over, simply changing the plot, maintaining the woman's character as the center of interest, as in *The Notorious Mrs. Ebbsmith,* Pinero's favorite of all his plays.

Pinero had the reputation for being a kind man—only when casting was he ruthless. He knew precisely whom he wanted for each part and would accept no substitute. He began the practice of casting plays to type, that is, putting actors in parts to which they were suited by appearance and manner. He believed that to expect one actor to be versatile enough to play a wide range of parts was to expect too much.

Although he was not as fiery-tempered as Henry A. Jones,

and avoided speaking in public, he also pioneered for a more realistic kind of play, for honest characterization and motivation. He was reticent and rather stoical, and did not involve himself violently as did Jones. He died in London on November 23, 1934.

When *The Second Mrs. Tanqueray* opened at the St. James Theatre, London, in 1893, it was an immediate success. Sir Herbert Beerbohm Tree had given the script to his brother Max to read and criticize. Max didn't like the play and advised his brother not to produce it. Sir Herbert, more keenly attuned to the demands of the popular theatre, ignored that advice and came up with a theatrical success. With Mrs. Patrick Campbell as Paula, the play had a rather long run—from May 27 to July 28. It was then taken to the provinces, and opened in New York in October of the same year. Mrs. Campbell revived it in Chicago, December 30, 1901, and it has often been revived since. Eleanora Duse played Paula in an Italian production.

In this play Pinero sets himself a genuinely challenging domestic problem: Is it possible for a woman of the lower classes and with a disreputable past to make a successful marriage with a man of high position and respectability? There is, as Shaw complains in his review of the printed play, rather obtrusive expository machinery in Act I. But Pinero does draw believable characters within believable situations. The crucial test comes when we are to see Paula Tanqueray as a sympathetic human being caught within an unsympathetic circumstance. That moment occurs in Act III, when Paula under Aubrey's questioning is made to face her two selves—the innately good person and the woman with a past. Here, as Shaw suggests, she should have remained true to her valid self, but instead, Pinero has the character and the play take a conventional turn. The original, authentic challenge disappears and the character and the play show that a woman of her sort is not capable of living the good life of the respectable classes.

PRINCIPAL DRAMATIC WORKS

Two Hundred a Year, 1877
The Money Spinner, 1881
The Magistrate, 1885
The Schoolmistress, 1886
Dandy Dick, 1887
Sweet Lavender, 1888
The Profligate, 1889
The Amazons, 1893
The Second Mrs. Tanqueray, 1893

The Notorious Mrs. Ebbsmith, 1895
Trelawney of the "Wells," 1898
The Gay Lord Quex, 1899
Iris, 1901
Letty, 1903
His House in Order, 1906
The Thunderbolt, 1908
Mid-Channel, 1909

The Second Mrs. Tanqueray

A PLAY IN FOUR ACTS

PERSONS

Aubrey Tanqueray
Paula
Ellean
Cayley Drummle
Mrs. Cortelyon
Captain Hugh Ardale
Gordon Jayne, M.D.
Frank Misquith, Q.C., M.P.
Sir George Orreyed, Bart.
Lady Orreyed
Morse

SCENE

The Present Day

The Scene of Act One is laid at MR. TANQUERAY'S
*rooms, No. 2 x, the Albany, in the month of November;
the occurrences of the succeeding Acts take place at his
house, "Highercoombe," near Willowmere, Surrey, during the early part of the following year.*

ACT ONE

AUBREY TANQUERAY'S *Chambers in the Albany—a richly and tastefully decorated room, elegantly and luxuriously furnished: on the right a large pair of doors opening into another room; on the left at the further end of the room a small door leading to a bed-chamber. A circular table is laid for a dinner for four persons, which has now reached the stage of dessert and coffee. Everything in the apartment suggests wealth and refinement. The fire is burning brightly.*

[AUBREY TANQUERAY, MISQUITH, *and* JAYNE *are seated at the dinner-table.* AUBREY *is forty-two, handsome, winning in manner, his speech and bearing retaining some of the qualities of young manhood.* MISQUITH *is about forty-seven, genial and portly.* JAYNE *is a year or two* MISQUITH'S *senior, soft-speaking and precise—in appearance a type of the prosperous town physician.* MORSE, AUBREY'S *servant, places a little cabinet of cigars and the spirit-lamp on the table beside* AUBREY *and goes out.*]

MISQUITH: Aubrey, it is a pleasant yet dreadful fact to contemplate, but it's nearly fifteen years since I first dined with you. You lodged in Piccadilly in those days, over a hatshop. Jayne, I met you at that dinner, and Cayley Drummle.

JAYNE: Yes, yes. What a pity it is that Cayley isn't here tonight.

AUBREY: Confound the old gossip! His empty chair has been staring us in the face all through dinner. I ought to have told Morse to take it away.

MISQUITH: Odd, his sending no excuse.

AUBREY: I'll walk round to his lodgings later on and ask after him.

MISQUITH: I'll go with you.

JAYNE: So will I.

AUBREY [*opening the cigar-cabinet*]: Doctor, it's useless to tempt you, I know. Frank—[MISQUITH *and* AUBREY *smoke.*] I particularly wished Cayley Drummle to be one of us tonight. You two fellows and Cayley are my closest, my best friends—

MISQUITH: My dear Aubrey!

JAYNE: I rejoice to hear you say so.

AUBREY: And I wanted to see the three of you round this table. You can't guess the reason.

MISQUITH: You desired to give

us a most excellent dinner.

JAYNE: Obviously.

AUBREY [*hesitatingly*]: Well—I—[*glancing at the clock*]—Cayley won't turn up now.

JAYNE: H'm, hardly.

AUBREY: Then you two shall hear it. Doctor, Frank, this is the last time we are to meet in these rooms.

JAYNE: The last time?

MISQUITH: You're going to leave the Albany?

AUBREY: Yes. You've heard me speak of a house I built in the country years ago, haven't you?

MISQUITH: In Surrey.

AUBREY: Well, when my wife died I cleared out of that house and let it. I think of trying the place again.

MISQUITH: But you'll go raving mad if ever you find yourself down there alone.

AUBREY: Ah, but I sha'n't be alone, and that's what I wanted to tell you. I'm going to be married.

JAYNE: Going to be married?

MISQUITH: Married?

AUBREY: Yes—tomorrow.

JAYNE: Tomorrow?

MISQUITH: You take my breath away! My dear fellow, I—I—of course, I congratulate you.

JAYNE: And—and—so do I—heartily.

AUBREY: Thanks—thanks.

[*There is a moment or two of embarrassment.*]

MISQUITH: Er—ah—this is an excellent cigar.

JAYNE: Ah—um—your coffee is remarkable.

AUBREY: Look here; I dare say you two old friends think this treatment very strange, very unkind. So I want you to understand me. You know a marriage often cools friendships. What's the usual course of things? A man's engagement is given out, he is congratulated, complimented upon his choice; the church is filled with troops of friends, and he goes away happily to a chorus of good wishes. He comes back, sets up house in town or country, and thinks to resume the old associations, the old companionships. My dear Frank, my dear good doctor, it's very seldom that it can be done. Generally, a worm has begun to eat its way into those hearty, unreserved, prenuptial friendships; a damnable constraint sets in and acts like a wasting disease; and so, believe me, in nine cases out of ten a man's marriage severs for him more close ties than it forms.

MISQUITH: Well, my dear Aubrey, I earnestly hope—

AUBREY: I know what you're going to say, Frank. I hope so, too. In the meantime let's face dangers. I've reminded you of the *usual* course of things, but my marriage isn't even the conventional sort of marriage likely to satisfy society. Now, Cayley's a bachelor, but you two men have wives. By-the-bye, my love to Mrs. Misquith and to Mrs. Jayne when you get home —don't forget that. Well, your wives may not—like—the lady I'm going to marry.

JAYNE: Aubrey, forgive me for suggesting that the lady you are going to marry may not like our wives—mine at least; I beg your pardon, Frank.

AUBREY: Quite so; then I must go the way my wife goes.

MISQUITH: Come, come, pray don't let us anticipate that either side will be called upon to make such a sacrifice.

AUBREY: Yes, yes, let us anticipate it. And let us make up our minds to have no slow bleeding-to-death of our friendship. We'll end a pleasant chapter here to-night, and after tonight start afresh. When my wife and I settle down at Willowmere it's possible that we shall all come together. But if this isn't to be, for Heaven's sake let us recognise that it is simply because it *can't* be, and not wear hypocritical faces and suffer and be wretched. Doctor, Frank—[*holding out his hands, one to* MISQUITH, *the other to* JAYNE]—good luck to all of us!

MISQUITH: But—but—do I understand we are to ask nothing? Not even the lady's name, Aubrey?

AUBREY: The lady, my dear Frank, belongs to the next chapter, and in that her name is Mrs. Aubrey Tanqueray.

JAYNE [*raising his coffee-cup*]: Then, in an old-fashioned way, I propose a toast. Aubrey, Frank, I give you "The Next Chapter!"

[*They drink the toast, saying, "The Next Chapter!"*]

AUBREY: Doctor, find a comfortable chair; Frank, you too. As we're going to turn out by-and-bye, let me scribble a couple of notes now while I think of them.

MISQUITH *and* JAYNE: Certainly—yes, yes.

AUBREY: It might slip my memory when I get back.

[AUBREY *sits at a writing-table at the other end of the room, and writes.*]

JAYNE [*to* MISQUITH *in a whisper*]: Frank— [MISQUITH *quietly leaves his chair, and sits nearer to* JAYNE.] What is all this? Simply a morbid crank of Aubrey's with regard to ante-nuptial acquaintances?

MISQUITH: H'm! Did you notice *one* expression he used?

JAYNE: Let me think—

MISQUITH: "My marriage is not even the conventional sort of marriage likely to satisfy society."

JAYNE: Bless me, yes! What does that suggest?

MISQUITH: That he has a particular rather than a general reason for anticipating estrangement from his friends, I'm afraid.

JAYNE: A horrible *mésalliance!* A dairymaid who has given him a glass of milk during a day's hunting, or a little anaemic shopgirl! Frank, I'm utterly wretched!

MISQUITH: My dear Jayne, speaking in absolute confidence, I have never been more profoundly depressed in my life.

[MORSE *enters.*]

MORSE [*announcing*]: Mr. Drummle.

[CAYLEY DRUMMLE *enters briskly.*

He is a neat little man of about five-and-forty, in manner bright, airy, debonair, but with an undercurrent of seriousness. MORSE *retires.*]

DRUMMLE: I'm in disgrace; nobody realises that more thoroughly than I do. Where's my host?

AUBREY [*who has risen*]: Cayley.

DRUMMLE [*shaking hands with him*]: Don't speak to me till I have tendered my explanation. A harsh word from anybody would unman me.

[MISQUITH *and* JAYNE *shake hands with* DRUMMLE.]

AUBREY: Have you dined?

DRUMMLE: No—unless you call a bit of fish, a cutlet, and a pancake dining.

AUBREY: Cayley, this is disgraceful.

JAYNE: Fish, a cutlet, and a pancake will require a great deal of explanation.

MISQUITH: Especially the pancake. My dear friend, your case looks miserably weak.

DRUMMLE: Hear me! hear me!

JAYNE: Now then!

MISQUITH: Come!

AUBREY: Well!

DRUMMLE: It so happens that tonight I was exceptionally early in dressing for dinner.

MISQUITH: For which dinner—the fish and cutlet?

DRUMMLE: For *this* dinner, of course—really, Frank! At a quarter to eight, in fact, I found myself trimming my nails, with ten minutes to spare. Just then, enter my man with a note—would I hasten, as fast as cab could carry me, to old Lady Orreyed in Bruton Street?—"sad trouble." Now, recollect, please, I had ten minutes on my hands, old Lady Orreyed was a very dear friend of my mother's, and was in some distress.

AUBREY: Cayley, come to the fish and cutlet!

MISQUITH *and* JAYNE: Yes, yes, and the pancake!

DRUMMLE: Upon my word! Well, the scene in Bruton Street beggars description; the women servants looked scared, the men drunk; and there was poor old Lady Orreyed on the floor of her boudoir like Queen Bess among her pillows.

AUBREY: What's the matter?

DRUMMLE [*to everybody*]: You know George Orreyed?

MISQUITH: Yes.

JAYNE: I've met him.

DRUMMLE: Well, he's a thing of the past.

AUBREY: Not dead!

DRUMMLE: Certainly, in the worst sense. He's married Mabel Hervey.

MISQUITH: What!

DRUMMLE: It's true—this morning. The poor mother showed me his letter—a dozen curt words, and some of those ill-spelt.

MISQUITH [*walking up to the fire-place*]: I'm very sorry.

JAYNE: Pardon my ignorance—who *was* Mabel Hervey?

DRUMMLE: You don't—? Oh, of course not. Miss Hervey—Lady Orreyed, as she now is—was a lady who would have been, perhaps has been, described in the reports of the Police or the Divorce Court as an actress.

Had she belonged to a lower stratum of our advanced civilisation she would, in the event of judicial inquiry, have defined her calling with equal justification as that of a dressmaker. To do her justice, she is a type of a class which is immortal. Physically, by the strange caprice of creation, curiously beautiful; mentally, she lacks even the strength of deliberate viciousness. Paint her portrait, it would symbolise a creature perfectly patrician; lance a vein of her superbly modelled arm, you would get the poorest *vin ordinaire!* Her affections, emotions, impulses, her very existence—a burlesque! Flaxen, five-and-twenty, and feebly frolicsome; anybody's, in less gentle society I should say everybody's, property! That, Doctor, was Miss Hervey who is the new Lady Orreyed. Dost thou like the picture?

MISQUITH: Very good, Cayley! Bravo!

AUBREY [*laying his hand on* DRUMMLE's *shoulder*]: You'd scarcely believe it, Jayne, but none of us really know anything about this lady, our gay young friend here, I suspect, least of all.

DRUMMLE: Aubrey, I applaud your chivalry.

AUBREY: And perhaps you'll let me finish a couple of letters which Frank and Jayne have given me leave to write. [*Returning to the writing-table.*] Ring for what you want, like a good fellow! [AUBREY *resumes his writing.*]

MISQUITH [*to* DRUMMLE]: Still,

the fish and cutlet remain unexplained.

DRUMMLE: Oh, the poor old woman was so weak that I insisted upon her taking some food, and felt there was nothing for it but to sit down opposite her. The fool! the blackguard!

MISQUITH: Poor Orreyed! Well, he's gone under for a time.

DRUMMLE: For a time! My dear Frank, I tell you he has absolutely ceased to be. [AUBREY, *who has been writing busily, turns his head towards the speakers and listens. His lips are set, and there is a frown upon his face.*] For all practical purposes you may regard him as the late George Orreyed. Tomorrow the very characteristics of his speech, as we remember them, will have become obsolete.

JAYNE: But surely, in the course of years, he and his wife will outlive—

DRUMMLE: No, no, Doctor, don't try to upset one of my settled beliefs. You may dive into many waters, but there is *one* social Dead Sea—!

JAYNE: Perhaps you're right.

DRUMMLE: Right! Good God! I wish you could prove me otherwise! Why, for years I've been sitting, and watching and waiting.

MISQUITH: You're in form tonight, Cayley. May we ask where you've been in the habit of squandering your useful leisure?

DRUMMLE: Where? On the shore of that same sea.

MISQUITH: And, pray, what have you been waiting for?

DRUMMLE: For some of my best friends *to come up*. [AUBREY

utters a half-stifled exclamation of impatience; then he hurriedly gathers up his papers from the writing-table. The three men turn to him.] Eh?

AUBREY: Oh, I—I'll finish my letters in the other room if you'll excuse me for five minutes. Tell Cayley the news. [*He goes out.*]

DRUMMLE [*hurrying to the door*]: My dear fellow, my jabbering has disturbed you! I'll never talk again as long as I live!

MISQUITH: Close the door, Cayley. [DRUMMLE *shuts the door.*]

JAYNE: Cayley—

DRUMMLE [*advancing to the dinner table*]: A smoke, a smoke, or I perish! [*Selects a cigar from the little cabinet.*]

JAYNE: Cayley, marriages are in the air.

DRUMMLE: Are they? Discover the bacillus, Doctor, and destroy it.

JAYNE: I mean, among our friends.

DRUMMLE: Oh, Nugent Warrinder's engagement to Lady Alice Tring. I've heard of that. They're not to be married till the spring.

JAYNE: Another marriage that concerns us a little takes place tomorrow.

DRUMMLE: Whose marriage?

JAYNE: Aubrey's.

DRUMMLE: Aub—! [*Looking towards* MISQUITH.] Is it a joke?

MISQUITH: No.

DRUMMLE [*looking from* MISQUITH *to* JAYNE]: To whom?

MISQUITH: He doesn't tell us.

JAYNE: We three were asked here tonight to receive the announcement. Aubrey has some theory that marriage is likely to alienate a man from his friends, and it seems to me he has taken the precaution to wish us good-bye.

MISQUITH: No, no.

JAYNE: Practically, surely.

DRUMMLE [*thoughtfully*]: Marriage in general, does he mean, or *this* marriage?

JAYNE: That's the point. Frank says—

MISQUITH: No, no, no; I feared it suggested—

JAYNE: Well, well. [*To* DRUMMLE.] What do you think of it?

DRUMMLE [*after a slight pause*]: Is there a light there? [*Lighting his cigar.*] He—wraps the lady —in mystery—you say?

MISQUITH: Most modestly.

DRUMMLE: Aubrey's—not—a very —young man.

JAYNE: Forty-three.

DRUMMLE: Ah! *L'age critique!*

MISQUITH: A dangerous age— yes, yes.

DRUMMLE: When you two fellows go home, do you mind leaving me behind here?

MISQUITH: Not at all.

JAYNE: By all means.

DRUMMLE: All right. [*Anxiously.*] Deuce take it, the man's second marriage mustn't be another mistake! [*With his head bent he walks up to the fireplace.*]

JAYNE: You knew him in his short married life, Cayley. Terribly unsatisfactory, wasn't it?

DRUMMLE: Well— [*Looking at the door.*] I quite closed that door?

MISQUITH: Yes. [*Settles himself on the sofa;* JAYNE *is seated in an armchair.*]

DRUMMLE [*smoking with his back to the fire*]: He married a Miss

Herriott; that was in the year eighteen—confound dates—twenty years ago. She was a lovely creature—by Jove, she was; by religion a Roman Catholic. She was one of your cold sort, you know—all marble arms and black velvet. I remember her with painful distinctness as the only woman who ever made me nervous.

MISQUITH: Ha, ha!

DRUMMLE: He loved her—to distraction, as they say. Jupiter, how fervently that poor devil courted her! But I don't believe she allowed him even to squeeze her fingers. She *was* an iceberg! As for kissing, the mere contact would have given him chapped lips. However, he married her and took her away, the latter greatly to my relief.

JAYNE: Abroad, you mean?

DRUMMLE: Eh? Yes. I imagine he gratified her by renting a villa in Lapland, but I don't know. After a while they returned, and then I saw how woefully Aubrey had miscalculated results.

JAYNE: Miscalculated—?

DRUMMLE: He had reckoned, poor wretch, that in the early days of marriage she would thaw. But she didn't. I used to picture him closing his doors and making up the fire in the hope of seeing her features relax. Bless her, the thaw never set in! I believe she kept a thermometer in her stays and always registered ten degrees below zero. However, in time a child came—a daughter.

JAYNE: Didn't that—?

DRUMMLE: Not a bit of it; it made matters worse. Frightened at her failure to stir up in him some sympathetic religious belief, she determined upon strong measures with regard to the child. He opposed her for a miserable year or so, but she wore him down, and the insensible little brat was placed in a convent, first in France, then in Ireland. Not long afterwards the mother died, strangely enough, of fever, the only warmth, I believe, that ever came to that woman's body.

MISQUITH: Don't, Cayley!

JAYNE: The child is living, we know.

DRUMMLE: Yes, if you choose to call it living. Miss Tanqueray—a young woman of nineteen now—is in the Loretto convent at Armagh. She professes to have found her true vocation in a religious life, and within a month or two will take final vows.

MISQUITH: He ought to have removed his daughter from the convent when the mother died.

DRUMMLE: Yes, yes, but absolutely at the end there was reconciliation between husband and wife, and she won his promise that the child should complete her conventual education. He reaped his reward. When he attempted to gain his girl's confidence and affection he was too late; he found he was dealing with the spirit of the mother. You remember his visit to Ireland last month?

JAYNE: Yes.

DRUMMLE: That was to wish his girl good-bye.

MISQUITH: Poor fellow!

DRUMMLE: He sent for me when he came back. I think he must have had a lingering hope that the girl would relent—would come to life, as it were—at the last moment, for, for an hour or so, in this room, he was terribly shaken. I'm sure he'd clung to that hope from the persistent way in which he kept breaking off in his talk to repeat one dismal word, as if he couldn't realise his position without dinning this damned word into his head.

JAYNE: What word was that?

DRUMMLE: Alone—alone.

[AUBREY *enters.*]

AUBREY: A thousand apologies!

DRUMMLE [*gaily*]: We are talking about you, my dear Aubrey.

[*During the telling of the story,* MISQUITH *has risen and gone to the fire, and* DRUMMLE *has thrown himself full-length on the sofa.* AUBREY *now joins* MISQUITH *and* JAYNE.]

AUBREY: Well, Cayley, are you surprised?

DRUMMLE: Surp—! I haven't been surprised for twenty years.

AUBREY: And you're not angry with me?

DRUMMLE: Angry! [*Rising.*] Because you considerately withhold the name of a lady with whom it is now the object of my life to become acquainted? My dear fellow, you pique my curiosity, you give zest to my existence! And as for a wedding, who on earth wants to attend that familiar and probably draughty function? Ugh! My cigar's out.

AUBREY: Let's talk about something else.

MISQUITH [*looking at his watch*]: Not tonight, Aubrey.

AUBREY: My dear Frank!

MISQUITH: I go up to Scotland tomorrow, and there are some little matters—

JAYNE: I am off too.

AUBREY: No, no.

JAYNE: I must: I have to give a look to a case in Clifford Street on my way home.

AUBREY [*going to the door*]: Well! [MISQUITH *and* JAYNE *exchange looks with* DRUMMLE. *Opening the door and calling.*] Morse, hats and coats! I shall write to you all next week from Genoa or Florence. Now, Doctor, Frank, remember, my love to Mrs. Misquith and to Mrs. Jayne!

[MORSE *enters with hats and coats.*]

MISQUITH *and* JAYNE: Yes, yes—yes, yes.

AUBREY: And your young people!

[*As* MISQUITH *and* JAYNE *put on their coats there is the clatter of careless talk.*]

JAYNE: Cayley, I meet you at dinner on Sunday.

DRUMMLE: At the Stratfields'. That's very pleasant.

MISQUITH [*putting on his coat with* AUBREY's *aid*]: Ah-h!

AUBREY: What's wrong?

MISQUITH: A twinge. Why didn't I go to Aix in August?

JAYNE [*shaking hands with* DRUMMLE]: Good night, Cayley.

DRUMMLE: Good night, my dear doctor!

MISQUITH [*shaking hands with*

DRUMMLE]: Cayley, are you in town for long?

DRUMMLE: Dear friend, I'm nowhere for long. Good night.

MISQUITH: Good night.

[AUBREY, JAYNE, *and* MISQUITH *go out, followed by* MORSE; *the hum of talk is continued outside.*]

AUBREY: A cigar, Frank?

MISQUITH: No, thank you.

AUBREY: Going to walk, Doctor?

JAYNE: If Frank will.

MISQUITH: By all means.

AUBREY: It's a cold night.

[*The door is closed.* DRUMMLE *remains standing with his coat on his arm and his hat in his hand.*]

DRUMMLE [*to himself, thoughtfully*]: Now then! What the devil—

[AUBREY *returns.*]

AUBREY [*eyeing* DRUMMLE *a little awkwardly*]: Well, Cayley?

DRUMMLE: Well, Aubrey?

[AUBREY *walks up to the fire and stands looking into it.*]

AUBREY: You're not going, old chap?

DRUMMLE [*sitting*]: No.

AUBREY [*after a slight pause, with a forced laugh*]: Hah! Cayley, I never thought I should feel—shy—with you.

DRUMMLE: Why do you?

AUBREY: Never mind.

DRUMMLE: Now, I can quite understand a man wishing to be married in the dark, as it were.

AUBREY: You can?

DRUMMLE: In your place I should very likely adopt the same course.

AUBREY: You think so?

DRUMMLE: And if I intended marrying a lady not prominently in society, as I presume you do—as I presume you do—

AUBREY: Well?

DRUMMLE: As I presume you do, I'm not sure that *I* should tender her for preliminary dissection at afternoon tea-tables.

AUBREY: No?

DRUMMLE: In fact, there is probably only one person—were I in your position tonight—with whom I should care to chat the matter over.

AUBREY: Who's that?

DRUMMLE: Yourself, of course. [*Going to* AUBREY *and standing beside him.*] Of course, yourself, old friend.

AUBREY [*after a pause*]: I must seem a brute to you, Cayley. But there are some acts which are hard to explain, hard to defend—

DRUMMLE: To defend—

AUBREY: Some acts which one must trust to time to put right.

[DRUMMLE *watches him for a moment, then takes up his hat and coat.*]

DRUMMLE: Well, I'll be moving.

AUBREY: Cayley! Confound you and your old friendship! Do you think I forget it? Put your coat down! Why did you stay behind here? Cayley, the lady I am going to marry is the lady—who is known as—Mrs. Jarman.

[*There is a pause.*]

DRUMMLE [*in a low voice*]: Mrs. Jarman! Are you serious? [*He walks up to the fireplace, where he leans upon the mantelpiece, uttering something like a groan.*]

AUBREY: As you've got this out of me, I give you leave to say all you care to say. Come, we'll be plain with each other. You know Mrs. Jarman?

DRUMMLE: I first met her at—what does it matter?

AUBREY: Yes, yes, everything! Come!

DRUMMLE: I met her at Homburg, two—three seasons ago.

AUBREY: Not as Mrs. Jarman?

DRUMMLE: No.

AUBREY: She was then—?

DRUMMLE: Mrs. Dartry.

AUBREY: Yes. She has also seen you in London, she says.

DRUMMLE: Certainly.

AUBREY: In Alford Street. Go on.

DRUMMLE: Please!

AUBREY: I insist.

DRUMMLE [*with a slight shrug of the shoulders*]: Some time last year I was asked by a man to sup at his house, one night after the theatre.

AUBREY: Mr. Selwyn Ethurst—a bachelor.

DRUMMLE: Yes.

AUBREY: You were surprised therefore to find Mr. Ethurst aided in his cursed hospitality by a lady.

DRUMMLE: I was unprepared.

AUBREY: The lady you had known as Mrs. Dartry? [DRUMMLE *inclines his head silently.*] There is something of a yachting cruise in the Mediterranean too, is there not?

DRUMMLE: I joined Peter Jarman's yacht at Marseilles, in the Spring, a month before he died.

AUBREY: Mrs. Jarman was on board?

DRUMMLE: She was a kind hostess.

AUBREY: And an old acquaintance?

DRUMMLE: Yes.

AUBREY: You have told your story.

DRUMMLE: With your assistance.

AUBREY: I have put you to the pain of telling it to show you that this is not the case of a blind man entrapped by an artful woman. Let me add that Mrs. Jarman has no legal right to that name; that she is simply Miss Ray—Miss Paula Ray.

DRUMMLE [*after a pause*]: I should like to express my regret, Aubrey, for the way in which I spoke of George Orreyed's marriage.

AUBREY: You mean you compare Lady Orreyed with Miss Ray? [DRUMMLE *is silent.*] Oh, of course! To you, Cayley, all women who have been roughly treated, and who dare to survive by borrowing a little of our philosophy, are alike. You see in the crowd of the ill-used only one pattern; you can't detect the shades of goodness, intelligence, even nobility there. Well, how should you? The crowd is dimly lighted! And, besides, yours is the way of the world.

DRUMMLE: My dear Aubrey, I *live* in the world.

AUBREY: The name we give our little parish of St. James's.

DRUMMLE [*laying a hand on AUBREY's shoulder*]: And you are quite prepared, my friend, to forfeit the esteem of your little parish?

AUBREY: I avoid mortification by shifting from one parish to another. I give up Pall Mall for the Surrey hills; leave off varnishing my boots, and double the thickness of the soles.

DRUMMLE: And your skin—do you

double the thickness of that
also?

AUBREY: I know you think me a
fool, Cayley—you needn't infer
that I'm a coward into the bargain. No! I know what I'm
doing, and I do it deliberately,
defiantly. I'm alone: I injure
no living soul by the step I'm
going to take; and so you can't
urge the one argument which
might restrain me. Of course, I
don't expect you to think com-
passionately, fairly even, of the
woman whom I—whom I am
drawn to—

DRUMMLE: My dear Aubrey, I
assure you I consider Mrs.—
Miss Jarman—Mrs. Ray—Miss
Ray—delightful. But I confess
there is a form of chivalry which
I gravely distrust, especially in
a man of—our age.

AUBREY: Thanks. I've heard you
say that from forty till fifty
a man is at heart either a stoic
or a satyr.

DRUMMLE [protestingly]: Ah!
now—

AUBREY: I am neither. I have a
temperate, honourable affection
for Mrs. Jarman. She has never
met a man who has treated her
well—I intend to treat her well.
That's all. And in a few years,
Cayley, if you've not quite forsaken me, I'll prove to you that
it's possible to rear a life of
happiness, of good repute, on
a—miserable foundation.

DRUMMLE [offering his hand]: Do
prove it!

AUBREY [taking his hand]: We
have spoken too freely of—of
Mrs. Jarman. I was excited—
angry. Please forget it!

DRUMMLE: My dear Aubrey, when
we next meet I shall remember
nothing but my respect for the
lady who bears your name.

[MORSE enters, closing the door
behind him carefully.]

AUBREY: What is it?

MORSE [hesitatingly]: May I speak
to you, sir? [In an undertone.]
Mrs. Jarman, sir.

AUBREY [softly to MORSE]: Mrs.
Jarman! Do you mean she is
at the lodge in her carriage?

MORSE: No, sir—here. [AUBREY
looks towards DRUMMLE, perplexed.] There's a nice fire in
your—in that room, sir. [Glanc-
ing in the direction of the door
leading to the bedroom.]

AUBREY [between his teeth, an-
grily]: Very well.

[MORSE retires.]

DRUMMLE [looking at his watch]:
A quarter to eleven—horrible!
[Taking up his hat and coat.]
Must get to bed—up late every
night this week. [AUBREY assists
DRUMMLE with his coat.] Thank
you. Well, good night, Aubrey. I
feel I've been deuced serious,
quite out of keeping with myself; pray overlook it.

AUBREY [kindly]: Ah, Cayley!

DRUMMLE [putting on a neck-hand-
kerchief]: And remember that,
after all, I'm merely a spectator
in life; nothing more than a man
at a play, in fact; only, like
the old-fashioned playgoer, I
love to see certain characters
happy and comfortable at the
finish. You understand?

AUBREY: I think I do.

DRUMMLE: Then, for as long as
you can, old friend, will you—
keep a stall for me?

AUBREY: Yes, Cayley.

DRUMMLE [*gaily*]: Ah, ha! Good night! [*Bustling to the door.*] Don't bother! I'll let myself out! Good night! God bless yer!

[*He goes out;* AUBREY *follows him.* MORSE *enters by the other door, carrying some unopened letters, which after a little consideration he places on the mantelpiece against the clock.* AUBREY *returns.*]

AUBREY: Yes?

MORSE: You hadn't seen your letters that came by the nine o'clock post, sir; I've put 'em where they'll catch your eye by-and-bye.

AUBREY: Thank you.

MORSE [*hesitatingly*]: Gunter's cook and waiter have gone, sir. Would you prefer me to go to bed?

AUBREY [*frowning*]: Certainly not.

MORSE: Very well, sir. [*He goes out.*]

AUBREY [*opening the upper door*]: Paula! Paula!

[PAULA *enters and throws her arms round his neck. She is a young woman of about twenty-seven: beautiful, fresh, innocent-looking. She is in superb evening dress.*]

PAULA: Dearest!

AUBREY: Why have you come here?

PAULA: Angry?

AUBREY: Yes—no. But it's eleven o'clock.

PAULA [*laughing*]: I know.

AUBREY: What on earth will Morse think?

PAULA: Do you trouble yourself about what servants *think*?

AUBREY: Of course.

PAULA: Goose! They're only machines made to wait upon people—and to give evidence in the Divorce Court. [*Looking round.*] Oh, indeed! A snug little dinner!

AUBREY: Three men.

PAULA [*suspiciously*]: Men?

AUBREY: Men.

PAULA [*penitently*]: Ah! [*Sitting at the table.*] I'm so hungry.

AUBREY: Let me get you some game pie, or some—

PAULA: No, no, hungry for this. What beautiful fruit! I love fruit when it's expensive. [*He clears a space on the table, places a plate before her, and helps her to fruit.*] I haven't dined, Aubrey dear.

AUBREY: My poor girl! Why?

PAULA: In the first place, I forgot to order any dinner, and my cook, who has always loathed me, thought he'd pay me out before he departed.

AUBREY: The beast!

PAULA: That's precisely what I—

AUBREY: No, Paula!

PAULA: What I told my maid to call him. What next will you think of me?

AUBREY: Forgive me. You must be starved.

PAULA [*eating fruit*]: *I* didn't care. As there was nothing to eat, I sat in my best frock, with my toes on the dining-room fender, and dreamt, oh, such a lovely dinner party.

AUBREY: Dear lonely little woman!

PAULA: It was perfect. I saw you at the end of a very long table, opposite me, and we exchanged sly glances now and again over the flowers. We were host and hostess, Aubrey, and had been married about five years.

AUBREY [*kissing her hand*]: Five years.

PAULA: And on each side of us was the nicest set imaginable—you know, dearest, the sort of men and women that can't be imitated.

AUBREY: Yes, yes. Eat some more fruit.

PAULA: But I haven't told you the best part of my dream.

AUBREY: Tell me.

PAULA: Well, although we had been married only such a few years, I seemed to know by the look on their faces that none of our guests had ever heard anything—anything—anything peculiar about the fascinating hostess.

AUBREY: That's just how it will be, Paula. The world moves so quickly. That's just how it will be.

PAULA [*with a little grimace*]: I wonder! [*Glancing at the fire.*] Ugh! Do throw another log on.

AUBREY [*mending the fire*]: There. But you mustn't be here long.

PAULA: Hospitable wretch! I've something important to tell you. No, stay where you are. [*Turning from him, her face averted.*] Look here, that was my dream, Aubrey; but the fire went out while I was dozing, and I woke up with a regular fit of the shivers. And the result of it all was that I ran upstairs and scribbled you a letter.

AUBREY: Dear baby!

PAULA: Remain where you are. [*Taking a letter from her pocket.*] This is it. I've given you an account of myself, furnished you with a list of my adventures since I—you know. [*Weighing the letter in her hand.*] I wonder if it would go for a penny. Most of it you're acquainted with; *I've* told you a good deal, haven't I?

AUBREY: Oh, Paula!

PAULA: What I haven't told you I dare say you've heard from others. But in case they've omitted anything—the dears—it's all here.

AUBREY: In Heaven's name, why must you talk like this tonight?

PAULA: It may save discussion by-and-bye, don't you think? [*Holding out the letter.*] There you are.

AUBREY: No, dear, no.

PAULA: Take it. [*He takes the letter.*] Read it through after I've gone, and then—read it again, and turn the matter over in your mind finally. And if, even at the very last moment, you feel you—oughtn't to go to church with me, send a messenger to Pont Street, any time before eleven tomorrow, telling me that you're afraid, and I—I'll take the blow.

AUBREY: Why, what—what do you think I am?

PAULA: That's it. It's because I know you're such a dear good fellow that I want to save you the chance of ever feeling sorry you married me. I really love you so much, Aubrey, that to save you that, I'd rather you treated me as—as the others have done.

AUBREY [*turning from her with a cry*]: Oh!

PAULA [*after a slight pause*]: I suppose I've shocked you. I can't help it if I have.

[*She sits, with assumed languor and indifference. He turns to her, advances, and kneels by her.*]

AUBREY: My dearest, you don't understand me. I—I can't bear to hear you always talking about —what's done with. I tell you I'll never remember it; Paula, can't you dismiss it? Try. Darling, if we promise each other to forget, to forget, we're bound to be happy. After all, it's a mechanical matter; the moment a wretched thought enters your head, you quickly think of something bright—it depends on one's will. Shall I burn this, dear? [*Referring to the letter he holds in his hand.*] Let me, let me!

PAULA [*with a shrug of the shoulders*]: I don't suppose there's much that's new to you in it— just as you like.

[*He goes to the fire and burns the letter.*]

AUBREY: There's an end of it. [*Returning to her.*] What's the matter?

PAULA [*rising, coldly*]: Oh, nothing! I'll go and put my cloak on.

AUBREY [*detaining her*]: What *is* the matter?

PAULA: Well, I think you might have said, "You're very generous, Paula," or at least, "Thank you, dear," when I offered to set you free.

AUBREY [*catching her in his arms*]: Ah!

PAULA: Ah! ah! Ha! ha! It's all very well, but you don't know what it cost me to make such an offer. I do so want to be married.

AUBREY: But you never imagined—?

PAULA: Perhaps not. And yet I *did* think of what I'd do at the end of our acquaintance if you had preferred to behave like the rest. [*Taking a flower from her bodice.*]

AUBREY: Hush!

PAULA: Oh, I forgot!

AUBREY: What would you have done when we parted?

PAULA: Why, killed myself.

AUBREY: Paula, dear!

PAULA: It's true. [*Putting the flower in his buttonhole.*] Do you know, I feel certain I should make away with myself if anything serious happened to me.

AUBREY: Anything serious! What, has nothing ever been serious to you, Paula?

PAULA: Not lately; not since a long while ago. I made up my mind then to have done with taking things seriously. If I hadn't, I— However, we won't talk about that.

AUBREY: But now, now, life will be different to you, won't it— quite different? Eh, dear?

PAULA: Oh, yes, now. Only, Aubrey, mind you keep me always happy.

AUBREY: I will try to.

PAULA: I know I couldn't swallow a second big dose of misery. I know that if ever I felt wretched again—truly wretched—I should take a leaf out of Connie Tirlemont's book. You remember? They found her— [*With a look of horror.*]

AUBREY: For God's sake, don't let your thoughts run on such things!

PAULA [*laughing*]: Ha, ha, how

scared you look! There, think of the time! Dearest, what will my coachman say? My cloak!

[*She runs off, gaily, by the upper door.* AUBREY *looks after her for a moment, then he walks up to the fire and stands warming his feet at the bars. As he does so he raises his head and observes the letters upon the mantelpiece. He takes one down quickly.*]

AUBREY: Ah! Ellean! [*Opening the letter and reading.*] "My dear father—A great change has come over me. I believe my mother in Heaven has spoken to me, and counselled me to turn to you in your loneliness. At any rate, your words have reached my heart, and I no longer feel fitted for this solemn life. I am ready to take my place by you. Dear father, will you receive me?— ELLEAN."

[PAULA *re-enters, dressed in a handsome cloak. He stares at her as if he hardly realised her presence.*]

PAULA: What are you staring at? Don't you admire my cloak?

AUBREY: Yes.

PAULA: Couldn't you wait till I'd gone before reading your letters?

AUBREY [*putting the letter away*]: I beg your pardon.

PAULA: Take me downstairs to the carriage. [*Slipping her arm through his.*] How I tease you! Tomorrow! I'm so happy! [*They go out.*]

ACT TWO

A morning-room in AUBREY TANQUERAY'S *house, "Higher-coombe," near Willowmere, Surrey—a bright and prettily furnished apartment of irregular shape, with double doors opening into a small hall at the back, another door on the left, and a large recessed window through which is obtained a view of extensive grounds. Everything about the room is charming and graceful. The fire is burning in the grate, and a small table is tastefully laid for breakfast. It is a morning in early spring, and the sun is streaming in through the window.*

[AUBREY *and* PAULA *are seated at breakfast, and* AUBREY *is silently reading his letters. Two servants, a man and a woman, hand dishes and then retire. After a little while* AUBREY *puts his letters aside and looks across to the window.*]

AUBREY: Sunshine! Spring!

PAULA [*glancing at the clock*]: Exactly six minutes.

AUBREY: Six minutes?

PAULA: Six minutes, Aubrey dear, since you made your last remark.

AUBREY: I beg your pardon: I

was reading my letters. Have you seen Ellean this morning?

PAULA [*coldly*]: Your last observation but one was about Ellean.

AUBREY: Dearest, what shall I talk about?

PAULA: Ellean breakfasted two hours ago, Morgan tells me, and then went out walking with her dog.

AUBREY: She wraps up warmly, I hope; this sunshine is deceptive.

PAULA: I ran about the lawn last night, after dinner, in satin shoes. Were you anxious about me?

AUBREY: Certainly.

PAULA [*melting*]: Really?

AUBREY: You make me wretchedly anxious; you delight in doing incautious things. You are incurable.

PAULA: Ah, what a beast I am! [*Going to him and kissing him, then glancing at the letters by his side.*] A letter from Cayley?

AUBREY: He is staying very near here, with Mrs.— Very near here.

PAULA: With the lady whose chimneys we have the honour of contemplating from our windows?

AUBREY: With Mrs. Cortelyon—yes.

PAULA: Mrs. Cortelyon! The woman who might have set the example of calling on me when we first threw out roots in this deadly-lively soil! Deuce take Mrs. Cortelyon!

AUBREY: Hush! my dear girl!

PAULA [*returning to her seat*]: Oh, I know she's an old acquaintance of yours—and of the first Mrs. Tanqueray. And she joins the rest of 'em in slapping the second Mrs. Tanqueray in the face. However, I have my re-

venge—she's six-and-forty, and I wish nothing worse to happen to any woman.

AUBREY: Well, she's going to town, Cayley says here, and his visit's at an end. He's coming over this morning to call on you. Shall we ask him to transfer himself to us? Do say yes.

PAULA: Yes.

AUBREY [*gladly*]: Ah, ha! old Cayley.

PAULA [*coldly*]: He'll amuse *you*.

AUBREY: And you too.

PAULA: Because you find a companion, shall I be boisterously hilarious?

AUBREY: Come, come! He talks London, and you know you like that.

PAULA: London! London or Heaven! Which is farther from me!

AUBREY: Paula!

PAULA: Oh! Oh, I am so bored, Aubrey!

AUBREY [*gathering up his letters and going to her, leaning over her shoulder*]: Baby, what can I do for you?

PAULA: I suppose, nothing. You have done all you can for me.

AUBREY: What do you mean?

PAULA: You have married me.

[*He walks away from her thoughtfully, to the writing table. As he places his letters on the table he sees an addressed letter, stamped for the post, lying on the blotting-book; he picks it up.*]

AUBREY [*in an altered tone*]: You've been writing this morning before breakfast?

PAULA [*looking at him quickly, then away again*]: Er—that letter.

AUBREY [*with the letter in his*

hand]: To Lady Orreyed. Why?

PAULA: Why not? Mabel's an old friend of mine.

AUBREY: Are you—corresponding?

PAULA: I heard from her yesterday. They've just returned from the Riviera. She seems happy.

AUBREY [*sarcastically*]: That's good news.

PAULA: Why are you always so cutting about Mabel? She's a kind-hearted girl. Everything's altered; she even thinks of letting her hair go back to brown. She's Lady Orreyed. She's married to George. What's the matter with her?

AUBREY [*turning away*]: Oh!

PAULA: You drive me mad sometimes with the tone you take about things! Great goodness, if you come to that, George Orreyed's wife isn't a bit worse than yours! [*He faces her suddenly.*] I suppose I needn't have made that observation.

AUBREY: No, there was scarcely a necessity. [*He throws the letter on to the table, and takes up the newspaper.*]

PAULA: I am very sorry.

AUBREY: All right, dear.

PAULA [*trifling with the letter*]: I —I'd better tell you what I've written. I meant to do so, of course. I—I've asked the Orreyeds to come and stay with us. [*He looks at her, and lets the paper fall to the ground in a helpless way.*] George was a great friend of Cayley's; I'm sure *he* would be delighted to meet them here.

AUBREY [*laughing mirthlessly*]: Ha, ha, ha! They say Orreyed has taken to tippling at dinner. Heavens above!

PAULA: Oh! I've no patience with you! You'll kill me with this life! [*She selects some flowers from a vase on the table, cuts and arranges them, and fastens them in her bodice.*] What is my existence, Sunday to Saturday? In the morning, a drive down to the village, with the groom, to give my orders to the tradespeople. At lunch, you and Ellean. In the afternoon, a novel, the newspapers: if fine, another drive—*if* fine! Tea—you and Ellean. Then two hours of dusk; then dinner—you and Ellean. Then a game of Bésique, you and I, while Ellean reads a religious book in a dull corner. Then a yawn from me, another from you, a sigh from Ellean; three figures suddenly rise—"Good night, good night, good night!" [*Imitating a kiss.*] "God bless you!" Ah!

AUBREY: Yes, yes, Paula—yes, dearest—that's what it is *now*. But by-and-bye, if people begin to come round us—

PAULA: Hah! That's where we've made the mistake, my friend Aubrey! [*Pointing to the window.*] Do you believe these people will *ever* come round us? Your former crony, Mrs. Cortelyon? Or the grim old vicar, or that wife of his whose huge nose is positively indecent? Or the Ullathornes, or the Gollans, or Lady William Petres? I know better! And when the young ones gradually take the place of the old, there will still remain the sacred tradition that the dreadful person who lives at the top of the hill is never, under any circumstances, to be called upon! And so we shall go on here, year in and year out, until the sap is run out of our lives, and we're stale and dry and withered from sheer, solitary respectability. Upon my word, I wonder we didn't see that we should have been far happier if we'd gone in for the devil-may-care, *café*-living sort of life in town! After all, *I* have a set, and you might have joined it. It's true, I did want, dearly, dearly, to be a married woman, but where's the pride in being a married woman among married women who are—married? If— [*Seeing that* AUBREY'S *head has sunk into his hands.*] Aubrey! My dear boy! You're not—crying?

[*He looks up, with a flushed face.* ELLEAN *enters, dressed very simply for walking. She is a low-voiced, grave girl of about nineteen, with a face somewhat resembling a Madonna. Towards* PAULA *her manner is cold and distant.*]

AUBREY [*in an undertone*]: Ellean!
ELLEAN: Good morning, papa. Good morning, Paula.

[PAULA *puts her arms round* EL-LEAN *and kisses her.* ELLEAN *makes little response.*]

PAULA: Good morning. [*Brightly.*] We've been breakfasting this side of the house, to get the sun.

[*She sits at the piano and rattles at a gay melody. Seeing that* PAULA'S *back is turned to them,* ELLEAN *goes to* AUBREY *and kisses him; he returns the kiss almost furtively. As they separate, the*

servants re-enter, and proceed to carry out the breakfast table.]

AUBREY [*to* ELLEAN]: I guess where you've been: there's some gorse clinging to your frock.
ELLEAN [*removing a sprig of gorse from her skirt*]: Rover and I walked nearly as far as Black Moor. The poor fellow has a thorn in his pad; I am going upstairs for my tweezers.
AUBREY: Ellean! [*She returns to him.*] Paula is a little depressed —out of sorts. She complains that she has no companion.
ELLEAN: I am with Paula nearly all the day, papa.
AUBREY: Ah, but you're such a little mouse. Paula likes cheerful people about her.
ELLEAN: I'm afraid I am naturally rather silent; and it's so difficult to seem to be what one is not.
AUBREY: I don't wish that, Ellean.
ELLEAN: I will offer to go down to the village with Paula this morning—shall I?
AUBREY [*touching her hand gently*]: Thank you—do.
ELLEAN: When I've looked after Rover, I'll come back to her.

[*She goes out;* PAULA *ceases playing, and turns on the music-stool, looking at* AUBREY.]

PAULA: Well, have you and Ellean had your little confidence?
AUBREY: Confidence?
PAULA: Do you think I couldn't feel it, like a pain between my shoulders?
AUBREY: Ellean is coming back in a few minutes to be with you. [*Bending over her.*] Paula, Paula

dear, is this how you keep your promise?

PAULA: Oh! [*Rising impatiently, and crossing swiftly to the settee, where she sits, moving restlessly.*] I *can't* keep my promise; I *am* jealous; it won't be smothered. I see you looking at her, watching her; your voice drops when you speak to her. I know how fond you are of that girl, Aubrey.

AUBREY: What would you have? I've no other home for her. She is my daughter.

PAULA: She is your saint. Saint Ellean!

AUBREY: You have often told me how good and sweet you think her.

PAULA: Good!—yes! Do you imagine *that* makes me less jealous? [*Going to him and clinging to his arm.*] Aubrey, there are two sorts of affection—the love for a woman you respect, and the love for the woman you—love. She gets the first from you: I never can.

AUBREY: Hush, hush! You don't realise what you say.

PAULA: If Ellean cared for me only a little, it would be different. I shouldn't be jealous then. Why doesn't she care for me?

AUBREY: She—she—she will, in time.

PAULA: You can't say that without stuttering.

AUBREY: Her disposition seems a little unresponsive; she resembles her mother in many ways; I can see it every day.

PAULA: She's marble. It's a shame. There's not the slightest excuse; for all she knows, I'm as much a saint as she—only married.

Dearest, help me to win her over!

AUBREY: Help you?

PAULA: You can. Teach her that it is her duty to love me; she hangs on to every word you speak. I'm sure, Aubrey, that the love of a nice woman who believed me to be like herself would do me a world of good. You'd get the benefit of it as well as I. It would soothe me; it would make me less horribly restless; it would take this—this—mischievous feeling from me. [*Coaxingly.*] Aubrey!

AUBREY: Have patience; everything will come right.

PAULA: Yes, if you help me.

AUBREY: In the meantime you will tear up your letter to Lady Orreyed, won't you?

PAULA [*kissing his hand*]: Of course I will—anything!

AUBREY: Ah, thank you, dearest! [*Laughing.*] Why, good gracious!—ha, ha!—just imagine "Saint Ellean" and that woman side by side!

PAULA [*going back with a cry*]: Ah!

AUBREY: What?

PAULA [*passionately*]: It's Ellean you're considering, not me? It's all Ellean with you! Ellean! Ellean!

[ELLEAN *re-enters.*]

ELLEAN: Did you call me, Paula? [*Clenching his hands,* AUBREY *turns away and goes out.*] Is papa angry?

PAULA: I drive him distracted sometimes. There, I confess it!

ELLEAN: Do you? Oh, why do you?

PAULA: Because I—because I'm jealous.

ELLEAN: Jealous?

PAULA: Yes—of you. [ELLEAN *is silent.*] Well, what do you think of that?

ELLEAN: I knew it; I've seen it. It hurts me dreadfully. What do you wish me to do? Go away?

PAULA: Leave us! [*Beckoning her with a motion of the head.*] Look here! [ELLEAN *goes to* PAULA *slowly and unresponsively.*] You could cure me of my jealousy very easily. Why don't you—like me?

ELLEAN: What do you mean by —like you? I don't understand.

PAULA: Love me.

ELLEAN: Love is not a feeling that is under one's control. I shall alter as time goes on, perhaps. I didn't begin to love my father deeply till a few months ago, and then I obeyed my mother.

PAULA: Ah, yes, you dream things, don't you—see them in your sleep? You fancy your mother speaks to you?

ELLEAN: When you have lost your mother it is a comfort to believe that she is dead only to this life, that she still watches over her child. I do believe that of my mother.

PAULA: Well, and so you haven't been bidden to love *me?*

ELLEAN [*after a pause, almost inaudibly*]: No.

PAULA: Dreams are only a hash-up of one's day-thoughts, I suppose you know. Think intently of anything, and it's bound to come back to you at night. I don't cultivate dreams myself.

ELLEAN: Ah, I knew you would only sneer!

PAULA: I'm not sneering; I'm speaking the truth. I say that if you cared for me in the day-time I should soon make friends with those nightmares of yours. Ellean, why don't you try to look on me as your second mother? Of course there are not many years between us, but I'm ever so much older than you—in experience. I shall have no children of my own, I know that; it would be a real comfort to me if you would make me feel we belonged to each other. Won't you? Perhaps you think I'm odd—not nice. Well, the fact is I've two sides to my nature, and I've let the one almost smother the other. A few years ago I went through some trouble, and since then I haven't shed a tear. I believe if you put your arms round me just once I should run upstairs and have a good cry. There, I've talked to you as I've never talked to a woman in my life. Ellean, you seem to fear me. Don't! Kiss me!

[*With a cry, almost of despair,* ELLEAN *turns from* PAULA *and sinks onto the settee, covering her face with her hands.*]

PAULA [*indignantly*]: Oh! Why is it! How dare you treat me like this? What do you mean by it? What do you mean?

[*A* SERVANT *enters.*]

SERVANT: Mr. Drummle, ma'am.

[CAYLEY DRUMMLE, *in riding-dress, enters briskly. The* SERVANT *retires.*]

PAULA [*recovering herself*]: Well, Cayley!

DRUMMLE [*shaking hands with her cordially*]: How are you? [*Shaking hands with* ELLEAN, *who rises.*] I saw you in the distance an hour ago, in the gorse near Stapleton's.

ELLEAN: I didn't see you, Mr. Drummle.

DRUMMLE: My dear Ellean, it is my experience that no charming young lady of nineteen ever does see a man of forty-five. [*Laughing.*] Ha, Ha!

ELLEAN [*going to the door*]: Paula, papa wishes me to drive down to the village with you this morning. Do you care to take me?

PAULA [*coldly*]: Oh, by all means. Pray tell Watts to balance the cart for three.

[ELLEAN *goes out.*]

DRUMMLE: How's Aubrey?

PAULA: Very well—when Ellean's about the house.

DRUMMLE: And you? I needn't ask.

PAULA [*walking away to the window*]: Oh, a dog's life, my dear Cayley, mine.

DRUMMLE: Eh?

PAULA: Doesn't that define a happy marriage? I'm sleek, well-kept, well-fed, never without a bone to gnaw and fresh straw to lie upon. [*Gazing out of the window.*] Oh, dear me!

DRUMMLE: H'm! Well, I heartily congratulate you on your kennel. The view from the terrace here is superb.

PAULA: Yes; I can see London.

DRUMMLE: London! Not quite so far, surely?

PAULA: *I* can. Also the Mediterranean, on a fine day. I wonder what Algiers looks like this morning from the sea! [*Impulsively.*] Oh, Cayley, do you remember those jolly times on board Peter Jarman's yacht when we lay off—? [*Stopping suddenly, seeing* DRUMMLE *staring at her.*] Good gracious! What are we talking about!

[AUBREY *enters.*]

AUBREY [*to* DRUMMLE]: Dear old chap! Has Paula asked you?

PAULA: Not yet.

AUBREY: We want you to come to us, now that you're leaving Mrs. Cortelyon—at once, today. Stay a month, as long as you please—eh, Paula?

PAULA: As long as you can possibly endure it—do, Cayley.

DRUMMLE [*looking at* AUBREY]: Delighted. [*To* PAULA.] Charming of you to have me.

PAULA: My dear man, you're a blessing. I must telegraph to London for more fish! A strange appetite to cater for! Something to do, to do, to do! [*She goes out in a mood of almost childish delight.*]

DRUMMLE [*eyeing* AUBREY]: Well?

AUBREY [*with a wearied anxious look*]: Well, Cayley?

DRUMMLE: How are you getting on?

AUBREY: My position doesn't grow less difficult. I told you, when I met you last week, of this feverish, jealous attachment of Paula's for Ellean?

DRUMMLE: Yes. I hardly know why, but I came to the conclusion that you don't consider it an altogether fortunate attachment.

AUBREY: Ellean doesn't respond to it.

DRUMMLE: These are early days. Ellean will warm towards your wife by-and-bye.

AUBREY: Ah, but there's the question, Cayley!

DRUMMLE: What question?

AUBREY: The question which positively distracts me. Ellean is so different from—most women; I don't believe a purer creature exists out of heaven. And I— I ask myself, am I doing right in exposing her to the influence of poor Paula's light, careless nature?

DRUMMLE: My dear Aubrey!

AUBREY: That shocks you! So it does me. I assure you I long to urge my girl to break down the reserve which keeps her apart from Paula, but somehow I can't do it—well, I don't do it. How can I make you understand? But when you come to us you'll understand quickly enough. Cayley, there's hardly a subject you can broach on which poor Paula hasn't some strange, out-of-the-way thought to give utterance to; some curious, warped notion. They are not mere worldly thoughts— unless, good God! they belong to the little hellish world which our blackguardism has created: no, her ideas have too little calculation in them to be called worldly. But it makes it the more dreadful that such thoughts should be ready, spontaneous; that expressing them has become a perfectly natural process; that her words, acts even, have almost lost their proper significance for her, and seem beyond her control. Ah, and the pain of listening to it all from the woman one loves, the woman one hoped to make happy and contented, who is really and truly a good woman, as it were, maimed! Well, this is my burden, and I shouldn't speak to you of it but for my anxiety about Ellean. Ellean! What is to be her future? It is in my hands; what am I to do? Cayley, when I remember how Ellean comes to me, from another world I always think—when I realise the charge that's laid on me, I find myself wishing, in a sort of terror, that my child were safe under the ground!

DRUMMLE: My dear Aubrey, aren't you making a mistake?

AUBREY: Very likely. What is it?

DRUMMLE: A mistake, not in regarding your Ellean as an angel, but in believing that, under any circumstances, it would be possible for her to go through life without getting her white robe —shall we say, a little dusty at the hem? Don't take me for a cynic. I am sure there are many women upon earth who are almost divinely innocent; but being on earth, they must send their robes to the laundry occasionally. Ah, and it's right that they should have to do so, for what can they learn from the checking of their little washing-bills but lessons of charity? Now I see but two courses open to you for the disposal of your angel.

AUBREY: Yes?

DRUMMLE: You must either restrict her to a paradise which is, like every earthly paradise, necessarily somewhat imperfect, or treat her as an ordinary flesh-and-blood young woman, and give her the advantages of that society to which she properly belongs.

AUBREY: Advantages?

DRUMMLE: My dear Aubrey, of all forms of innocence mere ignorance is the least admirable. Take my advice, let her walk and talk and suffer and be healed with the great crowd. Do it, and hope that she'll some day meet a good, honest fellow who'll make her life complete, happy, secure. Now you see what I'm driving at.

AUBREY: A sanguine programme, my dear Cayley! Oh, I'm not pooh-poohing it. Putting sentiment aside, of course I know that a fortunate marriage for Ellean would be the best—perhaps the only—solution of my difficulty. But you forget the danger of the course you suggest.

DRUMMLE: Danger?

AUBREY: If Ellean goes among men and women, how can she escape from learning, sooner or later, the history of—poor Paula's—old life?

DRUMMLE: H'm! You remember the episode of the Jeweller's Son in the Arabian Nights? Of course you don't. Well, if your daughter lives, she *can't* escape —what you're afraid of. [AUBREY *gives a half-stifled exclamation of pain.*] And when she does hear the story, surely it would be better that she should have some knowledge of the world to help her to understand it.

AUBREY: To understand!

DRUMMLE: To understand, to—philosophise.

AUBREY: To philosophise?

DRUMMLE: Philosophy is toleration, and it is only one step from toleration to forgiveness.

AUBREY: You're right, Cayley; I believe you always are. Yes, yes. But, even if I had the courage to attempt to solve the problem of Ellean's future in this way, I—I'm helpless.

DRUMMLE: How?

AUBREY: What means have I now of placing my daughter in the world I've left?

DRUMMLE: Oh, some friend—some woman friend.

AUBREY: I have none; they're gone.

DRUMMLE: You're wrong there; I know one—

AUBREY [*listening*]: That's Paula's cart. Let's discuss this again.

DRUMMLE [*going up to the window and looking out*]: It isn't the dog-cart. [*Turning to* AUBREY.] I hope you'll forgive me, old chap.

AUBREY: What for?

DRUMMLE: Whose wheels do you think have been cutting ruts in your immaculate drive?

[A SERVANT *enters.*]

SERVANT [*to* AUBREY]: Mrs. Cortelyon, sir.

AUBREY: Mrs. Cortelyon! [*After a short pause.*] Very well. [*The* SERVANT *withdraws.*] What on earth is the meaning of this?

DRUMMLE: Ahem! While I've been our old friend's guest, Aubrey, we have very naturally talked a good deal about you and yours.

AUBREY: Indeed, have you?

DRUMMLE: Yes; and Alice Cortelyon has arrived at the conclusion that it would have been far kinder had she called on Mrs. Tanqueray long ago. She's going abroad for Easter before settling down in London for the season, and I believe she has come over this morning to ask for Ellean's companionship.

AUBREY: Oh, I see! [*Frowning.*] Quite a friendly little conspiracy, my dear Cayley!

DRUMMLE: Conspiracy! Not at all, I assure you. [*Laughing.*] Ha, ha!

[ELLEAN *enters from the hall with* MRS. CORTELYON, *a handsome, good-humoured, spirited woman of about forty-five.*]

ELLEAN: Papa—

MRS. CORTELYON [*to* AUBREY, *shaking hands with him heartily*]: Well, Aubrey, how are you? I've just been telling this great girl of yours that I knew her when she was a sad-faced, pale baby. How is Mrs. Tanqueray? I have been a bad neighbour, and I'm here to beg forgiveness. Is she indoors?

AUBREY: She's upstairs putting on a hat, I believe.

MRS. CORTELYON [*sitting comfortably*]: Ah! [*She looks round:* DRUMMLE *and* ELLEAN *are talking together in the hall.*] We used to be very frank with each other, Aubrey. I suppose the old footing is no longer possible, eh?

AUBREY: If so, I'm not entirely to blame, Mrs. Cortelyon.

MRS. CORTELYON: Mrs. Cortelyon? H'm! No, I admit it. But you must make some little allowance for me, *Mr. Tanqueray.* Your first wife and I, as girls, were like two cherries on one stalk, and then I was the confidential friend of your married life. That post, perhaps, wasn't altogether a sinecure. And now—well, when a woman gets to my age I suppose she's a stupid, prejudiced, conventional creature. However, I've got over it and—[*giving him her hand*]—I hope you'll be enormously happy and let me be a friend once more.

AUBREY: Thank you, Alice.

MRS. CORTELYON: That's right. I feel more cheerful than I've done for weeks. But I suppose it would serve me right if the second Mrs. Tanqueray showed me the door. Do you think she will?

AUBREY [*listening*]: Here is my wife. [MRS. CORTELYON *rises, and* PAULA *enters, dressed for driving; she stops abruptly on seeing* MRS. CORTELYON.] Paula, dear, Mrs. Cortelyon has called to see you.

[PAULA *starts, looks at* MRS. CORTELYON *irresolutely, then after a slight pause barely touches* MRS. CORTELYON'S *extended hand.*]

PAULA [*whose manner now alternates between deliberate insolence and assumed sweetness*]: Mrs—? What name, Aubrey?

AUBREY: Mrs. Cortelyon.

PAULA: Cortelyon? Oh, yes. Cortelyon.

MRS. CORTELYON [*carefully guarding herself throughout against any expression of resentment*]: Aubrey ought to have told you that Alice Cortelyon and he are very old friends.

PAULA: Oh, very likely he has mentioned the circumstance. I have quite a wretched memory.

MRS. CORTELYON: You know we are neighbours, Mrs. Tanqueray.

PAULA: Neighbours? Are we really? Won't you sit down? [*They both sit.*] Neighbours! That's most interesting!

MRS. CORTELYON: Very near neighbours. You can see my roof from your windows.

PAULA: I fancy I *have* observed a roof. But you have been away from home; you have only just returned.

MRS. CORTELYON: I? What makes you think that?

PAULA: Why, because it is two months since we came to Highercoombe, and I don't remember your having called.

MRS. CORTELYON: Your memory is now terribly accurate. No, I've not been away from home, and it is to explain my neglect that I am here, rather unceremoniously, this morning.

PAULA: Oh, to explain—quite so. [*With mock solicitude.*] Ah, you've been very ill; I ought to have seen that before.

MRS. CORTELYON: Ill!

PAULA: You look dreadfully pulled down. We poor women show illness so plainly in our faces, don't we?

AUBREY [*anxiously*]: Paula dear, Mrs. Cortelyon is the picture of health.

MRS. CORTELYON [*with some asperity*]: I have never *felt* better in my life.

PAULA [*looking round innocently*]: Have I said anything awkward?

Aubrey, tell Mrs. Cortelyon how stupid and thoughtless I always am!

MRS. CORTELYON [*to* DRUMMLE, *who is now standing close to her*]: Really, Cayley—! [*He soothes her with a nod and smile and a motion of his finger to his lip.*] Mrs. Tanqueray, I am afraid my explanation will not be quite so satisfactory as either of those you have just helped me to. You may have heard—but, if you have heard, you have doubtless forgotten—that twenty years ago, when your husband first lived here, I was a constant visitor at Highercoombe.

PAULA: Twenty years ago—fancy! I was a naughty little child then.

MRS. CORTELYON: Possibly. Well, at that time, and till the end of her life, my affections were centred upon the lady of this house.

PAULA: Were they? That was very sweet of you.

[ELLEAN *approaches* MRS. CORTELYON, *listening intently to her.*]

MRS. CORTELYON: I will say no more on that score, but I must add this: when, two months ago, you came here, I realised, perhaps for the first time, that I was a middle-aged woman, and that it had become impossible for me to accept without some effort a breaking-in upon many tender associations. There, Mrs. Tanqueray, that is my confession. Will you try to understand it and pardon me?

PAULA [*watching* ELLEAN,—*sneeringly*]: Ellean dear, you appear to be very interested in Mrs.

Cortelyon's reminiscences; I don't think I can do better than make you my mouthpiece—there is such sympathy between us. What do you say—can we bring ourselves to forgive Mrs. Cortelyon for neglecting us for two weary months?

MRS. CORTELYON [*to* ELLEAN, *pleasantly*]: Well, Ellean? [*With a little cry of tenderness* ELLEAN *impulsively sits beside* MRS. CORTELYON *and takes her hand.*] My dear child!

PAULA [*in an undertone to* AUBREY]: Ellean isn't so very slow in taking to Mrs. Cortelyon!

MRS. CORTELYON [*to* PAULA *and* AUBREY]: Come, this encourages me to broach my scheme. Mrs. Tanqueray, it strikes me that you two good people are just now excellent company for each other, while Ellean would perhaps be glad of a little peep into the world you are anxious to avoid. Now, I'm going to Paris tomorrow for a week or two before settling down in Chester Square, so—don't gasp, both of you!—if this girl is willing, and you have made no other arrangements for her, will you let her come with me to Paris, and afterwards remain with me in town during the season? [ELLEAN *utters an exclamation of surprise.* PAULA *is silent.*] What do you say?

AUBREY: Paula—Paula dear. [*Hesitatingly.*] My dear Mrs. Cortelyon, this is wonderfully kind of you; I am really at a loss to—eh, Cayley?

DRUMMLE [*watching* PAULA *apprehensively*]: Kind! Now I must say I don't think so! I begged Alice to take *me* to Paris, and she declined. I am thrown over for Ellean! Ha! ha!

MRS. CORTELYON [*laughing*]: What nonsense you talk, Cayley!

[*The laughter dies out.* PAULA *remains quite still.*]

AUBREY: Paula dear.

PAULA [*slowly collecting herself*]: One moment. I—I don't quite—[*To* MRS. CORTELYON.] You propose that Ellean leaves Highercoombe almost at once, and remains with you some months?

MRS. CORTELYON: It would be a mercy to me. You can afford to be generous to a desolate old widow. Come, Mrs. Tanqueray, won't you spare her?

PAULA: Won't *I* spare her. [*Suspiciously.*] Have you mentioned your plan to Aubrey—before I came in?

MRS. CORTELYON: No, I had no opportunity.

PAULA: Nor to Ellean?

MRS. CORTELYON: Oh, no.

PAULA [*looking about her in suppressed excitement*]: This hasn't been discussed at all, behind my back?

MRS. CORTELYON: My dear Mrs. Tanqueray!

PAULA: Ellean, let us hear your voice in the matter!

ELLEAN: I should like to go with Mrs. Cortelyon—

PAULA: Ah!

ELLEAN: That is, if—if—

PAULA: If—what?

ELLEAN [*looking towards* AUBREY, *appealingly*]: Papa!

PAULA [*in a hard voice*]: Oh, of course—I forgot. [*To* AUBREY.] My dear Aubrey, it rests with you, naturally, whether I am— to lose—Ellean.

AUBREY: Lose Ellean! [*Advancing to* PAULA.] There is no question of losing Ellean. You would see Ellean in town constantly when she returned from Paris; isn't that so, Mrs. Cortelyon?

MRS. CORTELYON: Certainly.

PAULA [*laughing softly*]: Oh, I didn't know I should be allowed that privilege.

MRS. CORTELYON: Privilege, my dear Mrs. Tanqueray!

PAULA: Ha, ha! that makes all the difference, doesn't it?

AUBREY [*with assumed gaiety*]: All the difference? I should think so! [*To* ELLEAN, *laying his hand upon her head tenderly*.] And you are quite certain you wish to see what the world is like on the other side of Black Moor!

ELLEAN: If you are willing, papa, I am quite certain.

AUBREY [*looking at* PAULA *irresolutely, then speaking with an effort*]: Then I—I am willing.

PAULA [*rising and striking the table lightly with her clenched hand*]: That decides it! [*There is a general movement. Excitedly to* MRS. CORTELYON, *who advances towards her.*] When do you want her?

MRS. CORTELYON: We go to town this afternoon at five o'clock, and sleep tonight at Bayliss's. There is barely time for her to make her preparations.

PAULA: I will undertake that she is ready.

MRS. CORTELYON: I've a great deal to scramble through at home too, as you may guess. Good-bye!

PAULA [*turning away*]: Mrs. Cor-telyon is going. [PAULA *stands looking out of the window, with her back to those in the room.*]

MRS. CORTELYON [*to* DRUMMLE]: Cayley—

DRUMMLE [*to her*]: Eh?

MRS. CORTELYON: I've gone through it, for the sake of Aubrey and his child, but I— I feel a hundred. Is that a mad-woman?

DRUMMLE: Of course; all jealous women are mad. [*He goes out with* AUBREY.]

MRS. CORTELYON [*hesitatingly, to* PAULA]: Good-bye, Mrs. Tan-queray.

[PAULA *inclines her head with the slightest possible movement, then resumes her former position.* EL-LEAN *comes from the hall and takes* MRS. CORTELYON *out of the room. After a brief silence,* PAULA *turns with a fierce cry, and hurriedly takes off her coat and hat, and tosses them upon the settee.*]

PAULA: Who's that? Oh! Oh! Oh!

[*She drops into the chair as* AU-BREY *returns; he stands looking at her.*]

AUBREY: I—you have altered your mind about going out?

PAULA: Yes. Please to ring the bell.

AUBREY [*touching the bell*]: You are angry about Mrs. Cortelyon and Ellean. Let me try to explain my reasons—

PAULA: Be careful what you say to me just now! I have never felt like this—except once—in my life. Be careful what you say to me!

[*A* SERVANT *enters.*]

PAULA [*rising*]: Is Watts at the door with the cart?

SERVANT: Yes, ma'am.

PAULA: Tell him to drive down to the post-office directly with this. [*Picking up the letter which has been lying upon the table.*]

AUBREY: With that?

PAULA: Yes. My letter to Lady Orreyed. [*Giving the letter to the* SERVANT, *who goes out.*]

AUBREY: Surely you don't wish me to countermand any order of yours to a servant? Call the man back—take the letter from him!

PAULA: I have not the slightest intention of doing so.

AUBREY: I must, then. [*Going to the door. She snatches up her hat and coat and follows him.*] What are you going to do?

PAULA: If you stop that letter, I walk out of the house. [*He hesitates, then leaves the door.*]

AUBREY: I am right in believing that to be the letter inviting George Orreyed and his wife to stay here, am I not?

PAULA: Oh, yes—quite right.

AUBREY: Let it go; I'll write to him by-and-bye.

PAULA [*facing him*]: You dare!

AUBREY: Hush, Paula!

PAULA: Insult me again and, upon my word, I'll go straight out of the house!

AUBREY: Insult you?

PAULA: Insult me! What else is it? My God! what else is it?

What do you mean by taking Ellean from me?

AUBREY: Listen—!

PAULA: Listen to *me!* And how do you take her? You pack her off in the care of a woman who has deliberately held aloof from me, who's thrown mud at me! Yet this Cortelyon creature has only to put foot here once to be entrusted with the charge of the girl you know I dearly want to keep near me!

AUBREY: Paula dear! hear me—!

PAULA: Ah! of course, of course! I can't be so useful to your daughter as such people as this; and so I'm to be given the go-by for any town friend of yours who turns up and chooses to patronise us! Hah! Very well, at any rate, as you take Ellean from me you justify my looking for companions where I can most readily find 'em.

AUBREY: You wish me to fully appreciate your reason for sending that letter to Lady Orreyed?

PAULA: Precisely—I do.

AUBREY: And could you, after all, go back to associates of that order? It's not possible!

PAULA [*mockingly*]: What, not after the refining influence of these intensely respectable surroundings? [*Going to the door.*] We'll see!

AUBREY: Paula!

PAULA [*violently*]: We'll see! [*She goes out. He stands still, looking after her.*]

ACT THREE

The drawing-room at "Highercoombe." Facing the spectator are two large French windows, sheltered by a verandah, leading into the garden; on the right is a door opening into a small hall. The fireplace, with a large mirror above it, is on the left-hand side of the room, and higher up in the same wall are double doors recessed. The room is richly furnished, and everything betokens taste and luxury. The windows are open, and there is moonlight in the garden.

[LADY ORREYED, *a pretty, affected doll of a woman, with a mincing voice and flaxen hair, is sitting on the ottoman, her head resting against the drum, and her eyes closed.* PAULA, *looking pale, worn, and thoroughly unhappy, is sitting at a table. Both are in sumptuous dinner-gowns.*]

LADY ORREYED [*opening her eyes*]: Well, I never! I dropped off! [*Feeling her hair.*] Just fancy! Where are the men?
PAULA [*icily*]: Outside, smoking.

[*A* SERVANT *enters with coffee, which he hands to* LADY ORREYED. SIR GEORGE ORREYED *comes in by the window. He is a man of about thirty-five, with a low forehead, a receding chin, a vacuous expression, and an ominous redness about the nose.*]

LADY ORREYED [*taking coffee*]: Here's Dodo.
SIR GEORGE: I say, the flies under the verandah make you swear. [*The* SERVANT *hands coffee to* PAULA, *who declines it, then to* SIR GEORGE, *who takes a cup.*]

Hi! wait a bit! [*He looks at the tray searchingly, then puts back his cup.*] Never mind. [*Quietly to* LADY ORREYED.] I say, they're dooced sparin' with their liqueur, ain't they?

[*The* SERVANT *goes out at window.*]

PAULA [*to* SIR GEORGE]: Won't you take coffee, George?
SIR GEORGE: No, thanks. It's gettin' near time for a whiskey and potass. [*Approaching* PAULA, *regarding* LADY ORREYED *admiringly.*] I say, Birdie looks rippin' tonight, don't she?
PAULA: Your wife?
SIR GEORGE: Yaas—Birdie.
PAULA: Rippin'?
SIR GEORGE: Yaas.
PAULA: Quite—quite rippin'.

[*He moves round to the settee.* PAULA *watches him with distaste, then rises and walks away.* SIR GEORGE *falls asleep on the settee.*]

LADY ORREYED: Paula love, I fancied you and Aubrey were a little more friendly at dinner. You

114

haven't made it up, have you?

PAULA: We? Oh, no. We speak before others, that's all.

LADY ORREYED: And how long do you intend to carry on this game, dear?

PAULA [*turning away impatiently*]: I really can't tell you.

LADY ORREYED: Sit down, old girl; don't be so fidgety. [PAULA *sits on the upper seat of the ottoman, with her back to* LADY ORREYED.] Of course, it's my duty, as an old friend, to give you a good talking-to—[PAULA *glares at her suddenly and fiercely*]—but really I've found one gets so many smacks in the face through interfering in matrimonial squabbles that I've determined to drop it.

PAULA: I think you're wise.

LADY ORREYED: However, I must say that I do wish you'd look at marriage in a more solemn light—just as I do, in fact. It is such a beautiful thing—marriage, and if people in our position don't respect it, and set a good example by living happily with their husbands, what can you expect from the middle classes? When did this sad state of affairs between you and Aubrey actually begin?

PAULA: Actually, a fortnight and three days ago; I haven't calculated the minutes.

LADY ORREYED: A day or two before Dodo and I turned up—arrived.

PAULA: Yes. One always remembers one thing by another; we left off speaking to each other the morning I wrote asking you to visit us.

LADY ORREYED: Lucky for you I was able to pop down, wasn't it, dear?

PAULA [*glaring at her again*]: Most fortunate.

LADY ORREYED: A serious split with your husband without a pal on the premises—I should say, without a friend in the house—would be most unpleasant.

PAULA [*turning to her abruptly*]: This place must be horribly doleful for you and George just now. At least you ought to consider him before me. Why didn't you leave me to my difficulties?

LADY ORREYED: Oh, we're quite comfortable, dear, thank you—both of us. George and me are so wrapped up in each other, it doesn't matter where we are. I don't want to crow over you, old girl, but I've got a perfect husband.

[SIR GEORGE *is now fast asleep, his head thrown back and his mouth open, looking hideous.*]

PAULA [*glancing at* SIR GEORGE]: So you've given me to understand.

LADY ORREYED: Not that we don't have our little differences. Why, we fell out only this very morning. You remember the diamond and ruby tiara Charley Prestwick gave poor dear Connie Tirlemont years ago, don't you?

PAULA: No, I do not.

LADY ORREYED: No? Well, it's in the market. Benjamin of Piccadilly has got it in his shop window, and I've set my heart on it.

PAULA: You consider it quite necessary?

LADY ORREYED: Yes, because

what I say to Dodo is this—a lady of my station must smother herself with hair ornaments. It's different with you, love—people don't look for so much blaze from you, but I've got rank to keep up; haven't I?

PAULA: Yes.

LADY ORREYED: Well, that was the cause of the little set-to between I and Dodo this morning. He broke two chairs, he was in such a rage. I forgot they're your chairs; do you mind?

PAULA: No.

LADY ORREYED: You know, poor Dodo can't lose his temper without smashing something; if it isn't a chair, it's a mirror; if it isn't that, it's china—a bit of Dresden for choice. Dear old pet! he loves a bit of Dresden when he's furious. He doesn't really throw things *at* me, dear; he simply lifts them up and drops them, like a gentleman. I expect our room upstairs will look rather wrecky before I get that tiara.

PAULA: Excuse the suggestion; perhaps your husband can't afford it.

LADY ORREYED: Oh, how dreadfully changed you are, Paula! Dodo can always mortgage something, or borrow of his ma. What *is* coming to you!

PAULA: Ah! [*She sits at the piano and touches the keys.*]

LADY ORREYED: Oh, yes, do play! That's the one thing I envy you for.

PAULA: What shall I play?

LADY ORREYED: What was that heavenly piece you gave us last night, dear?

PAULA: A bit of Schubert. Would you like to hear it again?

LADY ORREYED: You don't know any comic songs, do you?

PAULA: I'm afraid not.

LADY ORREYED: I leave it to you.

[PAULA *plays.* AUBREY *and* CAYLEY DRUMMLE *appear outside the window; they look into the room.*]

AUBREY [*to* DRUMMLE]: You can see her face in that mirror. Poor girl, how ill and wretched she looks.

DRUMMLE: When are the Orreyeds going?

AUBREY: Heaven knows! [*Entering the room.*]

DRUMMLE: But *you're* entertaining them; what's it to do with heaven? [*Following* AUBREY.]

AUBREY: Do you know, Cayley, that even the Orreyeds serve a useful purpose? My wife actually speaks to me before our guests—think of that! I've come to rejoice at the presence of the Orreyeds!

DRUMMLE: I dare say; we're taught that beetles are sent for a benign end.

AUBREY: Cayley, talk to Paula again tonight.

DRUMMLE: Certainly, if I get the chance.

AUBREY: Let's contrive it. George is asleep; perhaps I can get that doll out of the way. [*As they advance into the room,* PAULA *abruptly ceases playing and finds interest in a volume of music.* SIR GEORGE *is now nodding and snoring apoplectically.*] Lady Orreyed, whenever you feel inclined for a game of billiards I'm at your service.

LADY ORREYED [*jumping up*]:

Charmed, I'm sure! I really thought you'd forgotten poor little me. Oh, look at Dodo!

AUBREY: No, no, don't wake him; he's tired.

LADY ORREYED: I must, he looks so plain. [*Rousing* SIR GEORGE.] Dodo! Dodo!

SIR GEORGE [*stupidly*]: 'Ullo!

LADY ORREYED: Dodo dear, you were snoring.

SIR GEORGE: Oh, I say, you could 'a told me that by-and-bye.

AUBREY: You want a cigar, George; come into the billiard-room. [*Giving his arm to* LADY ORREYED.] Cayley, bring Paula. [AUBREY *and* LADY ORREYED *go out.*]

SIR GEORGE [*rising*]: Hey, what! Billiard-room! [*Looking at his watch.*] How goes the—? Phew! 'Ullo, 'ullo! Whiskey and potass!

[*He goes rapidly after* AUBREY *and* LADY ORREYED. PAULA *resumes playing.*]

PAULA [*after a pause*]: Don't moon about after me, Cayley; follow the others.

DRUMMLE: Thanks, by-and-bye. [*Sitting.*] That's pretty.

PAULA [*after another pause, still playing*]: I wish you wouldn't stare so.

DRUMMLE: Was I staring? I'm sorry. [*She plays a little longer, then stops suddenly, rises, and goes to the window, where she stands looking out.* DRUMMLE *moves from the ottoman to the settee.*] A lovely night.

PAULA [*startled*]: Oh! [*Without turning to him.*] Why do you hop about like a monkey?

DRUMMLE: Hot rooms play the deuce with the nerves. Now, it would have done you good to have walked in the garden with us after dinner and made merry. Why didn't you?

PAULA: You know why.

DRUMMLE: Ah, you're thinking of the—difference between you and Aubrey?

PAULA: Yes, I *am* thinking of it.

DRUMMLE: Well, so am I. How long—?

PAULA: Getting on for three weeks.

DRUMMLE: Bless me, it must be! And this would have been such a night to have healed it! Moonlight, the stars, the scent of flowers; and yet enough darkness to enable a kind woman to rest her hand for an instant on the arm of a good fellow who loves her. Ah, ha! It's a wonderful power, dear Mrs. Aubrey, the power of an offended woman! Only realise it! Just that one touch—the mere tips of her fingers—and, for herself and another, she changes the colour of the whole world.

PAULA [*turning to him calmly*]: Cayley, my dear man, you talk exactly like a very romantic old lady. [*She leaves the window and sits playing with the knick-knacks on the table.*]

DRUMMLE [*to himself*]: H'm, that hasn't done it! Well—ha, ha!— I accept the suggestion. An old woman, eh?

PAULA: Oh, I didn't intend—

DRUMMLE: But why not! I've every qualification—well, almost. And I confess it would have given this withered bosom a throb of grandmotherly satisfaction if I could have seen you and Aubrey at peace before I take my leave tomorrow.

PAULA: Tomorrow, Cayley!

DRUMMLE: I must.

PAULA: Oh, this house is becoming unendurable.

DRUMMLE: You're very kind. But you've got the Orreyeds.

PAULA [*fiercely*]: The Orreyeds! I—I hate the Orreyeds! I lie awake at night, hating them!

DRUMMLE: Pardon me, I've understood that their visit is, in some degree, owing to—hem—your suggestion.

PAULA: Heavens! that doesn't make me like them better. Somehow or another, I—I've outgrown these people. This woman—I used to think her "jolly!" —sickens me. I can't breathe when she's near me: the whiff of her handkerchief turns me faint! And she patronises me by the hour, until I—I feel my nails growing longer with every word she speaks!

DRUMMLE: My dear lady, why on earth don't you say all this to Aubrey?

PAULA: Oh, I've been such an utter fool, Cayley!

DRUMMLE [*soothingly*]: Well, well, mention it to Aubrey!

PAULA: No, no, you don't understand. What do you think I've done?

DRUMMLE: Done! What, *since* you invited the Orreyeds?

PAULA: Yes; I must tell you—

DRUMMLE: Perhaps you'd better not.

PAULA: Look here! I've intercepted some letters from Mrs. Cortelyon and Ellean to—him. [*Producing three unopened letters from the bodice of her dress.*]

There are the accursed things! From Paris—two from the Cortelyon woman, the other from Ellean!

DRUMMLE: But why—why?

PAULA: I don't know. Yes, I do! I saw letters coming from Ellean to her father; not a line to me—not a line. And one morning it happened I was downstairs before he was, and I spied this one lying with his heap on the breakfast-table, and I slipped it into my pocket—out of malice, Cayley, pure deviltry! And a day or two afterwards I met Elwes the postman at the Lodge, and took the letters from him, and found these others amongst 'em. I felt simply fiendish when I saw them—fiendish! [*Returning the letters to her bodice.*] And now I carry them about with me, and they're scorching me like a mustard plaster!

DRUMMLE: Oh, this accounts for Aubrey not hearing from Paris lately!

PAULA: That's an ingenious conclusion to arrive at! Of course it does! [*With an hysterical laugh.*] Ha, ha!

DRUMMLE: Well, well! [*Laughing.*] Ha, ha, ha!

PAULA [*turning upon him*]: I suppose it *is* amusing!

DRUMMLE: I beg pardon.

PAULA: Heaven knows I've little enough to brag about! I'm a bad lot, but not in mean tricks of this sort. In all my life this is the most caddish thing I've done. How am I to get rid of these letters—that's what I want to know? How am I to get rid of them?

DRUMMLE: If I were you I should take Aubrey aside and put them into his hands as soon as possible.

PAULA: What! and tell him to his face that I—! No, thank you. I suppose *you* wouldn't like to—

DRUMMLE: No, no; I won't touch 'em!

PAULA: And you call yourself my friend?

DRUMMLE [*good-humouredly*]: No, I don't!

PAULA: Perhaps I'll tie them together and give them to his man in the morning.

DRUMMLE: That won't avoid an explanation.

PAULA [*recklessly*]: Oh, then he must miss them—

DRUMMLE: And trace them.

PAULA [*throwing herself upon the ottoman*]: I don't care!

DRUMMLE: I know you don't; but let me send him to you now, may I?

PAULA: Now! What do you think a woman's made of? I couldn't stand it, Cayley. I haven't slept for nights; and last night there was thunder, too! I believe I've got the horrors.

DRUMMLE [*taking the little hand-mirror from the table*]: You'll sleep well enough when you deliver those letters. Come, come, Mrs. Aubrey—a good night's rest! [*Holding the mirror before her face.*] It's quite time. [*She looks at herself for a moment, then snatches the mirror from him.*]

PAULA: You brute, Cayley, to show me that!

DRUMMLE: Then—may I? Be guided by a fr—a poor old woman! May I?

PAULA: You'll kill me, amongst you!

DRUMMLE: What do you say?

PAULA [*after a pause*]: Very well. [*He nods his head and goes out rapidly. She looks after him for a moment, and calls "Cayley! Cayley!" Then she again produces the letters, deliberately, one by one, fingering them with aversion. Suddenly she starts, turning her head towards the door.*] Ah!

[AUBREY *enters quickly.*]

AUBREY: Paula!

PAULA [*handing him the letters, her face averted*]: There! [*He examines the letters, puzzled, and looks at her enquiringly.*] They are many days old. I stole them, I suppose to make you anxious and unhappy. [*He looks at the letters again, then lays them aside on the table.*]

AUBREY [*gently*]: Paula, dear, it doesn't matter.

PAULA [*after a short pause*]: Why—why do you take it like this?

AUBREY: What did you expect?

PAULA: Oh, but I suppose silent reproaches are really the severest. And then, naturally, you are itching to open your letters. [*She crosses the room as if to go.*]

AUBREY: Paula! [*She pauses.*] Surely, surely, it's all over now?

PAULA: All over! [*Mockingly.*] Has my stepdaughter returned then? When did she arrive? I haven't heard of it!

AUBREY: You can be very cruel.

PAULA: That word's always on a man's lips; he uses it if his soup's cold. [*With another movement as if to go.*] Need we—

AUBREY: I know I've wounded you, Paula? But isn't there any way out of this?

PAULA: When does Ellean return? Tomorrow? Next week?

AUBREY [wearily]: Oh! Why should we grudge Ellean the little pleasure she is likely to find in Paris and in London?

PAULA: I grudge her nothing, if that's a hit at me. But with that woman—?

AUBREY: It must be that woman or another. You know that at present we are unable to give Ellean the opportunity of—of—

PAULA: Of mixing with respectable people.

AUBREY: The opportunity of gaining friends, experience, ordinary knowledge of the world. If you are interested in Ellean, can't you see how useful Mrs. Cortelyon's good offices are?

PAULA: May I put one question? At the end of the London season, when Mrs. Cortelyon has done with Ellean, is it quite understood that the girl comes back to us? [AUBREY is silent.] Is it? Is it?

AUBREY: Let us wait till the end of the season—

PAULA: Oh! I knew it. You're only fooling me; you put me off with any trash. I believe you've sent Ellean away, not for the reasons you give, but because you don't consider me a decent companion for her, because you're afraid she might get a little of her innocence rubbed off in my company? Come, isn't that the truth? Be honest! Isn't that it?

AUBREY: Yes. [There is a moment's silence on both sides.]

PAULA [with uplifted hands as if to strike him]: Oh!

AUBREY [taking her by the wrists]: Sit down. Sit down. [He puts her into a chair; she shakes herself free with a cry.] Now listen to me. Fond as you are, Paula, of harking back to your past, there's one chapter of it you always let alone. I've never asked you to speak of it; you've never offered to speak of it. I mean the chapter that relates to the time when you were—like Ellean. [She attempts to rise; he restrains her.] No, no.

PAULA: I don't choose to talk about that time. I won't satisfy your curiosity.

AUBREY: My dear Paula, I have no curiosity—I know what you were at Ellean's age. I'll tell you. You hadn't a thought that wasn't a wholesome one, you hadn't an impulse that didn't tend towards good, you never harboured a notion you couldn't have gossiped about to a parcel of children. [She makes another effort to rise: he lays his hand lightly on her shoulder.] And this was a very few years back—there are days now when you look like a schoolgirl—but think of the difference between the two Paulas. You'll have to think hard, because after a cruel life, one's perceptions grow a thick skin. But, for God's sake, do think till you get these two images clearly in your mind, and then ask yourself what sort of a friend such a woman as you are today would have been for the girl of seven or eight years ago.

PAULA [rising]: How dare you? I

could be almost as good a friend to Ellean as her own mother would have been had she lived. I know what you mean. How dare you?

AUBREY: You say that; very likely you believe it. But you're blind, Paula; you're blind. You! Every belief that a young, pure-minded girl holds sacred—that you once held sacred—you now make a target for a jest, a sneer, a paltry cynicism. I tell you, you're not mistress any longer of your thoughts or your tongue. Why, how often, sitting between you and Ellean, have I seen her cheeks turn scarlet as you've rattled off some tale that belongs by right to the club or the smoking-room! Have you noticed the blush? If you have, has the cause of it ever struck you? And this is the girl you say you love, I admit that you *do* love, whose love you expect in return! Oh, Paula, I make the best, the only, excuse for you when I tell you you're blind!

PAULA: Ellean—Ellean blushes easily.

AUBREY: You blushed as easily a few years ago.

PAULA [*after a short pause*]: Well! Have you finished your sermon?

AUBREY [*with a gesture of despair*]: Oh, Paula! [*Going up to the window, and standing with his back to the room.*]

PAULA [*to herself*]: A few—years ago! [*She walks slowly towards the door, then suddenly drops upon the ottoman in a paroxysm of weeping.*] O God! A few years ago!

AUBREY [*going to her*]: Paula!

PAULA [*sobbing*]: Oh, don't touch me!

AUBREY: Paula!

PAULA: Oh, go away from me! [*He goes back a few steps, and after a little while she becomes calmer and rises unsteadily; then in an altered tone.*] Look here—! [*He advances a step; she checks him with a quick gesture.*] Look here! Get rid of these people—Mabel and her husband—as soon as possible! I—I've done with them!

AUBREY [*in a whisper*]: Paula!

PAULA: And then—then—when the time comes for Ellean to leave Mrs. Cortelyon, give me—give me another chance! [*He advances again, but she shrinks away.*] No, no!

[*She goes out by the door on the right. He sinks onto the settee, covering his eyes with his hands. There is a brief silence, then a* SERVANT *enters.*]

SERVANT: Mrs. Cortelyon, sir, with Miss Ellean.

[AUBREY *rises to meet* MRS. CORTELYON, *who enters, followed by* ELLEAN, *both being in travelling dresses. The* SERVANT *withdraws.*]

MRS. CORTELYON [*shaking hands with* AUBREY]: Oh, my dear Aubrey!

AUBREY: Mrs. Cortelyon! [*Kissing* ELLEAN.] Ellean dear!

ELLEAN: Papa, is all well at home?

MRS. CORTELYON: We're shockingly anxious.

AUBREY: Yes, yes, all's well. This is quite unexpected. [*To* MRS. CORTELYON.] You've found Paris insufferably hot?

MRS. CORTELYON: Insufferably hot! Paris is pleasant enough. We've had no letter from you!

AUBREY: I wrote to Ellean a week ago.

MRS. CORTELYON: Without alluding to the subject I had written to you upon.

AUBREY [*thinking*]: Ah, of course—

MRS. CORTELYON: And since then we've both written, and you've been absolutely silent. Oh, it's too bad!

AUBREY [*picking up the letters from the table*]: It isn't altogether my fault. Here are the letters—

ELLEAN: Papa!

MRS. CORTELYON: They're unopened.

AUBREY: An accident delayed their reaching me till this evening. I'm afraid this has upset you very much.

MRS. CORTELYON: Upset me!

ELLEAN [*in an undertone to* MRS. CORTELYON]: Never mind. Not now, dear—not tonight.

AUBREY: Eh?

MRS. CORTELYON [*to* ELLEAN, *aloud*]: Child, run away and take your things off. She doesn't look as if she'd journeyed from Paris today.

AUBREY: I've never seen her with such a colour. [*Taking* ELLEAN'S *hands*.]

ELLEAN [*to* AUBREY, *in a faint voice*]: Papa, Mrs. Cortelyon has been so very, very kind to me, but I—I have come home. [*She goes out*.]

AUBREY: Come home! [*To* MRS. CORTELYON.] Ellean returns to us then?

MRS. CORTELYON: That's the very point I put to you in my letters, and you oblige me to travel from Paris to Willowmere on a warm day to settle it. I think perhaps it's right that Ellean should be with you just now, although I— My dear friend, circumstances are a little altered.

AUBREY: Alice, you're in some trouble.

MRS. CORTELYON: Well—yes, I *am* in trouble. You remember pretty little Mrs. Brereton who was once Caroline Ardale?

AUBREY: Quite well.

MRS. CORTELYON: She's a widow now, poor thing. She has the *entre-sol* of the house where we've been lodging in the Avenue de Friedland. Caroline's a dear chum of mine; she formed a great liking for Ellean.

AUBREY: I'm very glad.

MRS. CORTELYON: Yes, it's nice for her to meet her mother's friends. Er—that young Hugh Ardale the papers were full of some time ago—he's Caroline Brereton's brother, you know.

AUBREY: No, I didn't know. What did he do? I forget.

MRS. CORTELYON: Checked one of those horrid mutinies at some far-away station in India. Marched down with a handful of his men and a few faithful natives, and held the place until he was relieved. They gave him his company and a V.C. for it.

AUBREY: And he's Mrs. Brereton's brother?

MRS. CORTELYON: Yes. He's with his sister—*was*, rather—in Paris. He's home—invalided. Good gracious, Aubrey, why don't you help me out? Can't you guess what has occurred?

AUBREY: Alice!

MRS. CORTELYON: Young Ardale —Ellean!

AUBREY: An attachment?

MRS. CORTELYON: Yes, Aubrey. [*After a little pause.*] Well, I suppose I've got myself into sad disgrace. But really I didn't foresee anything of this kind. A serious, reserved child like Ellean, and a boyish, high-spirited soldier—it never struck me as being likely. [AUBREY *paces to and fro thoughtfully.*] I did all I could directly Captain Ardale spoke—wrote to you at once. Why on earth don't you receive your letters promptly, and when you do get them why can't you open them? I endured the anxiety till last night, and then made up my mind—home! Of course, it has worried me terribly. My head's bursting. Are there any salts about? [AUBREY *fetches a bottle from the cabinet and hands it to her.*] We've had one of those hateful smooth crossings that won't let you be properly indisposed.

AUBREY: My dear Alice, I assure you I've no thought of blaming you.

MRS. CORTELYON: That statement always precedes a quarrel.

AUBREY: I don't know whether this is the worst or the best luck. How will my wife regard it? Is Captain Ardale a good fellow?

MRS. CORTELYON: My dear Aubrey, you'd better read up the accounts of his wonderful heroism. Face to face with death for a whole week; always with a smile and a cheering word for the poor helpless souls depending on him! Of course it's that that has stirred the depths of your child's nature. I've watched her while we've been dragging the story out of him, and if angels look different from Ellean at that moment, I don't desire to meet any, that's all!

AUBREY: If you were in my position—? But you can't judge.

MRS. CORTELYON: Why, if I had a marriageable daughter of my own, and Captain Ardale proposed for her, naturally I should cry my eyes out all night—but I should thank Heaven in the morning.

AUBREY: You believe so thoroughly in him?

MRS. CORTELYON: Do you think I should have only a headache at this minute if I didn't! Look here, you've got to see me down the lane; that's the least you can do, my friend. Come into my house for a moment and shake hands with Hugh.

AUBREY: What, is he here?

MRS. CORTELYON: He came through with us, to present himself formally tomorrow. Where are my gloves? [AUBREY *fetches them from the ottoman.*] Make my apologies to Mrs. Tanqueray, please. She's well, I hope? [*Going towards the door.*] I can't feel sorry she hasn't seen me in this condition.

[ELLEAN *enters.*]

ELLEAN [*to* MRS. CORTELYON]: I've been waiting to wish you good night. I was afraid I'd missed you.

MRS. CORTELYON: Good night, Ellean.

ELLEAN [*in a low voice, embracing* MRS. CORTELYON]: I can't thank you. Dear Mrs. Cortelyon!

MRS. CORTELYON [*her arms round* ELLEAN, *in a whisper to* AUBREY]: Speak a word to her. [MRS. CORTELYON *goes out.*]

AUBREY [*to* ELLEAN]: Ellean, I'm going to see Mrs. Cortelyon home. Tell Paula where I am; explain, dear. [*Going to the door.*]

ELLEAN [*her head drooping*]: Yes. [*Quickly.*] Father! You are angry with me—disappointed?

AUBREY: Angry? No.

ELLEAN: Disappointed?

AUBREY [*smiling and going to her and taking her hand*]: If so, it's only because you've shaken my belief in my discernment. I thought you took after your poor mother a little, Ellean; but there's a look on your face tonight, dear, that I never saw on hers—never, never.

ELLEAN [*leaning her head on his shoulder*]: Perhaps I ought not to have gone away.

AUBREY: Hush! you're quite happy?

ELLEAN: Yes.

AUBREY: That's right. Then, as you are quite happy, there is something I particularly want you to do for me, Ellean.

ELLEAN: What is that?

AUBREY: Be very gentle with Paula. Will you?

ELLEAN: You think I have been unkind.

AUBREY [*kissing her upon the forehead*]: Be very gentle with Paula.

[*He goes out, and she stands looking after him; then, as she turns thoughtfully from the door, a rose is thrown through the window and falls at her feet. She picks up the flower wonderingly and goes to the window.*]

ELLEAN [*starting back*]: Hugh!

[HUGH ARDALE, *a handsome young man of about seven-and-twenty, with a boyish face and manner, appears outside the window.*]

HUGH: Nelly! Nelly dear!

ELLEAN: What's the matter?

HUGH: Hush! Nothing. It's only fun. [*Laughing.*] Ha, ha, ha! I've found out that Mrs. Cortelyon's meadow runs up to your father's plantation; I've come through a gap in the hedge.

ELLEAN: Why, Hugh?

HUGH: I'm miserable at The Warren: it's so different from the Avenue de Friedland. Don't look like that! Upon my word I meant just to peep at your home and go back, but I saw figures moving about here, and came nearer, hoping to get a glimpse of you. Was that your father? [*Entering the room.*]

ELLEAN: Yes.

HUGH: Isn't this fun! A rabbit ran across my foot while I was hiding behind that old yew.

ELLEAN: You must go away; it's not right for you to be here like this.

HUGH: But it's only fun, I tell you. You take everything so seriously. Do wish me good night.

ELLEAN: We have said good night.

HUGH: In the hall at The Warren, before Mrs. Cortelyon and a manservant. Oh, it's so different from the Avenue de Friedland!

ELLEAN [*giving him her hand hastily*]: Good night, Hugh.

HUGH: Is that all? We might be the merest acquaintances. [*He momentarily embraces her, but she releases herself.*]

ELLEAN: It's when you're like this that you make me feel utterly miserable. [*Throwing the rose from her angrily.*] Oh!

HUGH: I've offended you now, I suppose?

ELLEAN: Yes.

HUGH: Forgive me, Nelly. Come into the garden for five minutes; we'll stroll down to the plantation.

ELLEAN: No, no.

HUGH: For two minutes—to tell me you forgive me.

ELLEAN: I forgive you.

HUGH: Evidently. I sha'n't sleep a wink tonight after this. What a fool I am! Come down to the plantation. Make it up with me.

ELLEAN: There is somebody coming into this room. Do you wish to be seen here?

HUGH: I shall wait for you behind that yew tree. You must speak to me. Nelly!

[*He disappears.* PAULA *enters.*]

PAULA: Ellean!

ELLEAN: You—you are very surprised to see me, Paula, of course.

PAULA: Why are you here? Why aren't you with—your friend?

ELLEAN: I've come home—if you'll have me. We left Paris this morning; Mrs. Cortelyon brought me back. She was here a minute or two ago; papa has just gone with her to The Warren. He asked me to tell you.

PAULA: There are some people staying with us that I'd rather you didn't meet. It was hardly worth your while to return for a few hours.

ELLEAN: A few hours?

PAULA: Well, when do you go to London?

ELLEAN: I don't think I go to London, after all.

PAULA [*eagerly*]: You—you've quarrelled with her?

ELLEAN: No, no, no, not that; but—Paula! [*In an altered tone.*] Paula!

PAULA [*startled*]: Eh? [ELLEAN *goes deliberately to* PAULA *and kisses her.*] Ellean!

ELLEAN: Kiss me.

PAULA: What—what's come to you?

ELLEAN: I want to behave differently to you in the future. Is it too late?

PAULA: Too—late! [*Impulsively kissing* ELLEAN *and crying.*] No—no—no! No—no!

ELLEAN: Paula, don't cry.

PAULA [*wiping her eyes*]: I'm a little shaky; I haven't been sleeping. It's all right—talk to me.

ELLEAN: There is something I want to tell you—

PAULA: Is there—is there?

[*They sit together on the ottoman,* PAULA *taking* ELLEAN'S *hand.*]

ELLEAN: Paula, in our house in the Avenue de Friedland, on the floor below us, there was a Mrs. Brereton. She used to be a friend of my mother's. Mrs. Cortelyon and I spent a great deal of our time with her.

PAULA [*suspiciously*]: Oh! [*Letting* ELLEAN'S *hand fall.*] Is this lady going to take you up in place of Mrs. Cortelyon?

ELLEAN: No, no. Her brother is staying with her—*was* staying with her. Her brother— [*Breaking off in confusion.*]

PAULA: Well?

ELLEAN [*almost inaudibly*]: Paula— [*She rises and walks away,* PAULA *following her.*]

PAULA: Ellean! [*Taking hold of her.*] You're not in love! [ELLEAN *looks at* PAULA *appealingly.*] Oh, *you* in love! You! Oh, this is why you've come home! Of course, you can make friends with me now! You'll leave us for good soon, I suppose; so it doesn't much matter being civil to me for a little while!

ELLEAN: Oh, Paula!

PAULA: Why, how you have deceived us—all of us! We've taken you for a cold-blooded little saint. The fools you've made of us! Saint Ellean, Saint Ellean!

ELLEAN: Ah, I might have known you'd only mock me!

PAULA [*her tone changing*]: Eh?

ELLEAN: I—I can't talk to you. [*Sitting on the settee.*] You do nothing else but mock and sneer, nothing else.

PAULA: Ellean dear! Ellean! I didn't mean it. I'm so horribly jealous, it's a sort of curse on me. [*Kneeling beside* ELLEAN *and embracing her.*] My tongue runs away with me. I'm going to alter, I swear I am. I've made some good resolutions, and as God's above me, I'll keep them! If you are in love, if you do ever marry, that's no reason why we shouldn't be fond of each other. Come, you've kissed me of your own accord—you can't take it back. Now we're friends again, aren't we? Ellean dear! I want

to know everything, everything. Ellean dear, Ellean!

ELLEAN: Paula, Hugh has done something that makes me very angry. He came with us from Paris today, to see papa. He is staying with Mrs. Cortelyon and—I ought to tell you—

PAULA: Yes, yes. What?

ELLEAN: He has found his way by The Warren meadow through the plantation up to this house. He is waiting to bid me good night. [*Glancing towards the garden.*] He is—out there.

PAULA: Oh!

ELLEAN: What shall I do?

PAULA: Bring him in to see me! Will you?

ELLEAN: No, no.

PAULA: But I'm dying to know him. Oh, yes, you must. I shall meet him before Aubrey does. [*Excitedly running her hands over her hair.*] I'm so glad. [ELLEAN *goes out by the window.*] The mirror—mirror. What a fright I must look! [*Not finding the hand-glass on the table, she jumps onto the settee, and surveys herself in the mirror over the mantelpiece, then sits quietly down and waits.*] Ellean! Just fancy! Ellean!

[*After a pause* ELLEAN *enters by the window with* HUGH.]

ELLEAN: Paula, this is Captain Ardale—Mrs. Tanqueray.

[PAULA *rises and turns, and she and* HUGH *stand staring blankly at each other for a moment or two; then* PAULA *advances and gives him her hand.*]

PAULA [*in a strange voice, but calmly*]: How do you do?

HUGH: How do you do?

PAULA [*to* ELLEAN]: Mr. Ardale and I have met in London, Ellean. Er—Captain Ardale now?

HUGH: Yes.

ELLEAN: In London?

PAULA: They say the world's very small, don't they?

HUGH: Yes.

PAULA: Ellean, dear, I want to have a little talk about you to Mr. Ardale—Captain Ardale—alone. [*Putting her arms round* ELLEAN, *and leading her to the door.*] Come back in a little while. [ELLEAN *nods to* PAULA *with a smile and goes out, while* PAULA *stands watching her at the open door.*] In a little while—in a little— [*Closing the door and then taking a seat facing* HUGH.] Be quick! Mr. Tanqueray has only gone down to The Warren with Mr. Cortelyon. What is to be done?

HUGH [*blankly*]: Done?

PAULA: Done—done. Something must be done.

HUGH: I understood that Mr. Tanqueray had married a Mrs.—Mrs.—

PAULA: Jarman?

HUGH: Yes.

PAULA: I'd been going by that name. You didn't follow my doings after we separated.

HUGH: No.

PAULA [*sneeringly*]: No.

HUGH: I went out to India.

PAULA: What's to be done?

HUGH: Damn this chance!

PAULA: Oh, my God!

HUGH: Your husband doesn't know, does he?

PAULA: That you and I—?

HUGH: Yes.

PAULA: No. He knows about others.

HUGH: Not about me. How long were we—?

PAULA: I don't remember, exactly.

HUGH: Do you—do you think it matters?

PAULA: His—his daughter. [*With a muttered exclamation he turns away, and sits with his head in his hands.*] What's to be done?

HUGH: I wish I could think.

PAULA: Oh! Oh! What happened to that flat of ours in Ethelbert Street?

HUGH: I let it.

PAULA: All that pretty furniture?

HUGH: Sold it.

PAULA: I came across the key of the escritoire the other day in an old purse! [*Suddenly realising the horror and hopelessness of her position, and starting to her feet with an hysterical cry of rage.*] What am I maundering about?

HUGH: For God's sake, be quiet! Do let me think.

PAULA: This will send me mad! [*Suddenly turning and standing over him.*] You—you beast, to crop up in my life again like this!

HUGH: I always treated you fairly.

PAULA [*weakly*]: Oh! I beg your pardon—I know you did—I— [*She sinks on to the settee crying hysterically.*]

HUGH: Hush!

PAULA: She kissed me tonight! I'd won her over! I've had such a fight to make her love me! and now—just as she's beginning to love me, to bring this on her!

HUGH: Hush, hush! Don't break down!

PAULA [*sobbing*]: You don't know!

I—I haven't been getting on well in my marriage. It's been my fault. The life I used to lead spoilt me completely. But I'd made up my mind to turn over a new leaf from tonight. From tonight!

HUGH: Paula—

PAULA: Don't you call me that!

HUGH: Mrs. Tanqueray, there is no cause for you to despair in this way. It's all right, I tell you—it *shall* be all right.

PAULA [*shivering*]: What are we to do?

HUGH: Hold our tongues.

PAULA: Eh? [*Staring vacantly.*]

HUGH: The chances are a hundred to one against anyone ever turning up who knew us when we were together. Besides, no one would be such a brute as to split on us. If anybody did do such a thing we should have to lie! What are we upsetting ourselves like this for, when we've simply got to hold our tongues?

PAULA: You're as mad as I am!

HUGH: Can you think of a better plan?

PAULA: There's only one plan possible—let's come to our senses!—Mr. Tanqueray must be told.

HUGH: Your husband! What, and I lose Ellean! I lose Ellean!

PAULA: You've got to lose her.

HUGH: I won't lose her; I can't lose her!

PAULA: Didn't I read of your doing any number of brave things in India? Why, you seem to be an awful coward!

HUGH: That's another sort of pluck altogether; I haven't this sort of pluck.

PAULA: Oh, I don't ask *you* to tell Mr. Tanqueray. That's my job.

HUGH [*standing over her*]: You—you—you'd better! You—

PAULA [*rising*]: Don't bully me! I intend to.

HUGH [*taking hold of her; she wrenches herself free*]: Look here, Paula, I never treated you badly—you've owned it. Why should you want to pay me out like this? You don't know how I love·Ellean!

PAULA: Yes, that's just what I *do* know.

HUGH: I say you don't! She's as good as my own mother! I've been downright honest with her, too. I told her, in Paris, that I'd been a bit wild at one time, and, after a damned wretched day, she promised to forgive me because of what I'd done since in India. She's behaved like an angel to me! Surely I oughtn't to lose her, after all, just because I've been like other fellows! No; I haven't been half as rackety as a hundred men we could think of. Paula, don't pay me out for nothing; be fair to me, there's a good girl—be fair to me!

PAULA: Oh, I'm not considering you at all! I advise you not to stay here any longer. Mr. Tanqueray is sure to be back soon.

HUGH [*taking up his hat*]: What's the understanding between us, then? What have we arranged to do?

PAULA: I don't know what you're going to do; I've got to tell Mr. Tanqueray.

HUGH: By God, you shall do nothing of the sort! [*Approaching her fiercely.*]

PAULA: You shocking coward!

HUGH: If you dare! [*Going up to the window.*] Mind! If you dare!

PAULA [*following him*]: Why, what would you do?

HUGH [*after a short pause, sullenly*]: Nothing. I'd shoot my-self—that's nothing. Good night.

PAULA: Good night.

[*He disappears. She walks unsteadily to the ottoman, and sits; and as she does so her hand falls upon the little silver mirror, which she takes up, staring at her own reflection.*]

ACT FOUR

The drawing room at "Highercoombe," the same evening.

[PAULA *is still seated on the ottoman, looking vacantly before her, with the little mirror in her hand.* LADY ORREYED *enters.*]

LADY ORREYED: There you are! You never came into the billiard room. Isn't it maddening—Cayley Drummle gives me sixty out of a hundred, and beats me. I must be out of form, because I know I play remarkably well for a lady. Only last month— [PAULA *rises.*] Whatever is the matter with you, old girl?

PAULA: Why?

LADY ORREYED [*staring*]: It's the light, I suppose. [PAULA *replaces the mirror on the table.*] By Aubrey's bolting from the billiard table in that fashion I thought perhaps—

PAULA: Yes, it's all right.

LADY ORREYED: You've patched it up? [PAULA *nods.*] Oh, I am jolly glad—! I mean—

PAULA: Yes, I know what you mean. Thanks, Mabel.

LADY ORREYED [*kissing* PAULA]: Now take my advice; for the future—

PAULA: Mabel, if I've been disagreeable to you while you've been staying here, I—I beg your pardon. [*Walking away and sitting down.*]

LADY ORREYED: You disagreeable, my dear? I haven't noticed it. Dodo and me both consider you make a first-class hostess; but then you've had such practice, haven't you? [*Dropping on to the ottoman and gaping.*] Oh, talk about being sleepy—!

PAULA: Why don't you—!

LADY ORREYED: Why, dear, I must hang about for Dodo. You may as well know it; he's in one of his moods.

PAULA [*under her breath*]: Oh—!

LADY ORREYED: Now, it's not his fault; it was deadly dull for him while we were playing billiards. Cayley Drummle did ask him to mark, but I stopped that; it's so easy to make a gentleman look like a billiard-marker. This is just how it always is; if poor old Dodo has nothing to do, he loses count, as you may say.

PAULA: Hark!

[SIR GEORGE ORREYED *enters, walking slowly and deliberately; he looks pale and watery-eyed.*]

SIR GEORGE [*with mournful indistinctness*]: I'm 'fraid we've lef' you a grea' deal to yourself tonight, Mrs. Tanqueray. Attra'tions of billiards. I apol'gise. I say, where's ol' Aubrey?

PAULA: My husband has been obliged to go out to a neighbour's house.

SIR GEORGE: I want his advice on a rather pressing matter connected with my family—my family. [*Sitting.*] Tomorrow will do just as well.

LADY ORREYED [*to* PAULA]: This is the mood I hate so—drivelling about his precious family.

SIR GEORGE: The fact is, Mrs. Tanqueray, I am not easy in my min' 'bout the way I am treatin' my poor ol' mother.

LADY ORREYED [*to* PAULA]: Do you hear that? That's *his* mother, but *my* mother he won't so much as look at!

SIR GEORGE: I shall write to Bruton Street firs' thing in the morning.

LADY ORREYED [*to* PAULA]: Mamma has stuck to me through everything—well, you know!

SIR GEORGE: I'll get ol' Aubrey to figure out a letter. I'll drop line to Uncle Fitz too—dooced shame of the ol' feller to chuck me over in this manner. [*Wiping his eyes.*] All my family have chucked me over.

LADY ORREYED [*rising*]: Dodo!

SIR GEORGE: Jus' because I've married beneath me, to be chucked over! Aunt Lydia, the General, Hooky Whitgrave, Lady Sugnall—my own dear sister!—all turn their backs on me. It's more than I can stan'!

LADY ORREYED [*approaching him with dignity*]: Sir George, wish Mrs. Tanqueray good night at once, and come upstairs. Do you hear me?

SIR GEORGE [*rising angrily*]: Wha—!

LADY ORREYED: Be quiet!

SIR GEORGE: You presoom to order me about!

LADY ORREYED: You're making an exhibition of yourself.

SIR GEORGE: Look 'ere—!

LADY ORREYED: Come along, I tell you!

[*He hesitates, utters a few inarticulate sounds, then snatches up a fragile ornament from the table, and is about to dash it on the ground.* LADY ORREYED *retreats, and* PAULA *goes to him.*]

PAULA: George!

[*He replaces the ornament.*]

SIR GEORGE [*shaking* PAULA'S *hand*]: Good ni', Mrs. Tanqueray.

LADY ORREYED [*to* PAULA]: Good night, darling. Wish Aubrey good night for me. Now, Dodo? [*She goes out.*]

SIR GEORGE [*to* PAULA]: I say, are you goin' to sit up for ol' Aubrey?

PAULA: Yes.

SIR GEORGE: Shall I keep you comp'ny?

PAULA: No, thank you, George.

SIR GEORGE: Sure?

PAULA: Yes, sure.

SIR GEORGE [*shaking hands*]: Good night again.

PAULA: Good night.

[*She turns away. He goes out, steadying himself carefully.* DRUMMLE *appears outside the window, smoking.*]

DRUMMLE [*looking into the room and seeing* PAULA]: My last cigar. Where's Aubrey?

PAULA: Gone down to The Warren to see Mrs. Cortelyon home.

DRUMMLE [*entering the room*]: Eh? Did you say Mrs. Cortelyon?

PAULA: Yes. She has brought Ellean back.

DRUMMLE: Bless my soul! Why?

PAULA: I—I'm too tired to tell you, Cayley. If you stroll along the lane you'll meet Aubrey. Get the news from him.

DRUMMLE [*going up to the window*]: Yes, yes. [*Returning to* PAULA.] I don't want to bother you, only—the anxious old woman, you know. Are you and Aubrey—?

PAULA: Good friends again?

DRUMMLE [*nodding*]: Um.

PAULA [*giving him her hand*]: Quite, Cayley, quite.

DRUMMLE [*retaining her hand*]: That's capital. As I'm off so early tomorrow morning, let me say now—thank you for your hospitality. [*He bends over her hand gallantly, then goes out by the window.*]

PAULA [*to herself*]: "Are you and Aubrey—?" "Good friends again?" "Yes." "Quite, Cayley, quite."

[*There is a brief pause, then* AUBREY *enters hurriedly, wearing a light overcoat and carrying a cap.*]

AUBREY: Paula dear! Have you seen Ellean?

PAULA: I found her here when I came down.

AUBREY: She—she's told you?

PAULA: Yes, Aubrey.

AUBREY: It's extraordinary, isn't it! Not that somebody should fall in love with Ellean, or that Ellean herself should fall in love. All that's natural enough and was bound to happen, I suppose, sooner or later. But this young fellow! You know his history?

PAULA: His history?

AUBREY: You remember the papers were full of his name a few months ago?

PAULA: Oh, yes.

AUBREY: The man's as brave as a lion, there's no doubt about that; and, at the same time, he's like a big good-natured schoolboy, Mrs. Cortelyon says. Have you ever pictured the kind of man Ellean would marry some day?

PAULA: I can't say that I have.

AUBREY: A grave, sedate fellow I've thought about—hah! She has fallen in love with the way in which Ardale practically laid down his life to save those poor people shut up in the Residency. [*Taking off his coat.*] Well, I suppose if a man can do that sort of thing, one ought to be content. And yet—[*throwing his coat on the settee*] I should have met him tonight, but he'd gone out. Paula dear, tell me how you look upon this business.

PAULA: Yes, I will—I must. To begin with, I—I've seen Mr. Ardale.

AUBREY: Captain Ardale?

PAULA: Captain Ardale.

AUBREY: Seen him?

PAULA: While you were away he came up here, through our grounds, to try to get a word with Ellean. I made her fetch him in and present him to me.

AUBREY [*frowning*]: Doesn't Captain Ardale know there's a lodge and a front door to this place? Never mind! What is your impression of him?

PAULA: Aubrey, do you recollect my bringing you a letter—a letter giving you an account of myself—to the Albany late one night—the night before we got married?

AUBREY: A letter?

PAULA: You burnt it; don't you know?

AUBREY: Yes, I know.

PAULA: His name was in that letter.

AUBREY [*going back from her slowly, and staring at her*]: I don't understand.

PAULA: Well—Ardale and I once kept house together. [*He remains silent, not moving.*] Why don't you strike me? Hit me in the face—I'd rather you did! Hurt me! Hurt me!

AUBREY [*after a pause*]: What did you—and this man—say to each other—just now?

PAULA: I—hardly—know.

AUBREY: Think!

PAULA: The end of it all was that I—I told him I must inform you of—what had happened . . . he didn't want me to do that . . . I declared that I would . . . he dared me to. [*Breaking down.*] Let me alone!—oh!

AUBREY: Where was my daughter while this went on?

PAULA: I—I had sent her out of the room . . . that is all right.

AUBREY: Yes, yes—yes, yes. [*He turns his head towards the door.*]

PAULA: Who's that?

[*A* SERVANT *enters with a letter.*]

SERVANT: The coachman has just run up with this from The Warren, sir. [AUBREY *takes the letter.*] It's for Mrs. Tanqueray, sir; there's no answer.

[*The* SERVANT *withdraws.* AUBREY *goes to* PAULA *and drops the letter into her lap: she opens it with uncertain hands.*]

PAULA [*reading it to herself*]: It's from—him. He's going away—or gone—I think. [*Rising in a weak way.*] What does it say? I never could make out his writing. [*She gives the letter to* AUBREY, *and stands near him, looking at the letter over his shoulder as he reads.*]

AUBREY [*reading*]: "I shall be in Paris by tomorrow evening. Shall wait there, at Meurice's, for a week, ready to receive any communication you or your husband may address to me. Please invent some explanation to Ellean. Mrs. Tanqueray, for God's sake, do what you can for me."

[PAULA *and* AUBREY *speak in low voices, both still looking at the letter.*]

PAULA: Has he left The Warren, I wonder, already?

AUBREY: That doesn't matter.

PAULA: No, but I can picture him going quietly off. Very likely he's walking on to Bridgeford or Cottering tonight, to get the first train in the morning. A pleasant stroll for him.

AUBREY: We'll reckon he's gone, that's enough.

PAULA: That isn't to be answered in any way?

AUBREY: Silence will answer that.

PAULA: He'll soon recover his spirits, I know.

AUBREY: You know. [*Offering her the letter.*] You don't want this, I suppose?

PAULA: No.

AUBREY: It's done with—done with.

[*He tears the letter into small pieces. She has dropped the envelope; she searches for it, finds it, and gives it to him.*]

PAULA: Here!

AUBREY [*looking at the remnants of the letter*]: This is no good; I must burn it.

PAULA: Burn it in your room.

AUBREY: Yes.

PAULA: Put it in your pocket for now.

AUBREY: Yes. [*He does so.*]

[ELLEAN *enters, and they both turn, guilty, and stare at her.*]

ELLEAN [*after a short silence, wonderingly*]: Papa—

AUBREY: What do you want, Ellean?

ELLEAN: I heard from Willis that you had come in; I only want to wish you good night. [PAULA *steals away, without looking back.*] What's the matter? Ah! Of course, Paula has told you about Captain Ardale?

AUBREY: Well?

ELLEAN: Have you and he met?

AUBREY: No.

ELLEAN: You are angry with him; so was I. But tomorrow when he calls and expresses his regret—tomorrow—

AUBREY: Ellean—Ellean!

ELLEAN: Yes, papa?

AUBREY: I—I can't let you see this man again. [*He walks away from her in a paroxysm of distress, then, after a moment or two, he returns to her and takes her to his arms.*] Ellean! My child!

ELLEAN [*releasing herself*]: What has happened, papa? What is it?

AUBREY [*thinking out his words deliberately*]: Something has occurred, something has come to my knowledge, in relation to Captain Ardale, which puts any further acquaintanceship between you two out of the question.

ELLEAN: Any further acquaintanceship . . . out of the question?

AUBREY: Yes. [*Advancing to her quickly, but she shrinks from him.*]

ELLEAN: No, no—I am quite well. [*After a short pause.*] It's not an hour ago since Mrs. Cortelyon left you and me together here; you had nothing to urge against Captain Ardale then.

AUBREY: No.

ELLEAN: You don't know each other; you haven't even seen him this evening. Father!

AUBREY: I have told you he and I have not met.

ELLEAN: Mrs. Cortelyon couldn't have spoken against him to you just now. No, no, no; she's too good a friend to both of us. Aren't you going to give me some explanation? You can't take this position towards me—towards Captain Ardale—without affording me the fullest explanation.

AUBREY: Ellean, there are circumstances connected with Captain Ardale's career which you had better remain ignorant of. It must be sufficient for you that I consider these circumstances render him unfit to be your husband.

ELLEAN: Father!

AUBREY: You must trust me, Ellean; you must try to understand the depth of my love for you and the—the agony it gives me to hurt you. You must trust me.

ELLEAN: I will, father; but you must trust me a little too. Circumstances connected with Captain Ardale's career?

AUBREY: Yes.

ELLEAN: When he presents himself here tomorrow, of course you will see him and let him defend himself?

AUBREY: Captain Ardale will not be here tomorrow.

ELLEAN: Not! You have stopped his coming here?

AUBREY: Indirectly—yes.

ELLEAN: But just now he was talking to me at that window! Nothing had taken place then! And since then nothing can have—! Oh! Why—you have heard something against him from Paula.

AUBREY: From—Paula!

ELLEAN: She knows him.

AUBREY: She has told you so?

ELLEAN: When I introduced Captain Ardale to her she said she had met him in London. Of course! It is Paula who has done this!

AUBREY [*in a hard voice*]: I—I hope you—you'll refrain from rushing at conclusions. There's nothing to be gained by trying to avoid the main point, which is that you must drive Captain Ardale out of your thoughts. Understand that! You're able to obtain comfort from your religion, aren't you? I'm glad to think that's so. I talk to you in a harsh way, Ellean, but I feel your pain almost as acutely as you do. [*Going to the door.*] I—I can't say anything more to you tonight.

ELLEAN: Father! [*He pauses at the door.*] Father, I'm obliged to ask you this; there's no help for it—I've no mother to go to. Does what you have heard about Captain Ardale concern the time when he led a wild, a dissolute life in London?

AUBREY [*returning to her slowly and staring at her*]: Explain yourself!

ELLEAN: He has been quite honest with me. One day—in Paris —he confessed to me—what a man's life is—what his life had been.

AUBREY [*under his breath*]: Oh!

ELLEAN: He offered to go away, not to approach me again.

AUBREY: And you—you accepted his view of what a man's life is?

ELLEAN: As far as *I* could forgive him, I forgave him.

AUBREY [*with a groan*]: Why, when was it you left us? It hasn't taken you long to get your robe "just a little dusty at the hem!"

ELLEAN: What do you mean?

AUBREY: Hah! A few weeks ago my one great desire was to keep you ignorant of evil.

ELLEAN: Father, it is impossible

to be ignorant of evil. Instinct, common instinct, teaches us what is good and bad. Surely I am none the worse for knowing what is wicked and detesting it!

AUBREY: Detesting it! Why, you love this fellow!

ELLEAN: Ah, you don't understand! I have simply judged Captain Ardale as we all pray to be judged. I have lived in imagination through that one week in India when he deliberately offered his life back to God to save those wretched, desperate people. In his whole career I see now nothing but that one week; those few hours bring him nearer the saints, I believe, than fifty uneventful years of mere blamelessness would have done! And so, father, if Paula has reported anything to Captain Ardale's discredit—

AUBREY: Paula—!

ELLEAN: It must be Paula; it can't be anybody else.

AUBREY: You—you'll please keep Paula out of the question. Finally, Ellean, understand me—I have made up my mind. [*Again going to the door.*]

ELLEAN: But wait—listen! I have made up my mind also.

AUBREY: Ah! I recognise your mother in you now!

ELLEAN: You need not speak against my mother because you are angry with me!

AUBREY: I—I hardly know what I'm saying to you. In the morning—in the morning—

[*He goes out. She remains standing, and turns her head to listen. Then, after a moment's hesitation she goes softly to the window,*

and looks out under the verandah.]

ELLEAN [*in a whisper*]: Paula! Paula!

[PAULA *appears outside the window and steps into the room; her face is white and drawn, her hair is a little disordered.*]

PAULA [*huskily*]: Well?

ELLEAN: Have you been under the verandah all the while—listening?

PAULA: N—no.

ELLEAN: You *have* overheard us—I see you have. And it *is* you who have been speaking to my father against Captain Ardale. Isn't it? Paula, why don't you own it or deny it?

PAULA: Oh, I—I don't mind owning it; why should I?

ELLEAN: Ah! You seem to have been very, very eager to tell your tale.

PAULA: No, I wasn't eager, Ellean. I'd have given something not to have had to do it. I wasn't eager.

ELLEAN: Not! Oh, I think you might safely have spared us all for a little while.

PAULA: But Ellean, you forget I —I am your stepmother. It was my—my duty—to tell your father what I—what I knew—

ELLEAN: What you knew! Why, after all, what can you know? You can only speak from gossip, report, hearsay! How is it possible that you—! [*She stops abruptly. The two women stand staring at each other for a moment; then* ELLEAN *backs away from* PAULA *slowly.*] Paula!

PAULA: What—what's the matter?

ELLEAN: You—you knew Captain Ardale in London!

PAULA: Why—what do you mean?

ELLEAN: Oh! [*She makes for the door, but* PAULA *catches her by the wrist.*]

PAULA: You shall tell me what you mean!

ELLEAN: Ah! [*Suddenly, looking fixedly into* PAULA'S *face.*] You know what I mean.

PAULA: You accuse me!

ELLEAN: It's in your face!

PAULA [*hoarsely*]: You—you think I'm—that sort of creature, do you?

ELLEAN: Let me go!

PAULA: Answer me! You've always hated me! [*Shaking her.*] Out with it!

ELLEAN: You hurt me!

PAULA: You've always hated me! You shall answer me!

ELLEAN: Well, then, I have always—always—

PAULA: What?

ELLEAN: I have always known what you were!

PAULA: Ah! Who—who told you?

ELLEAN: Nobody but yourself. From the first moment I saw you I knew you were altogether unlike the good women I'd left; directly I saw you I knew what my father had done. You've wondered why I've turned from you! There— that's the reason! Oh, but this is a horrible way for the truth to come home to everyone! Oh!

PAULA: It's a lie! It's all a lie! [*Forcing* ELLEAN *down upon her knees.*] You shall beg my pardon for it. [ELLEAN *utters a loud shriek of terror.*] Ellean, I'm a good woman! I swear I am! I've always been a good woman! You dare to say I've ever been anything else! It's a lie!

[*Throwing her off violently.*]

[AUBREY *re-enters.*]

AUBREY: Paula! [PAULA *staggers back as* AUBREY *advances. Raising* ELLEAN.] What's this? What's this?

ELLEAN [*faintly*]: Nothing. It's— it's my fault. Father, I—I don't wish to see Captain Ardale again. [*She goes out,* AUBREY *slowly following her to the door.*]

PAULA: Aubrey, she—she guesses.

AUBREY: Guesses?

PAULA: About me—and Ardale.

AUBREY: About you—and Ardale?

PAULA: She says she suspected my character from the beginning . . . that's why she's always kept me at a distance . . . and now she sees through— [*She falters; he helps her to the otto- man, where she sits.*]

AUBREY [*bending over her*]: Paula, you must have said something —admitted something—

PAULA: I don't think so. It—it's in my face.

AUBREY: What?

PAULA: She tells me so. She's right! I'm tainted through and through; anybody can see it, anybody can find it out. You said much the same to me to- night.

AUBREY: If she has got this idea into her head we must drive it out, that's all. We must take steps to— What shall we do? We had better—better—what—what? [*Sitting and staring before him.*]

PAULA: Ellean! So meek, so de- mure! You've often said she re- minded you of her mother. Yes, I know now what your first mar- riage was like.

AUBREY: We must drive this

idea out of her head. We'll do something. What shall we do?

PAULA: She's a regular woman too. She could forgive *him* easily enough—but *me*! That's just a woman!

AUBREY: What *can* we do?

PAULA: Why, nothing! She'd have no difficulty in following up her suspicions. Suspicions! You should have seen how she looked at me! [*He buries his head in his hands. There is silence for a time, then she rises slowly, and goes and sits beside him.*] Aubrey.

AUBREY: Yes.

PAULA: I'm very sorry. [*Without meeting her eyes, he lays his hand on her arm for a moment.*]

AUBREY: Well, we must look things straight in the face. [*Glancing around.*] At any rate, we've done with this.

PAULA: I suppose so. [*After a brief pause.*] Of course, she and I can't live under the same roof any more. You know she kissed me tonight, of her own accord.

AUBREY: I asked her to alter towards you.

PAULA: That was it, then.

AUBREY: I—I'm sorry I sent her away.

PAULA: It was my fault; I made it necessary.

AUBREY: Perhaps now she'll propose to return to the convent— well, she must.

PAULA: Would you like to keep her with you and—and leave me?

AUBREY: Paula—!

PAULA: You needn't be afraid I'd go back to—what I was. I couldn't.

AUBREY: S—sh, for God's sake!

We—you and I—we'll get out of this place . . . What a fool I was to come here again!

PAULA: You lived here with your first wife!

AUBREY: We'll get out of this place and go abroad again, and begin afresh.

PAULA: Begin afresh?

AUBREY: There's no reason why the future shouldn't be happy for us—no reason that I can see—

PAULA: Aubrey!

AUBREY: Yes?

PAULA: You'll never forget this, you know.

AUBREY: This?

PAULA: Tonight, and everything that's led up to it. Our coming here, Ellean, our quarrels—cat and dog!—Mrs. Cortelyon, the Orreyeds, this man! What an everlasting nightmare for you!

AUBREY: Oh, we can forget it, if we choose.

PAULA: That was always your cry. How *can* one do it?

AUBREY: We'll make our calculations solely for the future, talk about the future, think about the future.

PAULA: I believe the future is only the past again, entered through another gate.

AUBREY: That's an awful belief.

PAULA: Tonight proves it. You must see now that, do what we will, go where we will, you'll be continually reminded of— what I was. I see it.

AUBREY: You're frightened tonight; meeting this man has frightened you. But that sort of thing isn't likely to recur. The world isn't quite so small as all that.

PAULA: Isn't it! The only great distances it contains are those we carry within ourselves—the distances that separate husbands and wives, for instance. And so it'll be with us. You'll do your best—oh, I know that—you're a good fellow. But circumstances will be too strong for you in the end, mark my words.

AUBREY: Paula—!

PAULA: Of course I'm pretty now—I'm pretty still—and a pretty woman, whatever else she may be, is always—well, endurable. But even now I notice that the lines of my face are getting deeper; so are the hollows about my eyes. Yes, my face is covered with little shadows that usen't to be there. Oh, I know I'm "going off." I hate paint and dye and those messes, but, by-and-bye, I shall drift the way of the others; I sha'n't be able to help myself. And then, some day—perhaps very suddenly, under a queer, fantastic light at night or in the glare of the morning—that horrid, irresistible truth that physical repulsion forces on men and women will come to you, and you'll sicken at me.

AUBREY: I—!

PAULA: You'll see me then, at last, with other people's eyes; you'll see me just as your daughter does now, as all wholesome folks see women like me. And I shall have no weapon to fight with—not one serviceable little bit of prettiness left me to defend myself with! A worn-out creature—broken up, very likely, some time before I ought to be—my hair bright, my eyes dull, my body too thin or too stout, my cheeks raddled and ruddled—a ghost, a wreck, a caricature, a candle that gutters, call such an end what you like! Oh, Aubrey, what shall I be able to say to you then? And this is the future you talk about! I know it—I know it! [*He is still sitting, staring forward; she rocks herself to and fro as if in pain.*] Oh, Aubrey! Oh! Oh!

AUBREY: Paula—! [*Trying to comfort her.*]

PAULA: Oh, and I wanted so much to sleep tonight! [*Laying her head upon his shoulder. From the distance, in the garden, there comes the sound of* DRUMMLE'S *voice; he is singing as he approaches the house.*] That's Cayley, coming back from The Warren. [*Starting up.*] He doesn't know, evidently. I—I won't see him!

[*She goes out quickly.* DRUMMLE'S *voice comes nearer.* AUBREY *rouses himself and snatches up a book from the table, making a pretence of reading. After a moment or two,* DRUMMLE *appears at the window and looks in.*]

DRUMMLE: Aha! my dear chap!

AUBREY: Cayley?

DRUMMLE [*coming into the room*]: I went down to The Warren after you.

AUBREY: Yes?

DRUMMLE: Missed you. Well—I've been gossiping with Mrs. Cortelyon. Confound you, I've heard the news!

AUBREY: What have you heard?

DRUMMLE: What have I heard!

Why—Ellean and young Ardale! [*Looking at* AUBREY *keenly.*] My dear Aubrey! Alice is under the impression that you are inclined to look on the affair favourably.

AUBREY [*rising and advancing to* DRUMMLE]: You've not—met—Captain Ardale?

DRUMMLE: No. Why do you ask? By-the-bye, I don't know that I need tell you—but it's rather strange. He's not at The Warren tonight.

AUBREY: No?

DRUMMLE: He left the house half an hour ago, to stroll about the lanes; just now a note came from him, a scribble in pencil, simply telling Alice that she would receive a letter from him tomorrow. What's the matter? There's nothing very wrong, is there? My dear chap, pray forgive me if I'm asking too much.

AUBREY: Cayley, you—you urged me to send her away!

DRUMMLE: Ellean! Yes, yes. But —but—by all accounts this is quite an eligible young fellow. Alice has been giving me the history—

AUBREY: Curse him! [*Hurling his book to the floor.*] Curse him! Yes, I do curse him—him and his class! Perhaps I curse myself too in doing it. He has only led "a man's life"—just as I, how many of us, have done! The misery he has brought on me and mine it's likely enough we, in our time, have helped to bring on others by this leading "a man's life"! But I do curse him for all that. My God, *I've* nothing more to fear—I've paid *my* fine! And so I can curse him

in safety. Curse him! Curse him!

DRUMMLE: In Heaven's name, tell me what's happened?

AUBREY [*gripping* DRUMMLE'S *arm*]: Paula! Paula!

DRUMMLE: What?

AUBREY: They met tonight here. They—they—they're not strangers to each other.

DRUMMLE: Aubrey!

AUBREY: Curse him! My poor, wretched wife! My poor, wretched wife!

[*The door opens and* ELLEAN *appears. The two men turn to her. There is a moment's silence.*]

ELLEAN: Father . . . father . . . !

AUBREY: Ellean?

ELLEAN: I—I want you. [*He goes to her.*] Father . . . go to Paula! [*He looks into her face, startled.*] Quickly—quickly! [*He passes her to go out; she seizes his arm, with a cry.*] No, no; don't go! [*He shakes her off and goes.* ELLEAN *staggers back towards* DRUMMLE.]

DRUMMLE [*to* ELLEAN]: What do you mean? What do you mean?

ELLEAN: I—I went to her room—to tell her I was sorry for something I had said to her. And I *was* sorry—I *was* sorry. I heard the fall. I—I've seen her. It's horrible.

DRUMMLE: She—she has—!

ELLEAN: Killed—herself? Yes—yes. So everybody will say. But I know—I helped to kill her. If I'd only been merciful! [*She faints upon the ottoman. He pauses for a moment irresolutely—then he goes to the door, opens it, and stands looking out.*]

Oscar Wilde
[1856-1900]

I TOOK THE DRAMA, the most objective form known to art, and made it as personal a mode of expression as the lyric or sonnet; at the same time I widened its range and enriched its characterization. . . . I treated art as the supreme reality and life as a mere mode of fiction." This is Oscar Wilde's own conception of what he brought to playwriting, an art form peculiarly well-suited to a great raconteur. His witty conversation found perfect expression in the dialogue of his plays.

He was born October 15, 1856, in Dublin, and grew up in a household where he heard much clever conversation. His father, a medical man, was rather overshadowed by his mother, who wrote under the name Speranza and was the center of a literary coterie. His older brother became a London journalist. Wilde was early interested in writing and while at Trinity College, Dublin, won a Gold Medal for his essay on Greek comic poets. He attended Oxford, from which he graduated in 1878 with a B.A. These years at Oxford he later spoke of as being the happiest of his life, because he then began to realize the extent to which he could influence society. While still at college he formulated his philosophy of art for art's sake and developed the reputation for being a poet, a wit, and an idler, although he was not idle. He was soon recognized as the leader of an aesthetic cult whose symbols were long hair, velveteen trousers, sunflowers, and exotic bric-à-brac.

In 1882 he toured the United States, giving some two hundred lectures, and was a greater success than had been anticipated. After his tour he returned to London and in 1884 married Constance Lloyd. During these years he was invited out constantly; he was the star of any gathering. He was able to take any suggested topic and enlarge on it wittily or perhaps relate an entire story which he improvised as he went along. Many of his witty remarks and epigrams he saved and used later in his published work. As he said of himself, "I summed up all systems in a phrase and all existence in an epigram." He wished to influence people and change society, and as a result he seized every opportunity to advertise himself. He said, "Fame comes from oneself. You must go about repeating how great you are till the dull crowd comes to believe it." He was heartily disliked by the middle class, who resented his intellectual freedom, contempt of conventions, and self-indulgence. He believed life should be all pleasure and whenever possible avoided any contact with pain or sorrow.

1888 to 1895 was a period of great literary activity for Wilde. He wrote *The Happy Prince and Other Tales,* fairy tales with a dash of satire; *Lord Arthur Savile's Crime and Other Stories; The Picture of Dorian Gray,* a short impressionistic novel full of epigrams; and another group of fairy tales, *A House of Pomegranates.* In 1891 he tried one blank verse tragedy, *The Duchess of Padua,* which was produced in New York, but in 1892 he found his real métier in light comedy. Before writing his first comedy, *Lady Windermere's Fan,* produced in 1892, he had had no theatrical experience; therefore he shut himself off from the society he loved for a fortnight and studied intensively the best French dramatists. His other plays, *A Woman of No Importance* (1893), *Salomé* (1893), *An Ideal Husband* (1895), and *The Importance of Being Earnest* (1895), followed within a period of four years. *The Importance of Being Earnest* he wrote in three weeks, and he remarked that if he needed the money, he could turn out a good play every two months. The stage, he said, ". . . is not merely the meeting-place of all the arts, but is also the return of art to life. The stage can combine in one exquisite presentation the illusion of actual life with the wonder of the unreal world. The true dramatist shows us life under the conditions of art, not art in the form of life."

Wilde's comedies were extremely successful; there were no other plays at the time whose polish and dexterity could compare with his. At last he was a power in society and could indulge himself as he liked. Unfortunately he let himself ". . . be lured into long spells of senseless and sensual ease." He called himself "a dandy, a man of fashion." Having surrounded himself with "the smaller natures and the meaner minds," he confessed, "I became the spendthrift of my own genius. . . ." His close friends remarked the change in him from a genial and generous man to a gross and hardened man. In 1895 he was goaded by a young friend, Lord Alfred Douglas, into bringing suit against Douglas' father, the Marquis of Queensberry. As a result he was arrested and brought to trial on a morals charge. He was cut by former friends, scorned and ridiculed publicly. He was found guilty in 1895 and sentenced to two years' hard labor and imprisonment. Imprisonment, particularly solitary confinement, was extremely hard on Wilde. He soon fell ill and was taken to the infirmary, where, as he said, he died, and was returned to prison a different man. Friends interceded for him and during the second year he was treated fairly well. He then began to write again and produced *De Profundis*, an explanation of his life and thought which was published posthumously in 1905. The treatment of prisoners, of children particularly, moved him to write two letters addressed to the editor of the *Daily Chronicle*. These letters were influential in helping to bring about badly needed prison reforms.

In May, 1897, he was released from prison and went to live in Paris on income given him by friends and his estranged wife. Although he wrote, "To regret one's own experience is to arrest one's own development," he nevertheless wrote only one complete work after his release, *The Ballad of Reading Gaol*. The firm resolutions he had made when leaving prison to live an orderly life and work hard faded rapidly away. He forgot the lesson he said he had learned about the value of sorrow and again wanted only the pleasures of the moment. After his friend, Alfred Douglas, betrayed him a second time, he lost all his joy of life, gave up all pretense at dignity, defied his doctor's orders, declined rapidly, and died in the spring of 1900 of cerebral meningitis in a Paris hotel.

The Importance of Being Earnest opened at St. James's Theatre in February, 1895. It was very well received, though not by drama critic Shaw, who considered it no more than an amusing trifle. In fact, Wilde had two successes going at the same time, *The Importance of Being Earnest* and *An Ideal Husband*. Both were playing during the time that Wilde's infamous trial was taking place. As a result of the public feeling generated against Wilde, his name was removed from the theatre program.

This play, *The Importance of Being Earnest,* one of the wittiest and most brilliant of the modern theatre, continues the tradition of Congreve and Sheridan; its language is sheer delight and its tongue-in-cheek construction is deft. Wilde is obviously using the technique of the well-made play, which he learned in a few weeks, but the whole is so delightful that the plotting simply adds to the comedy. Wilde's characters are insincere, but brilliant and always amusing; there is not one unpleasant character. The play may be viewed as a satire on the whole existence of insincere and superficial people of this society, but a moral tone never intrudes to mar the fun. Like their Restoration brothers, servants and masters are witty. Like Wilde himself, his characters would risk anything for the sake of a brilliant riposte. Max Beerbohm tells a story that illustrates how like his characters Wilde behaved. During the trial, which embarrassed and pained Wilde's friends, the principal actors who were performing in *An Ideal Husband* and *The Importance of Being Earnest* were walking down Piccadilly when they were hailed by Wilde, who was riding by in a cab. They were suddenly embarrassed and hoped he would drive on, but he stopped, got out, and inquired: "Have you heard what that swine Queensberry has had the effrontery to say?" The actors muttered and looked about in embarrassment. Wilde went relentlessly on, looking pointedly at Lewis Waller, the actor playing the lead in *An Ideal Husband:* "He actually had the effrontery to say that *The Importance of Being Earnest* is a better acted play than *An Ideal Husband!*" With that, he waved at them gaily, got back into the cab and drove off. That scene might easily have come out of an Oscar Wilde play.

One might look at *The Importance of Being Earnest* not only as a brilliant example of a modern comedy of manners but also as a kind of witty metaphor of Wilde's theory of art. As expressed in his essay, "The Decay of Lying," Wilde reverses the traditional notion that art holds the mirror up to nature. Life, says Wilde, is, if anything, an imitation of art. His brilliant characters are the most amusing liars, and finally, as it turns out, they aren't lying at all. They are artists and life, in its unexpected and convenient way, has brought to pass what the witty liars, especially the two young men, have invented on the inspiration of the moment.

The play continues to amuse and entertain contemporary audiences as much as it did the audience of 1895. It is often revived in the professional and non-professional theatre and a successful movie was made of it.

DRAMATIC WORKS

Vera, or The Nihilists, 1883
The Duchess of Padua, 1891
Lady Windermere's Fan, 1892
A Woman of No Importance, 1893

Salomé, 1894
The Importance of Being Earnest, 1895
An Ideal Husband, 1895

The
Importance
of Being Earnest

TO ROBERT BALDWIN ROSS IN APPRECIATION AND AFFECTION

★

THE PERSONS OF THE PLAY

JOHN WORTHING, J. P.

ALGERNON MONCRIEFF

REV. CANON CHASUBLE, D.D.

MERRIMAN, *Butler*

LANE, *Manservant*

LADY BRACKNELL

HON. GWENDOLEN FAIRFAX

CECILY CARDEW

MISS PRISM, *Governess*

THE SCENES OF THE PLAY

ACT I *Algernon Moncrieff's flat in Half-Moon Street, W.*

ACT II *The garden at the Manor House, Woolton*

ACT III *Drawing-room at the Manor House, Woolton*

TIME *The Present*

ACT ONE

Morning-room in Algernon's flat in Half-Moon Street. The room is luxuriously and artistically furnished. The sound of a piano is heard in the adjoining room.

[LANE *is arranging afternoon tea on the table and, after the music has ceased,* ALGERNON *enters.*]

ALGERNON: Did you hear what I was playing, Lane?

LANE: I didn't think it polite to listen, sir.

ALGERNON: I'm sorry for that, for your sake. I don't play accurately—anyone can play accurately—but I play with wonderful expression. As far as the piano is concerned, sentiment is my forte. I keep science for Life.

LANE: Yes, sir.

ALGERNON: And, speaking of the science of Life, have you got the cucumber sandwiches cut for Lady Bracknell?

LANE: Yes, sir. [*Hands them on a salver.*]

ALGERNON [*inspects them, takes two, and sits down on the sofa*]: Oh! . . . by the way, Lane, I see from your book that on Thursday night, when Lord Shoreman and Mr. Worthing were dining with me, eight bottles of champagne are entered as having been consumed.

LANE: Yes, sir; eight bottles and a pint.

ALGERNON: Why is it that at a bachelor's establishment the servants invariably drink the champagne? I ask merely for information.

LANE: I attribute it to the superior quality of the wine, sir. I have often observed that in married households the champagne is rarely of a first-rate brand.

ALGERNON: Good heavens! Is marriage so demoralizing as that?

LANE: I believe it *is* a very pleasant state, sir. I have had very little experience of it myself up to the present. I have only been married once. That was in consequence of a misunderstanding between myself and a young person.

ALGERNON [*languidly*]: I don't know that I am much interested in your family life, Lane.

LANE: No, sir; it is not a very interesting subject. I never think of it myself.

ALGERNON: Very natural, I am sure. That will do, Lane, thank you.

LANE: Thank you, sir.

[LANE *goes out.*]

ALGERNON: Lane's views on marriage seem somewhat lax. Really, if the lower orders don't set us a good example, what on earth is the use of them? They seem, as a class, to have absolutely no sense of moral responsibility.

[*Enter* LANE.]

LANE: Mr. Ernest Worthing.

[*Enter* JACK. LANE *goes out.*]

ALGERNON: How are you, my dear Ernest? What brings you up to town?

JACK: Oh, pleasure, pleasure! What else should bring one anywhere? Eating as usual, I see, Algy!

ALGERNON [*stiffly*]: I believe it is customary in good society to take some slight refreshment at five o'clock. Where have you been since last Thursday?

JACK [*sitting down on the sofa*]: In the country.

ALGERNON: What on earth do you do there?

JACK [*pulling off his gloves*]: When one is in town one amuses oneself. When one is in the country one amuses other people. It is excessively boring.

ALGERNON: And who are the people you amuse?

JACK [*airily*]: Oh, neighbours, neighbours.

ALGERNON: Got nice neighbours in your part of Shropshire?

JACK: Perfectly horrid! Never speak to one of them.

ALGERNON: How immensely you must amuse them! [*Goes over and takes sandwich.*] By the way, Shropshire is your county, is it not?

JACK: Eh? Shropshire? Yes, of course. Hallo! Why all these cups? Why cucumber sandwiches? Why such reckless extravagance in one so young? Who is coming to tea?

ALGERNON: Oh! merely Aunt Augusta and Gwendolen.

JACK: How perfectly delightful!

ALGERNON: Yes, that is all very well; but I am afraid Aunt Augusta won't quite approve of your being here.

JACK: May I ask why?

ALGERNON: My dear fellow, the way you flirt with Gwendolen is perfectly disgraceful. It is almost as bad as the way Gwendolen flirts with you.

JACK: I am in love with Gwendolen. I have come up to town expressly to propose to her.

ALGERNON: I thought you had come up for pleasure? . . . I call that business.

JACK: How utterly unromantic you are!

ALGERNON: I really don't see anything romantic in proposing. It is very romantic to be in love. But there is nothing romantic about a definite proposal. Why, one may be accepted. One usually is, I believe. Then the excitement is all over. The very essence of romance is uncertainty. If ever I get married, I'll certainly try to forget the fact.

JACK: I have no doubt about that, dear Algy. The Divorce Court was specially invented for people whose memories are so curiously constituted.

ALGERNON: Oh, there is no use speculating on that subject. Divorces are made in Heaven. [JACK *puts out his hand to take a sandwich.* ALGERNON *at once interferes.*] Please don't touch the cucumber sandwiches. They are ordered specially for Aunt Augusta. [*Takes one and eats it.*]

JACK: Well, you have been eating them all the time.

ALGERNON: That is quite a different matter. She is my aunt. [*Takes plate from below.*] Have some bread and butter. The bread and butter is for Gwendolen. Gwendolen is devoted to bread and butter.

JACK [*advancing to table and helping himself*]: And very good bread and butter it is too.

ALGERNON: Well, my dear fellow, you need not eat as if you were going to eat it all. You behave as if you were married to her already. You are not married to her already, and I don't think you ever will be.

JACK: Why on earth do you say that?

ALGERNON: Well, in the first place, girls never marry the men they flirt with. Girls don't think it right.

JACK: Oh, that is nonsense!

ALGERNON: It isn't. It is a great truth. It accounts for the extraordinary number of bachelors that one sees all over the place. In the second place, I don't give my consent.

JACK: Your consent!

ALGERNON: My dear fellow, Gwendolen is my first cousin. And before I allow you to marry her, you will have to clear up the whole question of Cecily. [*Rings bell.*]

JACK: Cecily! What on earth do you mean? What do you mean, Algy, by Cecily! I don't know any one of the name of Cecily.

[*Enter* LANE.]

ALGERNON: Bring me that cigarette case Mr. Worthing left in the smoking-room the last time he dined here.

LANE: Yes, sir.

[LANE *goes out.*]

JACK: Do you mean to say you have had my cigarette case all this time? I wish to goodness you had let me know. I have been writing frantic letters to Scotland Yard about it. I was very nearly offering a large reward.

ALGERNON: Well, I wish you would offer one. I happen to be more than usually hard up.

JACK: There is no good offering a large reward now that the thing is found.

[*Enter* LANE *with the cigarette case on a salver.* ALGERNON *takes it at once.* LANE *goes out.*]

ALGERNON: I think that is rather mean of you, Ernest, I must say. [*Opens case and examines it.*] However, it makes no matter, for, now that I look at the inscription inside, I find that the thing isn't yours after all.

JACK: Of course it's mine. [*Moving to him.*] You have seen me with it a hundred times, and you have no right whatsoever to read what is written inside. It is a very ungentlemanly thing to read a private cigarette case.

ALGERNON: Oh! it is absurd to have a hard and fast rule about what one should read and what one shouldn't. More than half of modern culture depends on what one shouldn't read.

JACK: I am quite aware of the fact, and I don't propose to discuss modern culture. It isn't the sort of thing one should talk of in private. I simply want my cigarette case back.

ALGERNON: Yes; but this isn't your cigarette case. This cigarette case is a present from someone of the name of Cecily, and you said you didn't know anyone of that name.

JACK: Well, if you want to know, Cecily happens to be my aunt.

ALGERNON: Your aunt!

JACK: Yes. Charming old lady she is, too. Lives at Tunbridge Wells. Just give it back to me, Algy.

ALGERNON [*retreating to back of sofa*]: But why does she call herself little Cecily if she is your aunt and lives at Tunbridge Wells? [*Reading.*] "From little Cecily with her fondest love."

JACK [*moving to sofa and kneeling upon it*]: My dear fellow, what on earth is there in that? Some aunts are tall, some aunts are not tall. That is a matter that surely an aunt may be allowed to decide for herself. You seem to think that every aunt should be exactly like your aunt! That is absurd. For Heaven's sake give me back my cigarette case. [*Follows* ALGERNON *round the room.*]

ALGERNON: Yes. But why does your aunt call you her uncle? "From little Cecily, with her fondest love to her dear Uncle Jack." There is no objection, I admit, to an aunt being a small aunt, but why an aunt, no matter what her size may be, should call her own nephew her uncle, I can't quite make out. Besides, your name isn't Jack at all; it is Ernest.

JACK: It isn't Ernest; it's Jack.

ALGERNON: You have always told me it was Ernest. I have introduced you to everyone as Ernest. You answer to the name of Ernest. You look as if your name was Ernest. You are the most earnest-looking person I ever saw in my life. It is perfectly absurd your saying that your name isn't Ernest. It's on your cards. Here is one of them. [*Taking it from case.*] "Mr. Ernest Worthing, B.4, The Albany." I'll keep this as a proof that your name is Ernest if ever you attempt to deny it to me, or to Gwendolen, or to anyone else. [*Puts the card in his pocket.*]

JACK: Well, my name is Ernest in town and Jack in the country, and the cigarette case was given to me in the country.

ALGERNON: Yes, but that does not account for the fact that your small Aunt Cecily, who lives at Tunbridge Wells, calls you her dear uncle. Come, old boy, you had much better have the thing out at once.

JACK: My dear Algy, you talk exactly as if you were a dentist. It is very vulgar to talk like a dentist when one isn't a dentist. It produces a false impression.

ALGERNON: Well, that is exactly what dentists always do. Now, go on! Tell me the whole thing. I may mention that I have always suspected you of being a confirmed and secret Bunbury-ist; and I am quite sure of it now.

JACK: Bunburyist? What on earth do you mean by a Bunbury-ist?

ALGERNON: I'll reveal to you the meaning of that incomparable expression as soon as you are kind enough to inform me why you are Ernest in town and Jack in the country.

JACK: Well, produce my ciga-rette case first.

ALGERNON: Here it is. [*Hands cigarette case.*] Now produce your explanation, and pray make it improbable. [*Sits on sofa.*]

JACK: My dear fellow, there is nothing improbable about my explanation at all. In fact it's perfectly ordinary. Old Mr. Thomas Cardew, who adopted me when I was a little boy, made me in his will guardian to his granddaughter, Miss Cecily Cardew. Cecily, who ad-dresses me as her uncle from motives of respect that you could not possibly appreciate, lives at my place in the coun-try under the charge of her ad-mirable governess, Miss Prism.

ALGERNON: Where is that place in the country, by the way?

JACK: That is nothing to you, dear boy. You are not going to be invited. . . . I may tell you candidly that the place is not in Shropshire.

ALGERNON: I suspected that, my dear fellow! I have Bunburyed all over Shropshire on two sepa-rate occasions. Now, go on. Why are you Ernest in town and Jack in the country?

JACK: My dear Algy, I don't know whether you will be able to understand my real motives. You are hardly serious enough. When one is placed in the position of guardian, one has to adopt a very high moral tone on all subjects. It's one's duty to do so. And as a high moral tone can hardly be said to conduce very much to either one's health or one's happiness, in order to get up to town I have always pre-tended to have a younger brother of the name of Ernest, who lives in the Albany, and gets into the most dreadful scrapes. That, my dear Algy, is the whole truth pure and simple.

ALGERNON: The truth is rarely pure and never simple. Modern life would be very tedious if it were either, and modern litera-ture a complete impossibility!

JACK: That wouldn't be at all a bad thing.

ALGERNON: Literary criticism is not your forte, my dear fellow. Don't try it. You should leave that to people who haven't been at a University. They do it so well in the daily papers. What you really are is a Bun-buryist. I was quite right in say-ing you were a Bunburyist. You are one of the most advanced Bunburyists I know.

JACK: What on earth do you mean?

ALGERNON: You have invented a very useful younger brother called Ernest, in order that you may be able to come up to town as often as you like. I have in-vented an invaluable perma-nent invalid called Bunbury, in order that I may be able to go down into the country when-ever I choose. Bunbury is perfectly invaluable. If it wasn't for Bunbury's extraordinary bad health, for instance, I wouldn't be able to dine with you at Willis's tonight, for I have been really engaged to Aunt Augusta for more than a week.

JACK: I haven't asked you to dine with me anywhere tonight.

ALGERNON: I know. You are absurdly careless about sending out invitations. It is very foolish of you. Nothing annoys people so much as not receiving invitations.

JACK: You had much better dine with your Aunt Augusta.

ALGERNON: I haven't the smallest intention of doing anything of the kind. To begin with, I dined there on Monday, and once a week is quite enough to dine with one's own relations. In the second place, whenever I do dine there I am always treated as a member of the family, and sent down with either no woman at all, or two. In the third place, I know perfectly well whom she will place me next to, tonight. She will place me next Mary Farquhar, who always flirts with her own husband across the dinner-table. That is not very pleasant. Indeed, it is not even decent . . . and that sort of thing is enormously on the increase. The amount of women in London who flirt with their own husbands is perfectly scandalous. It looks so bad. It is simply washing one's clean linen in public. Besides, now that I know you to be a confirmed Bunburyist I naturally want to talk to you about Bunburying. I want to tell you the rules.

JACK: I'm not a Bunburyist at all. If Gwendolen accepts me, I am going to kill my brother, indeed I think I'll kill him in any case. Cecily is a little too much interested in him. It is rather a bore. So I am going to get rid of Ernest. And I strongly advise you to do the same with Mr. . . . with your invalid friend who has the absurd name.

ALGERNON: Nothing will induce me to part with Bunbury, and if you ever get married, which seems to me extremely problematic, you will be very glad to know Bunbury. A man who marries without knowing Bunbury has a very tedious time of it.

JACK: That is nonsense. If I marry a charming girl like Gwendolen, and she is the only girl I ever saw in my life that I would marry, I certainly won't want to know Bunbury.

ALGERNON: Then your wife will. You don't seem to realize that in married life three is company and two is none.

JACK [*sententiously*]: That, my dear young friend, is the theory that the corrupt French Drama has been propounding for the last fifty years.

ALGERNON: Yes; and that the happy English home has proved in half the time.

JACK: For heaven's sake, don't try to be cynical. It's perfectly easy to be cynical.

ALGERNON: My dear fellow, it isn't easy to be anything nowadays. There's such a lot of beastly competition about. [*The sound of an electric bell is heard.*] Ah! that must be Aunt Augusta. Only relatives, or creditors, ever ring in that Wagnerian manner. Now, if I get her out of the way for ten minutes, so that you can have an opportunity for proposing to Gwendolen, may I dine with you tonight at Willis's?

JACK: I suppose so, if you want to.

ALGERNON: Yes, but you must be serious about it. I hate people who are not serious about meals. It is so shallow of them.

[*Enter* LANE.]

LANE: Lady Bracknell and Miss Fairfax.

[ALGERNON *goes forward to meet them. Enter* LADY BRACKNELL *and* GWENDOLEN.]

LADY BRACKNELL: Good afternoon, dear Algernon, I hope you are behaving very well.

ALGERNON: I'm feeling very well, Aunt Augusta.

LADY BRACKNELL: That's not quite the same thing. In fact the two things rarely go together. [*Sees* JACK *and bows to him with icy coldness.*]

ALGERNON [*to* GWENDOLEN]: Dear me, you are smart!

GWENDOLEN: I am always smart! Am I not, Mr. Worthing?

JACK: You're quite perfect, Miss Fairfax.

GWENDOLEN: Oh! I hope I am not that. It would leave no room for developments, and I intend to develop in many directions. [GWENDOLEN *and* JACK *sit down together in the corner.*]

LADY BRACKNELL: I'm sorry if we are a little late, Algernon,

but I was obliged to call on dear Lady Harbury. I hadn't been there since her poor husband's death. I never saw a woman so altered; she looks quite twenty years younger. And now I'll have a cup of tea, and one of those nice cucumber sandwiches you promised me.

ALGERNON: Certainly, Aunt Augusta. [*Goes over to tea-table.*]

LADY BRACKNELL: Won't you come and sit here, Gwendolen?

GWENDOLEN: Thanks, mamma, I'm quite comfortable where I am.

ALGERNON [*picking up empty plate in horror*]: Good heavens! Lane! Why are there no cucumber sandwiches? I ordered them specially.

LANE [*gravely*]: There were no cucumbers in the market this morning, sir. I went down twice.

ALGERNON: No cucumbers!

LANE: No, sir. Not even for ready money.

ALGERNON: That will do, Lane, thank you.

LANE: Thank you, sir. [*Goes out.*]

ALGERNON: I am greatly distressed, Aunt Augusta, about there being no cucumbers, not even for ready money.

LADY BRACKNELL: It really makes no matter, Algernon. I had some crumpets with Lady Harbury, who seems to me to be living entirely for pleasure now.

ALGERNON: I hear her hair has turned quite gold from grief.

LACY BRACKNELL: It certainly has changed its colour. From what cause I, of course, cannot say. [ALGERNON *crosses and hands tea.*] Thank you, I've quite a treat for you tonight, Algernon. I am going to send you down with Mary Farquhar. She is such a nice woman, and so attentive to her husband. It's delightful to watch them.

ALGERNON: I am afraid, Aunt Augusta, I shall have to give up the pleasure of dining with you tonight after all.

LADY BRACKNELL [*frowning*]: I hope not, Algernon. It would put my table completely out. Your uncle would have to dine upstairs. Fortunately he is accustomed to that.

ALGERNON: It is a great bore, and, I need hardly say, a terrible disappointment to me, but the fact is I have just had a telegram to say that my poor friend Bunbury is very ill again. [*Exchanges glances with* JACK.] They seem to think I should be with him.

LADY BRACKNELL: It is very strange. This Mr. Bunbury seems to suffer from curiously bad health.

ALGERNON: Yes; poor Bunbury is a dreadful invalid.

LADY BRACKNELL: Well, I must say, Algernon, that I think it is high time that Mr. Bunbury made up his mind whether he was going to live or to die. This shilly-shallying with the question is absurd. Nor do I in any way approve of the modern sympathy with invalids. I consider it morbid. Illness of any kind is hardly a thing to be encouraged in others. Health is the primary duty of life. I am always telling that to your poor uncle, but he never seems to take much notice . . . as far as any improvement in his ailment goes. I should be much obliged if you would ask Mr. Bunbury, from me, to be kind enough not to have a relapse on Saturday, for I rely on you to arrange my music for me. It is my last reception, and one wants something that will encourage conversation, particularly at the end of the season when everyone has practically said whatever they had to say, which, in most cases, was probably not much.

ALGERNON: I'll speak to Bunbury, Aunt Augusta, if he is still conscious, and I think I can promise you he'll be all right by Saturday. Of course the music is a great difficulty. You see, if one plays good music, people don't listen, and if one plays bad music people don't talk. But I'll run over the programme I've drawn out, if you will kindly come into the next room for a moment.

LADY BRACKNELL: Thank you, Algernon. It is very thoughtful of you. [*Rising, and following* ALGERNON.] I'm sure the programme will be delightful, after a few expurgations. French songs I cannot possibly allow. People always seem to think that they are improper, and either look shocked, which is vulgar, or laugh, which is worse. But German sounds a thoroughly respectable language, and, indeed I believe is so. Gwendolen, you will accompany me.

GWENDOLEN: Certainly, mamma.

[LADY BRACKNELL *and* ALGERNON *go into the music-room.* GWENDOLEN *remains behind.*]

JACK: Charming day it has been, Miss Fairfax.

GWENDOLEN: Pray don't talk to me about the weather, Mr. Worthing. Whenever people talk to me about the weather, I always feel quite certain that they mean something else. And that makes me so nervous.

JACK: I do mean something else.

GWENDOLEN: I thought so. In fact, I am never wrong.

JACK: And I would like to be allowed to take advantage of Lady Bracknell's temporary absence. . . .

GWENDOLEN: I would certainly advise you to do so. Mamma has a way of coming back suddenly into a room that I have often had to speak to her about.

JACK [nervously]: Miss Fairfax, ever since I met you I have admired you more than any girl . . . I have ever met since . . . I met you.

GWENDOLEN: Yes, I am quite well aware of the fact. And I often wish that in public, at any rate, you had been more demonstrative. For me you have always had an irresistible fascination. Even before I met you I was far from indifferent to you. [JACK looks at her in amazement.] We live, as I hope you know, Mr. Worthing, in an age of ideals. The fact is constantly mentioned in the more expensive monthly magazines, and has reached the provincial pulpits, I am told; and my ideal has always been to love someone of the name of Ernest. There is something in that name that inspires absolute confidence. The moment Algernon first mentioned to me that he had a friend called Ernest, I knew I was destined to love you.

JACK: You really love me, Gwendolen?

GWENDOLEN: Passionately!

JACK: Darling! You don't know how happy you've made me.

GWENDOLEN: My own Ernest!

JACK: But you don't really mean to say that you couldn't love me if my name wasn't Ernest?

GWENDOLEN: But your name is Ernest.

JACK: Yes, I know it is. But supposing it was something else? Do you mean to say you couldn't love me then?

GWENDOLEN [glibly]: Ah! that is clearly a metaphysical speculation, and like most metaphysical speculations has very little reference at all to the actual facts of real life, as we know them.

JACK: Personally, darling, to speak quite candidly, I don't much care about the name of Ernest. . . . I don't think the name suits me at all.

GWENDOLEN: It suits you perfectly. It is a divine name. It has music of its own. It produces vibrations.

JACK: Well, really, Gwendolen, I must say that I think there are lots of other much nicer names. I think Jack, for instance, a charming name.

GWENDOLEN: Jack? . . . No, there is very little music in the name Jack, if any at all, indeed. It does not thrill. It produces absolutely no vibrations. . . . I have known several Jacks, and they all, without exception, were more than usually plain. Besides, Jack is a notorious domesticity for John! And I pity any woman who is married to a man called John. She would probably never be allowed to know the entrancing pleasure of a single moment's solitude. The only really safe name is Ernest.

JACK: Gwendolen, I must get christened at once—I mean we must get married at once. There is no time to be lost.

GWENDOLEN: Married, Mr. Worthing?

JACK [astounded]: Well . . . surely. You know that I love you, and you led me to believe, Miss Fairfax, that you were not absolutely indifferent to me.

GWENDOLEN: I adore you. But you haven't proposed to me yet. Nothing has been said at all about marriage. The subject has not even been touched on.

JACK: Well . . . may I propose to you now?

GWENDOLEN: I think it would be an admirable opportunity. And to spare you any possible disappointment, Mr. Worthing, I think it only fair to tell you quite frankly beforehand that I am fully determined to accept you.

JACK: Gwendolen!

GWENDOLEN: Yes, Mr. Worthing, what have you got to say to me?

JACK: You know what I have got to say to you.

GWENDOLEN: Yes, but you don't say it.

JACK: Gwendolen, will you marry me? [Goes on his knees.]

GWENDOLEN: Of course I will, darling. How long you have been about it! I am afraid you have had very little experience in how to propose.

JACK: My own one, I have never loved anyone in the world but you.

GWENDOLEN: Yes, but men often propose for practice. I know my brother Gerald does. All my girl-friends tell me so. What wonderfully blue eyes you have, Ernest! They are quite, quite blue. I hope you will always look at me just like that, especially when there are other people present.

[Enter LADY BRACKNELL.]

LADY BRACKNELL: Mr. Worthing! Rise, sir, from this semi-recumbent posture. It is most indecorous.

GWENDOLEN: Mamma! [He tries to rise; she restrains him.] I must beg you to retire. This is no place for you. Besides, Mr. Worthing has not quite finished yet.

LADY BRACKNELL: Finished what, may I ask?

GWENDOLEN: I am engaged to Mr. Worthing, mamma. [They rise together.]

LADY BRACKNELL: Pardon me, you are not engaged to anyone. When you do become engaged to someone, I, or your father, should his health permit him, will inform you of the fact. An engagement should come on a young girl as a surprise, pleasant or unpleasant, as the case may be. It is hardly a matter that she could be allowed to arrange for herself. . . . And now I have a few questions to put to you, Mr. Worthing. While I am making these inquiries, you, Gwendolen, will wait for me below in the carriage.

GWENDOLEN [*reproachfully*]: Mamma!

LADY BRACKNELL: In the carriage, Gwendolen! [GWENDOLEN *goes to the door. She and* JACK *blow kisses to each other behind* LADY BRACKNELL'S *back.* LADY BRACKNELL *looks vaguely about as if she could not understand what the noise was. Finally turns round.*] Gwendolen, the carriage!

GWENDOLEN: Yes, mamma. [*Goes out, looking back at* JACK.]

LADY BRACKNELL [*sitting down*]: You can take a seat, Mr. Worthing. [*Looks in her pocket for note-book and pencil.*]

JACK: Thank you, Lady Bracknell, I prefer standing.

LADY BRACKNELL [*pencil and notebook in hand*]: I feel bound to tell you that you are not down on my list of eligible young men, although I have the same list as the dear Duchess of Bolton has. We work together, in fact. However, I am quite ready to enter your name, should your answers be what a really affectionate mother requires. Do you smoke?

JACK: Well, yes, I must admit I smoke.

LADY BRACKNELL: I am glad to hear it. A man should always have an occupation of some kind. There are far too many idle men in London as it is. How old are you?

JACK: Twenty-nine.

LADY BRACKNELL: A very good age to be married at. I have always been of opinion that a man who desires to get married should know either everything or nothing. Which do you know?

JACK [*after some hesitation*]: I know nothing, Lady Bracknell.

LADY BRACKNELL: I am pleased to hear it. I do not approve of anything that tampers with natural ignorance. Ignorance is like a delicate exotic fruit; touch it and the bloom is gone. The whole theory of modern education is radically unsound. Fortunately in England, at any rate, education produces no effect whatsoever. If it did, it would prove a serious danger to the upper classes, and probably lead to acts of violence in Grosvenor Square. What is your income?

JACK: Between seven and eight thousand a year.

LADY BRACKNELL [*makes a note in her book*]: In land, or in investments?

JACK: In investments, chiefly.

LADY BRACKNELL: That is satisfactory. What between the duties expected of one during one's lifetime, and the duties exacted from one after one's death, land has ceased to be either a profit or a pleasure. It gives one position, and prevents one from keeping it up. That's all that can be said about land.

JACK: I have a country house with some land, of course, attached to it, about fifteen hundred acres, I believe; but I don't depend on that for my real income. In fact, as far as I can make out, the poachers are the only people who make anything out of it.

LADY BRACKNELL: A country house! How many bedrooms? Well, that point can be cleared up afterwards. You have a town house, I hope? A girl with a simple, unspoiled nature, like Gwendolen, could hardly be expected to reside in the country.

JACK: Well, I own a house in Belgrave Square, but it is let by the year to Lady Bloxham. Of course, I can get it back whenever I like, at six months' notice.

LADY BRACKNELL: Lady Bloxham? I don't know her.

JACK: Oh, she goes about very little. She is a lady considerably advanced in years.

LADY BRACKNELL: Ah, nowadays that is no guarantee of respectability of character. What number in Belgrave Square?

JACK: 149.

LADY BRACKNELL [*shaking her head*]: The unfashionable side. I thought there was something. However, that could easily be altered.

JACK: Do you mean the fashion, or the side?

LADY BRACKNELL [*sternly*]: Both, if necessary, I presume. What are your politics?

JACK: Well, I am afraid I really have none. I am a Liberal Unionist.

LADY BRACKNELL: Oh, they count as Tories. They dine with us. Or come in the evening, at any rate. Now to minor matters. Are your parents living?

JACK: I have lost both my parents.

LADY BRACKNELL: To lose one parent, Mr. Worthing, may be regarded as a misfortune; to lose both looks like carelessness. Who was your father? He was evidently a man of some wealth. Was he born in what the Radical papers call the purple of commerce, or did he rise from the ranks of the aristocracy?

JACK: I am afraid I really don't know. The fact is, Lady Bracknell, I said I had lost my parents. It would be nearer the truth to say that my parents seem to have lost me. . . . I don't actually know who I am by birth. I was . . . well, I was found.

LADY BRACKNELL: Found!

JACK: The late Mr. Thomas Cardew, an old gentleman of a very charitable and kindly disposition, found me, and gave me the name of Worthing, because he happened to have a first-class ticket for Worthing in his pocket at the time. Worthing is a place in Sussex. It is a seaside resort.

LADY BRACKNELL: Where did the charitable gentleman who had a first-class ticket for this seaside resort find you?

JACK [*gravely*]: In a hand-bag.

LADY BRACKNELL: A hand-bag?

JACK [*very seriously*]: Yes, Lady Bracknell. I was in a hand-bag—a somewhat large, black leather hand-bag, with handles to it—an ordinary hand-bag in fact.

LADY BRACKNELL: In what locality did this Mr. James, or Thomas, Cardew come across this ordinary hand-bag?

JACK: In the cloak-room at Victoria Station. It was given to him in mistake for his own.

LADY BRACKNELL: The cloak-room at Victoria Station?

JACK: Yes. The Brighton line.

LADY BRACKNELL: The line is immaterial. Mr. Worthing, I confess I feel somewhat bewildered by what you have just told me. To be born, or at any rate bred, in a hand-bag, whether it had handles or not, seems to me to display a contempt for the ordinary decencies of family life that reminds one of the worst excesses of the French Revolution. And I presume you know what that unfortunate movement led to? As for the particular locality in which the hand-bag was found, a cloak-room at a railway station might serve to conceal a social indiscretion—has probably, indeed, been used for that purpose before now—but it could hardly be regarded as an assured basis for a recognized position in good society.

JACK: May I ask you then what you would advise me to do? I need hardly say I would do anything in the world to ensure Gwendolen's happiness.

LADY BRACKNELL: I would strongly advise you, Mr. Worthing, to try and acquire some relations as soon as possible, and to make a definite effort to produce at any rate one parent, of either sex, before the season is quite over.

JACK: Well, I don't see how I could possibly manage to do that. I can produce the hand-bag at any moment. It is in my dressing-room at home. I really think that should satisfy you, Lady Bracknell.

LADY BRACKNELL: Me, sir! What has it to do with me? You can hardly imagine that I and Lord Bracknell would dream of allowing our only daughter—a girl brought up with the utmost care—to marry into a cloak-room, and form an alliance with a parcel. Good morning, Mr. Worthing!

[LADY BRACKNELL *sweeps out in majestic indignation.*]

JACK: Good morning! [ALGERNON, *from the other room, strikes up the Wedding March.* JACK *looks perfectly furious, and goes to the door.*] For goodness' sake don't play that ghastly tune, Algy! How idiotic you are!

[*The music stops and* ALGERNON *enters cheerily.*]

ALGERNON: Didn't it go off all right, old boy? You don't mean to say Gwendolen refused you? I know it is a way she has. She is always refusing people. I think it is most ill-natured of her.

JACK: Oh, Gwendolen is as right as a trivet. As far as she is concerned, we are engaged. Her mother is perfectly unbearable. Never met such a Gorgon. . . . I don't really know what a Gorgon is like, but I am quite sure that Lady Bracknell is one. In any case, she is a monster, without being a myth, which is rather unfair. . . . I beg your pardon, Algy, I suppose I shouldn't talk about your own aunt in that way before you.

ALGERNON: My dear boy, I love hearing my relations abused. It is the only thing that makes me put up with them at all. Relations are simply a tedious pack of people, who haven't got the remotest knowledge of how to live, nor the smallest instinct about when to die.

JACK: Oh, that is nonsense!

ALGERNON: It isn't!

JACK: Well, I won't argue about the matter. You always want to argue about things.

ALGERNON: That is exactly what things were originally made for.

JACK: Upon my word, if I thought that, I'd shoot myself. . . . [*A pause.*] You don't think there is any chance of Gwendolen becoming like her mother in about a hundred and fifty years, do you, Algy?

ALGERNON: All women become like their mothers. That is their tragedy. No man does. That's his.

JACK: Is that clever?

ALGERNON: It is perfectly phrased! and quite as true as any observation in civilized life should be.

JACK: I am sick to death of cleverness. Everybody is clever nowadays. You can't go anywhere without meeting clever people. The thing has become an absolute public nuisance. I wish to goodness we had a few fools left.

ALGERNON: We have.

JACK: I should extremely like to meet them. What do they talk about?

ALGERNON: The fools? Oh! about the clever people, of course.

JACK: What fools.

ALGERNON: By the way, did you tell Gwendolen the truth about your being Ernest in town, and Jack in the country?

JACK [*in a very patronizing manner*]: My dear fellow, the truth isn't quite the sort of thing one tells to a nice, sweet, refined girl. What extraordinary ideas you have about the way to behave to a woman!

ALGERNON: The only way to behave to a woman is to make love to her, if she is pretty, and to someone else, if she is plain.

JACK: Oh, that is nonsense.

ALGERNON: What about your brother? What about the profligate Ernest?

JACK: Oh, before the end of the week I shall have got rid of him. I'll say he died in Paris of apoplexy. Lots of people die of apoplexy, quite suddenly, don't they?

ALGERNON: Yes, but it's hereditary, my dear fellow. It's a sort of thing that runs in families. You had much better say a severe chill.

JACK: You are sure a severe chill isn't hereditary, or anything of that kind?

ALGERNON: Of course it isn't!

JACK: Very well, then. My poor brother Ernest is carried off suddenly, in Paris, by a severe chill. That gets rid of him.

ALGERNON: But I thought you said that . . . Miss Cardew was a little too much interested in your poor brother Ernest? Won't she feel his loss a good deal?

JACK: Oh, that is all right. Cecily is not a silly romantic girl, I am glad to say. She has got a capital appetite, goes long walks, and pays no attention at all to her lessons.

ALGERNON: I would rather like to see Cecily.

JACK: I will take very good care you never do. She is excessively pretty, and she is only just eighteen.

ALGERNON: Have you told Gwendolen yet that you have an excessively pretty ward who is only just eighteen?

JACK: Oh! one doesn't blurt these things out to people. Cecily and Gwendolen are perfectly certain to be extremely great friends. I'll bet you anything you like that half an hour after they have met, they will be calling each other sister.

ALGERNON: Women only do that when they have called each other a lot of other things first. Now, my dear boy, if we want to get a good table at Willis's, we really must go and dress. Do you know it is nearly seven?

JACK [*irritably*]: Oh! It always is nearly seven.

ALGERNON: I'm hungry.

JACK: I never knew you when you weren't. . . .

ALGERNON: What shall we do after dinner? Go to a theatre?

JACK: Oh no! I loathe listening.

ALGERNON: Well, let us go to the Club.

JACK: Oh, no! I hate talking.

ALGERNON: Well, we might trot round to the Empire at ten?

JACK: Oh, no! I can't bear looking at things. It is so silly.

ALGERNON: Well, what shall we do?

JACK: Nothing!

ALGERNON: It is awfully hard work doing nothing. However, I don't mind hard work where there is no definite object of any kind.

[*Enter* LANE.]

LANE: Miss Fairfax.

[*Enter* GWENDOLEN. LANE *goes out.*]

ALGERNON: Gwendolen, upon my word!

GWENDOLEN: Algy, kindly turn your back. I have something very particular to say to Mr. Worthing.

ALGERNON: Really, Gwendolen, I don't think I can allow this at all.

GWENDOLEN: Algy, you always adopt a strictly immoral attitude towards life. You are not quite old enough to do that. [ALGERNON *retires to the fireplace.*]

JACK: My own darling!

GWENDOLEN: Ernest, we may never be married. From the expression on mamma's face I fear we never shall. Few parents nowadays pay any regard to what their children say to them. The old-fashioned respect for the young is fast dying out. Whatever influence I ever had over mamma, I lost at the age of three. But although she may prevent us from becoming man and wife, and I may marry someone else, and marry often, nothing that she can possibly do can alter my eternal devotion to you.

JACK: Dear Gwendolen!

GWENDOLEN: The story of your romantic origin, as related to me by mamma, with unpleasing comments, has naturally stirred the deeper fibres of my nature. Your Christian name has an irresistible fascination. The simplicity of your character makes you exquisitely incomprehensible to me. Your town address at the Albany I have. What is your address in the country?

JACK: The Manor House, Woolton, Hertfordshire.

[ALGERNON, *who has been carefully listening, smiles to himself, and writes the address on his shirt-cuff. Then picks up the Railway Guide.*]

GWENDOLEN: There is a good postal service, I suppose? It may be necessary to do something desperate. That of course will require serious consideration. I will communicate with you daily.

JACK: My own one!

GWENDOLEN: How long do you remain in town?

JACK: Till Monday.

GWENDOLEN: Good! Algy, you may turn round now.

ALGERNON: Thanks, I've turned round already.

GWENDOLEN: You may also ring the bell.

JACK: You will let me see you to your carriage, my own darling?

GWENDOLEN: Certainly.

JACK [*to* LANE, *who now enters*]: I will see Miss Fairfax out.

LANE: Yes, sir. [JACK *and* GWENDOLEN *go off.*]

[LANE *presents several letters on a salver, to* ALGERNON. *It is to be surmised that they are bills, as* ALGERNON, *after looking at the envelopes, tears them up.*]

ALGERNON: A glass of sherry, Lane.

LANE: Yes, sir.

ALGERNON: Tomorrow, Lane, I'm going Bunburying.

LANE: Yes, sir.

ALGERNON: I shall probably not be back till Monday. You can put up my dress clothes, my smoking jacket, and all the Bunbury suits . . .

LANE: Yes, sir. [*Handing sherry.*]

ALGERNON: I hope tomorrow will be a fine day, Lane.

LANE: It never is, sir.

ALGERNON: Lane, you're a perfect pessimist.

LANE: I do my best to give satisfaction, sir.

[*Enter* JACK. LANE *goes off.*]

JACK: There's a sensible, intellectual girl! the only girl I ever cared for in my life. [ALGERNON *is laughing immoderately.*] What on earth are you so amused at?

ALGERNON: Oh, I'm a little anxious about poor Bunbury, that is all.

JACK: If you don't take care, your friend Bunbury will get you into a serious scrape some day.

ALGERNON: I love scrapes. They are the only things that are never serious.

JACK: Oh, that's nonsense, Algy. You never talk anything but nonsense.

ALGERNON: Nobody ever does.

[JACK *looks indignantly at him, and leaves the room.* ALGERNON *lights a cigarette, reads his shirt-cuff, and smiles.*]

CURTAIN

ACT TWO

Garden at the Manor House. A flight of grey stone steps leads up to the house. The garden, an old-fashioned one, full of roses. Time of year, July. Basket chairs, and a table covered with books, are set under a large yew-tree.

[MISS PRISM *discovered seated at the table.* CECILY *is at the back, watering flowers.*]

MISS PRISM [*calling*]: Cecily, Cecily! Surely such a utilitarian occupation as the watering of flowers is rather Moulton's duty than yours? Especially at a moment when intellectual pleasures await you. Your German grammar is on the table. Pray open it at page fifteen. We will repeat yesterday's lesson.

CECILY [*coming over very slowly*]: But I don't like German. It isn't at all a becoming language. I know perfectly well that I look quite plain after my German lesson.

MISS PRISM: Child, you know how anxious your guardian is that you should improve yourself in every way. He laid particular stress on your German, as he was leaving for town yesterday. Indeed, he always lays stress on your German when he is leaving for town.

CECILY: Dear Uncle Jack is so very serious! Sometimes he is so serious that I think he cannot be quite well.

MISS PRISM [*drawing herself up*]: Your guardian enjoys the best of health, and his gravity of demeanour is especially to be commended in one so comparatively young as he is. I know no one who has a higher sense of duty and responsibility.

CECILY: I suppose that is why he often looks a little bored when we three are together.

MISS PRISM: Cecily! I am surprised at you. Mr. Worthing has many troubles in his life. Idle merriment and triviality would be out of place in his conversation. You must remember his constant anxiety about that unfortunate young man, his brother.

CECILY: I wish Uncle Jack would allow that unfortunate young man, his brother, to come down here sometimes. We might have a good influence over him, Miss Prism. I am sure you certainly would. You know German, and geology, and things of that kind influence a man very much. [CECILY *begins to write in her diary.*]

MISS PRISM [*shaking her head*]: I do not think that even I could produce any effect on a character that according to his own brother's admission is irretrievably weak and vacillating. Indeed I am not sure that I would desire to reclaim him. I am not in favour of this modern mania for turning bad people into good people at a moment's notice. As a man sows so let him reap. You must put away your diary, Cecily. I really don't see why you should keep a diary at all.

CECILY: I keep a diary in order to enter the wonderful secrets of my life. If I didn't write them down, I should probably forget all about them.

MISS PRISM: Memory, my dear Cecily, is the diary that we all carry about with us.

CECILY: Yes, but it usually chronicles the things that have never happened, and couldn't possibly have happened. I believe that Memory is responsible for nearly all the three-volume novels that Mudie sends us.

MISS PRISM: Do not speak slightingly of the three-volume novel, Cecily. I wrote one myself in earlier days.

CECILY: Did you really, Miss Prism? How wonderfully clever you are! I hope it did not end happily? I don't like novels that end happily. They depress me so much.

MISS PRISM: The good ended happily, and the bad unhappily. That is what Fiction means.

CECILY: I suppose so. But is seems very unfair. And was your novel ever published?

MISS PRISM: Alas! no. The manuscript unfortunately was abandoned. [CECILY *starts.*] I used the word in the sense of lost or mislaid. To your work, child, these speculations are profitless.

CECILY [*smiling*]: But I see dear Dr. Chasuble coming up through the garden.

MISS PRISM [*rising and advancing*]: Dr. Chasuble! This is indeed a pleasure.

[*Enter* CANON CHASUBLE.]

CHASUBLE: And how are we this morning? Miss Prism, you are, I trust, well?

CECILY: Miss Prism has just been complaining of a slight headache. I think it would do her so much good to have a short stroll with you in the Park, Dr. Chasuble.

MISS PRISM: Cecily, I have not mentioned anything about a headache.

CECILY: No, dear Miss Prism, I know that, but I felt instinctively that you had a headache. Indeed I was thinking about that, and not about my German lesson, when the Rector came in.

CHASUBLE: I hope, Cecily, you are not inattentive.

CECILY: Oh, I am afraid I am.

CHASUBLE: That is strange. Were I fortunate enough to be Miss Prism's pupil, I would hang upon her lips. [MISS PRISM *glares.*] I spoke metaphorically. —My metaphor was drawn from bees. Ahem! Mr. Worthing, I suppose, has not returned from town yet?

MISS PRISM: We do not expect him till Monday afternoon.

CHASUBLE: Ah yes, he usually likes to spend his Sunday in London. He is not one of those whose sole aim is enjoyment, as, by all accounts, that unfortunate young man his brother seems to be. But I must not disturb

Egeria and her pupil any longer.

MISS PRISM: Egeria? My name is Laetitia, Doctor.

CHASUBLE [*bowing*]: A classical allusion merely, drawn from the Pagan authors. I shall see you both no doubt at Evensong?

MISS PRISM: I think, dear Doctor, I will have a stroll with you. I find I have a headache after all, and a walk might do it good.

CHASUBLE: With pleasure, Miss Prism, with pleasure. We might go as far as the schools and back.

MISS PRISM: That would be delightful. Cecily, you will read your Political Economy in my absence. The chapter on the Fall of the Rupee you may omit. It is somewhat too sensational. Even these metallic problems have their melodramatic side. [*Goes down the garden with* DR. CHASUBLE.]

CECILY [*picks up books and throws them back on table*]: Horrid Political Economy! Horrid Geography! Horrid, horrid German!

[*Enter* MERRIMAN *with a card on a salver.*]

MERRIMAN: Mr. Ernest Worthing has just driven over from the station. He has brought his luggage with him.

CECILY [*takes the card and reads it*]: "Mr. Ernest Worthing, B.4, The Albany, W." Uncle Jack's brother! Did you tell him Mr. Worthing was in town?

MERRIMAN: Yes, Miss. He seemed very much disappointed. I mentioned that you and Miss Prism were in the garden. He said he was anxious to speak to you privately for a moment.

CECILY: Ask Mr. Ernest Worthing to come here. I suppose you had better talk to the housekeeper about a room for him.

MERRIMAN: Yes, Miss. [MERRIMAN *goes off.*]

CECILY: I have never met any really wicked person before. I feel rather frightened. I am so afraid he will look just like everyone else. [*Enter* ALGERNON, *very gay and debonair.*] He does!

ALGERNON [*raising his hat*]: You are my little cousin Cecily, I'm sure.

CECILY: You are under some strange mistake. I am not little. In fact, I believe I am more than usually tall for my age. [ALGERNON *is rather taken aback.*] But I am your cousin Cecily. You, I see from your card, are Uncle Jack's brother, my cousin Ernest, my wicked cousin Ernest.

ALGERNON: Oh! I am not really wicked at all, Cousin Cecily. You mustn't think that I am wicked.

CECILY: If you are not, then you have certainly been deceiving us all in a very inexcusable manner. I hope you have not been leading a double life, pretending to be wicked and being really good all the time. That would be hypocrisy.

ALGERNON [*looks at her in amazement*]: Oh! Of course I have been rather reckless.

CECILY: I am glad to hear it.

ALGERNON: In fact, now you mention the subject, I have been very bad in my own small way.

CECILY: I don't think you should be so proud of that, though I am sure it must have been very pleasant.

ALGERNON: It is much pleasanter being here with you.

CECILY: I can't understand how you are here at all. Uncle Jack won't be back till Monday afternoon.

ALGERNON: That is a great disappointment. I am obliged to go up by the first train on Monday morning. I have a business appointment that I am anxious . . . to miss!

CECILY: Couldn't you miss it anywhere but in London?

ALGERNON: No: the appointment is in London.

CECILY: Well, I know, of course, how important it is not to keep a business engagement, if one wants to retain any sense of the beauty of life, but still I think you had better wait till Uncle Jack arrives. I know he wants to speak to you about your emigrating.

ALGERNON: About my what?

CECILY: Your emigrating. He has gone up to buy your outfit.

ALGERNON: I certainly wouldn't let Jack buy my outfit. He has no taste in neckties at all.

CECILY: I don't think you will require neckties. Uncle Jack is sending you to Australia.

ALGERNON: Australia! I'd sooner die.

CECILY: Well, he said at dinner on Wednesday night, that you would have to choose between this world, the next world, and Australia.

ALGERNON: Oh, well! The accounts I have received of Australia and the next world are not particularly encouraging.

This world is good enough for me, Cousin Cecily.

CECILY: Yes, but are you good enough for it?

ALGERNON: I'm afraid I'm not that. That is why I want you to reform me. You might make that your mission, if you don't mind, Cousin Cecily.

CECILY: I'm afraid I've no time, this afternoon.

ALGERNON: Well, would you mind my reforming myself this afternoon?

CECILY: It is rather Quixotic of you. But I think you should try.

ALGERNON: I will. I feel better already.

CECILY: You are looking a little worse.

ALGERNON: That is because I am hungry.

CECILY: How thoughtless of me. I should have remembered that when one is going to lead an entirely new life, one requires regular and wholesome meals. Won't you come in?

ALGERNON: Thank you. Might I have a buttonhole first? I have never any appetite unless I have a buttonhole first.

CECILY: A Maréchal Niel? [*Picks up scissors.*]

ALGERNON: No, I'd sooner have a pink rose.

CECILY: Why? [*Cuts a flower.*]

ALGERNON: Because you are like a pink rose, Cousin Cecily.

CECILY: I don't think it can be right for you to talk to me like that. Miss Prism never says such things to me.

ALGERNON: Then Miss Prism is a short-sighted old lady. [CECILY *puts the rose in his buttonhole.*]

You are the prettiest girl I ever saw.

CECILY: Miss Prism says that all good looks are a snare.

ALGERNON: They are a snare that every sensible man would like to be caught in.

CECILY: Oh, I don't think I would care to catch a sensible man. I shouldn't know what to talk to him about.

[*They pass into the house.* MISS PRISM *and* DR. CHASUBLE *return.*]

MISS PRISM: You are too much alone, dear Dr. Chasuble. You should get married. A misanthrope I can understand—a womanthrope, never!

CHASUBLE [*with a scholar's shudder*]: Believe me, I do not deserve so neologistic a phrase. The precept as well as the practice of the Primitive Church was distinctly against matrimony.

MISS PRISM [*sententiously*]: That is obviously the reason why the Primitive Church has not lasted up to the present day. And you do not seem to realize, dear Doctor, that by persistently remaining single, a man converts himself into a permanent public temptation. Men should be more careful; this very celibacy leads weaker vessels astray.

CHASUBLE: But is a man not equally attractive when married?

MISS PRISM: No married man is ever attractive except to his wife.

CHASUBLE: And often, I've been told, not even to her.

MISS PRISM: That depends on the intellectual sympathies of the woman. Maturity can always be depended on. Ripeness can

be trusted. Young women are green. [DR. CHASUBLE *starts.*] I spoke horticulturally. My metaphor was drawn from fruits. But where is Cecily?

CHASUBLE: Perhaps she followed us to the schools.

[*Enter* JACK *slowly from the back of the garden. He is dressed in the deepest mourning, with crêpe hatband and black gloves.*]

MISS PRISM: Mr. Worthing!

CHASUBLE: Mr. Worthing?

MISS PRISM: This is indeed a surprise. We did not look for you till Monday afternoon.

JACK [*shakes* MISS PRISM'S *hand in a tragic manner*]: I have returned sooner than I expected. Dr. Chasuble, I hope you are well?

CHASUBLE: Dear Mr. Worthing, I trust this garb of woe does not betoken some terrible calamity?

JACK: My brother.

MISS PRISM: More shameful debts and extravagance?

CHASUBLE: Still leading his life of pleasure?

JACK [*shaking his head*]: Dead!

CHASUBLE: Your brother Ernest dead?

JACK: Quite dead.

MISS PRISM: What a lesson for him! I trust he will profit by it.

CHASUBLE: Mr. Worthing, I offer you my sincere condolence. You have at least the consolation of knowing that you are always the most generous and forgiving of brothers.

JACK: Poor Ernest! He had many faults, but it is a sad, sad blow.

CHASUBLE: Very sad indeed. Were you with him at the end?

JACK: No. He died abroad; in

Paris, in fact. I had a telegram last night from the manager of the Grand Hotel.

CHASUBLE: Was the cause of death mentioned?

JACK: A severe chill, it seems.

MISS PRISM: As a man sows, so shall he reap.

CHASUBLE [*raising his hand*]: Charity, dear Miss Prism, charity! None of us are perfect. I myself am peculiarly susceptible to draughts. Will the interment take place here?

JACK: No. He seems to have expressed a desire to be buried in Paris.

CHASUBLE: In Paris! [*Shakes his head.*] I fear that hardly points to any very serious state of mind at the last. You would no doubt wish me to make some slight allusion to this tragic domestic affliction next Sunday. [JACK *presses his hand convulsively.*] My sermon on the meaning of the manna in the wilderness can be adapted to almost any occasion, joyful, or, as in the present case, distressing. [*All sigh.*] I have preached it at harvest celebrations, christenings, confirmations, on days of humiliation and festal days. The last time I delivered it was in the Cathedral, as a charity sermon on behalf of the Society for the Prevention of Discontent among the Upper Orders. The Bishop, who was present, was much struck by some of the analogies I drew.

JACK: Ah! that reminds me, you mentioned christenings I think, Dr. Chasuble? I suppose you know how to christen all right? [DR. CHASUBLE *looks astounded.*]

I mean, of course, you are continually christening, aren't you?

MISS PRISM: It is, I regret to say, one of the Rector's most constant duties in this parish. I have often spoken to the poorer classes on the subject. But they don't seem to know what thrift is.

CHASUBLE: But is there any particular infant in whom you are interested, Mr. Worthing? Your brother was, I believe, unmarried, was he not?

JACK: Oh, yes.

MISS PRISM [*bitterly*]: People who live entirely for pleasure usually are.

JACK: But it is not for any child, dear Doctor. I am very fond of children. No! the fact is, I would like to be christened myself, this afternoon, if you have nothing better to do.

CHASUBLE: But surely, Mr. Worthing, you have been christened already?

JACK: I don't remember anything about it.

CHASUBLE: But have you any grave doubts on the subject?

JACK: I certainly intend to have. Of course I don't know if the thing would bother you in any way, or if you think I am a little too old now.

CHASUBLE: Not at all. The sprinkling, and, indeed, the immersion of adults is a perfectly canonical practice.

JACK: Immersion!

CHASUBLE: You need have no apprehensions. Sprinkling is all that is necessary, or indeed I think advisable. Our weather is so changeable. At what hour would you wish the ceremony performed?

JACK: Oh, I might trot round about five if that would suit you.

CHASUBLE: Perfectly, perfectly! In fact I have two similar ceremonies to perform at that time. A case of twins that occurred recently in one of the outlying cottages on your own estate. Poor Jenkins the carter, a most hard-working man.

JACK: Oh! I don't see much fun in being christened along with other babies. It would be childish. Would half-past five do?

CHASUBLE: Admirably! Admirably! [*Takes out watch.*] And now, dear Mr. Worthing, I will not intrude any longer into a house of sorrow. I would merely beg you not to be too much bowed down by grief. What seem to us bitter trials are often blessings in disguise.

MISS PRISM: This seems to me a blessing of an extremely obvious kind.

[*Enter* CECILY *from the house.*]

CECILY: Uncle Jack! Oh, I am pleased to see you back. But what horrid clothes you have got on. Do go and change them.

MISS PRISM: Cecily!

CHASUBLE: My child! my child. [CECILY *goes towards* JACK; *he kisses her brow in a melancholy manner.*]

CECILY: What is the matter, Uncle Jack? Do look happy! You look as if you had toothache, and I have got such a surprise for you. Who do you think is in the dining-room? Your brother!

JACK: Who?

CECILY: Your brother Ernest. He arrived about half an hour ago.

JACK: What nonsense! I haven't got a brother.

CECILY: Oh, don't say that. However badly he may have behaved to you in the past he is still your brother. You couldn't be so heartless as to disown him. I'll tell him to come out. And you will shake hands with him, won't you, Uncle Jack? [*Runs back into the house.*]

CHASUBLE: These are very joyful tidings.

MISS PRISM: After we had all been resigned to his loss, his sudden return seems to me peculiarly distressing.

JACK: My brother is in the dining-room? I don't know what it all means. I think it is perfectly absurd.

[*Enter* ALGERNON *and* CECILY *hand in hand. They come slowly up to* JACK.]

JACK: Good heavens! [*Motions* ALGERNON *away.*]

ALGERNON: Brother John, I have come down from town to tell you that I am very sorry for all the trouble I have given you, and that I intend to lead a better life in the future. [JACK *glares at him and does not take his hand.*]

CECILY: Uncle Jack, you are not going to refuse your own brother's hand?

JACK: Nothing will induce me to take his hand. I think his coming down here disgraceful. He knows perfectly well why.

CECILY: Uncle Jack, do be nice. There is some good in everyone. Ernest has just been telling me about his poor invalid friend

Mr. Bunbury whom he goes to visit so often. And surely there must be much good in one who is kind to an invalid, and leaves the pleasures of London to sit by a bed of pain.

JACK: Oh! he has been talking about Bunbury, has he?

CECILY: Yes, he has told me all about poor Mr. Bunbury, and his terrible state of health.

JACK: Bunbury! Well, I won't have him talk to you about Bunbury or about anything else. It is enough to drive one perfectly frantic.

ALGERNON: Of course I admit that the faults were all on my side. But I must say that I think that Brother John's coldness to me is peculiarly painful. I expected a more enthusiastic welcome, especially considering it is the first time I have come here.

CECILY: Uncle Jack, if you don't shake hands with Ernest I will never forgive you.

JACK: Never forgive me?

CECILY: Never, never, never!

JACK: Well, this is the last time I shall ever do it. [*Shakes hands with* ALGERNON *and glares.*]

CHASUBLE: It's pleasant, is it not, to see so perfect a reconciliation? I think we might leave the two brothers together.

MISS PRISM: Cecily, you will come with us.

CECILY: Certainly, Miss Prism. My little task of reconciliation is over.

CHASUBLE: You have done a beautiful action today, dear child.

MISS PRISM: We must not be premature in our judgements.

CECILY: I feel very happy. [*They*

all go off except JACK *and* ALGERNON.]

JACK: You young scoundrel, Algy, you must get out of this place as soon as possible. I don't allow any Bunburying here.

[*Enter* MERRIMAN.]

MERRIMAN: I have put Mr. Ernest's things in the room next to yours, sir. I suppose that is all right?

JACK: What?

MERRIMAN: Mr. Ernest's luggage, sir. I have unpacked it and put it in the room next to your own.

JACK: His luggage?

MERRIMAN: Yes, sir. Three portmanteaus, a dressing-case, two hatboxes, and a large luncheon-basket.

ALGERNON: I am afraid I can't stay more than a week this time.

JACK: Merriman, order the dog-cart at once. Mr. Ernest has been suddenly called back to town.

MERRIMAN: Yes, sir. [*Goes back into the house.*]

ALGERNON: What a fearful liar you are, Jack. I have not been called back to town at all.

JACK: Yes, you have.

ALGERNON: I haven't heard anyone call me.

JACK: Your duty as a gentleman calls you back.

ALGERNON: My duty as a gentleman has never interfered with my pleasures in the smallest degree.

JACK: I can quite understand that.

ALGERNON: Well, Cecily is a darling.

JACK: You are not to talk of Miss Cardew like that. I don't like it.

ALGERNON: Well, I don't like your clothes. You look perfectly ridiculous in them. Why on earth don't you go up and change? It is perfectly childish to be in deep mourning for a man who is actually staying for a whole week with you in your house as a guest. I call it grotesque.

JACK: You are certainly not staying with me for a whole week as a guest or anything else. You have got to leave . . . by the four-five train.

ALGERNON: I certainly won't leave you so long as you are in mourning. It would be most unfriendly. If I were in mourning you would stay with me, I suppose. I should think it very unkind if you didn't.

JACK: Well, will you go if I change my clothes?

ALGERNON: Yes, if you are not too long. I never saw anybody take so long to dress, and with such little result.

JACK: Well, at any rate, that is better than being always over-dressed as you are.

ALGERNON: If I am occasionally a little over-dressed, I make up for it by being always immensely over-educated.

JACK: Your vanity is ridiculous, your conduct an outrage, and your presence in my garden utterly absurd. However, you have got to catch the four-five, and I hope you will have a pleasant journey back to town. This Bunburying, as you call it, has not been a great success for you. [*Goes into the house.*]

ALGERNON: I think it has been a great success. I'm in love with Cecily, and that is everything. [*Enter* CECILY *at the back of the garden. She picks up the can and begins to water the flowers.*] But

I must see her before I go, and make arrangements for another Bunbury. Ah, there she is.

CECILY: Oh, I merely came back to water the roses. I thought you were with Uncle Jack.

ALGERNON: He's gone to order the dog-cart for me.

CECILY: Oh, is he going to take you for a nice drive?

ALGERNON: He's going to send me away.

CECILY: Then have we got to part?

ALGERNON: I am afraid so. It's a very painful parting.

CECILY: It is always painful to part from people whom one has known for a very brief space of time. The absence of old friends one can endure with equanimity. But even a momentary separation from anyone to whom one has just been introduced is almost unbearable.

ALGERNON: Thank you.

[*Enter* MERRIMAN.]

MERRIMAN: The dog-cart is at the door, sir.

[ALGERNON *looks appealingly at* CECILY.]

CECILY: It can wait, Merriman . . . for . . . five minutes.

MERRIMAN: Yes, miss.

[*Exit* MERRIMAN.]

ALGERNON: I hope, Cecily, I shall not offend you if I state quite frankly and openly that you seem to me to be in every way the visible personification of absolute perfection.

CECILY: I think your frankness does you great credit, Ernest. If you will allow me, I will copy your remarks into my diary. [*Goes over to table and begins writing in diary.*]

ALGERNON: Do you really keep a diary? I'd give anything to look at it. May I?

CECILY: Oh, no. [*Puts her hand over it.*] You see, it is simply a very young girl's record of her own thoughts and impressions, and consequently meant for publication. When it appears in volume form I hope you will order a copy. But pray, Ernest, don't stop. I delight in taking down from dictation, I have reached "absolute perfection." You can go on. I am quite ready for more.

ALGERNON [*somewhat taken aback*]: Ahem! Ahem!

CECILY: Oh, don't cough, Ernest. When one is dictating one should speak fluently and not cough. Besides, I don't know how to spell a cough. [*Writes as* ALGERNON *speaks.*]

ALGERNON [*speaking very rapidly*]: Cecily, ever since I first looked upon your wonderful and incomparable beauty, I have dared to love you wildly, passionately, devotedly, hopelessly.

CECILY: I don't think that you should tell me that you love me wildly, passionately, devotedly, hopelessly. Hopelessly doesn't seem to make much sense, does it?

ALGERNON: Cecily.

[*Enter* MERRIMAN.]

MERRIMAN: The dog-cart is waiting, sir.

ALGERNON: Tell it to come round next week, at the same hour.

MERRIMAN [*looks at* CECILY, *who makes no sign*]: Yes, sir.

[MERRIMAN *retires.*]

CECILY: Uncle Jack would be very much annoyed if he knew you were staying on till next week, at the same hour.

ALGERNON: Oh, I don't care about Jack. I don't care for anybody in the whole world but you. I love you, Cecily. You will marry me, won't you?

CECILY: You silly boy! Of course. Why, we have been engaged for the last three months.

ALGERNON: For the last three months?

CECILY: Yes, it will be exactly three months on Thursday.

ALGERNON: But how did we become engaged?

CECILY: Well, ever since dear Uncle Jack first confessed to us that he had a younger brother who was very wicked and bad, you of course have formed the chief topic of conversation between myself and Miss Prism. And of course a man who is much talked about is always very attractive. One feels there must be something in him, after all. I daresay it was foolish of me, but I fell in love with you, Ernest.

ALGERNON: Darling. And when was the engagement actually settled?

CECILY: On the 14th of February last. Worn out by your entire ignorance of my existence, I determined to end the matter one way or the other, and after a long struggle with myself I accepted you under this dear old tree here. The next day I bought this little ring in your name, and this is the little bangle with the true lover's knot I promised you always to wear.

ALGERNON: Did I give you this? It's very pretty, isn't it?

CECILY: Yes, you've wonderfully good taste, Ernest. It's the excuse I've always given for your leading such a bad life. And this is the box in which I keep all your dear letters. [*Kneels at table, opens box, and produces letters tied up with blue ribbon.*]

ALGERNON: My letters! But, my own sweet Cecily, I have never written you any letters.

CECILY: You need hardly remind me of that, Ernest. I remember only too well that I was forced to write your letters for you. I wrote always three times a week, and sometimes oftener.

ALGERNON: Oh, do let me read them, Cecily?

CECILY: Oh, I couldn't possibly. They would make you far too conceited. [*Replaces box.*] The three you wrote me after I had broken off the engagement are so beautiful, and so badly spelled, that even now I can hardly read them without crying a little.

ALGERNON: But was our engagement ever broken off?

CECILY: Of course it was. On the 22nd of last March. You can see the entry if you like. [*Shows diary.*] "Today I broke off my engagement with Ernest. I feel it is better to do so. The weather still continues charming."

ALGERNON: But why on earth did you break it off? What had I done? I had done nothing at all. Cecily, I am very much hurt indeed to hear you broke it off. Particularly when the weather was so charming.

CECILY: It would hardly have been a really serious engagement if it hadn't been broken off at least once. But I forgave you before the week was out.

ALGERNON [*crossing to her, and kneeling*]: What a perfect angel you are, Cecily.

CECILY: You dear romantic boy. [*He kisses her, she puts her fingers through his hair.*] I hope your hair curls naturally, does it?

ALGERNON: Yes, darling, with a little help from others.

CECILY: I am so glad.

ALGERNON: You'll never break off our engagement again, Cecily?

CECILY: I don't think I could break it off now that I have actually met you. Besides, of course, there is the question of your name.

ALGERNON: Yes, of course. [*Nervously.*]

CECILY: You must not laugh at me, darling, but it had always been a girlish dream of mine to love someone whose name was Ernest. [ALGERNON *rises*, CECILY *also.*] There is something in that name that seems to inspire absolute confidence. I pity any poor married woman whose husband is not called Ernest.

ALGERNON: But, my dear child, do you mean to say you could not love me if I had some other name?

CECILY: But what name?

ALGERNON: Oh, any name you like—Algernon—for instance . . .

CECILY: But I don't like the name of Algernon.

ALGERNON: Well, my own dear, sweet, loving little darling, I really can't see why you should object to the name of Algernon. It is not at all a bad name. In fact, it is rather an aristocratic name. Half of the chaps who get into the Bankruptcy Court are called Algernon. But seriously, Cecily . . . [*moving to her*] if my name was Algy, couldn't you love me?

CECILY [*rising*]: I might respect you, Ernest, I might admire your character, but I fear that I should not be able to give you my undivided attention.

ALGERNON: Ahem! Cecily! [*Picking up hat.*] Your Rector here is, I suppose, thoroughly experienced in the practice of all the rites and ceremonials of the Church?

CECILY: Oh, yes. Dr. Chasuble is a most learned man. He has never written a single book, so you can imagine how much he knows.

ALGERNON: I must see him at once on a most important christening—I mean on most important business.

CECILY: Oh!

ALGERNON: I shan't be away more than half an hour.

CECILY: Considering that we have been engaged since February the 14th, and that I only met you today for the first time, I think it is rather hard that you should leave me for so long a period as half an hour. Couldn't you make it twenty minutes?

ALGERNON: I'll be back in no time. [*Kisses her and rushes down the garden.*]

CECILY: What an impetuous boy he is! I like his hair so much. I must enter his proposal in my diary.

[*Enter* MERRIMAN.]

MERRIMAN: A Miss Fairfax has just called to see Mr. Worthing. On very important business, Miss Fairfax states.

CECILY: Isn't Mr. Worthing in his library?

MERRIMAN: Mr. Worthing went over in the direction of the Rectory some time ago.

CECILY: Pray ask the lady to come out here; Mr. Worthing is sure to be back soon. And you can bring tea.

MERRIMAN: Yes, Miss. [*Goes out.*]

CECILY: Miss Fairfax! I suppose one of the many good elderly women who are associated with Uncle Jack in some of his philanthropic work in London. I don't quite like women who are interested in philanthropic work. I think it is so forward of them.

[*Enter* MERRIMAN.]

MERRIMAN: Miss Fairfax.

[*Enter* GWENDOLEN. *Exit* MERRIMAN.]

CECILY [*advancing to meet her*]: Pray let me introduce myself to you. My name is Cecily Cardew.

GWENDOLEN: Cecily Cardew! [*Moving to her and shaking hands.*] What a very sweet name! Something tells me that we are going to be great friends. I like you already more than I can say. My first impressions of people are never wrong.

CECILY: How nice of you to like me so much after we have known each other such a comparatively short time. Pray sit down.

GWENDOLEN [*still standing up*]:

I may call you Cecily, may I not?

CECILY: With pleasure!

GWENDOLEN: And you will always call me Gwendolen, won't you?

CECILY: If you wish.

GWENDOLEN: Then that is all quite settled, is it not?

CECILY: I hope so. [*A pause. They both sit down together.*]

GWENDOLEN: Perhaps this might be a favourable opportunity for my mentioning who I am. My father is Lord Bracknell. You have never heard of papa, I suppose?

CECILY: I don't think so.

GWENDOLEN: Outside the family circle, papa, I am glad to say, is entirely unknown. I think that is quite as it should be. The home seems to me to be the proper sphere for the man. And certainly once a man begins to neglect his domestic duties he becomes painfully effeminate, does he not? And I don't like that. It makes men so very attractive. Cecily, mamma, whose views on education are remarkably strict, has brought me up to be extremely short-sighted; it is part of her system; so do you mind my looking at you through my glasses?

CECILY: Oh! not at all, Gwendolen. I am very fond of being looked at.

GWENDOLEN [*after examining* CECILY *carefully through a lorgnette*]: You are here on a short visit, I suppose.

CECILY: Oh, no! I live here.

GWENDOLEN [*severely*]: Really? Your mother, no doubt, or some female relative of advanced years, resides here also?

CECILY: Oh, no! I have no mother, nor, in fact, any relations.

GWENDOLEN: Indeed?

CECILY: My dear guardian, with the assistance of Miss Prism, has the arduous task of looking after me.

GWENDOLEN: Your guardian?

CECILY: Yes, I am Mr. Worthing's ward.

GWENDOLEN: Oh! It is strange he never mentioned to me that he had a ward. How secretive of him! He grows more interesting hourly. I am not sure, however, that the news inspires me with feelings of unmixed delight. [*Rising and going to her.*] I am very fond of you, Cecily; I have liked you ever since I met you! But I am bound to state that now that I know you are Mr. Worthing's ward, I cannot help expressing a wish you were—well, just a little older than you seem to be—and not quite so very alluring in appearance. In fact, if I may speak candidly—

CECILY: Pray do! I think that whenever one has anything unpleasant to say, one should always be quite candid.

GWENDOLEN: Well, to speak with perfect candour, Cecily, I wish that you were fully forty-two, and more than usually plain for your age. Ernest has a strong upright nature. He is the very soul of truth and honour. Disloyalty would be as impossible to him as deception. But even men of the noblest possible moral character are extremely susceptible to the influence of the physical charms of others. Modern, no less than Ancient History, supplies us with many most painful examples of what I refer to. If it were not so, indeed, History would be quite unreadable.

CECILY: I beg your pardon, Gwendolen, did you say Ernest?

GWENDOLEN: Yes.

CECILY: Oh, but it is not Mr. Ernest Worthing who is my guardian. It is his brother—his elder brother.

GWENDOLEN [*sitting down again*]: Ernest never mentioned to me that he had a brother.

CECILY: I am sorry to say they have not been on good terms for a long time.

GWENDOLEN: Ah! that accounts for it. And now that I think of it I have never heard any man mention his brother. The subject seems distasteful to most men. Cecily, you have lifted a load from my mind. I was growing almost anxious. It would have been terrible if any cloud had come across a friendship like ours, would it not? Of course you are quite, quite sure that it is not Mr. Ernest Worthing who is your guardian?

CECILY: Quite sure. [*A pause.*] In fact, I am going to be his.

GWENDOLEN [*inquiringly*]: I beg your pardon?

CECILY [*rather shy and confidingly*]: Dearest Gwendolen, there is no reason why I should make a secret of it to you. Our little county newspaper is sure to chronicle the fact next week. Mr. Ernest Worthing and I are engaged to be married.

GWENDOLEN [*quite politely, rising*]: My darling Cecily, I think there must be some slight error. Mr. Ernest Worthing is engaged to me. The announcement will appear in the *Morning Post* on Saturday at the latest.

CECILY [*very politely, rising*]: I am afraid you must be under some misconception. Ernest proposed to me exactly ten minutes ago. [*Shows diary.*]

GWENDOLEN [*examines diary through her lorgnette carefully*]: It is very curious, for he asked me to be his wife yesterday afternoon at 5:30. If you would care to verify the incident, pray do so. [*Produces diary of her own.*] I never travel without my diary. One should always have something sensational to read in the train. I am so sorry, dear Cecily, if it is any disappointment to you, but I am afraid I have the prior claim.

CECILY: It would distress me more than I can tell you, dear Gwendolen, if it caused you any mental or physical anguish, but I feel bound to point out that since Ernest proposed to you he clearly has changed his mind.

GWENDOLEN [*meditatively*]: If the poor fellow has been entrapped into any foolish promise I shall consider it my duty to rescue him at once, and with a firm hand.

CECILY [*thoughtfully and sadly*]: Whatever unfortunate entanglement my dear boy may have got into, I will never reproach him with it after we are married.

GWENDOLEN: Do you allude to me, Miss Cardew, as an entanglement? You are presumptuous. On an occasion of this kind it becomes more than a moral duty to speak one's mind. It becomes a pleasure.

CECILY: Do you suggest, Miss Fairfax, that I entrapped Ernest into an engagement? How dare you? This is no time for wearing the shallow mask of manners. When I see a spade I call it a spade.

GWENDOLEN [*satirically*]: I am glad to say that I have never seen a spade. It is obvious that our social spheres have been widely different.

[*Enter* MERRIMAN, *followed by the footman. He carries a salver, table cloth, and plate stand.* CECILY *is about to retort. The presence of the servants exercises a restraining influence, under which both girls chafe.*]

MERRIMAN: Shall I lay tea here as usual, Miss?

CECILY [*sternly, in a calm voice*]: Yes, as usual.

[MERRIMAN *begins to clear table and lay cloth. A long pause.* CECILY *and* GWENDOLEN *glare at each other.*]

GWENDOLEN: Are there many interesting walks in the vicinity, Miss Cardew?

CECILY: Oh! yes! a great many. From the top of one of the hills quite close one can see five counties.

GWENDOLEN: Five counties! I don't think I should like that; I hate crowds.

CECILY [*sweetly*]: I suppose that is why you live in town?

[GWENDOLEN *bites her lip, and beats her foot nervously with her parasol.*]

GWENDOLEN [*looking around*]: Quite a well-kept garden this is, Miss Cardew.

CECILY: So glad you like it, Miss Fairfax.

GWENDOLEN: I had no idea there were any flowers in the country.

CECILY: Oh, flowers are as common here, Miss Fairfax, as people are in London.

GWENDOLEN: Personally I cannot understand how anybody manages to exist in the country, if anybody who is anybody does. The country always bores me to death.

CECILY: Ah! This is what the newspapers call agricultural depression, is it not? I believe the aristocracy are suffering very much from it just at present. It is almost an epidemic amongst them, I have been told. May I offer you some tea, Miss Fairfax?

GWENDOLEN [*with elaborate politeness*]: Thank you. [*Aside.*] Detestable girl! But I require tea!

CECILY [*sweetly*]: Sugar?

GWENDOLEN [*superciliously*]: No, thank you. Sugar is not fashionable any more.

[CECILY *looks angrily at her, takes up the tongs and puts four lumps of sugar into the cup.*]

CECILY [*severely*]: Cake or bread and butter?

GWENDOLEN [*in a bored manner*]: Bread and butter, please. Cake is rarely seen at the best houses nowadays.

CECILY [*cuts a very large slice of cake and puts it on the tray*]: Hand that to Miss Fairfax.

[MERRIMAN *does so, and goes out*

with footman. GWENDOLEN *drinks the tea and makes a grimace. Puts down cup at once, reaches out her hand to the bread and butter, looks at it, and finds it is cake. Rises in indignation.*]

GWENDOLEN: You have filled my tea with lumps of sugar, and though I asked most distinctly for bread and butter, you have given me cake. I am known for the gentleness of my disposition, and the extraordinary sweetness of my nature, but I warn you, Miss Cardew, you may go too far.

CECILY [*rising*]: To save my poor, innocent, trusting boy from the machinations of any other girl there are no lengths to which I would not go.

GWENDOLEN: From the moment I saw you I distrusted you. I felt that you were false and deceitful. I am never deceived in such matters. My first impressions of people are invariably right.

CECILY: It seems to me, Miss Fairfax, that I am trespassing on your valuable time. No doubt you have many other calls of a similar character to make in the neighbourhood.

[*Enter* JACK.]

GWENDOLEN [*catching sight of him*]: Ernest! My own Ernest!

JACK: Gwendolen! Darling! [*Offers to kiss her.*]

GWENDOLEN [*drawing back*]: A moment! May I ask if you are engaged to be married to this young lady? [*Points to* CECILY.]

JACK [*laughing*]: To dear little Cecily! Of course not! What could have put such an idea

into your pretty little head?

GWENDOLEN: Thank you. You may! [*Offers her cheek.*]

CECILY [*very sweetly*]: I knew there must be some misunderstanding, Miss Fairfax. The gentleman whose arm is at present round your waist is my guardian, Mr. John Worthing.

GWENDOLEN: I beg your pardon?

CECILY: This is Uncle Jack.

GWENDOLEN [*receding*]: Jack! Oh!

[*Enter* ALGERNON.]

CECILY: Here is Ernest.

ALGERNON [*goes straight over to* CECILY *without noticing anyone else*]: My own love! [*Offers to kiss her.*]

CECILY [*drawing back*]: A moment, Ernest! May I ask you—are you engaged to be married to this young lady?

ALGERNON [*looking round*]: To what young lady? Good heavens! Gwendolen!

CECILY: Yes, to good heavens, Gwendolen, I mean to Gwendolen.

ALGERNON [*laughing*]: Of course not! What could have put such an idea into your pretty little head?

CECILY: Thank you. [*Presenting her cheek to be kissed.*] You may. [ALGERNON *kisses her.*]

GWENDOLEN: I felt there was some slight error, Miss Cardew. The gentleman who is now embracing you is my cousin, Mr. Algernon Moncrieff.

CECILY [*breaking away from Algernon*]: Algernon Moncrieff! Oh!

[*The two girls move towards each other and put their arms round each other's waists as if for protection.*]

CECILY: Are you called Algernon?

ALGERNON: I cannot deny it.

CECILY: Oh!

GWENDOLEN: Is your name really John?

JACK [*standing rather proudly*]: I could deny it if I liked. I could deny anything if I liked. But my name certainly is John. It has been John for years.

CECILY [*to* GWENDOLEN]: A gross deception has been practised on both of us.

GWENDOLEN: My poor wounded Cecily!

CECILY: My sweet wronged Gwendolen!

GWENDOLEN [*slowly and seriously*]: You will call me sister, will you not? [*They embrace.* JACK *and* ALGERNON *groan and walk up and down.*]

CECILY [*rather brightly*]: There is just one question I would like to be allowed to ask my guardian.

GWENDOLEN: An admirable idea! Mr. Worthing, there is just one question I would like to be permitted to put to you. Where is your brother Ernest? We are both engaged to be married to your brother Ernest, so it is a matter of some importance to us to know where your brother Ernest is at present.

JACK [*slowly and hesitatingly*]: Gwendolen—Cecily—it is very painful for me to be forced to speak the truth. It is the first time in my life that I have ever been reduced to such a painful position, and I am really quite inexperienced in doing anything of the kind. However, I will tell you quite frankly that I have no brother Ernest. I have no brother at all. I never had a brother in my life, and I certainly have not the smallest intention of ever having one in the future.

CECILY [*surprised*]: No brother at all?

JACK [*cheerily*]: None!

GWENDOLEN [*severely*]: Had you never a brother of any kind?

JACK [*pleasantly*]: Never. Not even of any kind.

GWENDOLEN: I am afraid it is quite clear, Cecily, that neither of us is engaged to be married to anyone.

CECILY: It is not a very pleasant position for a young girl suddenly to find herself in. Is it?

GWENDOLEN: Let us go into the house. They will hardly venture to come after us there.

CECILY: No, men are so cowardly, aren't they? [*They retire into the house with scornful looks.*]

JACK: This ghastly state of things is what you call Bunburying, I suppose?

ALGERNON: Yes, and a perfectly wonderful Bunbury it is. The most wonderful Bunbury I have ever had in my life.

JACK: Well, you've no right whatsoever to Bunbury here.

ALGERNON: That is absurd. One has a right to Bunbury anywhere one chooses. Every serious Bunburyist knows that.

JACK: Serious Bunburyist? Good heavens!

ALGERNON: Well, one must be serious about something, if one wants to have any amusement in life. I happen to be serious about Bunburying. What on earth you are serious about I haven't got the remotest idea. About everything, I should fancy. You have such an absolutely trivial nature.

JACK: Well, the only small satisfaction I have in the whole of this wretched business is that your friend Bunbury is quite exploded. You won't be able to run down to the country quite so often as you used to do, dear Algy. And a very good thing too.

ALGERNON: Your brother is a little off colour, isn't he, dear Jack? You won't be able to disappear to London quite so frequently as your wicked custom was. And not a bad thing either.

JACK: As for your conduct towards Miss Cardew, I must say that your taking in a sweet, simple, innocent girl like that is quite inexcusable. To say nothing of the fact that she is my ward.

ALGERNON: I can see no possible defence at all for your deceiving a brilliant, clever, thoroughly experienced young lady like Miss Fairfax. To say nothing of the fact that she is my cousin.

JACK: I wanted to be engaged to Gwendolen, that is all, I love her.

ALGERNON: Well, I simply wanted to be engaged to Cecily. I adore her.

JACK: There is certainly no chance of your marrying Miss Cardew.

ALGERNON: I don't think there is much likelihood, Jack, of you and Miss Fairfax being united.

JACK: Well, that is no business of yours.

ALGERNON: If it was my business,

I wouldn't talk about it. [*Begins to eat muffins.*] It is very vulgar to talk about one's business. Only people like stockbrokers do that, and then merely at dinner parties.

JACK: How you can sit there, calmly eating muffins when we are in this horrible trouble, I can't make out. You seem to me to be perfectly heartless.

ALGERNON: Well, I can't eat muffins in an agitated manner. The butter would probably get on my cuffs. One should always eat muffins quite calmly. It is the only way to eat them.

JACK: I say it's perfectly heartless your eating muffins at all, under the circumstances.

ALGERNON: When I am in trouble, eating is the only thing that consoles me. Indeed, when I am in really great trouble, as anyone who knows me intimately will tell you, I refuse everything except food and drink. At the present moment I am eating muffins because I am unhappy. Besides, I am particularly fond of muffins. [*Rising.*]

JACK [*rising*]: Well, there is no reason why you should eat them all in that greedy way. [*Takes muffins from Algernon.*]

ALGERNON [*offering tea-cake*]: I wish you would have tea-cake instead. I don't like tea-cake.

JACK: Good heavens! I suppose a man may eat his own muffins in his own garden.

ALGERNON: But you have just said it was perfectly heartless to eat muffins.

JACK: I said it was perfectly heartless of you, under the circumstances. That is a very different thing.

ALGERNON: That may be. But the muffins are the same. [*He seizes the muffin-dish from* JACK.]

JACK: Algy, I wish to goodness you would go.

ALGERNON: You can't possibly ask me to go without having some dinner. It's absurd. I never go without my dinner. No one ever does, except vegetarians and people like that. Besides I have just made arrangements with Dr. Chasuble to be christened at a quarter to six under the name of Ernest.

JACK: My dear fellow, the sooner you give up that nonsense the better. I made arrangements this morning with Dr. Chasuble to be christened myself at 5:30, and I naturally will take the name of Ernest. Gwendolen would wish it. We cannot both be christened Ernest. It's absurd. Besides, I have a perfect right to be christened if I like. There is no evidence at all that I have ever been christened by anybody. I should think it extremely probable I never was, and so does Dr. Chasuble. It is entirely different in your case. You have been christened already.

ALGERNON: Yes, but I have not been christened for years.

JACK: Yes, but you have been christened. That is the important thing.

ALGERNON: Quite so. So I know

my constitution can stand it. If you are not quite sure about your ever having been christened, I must say I think it rather dangerous your venturing on it now. It might make you very unwell. You can hardly have forgotten that someone very closely connected with you was very nearly carried off this week in Paris by a severe chill.

JACK: Yes, but you said yourself that a severe chill was not hereditary.

ALGERNON: It usen't to be, I know—but I daresay it is now. Science is always making wonderful improvements in things.

JACK [*picking up the muffin-dish*]: Oh, that is nonsense; you are always talking nonsense.

ALGERNON: Jack, you are at the muffins again! I wish you wouldn't. There are only two left. [*Takes them.*] I told you I was particularly fond of muffins.

JACK: But I hate tea-cake.

ALGERNON: Why on earth then do you allow tea-cake to be served up for your guests? What ideas you have on hospitality!

JACK: Algernon! I have already told you to go. I don't want you here. Why don't you go?

ALGERNON: I haven't quite finished my tea yet! and there is still one muffin left. [JACK *groans, and sinks into a chair.* ALGERNON *continues eating.*]

CURTAIN

ACT THREE

Drawing-room at the Manor House.

[GWENDOLEN *and* CECILY *are at the window, looking out into the garden.*]

GWENDOLEN: The fact that they did not follow us at once into the house, as anyone else would have done, seems to me to show that they have some sense of shame left.

CECILY: They have been eating muffins. That looks like repentance.

GWENDOLEN [*after a pause*]: They don't seem to notice us at all. Couldn't you cough?

CECILY: But I haven't got a cough.

GWENDOLEN: They're looking at us. What effrontery!

CECILY: They're approaching. That's very forward of them.

GWENDOLEN: Let us preserve a dignified silence.

CECILY: Certainly. It's the only thing to do now.

[*Enter* JACK *followed by* ALGERNON. *They whistle some dreadful popular air from a British Opera.*]

GWENDOLEN: This dignified silence seems to produce an unpleasant effect.

CECILY: A most distasteful one.

GWENDOLEN: But we will not be the first to speak.

CECILY: Certainly not.

GWENDOLEN: Mr. Worthing, I have something very particular to ask you. Much depends on your reply.

CECILY: Gwendolen, your common sense is invaluable. Mr. Moncrieff, kindly answer me the following question. Why did you pretend to be my guardian's brother?

ALGERNON: In order that I might have an opportunity of meeting you.

CECILY [*to* GWENDOLEN]: That certainly seems a satisfactory explanation, does it not?

GWENDOLEN: Yes, dear, if you can believe him.

CECILY: I don't. But that does not affect the wonderful beauty of his answer.

GWENDOLEN: True. In matters of grave importance, style, not sincerity, is the vital thing. Mr. Worthing, what explanation can you offer to me for pretending to have a brother? Was it in order that you might have an opportunity of coming up to town to see me as often as possible?

JACK: Can you doubt it, Miss Fairfax?

GWENDOLEN: I have the gravest doubts upon the subject. But I intend to crush them. This is not the moment for German scepticism. [*Moving to* CECILY.] Their explanations appear to be quite satisfactory, especially

Mr. Worthing's. That seems to me to have the stamp of truth upon it.

CECILY: I am more than content with what Mr. Moncrieff said. His voice alone inspires one with absolute credulity.

GWENDOLEN: Then you think we should forgive them?

CECILY: Yes. I mean no.

GWENDOLEN: True! I had forgotten. There are principles at stake that one cannot surrender. Which of us should tell them? The task is not a pleasant one.

CECILY: Could we not both speak at the same time?

GWENDOLEN: An excellent idea! I nearly always speak at the same time as other people. Will you take the time from me?

CECILY: Certainly. [GWENDOLEN *beats time with uplifted finger.*]

GWENDOLEN and CECILY [*speaking together*]: Your Christian names are still an insuperable barrier. That is all!

JACK and ALGERNON [*speaking together*]: Our Christian names! Is that all? But we are going to be christened this afternoon.

GWENDOLEN [*to* JACK]: For my sake you are prepared to do this terrible thing?

JSCK: I am.

CECILY [*to* ALGERNON]: To please me you are ready to face this fearful ordeal?

ALGERNON: I am!

GWENDOLEN: How absurd to talk of the equality of the sexes! Where questions of self-sacrifice are concerned, men are infinitely beyond us.

JACK: We are. [*Clasps hands with* ALGERNON.]

CECILY: They have moments of physical courage of which we women know absolutely nothing.

GWENDOLEN [*to* JACK]: Darling!

ALGERNON [*to* CECILY]: Darling! [*They fall into each other's arms.*]

[*Enter* MERRIMAN. *When he enters he coughs loudly, seeing the situation.*]

MERRIMAN: Ahem! Ahem! Lady Bracknell.

JACK: Good heavens!

[*Enter* LADY BRACKNELL. *The couples separate in alarm. Exit* MERRIMAN.]

LADY BRACKNELL: Gwendolen! What does this mean?

GWENDOLEN: Merely that I am engaged to be married to Mr. Worthing, mamma.

LADY BRACKNELL: Come here. Sit down. Sit down immediately. Hesitation of any kind is a sign of mental decay in the young, of physical weakness in the old. [*Turns to* JACK.] Apprised, sir, of my daughter's sudden flight by her trusty maid, whose confidence I purchased by means of a small coin, I followed her at once by a luggage train. Her unhappy father is, I am glad to say, under the impression that she is attending a more than usually lengthy lecture by the University Extension Scheme on the Influence of a permanent income on Thought. I do not propose to undeceive him. Indeed I have never undeceived him on any question. I would consider it wrong. But of course, you will clearly understand that all communication between yourself and my daughter must cease immediately from this moment. On this point, as indeed on all points, I am firm.

JACK: I am engaged to be married to Gwendolen, Lady Bracknell!

LADY BRACKNELL: You are nothing of the kind, sir. And now as regards Algernon! . . . Algernon!

ALGERNON: Yes, Aunt Augusta.

LADY BRACKNELL: May I ask if it is in this house that your invalid friend Mr. Bunbury resides?

ALGERNON [*stammering*]: Oh! No! Bunbury doesn't live here. Bunbury is somewhere else at present. In fact, Bunbury is dead.

LADY BRACKNELL: Dead! When did Mr. Bunbury die? His death must have been extremely sudden.

ALGERNON [*airily*]: Oh! I killed Bunbury this afternoon. I mean poor Bunbury died this afternoon.

LADY BRACKNELL: What did he die of?

ALGERNON: Bunbury? Oh, he was quite exploded.

LADY BRACKNELL: Exploded! Was he the victim of a revolutionary outrage? I was not aware that Mr. Bunbury was interested in social legislation. If so, he is well punished for his morbidity.

ALGERNON: My dear Aunt Augusta, I mean he was found out! The doctors found out that Bunbury could not live, that is what I mean—so Bunbury died.

LADY BRACKNELL: He seems to have had great confidence in the opinion of his physicians. I am glad, however, that he made up his mind at the last to some definite course of action, and acted under proper medical advice. And now that we have finally got rid of this Mr. Bunbury, may I ask, Mr. Worthing, who is that young person whose hand my nephew Algernon is now holding in what seems to me a peculiarly unnecessary manner?

JACK: That lady is Miss Cecily Cardew, my ward. [LADY BRACKNELL *bows coldly to* CECILY.]

ALGERNON: I am engaged to be married to Cecily, Aunt Augusta.

LADY BRACKNELL: I beg your pardon?

CECILY: Mr. Moncrieff and I are engaged to be married, Lady Bracknell.

LADY BRACKNELL [*with a shiver, crossing to the sofa and sitting down*]: I do not know whether there is anything peculiarly exciting in the air of this particular part of Hertfordshire, but the number of engagements that go on seems to me considerably above the proper average that statistics have laid down for our guidance. I think some preliminary inquiry on my part would not be out of place. Mr. Worthing, is Miss Cardew at all connected with any of the larger railway stations in London? I merely desire information. Until yesterday I had no idea that there were any families or persons whose origin was a Terminus.

[JACK *looks perfectly furious, but restrains himself.*]

JACK [*in a cold, clear voice*]: Miss Cardew is the granddaughter of the late Mr. Thomas Cardew of 149 Belgrave Square, S.W.; Gervase Park, Dorking, Surrey; and the Sporran, Fifeshire, N.B.

LADY BRACKNELL: That sounds not unsatisfactory. Three addresses always inspire confidence, even in tradesmen. But what proof have I of their authenticity?

JACK: I have carefully preserved the Court Guides of the period. They are open to your inspection, Lady Bracknell.

LADY BRACKNELL [*grimly*]: I have known strange errors in that publication.

JACK: Miss Cardew's family solicitors are Messrs. Markby, Markby, and Markby.

LADY BRACKNELL: Markby, Markby, and Markby? A firm of the very highest position in their profession. Indeed I am told that one of the Mr. Markby's is occasionally to be seen at dinner parties. So far I am satisfied.

JACK [*very irritably*]: How extremely kind of you, Lady Bracknell! I have also in my possession, you will be pleased to hear, certificates of Miss Cardew's birth, baptism, whooping cough, registration, vaccination, confirmation, and the measles; both the German and the English variety.

LADY BRACKNELL: Ah! A life crowded with incident, I see, though perhaps somewhat too exciting for a young girl. I am not myself in favour of premature experiences. [*Rises, looks at her watch.*] Gwendolen! the time approaches for our departure. We have not a moment to lose. As a matter of form, Mr. Worthing, I had better ask you if Miss Cardew has any little fortune?

JACK: Oh! about a hundred and thirty thousand pounds in the Funds. That is all. Good-bye, Lady Bracknell. So pleased to have seen you.

LADY BRACKNELL [*sitting down again*]: A moment, Mr. Worthing. A hundred and thirty thousand pounds! And in the Funds! Miss Cardew seems to me a most attractive young lady, now that I look at her. Few girls of the present day have any really solid qualities, any of the qualities that last, and improve with time. We live, I regret to say, in an age of surfaces. [*To* CECILY.] Come over here, dear. [CECILY *goes across.*] Pretty child! your dress is sadly simple, and your hair seems almost as Nature might have left it. But we can soon alter all that. A thoroughly experienced French maid produces a really marvellous result in a very brief space of time. I remember recommending one to young Lady Lancing, and after three months her own husband did not know her.

JACK: And after six months nobody knew her.

LADY BRACKNELL [*glares at* JACK *for a few moments. Then bends, with a practised smile, to* CECILY]: Kindly turn round, sweet child. [CECILY *turns completely round.*]

No, the side view is what I want. [CECILY *presents her profile.*] Yes, quite as I expected. There are distinct social possibilities in your profile. The two weak points in our age are its want of principle and its want of profile. The chin a little higher, dear. Style largely depends on the way the chin is worn. They are worn very high, just at present. Algernon!

ALGERNON: Yes, Aunt Augusta!

LADY BRACKNELL: There are distinct social possibilities in Miss Cardew's profile.

ALGERNON: Cecily is the sweetest, dearest, prettiest girl in the whole world. And I don't care twopence about social possibilities.

LADY BRACKNELL: Never speak disrespectfully of Society, Algernon. Only people who can't get into it do that. [*To* CECILY.] Dear child, of course you know that Algernon has nothing but his debts to depend upon. But I do not approve of mercenary marriages. When I married Lord Bracknell I had no fortune of any kind. But I never dreamed for a moment of allowing that to stand in my way. Well, I suppose I must give my consent.

ALGERNON: Thank you, Aunt Augusta.

LADY BRACKNELL: Cecily, you may kiss me!

CECILY [*kisses her*]: Thank you, Lady Bracknell.

LADY BRACKNELL: You may also address me as Aunt Augusta for the future.

CECILY: Thank you, Aunt Augusta.

LADY BRACKNELL: The marriage, I think, had better take place quite soon.

ALGERNON: Thank you, Aunt Augusta.

CECILY: Thank you, Aunt Augusta.

LADY BRACKNELL: To speak frankly, I am not in favour of long engagements. They give people the opportunity of finding out each other's character before marriage, which I think is never advisable.

JACK: I beg your pardon for interrupting you, Lady Bracknell, but this engagement is quite out of the question. I am Miss Cardew's guardian, and she cannot marry without my consent until she comes of age. That consent I absolutely decline to give.

LADY BRACKNELL: Upon what grounds, may I ask? Algernon is an extremely, I may almost say an ostentatiously, eligible young man. He has nothing, but he looks everything. What more can one desire?

JACK: It pains me very much to have to speak frankly to you, Lady Bracknell, about your nephew, but the fact is that I do not approve at all of his moral character. I suspect him of being untruthful. [ALGERNON *and* CECILY *look at him in indignant amazement.*]

LADY BRACKNELL: Untruthful! My nephew Algernon? Impossible! He is an Oxonian.

JACK: I fear there can be no possible doubt about the matter. This afternoon during my temporary absence in London on an important question of romance, he obtained admission to my house by means of the false pretence of being my brother. Under an assumed name he drank, I've just been informed by my butler, an entire pint bottle of my Perrier-Jouet, Brut, '89; wine I was specially reserving for myself. Continuing his disgraceful deception, he succeeded in the course of the afternoon in alienating the affections of my only ward. He subsequently stayed to tea, and devoured every single muffin. And what makes his conduct all the more heartless is, that he was perfectly well aware from the first that I have no brother, that I never had a brother, and that I don't intend to have a brother, not even of any kind. I distinctly told him so myself yesterday afternoon.

LADY BRACKNELL: Ahem! Mr. Worthing, after careful consideration I have decided entirely to overlook my nephew's conduct to you.

JACK: That is very generous of you, Lady Bracknell. My own decision, however, is unalterable. I decline to give my consent.

LADY BRACKNELL [to CECILY]: Come here, sweet child. [CECILY goes over.] How old are you, dear?

CECILY: Well, I am really only eighteen, but I always admit to twenty when I go to evening parties.

LADY BRACKNELL: You are perfectly right in making some slight alteration. Indeed, no woman should ever be quite accurate about her age. It looks so calculating. . . . [*In a medita-*

tive manner.] Eighteen, but admitting to twenty at evening parties. Well, it will not be very long before you are of age and free from the restraints of tutelage. So I don't think your guardian's consent is, after all, a matter of any importance.

JACK: Pray excuse me, Lady Bracknell, for interrupting you again, but it is only fair to tell you that according to the terms of her grandfather's will Miss Cardew does not come legally of age till she is thirty-five.

LADY BRACKNELL: That does not seem to me to be a grave objection. Thirty-five is a very attractive age. London society is full of women of the very highest birth who have, of their own free choice, remained thirty-five for years. Lady Dumbleton is an instance in point. To my own knowledge she has been thirty-five ever since she arrived at the age of forty, which was many years ago now. I see no reason why our dear Cecily should not be even still more attractive at the age you mention than she is at present. There will be a large accumulation of property.

CECILY: Algy, could you wait for me till I was thirty-five?

ALGERNON: Of course I could, Cecily. You know I could.

CECILY: Yes, I felt it instinctively, but I couldn't wait all that time. I hate waiting even five minutes for anybody. It always makes me rather cross. I am not punctual myself, I know, but I do like punctuality in others, and waiting, even to be married, is quite out of the question.

ALGERNON: Then what is to be done, Cecily?

CECILY: I don't know, Mr. Moncrieff.

LADY BRACKNELL: My dear Mr. Worthing, as Miss Cardew states positively that she cannot wait till she is thirty-five—a remark which I am bound to say seems to me to show a somewhat impatient nature—I would beg of you to reconsider your decision.

JACK: But my dear Lady Bracknell, the matter is entirely in your own hands. The moment you consent to my marriage with Gwendolen, I will most gladly allow your nephew to form an alliance with my ward.

LADY BRACKNELL [*rising and drawing herself up*]: You must be quite aware that what you propose is out of the question.

JACK: Then a passionate celibacy is all that any of us can look forward to.

LADY BRACKNELL: That is not the destiny I propose for Gwendolen. Algernon, of course, can choose for himself. [*Pulls out her watch.*] Come, dear [GWENDOLEN *rises*], we have already missed five, if not six, trains. To miss any more might expose us to comment on the platform.

[*Enter* DR. CHASUBLE.]

CHASUBLE: Everything is quite ready for the christenings.

LADY BRACKNELL: The christenings, sir! Is not that somewhat premature?

CHASUBLE [*looking rather puzzled, and pointing to* JACK *and* ALGERNON]: Both these gentlemen have expressed a desire for immediate baptism.

LADY BRACKNELL: At their age? The idea is grotesque and irreligious! Algernon, I forbid you to be baptized. I will not hear of such excesses. Lord Bracknell would be highly displeased if he learned that that was the way in which you wasted your time and money.

CHASUBLE: Am I to understand then that there are to be no christenings at all this afternoon?

JACK: I don't think that, as things are now, it would be of much practical value to either of us, Dr. Chasuble.

CHASUBLE: I am grieved to hear such sentiments from you, Mr. Worthing. They savour of the heretical views of the Anabaptists, views that I have completely refuted in four of my unpublished sermons. However, as your present mood seems to be one peculiarly secular, I will return to the church at once. Indeed, I have just been informed by the pew-opener that for the last hour and a half Miss Prism has been waiting for me in the vestry.

LADY BRACKNELL [*starting*]: Miss Prism! Did I hear you mention a Miss Prism?

CHASUBLE: Yes, Lady Bracknell. I am on my way to join her.

LADY BRACKNELL: Pray allow me to detain you for a moment. This matter may prove to be one of vital importance to Lord Bracknell and myself. Is this Miss Prism a female of repellent aspect, remotely connected with education?

CHASUBLE [*somewhat indignantly*]: She is the most cultivated of ladies, and the very picture of respectability.

LADY BRACKNELL: It is obviously the same person. May I ask what position she holds in your household?

CHASUBLE [*severely*]: I am a celibate, madam.

JACK [*interposing*]: Miss Prism, Lady Bracknell, has been for the last three years Miss Cardew's esteemed governess and valued companion.

LADY BRACKNELL: In spite of what I hear of her, I must see her at once. Let her be sent for.

CHASUBLE [*looking off*]: She approaches; she is nigh.

[*Enter* MISS PRISM *hurriedly.*]

MISS PRISM: I was told you expected me in the vestry, dear Canon. I have been waiting for you there for an hour and three-quarters. [*Catches sight of* LADY BRACKNELL, *who has fixed her with a stony glare.* MISS PRISM *grows pale and quails. She looks anxiously round as if desirous to escape.*]

LADY BRACKNELL [*in a severe, judicial voice*]: Prism! [MISS PRISM *bows her head in shame.*] Come here, Prism! [MISS PRISM *approaches in a humble manner.*] Prism! Where is that baby? [*General consternation. The Canon starts back in horror.* ALGERNON *and* JACK *pretend to be anxious to shield* CECILY *and* GWENDOLEN *from hearing the details of a terrible public scandal.*] Twenty-eight years ago, Prism, you left Lord Bracknell's house, Number 104, Upper Grosvenor Square, in charge of a perambulator that contained a baby of the male sex. You never returned. A few weeks later, through the elaborate investigations of the Metropolitan police, the perambulator was discovered at midnight standing by itself in a remote corner of Bayswater. It contained the manuscript of a three-volume novel of more than usually revolting sentimentality. [MISS PRISM *starts in involuntary indignation.*] But the baby was not there. [*Everyone looks at* MISS PRISM.] Prism! Where is that baby? [*A pause.*]

MISS PRISM: Lady Bracknell, I admit with shame that I do not know. I only wish I did. The plain facts of the case are these. On the morning of the day you mention, a day that is forever branded on my memory, I prepared as usual to take the baby out in its perambulator. I had also with me a somewhat old, but capacious hand-bag in which I had intended to place the manuscript of a work of fiction that I had written during my few unoccupied hours. In a moment of mental abstraction, for which I can never forgive myself, I deposited the manuscript in the bassinette and placed the baby in the hand-bag.

JACK [*who had been listening attentively*]: But where did you deposit the hand-bag?

MISS PRISM: Do not ask me, Mr. Worthing.

JACK: Miss Prism, this is a matter of no small importance to me. I insist on knowing where you deposited the hand-bag that contained that infant.

MISS PRISM: I left it in the cloak-room of one of the larger railway stations in London.

JACK: What railway station?

MISS PRISM [*quite crushed*]: Victoria. The Brighton line. [*Sinks into a chair.*]

JACK: I must retire to my room for a moment. Gwendolen, wait here for me.

GWENDOLEN: If you are not too long, I will wait here for you all my life. [*Exit* JACK *in great excitement.*]

CHASUBLE: What do you think this means, Lady Bracknell?

LADY BRACKNELL: I dare not even suspect, Dr. Chasuble. I need hardly tell you that in families of high position strange coincidences are not supposed to occur. They are hardly considered the thing.

[*Noises heard overhead as if someone was throwing trunks about. Everyone looks up.*]

CECILY: Uncle Jack seems strangely agitated.

CHASUBLE: Your guardian has a very emotional nature.

LADY BRACKNELL: This noise is extremely unpleasant. It sounds as if he was having an argument. I dislike arguments of any kind. They are always vulgar, and often convincing.

CHASUBLE [*looking up*]: It has stopped now. [*The noise is redoubled.*]

LADY BRACKNELL: I wish he would arrive at some conclusion.

GWENDOLEN: This suspense is terrible. I hope it will last.

[*Enter* JACK *with a hand-bag of black leather in his hand.*]

JACK [*rushing over to* MISS PRISM]: Is this the hand-bag, Miss Prism? Examine it carefully before you speak. The happiness of more than one life depends on your answer.

MISS PRISM [*calmly*]: It seems to be mine. Yes, here is the injury it received through the upsetting of a Gower Street omnibus in younger and happier days. Here is the stain on the lining caused by the explosion of a temperance beverage, an incident that occurred at Leamington. And here, on the lock, are my initials. I had forgotten that in an extravagant mood I had had them placed there. The bag is undoubtedly mine. I am delighted to have it so unexpectedly restored to me. It has been a great inconvenience being without it all these years.

JACK [*in a pathetic voice*]: Miss Prism, more is restored to you than this hand-bag. I was the baby you placed in it.

MISS PRISM [*amazed*]: You?

JACK [*embracing her*]: Yes . . . mother!

MISS PRISM [*recoiling in indignant astonishment*]: Mr. Worthing. I am unmarried!

JACK: Unmarried! I do not deny that is a serious blow. But after all, who has the right to cast a stone against one who has suffered? Cannot repentance wipe out an act of folly? Why should there be one law for men, and another for women? Mother, I forgive you. [*Tries to embrace her again.*]

MISS PRISM [*still more indignant*]: Mr. Worthing, there is some error. [*Pointing to* LADY BRACKNELL.] There is the lady who can tell you who you really are.

JACK [*after a pause*]: Lady Bracknell, I hate to seem inquisitive, but would you kindly inform me who I am?

LADY BRACKNELL: I am afraid that the news I have to give you will not altogether please you. You are the son of my poor sister, Mrs. Moncrieff, and consequently Algernon's elder brother.

JACK: Algy's elder brother! Then I have a brother after all. I knew I had a brother! I always said I had a brother! Cecily—how could you have ever doubted that I had a brother? [*Seizes hold of* ALGERNON.] Dr. Chasuble, my unfortunate brother. Miss Prism, my unfortunate brother. Gwendolen, my unfortunate brother. Algy, you young scoundrel, you will have to treat me with more respect in the future. You have never behaved to me like a brother in all your life.

ALGERNON: Well, not till today, old boy, I admit. I did my best, however, though I was out of practice. [*Shakes hands.*]

GWENDOLEN [*to* JACK]: My own! But what own are you? What is your Christian name, now that you have become someone else?

JACK: Good heavens! . . . I had quite forgotten that point. Your decision on the subject of my name is irrevocable, I suppose?

GWENDOLEN: I never change, except in my affections.

CECILY: What a noble nature you have, Gwendolen!

JACK: Then the question had better be cleared up at once. Aunt Augusta, a moment. At the time when Miss Prism left me in the hand-bag, had I been christened already?

LADY BRACKNELL: Every luxury that money could buy, including christening, had been lavished on you by your fond and doting parents.

JACK: Then I was christened! That is settled. Now, what name was I given? Let me know the worst.

LADY BRACKNELL: Being the eldest son you were naturally christened after your father.

JACK [*irritably*]: Yes, but what was my father's Christian name?

LADY BRACKNELL [*meditatively*]: I cannot at the present moment recall what the General's Christian name was. But I have no doubt he had one. He was eccentric, I admit. But only in later years. And that was the result of the Indian climate, and marriage, and indigestion, and other things of that kind.

JACK: Algy! Can't you recollect what our father's Christian name was?

ALGERNON: My dear boy, we were never even on speaking terms. He died before I was a year old.

JACK: His name would appear in the Army Lists of the period, I suppose, Aunt Augusta?

LADY BRACKNELL: The General was essentially a man of peace, except in his domestic life. But I have no doubt his name would appear in any military directory.

JACK: The Army Lists of the last forty years are here. These delightful records should have been my constant study. [*Rushes to bookcase and tears the books out.*] M. Generals . . . Mallam, Maxbohm, Magley—what ghastly names they have—Markby, Migsby, Mobbs, Moncrieff! Lieutenant 1840, Captain, Lieutenant-Colonel, Colonel, General 1869, Christian names, Ernest John. [*Puts book very quietly down and speaks quite calmly.*] I always told you, Gwendolen, my name was Ernest, didn't I? Well, it is Ernest after all. I mean it naturally is Ernest.

LADY BRACKNELL: Yes, I remember now that the General was called Ernest. I knew I had some particular reason for disliking the name.

GWENDOLEN: Ernest! My own Ernest! I felt from the first that you could have no other name!

JACK: Gwendolen, it is a terrible thing for a man to find out suddenly that all his life he has been speaking nothing but the truth. Can you forgive me?

GWENDOLEN: I can. For I feel that you are sure to change.

JACK: My own one!

CHASUBLE [*to* MISS PRISM]: Laetitia! [*Embraces her.*]

MISS PRISM [*enthusiastically*]: Frederick! At last!

ALGERNON: Cecily! [*Embraces her.*] At last!

JACK: Gwendolen! [*Embraces her.*] At last!

LADY BRACKNELL: My nephew, you seem to be displaying signs of triviality.

JACK: On the contrary, Aunt Augusta, I've now realized for the first time in my life the vital Importance of Being Earnest.

TABLEAU

CURTAIN

George Bernard Shaw
[1856-1950]

"M Y REPUTATION has been gained by my persistent struggle o force the public to reconsider its morals." That is the mature haw's description of his life's work, and it applies to all his vritings, not only plays, but his art and music criticism and his oolitical writing as well. He was born July 26, 1856, in Dublin nto a genteel but poor family, a family of downstarts, as Shaw aid. At the age of six he was shocked to discover that his ather, who professed to be a teetotaler, was actually an alco1olic. His father, however, had a sardonic humor and a fine appreciation of anti-climax which in his boyhood Shaw enjoyed and as a man put into his plays and conversations. "From my nother," said Shaw, "I derive my brains and character, which lo her credit." She was the strong force in the family; her great nterest was music and singing. Bernard and his two older sisters vere left to grow up as they could. Because of his father's drinkng the Shaws were generally excluded from the rest of the amily's social gatherings, and they came to depend largely upon 3eorge Lee, a singing teacher, for an adequate income.

Shaw said that he was compelled to develop his own character; he found comfort from his dismal, loveless home and ull, senseless schools in studying the paintings in the National art Gallery, in his love of music and in his father's books. He as a lazy, uninterested student, learning only what appealed o him, but he declared that he was born able to read without effort and between the ages of four and ten became very familiar with an illustrated copy of Shakespeare so that he could quote long passages before he had ever read the plays through. At seven he began to read Dickens and all the fairy tales he could lay hands on, being especially fond of Grimms' tales. He read Bunyan's *Pilgrim's Progress* aloud to his father, and while as a successful writer he was always loath to admit being influenced by anyone, these three, Shakespeare, Dickens, and Bunyan, were the writers who most affected him. His nurse, who, he said, was too poorly paid to be a good nurse, took him on walks—not in the parks as she was supposed to do, but through the tenement area and into the pubs. At an early age he was able to observe closely the appalling conditions of poverty which he was to fight all his life.

In 1872 Lee suddenly left Dublin for London. Without his support the Shaw family was unable to live, so with great resolution Bernard's mother took her two daughters and followed Lee to London, leaving her husband and Bernard to get on as best they could. Bernard then went to work at the age of fifteen for an estate agency; he began as an office boy, later rose to be a clerk responsible for large sums of money. Many years later he got from them a high recommendation which he no longer needed but was very proud of. He worked for this agency for five years, efficiently and accurately, meanwhile training the apprentices under him to sing opera in the wash room. On one occasion the elderly head of the firm walked in when one apprentice was passionately singing an aria from *Il Trovatore;* he listened in stunned silence for a moment, then ran from the room.

After five years as a clerk, Shaw determined to resign from what he felt was slave labor. He did so and made two resolutions: to become a great man and never to do an "honest day' work" again. In 1876 he went to London and joined his mother and older sister—his younger sister had just died of tuberculosis— and lived with them, earning little money but working constantly at writing. He bought cheap paper and wrote five sheet in quarto daily. If he reached the bottom of the last shee in the middle of a sentence, he stopped anyway; if he missed day, he made up those five sheets the next day by writing ten. He became, he said, as compulsive a writer as his father was a compulsive drinker. In five years he wrote five novels, none accepted for publication until fifty years later.

Shaw read Marx and later admitted being influenced by him. As a result of his political study, he became a Fabian Marxist or Socialist, which meant he advocated gradualism as a means of effecting social change. As a Socialist he needed to speak publicly, a difficult task for a shy and nervous young man. The singing lessons his mother had given him had taught him proper breathing; this training and his determination to speak effectively made him into a fine orator. He spoke in parks, on street corners, by bridges. He once spoke for four hours and on one occasion for an hour and a half in the rain to six policemen who had been sent to watch him. Getting and holding their attention was a challenge to him. He did amuse them and hold their attention, and he said years later that when he closed his eyes he could still see their black capes shining in the rain.

In 1885 his friend, William Archer, persuaded the editor of the *Pall Mall Gazette* to hire Shaw as reviewer of books, a position he held until 1888. In 1886 he became the art critic of the *World,* and in 1888 music critic of the *Star.* Shaw said the editor made him music critic to keep him from writing anything else and ruining his paper. His study of music and art from childhood on had well qualified him for both these positions, and his criticism still makes good reading. As a child he had been fascinated by the few plays he had seen and at the final curtain had had to be forcibly removed from the theatre, being convinced that the curtain would go up again. And so in 1892 he began to write for the theatre. Before he stopped, he wrote fifty-two plays and playlets. *Widowers' Houses* was performed in 1892 at the Royalty Theatre and was received with a fierce howl, only slightly less than that received by Ibsen's *Ghosts. Mrs. Warren's Profession* came next, but it was banned by the censor and was not performed until 1902. But these plays were done in other countries, America and Germany, and successfully. Richard Mansfield, an American actor, produced *Arms and the Man* in the United States in 1894. He also produced *The Devil's Disciple.*

In 1895 Shaw became the drama critic for *The Saturday Review*. From 1897 to 1903 he participated in the municipal government as vestryman and later as borough councillor, meanwhile working hard at his writing, so hard that in 1898 he had a physical collapse from over-work, too little food and exercise, and a foot injury which necessitated an operation. While he was bedridden, Charlotte Payne-Townsend, a friend, came to nurse him, was appalled at the discomfort in which he lived, and proposed to move him to her home. As Shaw expressed it, they were close friends with common interests and neither was concerned with "romantic love." Neither had any objections to giving up his freedom; thus they were married on June 1, 1898, when both were aged forty-two. Their marriage was extremely successful and happy, and when Charlotte died in 1943, Shaw said he missed her more profoundly than he would have thought possible.

Caesar and Cleopatra was written in 1898, *Man and Superman* in 1901–1903, and *Major Barbara* in 1905. The central theme of *Major Barbara* is that good physical environment is necessary before anything can be done to "raise the intelligence and morality of the average man." Barbara bribes the poor to be "saved"; Undershaft first saves them from the degradation of poverty. Despite Shaw's protestations that he owed no debt to Ibsen, his work shows definite traces of Ibsen and very early in his career he wrote the first full critical study of Ibsen in English, *The Quintessence of Ibsenism* (1891). He published his own plays and wrote a preface for each one, wanting, as he said, to give the public its money's worth, and to help it understand his meaning. Also he substituted readable descriptions for the technical stage directions, which practice was rather new. He declared that in writing a play there were two points on which probability and naturalness had to be discarded. The writer must make a reckless use of coincidence and his characters must be able to understand and describe themselves far better than real people ever can or do. Either by "self-portraiture or self-betrayal every character has to be defined to the audience." Doolittle is an example of a character who understands himself; Higgins exemplifies one who betrays himself without self-understanding.

In 1913 Shaw helped establish the *New Statesman*. He worked on *Heartbreak House* from 1913 to 1919. This play, thought to be Shaw's favorite, was performed in New York in 1920, but did not achieve production in England until 1921. *Saint Joan* was written in 1923. Shaw knew that the only way to attract the attention of the stolid British public was to attack "their sense of order and propriety." Consequently his plays did not consist of "occasional remarks to illustrate pictures," but were "verbal fencing matches between protagonists and antagonists." Shaw believed that the purpose of drama was to take life, unmeaning and haphazard, and so arrange it in an intelligible order that the audience is brought to think about it in a deeper way than it would otherwise.

In 1925 he received the Nobel prize and by 1928 he had resumed political writing. He and his wife traveled abroad a good deal before she became ill. After her death he settled at their home, Ayot St. Lawrence, where they had lived since 1906. He enjoyed his rose garden and his trees, which he insisted on pruning himself. In 1950 he fell when getting down from a tree and fractured his thigh. He was taken to a hospital where the fracture was satisfactorily set and was mending when an old infection of the kidney and bladder flared up. He asked to be taken home and died there peacefully on November 2, 1950. His and his wife's ashes were mingled and strewn over the garden.

Shaw's optimism, his belief in human progress (adapted partly from Bergson and Nietzsche), in the Life Force (which becomes the vital energy responsible for all human progress), is suggested in *Major Barbara*, established as Shavian doctrine in *Man and Superman*, and fully developed in *Back to Methuselah*, which Shaw called his Metabiological Pentateuch and his masterpiece. But *Back to Methuselah* proved to be Shaw's least successful major work and a kind of desperate act of will rather than a work of art. His optimistic attitude toward human progress and man's capacity to improve himself weakened. In his last two successful major works, *Heartbreak House* and *Saint Joan*, the optimism about human progress is all but gone. *Heartbreak House* concludes with the English Heartbreakers and Horsebackers waiting for more bombs to fall; *Saint Joan* concludes with Joan's despairing cry for the world's acceptance of saints: "How long, O Lord, how long?"

Major Barbara opened at the Court Theatre, November 28, 1905. The play expresses Shaw's principal ideas on Christianity, poverty, social progress, and charitable institutions and their relation to the economic institutions of the nation. In typical socialist fashion, Shaw sees charitable organizations as doing the dirty work of the oppressive economic forces by maintaining peace among the lower classes without bettering them economically, socially, or spiritually. They are simply made quiet and docile in their miserable poverty under the guise of being converted and saved by the Salvation Army.

The portrait of Undershaft, the munitions maker, is one of Shaw's greatest creations. Shaw's view of Undershaft is complex and grandiose: "diabolically subtle, gentle, self-possessed, powerful, stupendous, as well as amusing and interesting. There are the making of ten Hamlets and six Othellos in his mere leavings." Thus he described Undershaft to Louis Calvert, the actor who played Undershaft in the original production. As it turned out, Shaw was unhappy with Calvert's performance and lost no time in telling him so in a letter after opening night. Nevertheless, the play proved successful and was later produced by Grace George in America in 1915 and 1916. Shaw says his portrait of Adolphus Cusins is based on Gilbert Murray, Regius Professor of Greek at Oxford. Shaw has Cusins quote from Murray's translation of Euripides' *The Bacchae.* Lady Britomart is presumably based on Murray's mother-in-law.

Shaw brings to life significant social types of the time: the powerful industrialist in Undershaft, who is as enlightened as the most educated Fabian Socialist; the aristocratic liberal in Lady Britomart, who expresses the patrician spirit of *noblesse oblige* toward the poor; the energetic and idealistic young Christian reformer from the wealthy classes in Barbara; the blind leader of charitable institutions in Mrs. Baines, who unwittingly does the work of the Bodgers and the Undershafts in keeping the poor happy in their poverty; the enlightened member of the intelligentsia in Cusins. Among the Dickensian portraits of the poor, we have Peter Shirley, the poor made cowardly and docile by conscience and a crust of bread; Rummy Mitchens, for whom poverty is made tolerable by drink and small comforts; Snobby Price, whose petty thievery keeps him on the borderline of law and poverty; and Bill Walker, whose violence must be allayed and whose "conversion" is necessary to stave off any social eruption.

Nearly all of Shaw's principal interests and techniques are synthesized in the play. Shaw made use of the devices of the well-made play and of the characters and conflicts found in melodrama, but they appear in a new and vital form. The coincidence that makes Barbara's beloved Cousins the appropriate successor to Undershaft as a result of the last-minute discovery that he is a foundling is the well-made play at its best; the melodramatic Christian-Devil conflict in the Salvation Army versus the Munitions Works and the Satanic villain versus the innocent and Godly heroine are given a new dimension in the Barbara-Undershaft conflict. The conventional conclusion of that melodramatic conflict is reversed: The Satanic Undershaft converts the Christian Barbara to his doctrine of power and money. These effects and devices, combined with Shaw's paradoxical treatment of character and situation and his brilliant language, bring lasting life to the play and to Shaw's ideas about society, social institutions, and morality. As in the best of Shaw, the wit operates in a number of complex and penetrating ways. It disarms and defamiliarizes the audience response, as in the best satire; it alienates, by its reversals, the audience from its conventional attitudes; it makes ideas entertaining and even joyous; it reduces old attitudes and arguments to laughter and ridicule; it creates an aura of hyperconsciousness about the action of the play and the principal characters; it creates dramatic life and texture through surprise, paradox, antithesis, and parallel—all of which vibrate and reverberate throughout the play.

Obviously, Shaw's is an iconoclastic play. With keen marksmanship, he tumbles the social and religious icons of his day—the Christian work of charitable institutions; the idealism and altruism of Christians devoting their services to the poor, battling the devil in the streets, and uplifting and saving the poor by conversion; the effectiveness of Christian idealism and reformism in alleviating suffering and moral decay. The danger of the iconoclastic drama is that it will not survive its time, that it will become as stale and lifeless as the rubble it makes of those images. But Shaw's iconoclasm is as fresh, vigorous, and incisive now as the day it was first performed. The living expectation of dramatic conflict still pervades the scenes of confrontation and conversion. Shaw's characters, language, and ideas still breathe the life of vigorous drama. Like the work of the dramatist he most admired, Ibsen, the life of the plays continues beyond the time of social reform—the time when the immediate and topical social questions have been solved or satisfied. Like Ibsen, he caught, more than the social animal in his temporary predicament, the essential human animal in his perennial human predicament.

DRAMATIC WORKS

Widowers' Houses, 1892
The Philanderer, 1893
Mrs. Warren's Profession, 1894
Arms and the Man, 1894
Candida, 1895
The Man of Destiny, 1896
You Never Can Tell, 1897
The Devil's Disciple, 1897
Caesar and Cleopatra, 1898
Captain Brassbound's Conversion, 1899
The Admirable Bashville, 1901
Man and Superman, 1903
John Bull's Other Island, 1904
How He Lied to Her Husband, 1904
Major Barbara, 1905
Passion, Poison, and Petrifaction, 1905
The Doctor's Dilemma, 1906
The Interlude at the Playhouse, 1907
Getting Married, 1908
The Shewing-up of Blanco Posnet, 1909
Press Cuttings, 1909
The Fascinating Foundling, 1909
The Glimpse of Reality, 1909
Misalliance, 1910
The Dark Lady of the Sonnets, 1910
Fanny's First Play, 1911

Androcles and the Lion, 1912
Overruled, 1912
Pygmalion, 1912
Great Catherine, 1913
The Music-Cure, 1914
O'Flaherty, V.C., 1915
The Inca of Perusalem, 1916
Augustus Does His Bit, 1916
Annajanska, the Wild Grand Duchess, 1917
Heartbreak House, 1919
Back to Methuselah, 1920
Jitta's Atonement, 1922
Saint Joan, 1923
The Apple Cart, 1929
Too True to Be Good, 1931
Village Wooing, 1933
On the Rocks, 1933
The Simpleton of the Unexpected Isles, 1934
The Six of Calais, 1934
The Millionairess, 1935
Cymbeline Refinished, 1937
Geneva, 1938
In Good King Charles's Golden Days, 1939
Buoyant Billions, 1948
Farfetched Fables, 1948
Shakes Versus Shav, 1949
Why She Would Not, 1950

Major Barbara

★

*First produced in the United States at the Playhouse,
New York, on December 9, 1915.*

CAST

STEPHEN UNDERSHAFT

LADY BRITOMART

BARBARA UNDERSHAFT

SARAH UNDERSHAFT

ANDREW UNDERSHAFT

JENNY HILL

BILL WALKER

MORRISON

ADOLPHUS CUSINS

CHARLES LOMAX

RUMMY MITCHENS

SNOBBY PRICE

PETER SHIRLEY

BILTON

MRS BAINES

N.B. The Euripidean verses in the second act
of Major Barbara are not by me, nor even
directly by Euripides. They are by Professor
Gilbert Murray, whose English version of *The
Bacchae* came into our dramatic literature with
all the impulsive power of an original work
shortly before *Major Barbara* was begun. The
play, indeed, stands indebted to him in more
ways than one.
G.B.S.

ACT ONE

It is after dinner in January 1906, in the library in Lady Britomart Undershaft's house in Wilton Crescent. A large and comfortable settee is in the middle of the room, upholstered in dark leather. A person sitting on it (it is vacant at present) would have, on his right, Lady Britomart's writing table, with the lady herself busy at it; a smaller writing table behind him on his left; the door behind him on Lady Britomart's side; and a window with a window seat directly on his left. Near the window is an armchair.

Lady Britomart is a woman of fifty or thereabouts, well dressed and yet careless of her dress, well bred and quite reckless of her breeding, well mannered and yet appallingly outspoken and indifferent to the opinion of her interlocutors, amiable and yet peremptory, arbitrary, and high-tempered to the last bearable degree, and withal a very typical managing matron of the upper class, treated as a naughty child until she grew into a scolding mother, and finally settling down with plenty of practical ability and worldly experience, limited in the oddest way with domestic and class limitations, conceiving the universe exactly as if it were a large house in Wilton Crescent, though handling her corner of it very effectively on that assumption, and being quite enlightened and liberal as to the books in the library, the pictures on the walls, the music in the portfolios, and the articles in the papers.

Her son, Stephen, comes in. He is a gravely correct young man under 25, taking himself very seriously, but still in some awe of his mother, from childish habit and bachelor shyness rather than from any weakness of character.

STEPHEN: Whats the matter?

LADY BRITOMART: Presently, Stephen.

[*Stephen submissively walks to the settee and sits down. He takes up a Liberal weekly called* The Speaker].

LADY BRITOMART: Dont begin to read, Stephen. I shall require all your attention.

STEPHEN: It was only while I was waiting—

LADY BRITOMART: Dont make excuses, Stephen. [*He puts down* The Speaker]. Now! [*She fin-*

206

ishes her writing; rises; and comes to the settee]. I have not kept you waiting very long, I think.

STEPHEN: Not at all, mother.

LADY BRITOMART: Bring me my cushion. [*He takes the cushion from the chair at the desk and arranges it for her as she sits down on the settee*]. Sit down. [*He sits down and fingers his tie nervously*]. Dont fiddle with your tie, Stephen: there is nothing the matter with it.

STEPHEN: I beg your pardon. [*He fiddles with his watch chain instead*].

LADY BRITOMART: Now are you attending to me, Stephen?

STEPHEN: Of course, mother.

LADY BRITOMART: No: it's *not* of course. I want something much more than your everyday matter-of-course attention. I am going to speak to you very seriously, Stephen. I wish you would let that chain alone.

STEPHEN [*hastily relinquishing the chain*]: Have I done anything to annoy you, mother? If so, it was quite unintentional.

LADY BRITOMART [*astonished*]: Nonsense! [*With some remorse*] My poor boy, did you think I was angry with you?

STEPHEN: What is it, then, mother? You are making me very uneasy.

LADY BRITOMART [*squaring herself at him rather aggressively*]: Stephen: may I ask how soon you intend to realize that you are a grown-up man, and that I am only a woman?

STEPHEN [*amazed*]: Only a—

LADY BRITOMART: Dont repeat my words, please: it is a most aggravating habit. You must learn to face life seriously, Stephen. I really cannot bear the whole burden of our family affairs any longer. You must advise me: you must assume the responsibility.

STEPHEN: I!

LADY BRITOMART: Yes, you, of course. You were 24 last June. Youve been at Harrow and Cambridge. Youve been to India and Japan. You must know a lot of things, now; unless you have wasted your time most scandalously. Well, *advise* me.

STEPHEN [*much perplexed*]: You know I have never interfered in the household—

LADY BRITOMART: No: I should think not. I dont want you to order the dinner.

STEPHEN: I mean in our family affairs.

LADY BRITOMART: Well, you must interfere now; for they are getting quite beyond me.

STEPHEN [*troubled*]: I have thought sometimes that perhaps I ought; but really, mother, I know so little about them; and what I do know is so painful! it is so impossible to mention some things to you— [*he stops, ashamed*].

LADY BRITOMART: I suppose you mean your father.

STEPHEN [*almost inaudibly*]: Yes.

LADY BRITOMART: My dear: we cant go on all our lives not mentioning him. Of course you were quite right not to open the subject until I asked you to; but you are old enough now to be taken into my confidence, and to help me to deal with him about the girls.

STEPHEN: But the girls are all right. They are engaged.

LADY BRITOMART [*complacently*]: Yes: I have made a very good match for Sarah. Charles Lomax will be a millionaire at 35. But that is ten years ahead; and in the meantime his trustees cannot under the terms of his father's will allow him more than £800 a year.

STEPHEN: But the will says also that if he increases his income by his own exertions, they may double the increase.

LADY BRITOMART: Charles Lomax's exertions are much more likely to decrease his income than to increase it. Sarah will have to find at least another £800 a year for the next ten years; and even then they will be as poor as church mice. And what about Barbara? I thought Barbara was going to make the most brilliant career of all of you. And what does she do? Joins the Salvation Army; discharges her maid; lives on a pound a week; and walks in one evening with a professor of Greek whom she has picked up in the street, and who pretends to be a Salvationist, and actually plays the big drum for her in public because he has fallen head over ears in love with her.

STEPHEN: I was certainly rather taken aback when I heard they were engaged. Cusins is a very nice fellow, certainly: nobody would ever guess that he was born in Australia; but—

LADY BRITOMART: Oh, Adolphus Cusins will make a very good husband. After all, nobody can say a word against Greek: it stamps a man at once as an educated gentleman. And my family, thank Heaven, is not a pig-headed Tory one. We are Whigs, and believe in liberty. Let snobbish people say what they please: Barbara shall marry, not the man they like, but the man *I* like.

STEPHEN: Of course I was thinking only of his income. However, he is not likely to be extravagant.

LADY BRITOMART: Dont be too sure of that, Stephen. I know your quiet, simple, refined, poetic people like Adolphus: quite content with the best of everything! They cost more than your extravagant people, who are always as mean as they are second rate. No: Barbara will need at least £2000 a year. You see it means two additional households. Besides, my dear, *you* must marry soon. I dont approve of the present fashion of philandering bachelors and late marriages; and I am trying to arrange something for you.

STEPHEN: It's very good of you, mother; but perhaps I had better arrange that for myself.

LADY BRITOMART: Nonsense! you are much too young to begin matchmaking: you would be taken in by some pretty little nobody. Of course I dont mean that you are not to be consulted: you know that as well as I do. [*Stephen closes his lips and is silent*]. Now dont sulk, Stephen.

STEPHEN: I am not sulking, mother. What has all this got to do with—with—with my father?

LADY BRITOMART: My dear Stephen: where is the money to

come from? It is easy enough for you and the other children to live on my income as long as we are in the same house; but I cant keep four families in four separate houses. You know how poor my father is: he has barely seven thousand a year now; and really, if he were not the Earl of Stevenage, he would have to give up society. He can do nothing for us. He says, naturally enough, that it is absurd that he should be asked to provide for the children of a man who is rolling in money. You see, Stephen, your father must be fabulously wealthy, because there is always a war going on somewhere.

STEPHEN: You need not remind me of that, mother. I have hardly ever opened a newspaper in my life without seeing our name in it. The Undershaft torpedo! The Undershaft quick firers! The Undershaft ten inch! the Undershaft disappearing rampart gun! the Undershaft submarine! and now the Undershaft aerial battleship! At Harrow they called me the Woolwich Infant. At Cambridge it was the same. A little brute at King's who was always trying to get up revivals, spoilt my Bible—your first birthday present to me—by writing under my name, "Son and heir to Undershaft and Lazarus, Death and Destruction Dealers: address Christendom and Judea." But that was not so bad as the way I was kowtowed to everywhere because my father was making millions by selling cannons.

LADY BRITOMART: It is not only the cannons, but the war loans that Lazarus arranges under cover of giving credit for the cannons. You know, Stephen, it's perfectly scandalous. Those two men, Andrew Undershaft and Lazarus, positively have Europe under their thumbs. That is why your father is able to behave as he does. He is above the law. Do you think Bismarck or Gladstone or Disraeli could have openly defied every social and moral obligation all their lives as your father has? They simply wouldnt have dared. I asked Gladstone to take it up. I asked The Times to take it up. I asked the Lord Chamberlain to take it up. But it was just like asking them to declare war on the Sultan. They *wouldnt*. They said they couldnt touch him. I believe they were afraid.

STEPHEN: What could they do? He does not actually break the law.

LADY BRITOMART: Not break the law! He is always breaking the law. He broke the law when he was born: his parents were not married.

STEPHEN: Mother! Is that true?

LADY BRITOMART: Of course it's true: that was why we separated.

STEPHEN: He married without letting you know this!

LADY BRITOMART [*rather taken aback by this inference*]: Oh no. To do Andrew justice, that was not the sort of thing he did. Besides, you know the Undershaft motto: Unashamed. Everybody knew.

STEPHEN: But you said that was why you separated.

LADY BRITOMART: Yes, because he was not content with being a foundling himself: he wanted to disinherit you for another foundling. That was what I couldnt stand.

STEPHEN [*ashamed*]: Do you mean for—for—for—

LADY BRITOMART: Dont stammer, Stephen. Speak distinctly.

STEPHEN: But this is so frightful to me, mother. To have to speak to you about such things!

LADY BRITOMART: It's not pleasant for me, either, especially if you are still so childish that you must make it worse by a display of embarrassment. It is only in the middle classes, Stephen, that people get into a state of dumb helpless horror when they find that there are wicked people in the world. In our class, we have to decide what is to be done with wicked people; and nothing should disturb our self-possession. Now ask your question properly.

STEPHEN: Mother: have you no consideration for me? For Heaven's sake either treat me as a child, as you always do, and tell me nothing at all; or tell me everything and let me take it as best I can.

LADY BRITOMART: Treat you as a child! What do you mean? It is most unkind and ungrateful of you to say such a thing. You know I have never treated any of you as children. I have always made you my companions and friends, and allowed you perfect freedom to do and say whatever you liked, so long as you liked what I could approve of.

STEPHEN [*desperately*]: I daresay we have been the very imperfect children of a very perfect mother; but I do beg you to let me alone for once, and tell me about this horrible business of my father wanting to set me aside for another son.

LADY BRITOMART [*amazed*]: Another son! I never said anything of the kind. I never dreamt of such a thing. This is what comes of interrupting me.

STEPHEN: But you said—

LADY BRITOMART [*cutting him short*]: Now be a good boy, Stephen, and listen to me patiently. The Undershafts are descended from a foundling in the parish of St Andrew Undershaft in the city. That was long ago, in the reign of James the First. Well, this foundling was adopted by an armorer and gun-maker. In the course of time the foundling succeeded to the business; and from some notion of gratitude, or some vow or something, he adopted another foundling, and left the business to him. And that foundling did the same. Ever since that, the cannon business has always been left to an adopted foundling named Andrew Undershaft.

STEPHEN: But did they never marry? Were there no legitimate sons?

LADY BRITOMART: Oh yes: they married just as your father did; and they were rich enough to buy land for their own children and leave them well provided for. But they always adopted and trained some foundling to succeed them in the business; and of course they always quarrelled with their wives furiously over it. Your father was adopted in that way; and he pretends to consider himself bound to keep up the tradition and adopt somebody to leave the business to. Of course I was not going to stand that. There may have been some reason for it when the Undershafts could only marry women in their own class, whose sons were not fit to govern great estates. But there could be no excuse for passing over my son.

STEPHEN [*dubiously*]: I am afraid I should make a poor hand of managing a cannon foundry.

LADY BRITOMART: Nonsense! you could easily get a manager and pay him a salary.

STEPHEN: My father evidently had no great opinion of my capacity.

LADY BRITOMART: Stuff, child! you were only a baby: it had nothing to do with your capacity. Andrew did it on principle, just as he did every perverse and wicked thing on principle. When my father remonstrated, Andrew actually told him to his face that history tells us of only two successful institutions: one the Undershaft firm, and the other the Roman Empire under the Antonines. That was because the Antonine emperors all adopted their successors. Such rubbish! The Stevenages are as good as the Antonines, I hope; and you are a Stevenage. But that was Andrew all over. There you have the man! Always clever and unanswerable when he was defending nonsense and wickedness: always awkward and sullen when he had to behave sensibly and decently!

STEPHEN: Then it was on my account that your home life was broken up, mother. I am sorry.

LADY BRITOMART: Well, dear, there were other differences. I really cannot bear an immoral man. I am not a Pharisee, I hope; and I should not have minded his merely *doing* wrong things: we are none of us perfect. But your father didnt exactly *do* wrong things: he said them and thought them: that was what was so dreadful. He really had a sort of religion of wrongness. Just as one doesnt mind men practising immorality so long as they own that they are in the wrong by preaching morality; so I couldnt forgive Andrew for preaching immorality while he practised morality. You would all have grown up without principles, without any knowledge of right and wrong, if he had been in the house. You know, my dear, your father was a very attractive man in some ways. Children did not dislike him; and he took advantage of it to put the wickedest ideas into their heads, and make them quite unmanageable. I did not dislike him myself: very far from it; but nothing can bridge over moral disagreement.

STEPHEN: All this simply bewilders me, mother. People may differ about matters of opinion, or even about religion; but how can they differ about right and wrong? Right is right; and wrong is wrong; and if a man cannot distinguish them properly, he is either a fool or a rascal: thats all.

LADY BRITOMART [*touched*]: Thats my own boy [*she pats his cheek*]! Your father never could answer that: he used to laugh and get out of it under cover of some affectionate nonsense. And now that you understand the situation, what do you advise me to do?

STEPHEN: Well, what *can* you do?

LADY BRITOMART: I must get the money somehow.

STEPHEN: We cannot take money from him. I had rather go and live in some cheap place like Bedford Square or even Hampstead than take a farthing of his money.

LADY BRITOMART: But after all, Stephen, our present income comes from Andrew.

STEPHEN [*shocked*]: I never knew that.

LADY BRITOMART: Well, you surely didnt suppose your grandfather had anything to give me. The Stevenages could not do everything for you. We gave you social position. Andrew had to contribute *something*. He had a very good bargain, I think.

STEPHEN [*bitterly*]: We are utterly dependent on him and his cannons, then?

LADY BRITOMART: Certainly not: the money is settled. But he provided it. So you see it is not a question of taking money from him or not: it is simply a question of how much. I dont want any more for myself.

STEPHEN: Nor do I.

LADY BRITOMART: But Sarah does; and Barbara does. That is, Charles Lomax and Adolphus Cusins will cost them more. So I must put my pride in my pocket and ask for it, I suppose. That is your advice, Stephen, is it not?

STEPHEN: No.

LADY BRITOMART [*sharply*]: Stephen!

STEPHEN: Of course if you are determined—

LADY BRITOMART: I am not determined: I ask your advice; and I am waiting for it. I will not have all the responsibility thrown on my shoulders.

STEPHEN [*obstinately*]: I would die sooner than ask him for another penny.

LADY BRITOMART [*resignedly*]: You mean that *I* must ask him. Very well, Stephen: It shall be as you wish. You will be glad to know that your grandfather concurs. But he thinks I ought to ask Andrew to come here and see the girls. After all, he must have some natural affection for them.

STEPHEN: Ask him here!!!

LADY BRITOMART: Do *not* repeat my words, Stephen. Where else can I ask him?

STEPHEN: I never expected you to ask him at all.

LADY BRITOMART: Now dont tease, Stephen. Come! you see that it is necessary that he should pay us a visit, dont you?

STEPHEN [*reluctantly*]: I suppose so, if the girls cannot do without his money.

LADY BRITOMART: Thank you, Stephen: I knew you would give me the right advice when it was properly explained to you. I have asked your father to come this evening. [*Stephen bounds from his seat*]. Dont jump, Stephen: it fidgets me.

STEPHEN [*in utter consternation*]: Do you mean to say that my father is coming here tonight— that he may be here at any moment?

LADY BRITOMART [*looking at her watch*]: I said nine. [*He gasps. She rises*]. Ring the bell, please. [*Stephen goes to the smaller writing table; presses a button on it; and sits at it with his elbows on the table and his head in his hands, outwitted and overwhelmed*]. It is ten minutes to nine yet; and I have to prepare the girls. I asked Charles Lomax and Adolphus to dinner on purpose that they might be here. Andrew had better see them in case he should cherish any delusions as to their being capable of supporting their wives. [*The butler enters: Lady Britomart goes behind the settee to speak to him*]. Morrison: go up to the drawing room and tell everybody to come down here at once. [*Morrison withdraws. Lady Britomart turns to Stephen*]. Now remember, Stephen: I shall need all your countenance and authority. [*He rises and tries to recover some vestige of these attributes*]. Give me a chair, dear. [*He pushes a chair forward from the wall to where she stands, near the smaller writing table. She sits down; and he goes to the armchair, into

which he throws himself*]. I dont know how Barbara will take it. Ever since they made her a major in the Salvation Army she has developed a propensity to have her own way and order people about which quite cows me sometimes. It's not ladylike: I'm sure I dont know where she picked it up. Anyhow, Barbara shant bully me; but still it's just as well that your father should be here before she has time to refuse to meet him or make a fuss. Dont look nervous, Stephen: it will only encourage Barbara to make difficulties. *I* am nervous enough, goodness knows; but I dont shew it.

[*Sarah and Barbara come in with their respective young men, Charles Lomax and Adolphus Cusins. Sarah is slender, bored, and mundane. Barbara is robuster, jollier, much more energetic. Sarah is fashionably dressed: Barbara is in Salvation Army uniform. Lomax, a young man about town, is like many other young men about town. He is afflicted with a frivolous sense of humor which plunges him at the most inopportune moments into paroxysms of imperfectly suppressed laughter. Cusins is a spectacled student, slight, thin haired, and sweet voiced, with a more complex form of Lomax's complaint. His sense of humor is intellectual and subtle, and is complicated by an appalling temper. The lifelong struggle of a benevolent temperament and a high conscience against impulses of inhuman ridicule and fierce impatience has set up a chronic strain which has visibly wrecked his constitu-*

tion. He is a most implacable, determined, tenacious, intolerant person who by mere force of character presents himself as—and indeed actually is—considerate, gentle, explanatory, even mild and apologetic, capable possibly of murder, but not of cruelty or coarseness. By the operation of some instinct which is not merciful enough to blind him with the illusions of love, he is obstinately bent on marrying Barbara. Lomax likes Sarah and thinks it will be rather a lark to marry her. Consequently he has not attempted to resist Lady Britomart's arrangements to that end.

All four look as if they had been having a good deal of fun in the drawing room. The girls enter first, leaving the swains outside. Sarah comes to the settee. Barbara comes in after her and stops at the door].

BARBARA: Are Cholly and Dolly to come in?

LADY BRITOMART [*forcibly*]: Barbara: I will not have Charles called Cholly: the vulgarity of it positively makes me ill.

BARBARA: It's all right, mother: Cholly is quite correct nowadays. Are they to come in?

LADY BRITOMART: Yes, if they will behave themselves.

BARBARA [*through the door*]: Come in, Dolly; and behave yourself.

[*Barbara comes to her mother's writing table. Cusins enters smiling, and wanders towards Lady Britomart.*]

SARAH [*calling*]: Come in, Cholly. [*Lomax enters, controlling his features very imperfectly, and places himself vaguely between Sarah and Barbara*].

LADY BRITOMART [*peremptorily*]: Sit down, all of you. [*They sit. Cusins crosses to the window and seats himself there. Lomax takes a chair. Barbara sits at the writing table and Sarah on the settee*]. I dont in the least know what you are laughing at, Adolphus. I am surprised at you, though I expected nothing better from Charles Lomax.

CUSINS [*in a remarkably gentle voice*]: Barbara has been trying to teach me the West Ham Salvation March.

LADY BRITOMART: I see nothing to laugh at in that; nor should you if you are really converted.

CUSINS [*sweetly*]: You were not present. It was really funny, I believe.

LOMAX: Ripping.

LADY BRITOMART: Be quiet, Charles. Now listen to me, children. Your father is coming here this evening.

[*General stupefaction. Lomax, Sarah, and Barbara rise: Sarah scared, and Barbara amused and expectant*].

LOMAX [*remonstrating*]: Oh I say!

LADY BRITOMART: You are not called on to say anything, Charles.

SARAH: Are you serious, mother?

LADY BRITOMART: Of course I am serious. It is on your account, Sarah, and also on Charles's. [*Silence. Sarah sits, with a shrug. Charles looks painfully unworthy.*] I hope you are not going to object, Barbara.

BARBARA: I! why should I? My

father has a soul to be saved like anybody else. He's quite welcome as far as I am concerned. [*She sits on the table, and softly whistles "Onward, Christian Soldiers"*].

LOMAX [*still remonstrant*]: But really, dont you know! Oh I say!

LADY BRITOMART [*frigidly*]: What do you wish to convey, Charles?

LOMAX: Well, you must admit that this is a bit thick.

LADY BRITOMART [*turning with ominous suavity to Cusins*]: Adolphus: you are a professor of Greek. Can you translate Charles Lomax's remarks into reputable English for us?

CUSINS [*cautiously*]: If I may say so, Lady Brit, I think Charles has rather happily expressed what we all feel. Homer, speaking of Autolycus, uses the same phrase. πυκινὸν δόμον ἐλθεῖν means a bit thick.

LOMAX [*handsomely*]: Not that I mind, you know, if Sarah dont. [*He sits*].

LADY BRITOMART [*crushingly*]: Thank you. Have I *your* permission, Adolphus, to invite my own husband to my own house?

CUSINS [*gallantly*]: You have my unhesitating support in everything you do.

LADY BRITOMART: Tush! Sarah: have you nothing to say?

SARAH: Do you mean that he is coming regularly to live here?

LADY BRITOMART: Certainly not. The spare room is ready for him if he likes to stay for a day or two and see a little more of you; but there are limits.

SARAH: Well, he cant eat us, I suppose. *I* dont mind.

LOMAX [*chuckling*]: I wonder how the old man will take it.

LADY BRITOMART: Much as the old woman will, no doubt, Charles.

LOMAX [*abashed*]: I didnt mean—at least—

LADY BRITOMART: You didnt *think,* Charles. You never do; and the result is, you never mean anything. And now please attend to me, children. Your father will be quite a stranger to us.

LOMAX: I suppose he hasnt seen Sarah since she was a little kid.

LADY BRITOMART: Not since she was a little kid, Charles, as you express it with that elegance of diction and refinement of thought that seem never to desert you. Accordingly—er—[*impatiently*] Now I have forgotten what I was going to say. That comes of your provoking me to be sarcastic, Charles. Adolphus: will you kindly tell me where I was.

CUSINS [*sweetly*]: You were saying that as Mr Undershaft has not seen his children since they were babies, he will form his opinion of the way you have brought them up from their behavior tonight, and that therefore you wish us all to be particularly careful to conduct ourselves well, especially Charles.

LADY BRITOMART [*with emphatic approval*]: Precisely.

LOMAX: Look here, Dolly: Lady Brit didnt say that.

LADY BRITOMART [*vehemently*]: I did, Charles. Adolphus's recollection is perfectly correct. It is most important that you should be good; and I do beg you for once not to pair off into opposite corners and giggle and whisper while I am speaking to your father.

BARBARA: All right, mother. We'll do you credit. [*She comes off the table, and sits in her chair with ladylike elegance*].

LADY BRITOMART: Remember, Charles, that Sarah will want to feel proud of you instead of ashamed of you.

LOMAX: Oh I say! theres nothing to be exactly proud of, dont you know.

LADY BRITOMART: Well, try and look as if there was.

[*Morrison, pale and dismayed, breaks into the room in unconcealed disorder.*]

MORRISON: Might I speak a word to you, my lady?

LADY BRITOMART: Nonsense! Shew him up.

MORRISON: Yes, my lady. [*He goes*].

LOMAX: Does Morrison know who it is?

LADY BRITOMART: Of course. Morrison has always been with us.

LOMAX: It must be a regular corker for him, dont you know.

LADY BRITOMART: Is this a moment to get on my nerves, Charles, with your outrageous expressions?

LOMAX: But this is something out of the ordinary, really—

MORRISON [*at the door*]: The—er—Mr Undershaft. [*He retreats in confusion*].

[*Andrew Undershaft comes in. All rise. Lady Britomart meets him in the middle of the room behind the settee. Andrew is, on the surface, a stoutish, easygoing elderly man, with kindly patient manners, and an engaging simplicity of character. But he has a watchful, deliberate, waiting, listening face, and formidable reserves of power, both bodily and mental, in his capacious chest and long head. His gentleness is partly that of a strong man who has learnt by experience that his natural grip hurts ordinary people unless he handles them very carefully, and partly the mellowness of age and success. He is also a little shy in his present very delicate situation*].

LADY BRITOMART: Good evening, Andrew.

UNDERSHAFT: How d'ye do, my dear.

LADY BRITOMART: You look a good deal older.

UNDERSHAFT [*apologetically*]: I am somewhat older. [*Taking her hand with a touch of courtship*] Time has stood still with you.

LADY BRITOMART [*throwing away his hand*]: Rubbish! This is your family.

UNDERSHAFT [*surprised*]: Is it so large? I am sorry to say my memory is failing very badly in some things. [*He offers his hand with paternal kindness to Lomax*].

LOMAX [*jerkily shaking his hand*]: Ahdedoo.

UNDERSHAFT: I can see you are my eldest. I am very glad to meet you again, my boy.

LOMAX [*remonstrating*]: No, but look here dont you know—[*Overcome*] Oh I say!

LADY BRITOMART [*recovering from*

momentary speechlessness]: Andrew: do you mean to say that you dont remember how many children you have?

UNDERSHAFT: Well, I am afraid I—. They have grown so much—er. Am I making any ridiculous mistake? I may as well confess: I recollect only one son. But so many things have happened since, of course—er—

LADY BRITOMART [*decisively*]: Andrew: you are talking nonsense. Of course you have only one son.

UNDERSHAFT: Perhaps you will be good enough to introduce me, my dear.

LADY BRITOMART: That is Charles Lomax, who is engaged to Sarah.

UNDERSHAFT: My dear sir, I beg your pardon.

LOMAX: Notatall. Delighted, I assure you.

LADY BRITOMART: This is Stephen.

UNDERSHAFT [*bowing*]: Happy to make your acquaintance, Mr Stephen. Then [*going to Cusins*] you must be my son. [*Taking Cusins' hands in his*] How are you, my young friend? [*To Lady Britomart*] He is very like you, my love.

CUSINS: You flatter me, Mr Undershaft. My name is Cusins: engaged to Barbara. [*Very explicitly*] That is Major Barbara Undershaft, of the Salvation Army. That is Sarah, your second daughter. This is Stephen Undershaft, your son.

UNDERSHAFT: My dear Stephen, I *beg* your pardon.

STEPHEN: Not at all.

UNDERSHAFT: Mr Cusins: I am much indebted to you for explaining so precisely. [*Turning to Sarah*] Barbara, my dear—

SARAH [*prompting him*]: Sarah.

UNDERSHAFT: Sarah, of course. [*They shake hands. He goes over to Barbara*] Barbara—I am right this time, I hope?

BARBARA: Quite right. [*They shake hands*].

LADY BRITOMART [*resuming command*]: Sit down, all of you. Sit down, Andrew. [*She comes forward and sits on the settee. Cusins also brings his chair forward on her left. Barbara and Stephen resume their seats. Lomax gives his chair to Sarah and goes for another*].

UNDERSHAFT: Thank you, my love.

LOMAX [*conversationally, as he brings a chair forward between the writing table and the settee, and offers it to Undershaft*]: Takes you some time to find out exactly where you are, dont it?

UNDERSHAFT [*accepting the chair, but remaining standing*]: That is not what embarrasses me, Mr Lomax. My difficulty is that if I play the part of a father, I shall produce the effect of an intrusive stranger; and if I play the part of a discreet stranger, I may appear a callous father.

LADY BRITOMART: There is no need for you to play any part at all, Andrew. You had much better be sincere and natural.

UNDERSHAFT [*submissively*]: Yes, my dear: I daresay that will be best. [*He sits down comfortably*]. Well, here I am. Now what can I do for you all?

LADY BRITOMART: You need not do anything, Andrew. You are one of the family. You can sit with us and enjoy yourself.

[*A painfully conscious pause. Barbara makes a face at Lomax, whose too long suppressed mirth immediately explodes in agonized neighings*].

LADY BRITOMART [*outraged*]: Charles Lomax: if you can behave yourself, behave yourself. If not, leave the room.

LOMAX: I'm awfully sorry, Lady Brit; but really you know, upon my soul! [*He sits on the settee between Lady Britomart and Undershaft, quite overcome*].

BARBARA: Why dont you laugh if you want to, Cholly? It's good for your inside.

LADY BRITOMART: Barbara: you have had the education of a lady. Please let your father see that; and dont talk like a street girl.

UNDERSHAFT: Never mind me, my dear. As you know, I am not a gentleman; and I was never educated.

LOMAX [*encouragingly*]: Nobody'd know it, I assure you. You look all right, you know.

CUSINS: Let me advise you to study Greek, Mr Undershaft. Greek scholars are privileged men. Few of them know Greek; and none of them know anything else; but their position is unchallengeable. Other languages are the qualifications of waiters and commercial travellers: Greek is to a man of position what the hallmark is to silver.

BARBARA: Dolly: dont be insincere. Cholly: fetch your concertina and play something for us.

LOMAX [*jumps up eagerly, but checks himself to remark doubtfully to Undershaft*]: Perhaps that sort of thing isnt in your line, eh?

UNDERSHAFT: I am particularly fond of music.

LOMAX [*delighted*]: Are you? Then I'll get it. [*He goes upstairs for the instrument*].

UNDERSHAFT: Do you play, Barbara?

BARBARA: Only the tambourine. But Cholly's teaching me the concertina.

UNDERSHAFT: Is Cholly also a member of the Salvation Army?

BARBARA: No: he says it's bad form to be a dissenter. But I dont despair of Cholly. I made him come yesterday to a meeting at the dock gates, and take the collection in his hat.

UNDERSHAFT [*looks whimsically at his wife*]: !!

LADY BRITOMART: It is not my doing, Andrew. Barbara is old enough to take her own way. She has no father to advise her.

BARBARA: Oh yes she has. There are no orphans in the Salvation Army.

UNDERSHAFT: Your father there has a great many children and plenty of experience, eh?

BARBARA [*looking at him with quick interest and nodding*]: Just so. How did *you* come to understand that? [*Lomax is heard at the door trying the concertina*].

LADY BRITOMART: Come in, Charles. Play us something at once.

LOMAX: Righto! [*He sits down in his former place, and preludes*].

UNDERSHAFT: One moment, Mr Lomax. I am rather interested in the Salvation Army. Its motto might be my own: Blood and Fire.

LOMAX [*shocked*]: But not your sort of blood and fire, you know.

UNDERSHAFT: My sort of blood cleanses: my sort of fire purifies.

BARBARA: So do ours. Come down tomorrow to my shelter—the West Ham shelter—and see what we're doing. We're going to march to a great meeting in the Assembly Hall at Mile End. Come and see the shelter and then march with us: it will do you a lot of good. Can you play anything?

UNDERSHAFT: In my youth I earned pennies, and even shillings occasionally, in the streets and in public house parlors by my natural talent for stepdancing. Later on, I became a member of the Undershaft orchestral society, and performed passably on the tenor trombone.

LOMAX [*scandalized—putting down the concertina*]: Oh I say!

BARBARA: Many a sinner has played himself into heaven on the trombone, thanks to the Army.

LOMAX [*to Barbara, still rather shocked*]: Yes; but what about the cannon business, dont you know? [*To Undershaft*] Getting into heaven is not exactly in your line, is it?

LADY BRITOMART: Charles!!!

LOMAX: Well; but it stands to reason, dont it? The cannon business may be necessary and all that: we cant get on without cannons; but it isnt right, you know. On the other hand, there may be a certain amount of tosh about the Salvation Army—I belong to the Estab-lished Church myself—but still you cant deny that it's religion; and you cant go against religion, can you? At least unless youre downright immoral, dont you know.

UNDERSHAFT: You hardly appreciate my position, Mr Lomax—

LOMAX [*hastily*]: I'm not saying anything against you personally—

UNDERSHAFT: Quite so, quite so. But consider for a moment. Here I am, a profiteer in mutilation and murder. I find myself in a specially amiable humor just now because, this morning, down at the foundry, we blew twenty-seven dummy soldiers into fragments with a gun which formerly destroyed only thirteen.

LOMAX [*leniently*]: Well, the more destructive war becomes, the sooner it will be abolished, eh?

UNDERSHAFT: Not at all. The more destructive war becomes the more fascinating we find it. No, Mr Lomax: I am obliged to you for making the usual excuse for my trade; but I am not ashamed of it. I am not one of those men who keep their morals and their business in watertight compartments. All the spare money my trade rivals spend on hospitals, cathedrals, and other receptacles for conscience money, I devote to experiments and researches in improved methods of destroying life and property. I have always done so; and I always shall. Therefore your Christmas card moralities of peace on earth and goodwill among men are of no use to me. Your Christianity, which enjoins you to resist not evil, and to turn the other cheek, would make me a bankrupt. *My morality — my* religion — must have a place for cannons and torpedoes in it.

STEPHEN [*coldly—almost sullenly*]: You speak as if there were half a dozen moralities and religions to choose from, instead of one true morality and one true religion.

UNDERSHAFT: For me there is only one true morality; but it might not fit you, as you do not manufacture aerial battleships. There is only one true morality for every man; but every man has not the same true morality.

LOMAX [*overtaxed*]: Would you mind saying that again? I didnt quite follow it.

CUSINS: It's quite simple. As Euripides says, one man's meat is another man's poison morally as well as physically.

UNDERSHAFT: Precisely.

LOMAX: Oh, *that!* Yes, yes, yes. True. True.

STEPHEN: In other words, some men are honest and some are scoundrels.

BARBARA: Bosh! There are no scoundrels.

UNDERSHAFT: Indeed? Are there any good men?

BARBARA: No. Not one. There are neither good men nor scoundrels: there are just children of one Father; and the sooner they stop calling one another names the better. You neednt talk to me: I know them. Ive had scores of them through my hands: scoundrels, criminals, infidels, philanthropists, missionaries, county councillors, all sorts. Theyre all just the same sort of sinner; and theres the same salvation ready for them all.

UNDERSHAFT: May I ask have you ever saved a maker of cannons?

BARBARA: No. Will you let me try?

UNDERSHAFT: Well, I will make a bargain with you. If I go to see you tomorrow in your Salvation Shelter, will you come the day after to see me in my cannon works?

BARBARA: Take care. It may end in your giving up the cannons for the sake of the Salvation Army.

UNDERSHAFT: Are you sure it will not end in your giving up the Salvation Army for the sake of the cannons?

BARBARA: I will take my chance of that.

UNDERSHAFT: And I will take my chance of the other. [*They shake hands on it*]. Where is your shelter?

BARBARA: In West Ham. At the sign of the cross. Ask anybody in Canning Town. Where are your works?

UNDERSHAFT: In Perivale St Andrews. At the sign of the sword. Ask anybody in Europe.

LOMAX: Hadnt I better play something?

BARBARA: Yes. Give us Onward, Christian Soldiers.

LOMAX: Well, thats rather a strong order to begin with, dont you know. Suppose I sing Thourt passing hence, my brother. It's much the same tune.

BARBARA: It's too melancholy. You get saved, Cholly; and

youll pass hence, my brother, without making such a fuss about it.

LADY BRITOMART: Really, Barbara, you go on as if religion were a pleasant subject. Do have some sense of propriety.

UNDERSHAFT: I do not find it an unpleasant subject, my dear. It is the only one that capable people really care for.

LADY BRITOMART [*looking at her watch*]: Well, if you are determined to have it, I insist on having it in a proper and respectable way. Charles: ring for prayers.

[*General amazement. Stephen rises in dismay*].

LOMAX [*rising*]: Oh I say!

UNDERSHAFT [*rising*]: I am afraid I must be going.

LADY BRITOMART: You cannot go now, Andrew: it would be most improper. Sit down. What will the servants think?

UNDERSHAFT: My dear: I have conscientious scruples. May I suggest a compromise? If Barbara will conduct a little service in the drawing room, with Mr Lomax as organist, I will attend it willingly. I will even take part, if a trombone can be procured.

LADY BRITOMART: Dont mock, Andrew.

UNDERSHAFT [*shocked—to Barbara*]: You dont think I am mocking, my love, I hope.

BARBARA: No, of course not; and it wouldnt matter if you were: half the Army came to their first meeting for a lark. [*Rising*] Come along. [*She throws her arm round her father and sweeps

him out, calling to the others from the threshold*] Come, Dolly. Come, Cholly.

[*Cusins rises*].

LADY BRITOMART: I will not be disobeyed by everybody. Adolphus: sit down. [*He does not*]. Charles: you may go. You are not fit for prayers: you cannot keep your countenance.

LOMAX: Oh I say! [*He goes out*].

LADY BRITOMART [*continuing*]: But you, Adolphus, can behave yourself if you choose to. I insist on your staying.

CUSINS: My dear Lady Brit: there are things in the family prayer book that I couldnt bear to hear you say.

LADY BRITOMART: What things, pray?

CUSINS: Well, you would have to say before all the servants that we have done things we ought not to have done, and left undone things we ought to have done, and that there is no health in us. I cannot bear to hear you doing yourself such an injustice, and Barbara such an injustice. As for myself, I flatly deny it: I have done my best. I shouldnt dare to marry Barbara—I couldnt look you in the face—if it were true. So I must go to the drawing room.

LADY BRITOMART [*offended*]: Well, go. [*He starts for the door*]. And remember this, Adolphus [*he turns to listen*]: I have a very strong suspicion that you went to the Salvation Army to worship Barbara and nothing else. And I quite appreciate the very clever way in which you systematically humbug me. I have found you out. Take care Barbara doesnt. Thats all.

CUSINS [*with unruffled sweetness*]: Dont tell on me. [*He steals out*].

LADY BRITOMART: Sarah: if you want to go, go. Anything's better than to sit there as if you wished you were a thousand miles away.

SARAH [*languidly*]: Very well, mamma. [*She goes*].

[*Lady Britomart, with a sudden flounce, gives way to a little gust of tears*].

STEPHEN [*going to her*]: Mother: whats the matter?

LADY BRITOMART [*swishing away her tears with her handkerchief*]: Nothing. Foolishness. You can go with him, too, if you like, and leave me with 'the servants.

STEPHEN: Oh, you mustnt think that, mother. I—I dont like him.

LADY BRITOMART: The others do. That is the injustice of a woman's lot. A woman has to bring up her children; and that means to restrain them, to deny them things they want, to set them tasks, to punish them when they do wrong, to do all the unpleasant things. And then the father, who has nothing to do but pet them and spoil them, comes in when all her work is done and steals their affection from her.

STEPHEN: He has not stolen our affection from you. It is only curiosity.

LADY BRITOMART [*violently*]: I wont be consoled, Stephen. There is nothing the matter with me. [*She rises and goes towards the door*].

STEPHEN: Where are you going, mother?

LADY BRITOMART: To the drawing room, of course. [*She goes out. Onward, Christian Soldiers, on the concertina, with tambourine accompaniment, is heard when the door opens*]. Are you coming, Stephen?

STEPHEN: No. Certainly not. [*She goes. He sits down on the settee, with compressed lips and an expression of strong dislike*].

ACT TWO

The yard of the West Ham shelter of the Salvation Army is a cold place on a January morning. The building itself, an old warehouse, is newly whitewashed. Its gabled end projects into the yard in the middle, with a door on the ground floor, and another in the loft above it without any balcony or ladder, but with a pulley rigged over it for hoisting sacks. Those who come from this central gable end into the yard have the gateway leading to the street on their left, with a stone horse-trough just beyond it, and, on the right, a penthouse shielding a table from the weather.

*There are forms at the table; and on them are seated a man
and a woman, both much down on their luck, finishing a
meal of bread (one thick slice each, with margarine and
golden syrup) and diluted milk.*

*The man, a workman out of employment, is young, agile,
a talker, a poser, sharp enough to be capable of anything
in reason except honesty or altruistic considerations of any
kind. The woman is a commonplace old bundle of poverty
and hard-worn humanity. She looks sixty and probably is
forty-five. If they were rich people, gloved and muffed and
well wrapped up in furs and overcoats, they would be numbed
and miserable; for it is a. grindingly cold raw January day;
and a glance at the background of grimy warehouses and
leaden sky visible over the whitewashed walls of the yard
would drive any idle rich person straight to the Mediterranean.
But these two, being no more troubled with visions of the
Mediterranean than of the moon, and being compelled to
keep more of their clothes in the pawnshop, and less on
their persons, in winter than in summer, are not depressed
by the cold: rather are they stung into vivacity, to which
their meal has just now given an almost jolly turn. The
man takes a pull at his mug, and then gets up and moves
about the yard with his hands deep in his pockets, occasionally breaking into a stepdance.*

THE WOMAN: Feel better arter your meal, sir?

THE MAN: No. Call that a meal! Good enough for you, praps; but wot is it to me, an intelligent workin man.

THE WOMAN: Workin man! Wot are you?

THE MAN: Painter.

THE WOMAN [*sceptically*]: Yus, I dessay.

THE MAN: Yus, you dessay! I know. Every loafer that cant do nothink calls isself a painter. Well, I'm a real painter: grainer, finisher, thirty-eight bob a week when I can get it.

THE WOMAN: Then why dont you go and get it?

THE MAN: I'll tell you why. Fust: I'm intelligent—fffff! it's rotten cold here [*he dances a step or two*]—yes: intelligent beyond the station o life into which it has pleased the capitalists to call me; and they dont like a man that sees through em. Second, an intelligent bein needs a doo share of appiness; so I drink somethink cruel when I get the chawnce. Third, I stand by my class and do as little as I can so's to leave arf the job for me fellow workers. Fourth, I'm fly enough to know wots inside the law and wots outside it; and inside it I do as the capitalists do: pinch wot I can lay me ands on. In a proper state of society I am sober, industrious and honest: in Rome, so to speak, I do as the Romans do. Wots the consequence? When trade is bad—and it's rotten bad just now—and the employers az to sack arf their men, they generally start on me.

THE WOMAN: Whats your name?

THE MAN: Price. Bronterre O'Brien Price. Usually called Snobby Price, for short.

THE WOMAN: Snobby's a carpenter, aint it? You said you was a painter.

PRICE: Not that kind of a snob, but the genteel sort. I'm too uppish, owing to my intelligence, and my father being a Chartist and a reading, thinking man: a stationer, too. I'm none of your common hewers of wood and drawers of water; and dont you forget it. [*He returns to his seat at the table, and takes up his mug*]. Wots *your* name?

THE WOMAN: Rummy Mitchens, sir.

PRICE [*quaffing the remains of his milk to her*]: Your elth, Miss Mitchens.

RUMMY [*correcting him*]: Missis Mitchens.

PRICE: Wot! Oh Rummy, Rummy! Respectable married woman, Rummy, gittin rescued by the Salvation Army by pretendin to be a bad un. Same old game!

RUMMY: What am I to do? I cant starve. Them Salvation lasses is dear good girls; but the better you are, the worse they likes to think you were before they rescued you. Why shouldnt they av a bit o credit, poor loves? theyre worn to rags by their work. And where would they get the money to rescue us if we was to let on we're no worse than other people? You know what ladies and gentlemen are.

PRICE: Thievin swine! Wish I ad their job, Rummy, all the same. Wot does Rummy stand for? Pet name praps?

RUMMY: Short for Romola.

PRICE: For wot!?

RUMMY: Romola. It was out of a new book. Somebody me mother wanted me to grow up like.

PRICE: We're companions in misfortune, Rummy. Both on us got names that nobody cawnt pronounce. Consequently I'm Snobby and youre Rummy because Bill and Sally wasnt good enough for our parents. Such is life!

RUMMY: Who saved you, Mr Price? Was it Major Barbara?

PRICE: No: I come here on my own. I'm going to be Bronterre O'Brien Price, the converted painter. I know wot they like. I'll tell em how I blasphemed and gambled and wopped my poor old mother—

RUMMY [*shocked*]: Used you to beat your mother?

PRICE: Not likely. She used to beat me. No matter: you come and listen to the converted painter, and youll hear how she was a pious woman that taught me me prayers at er knee, an how I used to come home drunk and drag her out o bed be er snow white airs, an lam into er with the poker.

RUMMY: Thats whats so unfair to us women. Your confessions is just as big lies as ours: you dont tell what you really done no more than us; but you men can tell your lies right out at the meetins and be made much of for it; while the sort o confessions we az to make az to be wispered to one lady at a time. It aint right, spite of all their piety.

PRICE: Right! Do you spose the Army 'd be allowed if it went and did right? Not much. It combs our air and makes us good little blokes to be robbed and put upon. But I'll play the game as good as any of em. I'll see somebody struck by lightnin, or hear a voice sayin "Snobby Price: where will you spend eternity?" I'll av a time of it, I tell you.

RUMMY: You wont be let drink, though.

PRICE: I'll take it out in gorspellin, then. I dont want to drink if I can get fun enough any other way.

[*Jenny Hill, a pale, overwrought, pretty Salvation lass of 18, comes in through the yard gate, leading Peter Shirley, a half hardened, half worn-out elderly man, weak with hunger*].

JENNY [*supporting him*]: Come! pluck up. I'll get you something to eat. Youll be all right then.

PRICE [*rising and hurrying officiously to take the old man off Jenny's hands*]: Poor old man! Cheer up, brother: youll find rest and peace and appiness ere. Hurry up with the food, miss: e's fair done. [*Jenny hurries into the shelter*]. Ere, buck up, daddy! she's fetchin y'a thick slice o breadn treacle, an a mug o skyblue. [*He seats him at the corner of the table*].

RUMMY [*gaily*]: Keep up your old art! Never say die!

SHIRLEY: I'm not an old man. I'm ony 46. I'm as good as ever I was. The grey patch come in my hair before I was thirty. All it wants is three pennorth o hair dye: am I to be turned on the streets to starve for it? Holy God! Ive worked ten to twelve hours a day since I was thirteen, and paid my way all through; and now am I to be thrown into the gutter and my job given to a young man that can do it no better than me because Ive black hair that goes white at the first change?

PRICE [*cheerfully*]: No good jawrin about it. Youre ony a jumped-up, jerked-off, orspittle-turned-out incurable of an ole workin man: who cares about you? Eh? Make the thievin swine give you a meal: theyve stole many a one from you. Get a bit o your own back. [*Jenny returns with the usual meal*]. There you are, brother. Awsk a blessin an tuck that into you.

SHIRLEY [*looking at it ravenously but not touching it, and crying like a child*]: I never took anything before.

JENNY [*petting him*]: Come, come! the Lord sends it to you: he wasnt above taking bread from his friends; and why should you be? Besides, when we find you a job you can pay us for it if you like.

SHIRLEY [*eagerly*]: Yes, yes: thats true. I can pay you back: it's only a loan. [*Shivering*] Oh Lord! oh Lord! [*He turns to the table and attacks the meal ravenously*].

JENNY: Well, Rummy, are you more comfortable now?

RUMMY: God bless you, lovey! youve fed my body and saved my soul, havnt you? [*Jenny, touched, kisses her*]. Sit down and rest a bit: you must be ready to drop.

JENNY: Ive been going hard since morning. But theres more work than we can do. I mustnt stop.

RUMMY: Try a prayer for just two minutes. Youll work all the better after.

JENNY [*her eyes lighting up*]: Oh isnt it wonderful how a few minutes prayer revives you! I was quite lightheaded at twelve o'clock, I was so tired; but Major Barbara just sent me to pray for five minutes; and I was able to go on as if I had only just begun. [*To Price*] Did you have a piece of bread?

PRICE [*with unction*]: Yes, miss; but Ive got the piece that I value more; and thats the peace that passeth hall hannerstennin.

RUMMY [*fervently*]: Glory Hallelujah!

[*Bill Walker, a rough customer of about 25, appears at the yard gate and looks malevolently at Jenny*].

JENNY: That makes me so happy. When you say that, I feel wicked for loitering here. I must get to work again.

[*She is hurrying to the shelter, when the new-comer moves quickly up to the door and intercepts her. His manner is so threatening that she retreats as he comes at her truculently, driving her down the yard*].

BILL: Aw knaow you. Youre the one that took awy maw girl. Youre the one that set er agen me. Well, I'm gowin to ev er aht. Not that Aw care a carse for er or you: see? Bat Aw'll let er knaow; and Aw'll let *you* knaow. Aw'm gowing to give her a doin thatll teach er to cat awy from me. Nah in wiv you and tell er to cam aht afore Aw cam in and kick er aht. Tell er Bill Walker wants er. She'll knaow wot thet means; and if she keeps me witin itll be worse. You stop to jawr beck at me; and Aw'll stawt on you: d'ye eah? Theres your wy. In you gow. [*He takes her by the arm and slings her towards the door of the shelter. She falls on her hand and knee. Rummy helps her up again*].

PRICE [*rising, and venturing irresolutely towards Bill*]: Easy there, mate. She aint doin you no arm.

BILL: Oo are you callin mite? [*Standing over him threateningly*] Youre gowin to stend ap fer er, aw yer? Put ap your ends.

RUMMY [*running indignantly to him to scold him*]: Oh, you great brute— [*He instantly swings his left hand back against her face. She screams and reels back to the trough, where she sits down, covering her bruised face with her hands and rocking herself and moaning with pain*].

JENNY [*going to her*]: Oh, God forgive you! How could you strike an old woman like that?

BILL [*seizing her by the hair so violently that she also screams, and tearing her away from the old woman*]: You Gawd forgimme again an Aw'll Gawd forgive you one on the jawr thetll stop you pryin for a week. [*Holding her and turning fiercely on Price*] Ev you ennything to sy agen it?

PRICE [*intimidated*]: No, matey: she aint anything to do with me.

BILL: Good job for you! Aw'd pat two meals into you and fawt you with one finger arter, you stawved cur. [*To Jenny*] Nah are you gowin to fetch aht Mog Ebbijem; or em Aw to knock your fice off you and fetch her meself?

JENNY [*writhing in his grasp*]: Oh please someone go in and tell Major Barbara— [*She screams again as he wrenches her head down; and Price and Rummy flee into the shelter*].

BILL: You want to gow in and tell your Mijor of me, do you?

JENNY: Oh please dont drag my hair. Let me go.

BILL: Do you or downt you? [*She stifles a scream*]. Yus or nao?

JENNY: God give me strength—

BILL [*striking her with his fist in the face*]: Gow an shaow her thet, and tell her if she wants one lawk it to cam and interfere with me. [*Jenny, crying with pain, goes into the shed. He goes to the form and addresses the old man*]. Eah: finish your mess; an git aht o maw wy.

SHIRLEY [*springing up and facing him fiercely, with the mug in his hand*]: You take a liberty with me, and I'll smash you over the face with the mug and cut your eye out. Aint you satisfied— young whelps like you—with takin the bread out o the mouths of your elders that have brought you up and slaved for

you, but you must come shovin and cheekin and bullyin in here, where the bread o charity is sickenin in our stummicks?

BILL [*contemptuously, but backing a little*]: Wot good are you, you aold palsy mag? Wot good are you?

SHIRLEY: As good as you and better. I'll do a day's work agen you or any fat young soaker of your age. Go and take my job at Horrockses, where I worked for ten year. They want young men there: they cant afford to keep men over forty-five. Theyre very sorry—give you a character and happy to help you to get anything suited to your years— sure a steady man wont be long out of a job. Well, let em try *you*. Theyll find the differ. What do *you* know? Not as much as how to beeyave yourself—layin your dirty fist across the mouth of a respectable woman!

BILL: Downt provowk me to ly it acrost yours: d'ye eah?

SHIRLEY [*with blighting contempt*]: Yes: you like an old man to hit, dont you, when youve finished with the women. I aint seen you hit a young one yet.

BILL [*stung*]: You loy, you aold soupkitchener, you. There was a yang menn eah. Did Aw offer to itt him or did Aw not?

SHIRLEY: Was he starvin or was he not? Was he a man or only a crosseyed thief an a loafer? Would you hit my son-in-law's brother?

BILL: Oo's ee?

SHIRLEY: Todger Fairmile o Balls Pond. Him that won £20 off the Japanese wrastler at the music hall by standin out 17 minutes 4 seconds agen him.

BILL [*sullenly*]: Aw'm nao music awl wrastler. Ken he box?

SHIRLEY: Yes: an you cant.

BILL: Wot! Aw cawnt, cawnt Aw? Wots thet you sy [*threatening him*]?

SHIRLEY [*not budging an inch*]: Will you box Todger Fairmile if I put him on to you? Say the word.

BILL [*subsiding with a slouch*]: Aw'll stend ap to enny menn alawv, if he was ten Todger Fairmawls. But Aw dont set ap to be a perfeshnal.

SHIRLEY [*looking down on him with unfathomable disdain*]: *You* box! Slap an old woman with the back o your hand! You hadnt even the sense to hit her where a magistrate couldnt see the mark of it, you silly young lump of conceit and ignorance. Hit a girl in the jaw and ony make her cry! If Todger Fairmile'd done it, she wouldnt a got up inside o ten minutes, no more than you would if he got on to you. Yah! I'd set about you myself if I had a week's feedin in me instead o two months' starvation. [*He turns his back on him and sits down moodily at the table*].

BILL [*following him and stooping over him to drive the taunt in*]: You loy! youve the bread and treacle in you that you cam eah to beg.

SHIRLEY [*bursting into tears*]: Oh God! It's true: I'm only an old pauper on the scrap heap. [*Furiously*] But youll come to it yourself; and then youll know. Youll come to it sooner than a teetotaller like me, fillin your-self with gin at this hour o the mornin!

BILL: Aw'm nao gin drinker, you oald lawr; bat wen Aw want to give my girl a bloomin good awdin Aw lawk to ev a bit o devil in me: see? An eah Aw emm, talkin to a rotten aold blawter like you sted o givin her wot for. [*Working himself into a rage*] Aw'm gowin in there to fetch her aht. [*He makes vengefully for the shelter door*].

SHIRLEY: Youre going to the station on a stretcher, more likely; and theyll take the gin and the devil out of you there when they get you inside. You mind what youre about: the major here is the Earl o Stevenage's grand-daughter.

BILL [*checked*]: Garn!

SHIRLEY: Youll see.

BILL [*his resolution oozing*]: Well, Aw aint dan nathin to er.

SHIRLEY: Spose she said you did! who'd believe you?

BILL [*very uneasy, skulking back to the corner of the penthouse*]: Gawd! theres no jastice in this cantry. To think wot them people can do! Aw'm as good as er

SHIRLEY: Tell her so. It's jus what a fool like you would do

[*Barbara, brisk and businesslike comes from the shelter with a note book, and addresses herself to Shirley. Bill, cowed, sits down in the corner on a form, and turn his back on them*].

BARBARA: Good morning.

SHIRLEY [*standing up and taking off his hat*]: Good morning miss.

BARBARA: Sit down: make your self at home. [*He hesitates*

but she puts a friendly hand on his shoulder and makes him obey]. Now then! since youve made friends with us, we want to know all about you. Names and addresses and trades.

SHIRLEY: Peter Shirley. Fitter. Chucked out two months ago because I was too old.

BARBARA [*not at all surprised*]: Youd pass still. Why didnt you dye your hair?

SHIRLEY: I did. Me age come out at a coroner's inquest on me daughter.

BARBARA: Steady?

SHIRLEY: Teetotaller. Never out of a job before. Good worker. And sent to the knackers like an old horse!

BARBARA: No matter: if you did your part God will do his.

SHIRLEY [*suddenly stubborn*]: My religion's no concern of anybody but myself.

BARBARA [*guessing*]: *I* know. Secularist?

SHIRLEY [*hotly*]: Did I offer to deny it?

BARBARA: Why should you? My own father's a Secularist, I think. Our Father—yours and mine—fulfils himself in many ways; and I daresay he knew what he was about when he made a Secularist of you. So buck up, Peter! we can always find a job for a steady man like you. [*Shirley, disarmed and a little bewildered, touches his hat. She turns from him to Bill*]. Whats your name?

BILL [*insolently*]: Wots thet to you?

BARBARA [*calmly making a note*]: Afraid to give his name. Any trade?

BILL: Oo's afride to give is nime? [*Doggedly, with a sense of heroically defying the House of Lords in the person of Lord Stevenage*] If you want to bring a chawge agen me, bring it. [*She waits, unruffled*]. Moy nime's Bill Walker.

BARBARA [*as if the name were familiar: trying to remember how*]: Bill Walker? [*Recollecting*] Oh, I know: youre the man that Jenny Hill was praying for inside just now. [*She enters his name in her note book*].

BILL: Oo's Jenny Ill? And wot call as she to pry for me?

BARBARA: I dont know. Perhaps it was you that cut her lip.

BILL [*defiantly*]: Yus, it *was* me that cat her lip. Aw aint afride o *you*.

BARBARA: How could you be, since youre not afraid of God? Youre a brave man, Mr Walker. It takes some pluck to do *our* work here; but none of us dare lift our hand against a girl like that, for fear of her father in heaven.

BILL [*sullenly*]: I want nan o your kentin jawr. I spowse you think Aw cam eah to beg from you, like this demmiged lot eah. Not me. Aw downt want your bread and scripe and ketlep. Aw dont blieve in your Gawd, no more than you do yourself.

BARBARA [*sunnily apologetic and ladylike, as on a new footing with him*]: Oh, I beg your pardon for putting your name down, Mr Walker. I didnt understand. I'll strike it out.

BILL [*taking this as a slight, and deeply wounded by it*]: Eah! you let maw nime alown. Aint it good enaff to be in your book?

BARBARA [considering]: Well, you see, theres no use putting down your name unless I can do something for you, is there? Whats your trade?

BILL [still staring]: Thets nao concern o yours.

BARBARA: Just so. [Very business-like] I'll put you down as [writing] the man who—struck—poor little Jenny Hill—in the mouth.

BILL [rising threateningly]: See eah. Awve ed enaff o this.

BARBARA [quite sunny and fearless]: What did you come to us for?

BILL: Aw cam for maw gel, see? Aw cam to tike her aht o this and to brike er jawr for er.

BARBARA [complacently]: You see I was right about your trade. [Bill, on the point of retorting furiously, finds himself, to his great shame and terror, in danger of crying instead. He sits down again suddenly]. Whats her name?

BILL [dogged]: Er nime's Mog Ebbijem: thets wot her nime is.

BARBARA: Mog Habbijam! Oh, she's gone to Canning Town, to our barracks there.

BILL [fortified by his resentment of Mog's perfidy]: Is she? [Vindictively] Then Aw'm gowin to Kennintahn arter her. [He crosses to the gate; hesitates; finally comes back at Barbara]. Are you loyin to me to git shat o me?

BARBARA: I dont want to get shut of you. I want to keep you here and save your soul. Youd better stay: youre going to have a bad time today, Bill.

BILL: Oo's gowin to give it to me? You, preps?

BARBARA: Someone you dont believe in. But youll be glad afterwards.

BILL [slinking off]: Aw'll gow to Kennintahn to be aht o reach o your tangue. [Suddenly turning on her with intense malice] And if Aw downt fawnd Mog there, Aw'll cam beck and do two years for you, selp me Gawd if Aw downt!

BARBARA [a shade kindlier, if possible]: It's no use, Bill. She's got another bloke.

BILL: Wot!

BARBARA: One of her own converts. He fell in love with her when he saw her with her soul saved, and her face clean, and her hair washed.

BILL [surprised]: Wottud she wash it for, the carroty slat? It's red.

BARBARA: It's quite lovely now, because she wears a new look in her eyes with it. It's a pity youre too late. The new bloke has put your nose out of joint, Bill.

BILL: Aw'll put his nowse aht o joint for him. Not that Aw care a carse for er, mawned thet. But Aw'll teach her to drop me as if Aw was dirt. And Aw'll teach her to meddle with maw judy. Wots iz bleedin nime?

BARBARA: Sergeant Todger Fairmile.

SHIRLEY [rising with grim joy]: I'll go with him, miss. I want to see them two meet. I'll take him to the infirmary when it's over

BILL [to Shirley, with undissembled misgiving]: Is thet im you was speakin on?

SHIRLEY: Thats him.

BILL: Im that wrastled in the music awl?

SHIRLEY: The competitions at the National Sportin Club was worth nigh a hundred a year to him. He's gev em up now for religion; so he's a bit fresh for want of the exercise he was accustomed to. He'll be glad to see you. Come along.

BILL: Wots is wight?

SHIRLEY: Thirteen four. [*Bill's last hope expires*].

BARBARA: Go and talk to him, Bill. He'll convert you.

SHIRLEY: He'll convert your head into a mashed potato.

BILL [*sullenly*]: Aw aint afride of im. Aw aint afride of ennybody. Bat e can lick me. She's dan me. [*He sits down moodily on the edge of the horse trough*]:

SHIRLEY: You aint going. I thought not. [*He resumes his seat*].

BARBARA [*calling*]: Jenny!

JENNY [*appearing at the shelter door with a plaster on the corner of her mouth*]: Yes, Major.

BARBARA: Send Rummy Mitchens out to clear away here.

JENNY: I think she's afraid.

BARBARA [*her resemblance to her mother flashing out for a moment*]: Nonsense! she must do as she's told.

JENNY [*calling into the shelter*]: Rummy: the Major says you must come.

[*Jenny comes to Barbara, purposely keeping on the side next Bill, lest he should suppose that she shrank from him or bore malice*].

BARBARA: Poor little Jenny! Are you tired? [*Looking at the wounded cheek*] Does it hurt?

JENNY: No: it's all right now. It was nothing.

BARBARA [*critically*]: It was as hard as he could hit, I expect.

Poor Bill! You dont feel angry with him, do you?

JENNY: Oh no, no, no: indeed I dont, Major, bless his poor heart! [*Barbara kisses her; and she runs away merrily into the shelter. Bill writhes with an agonizing return of his new and alarming symptoms, but says nothing. Rummy Mitchens comes from the shelter*].

BARBARA [*going to meet Rummy*]: Now Rummy, bustle. Take in those mugs and plates to be washed; and throw the crumbs about for the birds.

[*Rummy takes the three plates and mugs; but Shirley takes back his mug from her, as there is still some milk left in it*].

RUMMY: There aint any crumbs. This aint a time to waste good bread on birds.

PRICE [*appearing at the shelter door*]: Gentleman come to see the shelter, Major. Says he's your father.

BARBARA: All right. Coming. [*Snobby goes back into the shelter, followed by Barbara*].

RUMMY [*stealing across to Bill and addressing him in a subdued voice, but with intense conviction*]: I'd av the lor of you, you flat eared pignosed potwalloper, if she'd let me. Youre no gentleman, to hit a lady in the face. [*Bill, with greater things moving in him, takes no notice*].

SHIRLEY [*following her*]: Here! in with you and dont get yourself into more trouble by talking.

RUMMY [*with hauteur*]: I aint ad the pleasure o being hintroduced to you, as I can remember.

[*She goes into the shelter with the plates*].

SHIRLEY: Thats the—

BILL [*savagely*]: Downt you talk to me, d'ye eah? You lea me alown, or Aw'll do you a mischief. Aw'm not dirt under *your* feet, ennywy.

SHIRLEY [*calmly*]: Dont you be afeerd. You aint such prime company that you need expect to be sought after. [*He is about to go into the shelter when Barbara comes out, with Undershaft on her right*].

BARBARA: Oh, there you are, Mr Shirley! [*Between them*] This is my father: I told you he was a Secularist, didnt I? Perhaps youll be able to comfort one another.

UNDERSHAFT [*startled*]: A Secularist! Not the least in the world: on the contrary, a confirmed mystic.

BARBARA: Sorry, I'm sure. By the way, papa, what *is* your religion? in case I have to introduce you again.

UNDERSHAFT: My religion? Well, my dear, I am a Millionaire. That is my religion.

BARBARA: Then I'm afraid you and Mr Shirley wont be able to comfort one another after all. Youre not a Millionaire, are you, Peter?

SHIRLEY: No; and proud of it.

UNDERSHAFT [*gravely*]: Poverty, my friend, is not a thing to be proud of.

SHIRLEY [*angrily*]: Who made your millions for you? Me and my like. Whats kep us poor? Keepin you rich. I wouldnt have your conscience, not for all your income.

UNDERSHAFT: I wouldnt have your income, not for all your conscience, Mr Shirley. [*He goes to the penthouse and sits down on a form*].

BARBARA [*stopping Shirley adroitly as he is about to retort*]: You wouldnt think he was my father, would you, Peter? Will you go into the shelter and lend the lasses a hand for a while: we're worked off our feet.

SHIRLEY [*bitterly*]: Yes: I'm in their debt for a meal, aint I?

BARBARA: Oh, not because youre in their debt, but for love of them, Peter, for love of them. [*He cannot understand, and is rather scandalized*]. There! dont stare at me. In with you; and give that conscience of yours a holiday [*bustling him into the shelter*].

SHIRLEY [*as he goes in*]: Ah! it's a pity you never was trained to use your reason, miss. Youd have been a very taking lecturer on Secularism.

[*Barbara turns to her father*].

UNDERSHAFT: Never mind me, my dear. Go about your work; and let me watch it for a while.

BARBARA: All right.

UNDERSHAFT: For instance, whats the matter with that outpatient over there?

BARBARA [*looking at Bill, whose attitude has never changed, and whose expression of brooding wrath has deepened*]: Oh, we shall cure him in no time. Just watch. [*She goes over to Bill and waits. He glances up at her and casts his eyes down again, uneasy, but grimmer than ever*]

It *would* be nice to just stamp on Mog Habbijam's face, wouldnt it, Bill?

BILL [*starting up from the trough in consternation*]: It's a loy: Aw never said so. [*She shakes her head*]. Oo taold you wot was in moy mawnd?

BARBARA: Only your new friend.

BILL: Wot new friend?

BARBARA: The devil, Bill. When he gets round people they get miserable, just like you.

BILL [*with a heartbreaking attempt at devil-may-care cheerfulness*]: Aw aint miserable. [*He sits down again, and stretches his legs in an attempt to seem indifferent*].

BARBARA: Well, if youre happy, why dont you look happy, as we do?

BILL [*his legs curling back in spite of him*]: Aw'm eppy enaff, Aw tell you. Woy cawnt you lea me alown? Wot ev I dan to *you?* Aw aint smashed *your* fice, ev Aw?

BARBARA [*softly: wooing his soul*]: It's not me thats getting at you, Bill.

BILL: Oo else is it?

BARBARA: Somebody that doesnt intend you to smash women's faces, I suppose. Somebody or something that wants to make a man of you.

BILL [*blustering*]: Mike a menn o me! Aint Aw a menn? eh? Oo sez Aw'm not a menn?

BARBARA: Theres a man in you somewhere, I suppose. But why did he let you hit poor little Jenny Hill? That wasnt very manly of him, was it?

BILL [*tormented*]: Ev dan wiv it, Aw tell you. Chack it. Aw'm sick o your Jenny Ill and er silly little fice.

BARBARA: Then why do you keep thinking about it? Why does it keep coming up against you in your mind? Youre not getting converted, are you?

BILL [*with conviction*]: Not ME. Not lawkly.

BARBARA: Thats right, Bill. Hold out against it. Put out your strength. Dont lets get you cheap. Todger Fairmile said he wrestled for three nights against his salvation harder than he ever wrestled with the Jap at the music hall. He gave in to the Jap when his arm was going to break. But he didnt give in to his salvation until his heart was going to break. Perhaps youll escape that. You havnt any heart, have you?

BILL: Wot d'ye mean? Woy aint Aw got a awt the sime as ennybody else?

BARBARA: A man with a heart wouldnt have bashed poor little Jenny's face, would he?

BILL [*almost crying*]: Ow, *will* you lea me alown? Ev Aw ever offered to meddle with *you,* that you cam neggin and provowkin me lawk this? [*He writhes convulsively from his eyes to his toes*].

BARBARA [*with a steady soothing hand on his arm and a gentle voice that never lets him go*]: It's your soul thats hurting you, Bill, and not me. Weve been through it all ourselves. Come with us, Bill. [*He looks wildly round*]. To brave manhood on earth and eternal glory in heaven. [*He is on the point of breaking down*]. Come. [*A drum is heard in the shelter; and Bill, with a gasp, escapes from the spell as Barbara turns quickly. Adolphus enters from the shelter with a big drum].* Oh! there you are, Dolly. Let me introduce a new friend of mine, Mr Bill Walker. This is my bloke, Bill: Mr Cusins. [*Cusins salutes with his drumstick*].

BILL: Gowin to merry im?

BARBARA: Yes.

BILL [*fervently*]: Gawd elp im! Gaw-aw-aw-awd elp im!

BARBARA: Why? Do you think he wont be happy with me?

BILL: Awve aony ed to stend it for a mawnin: e'll ev to stend it for a lawftawm.

CUSINS: That is a frightful reflecttion, Mr Walker. But I cant tear myself away from her.

BILL: Well, Aw ken. [*To Barbara*] Eah! do you knaow where Aw'm gowin to, and wot Aw'm gowin to do?

BARBARA: Yes: youre going to heaven; and youre coming back here before the week's out to tell me so.

BILL: You loy. Aw'm gowin to Kennintahn, to spit in Todger Fairmawl's eye. Aw beshed Jenny Ill's fice; an nar Aw'll git me aown fice beshed and cam beck and shaow it to er. Ee'll itt me ardern Aw itt her. Thatll mike us square. [*To Adolphus*] Is thet fair or is it not? Youre a genlmn: you oughter knaow.

BARBARA: Two black eyes wont make one white one, Bill.

BILL: Aw didnt awst *you*. Cawnt you never keep your mahth shat? Oy awst the genlmn.

CUSINS [*reflectively*]: Yes: I think youre right, Mr Walker. Yes: I should do it. It's curious: it's exactly what an ancient Greek would have done.

BARBARA: But what good will it do?

CUSINS: Well, it will give Mr Fairmile some exercise; and it will satisfy Mr Walker's soul.

BILL: Rot! there aint nao sach a thing as a saoul. Ah kin you tell wevver Awve a saoul or not? You never seen it.

BARBARA: Ive seen it hurting you when you went against it.

BILL [*with compressed aggravation*]: If you was maw gel and took the word aht o me mahth lawk thet, Aw'd give you sathink youd feel urtin, Aw would. [*To Adolphus*] You tike maw tip, mite. Stop er jawr; or youll doy afoah your tawm. [*With intense expression*] Wore aht: thets wot youll be: wore aht. [*He goes away through the gate*].

CUSINS [*looking after him*]: I wonder!

BARBARA: Dolly! [*indignant, in her mother's manner*].

CUSINS: Yes, my dear, it's very wearing to be in love with you. If it lasts, I quite think I shall die young.

BARBARA: Should you mind?

CUSINS: Not at all. [*He is suddenly softened, and kisses her over the drum, evidently not for the first time, as people cannot kiss over a big drum without practice. Undershaft coughs*].

BARBARA: It's all right, papa, weve not forgotten you. Dolly: explain the place to papa: I havnt time. [*She goes busily into the shelter*].

[*Undershaft and Adolphus now have the yard to themselves. Under-*

shaft, seated on a form, and still keenly attentive, looks hard at Adolphus. Adolphus looks hard at him].

UNDERSHAFT: I fancy you guess something of what is in my mind, Mr Cusins. [*Cusins flourishes his drumsticks as if in the act of beating a lively rataplan, but makes no sound*]. Exactly so. But suppose Barbara finds you out!

CUSINS: You know, I do not admit that I am imposing on Barbara. I am quite genuinely interested in the views of the Salvation Army. The fact is, I am a sort of collector of religions; and the curious thing is that I find I can believe them all. By the way, have you any religion?

UNDERSHAFT: Yes.

CUSINS: Anything out of the common?

UNDERSHAFT: Only that there are two things necessary to Salvation.

CUSINS [*disappointed, but polite*]: Ah, the Church Catechism. Charles Lomax also belongs to the Established Church.

UNDERSHAFT: The two things are—

CUSINS: Baptism and—

UNDERSHAFT: No. Money and gunpowder.

CUSINS [*surprised, but interested*]: That is the general opinion of our governing classes. The novelty is in hearing any man confess it.

UNDERSHAFT: Just so.

CUSINS: Excuse me: is there any place in your religion for honor, justice, truth, love, mercy and so forth?

UNDERSHAFT: Yes: they are the graces and luxuries of a rich, strong, and safe life.

CUSINS: Suppose one is forced to choose between them and money or gunpowder?

UNDERSHAFT: Choose money and gunpowder; for without enough of both you cannot afford the others.

CUSINS: That is your religion?

UNDERSHAFT: Yes.

[*The cadence of this reply makes a full close in the conversation. Cusins twists his face dubiously and contemplates Undershaft. Undershaft contemplates him*].

CUSINS: Barbara wont stand that. You will have to choose between your religion and Barbara.

UNDERSHAFT: So will you, my friend. She will find out that that drum of yours is hollow.

CUSINS: Father Undershaft: you are mistaken: I am a sincere Salvationist. You do not understand the Salvation Army. It is the army of joy, of love, of courage: it has banished the fear and remorse and despair of the old hell-ridden evangelical sects: it marches to fight the devil with trumpet and drum, with music and dancing, with banner and palm, as becomes a sally from heaven by its happy garrison. It picks the waster out of the public house and makes a man of him: it finds a worm wriggling in a back kitchen, and lo! a woman! Men and women of rank too, sons and daughters of the Highest. It takes the poor professor of Greek, the most artificial and self-suppressed of human creatures, from his meal of roots, and lets loose the rhapsodist in him; reveals the true worship of Dionysos to him; sends him down the public street drumming dithyrambs [*he plays a thundering flourish on the drum*].

UNDERSHAFT: You will alarm the shelter.

CUSINS: Oh, they are accustomed to these sudden ecstasies. However, if the drum worries you— [*He pockets the drumsticks; unhooks the drum; and stands it on the ground opposite the gateway*].

UNDERSHAFT: Thank you.

CUSINS: You remember what Euripides says about your money and gunpowder?

UNDERSHAFT: No.

CUSINS [*declaiming*]:

> One and another
> In money and guns may outpass his brother;
> And men in their millions float and flow
> And seethe with a million hopes as leaven;
> And they win their will; or they miss their will;
> And their hopes are dead or are pined for still;
> But who'er can know
> As the long days go
> That to live is happy, has found *his* heaven.

My translation: what do you think of it?

UNDERSHAFT: I think, my friend, that if you wish to know, as the long days go, that to live is happy, you must first acquire money enough for a decent life, and power enough to be your own master.

CUSINS: You are damnably discouraging. [*He resumes his declamation*].

> Is it so hard a thing to see
> That the spirit of God—whate'er it be—
> The law that abides and changes not, ages long,
> The Eternal and Nature-born: *these* things be strong?
> What else is Wisdom? What of Man's endeavor,
> Or God's high grace so lovely and so great?
> To stand from fear set free? to breathe and wait?
> To hold a hand uplifted over Fate?
> And shall not Barbara be loved for ever?

UNDERSHAFT: Euripides mentions Barbara, does he?

CUSINS: It is a fair translation. The word means Loveliness.

UNDERSHAFT: May I ask—as Barbara's father—how much a year she is to be loved for ever on?

CUSINS: As Barbara's father, that is more your affair than mine. I can feed her by teaching Greek: that is about all.

UNDERSHAFT: Do you consider it a good match for her?

CUSINS [*with polite obstinacy*]: Mr Undershaft: I am in many ways a weak, timid, ineffectual person; and my health is far from satisfactory. But whenever I feel that I must have anything, I get it, sooner or later. I feel that way about Barbara. I dont like marriage: I feel intensely afraid of it; and I dont know what I shall do with Barbara or what she will do with me. But I feel that I and nobody else must marry her. Please regard that as settled.—Not that I wish to be arbitrary; but why should I waste your time in discussing what is inevitable?

UNDERSHAFT: You mean that you will stick at nothing: not even the conversion of the Salvation Army to the worship of Dionysos.

CUSINS: The business of the Salvation Army is to save, not to wrangle about the name of the pathfinder. Dionysos or another: what does it matter?

UNDERSHAFT [*rising and approaching him*]: Professor Cusins: you are a young man after my own heart.

CUSINS: Mr Undershaft: you are, as far as I am able to gather, a most infernal old rascal; but you appeal very strongly to my sense of ironic humor. [*Undershaft mutely offers his hand. They shake*].

UNDERSHAFT [*suddenly concentrating himself*]: And now to business.

CUSINS: Pardon me. We are discussing religion. Why go back to such an uninteresting and unimportant subject as business?

UNDERSHAFT: Religion is our business at present, because it is through religion alone that we can win Barbara.

CUSINS: Have you, too, fallen in love with Barbara?

UNDERSHAFT: Yes, with a father's love.

CUSINS: A father's love for a grown-up daughter is the most dangerous of all infatuations. I apologize for mentioning my own pale, coy, mistrustful fancy in the same breath with it.

UNDERSHAFT: Keep to the point.

We have to win her; and we are neither of us Methodists.

CUSINS: That doesnt matter. The power Barbara wields here— the power that wields Barbara herself—is not Calvinism, not Presbyterianism, not Methodism—

UNDERSHAFT: Not Greek Paganism either, eh?

CUSINS: I admit that. Barbara is quite original in her religion.

UNDERSHAFT [*triumphantly*]: Aha! Barbara Undershaft would be. Her inspiration comes from within herself.

CUSINS: How do you suppose it got there?

UNDERSHAFT [*in towering excitement*]: It is the Undershaft inheritance. I shall hand on my torch to my daughter. She shall make my converts and preach my gospel—

CUSINS: What! Money and gunpowder!

UNDERSHAFT: Yes, money and gunpowder. Freedom and power. Command of life and command of death.

CUSINS [*urbanely: trying to bring him down to earth*]: This is extremely interesting, Mr Undershaft. Of course you know that you are mad.

UNDERSHAFT [*with redoubled force*]: And you?

CUSINS: Oh, mad as a hatter. You are welcome to my secret since I have discovered yours. But I am astonished. Can a madman make cannons?

UNDERSHAFT: Would anyone else than a madman make them? And now [*with surging energy*] question for question. Can a sane man translate Euripides?

CUSINS: No.

UNDERSHAFT [*seizing him by the shoulder*]: Can a sane woman make a man of a waster or a woman of a worm?

CUSINS [*reeling before the storm*]: Father Colossus — Mammoth Millionaire—

UNDERSHAFT [*pressing him*]: Are there two mad people or three in this Salvation shelter today?

CUSINS: You mean Barbara is as mad as we are?

UNDERSHAFT [*pushing him lightly off and resuming his equanimity suddenly and completely*]: Pooh, Professor! let us call things by their proper names. I am a millionaire; you are a poet: Barbara is a savior of souls. What have we three to do with the common mob of slaves and idolators? [*He sits down again with a shrug of contempt for the mob*].

CUSINS: Take care! Barbara is in love with the common people. So am I. Have you never felt the romance of that love?

UNDERSHAFT [*cold and sardonic*]: Have you ever been in love with Poverty, like St Francis? Have you ever been in love with Dirt, like St Simeon! Have you ever been in love with disease and suffering, like our nurses and philanthropists? Such passions are not virtues, but the most unnatural of all the vices. This love of the common people may please an earl's granddaughter and a university professor; but I have been a common man and a poor man; and it has no romance for me. Leave it to the poor to pretend that poverty is a blessing: leave it to the coward to make a religion of his cowardice by preaching humility: we know better than that. We three must stand together above the common people: how else can we help their children to climb up beside us? Barbara must belong to us, not to the Salvation Army.

CUSINS: Well, I can only say that if you think you will get her away from the Salvation Army by talking to her as you have been talking to me, you dont know Barbara.

UNDERSHAFT: My friend: I never ask for what I can buy.

CUSINS [*in a white fury*]: Do I understand you to imply that you can buy Barbara?

UNDERSHAFT: No; but I can buy the Salvation Army.

CUSINS: Quite impossible.

UNDERSHAFT: You shall see. All religious organizations exist by selling themselves to the rich.

CUSINS: Not the Army. That is the Church of the poor.

UNDERSHAFT: All the more reason for buying it.

CUSINS: I dont think you quite know what the Army does for the poor.

UNDERSHAFT: Oh yes I do. It draws their teeth: that is enough for me as a man of business.

CUSINS: Nonsense! It makes them sober—

UNDERSHAFT: I prefer sober workmen. The profits are larger.

CUSINS: —honest—

UNDERSHAFT: Honest workmen are the most economical.

CUSINS: —attached to their homes—

UNDERSHAFT: So much the better: they will put up with anything sooner than change their shop.

CUSINS: —happy—

UNDERSHAFT: An invaluable safeguard against revolution.

CUSINS: —unselfish—

UNDERSHAFT: Indifferent to their own interests, which suits me exactly.

CUSINS: —with their thoughts on heavenly things—

UNDERSHAFT [*rising*]: And not on Trade Unionism nor Socialism. Excellent.

CUSINS [*revolted*]: You really are an infernal old rascal.

UNDERSHAFT [*indicating Peter Shirley, who has just come from the shelter and strolled dejectedly down the yard between them*]: And this is an honest man!

SHIRLEY: Yes; and what av I got by it? [*He passes on bitterly and sits on the form, in the corner of the penthouse*].

[*Snobby Price, beaming sanctimoniously, and Jenny Hill, with a tambourine full of coppers, come from the shelter and go to the drum, on which Jenny begins to count the money*].

UNDERSHAFT [*replying to Shirley*]: Oh, your employers must have got a good deal by it from first to last.

[*He sits on the table, with one foot on the side form. Cusins, overwhelmed, sits down on the same form nearer the shelter. Barbara comes from the shelter to the middle of the yard. She is excited and a little over-wrought*].

BARBARA: Weve just had a splendid experience meeting at the other gate in Cripp's Lane. Ive

hardly ever seen them so much moved as they were by your confession, Mr Price.

PRICE: I could almost be glad of my past wickedness if I could believe that it would elp to keep hathers stright.

BARBARA: So it will, Snobby. How much, Jenny?

JENNY: Four and tenpence, Major.

BARBARA: Oh Snobby, if you had given your poor mother just one more kick, we should have got the whole five shillings!

PRICE: If she heard you say that, miss, she'd be sorry I didnt. But I'm glad. Oh what a joy it will be to her when she hears I'm saved!

UNDERSHAFT: Shall I contribute the odd twopence, Barbara? The millionaire's mite, eh? [*He takes a couple of pennies from his pocket*].

BARBARA: How did you make that twopence?

UNDERSHAFT: As usual. By selling cannons, torpedoes, submarines, and my new patent Grand Duke hand grenade.

BARBARA: Put it back in your pocket. You cant buy your salvation here for twopence: you must work it out.

UNDERSHAFT: Is twopence not enough? I can afford a little more, if you press me.

BARBARA: Two million millions would not be enough. There is bad blood on your hands; and nothing but good blood can cleanse them. Money is no use. Take it away. [*She turns to Cusins*]. Dolly: you must write another letter for me to the papers. [*He makes a wry face*].

Yes: I know you dont like it; but it must be done. The starvation this winter is beating us: everybody is unemployed. The General says we must close this shelter if we cant get more money. I force the collections at the meetings until I am ashamed: dont I, Snobby?

PRICE: It's a fair treat to see you work it, miss. The way you got them up for three-and-six to four-and-ten with that hymn, penny by penny and verse by verse, was a caution. Not a Cheap Jack on Mile End Waste could touch you at it.

BARBARA: Yes; but I wish we could do without it. I am getting at last to think more of the collection than of the people's souls. And what are those hatfuls of pence and halfpence? We want thousands! tens of thousands! hundreds of thousands! I want to convert people, not to be always begging for the Army in a way I'd die sooner than beg for myself.

UNDERSHAFT [*in profound irony*]: Genuine unselfishness is capable of anything, my dear.

BARBARA [*unsuspectingly, as she turns away to take the money from the drum and put it in a cash bag she carries*]: Yes, isnt it? [*Undershaft looks sardonically at Cusins*].

CUSINS [*aside to Undershaft*]: Mephistopheles! Machiavelli!

BARBARA [*tears coming into her eyes as she ties the bag and pockets it*]: How are we to feed them! I cant talk religion to a man with bodily hunger in his eyes. [*Almost breaking down*] It's frightful.

JENNY [*running to her*]: Major, dear—

BARBARA [*rebounding*]: No: dont comfort me. It will be all right. We shall get the money.

UNDERSHAFT: How?

JENNY: By praying for it, of course. Mrs Baines says she prayed for it last night; and she has never prayed for it in vain: never once. [*She goes to the gate and looks out into the street*].

BARBARA [*who has dried her eyes and regained her composure*]: By the way, dad, Mrs Baines has come to march with us to our big meeting this afternoon; and she is very anxious to meet you, for some reason or other. Perhaps she'll convert you.

UNDERSHAFT: I shall be delighted, my dear.

JENNY [*at the gate: excitedly*]: Major! Major! heres that man back again.

BARBARA: What man?

JENNY: The man that hit me. Oh, I hope he's coming back to join us.

[*Bill Walker, with frost on his jacket, comes through the gate, his hands deep in his pockets and his chin sunk between his shoulders, like a cleaned-out gambler. He halts between Barbara and the drum*].

BARBARA: Hullo, Bill! Back already!

BILL [*nagging at her*]: Bin talkin ever sence, ev you?

BARBARA: Pretty nearly. Well, has Todger paid you out for poor Jenny's jaw?

BILL: Nao e aint.

BARBARA: I thought your jacket looked a bit snowy.

BILL: Sao it is snaowy. You want to knaow where the snaow cam from, downt you?

BARBARA: Yes.

BILL: Well, it cam from orf the grahnd in Pawkinses Corner in Kennintahn. It got rabbed orf be maw shaoulders: see?

BARBARA: Pity you didnt rub some off with your knees, Bill! That would have done you a lot of good.

BILL [*with sour mirthless humor*]: Aw was sivin anather menn's knees at the tawm. E was kneelin on moy ed, e was.

JENNY: Who was kneeling on your head?

BILL: Todger was. E was pryin for me: pryin camfortable wiv me as a cawpet. Sow was Mog. Sao was the aol bloomin meetin. Mog she sez "Ow Lawd brike is stabborn sperrit; bat downt urt is dear art." Thet was wot she said. "Downt urt is dear art"! An er blowk—thirteen stun four!—kneelin wiv all is wight on me. Fanny, aint it?

JENNY: Oh no. We're so sorry, Mr Walker.

BARBARA [*enjoying it frankly*]: Nonsense! of course it's funny. Served you right, Bill! You must have done something to him first.

BILL [*doggedly*]: Aw did wot Aw said Aw'd do. Aw spit in is eye. E looks ap at the skoy and sez, "Ow that Aw should be fahnd worthy to be spit upon for the gospel's sike!" e sez; an Mog sez "Glaory Allelloolier!"; an then e called me Braddher, an dahned me as if Aw was a kid and e was me mather worshin me a Setterda nawt. Aw ednt jast

nao shaow wiv im at all. Arf the street pryed; an the tather arf larfed fit to split theirselves. [*To Barbara*] There! are you settisfawd nah?

BARBARA [*her eyes dancing*]: Wish I'd been there, Bill.

BILL: Yus: youd a got in a hextra bit o talk on me, wouldnt you?

JENNY: I'm so sorry, Mr. Walker.

BILL [*fiercely*]: Downt you gow being sorry for me: youve no call. Listen eah. Aw browk your jawr.

JENNY: No, it didnt hurt me: indeed it didn't, except for a moment. It was only that I was frightened.

BILL: Aw downt want to be forgive be you, or be ennybody. Wot Aw did Aw'll py for. Aw trawd to gat me aown jawr browk to settisfaw you—

JENNY [*distressed*]: Oh no—

BILL [*impatiently*]: Tell y' Aw did: cawnt you listen to wots bein taold you? All Aw got be it was bein mide a sawt of in the pablic street for me pines. Well, if Aw cawnt settisfaw you one wy, Aw ken anather. Listen eah! Aw ed two quid sived agen the frost; an Awve a pahnd of it left. A mite o mawn last week ed words with the judy e's gowing to merry. E give er wot-for; an e's bin fawnd fifteen bob. E ed a rawt to itt er cause they was gowin to be merrid; but Aw ednt nao rawt to itt you; sao put anather fawv bob on an call it a pahnd's worth. [*He produces a sovereign*]. Eahs the manney. Tike it; and lets ev no more o your forgivin an prying and your Mijor jawrin me. Let wot Aw dan be dan an pide for; and let there be a end of it.

JENNY: Oh, I couldnt take it, Mr Walker. But if you would give a shilling or two to poor Rummy Mitchens! you really did hurt her; and she's old.

BILL [*contemptuously*]: Not lawkly. Aw'd give her anather as soon as look at er. Let her ev the lawr o me as she threatened! *She* aint forgiven me: not mach. Wot Aw dan to er is not on me mawnd—wot she [*indicating Barbara*] mawt call on me conscience—no more than stickin a pig. It's this Christian gime o yours that Aw wownt ev plyed agen me: this bloomin forgivin an neggin an jawrin that mikes a menn thet sore that iz lawf's a burdn to im. Aw wownt ev it, Aw tell you; sao tike your manney and stop thraowin your silly beshed fice hap agen me.

JENNY: Major: may I take a little bit of it for the Army?

BARBARA: No: the Army is not to be bought. We want your soul, Bill; and we'll take nothing less.

BILL [*bitterly*]: Aw knaow. Me an maw few shillins is not good enaff for you. Youre a earl's grendorter, you are. Nathink less than a andered pahnd for you.

UNDERSHAFT: Come, Barbara! you could do a great deal of good with a hundred pounds. If you will set this gentleman's mind at ease by taking his pounds, I will give the other ninety-nine.

[*Bill, dazed by such opulence, instinctively touches his cap*].

BARBARA: Oh, youre too extravagant, papa. Bill offers twenty pieces of silver. All you need offer is the other ten. That will make the standard price to buy anybody who's for sale. I'm not; and the Army's not. [*To Bill*] Youll never have another quiet moment, Bill, until you come round to us. You cant stand out against your salvation.

BILL [*sullenly*]: Aw cawnt stend aht agen music awl wrastlers and awtful tangued women. Awve offered to py. Aw can do no more. Tike it or leave it. There it is. [*He throws the sovereign on the drum, and sits down on the horse-trough. The coin fascinates Snobby Price, who takes an early opportunity of dropping his cap on it*].

[*Mrs Baines comes from the shelter. She is dressed as a Salvation Army Commissioner. She is an earnest looking woman of about 40, with a caressing, urgent voice, and an appealing manner*].

BARBARA: This is my father, Mrs Baines. [*Undershaft comes from the table, taking his hat off with marked civility*]. Try what you can do with him. He wont listen to me, because he remembers what a fool I was when I was a baby. [*She leaves them together and chats with Jenny*].

MRS BAINES: Have you been shewn over the shelter, Mr Undershaft? You know the work we're doing, of course.

UNDERSHAFT [*very civilly*]: The whole nation knows it, Mrs Baines.

MRS BAINES: No, sir: the whole nation does not know it, or we should not be crippled as we are for want of money to carry our work through the length and breadth of the land. Let me tell you that there would have been rioting this winter in London but for us.

UNDERSHAFT: You really think so?

MRS BAINES: I know it. I remember 1886, when you rich gentlemen hardened your hearts against the cry of the poor. They broke the windows of your clubs in Pall Mall.

UNDERSHAFT [*gleaming with approval of their method*]: And the Mansion House Fund went up next day from thirty thousand pounds to seventy-nine thousand! I remember quite well.

MRS BAINES: Well, wont you help me to get at the people? They wont break windows then. Come here, Price. Let me shew you to this gentleman [*Price comes to be inspected*]. Do you remember the window breaking?

PRICE: My ole father thought it was the revolution, maam.

MRS BAINES: Would you break windows now?

PRICE: Oh no, maam. The windows of eaven av been opened to me. I know now that the rich man is a sinner like myself.

RUMMY [*appearing above at the loft door*]: Snobby Price!

SNOBBY: Wot is it?

RUMMY: Your mother's askin for you at the other gate in Cripps's Lane. She's heard about your confession [*Price turns pale*].

MRS BAINES: Go, Mr Price; and pray with her.

JENNY: You can go through the shelter, Snobby.

PRICE [*to Mrs Baines*]: I couldnt face her now, maam, with all the weight of my sins fresh on me. Tell her she'll find her son at ome, waitin for her in prayer. [*He skulks off through the gate, incidentally stealing the sovereign on his way out by picking up his cap from the drum*].

MRS BAINES [*with swimming eyes*]: You see how we take the anger and the bitterness against you out of their hearts, Mr Undershaft.

UNDERSHAFT: It is certainly most convenient and gratifying to all large employers of labor, Mrs Baines.

MRS BAINES: Barbara: Jenny: I have good news: most wonderful news. [*Jenny runs to her*]. My prayers have been answered. I told you they would, Jenny, didnt I?

JENNY: Yes, yes.

BARBARA [*moving nearer to the drum*]: Have we got money enough to keep the shelter open?

MRS BAINES: I hope we shall have enough to keep all the shelters open. Lord Saxmundham has promised us five thousand pounds—

BARBARA: Hooray!

JENNY: Glory!

MRS BAINES: —if—

BARBARA: "If!" If what?

MRS BAINES: —if five other gentlemen will give a thousand each to make it up to ten thousand.

BARBARA: Who is Lord Saxmundham? I never heard of him.

UNDERSHAFT [*who has pricked up*

his ears at the peer's name, and is now watching Barbara curiously]: A new creation, my dear. You have heard of Sir Horace Bodger?

BARBARA: Bodger! Do you mean the distiller? Bodger's whisky!

UNDERSHAFT: That is the man. He is one of the greatest of our public benefactors. He restored the cathedral at Hakington. They made him a baronet for that. He gave half a million to the funds of his party: they made him a baron for that.

SHIRLEY: What will they give him for the five thousand?

UNDERSHAFT: There is nothing left to give him. So the five thousand, I should think, is to save his soul.

MRS BAINES: Heaven grant it may! Oh Mr Undershaft, you have some very rich friends. Cant you help us towards the other five thousand? We are going to hold a great meeting this afternoon at the Assembly Hall in the Mile End Road. If I could only announce that one gentleman had come forward to support Lord Saxmundham, others would follow. Dont you know somebody? couldnt you? wouldnt you? [*her eyes fill with tears*] oh, think of those poor people, Mr Undershaft: think of how much it means to them, and how little to a great man like you.

UNDERSHAFT [*sardonically gallant*]: Mrs Baines: you are irresistible. I cant disappoint you; and I cant deny myself the satisfaction of making Bodger pay up. You shall have your five thousand pounds.

MRS BAINES: Thank God!

UNDERSHAFT: You dont thank me?

MRS BAINES: Oh sir, dont try to be cynical: dont be ashamed of being a good man. The Lord will bless you abundantly; and our prayers will be like a strong fortification round you all the days of your life. [*With a touch of caution*] You will let me have the cheque to shew at the meeting, wont you? Jenny: go in and fetch a pen and ink. [*Jenny runs to the shelter door*].

UNDERSHAFT: Do not disturb Miss Hill: I have a fountain pen [*Jenny halts. He sits at the table and writes the cheque. Cusins rises to make room for him. They all watch him silently*].

BILL [*cynically, aside to Barbara, his voice and accent horribly debased*]: Wot prawce selvytion nah?

BARBARA: Stop. [*Undershaft stops writing: they all turn to her in surprise*]. Mrs Baines: are you really going to take this money?

MRS BAINES [*astonished*]: Why not, dear?

BARBARA: Why not! Do you know what my father is? Have you forgotten that Lord Saxmundham is Bodger the whisky man? Do you remember how we implored the County Council to stop him from writing Bodger's Whisky in letters of fire against the sky; so that the poor drink-ruined creatures on the Embankment could not wake up from their snatches of sleep without being reminded of their deadly thirst by that wicked sky sign? Do you know that the worst thing I have had to fight here is not the devil, but Bodger, Bodger, Bodger, with his whisky, his distilleries, and his tied houses? Are you going to make our shelter another tied house for him, and ask me to keep it?

BILL: Rotten dranken whisky it is too.

MRS BAINES: Dear Barbara: Lord Saxmundham has a soul to be saved like any of us. If heaven has found the way to make a good use of his money, are we to set ourselves up against the answer to our prayers?

BARBARA: I know he has a soul to be saved. Let him come down here; and I'll do my best to help him to his salvation. But he wants to send his cheque down to buy us, and go on being as wicked as ever.

UNDERSHAFT [*with a reasonableness which Cusins alone perceives to be ironical*]: My dear Barbara: alcohol is a very necessary article. It heals the sick—

BARBARA: It does nothing of the sort.

UNDERSHAFT: Well, it assists the doctor: that is perhaps a less questionable way of putting it. It makes life bearable to millions of people who could not endure their existence if they were quite sober. It enables Parliament to do things at eleven at night that no sane person would do at eleven in the morning. Is it Bodger's fault that this inestimable gift is deplorably abused by less than one per cent of the poor? [*He turns again to the table; signs the cheque; and crosses it*].

MRS BAINES: Barbara: will there be less drinking or more if all those poor souls we are saving come tomorrow and find the doors of our shelters shut in their faces? Lord Saxmundham gives us the money to stop drinking—to take his own business from him.

CUSINS [*impishly*]: Pure self-sacrifice on Bodger's part, clearly! Bless dear Bodger! [*Barbara almost breaks down as Adolphus, too, fails her*].

UNDERSHAFT [*tearing out the cheque and pocketing the book as he rises and goes past Cusins to Mrs Baines*]: I also, Mrs Baines, may claim a little disinterestedness. Think of my business! think of the widows and orphans! the men and lads torn to pieces with shrapnel and poisoned with lyddite! [*Mrs Baines shrinks; but he goes on remorselessly*] the oceans of blood, not one drop of which is shed in a really just cause! the ravaged crops! the peaceful peasants forced, women and men, to till their fields under the fire of opposing armies on pain of starvation! the bad blood of the fierce little cowards at home who egg on others to fight for the gratification of their national vanity! All this makes money for me: I am never richer, never busier than when the papers are full of it. Well, it is your work to preach peace on earth and good will to men. [*Mrs Baines's face lights up again*]. Every convert you make is a vote against war. [*Her lips move in prayer*]. Yet I give you this money to help you to hasten my own commercial ruin. [*He gives her the cheque*].

CUSINS [*mounting the form in an ecstasy of mischief*]: The millennium will be inaugurated by the unselfishness of Undershaft and Bodger. Oh be joyful! [*He takes the drumsticks from his pocket and flourishes them*].

MRS BAINES [*taking the cheque*]: The longer I live the more proof I see that there is an Infinite Goodness that turns everything to the work of salvation sooner or later. Who would have thought that any good could have come out of war and drink? And yet their profits are brought today to the feet of salvation to do its blessed work. [*She is affected to tears*].

JENNY [*running to Mrs Baines and throwing her arms round her*]: Oh dear! how blessed, how glorious it all is!

CUSINS [*in a convulsion of irony*]: Let us seize this unspeakable moment. Let us march to the great meeting at once. Excuse me just an instant. [*He rushes into the shelter. Jenny takes her tambourine from the drum head*].

MRS BAINES: Mr Undershaft: have you ever seen a thousand people fall on their knees with one impulse and pray? Come with us to the meeting. Barbara shall tell them that the Army is saved, and saved through you.

CUSINS [*returning impetuously from the shelter with a flag and a trombone, and coming between Mrs Baines and Undershaft*]: You shall carry the flag down the first street, Mrs Baines [*he gives her the flag*]. Mr Under-

shaft is a gifted trombonist: he shall intone an Olympian diapason to the West Ham Salvation March. [*Aside to Undershaft, as he forces the trombone on him*] Blow, Machiavelli, blow.

UNDERSHAFT [*aside to him, as he takes the trombone*]: The trumpet in Zion! [*Cusins rushes to the drum, which he takes up and puts on. Undershaft continues, aloud*] I will do my best. I could vamp a bass if I knew the tune.

CUSINS: It is a wedding chorus from one of Donizetti's operas; but we have converted it. We convert everything to good here, including Bodger. You remember the chorus. "For thee immense rejoicing—immenso giubilo—immenso giubilo." [*With drum obbligato*] Rum tum ti tum tum, tum tum ti ta—

BARBARA: Dolly: you are breaking my heart.

CUSINS: What is a broken heart more or less here? Dionysos Undershaft has descended. I am possessed.

MRS BAINES: Come, Barbara: I must have my dear Major to carry the flag with me.

JENNY: Yes, yes, Major darling.

[*Cusins snatches the tambourine out of Jenny's hand and mutely offers it to Barbara*].

BARBARA [*coming forward a little as she puts the offer behind her with a shudder, whilst Cusins recklessly tosses the tambourine back to Jenny and goes to the gate*]: I cant come.

JENNY: Not come!

MRS BAINES [*with tears in her*

eyes]: Barbara: do you think I am wrong to take the money?

BARBARA [*impulsively going to her and kissing her*]: No, no: God help you, dear, you must: you are saving the Army. Go; and may you have a great meeting!

JENNY: But arnt you coming?

BARBARA: No. [*She begins taking off the silver S brooch from her collar*].

MRS BAINES: Barbara: what are you doing?

JENNY: Why are you taking your badge off? You cant be going to leave us, Major.

BARBARA [*quietly*]: Father: come here.

UNDERSHAFT [*coming to her*]: My dear! [*Seeing that she is going to pin the badge on his collar, he retreats to the penthouse in some alarm*].

BARBARA [*following him*]: Dont be frightened. [*She pins the badge on and steps back towards the table, shewing him to the others*] There! It's not much for £5000, is it?

MRS BAINES: Barbara: if you wont come and pray *with* us, promise me you will pray *for* us.

BARBARA: I cant pray now. Perhaps I shall never pray again.

MRS BAINES: Barbara!

JENNY: Major!

BARBARA [*almost delirious*]: I cant bear any more. Quick march!

CUSINS [*calling to the procession in the street outside*]: Off we go. Play up, there! *Immenso giubilo.* [*He gives the time with his drum; and the band strikes up the march, which rapidly becomes more distant as the procession moves briskly away*].

MRS BAINES: I must go, dear. Youre overworked: you will be all right tomorrow. We'll never lose you. Now Jenny: step out with the old flag. Blood and Fire! [*She marches out through the gate with her flag*].

JENNY: Glory Hallelujah! [*flourishing her tambourine and marching*].

UNDERSHAFT [*to Cusins, as he marches out past him easing the slide of his trombone*]: "My ducats and my daughter"!

CUSINS [*following him out*]: Money and gunpowder!

BARBARA: Drunkenness and Murder! My God: why hast thou forsaken me?

[*She sinks on the form with her face buried in her hands. The march passes away into silence. Bill Walker steals across to her*].

BILL [*taunting*]: Wot prawce selvytion nah?

SHIRLEY: Dont you hit her when she's down.

BILL: She itt me wen aw wiz dahn. Waw shouldnt Aw git a bit o me aown beck?

BARBARA [*raising her head*]: I didnt take *your* money, Bill. [*She crosses the yard to the gate and turns her back on the two men to hide her face from them*].

BILL [*sneering after her*]: Naow, it warnt enaff for you. [*Turning to the drum, he misses the money*] Ellow! If you aint took it sammun else ez. Weres it gorn? Bly me if Jenny Ill didnt tike it arter all!

RUMMY [*screaming at him from the loft*]: You lie, you dirty blackguard! Snobby Price pinched it off the drum when he took up his cap. I was up here all the time an see im do it.

BILL: Wot! Stowl maw manney! Waw didnt you call thief on him, you silly aold macker you?

RUMMY: To serve you aht for ittin me acrost the fice. It's cost y'pahnd, that az. [*Raising a paen of squalid triumph*] I done you. I'm even with you. Uve ad it aht *oy*— [*Bill snatches up Shirley's mug and hurls it at her. She slams the loft door and vanishes. The mug smashes against the door and falls in fragments*].

BILL [*beginning to chuckle*]: Tell us, aol menn, wot o'clock this mawnin was it wen im as they call Snobby Prawce was sived?

BARBARA [*turning to him more composedly, and with unspoiled sweetness*]: About half past twelve, Bill. And he pinched your pound at a quarter to two. *I* know. Well, you cant afford to lose it. I'll send it to you.

BILL [*his voice and accent suddenly improving*]: Not if Aw wiz to stawve for it. Aw aint to be bought.

SHIRLEY: Aint you? Youd sell yourself to the devil for a pint o beer; only there aint no devil to make the offer.

BILL [*unashamed*]: Sao Aw would, mite, and often ev, cheerful. But she cawnt baw me. [*Approaching Barbara*] You wanted maw saoul, did you? Well, you aint got it.

BARBARA: I nearly got it, Bill. But weve sold it back to you for ten thousand pounds.

SHIRLEY: And dear at the money!

BARBARA: No, Peter: it was worth more than money.

BILL [*salvationproof*]: It's nao good: you cawnt get rahnd me nah. Aw downt blieve in it; and Awve seen tody that Aw was rawt. [*Going*] Sao long, aol soupkitchener! Ta, ta, Mijor Earl's Grendorter! [*Turning at the gate*] Wot prawce selvytion nah? Snobby Prawce! Ha! ha!

BARBARA [*offering her hand*]: Goodbye, Bill.

BILL [*taken aback, half plucks his cap off; then shoves it on again defiantly*]: Git aht. [*Barbara drops her hand, discouraged. He has a twinge of remorse*]. But thets aw rawt, you knaow. Nathink pasnl. Naow mellice. Sao long, Judy. [*He goes*].

BARBARA: No malice. So long, Bill.

SHIRLEY [*shaking his head*]: You make too much of him, miss, in your innocence.

BARBARA [*going to him*]: Peter: I'm like you now. Cleaned out, and lost my job.

SHIRLEY: Youve youth an hope. Thats two better than me.

BARBARA: I'll get you a job, Peter. Thats hope for you: the youth will have to be enough for me. [*She counts her money*]. I have just enough left for two teas at Lockharts, a Rowton doss for you, and my tram and bus home. [*He frowns and rises with offended pride. She takes his arm*]. Dont be proud, Peter: it's sharing between friends. And promise me youll talk to me and not let me cry. [*She draws him towards the gate*].

SHIRLEY: Well, I'm not accustomed to talk to the like of you—

BARBARA [*urgently*]: Yes, yes: you must talk to me. Tell me about Tom Paine's books and Brad-

laugh's lectures. Come along.

SHIRLEY: Ah, if you would only read Tom Paine in the proper spirit, miss! [*They go out through the gate together*].

ACT THREE

Next day after lunch Lady Britomart is writing in the library in Wilton Crescent. Sarah is reading in the armchair near the window. Barbara, in ordinary fashionable dress, pale and brooding, is on the settee. Charles Lomax enters. He starts on seeing Barbara fashionably attired and in low spirits.

LOMAX: Youve left off your uniform!

[*Barbara says nothing; but an expression of pain passes over her face*].

LADY BRITOMART [*warning him in low tones to be careful*]: Charles!

LOMAX [*much concerned, coming behind the settee and bending sympathetically over Barbara*]: I'm awfully sorry, Barbara. You know I helped you all I could with the concertina and so forth. [*Momentously*] Still, I have never shut my eyes to the fact that there is a certain amount of tosh about the Salvation Army. Now the claims of the Church of England—

LADY BRITOMART: Thats enough, Charles. Speak of something suited to your mental capacity.

LOMAX: But surely the Church of England is suited to all our capacities.

BARBARA [*pressing his hand*]:

Thank you for your sympathy, Cholly. Now go and spoon with Sarah.

LOMAX [*dragging a chair from the writing table and seating himself affectionately by Sarah's side*]: How is my ownest today?

SARAH: I wish you wouldnt tell Cholly to do things, Barbara. He always comes straight and does them. Cholly: we're going to the works this afternoon.

LOMAX: What works?

SARAH: The cannon works.

LOMAX: What? your governor's shop!

SARAH: Yes.

LOMAX: Oh I say!

[*Cusins enters in poor condition. He also starts visibly when he sees Barbara without her uniform*].

BARBARA: I expected you this morning, Dolly. Didnt you guess that?

CUSINS [*sitting down beside her*]:

I'm sorry. I have only just breakfasted.

SARAH: But weve just finished lunch.

BARBARA: Have you had one of your bad nights?

CUSINS: No: I had rather a good night: in fact, one of the most remarkable nights I have ever passed.

BARBARA: The meeting?

CUSINS: No: after the meeting.

LADY BRITOMART: You should have gone to bed after the meeting. What were you doing?

CUSINS: Drinking.

LADY BRITOMART: Adolphus!
SARAH: Dolly!
BARBARA: Dolly!
LOMAX: Oh I say!

LADY BRITOMART: What were you drinking, may I ask?

CUSINS: A most devilish kind of Spanish burgundy, warranted free from added alcohol: a Temperance burgundy in fact. Its richness in natural alcohol made any addition superfluous.

BARBARA: Are you joking, Dolly?

CUSINS [*patiently*]: No. I have been making a night of it with the nominal head of this household: that is all.

LADY BRITOMART: Andrew made you drunk!

CUSINS: No: he only provided the wine. I think it was Dionysos who made me drunk. [*To Barbara*] I told you I was possessed.

LADY BRITOMART: Youre not sober yet. Go home to bed at once.

CUSINS: I have never before ventured to reproach you, Lady Brit; but how could you marry the Prince of Darkness?

LADY BRITOMART: It was much more excusable to marry him than to get drunk with him. That is a new accomplishment of Andrew's, by the way. He usent to drink.

CUSINS: He doesnt now. He only sat there and completed the wreck of my moral basis, the rout of my convictions, the purchase of my soul. He cares for you, Barbara. That is what makes him so dangerous to me.

BARBARA: That has nothing to do with it, Dolly. There are larger loves and diviner dreams than the fireside ones. You know that, dont you?

CUSINS: Yes: that is our understanding. I know it. I hold to it. Unless he can win me on that holier ground he may amuse me for a while; but he can get no deeper hold, strong as he is.

BARBARA: Keep to that; and the end will be right. Now tell me what happened at the meeting?

CUSINS: It was an amazing meeting. Mrs Baines almost died of emotion. Jenny Hill simply gibbered with hysteria. The Prince of Darkness played his trombone like a madman: its brazen roarings were like the laughter of the damned. 117 conversions took place then and there. They prayed with the most touching sincerity and gratitude for Bodger, and for the anonymous donor of the £5000. Your father would not let his name be given.

LOMAX: That was rather fine of the old man, you know. Most chaps would have wanted the advertisement.

CUSINS: He said all the charitable institutions would be down on him like kites on a battlefield if he gave his name.

LADY BRITOMART: Thats Andrew all over. He never does a proper thing without giving an improper reason for it.

CUSINS: He convinced me that I have all my life been doing improper things for proper reasons.

LADY BRITOMART: Adolphus: now that Barbara has left the Salvation Army, you had better leave it too. I will not have you playing that drum in the streets.

CUSINS: Your orders are already obeyed, Lady Brit.

BARBARA: Dolly: were you ever really in earnest about it? Would you have joined if you had never seen me?

CUSINS [*disingenuously*]: Well—er—well, possibly, as a collector of religions—

LOMAX [*cunningly*]: Not as a drummer, though, you know. You are a very clearheaded brainy chap, Dolly; and it must have been apparent to you that there is a certain amount of tosh about—

LADY BRITOMART: Charles: if you must drivel, drivel like a grown-up man and not like a schoolboy.

LOMAX [*out of countenance*]: Well, drivel is drivel, dont you know, whatever a man's age.

LADY BRITOMART: In good society in England, Charles, men drivel at all ages by repeating silly formulas with an air of wisdom. Schoolboys make their own formulas out of slang, like you. When they reach your age, and

get political private secretaryships and things of that sort, they drop slang and get their formulas out of the Spectator or The Times. *You* had better confine yourself to The Times. You will find that there is a certain amount of tosh about The Times; but at least its language is reputable.

LOMAX [*overwhelmed*]: You are so awfully strong-minded, Lady Brit—

LADY BRITOMART: Rubbish! [*Morrison comes in*]. What is it?

MORRISON: If you please, my lady, Mr Undershaft has just drove up to the door.

LADY BRITOMART: Well, let him in. [*Morrison hesitates*]. Whats the matter with you?

MORRISON: Shall I announce him, my lady; or is he at home here, so to speak, my lady?

LADY BRITOMART: Announce him.

MORRISON: Thank you, my lady. You wont mind my asking, I hope. The occasion is in a manner of speaking new to me.

LADY BRITOMART: Quite right. Go and let him in.

MORRISON: Thank you, my lady. [*He withdraws*].

LADY BRITOMART: Children: go and get ready. [*Sarah and Barbara go upstairs for their out-of-door wraps*]. Charles: go and tell Stephen to come down here in five minutes: you will find him in the drawing room. [*Charles goes*]. Adolphus: tell them to send round the carriage in about fifteen minutes. [*Adolphus goes*].

MORRISON [*at the door*]: Mr Undershaft. [*Undershaft comes in. Morrison goes out*].

UNDERSHAFT: Alone! How fortunate!

LADY BRITOMART [*rising*]: Dont be sentimental, Andrew. Sit down. [*She sits on the settee: he sits beside her, on her left. She comes to the point before he has time to breathe*]. Sarah must have £800 a year until Charles Lomax comes into his property. Barbara will need more, and need it permanently, because Adolphus hasnt any property.

UNDERSHAFT [*resignedly*]: Yes, my dear: I will see to it. Anything else? for yourself, for instance?

LADY BRITOMART: I want to talk to you about Stephen.

UNDERSHAFT [*rather wearily*]: Dont, my dear. Stephen doesnt interest me.

LADY BRITOMART: He does interest me. He is our son.

UNDERSHAFT: Do you really think so? He has induced us to bring him into the world; but he chose his parents very incongruously, I think. I see nothing of myself in him, and less of you.

LADY BRITOMART: Andrew: Stephen is an excellent son, and a most steady, capable, highminded young man. You are simply trying to find an excuse for disinheriting him.

UNDERSHAFT: My dear Biddy: the Undershaft tradition disinherits him. It would be dishonest of me to leave the cannon foundry to my son.

LADY BRITOMART: It would be most unnatural and improper of you to leave it to anyone else, Andrew. Do you suppose this wicked and immoral tradition can be kept up for ever? Do you pretend that Stephen could not carry on the foundry just as well as all the other sons of the big business houses?

UNDERSHAFT: Yes: he could learn the office routine without understanding the business, like all the other sons; and the firm would go on by its own momentum until the real Undershaft—probably an Italian or a German—would invent a new method and cut him out.

LADY BRITOMART: There is nothing that any Italian or German could do that Stephen could not do. And Stephen at least has breeding.

UNDERSHAFT: The son of a foundling! Nonsense!

LADY BRITOMART: My son, Andrew! And even you may have good blood in your veins for all you know.

UNDERSHAFT: True. Probably I have. That is another argument in favour of a foundling.

LADY BRITOMART: Andrew: dont be aggravating. And dont be wicked. At present you are both.

UNDERSHAFT: This conversation is part of the Undershaft tradition, Biddy. Every Undershaft's wife has treated him to it ever since the house was founded. It is mere waste of breath. If the tradition be ever broken it will be for an abler man than Stephen.

LADY BRITOMART [*pouting*]: Then go away.

UNDERSHAFT [*deprecatory*]: Go away!

LADY BRITOMART: Yes: go away. If you will do nothing for Stephen, you are not wanted here. Go to your foundling, whoever he is; and look after *him*.

UNDERSHAFT: The fact is, Biddy—

LADY BRITOMART: Dont call me Biddy. I dont call you Andy.

UNDERSHAFT: I will not call my wife Britomart: it is not good sense. Seriously, my love, the Undershaft tradition has landed me in a difficulty. I am getting on in years; and my partner Lazarus has at last made a stand and insisted that the succession must be settled one way or the other; and of course he is quite right. You see, I havent found a fit successor yet.

LADY BRITOMART [*obstinately*]: There is Stephen.

UNDERSHAFT: Thats just it: all the foundlings I can find are exactly like Stephen.

LADY BRITOMART: Andrew!!

UNDERSHAFT: I want a man with no relations and no schooling: that is, a man who would be out of the running altogether if he were not a strong man. And I cant find him. Every blessed foundling nowadays is snapped up in his infancy by Barnardo homes, or School Board officers, or Boards of Guardians; and if he shews the least ability he is fastened on by schoolmasters; trained to win scholarships like a racehorse; crammed with second-hand ideas; drilled and disciplined in docility and what they call good taste; and lamed for life so that he is fit for nothing but teaching. If you want to keep the foundry in the family, you had better find an eligible foundling and marry him to Barbara.

LADY BRITOMART: Ah! Barbara!

You pet! You would sacrifice Stephen to Barbara.

UNDERSHAFT: Cheerfully. And you, my dear, would boil Barbara to make soup for Stephen.

LADY BRITOMART: Andrew: this is not a question of our likings or dislikings: it is a question of duty. It is your duty to make Stephen your successor.

UNDERSHAFT: Just as much as it is your duty to submit to your husband. Come, Biddy! these tricks of the governing class are of no use with me. I am one of the governing class myself; and it is waste of time giving tracts to a missionary. I have the power in this matter; and I am not to be humbugged into using it for your purposes.

LADY BRITOMART: Andrew: you can talk my head off; but you cant change wrong into right. And your tie is all on one side. Put it straight.

UNDERSHAFT [*disconcerted*]: It wont stay unless it's pinned— [*He fumbles at it with childish grimaces*].

[*Stephen comes in*].

STEPHEN [*at the door*]: I beg your pardon [*about to retire*].

LADY BRITOMART: No: come in, Stephen. [*Stephen comes forward to his mother's writing table*].

UNDERSHAFT [*not very cordially*]: Good afternoon.

STEPHEN [*coldly*]: Good afternoon.

UNDERSHAFT [*to Lady Britomart*]: He knows all about the tradition, I suppose?

LADY BRITOMART: Yes. [*To Stephen*] It is what I told you last night, Stephen.

UNDERSHAFT [*sulkily*]: I understand you want to come into the cannon business.

STEPHEN: *I* go into trade! Certainly not.

UNDERSHAFT [*opening his eyes, greatly eased in mind and manner*]: Oh! in that case—

LADY BRITOMART: Cannons are not trade, Stephen. They are enterprise.

STEPHEN: I have no intention of becoming a man of business in any sense. I have no capacity for business and no taste for it. I intend to devote myself to politics.

UNDERSHAFT [*rising*]: My dear boy: this is an immense relief to me. And I trust it may prove an equally good thing for the country. I was afraid you would consider yourself disparaged and slighted. [*He moves towards Stephen as if to shake hands with him*].

LADY BRITOMART [*rising and interposing*]: Stephen: I cannot allow you to throw away an enormous property like this.

STEPHEN [*stiffly*]: Mother: there must be an end of treating me as a child, if you please. [*Lady Britomart recoils, deeply wounded by his tone*]. Until last night I did not take your attitude seriously, because I did not think you meant it seriously. But I find now that you left me in the dark as to matters which you should have explained to me years ago. I am extremely hurt and offended. Any further discussion of my intentions had better take place with my father, as between one man and another.

LADY BRITOMART: Stephen! [*She sits down again, her eyes filling with tears*].

UNDERSHAFT [*with grave compassion*]: You see, my dear, it is only the big men who can be treated as children.

STEPHEN: I am sorry, mother, that you have forced me—

UNDERSHAFT [*stopping him*]: Yes, yes, yes, yes: thats all right, Stephen. She wont interfere with you any more: your independence is achieved: you have won your latchkey. Dont rub it in; and above all, dont apologize. [*He resumes his seat*]. Now what about your future, as between one man and another—I beg your pardon, Biddy: as between two men and a woman.

LADY BRITOMART [*who has pulled herself together strongly*]: I quite understand, Stephen. By all means go your own way if you feel strong enough. [*Stephen sits down magisterially in the chair at the writing table with an air of affirming his majority*].

UNDERSHAFT: It is settled that you do not ask for the succession to the cannon business.

STEPHEN: I hope it is settled that I repudiate the cannon business.

UNDERSHAFT: Come, come! dont be so devilishly sulky: it's boyish. Freedom should be generous. Besides, I owe you a fair start in life in exchange for disinheriting you. You cant become prime minister all at once. Havnt you a turn for something? What about literature, art, and so forth?

STEPHEN: I have nothing of the artist about me, either in faculty or character, thank Heaven!

UNDERSHAFT: A philosopher, perhaps? Eh?

STEPHEN: I make no such ridiculous pretension.

UNDERSHAFT: Just so. Well, there is the army, the navy, the Church, the Bar. The Bar requires some ability. What about the Bar?

STEPHEN: I have not studied law. And I am afraid I have not the necessary push—I believe that is the name barristers give to their vulgarity—for success in pleading.

UNDERSHAFT: Rather a difficult case, Stephen. Hardly anything left but the stage, is there? [*Stephen makes an impatient movement*]. Well, come! is there *anything* you know or care for?

STEPHEN [*rising and looking at him steadily*]: I know the difference between right and wrong.

UNDERSHAFT [*hugely tickled*]: You dont say so! What! no capacity for business, no knowledge of law, no sympathy with art, no pretension to philosophy; only a simple knowledge of the secret that has puzzled all the philosophers, baffled all the lawyers, muddled all the men of business, and ruined most of the artists: the secret of right and wrong. Why, man, youre a genius, a master of masters, a god! At twenty-four, too!

STEPHEN [*keeping his temper with difficulty*]: You are pleased to be facetious. I pretend to nothing more than any honorable English gentleman claims as his birthright. [*He sits down angrily*].

UNDERSHAFT: Oh, thats everybody's birthright. Look at poor little Jenny Hill, the Salvation lassie! she would think you were laughing at her if you asked her to stand up in the street and teach grammar or geography or mathematics or even drawing room dancing; but it never occurs to her to doubt that she can teach morals and religion. You are all alike, you respectable people. You cant tell me the bursting strain of a ten-inch gun, which is a very simple matter; but you all think you can tell me the bursting strain of a man under temptation. You darent handle high explosives; but youre all ready to handle honesty and truth and justice and the whole duty of man, and kill one another at that game. What a country! What a world!

LADY BRITOMART [*uneasily*]: What do you think he had better do, Andrew?

UNDERSHAFT: Oh, just what he wants to do. He knows nothing and he thinks he knows everything. That points clearly to a political career. Get him a private secretaryship to someone who can get him an Under Secretaryship; and then leave him alone. He will find his natural and proper place in the end on the Treasury Bench.

STEPHEN [*springing up again*]: I am sorry, sir, that you force me to forget the respect due to you as my father. I am an Englishman and I will not hear the Government of my country insulted. [*He thrusts his hands in his pockets, and walks angrily across to the window*].

UNDERSHAFT [*with a touch of bru-*

tality]: The government of your country! *I* am the government of your country: I, and Lazarus. Do you suppose that you and half a dozen amateurs like you, sitting in a row in that foolish gabble shop, can govern Undershaft and Lazarus? No, my friend: you will do what pays *us*. You will make war when it suits us, and keep peace when it doesnt. You will find out that trade requires certain measures when we have decided on those measures. When I want anything to keep my dividends up, you will discover that my want is a national need. When other people want something to keep my dividends down, you will call out the police and military. And in return you shall have the support and applause of my newspapers, and the delight of imagining that you are a great statesman. Government of your country! Be off with you, my boy, and play with your caucuses and leading articles and historic parties and great leaders and burning questions and the rest of your toys. *I* am going back to my counting-house to pay the piper and call the tune.

STEPHEN [*actually smiling, and putting his hand on his father's shoulder with indulgent patronage*]: Really, my dear father, it is impossible to be angry with you. You dont know how absurd all this sounds to *me*. You are very properly proud of having been industrious enough to make money; and it is greatly to your credit that you have made so much of it. But it has kept you in circles where you are valued for your money and deferred to for it, instead of in the doubtless very old-fashioned and behind-the-times public school and university where I formed my habits of mind. It is natural for you to think that money governs England; but you must allow me to think I know better.

UNDERSHAFT: And what *does* govern England, pray?

STEPHEN: Character, father, character.

UNDERSHAFT: Whose character? Yours or mine?

STEPHEN: Neither yours nor mine, father, but the best elements in the English national character.

UNDERSHAFT: Stephen: Ive found your profession for you. Youre a born journalist. I'll start you with a high-toned weekly review. There!

[*Before Stephen can reply Sarah, Barbara, Lomax, and Cusins come in ready for walking. Barbara crosses the room to the window and looks out. Cusins drifts amiably to the armchair. Lomax remains near the door, whilst Sarah comes to her mother.*

Stephen goes to the smaller writing table and busies himself with his letters].

SARAH: Go and get ready, mamma: the carriage is waiting. [*Lady Britomart leaves the room*].

UNDERSHAFT [*to Sarah*]: Good day, my dear. Good afternoon, Mr Lomax.

LOMAX [*vaguely*]: Ahdedoo.

UNDERSHAFT [*to Cusins*]: Quite

well after last night, Euripides, eh?

CUSINS: As well as can be expected.

UNDERSHAFT: Thats right. [*To Barbara*] So you are coming to see my death and devastation factory, Barbara?

BARBARA [*at the window*]: You came yesterday to see my salvation factory. I promised you a return visit.

LOMAX [*coming forward between Sarah and Undershaft*]: Youll find it awfully interesting. Ive been through the Woolwich Arsenal; and it gives you a ripping feeling of security, you know, to think of the lot of beggars we could kill if it came to fighting. [*To Undershaft, with sudden solemnity*] Still, it must be rather an awful reflection for you, from the religious point of view as it were. Youre getting on, you know, and all that.

SARAH: You dont mind Cholly's imbecility, papa, do you?

LOMAX [*much taken aback*]: Oh I say!

UNDERSHAFT: Mr Lomax looks at the matter in a very proper spirit, my dear.

LOMAX: Just so. Thats all I meant, I assure you.

SARAH: Are you coming, Stephen?

STEPHEN: Well, I am rather busy —er— [*Magnanimously*] Oh well, yes: I'll come. That is, if there is room for me.

UNDERSHAFT: I can take two with me in a little motor I am experimenting with for field use. You wont mind its being rather unfashionable. It's not painted yet; but it's bullet proof.

LOMAX [*appalled at the prospect of confronting Wilton Crescent in an unpainted motor*]: Oh I say!

SARAH: The carriage for me, thank you. Barbara doesnt mind what she's seen in.

LOMAX: I say, Dolly, old chap: do you really mind the car being a guy? Because of course if you do I'll go in it. Still—

CUSINS: I prefer it.

LOMAX: Thanks awfully, old man. Come, my ownest. [*He hurries out to secure his seat in the carriage. Sarah follows him*].

CUSINS [*moodily walking across to Lady Britomart's writing table*]: Why are we two coming to this Works Department of Hell? that is what I ask myself.

BARBARA: I have always thought of it as a sort of pit where lost creatures with blackened faces stirred up smoky fires and were driven and tormented by my father. Is it like that, dad?

UNDERSHAFT [*scandalized*]: My dear! It is a spotlessly clean and beautiful hillside town.

CUSINS: With a Methodist chapel? Oh *do* say theres a Methodist chapel.

UNDERSHAFT: There are two: a Primitive one and a sophisticated one. There is even an Ethical Society; but it is not much patronized, as my men are all strongly religious. In the High Explosives Sheds they object to the presence of Agnostics as unsafe.

CUSINS: And yet they dont object to you!

BARBARA: Do they obey all your orders?

UNDERSHAFT: I never give them

any orders. When I speak to one of them it is "Well, Jones, is the baby doing well? and has Mrs Jones made a good recovery?" "Nicely, thank you, sir." And thats all.

CUSINS: But Jones has to be kept in order. How do you maintain discipline among your men?

UNDERSHAFT: I dont. They do. You see, the one thing Jones wont stand is any rebellion from the man under him, or any assertion of social equality between the wife of the man with 4 shillings a week less than himself, and Mrs Jones! Of course they all rebel against me, theoretically. Practically, every man of 'them keeps the man just below him in his place. I never meddle with them. I never bully them. I dont even bully Lazarus. I say that certain things are to be done; but I dont order anybody to do them. I dont say, mind you, that there is no ordering about and snubbing and even bullying. The men snub the boys and order them about; the carmen snub the sweepers; the artisans snub the unskilled laborers; the foremen drive and bully both the laborers and artisans; the assistant engineers find fault with the foremen; the chief engineers drop on the assistants; the departmental managers worry the chiefs; and the clerks have tall hats and hymnbooks and keep up the social tone by refusing to associate on equal terms with anybody. The result is a colossal profit, which comes to me.

CUSINS [*revolted*]: You really are

a—well, what I was saying yesterday.

BARBARA: What was he saying yesterday?

UNDERSHAFT: Never mind, my dear. He thinks I have made you unhappy. Have I?

BARBARA: Do you think I can be happy in this vulgar silly dress? I! who have worn the uniform. Do you understand what you have done to me? Yesterday I had a man's soul in my hand. I set him in the way of life with his face to salvation. But when we took your money he turned back to drunkenness and derision. [*With intense conviction*] I will never forgive you that. If I had a child, and you destroyed its body with your explosives—if you murdered Dolly with your horrible guns— I could forgive you if my forgiveness would open the gates of heaven to you. But to take a human soul from me, and turn it into the soul of a wolf! that is worse than any murder.

UNDERSHAFT: Does my daughter despair so easily? Can you strike a man to the heart and leave no mark on him?

BARBARA [*her face lighting up*]: Oh, you are right: he can never be lost now: where was my faith?

CUSINS: Oh, clever clever devil!

BARBARA: You may be a devil; but God speaks through you sometimes. [*She takes her father's hands and kisses them*]. You have given me back my happiness: I feel it deep down now, though my spirit is troubled.

UNDERSHAFT: You have learnt something. That always feels

at first as if you had lost something.

BARBARA: Well, take me to the factory of death; and let me learn something more. There must be some truth or other behind all this frightful irony. Come, Dolly. [*She goes out*].

CUSINS: My guardian angel! [*To Undershaft*] Avaunt! [*He follows Barbara*].

STEPHEN [*quietly, at the writing table*]: You must not mind Cusins, father. He is a very amiable good fellow; but he is a Greek scholar and naturally a little eccentric.

UNDERSHAFT: Ah, quite so. Thank you, Stephen. Thank you. [*He goes out*].

[*Stephen smiles patronizingly; buttons his coat responsibly; and crosses the room to the door. Lady Britomart, dressed for out-of-doors, opens it before he reaches it. She looks round for the others; looks at Stephen; and turns to go without a word*].

STEPHEN [*embarrassed*]: Mother—

LADY BRITOMART: Dont be apologetic, Stephen. And dont forget that you have outgrown your mother. [*She goes out*].

Perivale St Andrews lies between two Middlesex hills, half climbing the northern one. It is an almost smokeless town of white walls, roofs of narrow green slates or red tiles, tall trees, domes, campaniles, and slender chimney shafts, beautifully situated and beautiful in itself. The best view of it is obtained from the crest of a slope about half a mile to the east, where the high explosives are dealt with. The foundry lies hidden in the depths between, the tops of its chimneys sprouting like huge skittles into the middle distance. Across the crest runs an emplacement of concrete, with a firestep, and a parapet which suggests a fortification, because there is a huge cannon of the obsolete Woolwich Infant pattern peering across it at the town. The cannon is mounted on an experimental gun carriage: possibly the original model of the Undershaft disappearing rampart gun alluded to by Stephen. The firestep, being a convenient place to sit, is furnished here and there with straw disc cushions; and at one place there is the additional luxury of a fur rug.

Barbara is standing on the firestep, looking over the parapet towards the town. On her right is the cannon; on her left the end of a shed raised on piles, with a ladder of three or four steps up to the door, which opens outwards and has a little wooden landing at the threshold, with a fire bucket in the corner of the landing. Several dummy soldiers more or less mutilated, with straw protruding from their gashes, have been shoved out of the way under the landing. A few others are nearly upright against the shed; and one has fallen forward and lies, like a grotesque corpse, on the emplacement. The parapet stops short of the shed, leaving a gap which is the beginning of the path down the hill through the foundry to the town. The rug is on the firestep near this gap. Down on the emplacement behind the cannon is a trolley carrying a huge conical bombshell with a red band painted on it. Further to the right is the door of an office, which, like the sheds, is of the lightest possible construction.

[*Cusins arrives by the path from the town*].

BARBARA: Well?

CUSINS: Not a ray of hope. Everything perfect! wonderful! real! It only needs a cathedral to be a heavenly city instead of a hellish one.

BARBARA: Have you found out whether they have done anything for old Peter Shirley?

CUSINS: They have found him a job as gatekeeper and timekeeper. He's frightfully miserable. He calls the timekeeping brainwork, and says he isnt used to it; and his gate lodge is so splendid that he's ashamed to use the rooms, and skulks in the scullery.

BARBARA: Poor Peter!

[*Stephen arrives from the town. He carries a fieldglass*].

STEPHEN [*enthusiastically*]: Have you two seen the place? Why did you leave us?

CUSINS: I wanted to see everything I was not intended to see; and Barbara wanted to make the men talk.

STEPHEN: Have you found anything discreditable?

CUSINS: No. They call him Dandy Andy and are proud of his being a cunning old rascal; but it's all horribly, frightfully, immorally, unanswerably perfect.

[*Sarah arrives.*]

SARAH: Heavens! what a place! [*She crosses to the trolley*]. Did

you see the nursing home!? [*She sits down on the shell*].

STEPHEN: Did you see the libraries and schools!?

SARAH: Did you see the ball room and the banqueting chamber in the Town Hall!?

STEPHEN: Have you gone into the insurance fund, the pension fund, the building society, the various applications of co-operation!?

[*Undershaft comes from the office, with a sheaf of telegrams in his hand*].

UNDERSHAFT: Well, have you seen everything? I'm sorry I was called away. [*Indicating the telegrams*] Good news from Manchuria.

STEPHEN: Another Japanese victory?

UNDERSHAFT: Oh, I dont know. Which side wins does not concern us here. No: the good news is that the aerial battleship is a tremendous success. At the first trial it has wiped out a fort with three hundred soldiers in it.

CUSINS [*from the platform*]: Dummy soldiers?

UNDERSHAFT [*striding across to Stephen and kicking the prostrate dummy brutally out of his way*]: No: the real thing.

[*Cusins and Barbara exchange glances. Then Cusins sits on the step and buries his face in his hands. Barbara gravely lays her hand on his shoulder. He looks up at her in whimsical desperation*].

UNDERSHAFT: Well, Stephen, what do you think of the place?

STEPHEN: Oh, magnificent. A perfect triumph of modern industry. Frankly, my dear father, I have been a fool: I had no idea of what it all meant: of the wonderful forethought, the power of organization, the administrative capacity, the financial genius, the colossal capital it represents. I have been repeating to myself as I came through your streets "Peace hath her victories no less renowned than War." I have only one misgiving about it all.

UNDERSHAFT: Out with it.

STEPHEN: Well, I cannot help thinking that all this provision for every want of your workmen may sap their independence and weaken their sense of responsibility. And greatly as we enjoyed our tea at that splendid restaurant—how they gave us all that luxury and cake and jam and cream for threepence I really cannot imagine!—still you must remember that restaurants break up home life. Look at the continent, for instance! Are you sure so much pampering is really good for the men's characters?

UNDERSHAFT: Well you see, my dear boy, when you are organizing civilization you have to make up your mind whether trouble and anxiety are good things or not. If you decide that they are, then, I take it, you simply dont organize civilization; and there you are, with trouble and anxiety enough to make us all angels! But if you decide the other way, you may as well go through with it. However, Stephen, our characters are safe here. A sufficient dose of anxiety is always provided by the fact that we may be blown to smithereens at any moment.

SARAH: By the way, papa, where do you make the explosives?

UNDERSHAFT: In separate little sheds, like that one. When one of them blows up, it costs very little; and only the people quite close to it are killed.

[*Stephen, who is quite close to it, looks at it rather scaredly, and moves away quickly to the cannon. At the same moment the door of the shed is thrown abruptly open; and a foreman in overalls and list slippers comes out on the little landing and holds the door for Lomax, who appears in the doorway*].

LOMAX [*with studied coolness*]: My good fellow: you neednt get into a state of nerves. Nothing's going to happen to you; and I suppose it wouldnt be the end of the world if anything did. A little bit of British pluck is what *you* want, old chap. [*He descends and strolls across to Sarah*].

UNDERSHAFT [*to the foreman*]: Anything wrong, Bilton?

BILTON [*with ironic calm*]: Gentleman walked into the high explosives shed and lit a cigaret, sir: thats all.

UNDERSHAFT: Ah, quite so. [*Going over to Lomax*] Do you happen to remember what you did with the match?

LOMAX: Oh come! I'm not a fool. I took jolly good care to blow it out before I chucked it away.

BILTON: The top of it was red hot inside, sir.

LOMAX: Well, suppose it was! I didn't chuck it into any of your messes.

UNDERSHAFT: Think no more of it, Mr Lomax. By the way, would you mind lending me your matches.

LOMAX [*offering his box*]: Certainly.

UNDERSHAFT: Thanks. [*He pockets the matches*].

LOMAX [*lecturing to the company generally*]: You know, these high explosives dont go off like gunpowder, except when theyre in a gun. When theyre spread loose, you can put a match to them without the least risk: they just burn quietly like a bit of paper. [*Warming to the scientific interest of the subject*] Did you know that, Undershaft? Have you ever tried?

UNDERSHAFT: Not on a large scale, Mr Lomax. Bilton will give you a sample of gun cotton when you are leaving if you ask him. You can experiment with it at home. [*Bilton looks puzzled*].

SARAH: Bilton will do nothing of the sort, papa. I suppose it's your business to blow up the Russians and Japs; but you might really stop short of blowing up poor Cholly. [*Bilton gives it up and retires into the shed*].

LOMAX: My ownest, there is no danger. [*He sits beside her on the shell*].

[*Lady Britomart arrives from the town with a bouquet*].

LADY BRITOMART [*impetuously*]: Andrew: you shouldnt have let me see this place.

UNDERSHAFT: Why, my dear?

LADY BRITOMART: Never mind why: you shouldnt have: thats all. To think of all that [*indicating the town*] being yours! and that you have kept it to yourself all these years!

UNDERSHAFT: It does not belong to me. I belong to it. It is the Undershaft inheritance.

LADY BRITOMART: It is not. Your ridiculous cannons and that noisy banging foundry may be the Undershaft inheritance; but all that plate and linen, all that furniture and those houses and orchards and gardens belong to us. They belong to *me:* they are a man's business. I wont give them up. You must be out of your senses to throw them all away; and if you persist in such folly, I will call in a doctor.

UNDERSHAFT [*stooping to smell! the bouquet*]: Where did you get the flowers, my dear?

LADY BRITOMART: Your men presented them to me in your William Morris Labor Church.

CUSINS: Oh! It needed only that. A Labor Church! [*He mounts the firestep distractedly, and leans with his elbows on the parapet, turning his back to them*].

LADY BRITOMART: Yes, with Morris's words in mosaic letters ten feet high round the dome. NO MAN IS GOOD ENOUGH TO BE ANOTHER MAN'S MASTER. The cynicism of it!

UNDERSHAFT: It shocked the men at first, I am afraid. But now they take no more notice of it than of the ten commandments in church.

LADY BRITOMART: Andrew: you are trying to put me off the subject of the inheritance by profane jokes. Well, you shant. I dont ask it any longer for Stephen: he has inherited far too much of your perversity to be fit for it. But Barbara has rights as well as Stephen. Why should not Adolphus succeed to the inheritance? I could manage the town for him; and he can look after the cannons, if they are really necessary.

UNDERSHAFT: I should ask nothing better if Adolphus were a foundling. He is exactly the sort of new blood that is wanted in English business. But he's not a foundling; and theres an end of it. [*He makes for the office door*].

CUSINS [*turning to them*]: Not quite. [*They all turn and stare at him*]. I think— Mind! I am not committing myself in any way as to my future course—but I *think* the foundling difficulty can be got over. [*He jumps down to the emplacement*].

UNDERSHAFT [*coming back to him*]: What do you mean?

CUSINS: Well, I have something to say which is in the nature of a confession.

SARAH:
LADY BRITOMART:
BARBARA: Confession!
STEPHEN:

LOMAX: Oh I say!

CUSINS: Yes, a confession. Listen, all. Until I met Barbara I thought myself in the main an honorable, truthful man, because I wanted the approval of my conscience more than I wanted anything else. But the moment I saw Barbara, I wanted her far more than the approval of my conscience.

LADY BRITOMART: Adolphus!

CUSINS: It is true. You accused me yourself, Lady Brit, of joining the Army to worship Barbara; and so I did. She bought my soul like a flower at a street corner; but she bought it for herself.

UNDERSHAFT: What! Not for Dionysos or another?

CUSINS: Dionysos and all the others are in herself. I adored what was divine in her, and was therefore a true worshipper. But I was romantic about her too. I thought she was a woman of the people, and that a marriage with a professor of Greek would be far beyond the wildest social ambitions of her rank.

LADY BRITOMART: Adolphus!!

LOMAX: Oh I say!!!

CUSINS: When I learnt the horrible truth—

LADY BRITOMART: What do you mean by the horrible truth, pray?

CUSINS: That she was enormously rich; that her grandfather was an earl; that her father was the Prince of Darkness—

UNDERSHAFT: Chut!

CUSINS: —and that I was only an adventurer trying to catch a rich wife, then I stooped to deceive her about my birth.

BARBARA [*rising*]: Dolly!

LADY BRITOMART: Your birth! Now Adolphus, dont dare to make up a wicked story for the sake of these wretched cannons. Remember: I have seen photographs of your parents;

and the Agent General for South Western Australia knows them personally and has assured me that they are most respectable married people.

CUSINS: So they are in Australia; but here they are outcasts. Their marriage is legal in Australia, but not in England. My mother is my father's deceased wife's sister; and in this island I am consequently a foundling. [*Sensation*].

BARBARA: Silly! [*She climbs to the cannon, and leans, listening, in the angle it makes with the parapet*].

CUSINS: Is the subterfuge good enough, Machiavelli?

UNDERSHAFT [*thoughtfully*]: Biddy: this may be a way out of the difficulty.

LADY BRITOMART: Stuff! A man cant make cannons any the better for being his own cousin instead of his proper self. [*She sits down on the rug with a bounce that expresses her downright contempt for their casuistry*].

UNDERSHAFT [*to Cusins*]: You are an educated man. That is against the tradition.

CUSINS: Once in ten thousand times it happens that the schoolboy is a born master of what they try to teach him. Greek has not destroyed my mind: it has nourished it. Besides, I did not learn it at an English public school.

UNDERSHAFT: Hm! Well, I cannot afford to be too particular: you have cornered the foundling market. Let it pass. You are eligible, Euripides: you are eligible.

BARBARA: Dolly: yesterday morning, when Stephen told us all about the tradition, you became very silent; and you have been strange and excited ever since. Were you thinking of your birth then?

CUSINS: When the finger of Destiny suddenly points at a man in the middle of his breakfast, it makes him thoughtful.

UNDERSHAFT: Aha! You have had your eye on the business, my young friend, have you?

CUSINS: Take care! There is an abyss of moral horror between me and your accursed aerial battleships.

UNDERSHAFT: Never mind the abyss for the present. Let us settle the practical details and leave your final decision open. You know that you will have to change your name. Do you object to that?

CUSINS: Would any man named Adolphus—any man called Dolly!—object to be called something else?

UNDERSHAFT: Good. Now, as to money! I propose to treat you handsomely from the beginning. You shall start at a thousand a year.

CUSINS [*with sudden heat, his spectacles twinkling with mischief*]: A thousand! You dare offer a miserable thousand to the son-in-law of a millionaire! No, by Heavens, Machiavelli! you shall not cheat *me*. You cannot do without me; and I can do without you. I must have two thousand five hundred a year for two years. At the end of that time, if I am a failure, I go. But if I am a success, and stay on, you must give me the other five thousand.

UNDERSHAFT: What other five thousand?

CUSINS: To make the two years up to five thousand a year. The two thousand five hundred is only half pay in case I should turn out a failure. The third year I must have ten per cent on the profits.

UNDERSHAFT [*taken aback*]: Ten per cent! Why, man, do you know what my profits are?

CUSINS: Enormous, I hope: otherwise I shall require twenty-five per cent.

UNDERSHAFT: But, Mr Cusins, this is a serious matter of business. You are not bringing any capital into the concern.

CUSINS: What! no capital! Is my mastery of Greek no capital? Is my access to the subtlest thought, the loftiest poetry yet attained by humanity, no capital? My character! my intellect! my life! my career! what Barbara calls my soul! are these no capital? Say another word; and I double my salary.

UNDERSHAFT: Be reasonable—

CUSINS [*peremptorily*]: Mr Undershaft: you have my terms. Take them or leave them.

UNDERSHAFT [*recovering himself*]: Very well. I note your terms; and I offer you half.

CUSINS [*disgusted*]: Half!

UNDERSHAFT [*firmly*]: Half.

CUSINS: You call yourself a gentleman; and you offer me half!!

UNDERSHAFT: I do not call myself a gentleman; but I offer you half.

CUSINS: This to your future part-

ner! your successor! your son-in-law!

BARBARA: You are selling your own soul, Dolly, not mine. Leave me out of the bargain, please.

UNDERSHAFT: Come! I will go a step further for Barbara's sake. I will give you three fifths; but that is my last word.

CUSINS: Done!

LOMAX: Done in the eye! Why, *I* get only eight hundred, you know.

CUSINS: By the way, Mac, I am a classical scholar, not an arithmetical one. Is three fifths more than half or less?

UNDERSHAFT: More, of course.

CUSINS: I would have taken two hundred and fifty. How you can succeed in business when you are willing to pay all that money to a University don who is obviously not worth a junior clerk's wages!—well! What will Lazarus say?

UNDERSHAFT: Lazarus is a gentle romantic Jew who cares for nothing but string quartets and stalls at fashionable theatres. He will be blamed for your rapacity in money matters, poor fellow! as he has hitherto been blamed for mine. You are a shark of the first order, Euripides. So much the better for the firm!

BARBARA: Is the bargain closed, Dolly? Does your soul belong to him now?

CUSINS: No: the price is settled: that is all. The real tug of war is still to come. What about the moral question?

LADY BRITOMART: There is no moral question in the matter at all, Adolphus. You must simply sell cannons and weapons to people whose cause is right and just, and refuse them to foreigners and criminals.

UNDERSHAFT [*determinedly*]: No: none of that. You must keep the true faith of an Armorer, or you dont come in here.

CUSINS: What on earth is the true faith of an Armorer?

UNDERSHAFT: To give arms to all men who offer an honest price for them, without respect of persons or principles: to aristocrat and republican, to Nihilist and Tsar, to Capitalist and Socialist, to Protestant and Catholic, to burglar and policeman, to black man, white man and yellow man, to all sorts and conditions, all nationalities, all faiths, all follies, all causes and all crimes. The first Undershaft wrote up in his shop IF GOD GAVE THE HAND, LET NOT MAN WITHHOLD THE SWORD. The second wrote up ALL HAVE THE RIGHT TO FIGHT: NONE HAVE THE RIGHT TO JUDGE. The third wrote up TO MAN THE WEAPON: TO HEAVEN THE VICTORY. The fourth had no literary turn; so he did not write up anything; but he sold cannons to Napoleon under the nose of George the Third. The fifth wrote up PEACE SHALL NOT PREVAIL SAVE WITH A SWORD IN HER HAND. The sixth, my master, was the best of all. He wrote up NOTHING IS EVER DONE IN THIS WORLD UNTIL MEN ARE PREPARED TO KILL ONE ANOTHER IF IT IS NOT DONE. After that, there was nothing left for the seventh to say. So he wrote up, simply, UNASHAMED.

CUSINS: My good Machiavelli, I shall certainly write something up on the wall; only, as I shall write it in Greek, you wont be able to read it. But as to your Armorer's faith, if I take my neck out of the noose of my own morality I am not going to put it into the noose of yours. I shall sell cannons to whom I please and refuse them to whom I please. So there!

UNDERSHAFT: From the moment when you become Andrew Undershaft, you will never do as you please again. Dont come here lusting for power, young man.

CUSINS: If power were my aim I should not come here for it. You have no power.

UNDERSHAFT: None of my own, certainly.

CUSINS: I have more power than you, more will. You do not drive this place: it drives you. And what drives the place?

UNDERSHAFT [*enigmatically*]: A will of which I am a part.

BARBARA [*startled*]: Father! Do you know what you are saying; or are you laying a snare for my soul?

CUSINS: Dont listen to his metaphysics, Barbara. The place is driven by the most rascally part of society, the money hunters, the pleasure hunters, the military promotion hunters; and he is their slave.

UNDERSHAFT: Not necessarily. Remember the Armorer's Faith. I will take an order from a good man as cheerfully as from a bad one. If you good people prefer preaching and shirking to buying my weapons and fighting the rascals, dont blame me. I can make cannons: I cannot make courage and conviction. Bah! you tire me, Euripides, with your morality mongering. Ask Barbara: *she* understands. [*He suddenly reaches up and takes Barbara's hands, looking powerfully into her eyes*]. Tell him, my love, what power really means.

BARBARA [*hypnotized*]: Before I joined the Salvation Army, I was in my own power; and the consequence was that I never knew what to do with myself. When I joined it, I had not time enough for all the things I had to do.

UNDERSHAFT [*approvingly*]: Just so. And why was that, do you suppose?

BARBARA: Yesterday I should have said, because I was in the power of God. [*She resumes her self-possession, withdrawing her hands from his with a power equal to his own*]. But you came and shewed me that I was in the power of Bodger and Undershaft. Today I feel—oh! how can I put it into words? Sarah: do you remember the earthquake at Cannes, when we were little children—how little the surprise of the first shock mattered compared to the dread and horror of waiting for the second? That is how I feel in this place today. I stood on the rock I thought eternal; and without a word of warning it reeled and crumbled under me. I was safe with an infinite wisdom watching me, an army marching to Salvation with me; and in a moment, at a stroke of your pen in a cheque book, I stood alone; and the heavens were empty. That was the first shock of the earthquake: I am waiting for the second.

UNDERSHAFT: Come, come, my daughter! dont make too much of your little tinpot tragedy. What do we do here when we spend years of work and thought and thousands of pounds of solid cash on a new gun or an aerial battleship that turns out just a hairsbreadth wrong after all? Scrap it. Scrap it without wasting another hour or another pound on it. Well, you have made for yourself something that you call a morality or a religion or what not. It doesnt fit the facts. Well, scrap it. Scrap it and get one that does fit. That is what is wrong with the world at present. It scraps its obsolete steam engines and dynamos; but it wont scrap its old prejudices and its old moralities and its old religions and its old political constitutions. Whats the result? In machinery it does very well; but in morals and religion and politics it is working at a loss that brings it nearer bankruptcy every year. Dont persist in that folly. If your old religion broke down yesterday, get a newer and a better one for tomorrow.

BARBARA: Oh how gladly I would take a better one to my soul! But you offer me a worse one. [*Turning on him with sudden vehemence*]. Justify yourself: shew me some light through the darkness of this dreadful place, with its beautifully clean workshops, and respectable workmen, and model homes.

UNDERSHAFT: Cleanliness and respectability do not need justification, Barbara: they justify themselves. I see no darkness here, no dreadfulness. In your Salvation shelter I saw poverty, misery, cold and hunger. You gave them bread and treacle and dreams of heaven. I give from thirty shillings a week to twelve thousand a year. They find their own dreams; but I look after the drainage.

BARBARA: And their souls?

UNDERSHAFT: I save their souls just as I saved yours.

BARBARA [revolted]: You saved my soul! What do you mean?

UNDERSHAFT: I fed you and clothed you and housed you. I took care that you should have money enough to live handsomely—more than enough; so that you could be wasteful, careless, generous. That saved your soul from the seven deadly sins.

BARBARA [bewildered]: The seven deadly sins!

UNDERSHAFT: Yes, the deadly seven. [Counting on his fingers] Food, clothing, firing, rent, taxes, respectability and children. Nothing can lift those seven millstones from Man's neck but money; and the spirit cannot soar until the millstones are lifted. I lifted them from your spirit. I enabled Barbara to become Major Barbara; and I saved her from the crime of poverty.

CUSINS: Do you call poverty a crime?

UNDERSHAFT: The worst of crimes. All the other crimes are virtues beside it: all the other dishonors are chivalry itself by comparison. Poverty blights whole cities; spreads horrible pestilences; strikes dead the very souls of all who come within sight, sound, or smell of it. What you call crime is nothing: a murder here and a theft there, a blow now and a curse then: what do they matter? they are only the accidents and illnesses of life: there are not fifty genuine professional criminals in London. But there are millions of poor people, abject people, dirty people, ill fed, ill clothed people. They poison us morally and physically: they kill the happiness of society: they force us to do away with our own liberties and to organize unnatural cruelties for fear they should rise against us and drag us down into their abyss. Only fools fear crime: we all fear poverty. Pah! [turning on Barbara] you talk of your half-saved ruffian in West Ham: you accuse me of dragging his soul back to perdition. Well, bring him to me here; and I will drag his soul back again to salvation for you. Not by words and dreams; but by thirty-eight shillings a week, a sound house in a handsome street, and a permanent job. In three weeks he will have a fancy waistcoat; in three months a tall hat and a chapel sitting; before the end of the year he will shake hands with a duchess at a Primrose League meeting, and join the Conservative Party.

BARBARA: And will he be the better for that?

UNDERSHAFT: You know he will. Dont be a hypocrite, Barbara. He will be better fed, better housed, better clothed, better behaved; and his children will be pounds heavier and bigger. That will be better than an American cloth mattress in a shelter, chopping firewood, eating bread and treacle, and being forced to kneel down from time to time to thank heaven for it: knee drill, I think you call it. It is cheap work converting starving men with a Bible in one hand and a slice of bread in the other. I will undertake to convert West Ham to Mahometanism on the same terms. Try your hand on *my* men: their souls are hungry because their bodies are full.

BARBARA: And leave the east end to starve?

UNDERSHAFT [*his energetic tone dropping into one of bitter and brooding remembrance*]: *I* was an east ender. I moralized and starved until one day I swore that I would be a full-fed free man at all costs; that nothing should stop me except a bullet, neither reason nor morals nor the lives of other men. I said "Thou shalt starve ere I starve"; and with that word I became free and great. I was a dangerous man until I had my will: now I am a useful, beneficent, kindly person. That is the history of most self-made millionaires, I fancy. When it is the history of every Englishman we shall have an England worth living in.

LADY BRITOMART: Stop making speeches, Andrew. This is not the place for them.

UNDERSHAFT [*punctured*]: My dear: I have no other means of conveying my ideas.

LADY BRITOMART: Your ideas are nonsense. You got on because you were selfish and unscrupulous.

UNDERSHAFT: Not at all. I had the strongest scruples about poverty and starvation. Your moralists are quite unscrupulous about both: they make virtues of them. I had rather be a thief than a pauper. I had rather be a murderer than a slave. I dont want to be either; but if you force the alternative on me, then, by Heaven, I'll chose the braver and more moral one. I hate poverty and slavery worse than any other crimes whatsoever. And let me tell you this. Poverty and slavery have stood up for centuries to your sermons and leading articles: they will not stand up to my machine guns. Dont preach at them: dont reason with them. Kill them.

BARBARA: Killing. Is that your remedy for everything?

UNDERSHAFT: It is the final test of conviction, the only lever strong enough to overturn a social system, the only way of saying Must. Let six hundred and seventy fools loose in the streets; and three policemen can scatter them. But huddle them together in a certain house in Westminster; and let them go through certain ceremonies and call themselves certain names until at last they get the courage to kill; and your six hundred and seventy fools become a government. Your pious mob fills up ballot papers and imagines it is governing its masters; but the ballot paper that really governs is the paper that has a bullet wrapped up in it.

CUSINS: That is perhaps why, like most intelligent people, I never vote.

UNDERSHAFT: Vote! Bah! When you vote, you only change the names of the cabinet. When you shoot, you pull down governments, inaugurate new epochs, abolish old orders and set up new. Is that historically true, Mr. Learned Man, or is it not?

CUSINS: It is historically true. I loathe having to admit it. I repudiate your sentiments. I abhor your nature. I defy you in every possible way. Still, it is true. But it ought not to be true.

UNDERSHAFT: Ought! ought! ought! ought! ought! Are you going to spend your life saying ought, like the rest of our moralists? Turn your oughts into shalls, man. Come and make explosives with me. Whatever can blow men up can blow society up. The history of the world is the history of those who had courage enough to embrace this truth. Have you the courage to embrace it, Barbara?

LADY BRITOMART: Barbara: I positively forbid you to listen to your father's abominable wickedness. And you, Adolphus, ought to know better than to go about saying that wrong things are true. What does it matter whether they are true if they are wrong?

UNDERSHAFT: What does it mat-

ter whether they are wrong if they are true?

LADY BRITOMART [*rising*]: Children: come home instantly. Andrew: I am exceedingly sorry I allowed you to call on us. You are wickeder than ever. Come at once.

BARBARA [*shaking her head*]: It's no use running away from wicked people, mamma.

LADY BRITOMART: It is every use. It shews your disapprobation of them.

BARBARA: It does not save them.

LADY BRITOMART: I can see that you are going to disobey me. Sarah: are you coming home or are you not?

SARAH: I daresay it's very wicked of papa to make cannons; but I dont think I shall cut him on that account.

LOMAX [*pouring oil on the troubled waters*]: The fact is, you know, there is a certain amount of tosh about this notion of wickedness. It doesnt work. You must look at facts. Not that I would say a word in favor of anything wrong; but then, you see, all sorts of chaps are always doing all sorts of things; and we have to fit them in somehow, dont you know. What I mean is that you cant go cutting everybody; and thats about what it comes to. [*Their rapt attention to his eloquence makes him nervous*]. Perhaps I dont make myself clear.

LADY BRITOMART: You are lucidity itself, Charles. Because Andrew is successful and has plenty of money to give to Sarah, you will flatter him and encourage him in his wickedness.

LOMAX [*unruffled*]: Well, where the carcase is, there will the eagles be gathered, dont you know. [*To Undershaft*] Eh? What?

UNDERSHAFT: Precisely. By the way, may I call you Charles?

LOMAX: Delighted. Cholly is the usual ticket.

UNDERSHAFT [*to Lady Britomart*]: Biddy—

LADY BRITOMART [*violently*]: Dont dare call me Biddy. Charles Lomax: you are a fool. Adolphus Cusins: you are a Jesuit. Stephen: you are a prig. Barbara: you are a lunatic. Andrew: you are a vulgar tradesman. Now you all know my opinion; and my conscience is clear, at all events. [*She sits down with a vehemence that the rug fortunately softens*].

UNDERSHAFT: My dear: you are the incarnation of morality. [*She snorts*]. Your conscience is clear and your duty done when you have called everybody names. Come, Euripides! it is getting late; and we all want to go home. Make up your mind.

CUSINS: Understand this, you old demon—

LADY BRITOMART: Adolphus!

UNDERSHAFT: Let him alone, Biddy. Proceed, Euripides.

CUSINS: You have me in a horrible dilemma. I want Barbara.

UNDERSHAFT: Like all young men, you greatly exaggerate the difference between one young woman and another.

BARBARA: Quite true, Dolly.

CUSINS: I also want to avoid being a rascal.

UNDERSHAFT [*with biting contempt*]: You lust for personal righteousness, for self-approval, for what you call a good conscience, for what Barbara calls salvation, for what I call patronizing people who are not so lucky as yourself.

CUSINS: I do not: all the poet in me recoils from being a good man. But there are things in me that I must reckon with. Pity—

UNDERSHAFT: Pity! The scavenger of misery.

CUSINS: Well, love.

UNDERSHAFT: I know. You love the needy and the outcast: you love the oppressed races, the negro, the Indian ryot, the underdog everywhere. Do you love the Japanese? Do you love the French? Do you love the English?

CUSINS: No. Every true Englishman detests the English. We are the wickedest nation on earth; and our success is a moral horror.

UNDERSHAFT: That is what comes of your gospel of love, is it?

CUSINS: May I not love even my father-in-law?

UNDERSHAFT: Who wants your love, man? By what right do you take the liberty of offering it to me? I will have your due heed and respect, or I will kill you. But your love! Damn your impertinence!

CUSINS [*grinning*]: I may not be able to control my affections, Mac.

UNDERSHAFT: You are fencing, Euripides. You are weakening: your grip is slipping. Come! try your last weapon. Pity and love have broken in your hand: forgiveness is still left.

CUSINS: No: forgiveness is a beggar's refuge. I am with you there: we must pay our debts.

UNDERSHAFT: Well said. Come! you will suit me. Remember the words of Plato.

CUSINS [*starting*]: Plato! *You* dare quote Plato to *me!*

UNDERSHAFT: Plato says, my friend, that society cannot be saved until either the Professors of Greek take to making gunpowder, or else the makers of gunpowder become Professors of Greek.

CUSINS: Oh, tempter, cunning tempter!

UNDERSHAFT: Come! choose, man, choose.

CUSINS: But perhaps Barbara will not marry me if I make the wrong choice.

BARBARA: Perhaps not.

CUSINS [*desperately perplexed*]: You hear!

BARBARA: Father: do you love nobody?

UNDERSHAFT: I love my best friend.

LADY BRITOMART: And who is that, pray?

UNDERSHAFT: My bravest enemy. That is the man who keeps me up to the mark.

CUSINS: You know, the creature is really a sort of poet in his way. Suppose he is a great man, after all!

UNDERSHAFT: Suppose you stop talking and make up your mind, my young friend.

CUSINS: But you are driving me against my nature. I hate war.

UNDERSHAFT: Hatred is the coward's revenge for being in-

timidated. Dare you make war on war? Here are the means: my friend Mr Lomax is sitting on them.

LOMAX [*springs up*]: Oh I say! You dont mean that this thing is loaded, do you? My ownest: come off it.

SARAH [*sitting placidly on the shell*]: If I am to be blown up, the more thoroughly it is done the better. Dont fuss, Cholly.

LOMAX [*to Undershaft, strongly remonstrant*]: Your own daughter, you know!

UNDERSHAFT: So I see. [*To Cusins*] Well, my friend, may we expect you here at six tomorrow morning?

CUSINS [*firmly*]: Not on any account. I will see the whole establishment blown up with its own dynamite before I will get up at five. My hours are healthy, rational hours: eleven to five.

UNDERSHAFT: Come when you please: before a week you will come at six and stay until I turn you out for the sake of your health. [*Calling*] Bilton! [*He turns to Lady Britomart, who rises*]. My dear: let us leave these two young people to themselves for a moment. [*Bilton comes from the shed*]. I am going to take you through the gun cotton shed.

BILTON [*barring the way*]: You cant take anything explosive in here, sir.

LADY BRITOMART: What do you mean? Are you alluding to me?

BILTON [*unmoved*]: No, maam. Mr Undershaft has the other gentleman's matches in his pocket.

LADY BRITOMART [*abruptly*]: Oh!

I beg your pardon. [*She goes into the shed*].

UNDERSHAFT: Quite right, Bilton, quite right: here you are. [*He gives Bilton the box of matches*]. Come, Stephen. Come, Charles. Bring Sarah. [*He passes into the shed*].

[*Bilton opens the box and deliberately drops the matches into the fire-bucket*].

LOMAX: Oh! I say. [*Bilton stolidly hands him the empty box*]. Infernal nonsense! Pure scientific ignorance! [*He goes in*].

SARAH: Am I all right, Bilton?

BILTON: Youll have to put on list slippers, miss: thats all. Weve got em inside. [*She goes in*].

STEPHEN [*very seriously to Cusins*]: Dolly, old fellow, think. Think before you decide. Do you feel that you are a sufficiently practical man? It is a huge undertaking, an enormous responsibility. All this mass of business will be Greek to you.

CUSINS: Oh, I think it will be much less difficult than Greek.

STEPHEN: Well, I just want to say this before I leave you to yourselves. Dont let anything I have said about right and wrong prejudice you against this great chance in life. I have satisfied myself that the business is one of the highest character and a credit to our country. [*Emotionally*] I am very proud of my father. I— [*Unable to proceed, he presses Cusins' hand and goes hastily into the shed, followed by Bilton*].

[*Barbara and Cusins, left alone together, look at one another silently*].

CUSINS: Barbara: I am going to accept this offer.

BARBARA: I thought you would.

CUSINS: You understand, dont you, that I had to decide without consulting you. If I had thrown the burden of the choice on you, you would sooner or later have despised me for it.

BARBARA: Yes: I did not want you to sell your soul for me any more than for this inheritance.

CUSINS: It is not the sale of my soul that troubles me: I have sold it too often to care about that. I have sold it for a professorship. I have sold it for an income. I have sold it to escape being imprisoned for refusing to pay taxes for hangmen's ropes and unjust wars and things that I abhor. What is all human conduct but the daily and hourly sale of our souls for trifles? What I am now selling it for is neither money nor position nor comfort, but for reality and for power.

BARBARA: You know that you will have no power, and that he has none.

CUSINS: I know. It is not for myself alone. I want to make power for the world.

BARBARA: I want to make power for the world too; but it must be spiritual power.

CUSINS: I think all power is spiritual: these cannons will not go off by themselves. I have tried to make spiritual power by teaching Greek. But the world can never be really touched by a dead language and a dead civilization. The people must have power; and the people cannot have Greek. Now the power that is made here can be wielded by all men.

BARBARA: Power to burn women's houses down and kill their sons and tear their husbands to pieces.

CUSINS: You cannot have power for good without having power for evil too. Even mother's milk nourishes murderers as well as heroes. This power which only tears men's bodies to pieces has never been so horribly abused as the intellectual power, the imaginative power, the poetic, religious power that can enslave men's souls. As a teacher of Greek I gave the intellectual man weapons against the common man. I now want to give the common man weapons against the intellectual man. I love the common people. I want to arm them against the lawyers, the doctors, the priests, the literary men, the professors, the artists, and the politicians, who, once in authority, are more disastrous and tyrannical than all the fools, rascals, and impostors. I want a power simple enough for common men to use, yet strong enough to force the intellectual oligarchy to use its genius for the general good.

BARBARA: Is there no higher power than that [*pointing to the shell*]?

CUSINS: Yes; but that power can destroy the higher powers just as a tiger can destroy a man: therefore Man must master that power first. I admitted this when the Turks and Greeks were last at war. My best pupil went out to fight for Hellas. My parting gift to him was not a copy of Plato's Republic, but a revolver and a hundred Undershaft cartridges. The blood of every Turk he shot—if he shot any—is on my head as well as on Undershaft's. That act committed me to this place for ever. Your father's challenge has beaten me. Dare I make war on war? I must. I will. And now, is it all over between us?

BARBARA [*touched by his evident dread of her answer*]: Silly baby Dolly! How could it be!

CUSINS [*overjoyed*]: Then you— you—you— Oh for my drum! [*He flourishes imaginary drumsticks*].

BARBARA [*angered by his levity*]: Take care, Dolly, take care. Oh, if only I could get away from you and from father and from it all! if I could have the wings of a dove and fly away to heaven!

CUSINS: And leave *me!*

BARBARA: Yes, you, and all the other naughty mischievous children of men. But I cant. I was happy in the Salvation Army for a moment. I escaped from the world into a paradise of enthusiasm and prayer and soul saving; but the moment our money ran short, it all came back to Bodger: it was he who saved our people: he, and the Prince of Darkness, my papa. Undershaft and Bodger: their hands stretch everywhere: when we feed a starving fellow creature, it is with their bread, because there is no other bread; when we tend the sick, it is in the hospitals they endow; if we turn from the churches they build, we must kneel on the stones of the streets they pave.

As long as that lasts, there is no getting away from them. Turning our backs on Bodger and Undershaft is turning our backs on life.

CUSINS: I thought you were determined to turn your back on the wicked side of life.

BARBARA: There is no wicked side: life is all one. And I never wanted to shirk my share in whatever evil must be endured, whether it be sin or suffering. I wish I could cure you of middle-class ideas, Dolly.

CUSINS [*gasping*]: Middle cl—! A snub! A social snub to *me!* from the daughter of a foundling!

BARBARA: That is why I have no class, Dolly: I come straight out of the heart of the whole people. If I were middle-class I should turn my back on my father's business; and we should both live in an artistic drawing room, with you reading the reviews in one corner, and I in the other at the piano, playing Schumann: both very superior persons, and neither of us a bit of use. Sooner than that, I would sweep out the guncotton shed, or be one of Bodger's barmaids. Do you know what would have happened if you had refused papa's offer?

CUSINS: I wonder!

BARBARA: I should have given you up and married the man who accepted it. After all, my dear old mother has more sense than any of you. I felt like her when I saw this place—felt that I must have it—that never, never, never could I let it go; only she thought it was the houses and the kitchen ranges and the linen and china, when it was really all the human souls to be saved: not weak souls in starved bodies, sobbing with gratitude for a scrap of bread and treacle, but fullfed, quarrelsome, snobbish, uppish creatures, all standing on their little rights and dignities, and thinking that my father ought to be greatly obliged to them for making so much money for him—and so he ought. That is where salvation is really wanted. My father shall never throw it in my teeth again that my converts were bribed with bread. [*She is transfigured*]. I have got rid of the bribe of bread. I have got rid of the bribe of heaven. Let God's work be done for its own sake: the work he had to create us to do because it cannot be done except by living men and women. When I die, let him be in my debt, not I in his; and let me forgive him as becomes a woman of my rank.

CUSINS: Then the way of life lies through the factory of death?

BARBARA: Yes, through the raising of hell to heaven and of man to God, through the unveiling of an eternal light in the Valley of The Shadow. [*Seizing him with both hands*] Oh, did you think my courage would never come back? did you believe that I was a deserter? that I, who have stood in the streets, and taken my people to my heart, and talked of the holiest and greatest things with them, could ever turn back and chatter foolishly to fashionable people about nothing in a drawing room? Never, never, never, never: Major Barbara will die with the colors. Oh! and I have my dear little Dolly boy still; and he has found me my place and my work. Glory Hallelujah! [*She kisses him*].

CUSINS: My dearest: consider my delicate health. I cannot stand as much happiness as you can.

BARBARA: Yes: it is not easy work being in love with me, is it? But it's good for you. [*She runs to the shed, and calls, childlike*] Mamma! Mamma! [*Bilton comes out of the shed, followed by Undershaft*]. I want Mamma.

UNDERSHAFT: She is taking off her list slippers, dear. [*He passes on to Cusins*]. Well? What does she say?

CUSINS: She has gone right up into the skies.

LADY BRITOMART [*coming from the shed and stopping on the steps, obstructing Sarah, who*

follows with Lomax. Barbara clutches like a baby at her mother's skirt]: Barbara: when will you learn to be independent and to act and think for yourself? I know as well as possible what that cry of "Mamma, Mamma," means. Always running to me!

SARAH [*touching Lady Britomart's ribs with her finger tips and imitating a bicycle horn*]: Pip! pip!

LADY BRITOMART [*highly indignant*]: How dare you say Pip! pip! to me, Sarah? You are both very naughty children. What do you want, Barbara?

BARBARA: I want a house in the village to live in with Dolly. [*Dragging at the skirt*] Come and tell me which one to take.

UNDERSHAFT [*to Cusins*]: Six o'clock tomorrow morning, Euripides.

THE END

Sir James Matthew Barrie
[1860-1937]

Sir James Barrie was born May 9, 1860, at Kirriemuir, Scotland, the ninth child and youngest son of a hand-loom weaver. His childhood was happy; the first sorrow that touched it was the accidental death of his older brother, a blow from which his mother never really recovered and which caused Barrie to swear to her that he would always care for her and try to make up for her loss. He was a small child, but very athletic. He developed a love for cricket, a game which he played into his adult years, and, although he was only five feet, one inch tall, he was considered a fierce player. He was also extremely imaginative and was always the one who made up the games and stories that the other children played. Even as a child he recognized the responsibilities and sorrows that burdened adults and said that, "The horror of my childhood was that I knew a time would come when I also must give up the games, and how it was to be done I saw not. . . . I felt that I must continue playing in secret. . . ." He attended the Glasgow Academy and graduated from Edinburgh University in 1882 with an M.A. He was not an outstanding student and was never at the head of his class. He found the professors and students much more interesting than his studies. Even as a boy he was determined to write and by 1883 was appointed leader-writer and sub-editor on the Nottingham *Journal.* Besides this he wrote constantly—sketches, short stories, and articles.

In 1885 he moved to London, where he wrote for many magazines and published stories serially under the name Gavin Ogilvy. During 1888–89 he published his Scottish sketches and episodes, all of them drawn directly from places, people, and events he had either experienced himself or heard from his mother. No detail of his childhood had been lost on him. Although he did not always feel well—he was given all his life to severe headaches and fits of depression—he wrote assiduously and his advice to younger writers was, "Concentrate, though your coat-tails are on fire." From 1891 on he began to have an increasing interest in the stage. A three-act farce, *Walker, London,* ran for five hundred and eleven performances in 1892. Barrie's fancy was often taken by the actresses he encountered, and in 1894 he married Mary Ansell, a young actress. They had no children and were divorced in 1909. He maintained close relationships with his parents, sisters, and brothers, visiting his home frequently, always if anyone was ill. As his income increased he gave them much financial support. He wrote *Margaret Ogilvy* as a tribute to his mother and some of the characters in his novels were patterned after his sisters.

A dramatization of his successful novel, *The Little Minister,* first produced in 1897 in Washington, D.C., with Maude Adams, was his first great stage hit. After that came *Quality Street,* first performed in Toledo, Ohio, in 1901. It was at this time that he moved to an apartment across from Kensington Gardens and began spending many hours sitting in the park with his Newfoundland dog, Luath, dreaming about Peter Pan. Here also he encountered children, for whom he had an affinity. They were charmed by him and listened enraptured to the stories he never tired of telling them. *The Admirable Crichton,* produced in England in 1902, was his first play to have a touch of satire in it. It was a success, and people became so engrossed with Crichton that they wanted to know what happened to him later. As a result Barrie wrote a book called *The Case Is Altered,* designed to follow the play. He wrote many other plays, both one-act and full-length, which met with varying success. *What Every Woman Knows,* a full-length play with a political environment, was one of his greatest successes.

In 1912 he had a statue of Peter Pan blowing his pipes placed in Kensington Gardens. This statue was a surprise to everyone, including the city officials, but everyone agreed that it should remain where Barrie wanted it.

His love and sympathy for people, especially children, were strong, although he could never express them except through his writing. When a close friend of his died Barrie gladly undertook the support of the wife and her sons and later on the son of still another friend. The fate of these boys was very close to him; thus World War I was an immediate and constant worry to him. During the last years of his life he was very unwell and in constant emotional turmoil over his last play, *The Boy David,* which he had written for Elisabeth Bergner. After much time and many difficulties it was finally produced, but it was not a success. David seemed to be Peter Pan over again. This, perhaps, was not surprising. Barrie had recognized some years earlier that nothing had influenced him and that he had, as he said, simply a little box inside him containing a few trifles that he played games with for many years until both he and the public tired of it. He died in London on June 19, 1937.

The Admirable Crichton was first produced at the Duke of York's Theatre in 1902; it was not published in book form until 1915. Before it was published, Barrie changed the ending, which had created some controversy. The original version had Crichton marry Tweeny and open a bar at the fashionable end of Harrow Road. In the final version (used here), Crichton leaves service and goes off without Tweeny. The revised ending is more in character for Crichton. One cannot imagine a man of Crichton's mind and disposition settling down happily with Tweeny. His attraction to Tweeny seems more whimsical and amusing than credible, especially after his experience on the island. We must assume that that experience determines what he does or does not do afterward. The logic of the play certainly demands it. He could not remain with Lord Loam's household and surely, after nearly marrying the lovely and well-bred Lady Mary, he could not possibly go back to Tweeny, who, though a faithful and dependable servant, would hardly make Crichton an adequate wife. Barrie's inventive skill saves the last act from being expository and undramatic. When he introduces Lady Brocklehurst and her trouble-some questions about life on the island, this act is, instead, quite comic and witty.

The play seems an odd one for Barrie to have written. The idea for the play first came to him when he read a notice in the news-paper that a wealthy gentleman had given a dinner party for his servants. The development of this germ into a social comedy on the question of social equality seems more suitable to Galsworthy or Shaw than to Barrie. Barrie's style is more inclined toward the fanciful and whimsical, as in *Peter Pan* and *Dear Brutus,* than toward more serious themes. However, though the theme may be Shaw's or Galsworthy's, the treatment is Barrie's. He treats the social theme with wit, comedy, and his usual fancy. He takes a servant-master situation in London, and then, typical of his manner, transports them to a desert island to put the ques-tion of equality to the natural test. After he has made his test, he transports them back to civilized London. The scenes on the island have much of the tone and romance of Barrie's other plays. They suggest, more than anything, Barrie's grown-up boys and girls in the woods. It utilizes the same structural device to be found later in *Dear Brutus.* In *Dear Brutus,* Barrie raises the question: Would the lives of these people be different if they were given a second chance? Like the fanciful transportation of his characters to a desert island in *Crichton,* he transports his characters to an enchanted wood in *Dear Brutus.*

Barrie gives a half-serious and half-humorous answer to that question of equality: Master and servant in civilized London are made so by established tradition and it has nothing to do with natural endowment; master and servant on the desert island are made so by natural endowment and it has nothing to do with tradition. The play performs very well and is constantly revived in England and America.

DRAMATIC WORKS

Walker, London, 1892
The Professor's Love Story, 1894
The Little Minister, 1897
Quality Street, 1901
The Admirable Crichton, 1902
Little Mary, 1903
Peter Pan, 1904
Alice Sit-by-the-Fire, 1905
Pantaloon, 1905
Josephine, 1906
Punch, 1906
What Every Woman Knows, 1908
The Twelve Pound Look, 1910
A Slice of Life, 1910

Rosalind, 1912
The Will, 1913
Rosy Rapture, 1915
A Kiss for Cinderella, 1916
The Old Lady Shows Her Medals,
  1917
Dear Brutus, 1917
A Well Remembered Voice, 1918
The Truth About the Russian Dancers, 1920
Mary Rose, 1920
Shall We Join the Ladies? 1922
The Boy David, 1936

The
Admirable Crichton

★

CAST

HON. ERNEST WOOLLEY, *nephew of the* EARL OF LOAM
CRICHTON, the Earl of Loam's butler
LADY AGATHA LASENBY } *daughters of*
LADY CATHERINE LASENBY } *the* EARL OF
LADY MARY LASENBY } LOAM
REV. JOHN TREHERNE
THE EARL OF LOAM
LORD BROCKLEHURST
MRS. PERKINS, *the* EARL OF LOAM'*s housekeeper*
FLEURY, *the chef*
ROLLESTON, *the valet*
TOMPSETT, *the coachman*
FISHER, LADY MARY'S *maid*
SIMMONS, *a maid*
JEANNE, *a maid*
THOMAS, *the first footman*
JOHN, *the second footman*
JANE, *a parlor maid*
GLADYS, *another parlor maid*
"TWEENY," *a kitchen maid*
A Stable-Boy
A Page
A Naval Officer
THE COUNTESS OF BROCKLEHURST, *mother of*
LORD BROCKLEHURST

ACT ONE

At Loam House, Mayfair.

A moment before the curtain rises, the HON. ERNEST
WOOLLEY *drives up to the door of Loam House in Mayfair. There is a happy smile on his pleasant, insignificant
face, and this presumably means that he is thinking of himself. He is too busy over nothing, this man about town, to
be always thinking of himself, but, on the other hand, he
almost never thinks of any other person. Probably* ERNEST'S
*great moment is when he wakes of a morning and realises
that he really is* ERNEST, *for we must all wish to be that
which is our ideal. We can conceive him springing out of
bed light-heartedly and waiting for his man to do the rest.
He is dressed in excellent taste, with just the little bit more
which shows that he is not without a sense of humour: the
dandiacal are often saved by carrying a smile at the whole
thing in their spats, let us say.* ERNEST *left Cambridge the
other day, a member of the Athenaeum* (which he would
be sorry to have you confound with a club in London of the
same name). He is a bachelor, but not of arts, no mean
epigrammatist (as you shall see), and a favourite of the
ladies. He is almost a celebrity in restaurants, where he
dines frequently, returning to sup; and during this last year
he has probably paid as much in them for the privilege of
handing his hat to an attendant as the rent of a working-
man's flat. He complains brightly that he is hard up, and
that if somebody or other at Westminster does not look out
the country will go to the dogs. He is no fool. He has the
shrewdness to float with the current because it is a labour-
saving process, but he has sufficient pluck to fight, if fight
he must (a brief contest, for he would soon be toppled over).
He has a light nature, which would enable him to bob up
cheerily in new conditions and return unaltered to the old
ones. His selfishness is his most endearing quality. If he*

---

*Athenæum. The Athenæum Club of London, a famous literary
and scientific organization, was founded by Sir Walter Scott,
Thomas Moore, and others in 1824. According to John Steeg-
mann's *Cambridge* (Batsford, London, 1940), "the absurdly named
Athenaeum" of Cambridge "was largely composed of rich Etonians
and Wykehamists and the hunting crowd."

has his way he will spend his life like a cat in pushing his betters out of the soft places, and until he is old he will be fondled in the process.

He gives his hat to one footman and his cane to another, and mounts the great staircase unassisted and undirected. As a nephew of the house he need show no credentials even to CRICHTON, *who is guarding a door above.*

It would not be good taste to describe CRICHTON, *who is only a servant; if to the scandal of all good houses he is to stand out as a figure in the play, he must do it on his own, as they say in the pantry and the boudoir. We are not going to help him. We have had misgivings ever since we found his name in the title, and we shall keep him out of his rights as long as we can. Even though we softened to him he would not be a hero in these clothes of servitude; and he loves his clothes. How to get him out of them? It would require a cataclysm. To be an indoor servant at all is to* CRICHTON *a badge of honour; to be a butler at thirty is the realisation of his proudest ambitions. He is devotedly attached to his master, who, in his opinion, has but one fault, he is not sufficiently contemptuous of his inferiors. We are immediately to be introduced to this solitary failing of a great English peer.*

This perfect butler, then, opens a door, and ushers ERNEST *into a certain room. At the same moment the curtain rises on this room, and the play begins.*

It is one of several reception-rooms in Loam House, not the most magnificent but quite the softest; and of a warm afternoon all that those who are anybody crave for is the softest. The larger rooms are magnificent and bare, carpetless, so that it is an accomplishment to keep one's feet on them; they are sometimes lent for charitable purposes; they are also all in use on the night of a dinner-party, when you may find yourself alone in one, having taken a wrong turning; or alone, save for two others who are within hailing distance. This room, however, is comparatively small and very soft. There are so many cushions in it that you wonder why, if you are an outsider and don't know that it needs six cushions to make one fair head comfy. The couches themselves are cushions as large as beds, and there is an art of sinking into them and of waiting to be helped out of them. There are several famous paintings on the walls, of which you may say "Jolly thing that," without losing caste as knowing too much; and in cases there are glorious miniatures, but the daughters of the house cannot tell you of whom; "there is a catalogue somewhere." There are a thousand or so of roses in basins, several library novels, and a row of weekly illustrated newspapers lying against each other like fallen soldiers. If any one disturbs this row CRICHTON *seems to know of it from afar and appears noiselessly and replaces the wanderer. One thing unexpected in such a room is a great array of tea things.* ERNEST *spots them with a twinkle, and has his epigram at once unsheathed. He dallies, however, before delivering the thrust.*

ERNEST: I perceive, from the tea cups, Crichton, that the great function is to take place here.

CRICHTON [*with a respectful sigh*]: Yes, sir.

ERNEST [*chuckling heartlessly*]: The servants' hall coming up to have tea in the drawing-room! [*With terrible sarcasm*] No wonder you look happy, Crichton.

CRICHTON [*under the knife*]: No, sir.

ERNEST: Do you know, Crichton, I think that with an effort you might look even happier. [CRICHTON *smiles wanly.*] You don't approve of his lordship's compelling his servants to be his equals—once a month?

CRICHTON: It is not for me, sir, to disapprove of his lordship's Radical views.

ERNEST: Certainly not. And, after all, it is only once a month that he is affable to you.

CRICHTON: On all other days of the month, sir, his lordship's treatment of us is everything that could be desired.

ERNEST [*this is the epigram*]: Tea cups! Life, Crichton, is like a cup of tea; the more heartily we drink, the sooner we reach the dregs.

CRICHTON [*obediently*]: Thank you, sir.

ERNEST [*becoming confidential, as we do when we have need of an ally*]: Crichton, in case I should be asked to say a few words to the servants, I have strung together a little speech. [*His hand strays to his pocket.*] I was wondering where I should stand.

[*He tries various places and postures, and comes to rest leaning over a high chair, whence, in dumb show, he addresses a gathering.* CRICHTON, *with the best intentions, gives him a footstool to stand on, and departs, happily unconscious that* ERNEST *in some dudgeon has kicked the footstool across the room.*]

ERNEST [*addressing an imaginary audience, and desirous of startling them at once*]: Suppose you were all little fishes at the bottom of the sea—

[*He is not quite satisfied with his position, though sure that the fault must lie with the chair for being too high, not with him for being too short.* CRICHTON'S *suggestion was not perhaps a bad one after all. He lifts the stool, but hastily conceals it behind him on the entrance of the* LADIES CATHERINE *and* AGATHA, *two daughters of the house.* CATHERINE *is twenty, and* AGATHA *two years younger. They are very fashionable young women indeed, who might wake up for a dance, but they are very lazy,* CATHERINE *being two years lazier than* AGATHA.]

ERNEST [*uneasily jocular, because he is concealing the footstool*]: And how are my little friends today?

AGATHA [*contriving to reach a settee*]: Don't be silly, Ernest. If you want to know how we are, we are dead. Even to think of entertaining the servants is so exhausting.

CATHERINE [*subsiding nearer the door*]: Besides which, we have had to decide what frocks to take with us on the yacht, and that is such a mental strain.

ERNEST: You poor over-worked things. [*Evidently* AGATHA *is his favourite, for he helps her to put her feet on the settee, while* CATHERINE *has to dispose of her own feet.*] Rest your weary limbs.

CATHERINE [*perhaps in revenge*]: But why have you a footstool in your hand?

AGATHA: Yes?

ERNEST: Why? [*Brilliantly; but to be sure he has had time to think it out.*] You see, as the servants are to be the guests I must be butler. I was practising. This is a tray, observe. [*Holding the footstool as a tray, he minces across the room like an accomplished footman. The gods favour him, for just here* LADY MARY *enters, and he holds out the footstool to her.*] Tea, my lady?

[LADY MARY *is a beautiful creature of twenty-two, and is of a natural hauteur which is at once the fury and the envy of her sisters. If she chooses she can make you seem so insignificant that you feel you might be swept away with the crumb-brush. She seldom chooses,* because of the trouble of preening herself as she does it; she is usually content to show that you merely tire her eyes. She often seems to be about to go to sleep in the middle of a remark: there is quite a long and anxious pause, and then she continues, like a clock that hesitates, bored in the middle of its strike.]

LADY MARY [*arching her brows*]: It is only you, Ernest; I thought there was some one here. [*And she also bestows herself on cushions.*]

ERNEST [*a little piqued, and deserting the footstool*]: Had a very tiring day also, Mary?

LADY MARY [*yawning*]: Dreadfully. Been trying on engagement-rings all the morning.

ERNEST [*who is as fond of gossip as the oldest club member*]: What's that? [*To* AGATHA.] Is it Brocklehurst? [*The energetic* AGATHA *nods.*] You have given your warm young heart to Brocky? [LADY MARY *is impervious to his humour, but he continues bravely.*] I don't wish to fatigue you, Mary, by insisting on a verbal answer, but if, without straining yourself, you can signify Yes or No, won't you make the effort? [*She indolently flashes a ring on her most important finger, and he starts back melodramatically.*] The ring! Then I am too late, too late! [*Fixing* LADY MARY *sternly, like a prosecuting counsel.*] May I ask, Mary, does Brocky know? Of course, it was that terrible mother of his who pulled this through. Mother does everything for Brocky. Still, in the eyes of the law you will be, not her wife, but his, and, therefore, I hold that Brocky ought to be informed. Now— [*He discovers that their languorous eyes have closed.*] If you girls are shamming sleep in the expectation that I shall awaken you in the manner beloved of ladies, abandon all such hopes.

[CATHERINE *and* AGATHA *look up without speaking.*]

LADY MARY [*speaking without looking up*]: You impertinent boy.

ERNEST [*eagerly plucking another epigram from his quiver*]: I knew that was it, though I don't know everything. Agatha, I'm not young enough to know everything. [*He looks hopefully from one to another, but though they try to grasp this, his brilliance baffles them.*]

AGATHA [*his secret admirer*]: *Young* enough?

ERNEST [*encouragingly*]: Don't you see? I'm not young enough to know everything.

AGATHA: I'm sure it's awfully clever, but it's so puzzling.

[*Here* CRICHTON *ushers in an athletic, pleasant-faced young clergyman,* MR. TREHERNE, *who greets the company.*]

CATHERINE: Ernest, say it to Mr. Treherne.

ERNEST: Look here, Treherne, I'm not young enough to know everything.

TREHERNE: How do you mean, Ernest?

ERNEST [*a little nettled*]: I mean what I say.

LADY MARY: Say it again; say it more slowly.

ERNEST: I'm—not—young—enough —to—know—everything.

TREHERNE: *I* see. What you really mean, my boy, is that you are not old enough to know everything.

ERNEST: No, I don't.

TREHERNE: I assure you that's it.

LADY MARY: Of course it is.

CATHERINE: Yes, Ernest, that's it.

[ERNEST, *in desperation, appeals to* CRICHTON.]

ERNEST: I am not young enough, Crichton, to know everything.

[*It is an anxious moment, but a smile is at length extorted from* CRICHTON *as with a corkscrew.*]

CRICHTON: Thank you, sir. [*He goes.*]

ERNEST [*relieved*]: Ah, if you had that fellow's head, Treherne, you would find something better to do with it than play cricket. I hear you bowl with your head.

TREHERNE [*with proper humility*]: I'm afraid cricket is all I'm good for, Ernest.

CATHERINE [*who thinks he has a heavenly nose*]: Indeed, it isn't. You are sure to get on, Mr. Treherne.

TREHERNE: Thank you, Lady Catherine.

CATHERINE: But it was the bishop who told me so. He said a clergyman who breaks both ways* is sure to get on in England.

TREHERNE: I'm jolly glad.

*breaks both ways. A "break" in cricket is comparable to a curved pitch in baseball, except that the curve becomes important after the ball hits the ground.

[*The master of the house comes in, accompanied by* LORD BROCKLEHURST. *The* EARL OF LOAM *is a widower, a philanthropist, and a peer of advanced ideas. As a widower he is at least able to interfere in the domestic concerns of his house—to rummage in the drawers, so to speak, for which he has felt an itching all his blameless life; his philanthropy has opened quite a number of other drawers to him; and his advanced ideas have blown out his figure. He takes in all the weightiest monthly reviews, and prefers those that are uncut, because he perhaps never looks better than when cutting them; but he does not read them, and save for the cutting it would suit him as well merely to take in the covers. He writes letters to the papers, which are printed in a type to scale with himself, and he is very jealous of those other correspondents who get his type. Let laws and learning, art and commerce die, but leave the big type to an intellectual aristocracy. He is really the reformed House of Lords which will come some day.*

Young LORD BROCKLEHURST *is nothing save for his rank. You could pick him up by the handful any day in Piccadilly or Holborn, buying socks—or selling them.*]

LORD LOAM [*expansively*]: You are here, Ernest. Feeling fit for the voyage, Treherne?

TREHERNE: Looking forward to it enormously.

LORD LOAM: That's right. [*He chases his children about as if they were chickens.*] Now then, Mary, up and doing, up and doing. Time we had the servants in. They enjoy it so much.

LADY MARY: They hate it.

LORD LOAM: Mary, to your duties. [*And he points severely to the tea-table.*]

ERNEST [*twinkling*]: Congratulations, Brocky.

LORD BROCKLEHURST [*who detests humour*]: Thanks.

ERNEST: Mother pleased?

LORD BROCKLEHURST [*with dignity*]: Mother is very pleased.

ERNEST: That's good. Do you go on the yacht with us?

LORD BROCKLEHURST: Sorry I can't. And look here, Ernest, I will *not* be called Brocky.

ERNEST: Mother don't like it?

LORD BROCKLEHURST: She does not. [*He leaves* ERNEST, *who forgives him and begins to think about his speech.* CRICHTON *enters.*]

LORD LOAM [*speaking as one man to another*]: We are quite ready, Crichton.

[CRICHTON *is distressed.*]

LADY MARY [*sarcastically*]: How Crichton enjoys it.!

LORD LOAM [*frowning*]: He is the only one who doesn't; pitiful creature.

CRICHTON [*shuddering under his lord's displeasure*]: I can't help being a Conservative, my lord.

LORD LOAM: Be a man, Crichton. You are the same flesh and blood as myself.

CRICHTON [*in pain*]: Oh, my lord!

LORD LOAM [*sharply*]: Show them in; and, by the way, they were not all here last time.

CRICHTON: All, my lord, except the merest trifles.

LORD LOAM: It must be every one.

[*Lowering.*] And remember this, Crichton, for the time being you are my equal. [*Testily.*] I shall soon show you whether you are not my equal. Do as you are told. [CRICHTON *departs to obey, and his lordship is now a general. He has no pity for his daughters, and uses a terrible threat.*] And girls, remember, no condescension. The first who condescends recites. [*This sends them scurrying to their labours.*] By the way, Brocklehurst, can you do anything?

LORD BROCKLEHURST: How do you mean?

LORD LOAM: Can you do anything—with a penny or a handkerchief, make them disappear, for instance?

LORD BROCKLEHURST: Good heavens, no.

LORD LOAM: It's a pity. Every one in our position ought to be able to do something. Ernest, I shall probably ask you to say a few words; something bright and sparkling.

ERNEST: But, my dear uncle, I have prepared nothing.

LORD LOAM: Anything impromptu will do.

ERNEST: Oh—well—if anything strikes me on the spur of the moment. [*He unostentatiously gets the footstool into position behind the chair.* CRICHTON *reappears to announce the guests, of whom the first is the housekeeper.*]

CRICHTON [*reluctantly*]: Mrs. Perkins.

LORD LOAM [*shaking hands*]: Very delighted, Mrs. Perkins. Mary, our friend, Mrs. Perkins.

LADY MARY: How do you do, Mrs. Perkins? Won't you sit here?

LORD LOAM [*threateningly*]: Agatha!

AGATHA [*hastily*]: How do you do? Won't you sit down?

LORD LOAM [*introducing*]: Lord Brocklehurst—my valued friend, Mrs. Perkins.

[LORD BROCKLEHURST *bows and escapes. He has to fall back on* ERNEST.]

LORD BROCKLEHURST: For heaven's sake, Ernest, don't leave me for a moment; this sort of thing is utterly opposed to all my principles.

ERNEST [*airily*]: You stick to me, Brocky, and I'll pull you through.

CRICHTON: Monsieur Fleury.

ERNEST: The chef.

LORD LOAM [*shaking hands with the chef*]: Very charmed to see you, Monsieur Fleury.

FLEURY: Thank you very much. [FLEURY *bows to* AGATHA, *who is not effusive.*]

LORD LOAM [*warningly*]: Agatha—recitation?

[*She tosses her head, but immediately finds a seat and tea for* M. FLEURY. TREHERNE *and* ERNEST *move about, making themselves amiable.* LADY MARY *is presiding at the tea-tray.*]

CRICHTON: Mr. Rolleston.

LORD LOAM [*shaking hands with his valet*]: How do you do, Rolleston?

[CATHERINE *looks after the wants of* ROLLESTON.]

CRICHTON: Mr. Tompsett.

[TOMPSETT, *the coachman, is re-*

*ceived with honours, from which
he shrinks.*]

CRICHTON: Miss Fisher.

[*This superb creature is no less
than* LADY MARY'S *maid, and even*
LORD LOAM *is a little nervous.*]

LORD LOAM: This is a pleasure,
Miss Fisher.

ERNEST [*unabashed*]: If I might
venture, Miss Fisher. [*And he
takes her unto himself.*]

CRICHTON: Miss Simmons.

LORD LOAM [*to* CATHERINE'S *maid*]:
You are always welcome, Miss
Simmons.

ERNEST [*perhaps to kindle jealousy
in* MISS FISHER]: At last we meet.
Won't you sit down?

CRICHTON: Mademoiselle Jeanne.

LORD LOAM: Charmed to see you,
Mademoiselle Jeanne.

[*A place is found for* AGATHA'S
*maid, and the scene is now an
animated one; but still our host
thinks his girls are not sufficiently
sociable. He frowns on* LADY MARY.]

LADY MARY [*in alarm*]: Mr. Treherne, this is Fisher, my maid.

LORD LOAM [*sharply*]: Your what,
Mary?

LADY MARY: My friend.

CRICHTON: Thomas.

LORD LOAM: How do you do,
Thomas?

[*The first footman gives him a
reluctant hand.*]

CRICHTON: John.

LORD LOAM: How do you do,
John?

[ERNEST *signs to* LORD BROCKLE-
HURST, *who hastens to him.*]

ERNEST [*introducing*]: Brocklehurst, this is John. I think you

have already met on the doorstep.

CRICHTON: Jane.

[*She comes, wrapping her hands
miserably in her apron.*]

LORD LOAM [*doggedly*]: Give me
your hand, Jane.

CRICHTON: Gladys.

ERNEST: How do you do, Gladys.
You know my uncle?

LORD LOAM: Your hand, Gladys.

[*He bestows her on* AGATHA.]

CRICHTON: Tweeny.

[*She is a very humble and frightened kitchenmaid, of whom we are
to see more.*]

LORD LOAM: So happy to see you.

FISHER: John, I saw you talking
to Lord Brocklehurst just now;
introduce me.

LORD BROCKLEHURST [*at the same
moment to* ERNEST]: That's an
uncommon pretty girl; if I must
feed one of them, Ernest, that's
the one.

[*But* ERNEST *tries to part him and*
FISHER *as they are about to shake
hands.*]

ERNEST: No you don't, it won't
do, Brocky. [*To* MISS FISHER.]
You are too pretty, my dear.
Mother wouldn't like it. [*Dis-
covering* TWEENY.] Here's something safer. Charming girl,
Brocky, dying to know you; let
me introduce you. Tweeny, Lord
Brocklehurst—Lord Brocklehurst, Tweeny.

[BROCKLEHURST *accepts his fate;
but he still has an eye for* FISHER,
and something may come of this.]

LORD LOAM [*severely*]: They are not all here, Crichton.

CRICHTON [*with a sigh*]: Odds and ends.

[*A* STABLE-BOY *and a* PAGE *are shown in, and for a moment no daughter of the house advances to them.*]

LORD LOAM [*with a roving eye on his children*]: Which is to recite?

[*The last of the company are, so to say, embraced.*]

LORD LOAM [*to* TOMPSETT, *as they partake of tea together*]: And how are all at home?

TOMPSETT: Fairish, my lord, if 'tis the horses you are inquiring for?

LORD LOAM: No, no, the family. How's the baby?

TOMPSETT: Blooming, your lordship.

LORD LOAM: A very fine boy. I remember saying so when I saw him; nice little fellow.

TOMPSETT [*not quite knowing whether to let it pass*]: Beg pardon, my lord, it's a girl.

LORD LOAM: A girl? Aha! ha! ha! exactly what I said. I distinctly remember saying, If it's spared it will be a girl.

[CRICHTON *now comes down.*]

LORD LOAM: Very delighted to see you, Crichton. [CRICHTON *has to shake hands.*] Mary, you know Mr. Crichton? [*He wanders off in search of other prey.*]

LADY MARY: Milk and sugar, Crichton?

CRICHTON: I'm ashamed to be seen talking to you, my lady.

LADY MARY: To such a perfect servant as you all this must be most distasteful. [CRICHTON *i too respectful to answer.*] Oh please do speak, or I shall hav to recite. You do hate it, don' you?

CRICHTON: It pains me, you ladyship. It disturbs the eti quette of the servants' hall After last month's meeting th pageboy, in a burst of equality called me Crichton. He wa dismissed.

LADY MARY: I wonder—I reall do—how you can remain wit us.

CRICHTON: I should have fe compelled to give notice, m lady, if the master had not ha a seat in the Upper House. cling to that.

LADY MARY: Do go on speakin Tell me, what did Mr. Erne mean by saying he was not youn enough to know everything?

CRICHTON: I have no idea, m lady.

LADY MARY: But you laughed.

CRICHTON: My lady, he is th second son of a peer.

LADY MARY: Very proper sent ments. You are a good sou Crichton.

LORD BROCKLEHURST [*desperate to* TWEENY]: And now tell m have you been to the Oper What sort of weather have yc been having in the kitche [TWEENY *gurgles.*] For heaven sake, woman, be articulate.

CRICHTON [*still talking to* LAD MARY]: No, my lady; his lor ship may compel us to be equ upstairs, but there will never b equality in the servants' hall.

LORD LOAM [*overhearing this* What's that? No equality? Can you see, Crichton, that our div

sions into classes are artificial, that if we were to return to Nature, which is the aspiration of my life, all would be equal?

CRICHTON: If I may make so bold as to contradict your lordship—

LORD LOAM [*with an effort*]: Go on.

CRICHTON: The divisions into classes, my lord, are not artificial. They are the natural outcome of a civilised society. [*To* LADY MARY.] There must always be a master and servants in all civilised communities, my lady, for it is natural, and whatever is natural is right.

LORD LOAM [*wincing*]: It is very unnatural for me to stand here and allow you to talk such nonsense.

CRICHTON [*eagerly*]: Yes, my lord, it is. That is what I have been striving to point out to your lordship.

AGATHA [*to* CATHERINE]: What is the matter with Fisher? She is looking daggers.

CATHERINE: The tedious creature; some question of etiquette, I suppose. [*She sails across to* FISHER.] How are you, Fisher?

FISHER [*with a toss of her head*]: I am nothing, my lady, I am nothing at all.

AGATHA: Oh dear, who says so?

FISHER [*affronted*]: His lordship has asked that kitchen wench to have a second cup of tea.

CATHERINE: But why not?

FISHER: If it pleases his lordship to offer it to *her* before offering it to *me*—

AGATHA: So that is it. Do you want another cup of tea, Fisher?

FISHER: No, my lady—but my po-

sition—I should have been asked first.

AGATHA: Oh dear.

[*All this has taken some time, and by now the feeble appetites of the uncomfortable guests have been satiated. But they know there is still another ordeal to face—his lordship's monthly speech. Every one awaits it with misgiving—the servants lest they should applaud, as last time, in the wrong place, and the daughters because he may be personal about them, as the time before.* ERNEST *is annoyed that there should be this speech at all when there is such a much better one coming, and* BROCKLEHURST *foresees the degradation of the peerage. All are thinking of themselves alone save* CRICHTON, *who knows his master's weakness, and fears he may stick in the middle.* LORD LOAM, *however, advances cheerfully to his doom. He sees* ERNEST'S *stool, and artfully stands on it, to his nephew's natural indignation. The three ladies knit their lips, the servants look down their noses, and the address begins.*]

LORD LOAM: My friends, I am glad to see you all looking so happy. It used to be predicted by the scoffer that these meetings would prove distasteful to you. Are they distasteful? I hear you laughing at the question. [*He has not heard them, but he hears them now, the watchful* CRICHTON *giving them a lead.*] No harm in saying that among us today is one who was formerly hostile to the movement, but who today has been won over. I refer to Lord Brocklehurst, who, I am sure, will presently say to me that if the charming lady now by his side has derived as much pleasure from his company as he has derived from hers, he will be more than satisfied. [*All look at* TWEENY, *who trembles.*] For the time being the artificial and unnatural—I say unnatural—[*Glaring at* CRICHTON, *who bows slightly.*]—barriers of society are swept away. Would that they could be swept away for ever. [*The* PAGEBOY *cheers, and has the one moment of prominence in his life. He grows up, marries, and has children, but is never really heard of again.*] But that is entirely and utterly out of the question. And now for a few months we are to be separated. As you know, my daughters and Mr. Ernest and Mr. Treherne are to accompany me on my yacht, on a voyage to distant parts of the earth. In less than forty-eight hours we shall be under weigh. [*But for* CRICHTON'S *eye the reckless* PAGEBOY *would repeat his success.*] Do not think our life on the yacht is to be one long idle holiday. My views on the excessive luxury of the day are well known, and what I preach I am resolved to practise. I have therefore decided that my daughters, instead of having one maid each as a present, shall on this voyage have but one maid between them.

[*Three maids rise; also three mistresses.*]

CRICHTON: My lord!
LORD LOAM: My mind is made up.
ERNEST: I cordially agree.
LORD LOAM: And now, my friends,

I should like to think that there is some piece of advice I might give you, some thought, some noble saying over which you might ponder in my absence. In this connection I remember a proverb, which has had a great effect on my own life. I first heard it many years ago. I have never forgotten it. It constantly cheers and guides me. That proverb is—that proverb was—the proverb I speak of— [*He grows pale and taps his forehead.*]

LADY MARY: Oh dear, I believe he has forgotten it.

LORD LOAM [*desperately*]: The proverb—that proverb to which I refer— [*Alas, it has gone. The distress is general. He has not even the sense to sit down. He gropes for the proverb in the air. They try applause, but it is no help.*] I have it now—[*Not he.*]

LADY MARY [*with confidence*]: Crichton.

[*He does not fail her. As quietly as if he were in goloshes, mind as well as feet, he dismisses the domestics; they go according to precedence as they entered, yet, in a moment, they are gone. Then he signs to* MR. TREHERNE, *and they conduct* LORD LOAM *with dignity from the room. His hands are still catching flies; he still mutters, "The proverb—that proverb"; but he continues, owing to* CRICHTON'S *skilful treatment, to look every inch a peer. The ladies have now an opportunity to air their indignation.*]

LADY MARY: One maid among three grown women!

LORD BROCKLEHURST: Mary,

think I had better go. That dreadful kitchenmaid—

LADY MARY: I can't blame you, George.

[*He salutes her.*]

LORD BROCKLEHURST: Your father's views are shocking to me, and I am glad I am not to be one of the party on the yacht. My respect for myself, Mary, my natural anxiety as to what mother will say. I shall see you, darling, before you sail. [*He bows to the others and goes.*]

ERNEST: Selfish brute, only thinking of himself. What about my speech?

LADY MARY: One maid among three of us. What's to be done?

ERNEST: Pooh! You must do for yourselves, that's all.

LADY MARY: Do for ourselves. How can we know where our things are kept?

AGATHA: Are you aware that dresses button up the back?

CATHERINE: How are we to get into our shoes and be prepared for the carriage?

LADY MARY: Who is to put us to bed, and who is to get us up, and how shall we ever know it's morning if there is no one to pull up the blinds?

[CRICHTON *crosses on his way out.*]

ERNEST: How is his lordship now?

CRICHTON: A little easier, sir.

LADY MARY: Crichton, send Fisher to me.

[*He goes.*]

ERNEST: I have no pity for you girls, I—

LADY MARY: Ernest, go away, and don't insult the broken-hearted.

ERNEST: And uncommon glad I am to go. Ta-ta, all of you. He asked me to say a few words. I came here to say a few words, and I'm not at all sure that I couldn't bring an action against him. [*He departs, feeling that he has left a dart behind him. The girls are alone with their tragic thoughts.*]

LADY MARY [*become a mother to the younger ones at last*]: My poor sisters, come here. [*They go to her doubtfully.*] We must make this draw us closer together. I shall do my best to help you in every way. Just now I cannot think of myself at all.

AGATHA: But how unlike you, Mary.

LADY MARY: It is my duty to protect my sisters.

CATHERINE: I never knew her so sweet before, Agatha. [*Cautiously.*] What do you propose to do, Mary?

LADY MARY: I propose when we are on the yacht to lend Fisher to you when I don't need her myself.

AGATHA: Fisher?

LADY MARY [*who has the most character of the three*]: Of course, as the eldest, I have decided that it is *my* maid we shall take with us.

CATHERINE [*speaking also for* AGATHA]: Mary, you toad.

AGATHA: Nothing on earth would induce Fisher to lift her hand for either me or Catherine.

LADY MARY: I was afraid of it, Agatha. That is why I am so sorry for you.

[*The further exchange of pleas-*

antries is interrupted by the arrival of FISHER.]

LADY MARY: Fisher, you heard what his lordship said?

FISHER: Yes, my lady.

LADY MARY [*coldly, though the others would have tried blandishment*]: You have given me some satisfaction of late, Fisher, and to mark my approval I have decided that you shall be the maid who accompanies us.

FISHER [*acidly*]: I thank you, my lady.

LADY MARY: That is all; you may go.

FISHER [*rapping it out*]: If you please, my lady, I wish to give notice.

[CATHERINE *and* AGATHA *gleam, but* LADY MARY *is of sterner stuff.*]

LADY MARY [*taking up a book*]: Oh, certainly—you may go.

CATHERINE: But why, Fisher?

FISHER: I could not undertake, my lady, to wait upon three. *We* don't do it. [*In an indignant outburst to* LADY MARY.] Oh, my lady, to think that this affront—

LADY MARY [*looking up*]: I thought I told you to go, Fisher.

[FISHER *stands for a moment irresolute; then goes. As soon as she has gone* LADY MARY *puts down her book and weeps. She is a pretty woman, but this is the only pretty thing we have seen her do yet.*]

AGATHA [*succinctly*]: Serves you right.

[CRICHTON *comes.*]

CATHERINE: It will be Simmons after all. Send Simmons to me.

CRICHTON [*after hesitating*]: My lady, might I venture to speak?

CATHERINE: What is it?

CRICHTON: I happen to know, your ladyship, that Simmons desires to give notice for the same reason as Fisher.

CATHERINE: Oh!

AGATHA [*triumphant*]: Then, Catherine, we take Jeanne.

CRICHTON: And Jeanne also, my lady.

[LADY MARY *is reading, indifferent though the heavens fall, but her sisters are not ashamed to show their despair to* CRICHTON.]

AGATHA: We can't blame them. Could any maid who respected herself be got to wait upon three?

LADY MARY [*with languid interest*]: I suppose there are such persons, Crichton?

CRICHTON [*guardedly*]: I have heard, my lady, that there are such.

LADY MARY [*a little desperate*]: Crichton, what's to be done? We sail in two days; could one be discovered in the time?

AGATHA [*frankly a supplicant*]: Surely you can think of some one?

CRICHTON [*after hesitating*]: There is in this establishment, your ladyship, a young woman—

LADY MARY: Yes?

CRICHTON: A young woman, on whom I have for some time cast an eye.

CATHERINE [*eagerly*]: Do you mean as a possible lady's-maid?

CRICHTON: I had thought of her, my lady, in another connection.

LADY MARY: Ah!

CRICHTON: But I believe she is quite the young person you require. Perhaps if you could see her, my lady—

LADY MARY: I shall certainly see her. Bring her to me. [*He goes.*] You two needn't wait.

CATHERINE: Needn't we? We see your little game, Mary.

AGATHA: We shall certainly remain and have our two thirds of her.

[*They sit there doggedly until* CRICHTON *returns with* TWEENY, *who looks scared.*]

CRICHTON: This, my lady, is the young person.

CATHERINE [*frankly*]: Oh dear!

[*It is evident that all three consider her quite unsuitable.*]

LADY MARY: Come here, girl. Don't be afraid.

[TWEENY *looks imploringly at her idol.*]

CRICHTON: Her appearance, my lady, is homely, and her manners, as you may have observed, deplorable, but she has a heart of gold.

LADY MARY: What is your position downstairs?

TWEENY [*bobbing*]: I'm a tweeny, your ladyship.

CATHERINE: A what?

CRICHTON: A tweeny; that is to say, my lady, she is not at present, strictly speaking, anything; a *between* maid; she helps the vegetable maid. It is she, my lady, who conveys the dishes from the one end of the kitchen table, where they are placed by the cook, to the other end, where they enter into the charge of Thomas and John.

LADY MARY: I see. And you and Crichton are—ah—keeping company?

[CRICHTON *draws himself up.*]

TWEENY [*aghast*]: A butler don't keep company, my lady.

LADY MARY [*indifferently*]: Does he not?

CRICHTON: No, your ladyship, we butlers may—[*He makes a gesture with his arms.*]—but we do not keep company.

AGATHA: I know what it is; you are engaged?

[TWEENY *looks longingly at* CRICHTON.]

CRICHTON: Certainly not, my lady. The utmost I can say at present is that I have cast a favourable eye.

[*Even this is much to* TWEENY.]

LADY MARY: As you choose. But I am afraid, Crichton, she will not suit us.

CRICHTON: My lady, beneath this simple exterior are concealed a very sweet nature and rare womanly gifts.

AGATHA: Unfortunately, that is not what we want.

CRICHTON: And it is she, my lady, who dresses the hair of the ladies'-maids for our evening meals.

[*The ladies are interested at last.*]

LADY MARY: She dresses Fisher's hair?

TWEENY: Yes, my lady, and I does them up when they goes to parties.

CRICHTON [*pained, but not scolding*]: *Does!*

TWEENY: Doos. And it's me what alters your gowns to fit them.

CRICHTON: *What* alters?

TWEENY: Which alters.

AGATHA: Mary?

LADY MARY: I shall certainly have her.

CATHERINE: *We* shall certainly have her. Tweeny, we have decided to make a lady's-maid of you.

TWEENY: Oh lawks!

AGATHA: We are doing this for you so that your position socially may be more nearly akin to that of Crichton.

CRICHTON [*gravely*]: It will undoubtedly increase the young person's chances.

LADY MARY: Then if I get a good character for you from Mrs. Perkins, she will make the necessary arrangements.

[*She resumes reading.*]

TWEENY [*elated*]: My lady!

LADY MARY: By the way, I hope you are a good sailor.

TWEENY [*startled*]: You don't mean, my lady, I'm to go on the ship?

LADY MARY: Certainly.

TWEENY: But— [*To* CRICHTON.] You ain't going, sir?

CRICHTON: No.

TWEENY [*firm at last*]: Then neither ain't I.

AGATHA: You must.

TWEENY: Leave him! Not me.

LADY MARY: Girl, don't be silly. Crichton will be—considered in your wages.

TWEENY: I ain't going.

CRICHTON: I feared this, my lady.

TWEENY: Nothing'll budge me.

LADY MARY: Leave the room.

[CRICHTON *shows* TWEENY *out with marked politeness.*]

AGATHA: Crichton, I think you might have shown more displeasure with her.

CRICHTON [*contrite*]: I was touched, my lady. I see, my lady, that to part from her would be a wrench to me, though I could not well say so in her presence, not having yet decided how far I shall go with her. [*He is about to go when* LORD LOAM *returns, fuming.*]

LORD LOAM: The ingrate! The smug! The fop!

CATHERINE: What is it now, father?

LORD LOAM: That man of mine, Rolleston, refuses to accompany us because you are to have but one maid.

AGATHA: Hurrah!

LADY MARY [*in better taste*]: Darling father, rather than you should lose Rolleston, we will consent to take all the three of them.

LORD LOAM: Pooh, nonsense! Crichton, find me a valet who can do without three maids.

CRICHTON: Yes, my lord. [*Troubled.*] In the time—the more suitable the party, my lord, the less willing will he be to come without the—the usual perquisites.

LORD LOAM: Any one will do.

CRICHTON [*shocked*]: My lord!

LORD LOAM: The ingrate! The puppy!

[AGATHA *has an idea, and whispers to* LADY MARY.]

LADY MARY: I ask a favour of a servant?—never!

AGATHA: Then I will. Crichton, would it not be very distressing to you to let his lordship go, attended by a valet who might

prove unworthy? It is only for
three months; don't you think
that you—you yourself—you—
[*As* CRICHTON *sees what she
wants he pulls himself up with
noble, offended dignity, and she
is appalled.*] I beg your pardon.
[*He bows stiffly.*]

CATHERINE [*to* CRICHTON]: But
think of the joy to Tweeny.

[CRICHTON *is moved, but he shakes
his head.*]

LADY MARY [*so much the cleverest*]:
Crichton, do you think it safe
to let the master you love go so
far away without you while he
has these dangerous views about
equality?

[CRICHTON *is profoundly stirred.
After a struggle he goes to his master, who has been pacing the room.*]

CRICHTON: My lord, I have found
a man.

LORD LOAM: Already? Who is he?
[CRICHTON *presents himself with
a gesture.*] Yourself?

CATHERINE: Father, how good of
him.

LORD LOAM [*pleased, but thinking
it a small thing*]: Uncommon
good. Thank you, Crichton. This
helps me nicely out of a hole;
and how it will annoy Rolleston!
Come with me, and we shall tell
him. Not that I think you have
lowered yourself in any way.
Come along. [*He goes, and
CRICHTON is to follow him, but
is stopped by AGATHA impulsively
offering him her hand.*]

CRICHTON [*who is much shaken*]:
My lady—a valet's hand!

AGATHA: I had no idea you would
feel it so deeply; why did you
do it?

[CRICHTON *is too respectful to
reply.*]

LADY MARY [*regarding him*]:
Crichton, I am curious. I insist
upon an answer.

CRICHTON: My lady, I am the son
of a butler and a lady's-maid—
perhaps the happiest of all
combinations, and to me the
most beautiful thing in the world
is a haughty, aristocratic English house, with every one kept
in his place. Though I were
equal to your ladyship, where
would be the pleasure to me?
It would be counterbalanced
by the pain of feeling that
Thomas and John were equal
to me.

CATHERINE: But father says if we
were to return to Nature—

CRICHTON: If we did, my lady,
the first thing we should do
would be to elect a head. Circumstances might alter cases;
the same person might not be
master; the same persons might
not be servants. I can't say as
to that, nor should we have the
deciding of it. Nature would
decide for us.

LADY MARY: You seem to have
thought it all out carefully,
Crichton.

CRICHTON: Yes, my lady.

CATHERINE: And you have done
this for us, Crichton, because
you thought that—that father
needed to be kept in his place?

CRICHTON: I should prefer to
say, my lady, that I have done
it for the house.

AGATHA: Thank you, Crichton.
Mary, be nicer to him. [*But
LADY MARY has begun to read
again.*] If there was any way

in which we could show our gratitude.

CRICHTON: If I might venture, my lady, would you kindly show it by becoming more like Lady Mary. That disdain is what we like from our superiors. Even so do we, the upper servants, disdain the lower servants, while they take it out of the odds and ends. [*He goes, and they bury themselves in cushions.*]

AGATHA: Oh dear, what a tiring day.

CATHERINE: I feel dead. Tuck in your feet, you selfish thing.

[LADY MARY *is lying reading on another couch.*]

LADY MARY: I wonder what he meant by circumstances might alter cases.

AGATHA [*yawning*]: Don't talk, Mary, I was nearly asleep.

LADY MARY: I wonder what he meant by the same person might not be master, and the same persons might not be servants.

CATHERINE: Do be quiet, Mary, and leave it to Nature; he said Nature would decide.

LADY MARY: I wonder— [*But she does not wonder very much. She would wonder more if she knew what was coming. Her book slips unregarded to the floor. The ladies are at rest until it is time to dress.*]

LADY MARY: I wonder what he

END OF ACT I

ACT TWO

The island.

Two months have elapsed, and the scene is a desert island in the Pacific, on which our adventurers have been wrecked.

The curtain rises on a sea of bamboo, which shuts out all view save the foliage of palm trees and some gaunt rocks. Occasionally CRICHTON *and* TREHERNE *come momentarily into sight, hacking and hewing the bamboo, through which they are making a clearing between the ladies and the shore; and by and by, owing to their efforts, we shall have an unrestricted outlook on to a sullen sea that is at present hidden. Then we shall also be able to note a mast standing out of the water—all that is left, saving floating wreckage, of the ill-fated yacht the* Bluebell. *The beginnings of a hut will also be seen, with* CRICHTON *driving its walls into the ground or astride its roof of saplings, for at present he is doing more than one thing at a time. In a red shirt, with the ends of his sailor's breeches thrust into wading-boots, he looks a man for the moment; we suddenly remember some one's saying— perhaps it was ourselves—that a cataclysm would be needed* to get him out of his servant's clothes, and apparently it has been forthcoming. It is no longer beneath our dignity to cast an inquiring eye on his appearance. His features are not distinguished, but he has a strong jaw and green eyes, in which a yellow light burns that we have not seen before. His dark hair, hitherto so decorously sleek, has been ruffled this way and that by wind and weather, as if they were part of the cataclysm and wanted to help his chance. His muscles must be soft and flabby still, but though they shriek aloud to him to desist, he rains lusty blows with his axe, like one who has come upon the open for the first time in his life, and likes it. He is as yet far from being an expert woods-man—mark the blood on his hands at places where he has hit them instead of the tree; but note also that he does not waste time in bandaging them—he rubs them in the earth and goes on. His face is still of the discreet pallor that be-fits a butler, and he carries the smaller logs as if they were a salver; not in a day or a month will he shake off the badge of servitude, but without knowing it he has begun.

But for the hatchets at work, and an occasional something horrible falling from a tree into the ladies' laps, they hear nothing save the mournful surf breaking on a coral shore.

They sit or recline huddled together against a rock, and they are farther from home, in every sense of the word, than ever before. Thirty-six hours ago, they were given three minutes in which to dress, without a maid, and reach the boats, and they have not made the best of that valuable time. None of them has boots, and had they known this prickly island they would have thought first of boots. They have a sufficiency of garments, but some of them were gifts dropped into the boat—LADY MARY'S tarpaulin coat and hat, for instance, and CATHERINE'S blue jersey and red cap, which certify that the two ladies were lately before the mast. AGATHA is too gay in ERNEST'S dressing-gown, and clutches it to her person with both hands as if afraid that it may be claimed by its rightful owner. There are two pairs of bath slippers between the three of them, and their hair cries aloud and in vain for hairpins.

By their side, on an inverted bucket, sits ERNEST, clothed neatly in the garments of day and night, but, alas, bare-footed. He is the only cheerful member of this company of four, but his brightness is due less to a manly desire to suc-cour the helpless than to his having been lately in the throes of composition, and to his modest satisfaction with the re-sult. He reads to the ladies, and they listen, each with one scared eye to the things that fall from trees.

ERNEST [*who has written on the fly-leaf of the only book saved from the wreck*]: This is what I have written. "Wrecked, wrecked, wrecked! on an island in the Tropics, the following: the Hon. Ernest Woolley, the Rev. John Treherne, the Ladies Mary, Catherine, and Agatha Lasenby, with two servants. We are the sole survivors of Lord Loam's steam yacht *Bluebell*, which encountered a fearful gale in these seas, and soon became a total wreck. The crew behaved gallantly, putting us all into the first boat. What became of them I cannot tell, but we, after dreadful sufferings, and insufficiently clad, in whatever garments we could lay hold of in the dark"—

LADY MARY: Please don't describe our garments.

ERNEST: —"succeeded in reaching this island, with the loss of only one of our party, namely, Lord Loam, who flung away his life in a gallant attempt to save a servant who had fallen overboard."

[*The ladies have wept long and sore for their father, but there is something in this last utterance that makes them look up.*]

AGATHA: But, Ernest, it was Crichton who jumped overboard trying to save father.

ERNEST [*with the candour that is one of his most engaging qualities*]: Well, you know, it was rather silly of uncle to fling away his life by trying to get into the boat first; and as this document may be printed in the English

papers, it struck me, an English peer, you know—

LADY MARY [*every inch an English peer's daughter*]: Ernest, that is very thoughtful of you.

ERNEST [*continuing, well pleased*]: —"By night the cries of wild cats and the hissing of snakes terrify us extremely"—[*This does not satisfy him so well, and he makes a correction.*]—"terrify the ladies extremely. Against these we have no weapons except one cutlass and a hatchet. A bucket washed ashore is at present our only comfortable seat"—

LADY MARY [*with some spirit*]: And Ernest is sitting on it.

ERNEST: H'sh! Oh, do be quiet. —"To add to our horrors, night falls suddenly in these parts, and it is then that savage animals begin to prowl and roar."

LADY MARY: Have you said that vampire bats suck the blood from our toes as we sleep?

ERNEST: No, that's all. I end up, "Rescue us or we perish. Rich reward. Signed Ernest Woolley, in command of our little party." This is written on a leaf taken out of a book of poems that Crichton found in his pocket. Fancy Crichton being a reader of poetry. Now I shall put it into the bottle and fling it into the sea. [*He pushes the precious document into a soda-water bottle, and rams the cork home. At the same moment, and with effort, he gives birth to one of his most characteristic epigrams.*] The tide is going out, we mustn't miss the post. [*They are so unhappy that they fail to grasp it, and a little petulantly he calls* for CRICHTON, *ever his stand-by in the hour of epigram.* CRICHTON *breaks through the undergrowth quickly, thinking the ladies are in danger.*]

CRICHTON: Anything wrong, sir?

ERNEST [*with fine confidence*]: The tide, Crichton, is a postman who calls at our island twice a day for letters.

CRICHTON [*after a pause*]: Thank you, sir. [*He returns to his labours, however, without giving the smile which is the epigrammatist's right, and* ERNEST *is a little disappointed in him.*]

ERNEST: Poor Crichton! I sometimes think he is losing his sense of humour. Come along, Agatha. [*He helps his favourite up the rocks, and they disappear gingerly from view.*]

CATHERINE: How horribly still it is.

LADY MARY [*remembering some recent sounds*]: It is best when it is still.

CATHERINE [*drawing closer to her*]: Mary, I have heard that they are always very still just before they jump.

LADY MARY: Don't.

[*A distinct chopping is heard, and they are startled.*]

LADY MARY [*controlling herself*]: It is only Crichton knocking down trees.

CATHERINE [*almost imploringly*]: Mary, let us go and stand beside him.

LADY MARY [*coldly*]: Let a servant see that I am afraid!

CATHERINE: Don't, then; but remember this, dear, they often drop on one from above. [*She moves away, nearer to the friendly sound of the axe, and* LADY MARY *is left alone. She is the most courageous of them as well as the haughtiest, but when something she had thought to be a stick glides toward her, she forgets her dignity and screams.*]

LADY MARY [*calling*]: Crichton, Crichton!

[*It must have been* TREHERNE *who was tree-felling, for* CRICHTON *comes to her from the hut, drawing his cutlass.*]

CRICHTON [*anxious*]: Did you call, my lady?

LADY MARY [*herself again, now that he is there*]: I! Why should I?

CRICHTON: I made a mistake, your ladyship. [*Hesitating.*] If you are afraid of being alone, my lady—

LADY MARY: Afraid! Certainly not. [*Doggedly.*] You may go. [*But she does not complain when he remains within eyesight cutting the bamboo. It is heavy work, and she watches him silently.*]

LADY MARY: I wish, Crichton, you could work without getting so hot.

CRICHTON [*mopping his face*]: I wish I could, my lady. [*He continues his labours.*]

LADY MARY [*taking off her oilskins*]: It makes me hot to look at you.

CRICHTON: It almost makes me cool to look at your ladyship.

LADY MARY [*who perhaps thinks he is presuming*]: Anything I can do for you in that way, Crichton, I shall do with pleasure.

CRICHTON [*quite humbly*]: Thank you, my lady.

[*By this time most of the bamboo has been cut, and the shore and sea are visible, except where they are hidden by the half completed hut. The mast rising solitary from the water adds to the desolation of the scene, and at last tears run down* LADY MARY'S *face.*]

CRICHTON: Don't give way, my lady, things might be worse.

LADY MARY: My poor father.

CRICHTON: If I could have given my life for his.

LADY MARY: You did all a man could do. Indeed I thank you, Crichton. [*With some admiration and more wonder.*] You are a man.

CRICHTON: Thank you, my lady.

LADY MARY: But it is all so awful. Crichton, is there any hope of a ship coming?

CRICHTON [*after hesitation*]: Of course there is, my lady.

LADY MARY [*facing him bravely*]: Don't treat me as a child. I have got to know the worst, and to face it. Crichton, the truth.

CRICHTON [*reluctantly*]: We were driven out of our course, my lady; I fear far from the track of commerce.

LADY MARY: Thank you; I understand. [*For a moment, however, she breaks down. Then she clenches her hands and stands erect.*]

CRICHTON [*watching her, and forgetting perhaps for the moment that they are not just a man and woman*]: You're a good plucky 'un, my lady.

LADY MARY [*falling into the same error*]: I shall try to be. [*Extricating herself.*] Crichton, how dare you?

CRICHTON: I beg your ladyship's pardon; but you are. [*She smiles, as if it were a comfort to be told this even by* CRICHTON.] And until a ship comes we are three men who are going to do our best for you ladies.

LADY MARY [*with a curl of the lip*]: Mr. Ernest does no work.

CRICHTON [*cheerily*]: But he will, my lady.

LADY MARY: I doubt it.

CRICHTON [*confidently, but perhaps thoughtlessly*]: No work—no dinner—will make a great change in Mr. Ernest.

LADY MARY: No work—no dinner. When did you invent that rule, Crichton?

CRICHTON [*loaded with bamboo*]: I didn't invent it, my lady. I seem to see it growing all over the island.

LADY MARY [*disquieted*]: Crichton, your manner strikes me as curious.

CRICHTON [*pained*]: I hope not, your ladyship.

LADY MARY [*determined to have it out with him*]: You are not implying anything so unnatural, I presume, as that if I and my sisters don't work there will be no dinner for *us?*

CRICHTON [*brightly*]: If it is unnatural, my lady, that is the end of it.

LADY MARY: If? Now I understand. The perfect servant at home holds that we are all equal now. I see.

CRICHTON [*wounded to the quick*]: My lady, can you think me so inconsistent?

LADY MARY: That is it.

CRICHTON [*earnestly*]: My lady, I disbelieved in equality at home because it was against nature, and for that same reason I as utterly disbelieve in it on an island.

LADY MARY [*relieved by his obvious sincerity*]: I apologise.

CRICHTON [*continuing unfortunately*]: There must always, my lady, be one to command and others to obey.

LADY MARY [*satisfied*]: One to command, others to obey. Yes. [*Then suddenly she realises that there may be a dire meaning in his confident words.*] Crichton!

CRICHTON [*who has intended no dire meaning*]: What is it, my lady?

[*But she only stares into his face and then hurries from him. Left alone, he is puzzled, but being a practical man he busies himself gathering firewood, until* TWEENY *appears excitedly carrying cocoanuts in her skirt. She has made better use than the ladies of her three minutes' grace for dressing.*]

TWEENY [*who can be happy even on an island if* CRICHTON *is with her*]: Look what I found.

CRICHTON: Cocoa-nuts. Bravo!

TWEENY: They grows on trees.

CRICHTON: Where did you think they grew?

TWEENY: I thought as how they grew in rows on top of little sticks.

CRICHTON [*wrinkling his brows*]: Oh Tweeny, Tweeny!

TWEENY [*anxiously*]: Have I offended of your feelings again, sir?

CRICHTON: A little.

TWEENY [*in a despairing outburst*]: I'm full o' vulgar words and ways; and though I may keep

them in their holes when you are by, as soon as I'm by myself out they comes in a rush like beetles when the house is dark. I says them gloating-like, in my head—"Blooming" I says, and "All my eye," and "Ginger," and "Nothink"; and all the time we was being wrecked I was praying to myself, "Please the Lord it may be an island as it's natural to be vulgar on." [*A shudder passes through* CRICHTON, *and she is abject.*] That's the kind I am, sir. I'm 'opeless. You'd better give me up. [*She is a pathetic, forlorn creature, and his manhood is stirred.*]

CRICHTON [*wondering a little at himself for saying it*]: I won't give you up. It is strange that one so common should attract one so fastidious; but so it is. [*Thoughtfully.*] There is something about you, Tweeny, there is a *je ne sais quoi* about you.

TWEENY [*knowing only that he has found something in her to commend*]: Is there, is there? Oh, I am glad.

CRICHTON [*putting his hand on her shoulder like a protector*]: We shall fight your vulgarity together. [*All this time he has been arranging sticks for his fire.*] Now get some dry grass. [*She brings him grass, and he puts it under the sticks. He produces an odd lens from his pocket, and tries to focus the sun's rays.*]

TWEENY: Why, what's that?

CRICHTON [*the ingenious creature*]: That's the glass from my watch and one from Mr. Treherne's, with a little water between them. I'm hoping to kindle a fire with it.

TWEENY [*properly impressed*]: Oh sir!

[*After one failure the grass takes fire, and they are blowing on it when excited cries near by bring them sharply to their feet.* AGATHA *runs to them, white of face, followed by* ERNEST.]

ERNEST: Danger! Crichton, a tiger-cat!

CRICHTON [*getting his cutlass*]: Where?

AGATHA: It is at our heels.

ERNEST: Look out, Crichton.

CRICHTON: H'sh!

[TREHERNE *comes to his assistance, while* LADY MARY *and* CATHERINE *join* AGATHA *in the hut.*]

ERNEST: It will be on us in a moment. [*He seizes the hatchet and guards the hut. It is pleasing to see that* ERNEST *is no coward.*]

TREHERNE: Listen!

ERNEST: The grass is moving. It's coming.

[*It comes. But it is no tiger-cat; it is* LORD LOAM *crawling on his hands and knees, a very exhausted and dishevelled peer, wondrously attired in rags. The girls see him, and with glad cries rush into his arms.*]

LADY MARY: Father.

LORD LOAM: Mary—Catherine—Agatha. Oh dear, my dears, my dears, oh dear!

LADY MARY: Darling.

AGATHA: Sweetest.

CATHERINE: Love.

TREHERNE: Glad to see you, sir.

ERNEST: Uncle, uncle, dear old uncle.

[*For a time such happy cries fill the air, but presently* TREHERNE *is thoughtless.*]

TREHERNE: Ernest thought you were a tiger-cat.

LORD LOAM [*stung somehow to the quick*]: Oh, did you? I knew you at once, Ernest; I knew you by the way you ran.

[ERNEST *smiles forgivingly.*]

CRICHTON [*venturing forward at last*]: My lord, I am glad.

ERNEST [*with upraised finger*]: But you are also idling, Crichton. [*Making himself comfortable on the ground.*] We mustn't waste time. To work, to work.

CRICHTON [*after contemplating him without rancour*]: Yes, sir. [*He gets a pot from the hut and hangs it on a tripod over the fire, which is now burning brightly.*]

TREHERNE: Ernest, you be a little more civil. Crichton, let me help. [*He is soon busy helping* CRICHTON *to add to the strength of the hut.*]

LORD LOAM [*gazing at the pot as ladies are said to gaze on precious stones*]: Is that—but I suppose I'm dreaming again. [*Timidly.*] It isn't by any chance a pot on top of a fire, is it?

LADY MARY: Indeed, it is, dearest. It is our supper.

LORD LOAM: I have been dreaming of a pot on a fire for two days. [*Quivering.*] There's nothing in it, is there?

ERNEST: Sniff, uncle. [LORD LOAM *sniffs.*]

LORD LOAM [*reverently*]: It smells of onions!

[*There is a sudden diversion.*]

CATHERINE: Father, you have boots!

LADY MARY: So he has.

LORD LOAM: Of course I have.

ERNEST [*with greedy cunning*]: You are actually wearing boots, uncle. It's very unsafe, you know, in this climate.

LORD LOAM: Is it?

ERNEST: We have all abandoned them, you observe. The blood, the arteries, you know.

LORD LOAM: I hadn't a notion. [*He holds out his feet, and* ERNEST *kneels.*]

ERNEST: O Lord, yes. [*In another moment those boots will be his.*]

LADY MARY [*quickly*]: Father, he is trying to get your boots from you. There is nothing in the world we wouldn't give for boots.

ERNEST [*rising haughtily, a proud spirit misunderstood*]: I only wanted the loan of them.

AGATHA [*running her fingers along them lovingly*]: If you lend them to any one, it will be to us, won't it, father?

LORD LOAM: Certainly, my child.

ERNEST: Oh, very well. [*He is leaving these selfish ones.*] I don't want your old boots. [*He gives his uncle a last chance.*] You don't think you could spare me *one* boot?

LORD LOAM [*tartly*]: I do not.

ERNEST: Quite so. Well, all I can say is I'm sorry for you. [*He departs to recline elsewhere.*]

LADY MARY: Father, we thought we should never see you again.

LORD LOAM: I was washed ashore, my dear, clinging to a hencoop. How awful that first night was.

LADY MARY: Poor father.

LORD LOAM: When I woke, I wept. Then I began to feel extremely hungry. There was a large turtle on the beach. I remembered from the *Swiss Family Robinson* that if you turn a turtle over he is helpless. My dears, I crawled towards him, I flung myself upon him—[*here he pauses to rub his leg*]—the nasty, spiteful brute.

LADY MARY: You didn't turn him over?

LORD LOAM [*vindictively, though he is a kindly man*]: Mary, the senseless thing wouldn't wait; I found that none of them would wait.

CATHERINE: We should have been as badly off if Crichton hadn't—

LADY MARY [*quickly*]: Don't praise Crichton.

LORD LOAM: And then those beastly monkeys. I always understood that if you flung stones at them they would retaliate by flinging cocoa-nuts at you. Would you believe it, I flung a hundred stones, and not one monkey had sufficient intelligence to grasp my meaning. How I longed for Crichton.

LADY MARY [*wincing*]: For us also, father?

LORD LOAM: For you also. I tried for hours to make a fire. The authors say that when wrecked on an island you can obtain a light by rubbing two pieces of stick together. [*With feeling.*] The liars!

LADY MARY: And all this time you thought there was no one on the island but yourself?

LORD LOAM: I thought so until this morning. I was searching the pools for little fishes, which I caught in my hat, when suddenly I saw before me—on the sand—

CATHERINE: What?

LORD LOAM: A hairpin.

LADY MARY: A hairpin! It must be one of ours. Give it me, father.

AGATHA: No, it's mine.

LORD LOAM: I didn't keep it.

LADY MARY [speaking for all three]: Didn't keep it? Found a hairpin on an island, and didn't keep it?

LORD LOAM [humbly]: My dears.

AGATHA [scarcely to be placated]: Oh father, we have returned to nature more than you bargained for.

LADY MARY: For shame, Agatha. [She has something on her mind.] Father, there is something I want you to do at once—I mean to assert your position as the chief person on the island.

[They are all surprised.]

LORD LOAM: But who would presume to question it?

CATHERINE: She must mean Ernest.

LADY MARY: Must I?

AGATHA: It's cruel to say anything against Ernest.

LORD LOAM [firmly]: If any one presumes to challenge my position, I shall make short work of him.

AGATHA: Here comes Ernest; now see if you can say these horrid things to his face.

LORD LOAM: I shall teach him his place at once.

LADY MARY [anxiously]: But how?

LORD LOAM [chuckling]: I have just thought of an extremely amusing way of doing it. [As ERNEST approaches.] Ernest.

ERNEST [loftily]: Excuse me, uncle, I'm thinking. I'm planning out the building of this hut.

LORD LOAM: I also have been thinking.

ERNEST: That don't matter.

LORD LOAM: Eh?

ERNEST: Please, please, this is important.

LORD LOAM: I have been thinking that I ought to give you my boots.

ERNEST: What!

LADY MARY: Father.

LORD LOAM [genially]: Take them, my boy. [With a rapidity we had not thought him capable of, ERNEST becomes the wearer of the boots.] And now I dare say you want to know why I give them to you, Ernest?

ERNEST [moving up and down in them deliciously]: Not at all. The great thing is, "I've got 'em, I've got 'em."

LORD LOAM [majestically, but with a knowing look at his daughters]: My reason is that, as head of our little party, you, Ernest, shall be our hunter, you shall clear the forests of those savage beasts that make them so dangerous. [Pleasantly.] And now you know, my dear nephew, why I have given you my boots.

ERNEST: This is my answer. [He kicks off the boots.]

LADY MARY [still anxious]: Father, assert yourself.

LORD LOAM: I shall now assert myself. [But how to do it? He has a happy thought.] Call Crichton.

LADY MARY: Oh father.

[CRICHTON comes in answer to a summons, and is followed by TREHERNE.]

ERNEST [*wondering a little at* LADY MARY'S *grave face*]: Crichton, look here.

LORD LOAM [*sturdily*]: Silence! Crichton, I want your advice as to what I ought to do with Mr. Ernest. He has defied me.

ERNEST: Pooh!

CRICHTON [*after considering*]: May I speak openly, my lord?

LADY MARY [*keeping her eyes fixed on him*]: That is what we desire.

CRICHTON [*quite humbly*]: Then I may say, your lordship, that I have been considering Mr. Ernest's case at odd moments ever since we were wrecked.

ERNEST: My case?

LORD LOAM [*sternly*]: Hush.

CRICHTON: Since we landed on the island, my lord, it seems to me that Mr. Ernest's epigrams have been particularly brilliant.

ERNEST [*gratified*]: Thank you, Crichton.

CRICHTON: But I find—I seem to find it growing wild, my lord, in the woods, that sayings which would be justly admired in England are not much use on an island. I would therefore most respectfully propose that henceforth every time Mr. Ernest favours us with an epigram his head should be immersed in a bucket of cold spring water.

[*There is a terrible silence.*]

LORD LOAM [*uneasily*]: Serve him right.

ERNEST: I should like to see you try to do it, uncle.

CRICHTON [*ever ready to come to the succour of his lordship*]: My feeling, my lord, is that at the next offence I should convey him to a retired spot, where I shall carry out the undertaking in as respectful a manner as is consistent with a thorough immersion. [*Though his manner is most respectful, he is firm; he evidently means what he says.*]

LADY MARY [*a ramrod*]: Father, you must not permit this; Ernest is your nephew.

LORD LOAM [*with his hand to his brow*]: After all, he is my nephew, Crichton; and, as I am sure, he now sees that I am a strong man—

ERNEST [*foolishly in the circumstances*]: A strong man. You mean a stout man. You are one of mind to two of matter. [*He looks round in the old way for approval. No one has smiled, and to his consternation he sees that* CRICHTON *is quietly turning up his sleeves.* ERNEST *makes an appealing gesture to his uncle; then he turns defiantly to* CRICHTON.]

CRICHTON: Is it to be before the ladies, Mr. Ernest, or in the privacy of the wood? [*He fixes* ERNEST *with his eye.* ERNEST *is cowed.*] Come.

ERNEST [*affecting bravado*]: Oh, all right.

CRICHTON [*succinctly*]: Bring the bucket.

[ERNEST *hesitates. He then lifts the bucket and follows* CRICHTON *to the nearest spring.*]

LORD LOAM [*rather white*]: I'm sorry for him, but I had to be firm.

LADY MARY: Oh father, it wasn't you who was firm. Crichton did it himself.

LORD LOAM: Bless me, so he did.

LADY MARY: Father, be strong.

LORD LOAM [*bewildered*]: You can't mean that my faithful Crichton—

LADY MARY: Yes, I do.

TREHERNE: Lady Mary, I stake my word that Crichton is incapable of acting dishonourably.

LADY MARY: I know that; I know it as well as you. Don't you see that that is what makes him so dangerous?

TREHERNE: By Jove, I—I believe I catch your meaning.

CATHERINE: He is coming back.

LORD LOAM [*who has always known himself to be a man of ideas*]: Let us all go into the hut, just to show him at once that it is *our* hut.

LADY MARY [*as they go*]: Father, I implore you, assert yourself now and for ever.

LORD LOAM: I will.

LADY MARY: And, please, don't ask him how you are to do it.

[CRICHTON *returns with sticks to mend the fire.*]

LORD LOAM [*loftily, from the door of the hut*]: Have you carried out my instructions, Crichton?

CRICHTON [*deferentially*]: Yes, my lord.

[ERNEST *appears, mopping his hair, which has become very wet since we last saw him. He is not bearing malice, he is too busy drying, but* AGATHA *is specially his champion.*]

AGATHA: It's infamous, infamous.

LORD LOAM [*strongly*]: *My* orders, Agatha.

LADY MARY: Now, father, please.

LORD LOAM [*striking an attitude*]: Before I give you any further orders, Crichton—

CRICHTON: Yes, my lord.

LORD LOAM [*delighted*]: Pooh! It's all right.

LADY MARY: No. Please go on.

LORD LOAM: Well, well. This question of the leadership; what do you think now, Crichton?

CRICHTON: My lord, I feel it is a matter with which *I* have nothing to do.

LORD LOAM: Excellent. Ha, Mary? That settles it, I think.

LADY MARY: It seems to, but—I'm not sure.

CRICHTON: It will settle itself naturally, my lord, without any interference from us.

[*The reference to Nature gives general dissatisfaction.*]

LADY MARY: Father.

LORD LOAM [*a little severely*]: It settled itself long ago, Crichton, when I was born a peer, and you, for instance, were born a servant.

CRICHTON [*acquiescing*]: Yes, my lord, that was how it all came about quite naturally in England. We had nothing to do with it there, and we shall have as little to do with it here.

TREHERNE [*relieved*]: That's all right.

LADY MARY [*determined to clinch the matter*]: One moment. In short, Crichton, his lordship will continue to be our natural head.

CRICHTON: I dare say, my lady, I dare say.

CATHERINE: But you must *know*.

CRICHTON: Asking your pardon, my lady, one can't be sure—on an island.

[*They look at each other uneasily.*]

LORD LOAM [*warningly*]: Crichton, I don't like this.

CRICHTON [*harassed*]: The more I think of it, your lordship, the more uneasy I become myself. When I heard, my lord, that you had left that hairpin behind— [*He is pained.*]

LORD LOAM [*feebly*]: One hairpin among so many would only have caused dissension.

CRICHTON [*very sorry to have to contradict him*]: Not so, my lord. From that hairpin we could have made a needle; with that needle we could, out of skins, have sewn trousers—of which your lordship is in need; indeed, we are all in need of them.

LADY MARY [*suddenly self-conscious*]: All?

CRICHTON: On an island, my lady.

LADY MARY: Father.

CRICHTON [*really more distressed by the prospect than she*]: My lady, if Nature does not think them necessary, you may be sure she will not ask you to wear them. [*Shaking his head.*] But among all this undergrowth—

LADY MARY: Now you see this man in his true colours.

LORD LOAM [*violently*]: Crichton, you will either this moment say, "Down with Nature," or—

CRICHTON [*scandalised*]: My Lord!

LORD LOAM [*loftily*]: Then this is my last word to you; take a month's notice. [*If the hut had a door he would now shut it to indicate that the interview is closed.*]

CRICHTON [*in great distress*]: Your lordship, the disgrace—

LORD LOAM [*swelling*]: Not another word: you may go.

LADY MARY [*adamant*]: And don't come to me, Crichton, for a character.

ERNEST [*whose immersion has cleared his brain*]: Aren't you all forgetting that this is an island?

[*This brings them to earth with a bump.* LORD LOAM *looks to his eldest daughter for the fitting response.*]

LADY MARY [*equal to the occasion*]: It makes only this difference— that you may go at once, Crichton, to some other part of the island.

[*The faithful servant has been true to his superiors ever since he was created, and never more true than at this moment; but his fidelity is founded on trust in Nature, and to be untrue to it would be to be untrue to them. He lets the wood he has been gathering slip to the ground, and bows his sorrowful head. He turns to obey. Then affection for these great ones wells up in him.*]

CRICHTON: My lady, let me work for you.

LADY MARY: Go.

CRICHTON: You need me so sorely; I can't desert you; I won't.

LADY MARY [*in alarm, lest the others may yield*]: Then, father, there is but one alternative, *we* must leave him.

[LORD LOAM *is looking yearningly at* CRICHTON.]

TREHERNE: It seems a pity.

CATHERINE [*forlornly*]: *You* will work for us?

TREHERNE: Most willingly. But I must warn you all that, so far,

Crichton has done nine-tenths of the scoring.

LADY MARY: The question is, are we to leave this man?

LORD LOAM [*wrapping himself in his dignity*]: Come, my dears.

CRICHTON: My lord!

LORD LOAM: Treherne—Ernest—get our things.

ERNEST: We don't have any, uncle. They all belong to Crichton.

TREHERNE: Everything we have he brought from the wreck—he went back to it before it sank. He risked his life.

CRICHTON: My lord, anything you would care to take is yours.

LADY MARY [*quickly*]: Nothing.

ERNEST: Rot! If I could have your socks, Crichton—

LADY MARY: Come, father; we are ready. [*Followed by the others, she and* LORD LOAM *pick their way up the rocks. In their indignation they scarcely notice that daylight is coming to a sudden end.*]

CRICHTON: My lord, I implore you—*I* am not desirous of being head. Do you have a try at it, my lord.

LORD LOAM [*outraged*]: A try at it!

CRICHTON [*eagerly*]: It may be that you will prove to be the best man.

LORD LOAM: *May* be! My children, come.

[*They disappear proudly in single file.*]

TREHERNE: Crichton, I'm sorry; but of course I must go with them.

CRICHTON: Certainly, sir. [*He calls to* TWEENY, *and she comes from behind the hut, where she has been watching breathlessly.*] Will you be so kind, sir, as to take her to the others?

TREHERNE: Assuredly.

TWEENY: But what do it all mean?

CRICHTON: Does, Tweeny, does. [*He passes her up the rocks to* TREHERNE.] We shall meet again soon, Tweeny. Good night, sir.

TREHERNE: Good night. I dare say they are not far away.

CRICHTON [*thoughtfully*]: They went westward, sir, and the wind is blowing in that direction. That may mean, sir, that Nature is already taking the matter into her own hands. They are all hungry, sir, and the pot has come a-boil. [*He takes off the lid.*]: The smell will be borne westward. That pot is full of Nature, Mr. Treherne. Good night, sir.

TREHERNE: Good night.

[*He mounts the rocks with* TWEENY, *and they are heard for a little time after their figures are swallowed up in the fast growing darkness.* CRICHTON *stands motionless, the lid in his hand, though he has forgotten it, and his reason for taking it off the pot. He is deeply stirred, but presently is ashamed of his dejection, for it is as if he doubted his principles. Bravely true to his faith that Nature will decide now as ever before, he proceeds manfully with his preparations for the night. He lights a ship's lantern, one of several treasures he has brought ashore, and is filling his pipe with crumbs of tobacco from various pockets, when the stealthy movements of some animal in the grass startles him. With the lantern*] in one hand and his cutlass in the other, he searches the ground around the hut. He returns, lights his pipe, and sits down by the fire, which casts weird moving shadows. There is a red gleam on his face; in the darkness he is a strong and perhaps rather sinister figure. In the great stillness that has fallen over the land, the wash of the surf seems to have increased in volume. The sound is indescribably mournful. Except where the fire is, desolation has fallen on the island like a pall.

Once or twice, as Nature dictates, CRICHTON leans forward to stir the pot, and the smell is borne westward. He then resumes his silent vigil.

Shadows other than those cast by the fire begin to descend the rocks. They are the adventurers returning. One by one they steal nearer to the pot until they are squatted round it, with their hands out to the blaze. LADY MARY only is absent. Presently she comes within sight of the others, then stands against a tree with her teeth clenched. One wonders, perhaps, what Nature is to make of her.]

END OF ACT II

ACT THREE

The happy home.

The scene is the hall of their island home two years later. This sturdy log-house is no mere extension of the hut we have seen in process of erection, but has been built a mile or less to the west of it, on higher ground and near a stream. When the master chose this site, the others thought that all he expected from the stream was a sufficiency of drinking water. They know better now every time they go down to the mill or turn on the electric light.

This hall is the living-room of the house, and walls and roof are of stout logs. Across the joists supporting the roof are laid many home-made implements, such as spades, saws, fishing-rods, and from hooks in the joists are suspended cured foods, of which hams are specially in evidence. Deep recesses half way up the walls contain various provender in barrels and sacks. There are some skins, trophies of the chase, on the floor, which is otherwise bare. The chairs and tables are in some cases hewn out of the solid wood, and in others the result of rough but efficient carpentering. Various pieces of wreckage from the yacht have been turned to novel uses: thus the steering-wheel now hangs from the centre of the

roof, with electric lights attached to it encased in bladders.
A lifebuoy has become the back of a chair. Two barrels have
been halved and turn coyly from each other as a settee.

The farther end of the room is more strictly the kitchen,
and is a great recess, which can be shut off from the hall
by folding doors. There is a large open fire in it. The chimney
is half of one of the boats of the yacht. On the walls of the
kitchen proper are many plate-racks, containing shells; there
are rows of these of one size and shape, which mark them
off as dinner plates or bowls; others are as obviously tureens.
They are arranged primly as in a well-conducted kitchen;
indeed, neatness and cleanliness are the note struck every-
where, yet the effect of the whole is romantic and barbaric.

The outer door into this hall is a little peculiar on an
island. It is covered with skins and is in four leaves, like
the swing doors of fashionable restaurants, which allow you
to enter without allowing the hot air to escape. During the
winter season our castaways have found the contrivance
useful, but CRICHTON'S *brain was perhaps a little lordly*
when he conceived it. Another door leads by a passage to
the sleeping-rooms of the house, which are all on the ground-
floor, and to Crichton's work-room, where he is at this
moment, and whither we should like to follow him, but in
a play we may not, as it is out of sight. There is a large
window space without a window, which, however, can be
shuttered, and through this we have a view of cattle-sheds,
fowl-pens, and a field of grain. It is a fine summer evening.

TWEENY *is sitting there, very busy plucking the feathers off*
a bird and dropping them on a sheet placed for that purpose
on the floor. She is trilling to herself in the lightness of her
heart. We may remember that TWEENY, *alone among the*
women, had dressed wisely for an island when they fled the
yacht, and her going-away gown still adheres to her, though
in fragments. A score of pieces have been added here and
there as necessity compelled, and these have been patched
and repatched in incongruous colours; but, when all is said
and done, it can still be maintained that TWEENY *wears a*
skirt. She is deservedly proud of her skirt, and sometimes
lends it on important occasions when approached in the
proper spirit.

Some one outside has been whistling to TWEENY; *the*
guarded whistle which, on a less savage island, is some-
times assumed to be an indication to cook that the constable
is willing, if the coast is clear. TWEENY, *however, is en-*
grossed, or perhaps she is not in the mood for a follower, so
he climbs in at the window undaunted, to take her willy
nilly. He is a jolly-looking labouring man, who answers to

the name of Daddy, and— *But though that may be his island name, we recognise him at once. He is* LORD LOAM, *settled down to the new conditions, and enjoying life heartily as handyman about the happy home. He is comfortably attired in skins. He is still stout, but all the flabbiness has dropped from him; gone too is his pomposity; his eye is clear, brown his skin; he could leap a gate.*

In his hands he carries an island-made concertina, and such is the exuberance of his spirits that, as he lights on the floor, he bursts into music and song, something about his being a chickety chickety chick chick, and will TWEENY *please to tell him whose chickety chick she is. Retribution follows sharp. We hear a whir, as if from insufficiently oiled machinery, and over the passage door appears a placard showing the one word "Silence." His lordship stops, and steals to* TWEENY *on his tiptoes.*

LORD LOAM: I thought the Gov. was out.

TWEENY: Well, you see he ain't. And if he were to catch you here idling—

[LORD LOAM *pales. He lays aside his musical instrument and hurriedly dons an apron.* TWEENY *gives him the bird to pluck, and busies herself laying the table for dinner.*]

LORD LOAM [*softly*]: What is he doing now?

TWEENY: I think he's working out that plan for laying on hot and cold.

LORD LOAM [*proud of his master*]: And he'll manage it too. The man who could build a blacksmith's forge without tools—

TWEENY [*not less proud*]: He made the tools.

LORD LOAM: Out of half a dozen rusty nails. The saw-mill, Tweeny; the speaking-tube; the electric lighting; and look at the use he has made of the bits

of the yacht that were washed ashore. And all in two years. He's a master I'm proud to pluck for. [*He chirps happily at his work, and she regards him curiously.*]

TWEENY: Daddy, you're of little use, but you're a bright, cheerful creature to have about the house. [*He beams at this commendation.*] Do you ever think of old times now? We was a bit different.

LORD LOAM [*pausing*]: Circumstances alter cases. [*He resumes his plucking contentedly.*]

TWEENY: But, Daddy, if the chance was to come of getting back?

LORD LOAM: I have given up bothering about it.

TWEENY: You bothered that day long ago when we saw a ship passing the island. How we all ran like crazy folk into the water, Daddy, and screamed and held out our arms. [*They are both a little agitated.*] But it sailed away, and we've never seen another.

LORD LOAM: If we had had the

electrical contrivance we have now we could have attracted that ship's notice. [*Their eyes rest on a mysterious apparatus that fills a corner of the hall.*] A touch on that lever, Tweeny, and in a few moments bonfires would be blazing all round the shore.

TWEENY [*backing from the lever as if it might spring at her*]: It's the most wonderful thing he has done.

LORD LOAM [*in a reverie*]: And then—England—home!

TWEENY [*also seeing visions*]: London of a Saturday night!

LORD LOAM: My lords, in rising once more to address this historic chamber—

TWEENY: There was a little ham and beef shop off the Edgware Road—

[*The visions fade; they return to the practical.*]

LORD LOAM: Tweeny, do you think I could have an egg to my tea?

[*At this moment a wiry, athletic figure in skins darkens the window. He is carrying two pails, which are suspended from a pole on his shoulder, and he is* ERNEST. *We should say that he is* ERNEST *completely changed if we were of those who hold that people change. As he enters by the window he has heard* LORD LOAM'S *appeal, and is perhaps justifiably indignant.*]

ERNEST: What is that about an egg? Why should you have an egg?

LORD LOAM [*with hauteur*]: That is my affair, sir. [*With a Parthian shot* as he withdraws stiffly from the room.*] The Gov. has never put *my* head in a bucket.

ERNEST [*coming to rest on one of his buckets, and speaking with excusable pride. To* TWEENY]: Nor mine for nearly three months. It was only last week, Tweeny, that he said to me, "Ernest, the water cure has worked marvels in you, and I question whether I shall require to dip you any more." [*Complacently.*] Of course that sort of thing encourages a fellow.

TWEENY [*who has now arranged the dinner table to her satisfaction*]: I will say, Erny, I never seen a young chap more improved.

ERNEST [*gratified*]: Thank you, Tweeny, that's very precious to me. [*She retires to the fire to work the great bellows with her foot, and* ERNEST *turns to* TREHERNE, *who has come in looking more like a cow-boy than a clergyman. He has a small box in his hand which he tries to conceal.*] What have you got there, John?

TREHERNE: Don't tell anybody. It is a little present for the Gov.; a set of razors. One for each day in the week.

ERNEST [*opening the box and examining its contents*]: Shells! He'll like that. He likes sets of things.

TREHERNE [*in a guarded voice*]: Have you noticed that?

ERNEST: Rather.

TREHERNE: He's becoming a bit magnificent in his ideas.

---

*Parthian shot, having the last word, as the Parthians were supposed to shoot missiles backward as they fled.

ERNEST [*huskily*]: John, it sometimes gives me the creeps.

TREHERNE [*making sure that* TWEENY *is out of hearing*]: What do you think of that brilliant robe he got the girls to make for him?

ERNEST [*uncomfortably*]: I think he looks too regal in it.

TREHERNE: Regal! I sometimes fancy that that's why he's so fond of wearing it. [*Practically.*] Well, I must take these down to the grindstone and put an edge on them.

ERNEST [*button-holing him*]: I say, John, I want a word with you.

TREHERNE: Well?

ERNEST [*become suddenly diffident*]: Dash it all, you know, you're a clergyman.

TREHERNE: One of the best things the Gov. has done is to insist that none of you forget it.

ERNEST [*taking his courage in his hands*]: Then—would you, John?

TREHERNE: What?

ERNEST [*wistfully*]: Officiate at a marriage ceremony, John?

TREHERNE [*slowly*]: Now, that's really odd.

ERNEST: Odd? Seems to me it's natural. And whatever is natural, John, is right.

TREHERNE: I mean that same question has been put to me today already.

ERNEST [*eagerly*]: By one of the women?

TREHERNE: Oh no; they all put it to me long ago. This was by the Gov. himself.

ERNEST: By Jove! [*Admiringly.*] I say, John, what an observant beggar he is.

TREHERNE: Ah! You fancy he was thinking of you?

ERNEST: I do not hesitate to affirm, John, that he has seen the love-light in my eyes. You answered—

TREHERNE: I said Yes, I thought it would be my duty to officiate if called upon.

ERNEST: You're a brick.

TREHERNE [*still pondering*]: But I wonder whether he *was* thinking of you?

ERNEST: Make your mind easy about that.

TREHERNE: Well, my best wishes. Agatha is a very fine girl.

ERNEST: Agatha! What made you think it was Agatha?

TREHERNE: Man alive, you told me all about it soon after we were wrecked.

ERNEST: Pooh! Agatha's all very well in her way, John, but I'm flying at bigger game.

TREHERNE: Ernest, which is it?

ERNEST: Tweeny, of course.

TREHERNE: Tweeny? [*Reprovingly.*] Ernest, I hope her cooking has nothing to do with this.

ERNEST [*with dignity*]: Her cooking has very little to do with it.

TREHERNE: But does she return your affection?

ERNEST [*simply*]: Yes, John, I believe I may say so. I am unworthy of her, but I think I have touched her heart.

TREHERNE [*with a sigh*]: Some people seem to have all the luck. As you know, Catherine won't look at me.

ERNEST: I'm sorry, John.

TREHERNE: It's my deserts; I'm a second eleven* sort of chap.

---

*second eleven, second team in cricket.

Well, my heartiest good wishes, Ernest.

ERNEST: Thank you, John. How's the little black pig today?

TREHERNE [*departing*]: He has begun to eat again.

[*After a moment's reflection* ERNEST *calls to* TWEENY.]

ERNEST: Are you very busy, Tweeny?

TWEENY [*coming to him good-naturedly*]: There's always work to do; but if you want me, Ernest—

ERNEST: There's something I should like to say to you if you could spare a moment.

TWEENY: Willingly. What is it?

ERNEST: What an ass I used to be, Tweeny.

TWEENY [*tolerantly*]: Oh, let bygones be bygones.

ERNEST [*sincerely, and at his very best*]: I'm no great shakes even now. But listen to this, Tweeny; I have known many women, but until I knew you I never knew any woman.

TWEENY [*to whose uneducated ears this sounds dangerously like an epigram*]: Take care—the bucket.

ERNEST [*hurriedly*]: I didn't mean it in that way. [*He goes chivalrously on his knees.*] Ah, Tweeny, I don't undervalue the bucket, but what I want to say now is that the sweet refinement of a dear girl has done more for me than any bucket could do.

TWEENY [*with large eyes*]: Are you offering to walk out with me, Erny?

ERNEST [*passionately*]: More than that. I want to build a little house for you—in the sunny glade down by Porcupine Creek. I want to make chairs for you and tables; and knives and forks, and a sideboard for you.

TWEENY [*who is fond of language*]: I like to hear you. [*Eyeing him.*] Would there be any one in the house except myself, Ernest?

ERNEST [*humbly*]: Not often; but just occasionally there would be your adoring husband.

TWEENY [*decisively*]: It won't do, Ernest.

ERNEST [*pleading*]: It isn't as if I should be much there.

TWEENY: I know, I know; but I don't love you, Ernest. I'm that sorry.

ERNEST [*putting his case cleverly*]: Twice a week I should be away altogether—at the dam. On the other days you would never see me from breakfast time to supper. [*With the self-abnegation of the true lover.*] If you like I'll even go fishing on Sundays.

TWEENY: It's no use, Erny.

ERNEST [*rising manfully*]: Thank you, Tweeny; it can't be helped. [*Then he remembers.*] Tweeny, we shall be disappointing the Gov.

TWEENY [*with a sinking*]: What's that?

ERNEST: He wanted us to marry.

TWEENY [*blankly*]: You and me? the Gov.! [*Her head droops woefully. From without is heard the whistling of a happier spirit, and* TWEENY *draws herself up fiercely.*] That's her; that's the thing what has stole his heart from me. [*A stalwart youth appears at the window, so handsome and tingling with vitality that, glad to depose* CRICHTON, *we cry thankfully,* "The hero at last." *But it is not the hero; it is the heroine. This splendid boy, clad in skins, is what Nature has done for* LADY MARY. *She carries bow and arrows and a blow-pipe, and over her shoulder is a fat buck, which she drops with a cry of triumph. Forgetting to enter demurely, she leaps through the window. Sourly.*] Drat you, Polly, why don't you wipe your feet?

LADY MARY [*good-naturedly*]: Come, Tweeny, be nice to me. It's a splendid buck.

[*But* TWEENY *shakes her off, and retires to the kitchen fire.*]

ERNEST: Where did you get it?

LADY MARY [*gaily*]: I sighted a herd near Penguin's Creek, but had to creep round Silver Lake to get to windward of them. However, they spotted me and then the fun began. There was nothing for it but to try and run them down, so I singled out a fat buck and away we went down the shore of the lake, up the valley of rolling stones; he doubled into Brawling River and took to the water, but I swam after him; the river is only half a mile broad there, but it runs strong. He went spinning down the rapids, down I went in pursuit; he clambered ashore, I clambered ashore; away we tore helter-skelter up the hill and down again. I lost him in the marshes, got on his track again near Bread Fruit Wood, and brought him down with an arrow in Firefly Grove.

TWEENY [*staring at her*]: Aren't you tired?

LADY MARY: Tired! It was gor-

geous. [*She runs up a ladder and deposits her weapons on the joists. She is whistling again.*]

TWEENY [*snapping*]: I can't abide a woman whistling.

LADY MARY [*indifferently*]: I like it.

TWEENY [*stamping her foot*]: Drop it, Polly, I tell you.

LADY MARY [*stung*]: I won't. I'm as good as you are.

[*They are facing each other defiantly.*]

ERNEST [*shocked*]: Is this necessary? Think how it would pain him.

[LADY MARY'S *eyes take a new expression. We see them soft for the first time.*]

LADY MARY [*contritely*]: Tweeny, I beg your pardon. If my whistling annoys you, I shall try to cure myself of it. [*Instead of calming* TWEENY, *this floods her face in tears.*] Why, how can that hurt you, Tweeny dear?

TWEENY: Because I can't make you lose your temper.

LADY MARY [*divinely*]: Indeed, I often do. Would that I were nicer to everybody.

TWEENY: There you are again. [*Wistfully.*] What makes you want to be so nice, Polly?

LADY MARY [*with fervour*]: Only thankfulness, Tweeny. [*She exults.*] It is such fun to be alive.

[*So also seem to think* CATHERINE *and* AGATHA, *who bounce in with fishing-rods and creel. They, too, are in manly attire.*]

CATHERINE: We've got some ripping fish for the Gov.'s dinner.

Are we in time? We ran all the way.

TWEENY [*tartly*]: You'll please to cook them yourself, Kitty, and look sharp about it. [*She retires to her hearth, where* AGATHA *follows her.*]

AGATHA [*yearning*]: Has the Gov. decided who is to wait upon him today?

CATHERINE [*who is cleaning her fish*]: It's my turn.

AGATHA [*hotly*]: I don't see that.

TWEENY [*with bitterness*]: It's to be neither of you, Aggy; he wants Polly again.

[LADY MARY *is unable to resist a joyous whistle.*]

AGATHA [*jealously*]: Polly, you toad.

[*But they cannot make* LADY MARY *angry.*]

TWEENY [*storming*]: How dare you look so happy?

LADY MARY [*willing to embrace her*]: I wish, Tweeny, there was anything I could do to make you happy also.

TWEENY: Me! Oh, I'm happy. [*She remembers* ERNEST, *whom it is easy to forget on an island.*] I've just had a proposal, I tell you.

[LADY MARY *is shaken at last, and her sisters with her.*]

AGATHA: A proposal?

CATHERINE [*going white*]: Not— not— [*She dare not say his name.*]

ERNEST [*with singular modesty*]: You needn't be alarmed; it's only me.

LADY MARY [*relieved*]: Oh, you!

AGATHA [*happy again*]: Ernest,

you dear, I got such a shock.

CATHERINE: It was only Ernest. [*Showing him her fish in thankfulness.*] They are beautifully fresh; come and help me to cook them.

ERNEST [*with simple dignity*]: Do you mind if I don't cook fish tonight? [*She does not mind in the least. They have all forgotten him. A lark is singing in three hearts.*] I think you might all be a little sorry for a chap. [*But they are not even sorry, and he addresses* AGATHA *in these winged words.*] I'm particularly disappointed in you, Aggy; seeing that I was half engaged to you, I think you might have had the good feeling to be a little more hurt.

AGATHA: Oh, bother.

ERNEST [*summing up the situation in so far as it affects himself*]: I shall now go and lie down for a bit. [*He retires coldly but unregretted.* LADY MARY *approaches* TWEENY *with her most insinuating smile.*]

LADY MARY: Tweeny, as the Gov. has chosen me to wait on him, please may I have the loan of it again?

[*The reference made with such charming delicacy is evidently to* TWEENY'S *skirt.*]

TWEENY [*doggedly*]: No, you mayn't.

AGATHA [*supporting* TWEENY]: Don't you give it to her.

LADY MARY [*still trying sweet persuasion*]: You know quite well that he prefers to be waited on in a skirt.

TWEENY: I don't care. Get on for yourself.

LADY MARY: It is the only one on the island.

TWEENY: And it's mine.

LADY MARY [*an aristocrat after all*]: Tweeny, give me that skirt directly.

CATHERINE: Don't.

TWEENY: I won't.

LADY MARY [*clearing for action*]: I shall make you.

TWEENY: I should like to see you try.

[*An unseemly fracas appears to be inevitable, but something happens. The whir is again heard, and the notice is displayed "Dogs delight to bark and bite." Its effect is instantaneous and cheering. The ladies look at each other guiltily and immediately proceed on tiptoe to their duties. These are all concerned with the master's dinner.* CATHERINE *attends to his fish.* AGATHA *fills a quaint toast-rack and brings the menu, which is written on a shell.* LADY MARY *twists a wreath of green leaves around her head, and places a flower beside the master's plate.* TWEENY *signs that all is ready, and she and the younger sisters retire into the kitchen, drawing the screen that separates it from the rest of the room.* LADY MARY *beats a tom-tom, which is the dinner bell. She then gently works a punkah, which we have not hitherto observed, and stands at attention. No doubt she is in hopes that the Gov. will enter into conversation with her, but she is too good a parlour-maid to let her hopes appear in her face. We may watch her manner with complete approval. There is not one of us who would not give her £26 a year.*

The master comes in quietly, a book in his hand, still the only book on the island, for he has not thought it worth while to build a printing-press. His dress is not noticeably different from that of the others, the skins are similar, but perhaps these are a trifle more carefully cut or he carries them better. One sees somehow that he has changed for his evening meal. There is an odd suggestion of a dinner jacket about his doeskin coat. It is, perhaps, too grave a face for a man of thirty-two, as if he were over much immersed in affairs, yet there is a sunny smile left to lighten it at times and bring back its youth; perhaps too intellectual a face to pass as strictly handsome, not sufficiently suggestive of oats. His tall figure is very straight, slight rather than thick-set, but nobly muscular. His big hands, firm and hard with labour though they be, are finely shaped —note the fingers so much more tapered, the nails better tended than those of his domestics; they are one of many indications that he is of a superior breed. Such signs, as has often been pointed out, are infallible. A romantic figure, too. One can easily see why the women-folks of this strong man's house both adore and fear him.

He does not seem to notice who is waiting on him tonight, but inclines his head slightly to whoever it is, as she takes her place at the back of his chair. LADY MARY *respectfully places the menu-shell before him, and he glances at it.*]

CRICHTON: Clear, please.

[LADY MARY *knocks on the screen,*

and a serving hutch in it opens, through which TWEENY *offers two soup plates.* LADY MARY *selects the clear, and the aperture is closed. She works the punkah while the master partakes of the soup.*]

CRICHTON [*who always gives praise where it is due*]: An excellent soup, Polly, but still a trifle too rich.

LADY MARY: Thank you.

[*The next course is the fish, and while it is being passed through the hutch we have a glimpse of three jealous women.* LADY MARY'S *movements are so deft and noiseless that any observant spectator can see that she was born to wait at table.*]

CRICHTON [*unbending as he eats*]: Polly, you are a very smart girl.

LADY MARY [*brindling, but naturally gratified*]: La!

CRICHTON [*smiling*]: And I'm not the first you've heard it from, I'll swear.

LADY MARY [*wriggling*]: Oh Gov.!

CRICHTON: Got any followers on the island, Polly?

LADY MARY [*tossing her head*]: Certainly not.

CRICHTON: I thought that perhaps John or Ernest—

LADY MARY [*tilting her nose*]: I don't say that it's for want of asking.

CRICHTON [*emphatically*]: I'm sure it isn't. [*Perhaps he thinks he has gone too far.*] You may clear.

[*Flushed with pleasure, she puts before him a bird and vegetables, sees that his beaker is filled with wine, and returns to the punkah. She*

would love to continue their conversation, but it is for him to decide. For a time he seems to have forgotten her.]

CRICHTON: Did you lose any arrows today?

LADY MARY: Only one in Firefly Grove.

CRICHTON: You were as far as that? How did you get across the Black Gorge?

LADY MARY: I went across on the rope.

CRICHTON: Hand over hand?

LADY MARY [*swelling at the implied praise*]: I wasn't in the least dizzy.

CRICHTON [*moved*]: You brave girl! [*He sits back in his chair a little agitated.*] But never do that again.

LADY MARY [*pouting*]: It is such fun, Gov.

CRICHTON [*decisively*]: I forbid it.

LADY MARY [*the little rebel*]: I shall.

CRICHTON [*surprised*]: Polly! [*He signs to her sharply to step forward, but for a moment she holds back petulantly, and even when she does come it is less obediently than like a naughty, sulky child. Nevertheless, with the forbearance that is characteristic of the man, he addresses her with grave gentleness rather than severely.*] You must do as I tell you, you know.

LADY MARY [*strangely passionate*]: I shan't.

CRICHTON [*smiling at her fury*]: We shall see. Frown at me, Polly; there, you do it at once. Clench your little fists, stamp your feet, bite your ribbons— [*A student of women, or at least of this woman, he knows that she is about to do those things, and thus she seems to do them to order.* LADY MARY *screws up her face like a baby and cries. He is immediately kind.*] You child of Nature; was it cruel of me to wish to save you from harm?

LADY MARY [*drying her eyes*]: I'm an ungracious wretch. Oh Gov., I don't try half hard enough to please you. I'm even wearing— [*she looks down sadly*]—when I know you prefer *it*.

CRICHTON [*thoughtfully*]: I admit I do prefer *it*. Perhaps I am a little old-fashioned in these matters. [*Her tears again threaten.*] Ah, don't, Polly; that's nothing.

LADY MARY: If I could only please you, Gov.

CRICHTON [*slowly*]: You do please me, child, very much—[*he half rises*]—very much indeed. [*If he meant to say more he checks himself. He looks at his plate.*] No more, thank you.

[*The simple island meal is ended, save for the walnuts and the wine, and* CRICHTON *is too busy a man to linger long over them. But he is a stickler for etiquette, and the table is cleared charmingly, though with dispatch, before they are placed before him.* LADY MARY *is an artist with the crumb-brush, and there are few arts more delightful to watch. Dusk has come sharply, and she turns on the electric light. It awakens* CRICHTON *from a reverie in which he has been regarding her.*]

CRICHTON: Polly, there is only one thing about you that I don't quite like. [*She looks up, making a moue, if that can be said of one who so well knows her place. He explains.*] That action of the hands.

LADY MARY: What do I do?

CRICHTON: So—like one washing them. I have noticed that the others tend to do it also. It seems odd.

LADY MARY [*archly*]: Oh Gov., have you forgotten?

CRICHTON: What?

LADY MARY: That once upon a time a certain other person did that.

CRICHTON [*groping*]: You mean myself? [*She nods, and he shudders.*] Horrible!

LADY MARY [*afraid she has hurt him*]: You haven't for a very long time. Perhaps it is natural for servants.

CRICHTON: That must be it. [*He rises.*] Polly! [*She looks up expectantly, but he only sighs and turns away.*]

LADY MARY [*gently*]: You sighed, Gov.

CRICHTON: Did I? I was thinking. [*He paces the room and then turns to her agitatedly, yet with control over his agitation. There is some mournfulness in his voice.*] I have always tried to do the right thing on this island. Above all, Polly, I want to do the right thing by you.

LADY MARY [*with shining eyes*]: How we all trust you. That is your reward, Gov.

CRICHTON [*who is having a fight with himself*]: And now I want a greater reward. Is it fair to you? Am I playing the game? Bill Crichton would like always to play the game. If we were in

England— [*He pauses so long that she breaks in softly.*]

LADY MARY: We know now that we shall never see England again.

CRICHTON: I am thinking of two people whom neither of us has seen for a long time—Lady Mary Lasenby, and one Crichton, a butler. [*He says the last word bravely, a word he once loved, though it is the most horrible of all words to him now.*]

LADY MARY: That cold, haughty, insolent girl. Gov., look around you and forget them both.

CRICHTON: I had nigh forgotten them. He has had a chance, Polly—that butler—in these two years of becoming a man, and he has tried to take it. There have been many failures, but there has been some success, and with it I have let the past drop off me, and turned my back on it. That butler seems a faraway figure to me now, and not myself. I hail him, but we scarce know each other. If I am to bring him back it can only be done by force, for in my soul he is now abhorrent to me. But if I thought it best for you I'd haul him back; I swear as an honest man, I would bring him back with all his obsequious ways and deferential airs, and let you see the man you call your Gov. melt for ever into 'him who was your servant.

LADY MARY [*shivering*]: You hurt me. You say these things, but you say them like a king. To me it is the past that was not real.

CRICHTON [*too grandly*]: A king! I sometimes feel— [*For a moment the yellow light gleams in his green eyes. We remember suddenly what* TREHERNE *and* ERNEST *said about his regal look. He checks himself.*] I say it harshly, it is so hard to say, and all the time there is another voice within me crying— [*He stops.*]

LADY MARY [*trembling but not afraid*]: If it is the voice of Nature—

CRICHTON [*strongly*]: I know it to be the voice of Nature.

LADY MARY [*in a whisper*]: Then, if you want to say it very much, Gov., please say it to Polly Lasenby.

CRICHTON [*again in the grip of an idea*]: A king! Polly, some people hold that the soul but leaves one human tenement for another, and so lives on through all the ages. I have occasionally thought of late that, in some past existence, I may have been a king. It has all come to me so naturally, not as if I had had to work it out, but—as—if—I—remembered.

"Or ever the knightly years were gone,
With the old world to the grave,
I was a *king* in Babylon,
And you were a Christian slave." *

It may have been; you hear me, it may have been.

LADY MARY [*who is as one fascinated*]: It may have been.

CRICHTON: I am lord over all. They are but hewers of wood and drawers of water for me. These shores are mine. Why should I hesitate; I have no

*Or . . . slave. The quotation is from *Echoes XXXVII* by W. E. Henley, whose poems, Crichton explains later, he had with him on the island.

longer any doubt. I do believe I am doing the right thing. Dear Polly, I have grown to love you; are you afraid to mate with me? [*She rocks her arms; no words will come from her.*]

"I was a king in Babylon,
And you were a Christian slave."

LADY MARY [*bewitched*]: You are the most wonderful man I have ever known, and I am not afraid. [*He takes her to him reverently. Presently he is seated, and she is at his feet looking up adoringly in his face. As the tension relaxes she speaks with a smile.*] I want you to tell me—every woman likes to know—when was the first time you thought me nicer than the others?

CRICHTON [*who, like all big men, is simple*]: I think a year ago. We were chasing goats on the Big Slopes, and you out-distanced us all; you were the first of our party to run a goat down; I was proud of you that day.

LADY MARY [*blushing with pleasure*]: Oh Gov., I only did it to please you. Everything I have done has been out of the desire to please you. [*Suddenly anxious.*] If I thought that in taking a wife from among us you were imperilling your dignity—

CRICHTON [*perhaps a little masterful*]: Have no fear of that, dear. I have thought it all out. The wife, Polly, always takes the same position as the husband.

LADY MARY: But I am so unworthy. It was sufficient to me that I should be allowed to wait on you at that table.

CRICHTON: You shall wait on me no longer. At whatever table I

sit, Polly, you shall soon sit there also. [*Boyishly.*] Come, let us try what it will be like.

LADY MARY: As your servant at you feet.

CRICHTON: No, as my consort by my side.

[*They are sitting thus when the hatch is again opened and coffee offered. But LADY MARY is no longer there to receive it. Her sisters peep through in consternation. In vain they rattle the cup and saucer. AGATHA brings the coffee to CRICHTON.*]

CRICHTON [*forgetting for the moment that it is not a month hence*]: Help your mistress first, girl. [*Three women are bereft of speech, but he does not notice it. He addresses CATHERINE vaguely.*] Are you a good girl, Kitty?

CATHERINE [*when she finds her tongue*]: I try to be, Gov.

CRICHTON [*still more vaguely*]: That's right. [*He takes command of himself again, and signs to them to sit down. ERNEST comes in cheerily, but finding CRICHTON here is suddenly weak. He subsides on a chair, wondering what has happened.*]

CRICHTON [*surveying him*]: Ernest. [*ERNEST rises.*] You are becoming a little slovenly in your dress, Ernest; I don't like it.

ERNEST [*respectfully*]: Thank you. [*ERNEST sits again. DADDY and TREHERNE arrive.*]

CRICHTON: Daddy, I want you.

LORD LOAM [*with a sinking*]: Is it because I forgot to clean out the dam?

CRICHTON [*encouragingly*]: No, no. [*He pours some wine into a goblet.*] A glass of wine with you, Daddy.

LORD LOAM [*hastily*]: Your health, Gov. [*He is about to drink, but the master checks him.*]

CRICHTON: And hers. Daddy, this lady has done me the honour to promise to be my wife.

LORD LOAM [*astounded*]: Polly!

CRICHTON [*a little perturbed*]: I ought first to have asked your consent. I deeply regret—but Nature; may I hope I have your approval?

LORD LOAM: May you, Gov.? [*Delighted.*] Rather! Polly! [*He puts his proud arms round her.*]

TREHERNE: We all congratulate you, Gov., most heartily.

ERNEST: Long life to you both, sir.

[*There is much shaking of hands, all of which is sincere.*]

TREHERNE: When will it be, Gov.?

CRICHTON [*after turning to* LADY MARY, *who whispers to him*]: As soon as the bridal skirt can be prepared. [*His manner has been most indulgent, and without the slightest suggestion of patronage. But he knows it is best for all that he should keep his place, and that his presence hampers them.*] My friends, I thank you for your good wishes, I thank you all. And now, perhaps you would like me to leave you to yourselves. Be joyous. Let there be song and dance tonight. Polly, I shall take my coffee in the parlour—you understand. [*He retires with pleasant dignity. Immediately there is a rush of two girls at* LADY MARY.]

LADY MARY: Oh, oh! Father, they are pinching me.

LORD LOAM [*taking her under his protection*]: Agatha, Catherine, never presume to pinch your sister again. On the other hand, she may pinch you henceforth as much as ever she chooses.

[*In the meantime* TWEENY *is weeping softly, and the two are not above using her as a weapon.*]

CATHERINE: Poor Tweeny, it's a shame.

AGATHA: After he had almost promised *you*.

TWEENY [*loyally turning on them*]: No, he never did. He was always honourable as could be. 'Twas me as was too vulgar. Don't you dare say a word agin that man.

ERNEST [*to* LORD LOAM]: You'll get a lot of tit-bits out of this, Daddy.

LORD LOAM: That's what I was thinking.

ERNEST [*plunged in thought*]: I dare say *I* shall have to clean out the dam now.

LORD LOAM [*heartlessly*]: I dare say. [*His gay old heart makes him again proclaim that he is a chickety chick. He seizes the concertina.*]

TERHERNE [*eagerly*]: That's the proper spirit. [*He puts his arm round* CATHERINE, *and in another moment they are all dancing to Daddy's music. Never were people happier on an island. A moment's pause is presently created by the return of* CRICHTON *wearing the wonderful robe of which we have already had dark mention. Never has he looked more regal, never perhaps felt*

so regal. We need not grudge
him the one foible of his rule,
for it is all coming to an end.]
CRICHTON [*graciously, seeing them
hesitate*]: No, no; I am delighted
to see you all so happy. Go on.
TREHERNE: We don't like to before you, Gov.
CRICHTON [*his last order*]: It is
my wish.

[*The merrymaking is resumed, and
soon* CRICHTON *himself joins in
the dance. It is when the fun is at
its fastest and most furious that
all stop abruptly as if turned to
stone. They have heard the boom
of a gun. Presently they are alive
again.* ERNEST *leaps to the window.*]

TREHERNE [*huskily*]: It was a ship's
gun. [*They turn to* CRICHTON
*for confirmation; even in that
hour they turn to* CRICHTON.]
Gov.?
CRICHTON: Yes.

[*In another moment* LADY MARY
and LORD LOAM *are alone.*]

LADY MARY [*seeing that her father
is unconcerned*]: Father, you
heard.
LORD LOAM [*placidly*]: Yes, my
child.
LADY MARY [*alarmed by his unnatural calmness*]: But it was
a gun, father.
LORD LOAM [*looking an old man
now, and shuddering a little*]:
Yes—a gun—I have often heard
it. It's only a dream, you know;
why don't we go on dancing?

[*She takes his hands, which have
gone cold.*]

LADY MARY: Father. Don't you
see, they have all rushed down
to the beach? Come.

LORD LOAM: Rushed down to the
beach; yes, always that—I often
dream it.
LADY MARY: Come, father, come.
LORD LOAM: Only a dream, my
poor girl.

[CRICHTON *returns. He is pale
but firm.*]

CRICHTON: We can see lights
within a mile of the shore—a
great ship.
LORD LOAM: A ship—always a
ship.
LADY MARY: Father, this is no
dream.
LORD LOAM [*looking timidly at*
CRICHTON]: It's a dream, isn't
it? There's no ship?
CRICHTON [*soothing him with a
touch*]: You are awake, Daddy,
and there is a ship.
LORD LOAM [*clutching him*]: You
are not deceiving me?
CRICHTON: It is the truth.
LORD LOAM [*reeling*]: True?—a
ship—at last! [*He goes after the
others pitifully.*]
CRICHTON [*quietly*]: There is a
small boat between it and the
island; they must have sent it
ashore for water.
LADY MARY: Coming in?
CRICHTON: No. That gun must
have been a signal to recall it.
It is going back. They can't
hear our cries.
LADY MARY [*pressing her temples*]:
Going away. So near—so near.
[*Almost to herself.*] I think I'm
glad.
CRICHTON [*cheerily*]: Have no
fear. I shall bring them back.
[*He goes towards the table on
which is the electrical apparatus.*]
LADY MARY [*standing on guard as it
were between him and the table*]:

What are you going to do?

CRICHTON: To fire the beacons.

LADY MARY: Stop! [*She faces him.*] Don't you see what it means?

CRICHTON [*firmly*]: It means that our life on the island has come to a natural end.

LADY MARY [*huskily*]: Gov., let the ship go.

CRICHTON: The old man—you saw what it means to him.

LADY MARY: But I am afraid.

CRICHTON [*adoringly*]: Dear Polly.

LADY MARY: Gov., let the ship go.

CRICHTON [*she clings to him, but though it is his death sentence he loosens her hold*]: Bill Crichton has got to play the game. [*He pulls the levers. Soon through the window one of the beacons is seen flaring red. There is a long pause. Shouting is heard. ERNEST is the first to arrive.*]

ERNEST: Polly, Gov., the boat has turned back. They are English sailors; they have landed! We are rescued, I tell you, rescued!

LADY MARY [*wanly*]: Is it anything to make so great a to-do about?

ERNEST [*staring*]: Eh?

LADY MARY: Have we not been happy here?

ERNEST: Happy? lord, yes.

LADY MARY [*catching hold of his sleeve*]: Ernest, we must never forget all that the Gov. has done for us.

ERNEST [*stoutly*]: Forget it? The man who could forget it would be a selfish wretch and a— But I say, this makes a difference!

LADY MARY [*quickly*]: No, it doesn't.

ERNEST [*his mind tottering*]: A mighty difference!

[*The others come running in, some weeping with joy, others boisterous. We see blue-jackets gazing through the window at the curious scene. LORD LOAM comes accompanied by a naval officer, whom he is continually shaking by the hand.*]

LORD LOAM: And here, sir, is our little home. Let me thank you in the name of us all, again and again and again.

OFFICER: Very proud, my lord. It is indeed an honour to have been able to assist so distinguished a gentleman as Lord Loam.

LORD LOAM: A glorious, glorious day. I shall show you our other room. Come, my pets. Come, Crichton. [*He has not meant to be cruel. He does not know he has said it. It is the old life that has come back to him. They all go. All leave CRICHTON except LADY MARY.*]

LADY MARY [*stretching out her arms to him*]: Dear Gov., I will never give you up.

[*There is a salt smile on his face as he shakes his head to her. He lets the cloak slip to the ground. She will not take this for an answer; again her arms go out to him. Then comes the great renunciation. By an effort of will he ceases to be an erect figure; he has the humble bearing of a servant. His hands come together as if he were washing them.*]

CRICHTON [*it is the speech of his life*]: My lady.

[*She goes away. There is none to salute him now, unless we do it.*]

END OF ACT III

ACT FOUR

The other island.

Some months have elapsed, and we have again the honour of waiting upon LORD LOAM *in his London home. It is the room of the first act, but with a new scheme of decoration, for on the walls are exhibited many interesting trophies from the island, such as skins, stuffed birds, and weapons of the chase, labelled "shot by Lord Loam," "Hon. Ernest Woolley's Blowpipe," etc. There are also two large glass cases containing other odds and ends, including, curiously enough, the bucket in which* ERNEST *was first dipped, but there is no label calling attention to the incident.*

It is not yet time to dress for dinner, and his lordship is on a couch, hastily yet furtively cutting the pages of a new book. With him are his two younger daughters and his nephew, and they also are engaged in literary pursuits; that is to say, the ladies are eagerly but furtively reading the evening papers, of which ERNEST *is sitting complacently but furtively on an endless number, and doling them out as called for. Note the frequent use of the word "furtive." It implies that they do not wish to be discovered by their butler, say, at their otherwise delightful task.*

AGATHA [*reading aloud, with emphasis on the wrong words*]: "In conclusion, we most heartily congratulate the Hon. Ernest Woolley. This book of his, regarding the adventures of himself and his brave companions on a desert isle, stirs the heart like a trumpet." [*Evidently the book referred to is the one in* LORD LOAM'S *hands.*]

ERNEST [*handing her a pink paper*]: Here is another.

CATHERINE [*reading*]: "From the first to the last of Mr. Woolley's engrossing pages it is evident that he was an ideal man to be wrecked with, and a true hero." [*Large-eyed.*] Ernest!

ERNEST [*calmly*]: That's how it strikes *them,* you know. Here's another one.

AGATHA [*reading*]: "There are many kindly references to the two servants who were wrecked with the family, and Mr. Woolley pays the butler a glowing tribute in a footnote."

[*Some one coughs uncomfortably.*]

LORD LOAM [*who has been searching the index for the letter L*]: Excellent, excellent. At the same time I must say, Ernest, that the whole book is about yourself.

ERNEST [*genially*]: As the author—

LORD LOAM: Certainly, certainly. Still, you know, as a peer of the realm—[*with dignity*]—I think, Ernest, you might have given me one of your adventures.

ERNEST: I say it was you who taught us how to obtain a fire by rubbing two pieces of stick together.

LORD LOAM [*beaming*]: Do you, do you? I call that very handsome. What page?

[*Here the door opens, and the well-bred* CRICHTON *enters with the evening papers as subscribed for by the house. Those we have already seen have perhaps been introuced by* ERNEST *up his waistcoat. Every one except the intruder is immediately self-conscious, and when he withdraws there is a general sigh of relief. They pounce on the new papers.* ERNEST *evidently gets a shock from one, which he casts contemptuously on the floor.*]

AGATHA [*more fortunate*]: Father, see page 81. "It was a tiger-cat," says Mr. Woolley, "of the largest size. Death stared Lord Loam in the face, but he never flinched."

LORD LOAM [*searching his book eagerly*]: Page 81.

AGATHA: "With presence of mind only equalled by his courage, he fixed an arrow in his bow."

LORD LOAM: Thank you, Ernest; thank you, my boy.

AGATHA: "Unfortunately he missed."

LORD LOAM: Eh?

AGATHA: "But by great good luck I heard his cries"—

LORD LOAM: My cries?

AGATHA: —"and rushing forward with drawn knife, I stabbed the monster to the heart."

[LORD LOAM *shuts his book with a pettish slam. There might be a scene here were it not that* CRICHTON *reappears and goes to one of the glass cases. All are at once on the alert, and his lordship is particularly sly.*]

LORM LOAM: Anything in the papers, Catherine?

CATHERINE: No, father, nothing—nothing at all.

ERNEST [*it pops out as of yore*]: The papers! The papers are guides that tell us what we ought to do, and then we don't do it.

[CRICHTON *having opened the glass case has taken out the bucket, and* ERNEST, *looking round for applause, sees him carrying it off and is undone. For a moment of time he forgets that he is no longer on the island, and with a sigh he is about to follow* CRICHTON *and the bucket to a retired spot. The door closes, and* ERNEST *comes to himself.*]

LORD LOAM [*uncomfortably*]: I told him to take it away.

ERNEST: I thought—[*he wipes his brow*]—I shall go and dress. [*He goes.*]

CATHERINE: Father, it's awful having Crichton here. It's like living on tiptoe.

LORD LOAM [*gloomily*]: While he is here we are sitting on a volcano.

AGATHA: How mean of you! I am sure he has only stayed on

with us to—to help us through. It would have looked so suspicious if he had gone at once.

CATHERINE [*revelling in the worst*]: But suppose Lady Brocklehurst were to get at him and pump him. She's the most terrifying, suspicious old creature in England; and Crichton simply can't tell a lie.

LORD LOAM: My dear, that is the volcano to which I was referring. [*He has evidently something to communicate.*] It's all Mary's fault. She said to me yesterday that she would break her engagement with Brocklehurst unless I told him about—you know what.

[*All conjure up the vision of* CRICHTON.]

AGATHA: Is she mad?

LORD LOAM: She calls it common honesty.

CATHERINE: Father, have you told him?

LORD LOAM [*heavily*]: She thinks I have, but I couldn't. She's sure to find out tonight. [*Unconsciously he leans on the island concertina, which he has perhaps been lately showing to an interviewer as something he made for* TWEENY. *It squeaks, and they all jump.*]

CATHERINE: It's like a bird of ill-omen.

LORD LOAM [*vindictively*]: I must have it taken away; it has done that twice.

[LADY MARY *comes in. She is in evening dress. Undoubtedly she meant to sail in, but she forgets, and despite her garments it is a manly entrance. She is properly* ashamed of herself. *She tries again, and has an encouraging success. She indicates to her sisters that she wishes to be alone with papa.*]

AGATHA: All right, but we know what it's about. Come along, Kit.

[*They go.* LADY MARY *thoughtlessly sits like a boy, and again corrects herself. She addresses her father, but he is in a brown study, and she seeks to draw his attention by whistling. This troubles them both.*]

LADY MARY: How horrid of me!

LORD LOAM [*depressed*]: If you would try to remember—

LADY MARY [*sighing*]: I do; but there are so many things to remember.

LORD LOAM [*sympathetically*]: There are— [*In a whisper.*] Do you know, Mary, I constantly find myself secreting hairpins.

LADY MARY: I find it so difficult to go up steps one at a time.

LORD LOAM: I was dining with half a dozen members of our party last Thursday, Mary, and they were so eloquent that I couldn't help wondering all the time how many of their heads *he* would have put in the bucket.

LADY MARY: I use so many of his phrases. And my appetite is so scandalous. Father, I usually have a chop before we sit down to dinner.

LORD LOAM: As for my clothes— [*Wriggling.*] My dear, you can't think how irksome collars are to me nowadays.

LADY MARY: They can't be half such an annoyance, father, as—

[*She looks dolefully at her skirt.*]

LORD LOAM [*hurriedly*]: Quite so—quite so. You have dressed early tonight, Mary.

LADY MARY: That reminds me; I had a note from Brocklehurst saying that he would come a few minutes before his mother as—as he wanted to have a talk with me. He didn't say what about, but of course we know. [*His lordship fidgets. With feeling.*] It was good of you to tell him, father. Oh, it is horrible to me— [*Covering her face.*] It seemed so natural at the time.

LORD LOAM [*petulantly*]: Never again make use of that word in this house, Mary.

LADY MARY [*with an effort*]: Father, Brocklehurst has been so loyal to me for these two years that I should despise myself were I to keep my—my extraordinary lapse from him. Had Brocklehurst been a little less good, then you need not have told him my strange little secret.

LORD LOAM [*weakly*]: Polly—I mean Mary—it was all Crichton's fault, he—

LADY MARY [*with decision*]: No, father, no; not a word against him though. I haven't the pluck to go on with it; I can't even understand how it ever was. Father, do you not still hear the surf? Do you see the curve of the beach?

LORD LOAM: I have begun to forget— [*In a low voice.*] But they were happy days; there was something magical about them.

LADY MARY: It was glamour. Father, I have lived Arabian nights. I have sat out a dance with the evening star. But it was all in a past existence, in the days of Babylon, and I am myself again. But he has been chivalrous always. If the slothful, indolent creature I used to be has improved in any way, I owe it all to him. I am slipping back in many ways, but I am determined not to slip back altogether—in memory of him and his island. That is why I insisted on your telling Brocklehurst. He can break our engagement if he chooses. [*Proudly.*] Mary Lasenby is going to play the game.

LORD LOAM: But my dear—

[LORD BROCKLEHURST *is announced.*]

LADY MARY [*meaningly*]: Father, dear, oughtn't you to be dressing?

LORD LOAM [*very unhappy*]: The fact is—before I go—I want to say—

LORD BROCKLEHURST: Loam, if you don't mind, I wish very specially to have a word with Mary before dinner.

LORD LOAM: But—

LADY MARY: Yes, father. [*She induces him to go, and thus courageously faces* LORD BROCKLEHURST *to hear her fate.*] I am ready, George.

LORD BROCKLEHURST [*who is so agitated that she ought to see he is thinking not of her but of himself*]: It is a painful matter— I wish I could have spared you this, Mary.

LADY MARY: Please go on.

LORD BROCKLEHURST: In common fairness, of course, this should be remembered, that two years had elapsed. You and I had no reason to believe that we should ever meet again.

[*This is more considerate than she had expected.*]

LADY MARY [*softening*]: I was so lost to the world, George.

LORD BROCKLEHURST [*with a groan*]: At the same time, the thing is utterly and absolutely inexcusable—

LADY MARY [*recovering her hauteur*]: Oh!

LORD BROCKLEHURST: And so I have already said to mother.

LADY MARY [*disdaining him*]: You have told her?

LORD BROCKLEHURST: Certainly, Mary, certainly; I tell mother everything.

LADY MARY [*curling her lip*]: And what did she say?

LORD BROCKLEHURST: To tell the truth, mother rather poohpoohed the whole affair.

LADY MARY [*incredulous*]: Lady Brocklehurst pooh-poohed the whole affair!

LORD BROCKLEHURST: She said, "Mary and I will have a good laugh over this."

LADY MARY [*outraged*]: George, your mother is a hateful, depraved old woman.

LORD BROCKLEHURST: Mary!

LADY MARY [*turning away*]: Laugh indeed, when it will always be such a pain to me.

LORD BROCKLEHURST [*with strange humility*]: If only you would let me bear all the pain, Mary.

LADY MARY [*who is taken aback*]: George, I think you are the noblest man— [*She is touched, and gives him both her hands. Unfortunately he simpers.*]

LORD BROCKLEHURST: She was a pretty little thing. [*She stares, but he marches to his doom.*] Ah, not beautiful like you. I assure you it was the merest flirtation; there were a few letters, but we have got them back. It was all owing to the boat being so late at Calais. You see, she had such large, helpless eyes.

LADY MARY [*fixing him*]: George, when you lunched with father today at the club—

LORD BROCKLEHURST: I didn't. He wired me that he couldn't come.

LADY MARY [*with a tremor*]: But he wrote you?

LORD BROCKLEHURST: No.

LADY MARY [*a bird singing in her breast*]: You haven't seen him since?

LORD BROCKLEHURST: No.

[*She is saved. Is he to be let off also? Not at all. She bears down on him like a ship of war.*]

LADY MARY: George, who and what is this woman?

LORD BROCKLEHURST [*cowering*]: She was—she is—the shame of it —a lady's-maid.

LADY MARY [*properly horrified*]: A what?

LORD BROCKLEHURST: A lady's-maid. A mere servant, Mary. [LADY MARY *whirls round so that he shall not see her face.*] I first met her at this house when you were entertaining the servants; so you see it was largely your father's fault.

LADY MARY [*looking him up and down*]: A lady's-maid?

LORD BROCKLEHURST [*degraded*]: Her name was Fisher.

LADY MARY: My maid!

LORD BROCKLEHURST [*with open*

hands]: Can you forgive me, Mary?

LADY MARY: Oh George, George!

LORD BROCKLEHURST: Mother urged me not to tell you anything about it; but—

LADY MARY [*from her heart*]: I am so glad you told me.

LORD BROCKLEHURST: You see there was nothing wrong in it.

LADY MARY [*thinking perhaps of another incident*]: No, indeed.

LORD BROCKLEHURST [*inclined to simper again*]: And she behaved awfully well. She quite saw that it was because the boat was late. I suppose the glamour to a girl in service of a man in high position—

LADY MARY: Glamour!—yes, yes, that was it.

LORD BROCKLEHURST: Mother says that a girl in such circumstances is to be excused if she loses her head.

LADY MARY [*impulsively*]: George, I am so sorry if I said any thing against your mother. I am sure she is the dearest old thing.

LORD BROCKLEHURST [*in calm waters at last*]: Of course for women of our class she has a very different standard.

LADY MARY [*grown tiny*]: Of course.

LORD BROCKLEHURST: You see, knowing how good a woman she is herself, she was naturally anxious that I should marry some one like her. That is what has made her watch your conduct so jealously, Mary.

LADY MARY [*hurriedly thinking things out*]: I know. I—I think, George, that before your mother comes I should like to say a word to father.

LORD BROCKLEHURST [*nervously*]: About this?

LADY MARY: Oh no; I shan't tell him of this. About something else.

LORD BROCKLEHURST: And you do forgive me, Mary?

LADY MARY [*smiling on him*]: Yes, yes. I—I am sure the boat was *very* late, George.

LORD BROCKLEHURST [*earnestly*]: It really was.

LADY MARY: I am even relieved to know that you are not quite perfect, dear. [*She rests her hands on his shoulders. She has a moment of contrition.*] George, when we are married, we shall try to be not an entirely frivolous couple, won't we? We must endeavour to be of some little use, dear.

LORD BROCKLEHURST [*the ass*]: *Noblesse oblige.*

LADY MARY [*haunted by the phrases of a better man*]: Mary Lasenby is determined to play the game, George. [*Perhaps she adds to herself, "Except just this once."* A kiss closes this episode of the two lovers; and soon after the departure of* LADY MARY *the* COUNTESS OF BROCKLEHURST *is announced. She is a very formidable old lady.*]

LADY BROCKLEHURST: Alone, George?

LORD BROCKLEHURST: Mother, I told her all; she has behaved magnificently.

LADY BROCKLEHURST [*who has not shared his fears*]: Silly boy. [*She casts a supercilious eye on the island trophies.*] So these are the wonders they brought back with them. Gone away to dry her eyes, I suppose?

LORD BROCKLEHURST [*proud of his mate*]: She didn't cry, mother.

LADY BROCKLEHURST: No? [*She reflects.*] You're quite right. I wouldn't have cried. Cold, icy. Yes, that was it.

LORD BROCKLEHURST [*who has not often contradicted her*]: I assure you, mother, that wasn't it at all. She forgave me at once.

LADY BROCKLEHURST [*opening her eyes sharply to the full*]: Oh!

LORD BROCKLEHURST: She was awfully nice about the boat being late; she even said she was relieved to find that I wasn't quite perfect.

LADY BROCKLEHURST [*pouncing*]: She said that?

LORD BROCKLEHURST: She really did.

LADY BROCKLEHURST: I mean *I* wouldn't. Now if *I* had said that, what would have made me say it? [*Suspiciously.*] George, is Mary all we think her?

LORD BROCKLEHURST [*with unexpected spirit*]: If she wasn't, mother, you would know it.

LADY BROCKLEHURST: Hold your tongue, boy. We don't really know what happened on that island.

LORD BROCKLEHURST: You were reading the book all the morning.

LADY BROCKLEHURST: How can I be sure that the book is true?

LORD BROCKLEHURST: They all talk of it as true.

LADY BROCKLEHURST: How do I know that they are not lying?

LORD BROCKLEHURST: Why should they lie?

LADY BROCKLEHURST: Why shouldn't they? [*She reflects again.*] If I had been wrecked on an island, I think it highly probable that I should have lied when I came back. Weren't some servants with them?

LORD BROCKLEHURST: Crichton, the butler. [*He is surprised to see her ring the bell.*] Why, mother, you are not going to—

LADY BROCKLEHURST: Yes, I am. [*Pointedly.*] George, watch whether Crichton begins any of his answers to my questions with "The fact is."

LORD BROCKLEHURST: Why?

LADY BROCKLEHURST: Because that is usually the beginning of a lie.

LORD BROCKLEHURST [*as* CRICHTON *opens the door*]: Mother, you can't do these things in other people's houses.

LADY BROCKLEHURST [*coolly, to* CRICHTON]: It was I who rang. [*Surveying him through her eyeglass.*] So you were one of the castaways, Crichton?

CRICHTON: Yes, my lady.

LADY BROCKLEHURST: Delightful book Mr. Woolley has written about your adventures. [CRICHTON *bows.*] Don't you think so?

CRICHTON: I have not read it, my lady.

LADY BROCKLEHURST: Odd that they should not have presented you with a copy.

LORD BROCKLEHURST: Presumably Crichton is no reader.

LADY BROCKLEHURST: By the way, Crichton, were there any books on the island?

CRICHTON: I had one, my lady—Henley's poems.

LORD BROCKLEHURST: Never heard of him.

[CRICHTON *again bows.*]

LADY BROCKLEHURST [*who has not heard of him either*]: I think you were not the only servant wrecked?

CRICHTON: There was a young woman, my lady.

LADY BROCKLEHURST: I want to see her. [CRICHTON *bows, but remains.*] Fetch her up.

[*He goes.*]

LORD BROCKLEHURST [*almost standing up to his mother*]: This is scandalous.

LADY BROCKLEHURST [*defining her position*]: I am a mother. [CATHERINE *and* AGATHA *enter in dazzling confections, and quake in secret to find themselves practically alone with* LADY BROCKLEHURST. *Even as she greets them.*] How d' you do, Catherine—Agatha? You didn't dress like this on the island, I expect! By the way, how did you dress?

[*They have thought themselves prepared, but—*]

AGATHA: Not—not so well, of course, but quite the same idea.

[*They are relieved by the arrival of* TREHERNE, *who is in clerical dress.*]

LADY BROCKLEHURST: How do you do, Mr. Treherne? There is not so much of you in the book as I had hoped.

TREHERNE [*modestly*]: There wasn't very much of me on the island, Lady Brocklehurst.

LADY BROCKLEHURST: How d' ye mean?

[*He shrugs his honest shoulders.*]

LORD BROCKLEHURST: I hear you have got a living, Treherne. Congratulations.

TREHERNE: Thanks.

LORD BROCKLEHURST: Is it a good one?

TREHERNE: So-so. They are rather weak in bowling, but it's a good bit of turf.

[*Confidence is restored by the entrance of* ERNEST, *who takes in the situation promptly, and, of course, knows he is a match for any old lady.*]

ERNEST [*with ease*]: How do you do, Lady Brocklehurst.

LADY BROCKLEHURST: Our brilliant author!

ERNEST [*impervious to satire*]: Oh, I don't know.

LADY BROCKLEHURST: It is as engrossing, Mr. Woolley, as if it were a work of fiction.

ERNEST [*suddenly uncomfortable*]: Thanks, awfully. [*Recovering.*] The fact is— [*He is puzzled by seeing the Brocklehurst family exchange meaning looks.*]

CATHERINE [*to the rescue*]: Lady Brocklehurst, Mr. Treherne and I—we are engaged.

AGATHA: And Ernest and I.

LADY BROCKLEHURST [*grimly*]: I see, my dears; thought it wise to keep the island in the family.

[*An awkward moment this for the entrance of* LORD LOAM *and* LADY MARY, *who, after a private talk upstairs, are feeling happy and secure.*]

LORD LOAM [*with two hands for his distinguished guest*]: Aha! ha, ha! younger than any of them, Emily.

LADY BROCKLEHURST: Flatterer. [*To* LADY MARY.] You seem in high spirits, Mary.

LADY MARY [*gaily*]: I am.

LADY BROCKLEHURST [*with a significant glance at* LORD BROCKLEHURST]: After—

LADY MARY: I—I mean. The fact is—

[*Again that disconcerting glance between the* COUNTESS *and her son.*]

LORD LOAM [*humorously*]: She hears wedding bells, Emily, ha, ha!

LADY BROCKLEHURST [*coldly*]: Do you, Mary? Can't say I do; but I'm hard of hearing.

LADY MARY [*instantly her match*]: If you don't, Lady Brocklehurst, I'm sure I don't.

LORD LOAM [*nervously*]: Tut, tut. Seen our curios from the island, Emily; I should like you to examine them.

LADY BROCKLEHURST: Thank you, Henry. I am glad you say that, for I have just taken the liberty of asking two of them to step upstairs.

[*There is an uncomfortable silence, which the entrance of* CRICHTON *with* TWEENY *does not seem to dissipate.* CRICHTON *is impenetrable, but* TWEENY *hangs back in fear.*]

LORD BROCKLEHURST [*stoutly*]: Loam, I have no hand in this.

LADY BROCKLEHURST [*undisturbed*]: Pooh, what have I done? You always begged me to speak to the servants, Henry, and I merely wanted to discover whether the views you used to

hold about equality were adopted on the island; it seemed a splendid opportunity, but Mr. Woolley has not a word on the subject.

[*All eyes turn to* ERNEST.]

ERNEST [*with confidence*]: The fact is— [*The fatal words again.*]

LORD LOAM [*not quite certain what he is to assure her of*]: I assure you, Emily—

LADY MARY [*as cold as steel*]: Father, nothing whatever happened on the island of which I, for one, am ashamed, and I hope Crichton will be allowed to answer Lady Brocklehurst's questions.

LADY BROCKLEHURST: To be sure. There's nothing to make a fuss about, and we're a family party. [*To* CRICHTON.] Now, truthfully, my man.

CRICHTON [*calmly*]: I promise that, my lady.

[*Some hearts sink, the hearts that could never understand a* CRICHTON.]

LADY BROCKLEHURST [*sharply*]: Well, were you all equal on the island?

CRICHTON: No, my lady. I think I may say there was as little equality there as elsewhere.

LADY BROCKLEHURST: All the social distinctions were preserved?

CRICHTON: As at home, my lady.

LADY BROCKLEHURST: The servants?

CRICHTON: They had to keep their place.

LADY BROCKLEHURST: Wonderful. How was it managed? [*With*

an inspiration.] You, girl, tell me that?

[*Can there be a more critical moment?*]

TWEENY [*in agony*]: If you please, my lady, it was all the Gov.'s doing.

[*They give themselves up for lost.* LORD LOAM *tries to sink out of sight.*]

CRICHTON: In the regrettable slang of the servants' hall, my lady, the master is usually referred to as the Gov.

LADY BROCKLEHURST: I see. [*She turns to* LORD LOAM.] You—

LORD LOAM [*reappearing*]: Yes, I understand that is what they call me.

LADY BROCKLEHURST [*to* CRICHTON]: You didn't even take your meals with the family?

CRICHTON: No, my lady, I dined apart.

[*Is all safe?*]

LADY BROCKLEHURST [*alas*]: You, girl, also? Did you dine with Crichton?

TWEENY [*scared*]: No, your ladyship.

LADY BROCKLEHURST [*fastening on her*]: With whom?

TWEENY: I took my bit of supper with—with Daddy and Polly and the rest.

[*Vae victis.* *]

ERNEST [*leaping into the breach*]: Dear old Daddy—he was our monkey. You remember our monkey, Agatha?

AGATHA: Rather! What a funny old darling he was.

---

* *Vae victis,* woe to the vanquished.

CATHERINE [*thus encouraged*]: And don't you think Polly was the sweetest little parrot, Mary?

LADY BROCKLEHURST: Ah! I understand; animals you had domesticated?

LORD LOAM [*heavily*]: Quite so—quite so.

LADY BROCKLEHURST: The servants' teas that used to take place here once a month—

CRICHTON: They did not seem natural on the island, my lady, and were discontinued by the Gov.'s orders.

LORD BROCKLEHURST: A clear proof, Loam, that they were a mistake here.

LORD LOAM [*seeing the opportunity for a diversion*]: I admit it frankly. I abandon them. Emily, as the result of our experiences on the island, I think of going over to the Tories.

LADY BROCKLEHURST: I am delighted to hear it.

LORD LOAM [*expanding*]: Thank you, Crichton, thank you; that is all.

[*He motions to them to go, but the time is not yet.*]

LADY BROCKLEHURST: One moment. [*There is a universal but stifled groan.*] Young people, Crichton, will be young people, even on an island; now, I suppose there was a certain amount of—shall we say sentimentalising, going on?

CRICHTON: Yes, my lady, there was.

LORD BROCKLEHURST [*ashamed*]: Mother!

LADY BROCKLEHURST [*disregarding him*]: Which gentleman? [*To* TWEENY.] You, girl, tell me.

TWEENY [*confused*]: If you please, my lady—

ERNEST [*hurriedly*]: The fact is—

[*He is checked as before, and probably says "D—n" to himself, but he has saved the situation.*]

TWEENY [*gasping*]: It was him—Mr. Ernest, your ladyship.

LADY BROCKLEHURST [*counsel for the prosecution*]: With which lady?

AGATHA: I have already told you, Lady Brocklehurst, that Ernest and I—

LADY BROCKLEHURST: Yes, *now;* but you were two years on the island. [*Looking at* LADY MARY.] Was it this lady?

TWEENY: No, your ladyship.

LADY BROCKLEHURST: Then I don't care which of the others it was. [TWEENY *gurgles.*] Well, I suppose that will do.

LORD BROCKLEHURST: Do! I hope you are ashamed of yourself, mother. [*To* CRICHTON, *who is going.*] You are an excellent fellow, Crichton; and if, after we are married, you ever wish to change your place, come to us.

LADY MARY [*losing her head for the only time*]: Oh no, impossible.

LADY BROCKLEHURST [*at once suspicious*]: Why impossible? [LADY MARY *cannot answer, or perhaps she is too proud.*] Do you see why it should be impossible, my man?

[*He can make or mar his unworthy* MARY *now. Have you any doubt of him?*]

CRICHTON: Yes, my lady. I had not told you, my lord, but as soon as your lordship is suited I wish to leave service.

[*They are all immensely relieved, except poor* TWEENY.]

TREHERNE [*the only curious one*]: What will you do, Crichton?

[CRICHTON *shrugs his shoulders; "God knows," it may mean.*]

CRICHTON: Shall I withdraw, my lord?

[*He withdraws without a tremor,* TWEENY *accompanying him. They can all breathe again; the thunderstorm is over.*]

LADY BROCKLEHURST [*thankful to have made herself unpleasant*]: Horrid of me, wasn't it? But if one wasn't disagreeable now and again, it would be horribly tedious to be an old woman. He will soon be yours, Mary, and then—think of the opportunities you will have of being disagreeable to me. On that understanding, my dear, don't you think we might—?

[*Their cold lips meet.*]

LORD LOAM [*vaguely*]: Quite so—quite so.

[CRICHTON *announces dinner, and they file out.* LADY MARY *stays behind a moment and impulsively holds out her hand.*]

LADY MARY: To wish you every dear happiness.

CRICHTON [*an enigma to the last*]: The same to you, my lady.

LADY MARY: Do you despise me, Crichton? [*The man who could never tell a lie makes no answer.*] You are the best man among us.

CRICHTON: On an island, my lady, perhaps; but in England, no.

LADY MARY: Then there's something wrong with England.

CRICHTON: My lady, not even from you can I listen to a word against England.

LADY MARY: Tell me one thing: you have not lost your courage?

CRICHTON: No, my lady.

[*She goes. He turns out the lights.*]

THE END

John Galsworthy
[1867-1933]

J OHN GALSWORTHY was born at Kingston Hill, Surrey, on the 14th of August, 1867, like Pinero, the son of a solicitor. He was educated at Harrow, where he proved himself a very good athlete. He obtained a law degree and was called to the bar in 1890. He decided to specialize in marine law and, to gain experience in that field, he traveled to the Near East in a merchant ship. It was on such a ship that he first caught sight of a new mate, very dirty and angry and ill-spoken. This mate turned out to be Joseph Conrad who became Galsworthy's life-long friend. In 1905 he married Ada Pearson; they had no children.

He began writing short stories and novels under the name of John Sinjohn, but his first success in 1906 was the result of a novel and a play. The novel was *The Man of Property,* which led him ultimately into writing the *Forsyte Saga,* and the play was *The Silver Box,* produced by Granville-Barker. Galsworthy had written the play with slight hope of getting it produced, particularly as he had had no theatrical experience or training. His novel was a critical, objective description of Victorian upper-class commercial society, narrow in its outlook but determined and prudent. Galsworthy brought much the same objectivity to his plays.

He believed that drama should not draw a distorted moral because doing so would turn it into a caricature. He said three courses were open to the playwright: he could give the public what it already believes; he could give the public what he believes; or he could show the public the phenomena of life and character just as it is, but selected and combined—not distorted by any prejudice—and leave the public to draw whatever moral it can. Galsworthy judged the third course to be the ideal one and realized that it required detachment, sympathy, and industry on the part of the writer, who should expect no practical result from his play. Galsworthy belonged to no political party and held no particular social ideals, which, while making it easier, perhaps, for him to be more "objective" than Shaw, also resulted in his being a less vital writer. He was not philosophic, humorous, or romantic. He did have pity for people and for animals, but showed himself in his writing to be most moved by young love and beauty. The cardinal sin in drama, he said, was to hang characters on the plot; rather the plot should hang on the characters. The dialogue should reflect the characters and serve to advance the play. Accordingly his dialogue was not stagy, or witty, or filled with brilliant epigrams. It was lifelike and suited the characters. His plots were simple and honestly worked out, no one character being entirely right or wrong. He tried to avoid theatricality and cheap sensationalism. Also, he offered no remedies or happy endings, so that sometimes his plays depressed even him. After seeing a production of *Justice,* he remarked that he never wanted to see that damned play again.

The Silver Box shows how a wealthy man with a good lawyer can win a lawsuit, whereas a poor man goes to jail. Even so, there is right and wrong on both sides. Galsworthy's view was not so revolutionary as it was conscientious. By 1906 the public was ready for social problem plays, and this play was a success. In 1909 he wrote *Strife,* a play about management and labor disputes, which preceded the great labor strikes by some years and presented the views of both sides fairly. In 1910 *Justice* was produced. This play showed how it was possible for the law to so crush a weak criminal that he was driven to suicide. Galsworthy spent hours examining prisons and cells in an effort to give the play authenticity and depicted conditions so well that after Winston Churchill saw the play he instituted a reform of solitary confinement. This play particularly made Galsworthy unhappy in that he could see no valid solution to the problem it posed. He wrote another play, *The Mob,* which dealt with the South African war and the moneyed interests involved, and gave a picture of totalitarianism, but this play he later jokingly said should be avoided. Galsworthy believed that the drama in his time was renascent because of a new spirit—an awakened humanity and conscience—and he foresaw two developing channels for the drama: naturalism and a poetic verse drama.

He died at Hampstead on January 31, 1933.

Galsworthy's sincere interest and concern with the problem of justice and of the individual in a losing battle with his society is dramatized in all of his plays. *The Silver Box* was his first and one of his most successful treatments of this problem of justice and of what Galsworthy would call the "erring individual" face to face with his society. When it was produced in 1906, it established Galsworthy as a serious dramatist at a time when the drama of social conflict was on the rise in England. Galsworthy believed that men lived among men in a disharmonic, a perpetually ironic state. Thus he handles dramatic irony with much of the skill of Ibsen. He defines the helplessness of the individual against the immense odds of the powerful social machinery and the self-deceiving, self-righteous, and self-approving managers who look on with satisfaction and even a sense of generosity at the destruction of human beings.

Like Ibsen, Galsworthy made use of the devices of the well-made play, but sometimes these devices are more obtrusive. The exposition in the first act, for instance, is rather obvious in the exchange between the two servants; the coincidental parallel of thefts—young Barthwick's and Jones's—is a little too neatly worked out to accommodate the thematic development; the entrance of the policeman in Act II to discover the box in plain view is also rather too convenient for the climax; and the pathetic end of the second act is much too sentimental for an otherwise rather tough-minded play. Aside from these faults, the play is tightly and powerfully constructed; the realistic dialogue is hard-hitting and the theme is as topical today as it was at the turn of the century. The play has the impact of an Ibsen drama, though it has few of the powerful overtones that make Ibsen a giant in the modern theatre.

Nevertheless the play achieves considerable life and generates ironic power. Few social problem plays in the modern theatre can match the mounting irony from first act to last: Beginning with Mrs. Jones's cross-examination by Barthwick to the Judge's cross-examination of Jones, the couple convict themselves by revealing the dismal circumstances of their poverty; the court's final victimization of them because of their poverty and the action of leaving them more destitute and miserable than it found them is capped by the final ironic touch—the Judge and Mr. Barthwick consider the action an act of charity. These are considerable claims to make for any dramatist. What tends to date the play, perhaps, is a combination of the obtrusive devices and some of the realistic dialogue. However, the characters are sharply and surely drawn and the play demonstrates that Galsworthy's skill as a social thesis dramatist is equal to that of any of the social thesis dramatists of the contemporary theatre.

DRAMATIC WORKS

The Silver Box, 1906
Joy, 1907
Strife, 1909
Justice, 1910
The Little Dream, 1911
The Eldest Son, 1912
The Pigeon, 1912

The Fugitive, 1913
The Mob, 1914
The Skin Game, 1920
Loyalties, 1922
Windows, 1922
The Forest, 1924
Escape, 1926

The Silver Box

★

CAST

JOHN BARTHWICK, M.P., *a wealthy Liberal*
MRS. BARTHWICK, *his wife*
JACK BARTHWICK, *their son*
ROPER, *their solicitor*
MRS. JONES, *their charwoman*
MARLOW, *their manservant*
WHEELER, *their maidservant*
JONES, *the stranger within their gates*
MRS. SEDDON, *a landlady*
SNOW, *a detective*
JULIUS HOLDEN, *a Police Magistrate*
AN UNKNOWN LADY, *from beyond*
TWO LITTLE GIRLS, *homeless*
LIVENS, *their father*
RELIEVING OFFICER
MAGISTRATE'S CLERK
USHER
CLERK OF COURT
SWEARING CLERK
CONSTABLE
Policemen, Clerks, and others

TIME: *The present. The action of the first two Acts takes place on Easter Tuesday; the action of the third on Easter Wednesday week.*

ACT I
SCENE I: *Rockingham Gate.*
John Barthwick's Dining-room.
SCENE II: *The Same.*
SCENE III: *The Same.*

ACT II
SCENE I: *The Jones's Lodgings, Merthyr Street.*
SCENE II: *John Barthwick's Dining-room.*

ACT III
A London Police Court.

ACT ONE

SCENE FIRST: *The curtain rises on the* BARTHWICKS' *dining-room, large, modern, and well furnished; the window curtains drawn. Electric light is burning. On the large round dining-table is set out a tray with whisky, a syphon, and a silver cigarette-box. It is past midnight.*

[*A fumbling is heard outside the door. It is opened suddenly;* JACK BARTHWICK *seems to fall into the room. He stands holding by the door knob, staring before him, with a beatific smile. He is in evening dress and opera hat, and carries in his hand a sky-blue velvet lady's reticule. His boyish face is freshly coloured and clean-shaven. An overcoat is hanging on his arm.*]

JACK: Hello! I've got home all ri— [*Defiantly.*] Who says I sh'd never 've opened th' door without 'sistance. [*He staggers in, fumbling with the reticule. A lady's handkerchief and purse of crimson silk fall out.*] Serve her joll' well right—everything droppin' out. Th' cat. I've scored her off—I've got her bag. [*He swings the reticule.*] Serves her joll' well right. [*He takes a cigarette out of the silver box and puts it in his mouth.*] Never gave tha' fellow anything! [*He hunts through all his pockets and pulls a shilling out; it drops and rolls away. He looks for it.*] Beastly shilling! [*He looks again.*] Base ingratitude! Absolutely nothing.

[*He laughs.*] Mus' tell him I've got absolutely nothing.

[*He lurches through the door and down a corridor, and presently returns, followed by* JONES, *who is advanced in liquor.* JONES, *about thirty years of age, has hollow cheeks, black circles round his eyes, and rusty clothes. He looks as though he might be unemployed, and enters in a hang-dog manner.*]

JACK: Sh! sh! sh! Don't you make a noise, whatever you do. Shu' the door, an' have a drink. [*Very solemnly.*] You helped me to open the door—I've got nothin' for you. This is my house. My father's name's Barthwick; he's Member of Parliament—Liberal Member of Parliament: I've told you that before. Have a drink! [*He pours out whisky and drinks it up.*] I'm not drunk — [*Subsiding on a sofa.*] Tha's all right. Wha's your name? My name's Barthwick, so's my father's; *I'm* a Liberal too—wha're you?

JONES [*in a thick, sardonic voice*]: I'm a bloomin' Conser*vative*. My name's Jones! My wife works

347

'ere; she's the char; she works 'ere.

JACK: Jones? [*He laughs.*] There's 'nother Jones at College with me. I'm not a Socialist myself; I'm a Liberal—there's ve-lill difference, because of the principles of the Lib—Liberal Party. We're all equal before the law—tha's rot, tha's silly. [*Laughs.*] Wha' was I about to say? Give me some whisky. [JONES *gives him the whisky he desires, together with a squirt of syphon.*] Wha' I was goin' tell you was—I've had a row with her. [*He waves the reticule.*] Have a drink, Jones—sh'd never have got in without you—tha's why I'm giving you a drink. Don' care who knows I've scored her off. Th' cat! [*He throws his feet up on the sofa.*] Don' you make a noise, whatever you do. You pour out a drink—you make yourself good long, long drink —you take cigarette—you take anything you like. Sh'd never have got in without you. [*Closing his eyes.*] You're a Tory— you're a Tory Socialist. I'm Liberal myself—have a drink— I'm an excel'nt chap.

[*His head drops back. He, smiling, falls asleep, and* JONES *stands looking at him; then, snatching up* JACK'S *glass, he drinks it off. He picks the reticule from off* JACK'S *shirt-front, holds it to the light, and smells at it.*]

JONES: Been on the tiles and brought 'ome some of yer cat's fur.

[*He stuffs it into* JACK'S *breast pocket.*]

JACK [*murmuring*]: I've scored you off! You cat!

[JONES *looks around him furtively; he pours out whisky and drinks it. From the silver box he takes a cigarette, puffs at it, and drinks more whisky. There is no sobriety left in him.*]

JONES: Fat lot o' things they've got 'ere! [*He sees the crimson purse lying on the floor.*] More cat's fur. Puss, puss! [*He fingers it, drops it on the tray, and looks at* JACK.] Calf! Fat calf! [*He sees his own presentment in a mirror. Lifting his hands, with fingers spread, he stares at it; then looks again at* JACK, *clenching his fist as if to batter in his sleeping, smiling face. Suddenly he tilts the rest of the whisky into the glass and drinks it. With cunning glee he takes the silver box and purse and pockets them.*] I'll score *you* off too, that's wot I'll do!

[*He gives a little snarling laugh and lurches to the door. His shoulder rubs against the switch; the light goes out. There is a sound as of a closing outer door.*]

[*The curtain falls.*]

[*The curtain rises again at once.*]

SCENE SECOND: *In the* BARTHWICKS' *dining-room.* JACK *is still asleep; the morning light is coming through the curtains. The time is half-past eight.* WHEELER, *brisk person, enters with a dust-pan, and* MRS. JONES *more slowly with a scuttle.*

WHEELER [*drawing the curtains*]: That precious husband of yours was round for you after you'd gone yesterday, Mrs. Jones. Wanted your money for drink, I suppose. He hangs about the corner here half the time. I saw him outside the "Goat and Bells" when I went to the post last night. If I were you I wouldn't live with him. I wouldn't live with a man that raised his hand to me. I wouldn't put up with it. Why don't you take your children and leave him? If you put up with 'im it'll only make him worse. I never can see why, because a man's married you, he should knock you about.

MRS. JONES [*slim, dark-eyed, and dark-haired; oval-faced, and with a smooth, soft, even voice; her manner patient, her way of talking quite impersonal; she wears a blue linen dress, and boots with holes*]: It was nearly two last night before he come home, and he wasn't himself. He made me get up, and he knocked me about; he didn't seem to know *what* he was saying or doing. Of course I *would* leave him, but I'm really afraid of what he'd do to me. He's such a violent man when he's not himself.

WHEELER: Why don't you get him locked up? You'll never have any peace until you get him locked up. If I were you I'd go to the police court tomorrow. That's what I would do.

MRS. JONES: Of course I ought to go, because he does treat me so badly when he's not himself. But you see, Bettina, he has a very hard time—he's been out

of work two months, and it preys upon his mind. When he's in work he behaves himself much better. It's when he's out of work that he's so violent.

WHEELER: Well, if you won't take any steps you'll never get rid of him.

MRS. JONES: Of course it's very wearing to me; I don't get my sleep at nights. And it's not as if I were getting help from him, because I have to do for the children and all of us. And he throws such dreadful things up at me, talks of my having men to follow me about. Such a thing never happens; no man ever speaks to me. And of course it's just the other way. It's what he does that's wrong and makes me so unhappy. And then he's always threatenin' to cut my throat if I leave him. It's all the drink, and things preying on his mind; he's not a bad man really. Sometimes he'll speak quite kind to me, but I've stood so much from him, I don't feel it in me to speak kind back, but just keep myself to myself. And he's all right with the children too, except when he's not himself.

WHEELER: You mean when he's drunk, the beauty.

MRS. JONES: Yes. [*Without change of voice.*] There's the young gentleman asleep on the sofa.

[*The both look silently at* JACK.]

MRS. JONES [*at last, in her soft voice*]: He doesn't look quite himself.

WHEELER: He's a young limb, that's what he is. It's my belief he was tipsy last night, like your husband. It's another kind of bein' out of work that sets *him* to drink. I'll go and tell Marlow. This is his job. [*She goes.*]

[MRS. JONES, *upon her knees, begins a gentle sweeping.*]

JACK [*waking*]: Who's there? What is it?

MRS. JONES: It's me, sir, Mrs. Jones.

JACK [*sitting up and looking round*]: Where is it—what—what time is it?

MRS. JONES: It's getting on for nine o'clock, sir.

JACK: For nine! Why—what! [*Rising, and loosening his tongue; putting hand to his head, and staring hard at* MRS. JONES.] Look here, you, Mrs.—Mrs. Jones— don't you say you caught me asleep here.

MRS. JONES: No, sir, of course I won't, sir.

JACK: It's quite an accident; I don't know how it happened. I must have forgotten to go to bed. It's a queer thing. I've got a most beastly headache. Mind you don't say anything, Mrs. Jones.

[*Goes out and passes* MARLOW *in the doorway.* MARLOW *is young and quiet; he is clean-shaven, and his hair is brushed high from his forehead in a coxcomb. Incidentally a butler, he is first a man. He looks at* MRS. JONES, *and smiles a private smile.*]

MARLOW: Not the first time, and won't be the last. Looked a bit dicky, eh, Mrs. Jones?

MRS. JONES: He didn't look quite himself. Of course I didn't take notice.

MARLOW: You're used to them. How's your old man?

MRS. JONES [*softly as throughout*]: Well, he was very bad last night; he didn't seem to know what he was about. He was very late, and he was most abusive. But now, of course, he's asleep.

MARLOW: That's his way of finding a job, eh?

MRS. JONES: As a rule, Mr. Marlow, he goes out early every morning looking for work, and sometimes he comes in fit to drop—and of course I can't say he doesn't try to get it, because he does. Trade's very bad. [*She stands quite still, her pan and brush before her, at the beginning and the end of long vistas of experience, traversing them with her impersonal eye.*] But he's not a good husband to me— last night he hit me, and he was so dreadfully abusive.

MARLOW: Bank 'oliday, eh! He's too fond of the "Goat and Bells," that's what's the matter with him. I see him at the corner late every night. He hangs about.

MRS. JONES: He gets to feeling very low walking about all day after work, and being refused so often, and then when he gets a drop in him it goes to his head. But he shouldn't treat his wife as he treats me. Sometimes I've had to go and walk about at night, when he wouldn't let me stay in the room; but he's sorry for it afterwards. And he hangs about after me, he waits for me in the street; and I don't think he ought to, because I've always been a good wife to him. And I tell him Mrs. Barthwick wouldn't like him coming about the place.

But that only makes him angry, and he says dreadful things about the gentry. Of course it was through me that he first lost his place, through his not treating me right; and that's made him bitter against the gentry. He had a very good place as groom in the country; but it made such a stir, because of course he didn't treat me right.

MARLOW: Got the sack?

MRS. JONES: Yes; his employer said he couldn't keep him, because there was a great deal of talk; and he said it was such a bad example. But it's very important for me to keep my work here; I have the three children, and I don't want him to come about after me in the streets, and make a disturbance as he sometimes does.

MARLOW [*holding up the empty decanter*]: Not a drain! Next time he hits you get a witness and go down to the court—

MRS. JONES: Yes, I think I've made up my mind. I think I ought to.

MARLOW: That's right. Where's the ciga—? [*He searches for the silver box; he looks at* MRS. JONES, *who is sweeping on her hands and knees; he checks himself and stands reflecting. From the tray he picks two half-smoked cigarettes, and reads the name on them.*] Nestor—where the deuce—?

[*With a meditative air he looks again at* MRS. JONES *and, taking up* JACK'S *overcoat, he searches in the pockets.* WHEELER, *with a tray of breakfast things, comes in.*]

MARLOW [*aside to* WHEELER]: Have you seen the cigarette-box?

WHEELER: No.

MARLOW: Well, it's gone. I put it on the tray last night. And he's been smoking. [*Showing her the ends of cigarettes.*] It's not in these pockets. He can't have taken it upstairs this morning! Have a good look in his room when he comes down. Who's been in here?

WHEELER: Only me and Mrs. Jones.

MRS. JONES: I've finished here; shall I do the drawing-room now?

WHEELER [*looking at her doubtfully*]: Have you seen— Better do the boudwower first.

[MRS. JONES *goes out with pan and brush.* MARLOW *and* WHEELER *look each other in the face.*]

MARLOW: It'll turn up.

WHEELER [*hesitatingly*]: You don't think *she—*[*Nodding at the door.*]

MARLOW [*stoutly*]: I don't—I never believes anything of anybody.

WHEELER: But the master'll have to be told.

MARLOW: You wait a bit, and see if it don't turn up. Suspicion's no business of ours. I set my mind against it.

[*The curtain falls.*]

[*The curtain rises again at once.*]

SCENE THIRD: BARTHWICK *and* MRS. BARTHWICK *are seated at the breakfast table. He is a man between fifty and sixty; quietly important, with a bald forehead, and pince-nez, and the "Times" in his hand. She is a lady of nearly fifty, well dressed, with greyish hair, good features, and a decided manner. They face each other.*

BARTHWICK [*from behind his paper*]: The Labour man has got in at the by-election for Barnside, my dear.

MRS. BARTHWICK: Another Labour? I can't think what on earth the country is about.

BARTHWICK: I predicted it. It's not a matter of vast importance.

MRS. BARTHWICK: Not? How can you take it so calmly, John? To me it's simply outrageous. And there you sit, you Liberals, and pretend to encourage these people!

BARTHWICK [*frowning*]: The representation of all parties is necessary for any proper reform, for any proper social policy.

MRS. BARTHWICK: I've no patience with your talk of reform—all that nonsense about social policy. We know perfectly well what it is they want; they want things for themselves. Those Socialists and Labour men are an absolutely selfish set of people. They have no sense of patriotism, like the upper classes; *they simply want what we've got.*

BARTHWICK: Want what we've got! [*He stares into space.*] My dear, what are you talking about? [*With a contortion.*] I'm no alarmist.

MRS. BARTHWICK: Cream? Quite uneducated men! Wait until they begin to tax our investments. I'm convinced that when they once get a chance they will tax everything—they've no feeling for the country. You Liberals and Conservatives, you're all alike; you don't see an inch before your noses. You've no imagination, not a scrap of imagination between you. You ought to join hands and nip it in the bud.

BARTHWICK: You're talking nonsense! How is it possible for Liberals and Conservatives to join hands, as you call it? That shows how absurd it is for women— Why, the very essence of a Liberal is to trust in the people!

MRS. BARTHWICK: Now, John, eat your breakfast. As if there were any real difference between you and the Conservatives. All the upper classes have the same interests to protect, and the same principles. [*Calmly.*] Oh! you're sitting upon a volcano, John.

BARTHWICK: What!

MRS. BARTHWICK: I read a letter in the paper yesterday. I forget the man's name, but it made the whole thing perfectly clear. You don't look things in the face.

BARTHWICK: Indeed! [*Heavily.*] I am a Liberal! Drop the subject, please!

MRS. BARTHWICK: Toast? I quite agree with what this man says: Education is simply ruining the lower classes. It unsettles them, and that's the worst thing for us all. I see an enormous difference in the manner of servants.

BARTHWICK [*with suspicious emphasis*]: I welcome any change that will lead to something better. [*He opens a letter.*] H'm! This is that affair of Master Jack's again. "High Street, Oxford. Sir, We have received Mr. John Barthwick, Senior's, draft for forty pounds!" Oh! the letter's to him! "We now enclose the cheque you cashed with us, which, as we stated in our previous letter, was not met on presentation at your bank. We are, Sir, yours obediently, Moss and Sons, Tailors." H'm! [*Staring at the cheque.*] A pretty business altogether! The boy might have been prosecuted.

MRS. BARTHWICK: Come, John, you know Jack didn't mean anything; he only thought he was overdrawing. I still think his bank ought to have cashed that cheque. They must know your position.

BARTHWICK [*replacing in the envelope the letter and the cheque*]: Much good that would have done him in a court of law.

[*He stops as* JACK *comes in, fastening his waistcoat and staunching a razor cut upon his chin.*]

JACK [*sitting down between them, and speaking with an artificial joviality*]: Sorry I'm late. [*He looks lugubriously at the dishes.*] Tea, please, mother. Any letters for me? [BARTHWICK *hands the letter to him.*] But look here, I say, this has been opened! I do wish you wouldn't—

BARTHWICK [*touching the envelope*]: I suppose I'm entitled to this name.

JACK [*sulkily*]: Well, I can't help having your name, father! [*He reads the letter, and mutters.*] Brutes!

BARTHWICK [*eying him*]: You don't deserve to be so well out of that.

JACK: Haven't you ragged me enough, dad?

MRS. BARTHWICK: Yes, John, let Jack have his breakfast.

BARTHWICK: If you hadn't had me to come to, where would you have been? It's the merest accident—suppose you had been the son of a poor man or a clerk? Obtaining money with a cheque you knew your bank could not meet. It might have ruined you for life. I can't see what's to become of you if these are your principles. I never did anything of the sort myself.

JACK: I expect you always had lots of money. If you've got plenty of money, of course—

BARTHWICK: On the contrary, I had not your advantages. My father kept me very short of money.

JACK: How much had you, dad?

BARTHWICK: It's not material. The question is, do you feel the gravity of what you did?

JACK: I don't know about the gravity. Of course, I'm very sorry if you think it was wrong. Haven't I said so! I should never have done it at all if I hadn't been so jolly hard up.

BARTHWICK: How much of that forty pounds have you got left, Jack?

JACK [*hesitating*]: I don't know—not much.

BARTHWICK: How much?

JACK [*desperately*]: I haven't got any.

BARTHWICK: What?

JACK: I know I've got the most beastly headache. [*He leans his head on his hand.*]

MRS. BARTHWICK: Headache? My dear boy! Can't you eat any breakfast?

JACK [*drawing in his breath*]: Too jolly bad!

MRS. BARTHWICK: I'm so sorry. Come with me, dear; I'll give you something that will take it away at once.

[*They leave the room; and* BARTHWICK, *tearing up the letter, goes to the fireplace and puts the pieces in the fire. While he is doing this* MARLOW *comes in, and looking round him, is about quietly to withdraw.*]

BARTHWICK: What's that? What d' you want?

MARLOW: I was looking for Mr. John, sir.

BARTHWICK: What d' you want Mr. John for?

MARLOW [*with hesitation*]: I thought I should find him here, sir.

BARTHWICK [*suspiciously*]: Yes, but what do you want him for?

MARLOW [*offhandedly*]: There's a lady called—asked to speak to him for a minute, sir.

BARTHWICK: A lady, at this time in the morning. What sort of a lady?

MARLOW [*without expression in his voice*]: I can't tell, sir; no particular sort. She might be after charity. She might be a Sister of Mercy, I should think, sir.

BARTHWICK: Is she dressed like one?

MARLOW: No, sir, she's in plain clothes, sir.

BARTHWICK: Didn't she say what she wanted?

MARLOW: No, sir.

BARTHWICK: Where did you leave her?

MARLOW: In the hall, sir.

BARTHWICK: In the hall? How do you know she's not a thief—no got designs on the house?

MARLOW: No, sir, I don't fancy so, sir.

BARTHWICK: Well, show her in here; I'll see her myself.

[MARLOW *goes out with a private gesture of dismay. He soon returns, ushering in a young pale lady with dark eyes and pretty figure, in a modish, black, but rather shabby dress, a black and white trimmed hat with a bunch of Parma violets wrongly placed, and fuzzy-spotted veil. At the sight of* MR. BARTHWICK *she exhibits every sign of nervousness.* MARLOW *goes out.*]

UNKNOWN LADY: Oh! but—I beg pardon—there's some mistake—I— [*She turns to fly.*]

BARTHWICK: Whom did you want to see, madam?

UNKNOWN [*stopping and looking back*]: It was Mr. *John* Barthwick I wanted to see.

BARTHWICK: I am John Barthwick, madam. What can I have the pleasure of doing for you?

UNKNOWN: Oh! I—I don't— [*She drops her eyes.* BARTHWICK *scrutinizes her, and purses his lips.*]

BARTHWICK: It was my son, perhaps, you wished to see?

UNKNOWN [*quickly*]: Yes, of course, it's your son.

BARTHWICK: May I ask whom I have the pleasure of speaking to?

UNKNOWN [*appeal and hardiness upon her face*]: My name is—oh! it doesn't matter—I don't want to make any fuss. I just want to see your son for a minute. [*Boldly.*] In fact, I *must* see him.

BARTHWICK [*controlling his uneasiness*]: My son is not very well. If necessary, no doubt I could attend to the matter; be so kind as to let me know—

UNKNOWN: Oh! but I *must* see him—I've come on purpose—[*She bursts our nervously.*] I don't want to make any fuss, but the fact is, last—last night your son took away—he took away my— [*She stops.*]

BARTHWICK [*severely*]: Yes, madam, what?

UNKNOWN: He took away my—my reticule.

BARTHWICK: Your reti—?

UNKNOWN: I don't care about the reticule; it's not *that* I want—I'm sure I don't want to make any fuss—[*her face is quivering*]—but—but—all my money was in it!

BARTHWICK: In what—in what?

UNKNOWN: In my purse, in the reticule. It was a crimson silk purse. Really, I wouldn't have come—I don't want to make any fuss. But I must get my money back—mustn't I?

BARTHWICK: Do you tell me that my son—?

UNKNOWN: Oh! well, you see, he wasn't quite—I mean he was— [*She smiles mesmerically.*]

BARTHWICK: I beg your pardon.

UNKNOWN [*stamping her foot*]: Oh! don't you see—tipsy! We had a quarrel.

BARTHWICK [*scandalised*]: How? Where?

UNKNOWN [*defiantly*]: At my place. We'd had supper at the—and your son—

BARTHWICK [*pressing the bell*]: May I ask how you knew this house? Did he give you his name and address?

UNKNOWN [*glancing sidelong*]: I got it out of his overcoat.

BARTHWICK [*sardonically*]: Oh! you got it out of his overcoat. And may I ask if my son will know you by daylight?

UNKNOWN: Know me? I should jolly— I mean, of course he will!

[MARLOW *comes in.*]

BARTHWICK: Ask Mr. John to come down. [MARLOW *goes out, and* BARTHWICK *walks uneasily about.*] And how long have you enjoyed his acquaintanceship?

UNKNOWN: Only since—only since Good Friday.

BARTHWICK: I am at a loss—I repeat I am at a loss—

[*He glances at this unknown lady, who stands with eyes cast down, twisting her hands. And suddenly* JACK *appears. He stops on seeing who is here, and the unknown lady hysterically giggles. There is a silence.*]

BARTHWICK [*portentously*]: This young—er—lady says that last night—I think you said last night, madam,—you took away—

UNKNOWN [*impulsively*]: My reticule, and all my money was in a crimson silk purse.

JACK: Reticule. [*Looking round for any chance to get away.*] I don't know anything about it.

BARTHWICK [*sharply*]: Come, do you deny seeing this young lady last night?

JACK: Deny? No, of course. [*Whispering.*] Why did you give me away like this? What on earth did you come here for?

UNKNOWN [*tearfully*]: I'm sure

I didn't want to—it's not likely, is it? You snatched it out of my hand—you know you did—and the purse had all my money in it. I didn't follow you last night because I didn't want to make a fuss and it was so late, and you were so—

BARTHWICK: Come, sir, don't turn your back on me—explain!

JACK [desperately]: I don't remember anything about it. [In a low voice to his friend.] Why on earth couldn't you have written?

UNKNOWN [sullenly]: I want it now; I must have it—I've got to pay my rent today. [She looks at BARTHWICK.] They're only too glad to jump on people who are not—not well off.

JACK: I don't remember anything about it, really. I don't remember anything about last night at all. [He puts his hand up to his head.] It's all—cloudy, and I've got such a beastly headache.

UNKNOWN: But you took it; you know you did. You said you'd score me off.

JACK: Well, then, it must be here. I remember now—I remember something. Why did I take the beastly thing?

BARTHWICK: Yes, why did you take the beastly— [He turns abruptly to the window.]

UNKNOWN [with her mesmeric smile]: You weren't quite—were you?

JACK [smiling pallidly]: I'm awfully sorry. If there's anything I can do—

BARTHWICK: Do? You can restore this property, I suppose.

JACK: I'll go and have a look, but I really don't think I've got it.

[He goes out hurriedly. And BARTHWICK, placing a chair, motions to the visitor to sit; then, with pursed lips, he stands and eyes her fixedly. She sits, and steals a look at him; then turns away, and, drawing up her veil, stealthily wipes her eyes. And JACK comes back.]

JACK [ruefully holding out the empty reticule]: Is that the thing? I've looked all over—I can't find the purse anywhere. Are you sure it was there?

UNKNOWN [tearfully]: Sure? Of course I'm sure. A crimson silk purse. It was all the money I had.

JACK: I really am awfully sorry—my head's so jolly bad. I've asked the butler, but he hasn't seen it.

UNKNOWN: I must have my money—

JACK: Oh! Of course—that'll be all right; I'll see that that's all right. How much?

UNKNOWN [sullenly]: Seven pounds—twelve—it's all I've got in the world.

JACK: That'll be all right; I'll send you a—cheque.

UNKNOWN [eagerly]: No; now please. Give me what was in my purse; I've got to pay my rent this morning. They won't give me another day; I'm a fortnight behind already.

JACK [blankly]: I'm awfully sorry; I really haven't a penny in my pocket. [He glances stealthily at BARTHWICK.]

UNKNOWN [excitedly]: Come, say you must—it's my money and you took it. I'm not going away without it. They'll turn me out of my place.

JACK [clasping his head]: But I can't

give you what I haven't got. Don't I tell you I haven't a beastly cent?

UNKNOWN [*tearing at her hand-kerchief*]: Oh! do give it me! [*She puts her hands together in appeal; then, with sudden fierceness.*] If you don't I'll summons you. It's stealing, that's what it is!

BARTHWICK [*uneasily*]: One moment, please. As a matter of—er—principle, I shall settle this claim. [*He produces money.*] Here is eight pounds; the extra will cover the value of the purse and your cab fares. I need make no comment—no thanks are necessary.

[*Touching the bell, he holds the door ajar in silence. The unknown lady stores the money in her reticule, she looks from* JACK *to* BARTHWICK, *and her face is quivering faintly with a smile. She hides it with her hand, and steals away. Behind her* BARTHWICK *shuts the door.*]

BARTHWICK [*with solemnity*]: H'm! This is a nice thing to happen!

JACK [*impersonally*]: What awful luck!

BARTHWICK: So this is the way that forty pounds has gone! One thing after another! Once more I should like to know where you'd have been if it hadn't been for me! You don't seem to have any principles. You—you're one of those who are a nuisance to society; you—you're dangerous! What your mother would say I don't know. Your conduct, as far as I can see, is absolutely unjustifiable. It's—it's criminal. Why, a poor man

who behaved as you've done . . . d'you think he'd have any mercy shown him? What you want is a good lesson. You and your sort are—[*he speaks with feeling*]—a nuisance to the community. Don't ask me to help you next time. You're not fit to be helped.

JACK [*turning upon his sire, with unexpected fierceness*]: All right, I won't then, and see how you like it. You wouldn't have helped me this time, I know, if you hadn't been scared the thing would get into the papers. Where are the cigarettes?

BARTHWICK [*regarding him uneasily*]: Well—I'll say no more about it. [*He rings the bell.*] I'll pass it over for this once, but— [MARLOW *comes in.*] You can clear away. [*He hides his face behind the "Times."*]

JACK [*brightening*]: I say, Marlow, where are the cigarettes?

MARLOW: I put the box out with the whisky bottle last night, sir, but this morning I can't find it anywhere.

JACK: Did you look in my room?

MARLOW: Yes, sir; I've looked all over the house. I found two Nestor ends in the tray this morning, so you must have been smokin' last night, sir. [*Hesitating.*] I'm really afraid some one's purloined the box.

JACK [*uneasily*]: Stolen it!

BARTHWICK: What's that! The cigarette-box! Is anything else missing?

MARLOW: No, sir; I've been through the plate.

BARTHWICK: Was the house all right this morning? None of the windows open?

MARLOW: No, sir. [*Quietly to* JACK.] You left your latch-key in the door last night, sir. [*He hands it back, unseen by* BARTHWICK.]

JACK: Tst!

BARTHWICK: Who's been in the room this morning?

MARLOW: Me and Wheeler, and Mrs. Jones is all, sir, as far as I know.

BARTHWICK: Have you asked Mrs. Barthwick? [*To* JACK.] Go and ask your mother if she's had it; ask her to look and see if she's missed anything else. [JACK *goes upon this mission.*] Nothing is more disquieting than losing things like this.

MARLOW: No, sir.

BARTHWICK: Have you any suspicions?

MARLOW: No, sir.

BARTHWICK: This Mrs. Jones—how long has she been working here?

MARLOW: Only this last month, sir.

BARTHWICK: What sort of person?

MARLOW: I don't know much about her, sir; seems a very quiet, respectable woman.

BARTHWICK: Who did the room this morning?

MARLOW: Wheeler and Mrs. Jones, sir.

BARTHWICK [*with his forefinger upraised*]: Now, was this Mrs. Jones in the room alone at any time?

MARLOW [*expressionless*]: Yes, sir.

BARTHWICK: How do you know that?

MARLOW [*reluctantly*]: I found her here, sir.

BARTHWICK: And has Wheeler been in the room alone?

MARLOW: No, sir, she's not, sir I should say, sir, that Mrs. Jones seems a very honest—

BARTHWICK [*holding up his hand*]: I want to know this: Has this Mrs. Jones been here the whole morning?

MARLOW: Yes, sir—no, sir—she stepped over to the greengrocer's for cook.

BARTHWICK: H'm! Is she in the house now?

MARLOW: Yes, sir.

BARTHWICK: Very good. I shall make a point of clearing this up On principle I shall make a point of fixing the responsibility; it goes to the foundations of security. In all you interests—

MARLOW: Yes, sir.

BARTHWICK: What sort of circumstances is this Mrs. Jones in? Is her husband in work?

MARLOW: I believe not, sir.

BARTHWICK: Very well. Say nothing about it to any one. Tell Wheeler not to speak of it and ask Mrs. Jones to step up here.

MARLOW: Very good, sir.

[MARLOW *goes out, his face concerned; and* BARTHWICK *stays his face judicial and a little pleased as befits a man conducting an inquiry.* MRS. BARTHWICK *and he son come in.*]

BARTHWICK: Well, my dear, you'v not seen it, I suppose?

MRS. BARTHWICK: No. But wha an extraordinary thing, John Marlow, of course, is out of th question. I'm certain none o the maids—as for cook!

BARTHWICK: Oh, cook!

MRS. BARTHWICK: Of course! It'

perfectly detestable to me to suspect anybody.

BARTHWICK: It is not a question of one's feelings. It's a question of justice. On principle—

MRS. BARTHWICK: I shouldn't be a bit surprised if the charwoman knew something about it. It was Laura who recommended her.

BARTHWICK [*judicially*]: I am going to have Mrs. Jones up. Leave it to me; and—er—remember that nobody is guilty until they're proved so. I shall be careful. I have no intention of frightening her; I shall give her every chance. I hear she's in poor circumstances. If we are not able to do much for them we are bound to have the greatest sympathy with the poor. [MRS. JONES *comes in.*] [*Pleasantly.*] Oh! good morning, Mrs. Jones.

MRS. JONES [*soft, and even, unemphatic*]: Good morning, sir! Good morning, ma'am!

BARTHWICK: About your husband —he's not in work, I hear?

MRS. JONES: No, sir; of course he's not in work just now.

BARTHWICK: Then I suppose he's earning nothing.

MRS. JONES: No, sir; he's not earning anything just now, sir.

BARTHWICK: And how many children have you?

MRS. JONES: Three children; but of course they don't eat very much, sir.

[*A little silence.*]

BARTHWICK: And how old is the eldest?

MRS. JONES: Nine years old, sir.

BARTHWICK: Do they go to school?

MRS. JONES: Yes, sir, they all three go to school every day.

BARTHWICK [*severely*]: And what about their food when you're out at work?

MRS. JONES: Well, sir, I have to give them their dinner to take with them. Of course I'm not always able to give them anything; sometimes I have to send them without; but my husband is very good about the children when he's in work. But when he's not in work of course he's a very difficult man.

BARTHWICK: He drinks, I suppose?

MRS. JONES: Yes, sir. Of course I can't say he doesn't drink, because he does.

BARTHWICK: And I suppose he takes all your money?

MRS. JONES: No, sir, he's very good about my money, except when he's not himself, and then, of course, he treats me very badly.

BARTHWICK: Now what is he— your husband?

MRS. JONES: By profession, sir, of course he's a groom.

BARTHWICK: A groom! How came he to lose his place?

MRS. JONES: He lost his place a long time ago, sir, and he's never had a very long job since; and now, of course, the motor-cars are against him.

BARTHWICK: When were you married to him, Mrs. Jones?

MRS. JONES: Eight years ago, sir— that was in—

MRS. BARTHWICK [*sharply*]: Eight? You said the eldest child was nine.

MRS. JONES: Yes, ma'am; of course that was why he lost his place. He didn't treat me rightly, and of course his employer said he couldn't keep him because of the example.

BARTHWICK: You mean he—ahem—

MRS. JONES: Yes, sir; and of course after he lost his place he married me.

MRS. BARTHWICK: You actually mean to say you—you were—

BARTHWICK: My dear—

MRS. BARTHWICK [*indignantly*]: How disgraceful!

BARTHWICK [*hurriedly*]: And where are you living now, Mrs. Jones?

MRS. JONES: We've not got a home, sir. Of course we've been obliged to put away most of our things.

BARTHWICK: Put your things away! You mean to—to—er—to pawn them?

MRS. JONES: Yes, sir, to put them away. We're living in Merthyr Street—that is close by here, sir—at No. 34. We just have the one room.

BARTHWICK: And what do you pay a week?

MRS. JONES: We pay six shillings a week, sir, for a furnished room.

BARTHWICK: And I suppose you're behind in the rent?

MRS. JONES: Yes, sir, we're a little behind in the rent.

BARTHWICK: But *you're* in good work, aren't you?

MRS. JONES: Well, sir, I have a day in Stamford Place Thursdays. And Mondays and Wednesdays and Fridays I come here. But today, of course, is a half-day, because of yesterday's Bank Holiday.

BARTHWICK: I see; four days a week, and you get half a crown a day, is that it?

MRS. JONES: Yes, sir, and my din-

ner; but sometimes it's only half a day, and that's eighteen-pence.

BARTHWICK: And when your husband earns anything he spends it in drink, I suppose?

MRS. JONES: Sometimes he does, sir, and sometimes he gives it to me for the children. Of course he would work if he could get it, sir, but it seems there are a great many people out of work.

BARTHWICK: Ah! Yes. We—er—won't go into that. [*Sympathetically.*] And how about your work here? Do you find it hard?

MRS. JONES: Oh! no, sir, not very hard, sir; except of course, when I don't get my sleep at night.

BARTHWICK: Ah! And you help do all the rooms? And sometimes, I suppose, you go out for cook?

MRS. JONES: Yes, sir.

BARTHWICK: And you've been out this morning?

MRS. JONES: Yes, sir, of course I had to go to the greengrocer's.

BARTHWICK: Exactly. So your husband earns nothing? And he's a bad character.

MRS. JONES: No, sir, I don't say that, sir. I think there's a great deal of good in him; though he does treat me very bad sometimes. And of course I don't like to leave him, but I think I ought to, because really I hardly know how to stay with him. He often raises his hand to me. Not long ago he gave me a blow here [*touches her breast*] and I can feel it now. So I think I ought to leave him, don't *you*, sir?

BARTHWICK: Ah! I can't help you there. It's a very serious thing to leave your husband. Very serious thing.

MRS. JONES: Yes, sir, of course I'm afraid of what he might do to me if I were to leave him; he can be so very violent.

BARTHWICK: H'm! Well, that I can't pretend to say anything about. It's the bad principle I'm speaking of—

MRS. JONES: Yes, sir; I know nobody can help me. I know I must decide for myself, and of course I know that he has a very hard life. And he's fond of the children, and it's very hard for him to see them going without food.

BARTHWICK [*hastily*]: Well—er—thank you, I just wanted to hear about you. I don't think I need detain you any longer, Mrs.—Jones.

MRS. JONES: No, sir, thank you, sir.

BARTHWICK: Good morning, then.

MRS. JONES: Good morning, sir; good morning, ma'am.

BARTHWICK [*exchanging glances with his wife*]: By the way, Mrs. Jones—I think it is only fair to tell you, a silver cigarette-box—er—is missing.

MRS. JONES [*looking from one face to the other*]: I am very sorry, sir.

BARTHWICK: Yes; you have not seen it, I suppose?

MRS. JONES [*realising that suspicion is upon her; with an uneasy movement*]: Where was it, sir; if you please, sir?

BARTHWICK [*evasively*]: Where did Marlow say? Er—in this room, yes, in *this* room.

MRS. JONES: No, sir, I haven't seen it—of course if I'd seen it I should have noticed it.

BARTHWICK [*giving her a rapid glance*]: You—you are sure of that?

MRS. JONES [*impassively*]: Yes, sir. [*With a slow nodding of her head.*] I have not seen it, and of course I *don't* know where it is. [*She turns and goes quietly out.*]

BARTHWICK: H'm!

[*The three* BARTHWICKS *avoid each other's glances.*]

[*The curtain falls.*]

ACT TWO

SCENE FIRST: *The* JONES'S *lodgings, Merthyr Street, at half-past two o'clock.*

[*The bare room, with tattered oil-cloth and damp, distempered walls, has an air of tidy wretchedness. On the bed lies* JONES, *half-dressed; his coat is thrown across his feet, and muddy boots are lying on the floor close by. He is asleep. The door is opened and* MRS. JONES *comes in, dressed in a pinched black jacket and old black sailor hat; she carries a parcel wrapped up in the "Times." She puts her parcel down, unwraps an apron, half a loaf, two onions, three potatoes, and a tiny piece of bacon. Taking a teapot from the cupboard, she rinses it, shakes into it some powdered tea out of a screw of paper, puts it on the hearth, and sitting in a wooden chair quietly begins to cry.*]

JONES [*stirring and yawning*]: That you? What's the time?

MRS. JONES [*drying her eyes, and in her usual voice*]: Half-past two.

JONES: What you back so soon for?

MRS. JONES: I only had the half day today, Jem.

JONES [*on his back, and in a drowsy voice*]: Got anything for dinner?

MRS. JONES: Mrs. Barthwick's cook gave me a little bit of bacon. I'm going to make a stew. [*She prepares for cooking.*] There's fourteen shillings owing for rent, James, and of course I've only got two and fourpence. They'll be coming for it today.

JONES [*turning towards her on his elbow*]: Let 'em come and find my surprise packet. I've had enough o' this tryin' for work. Why should I go round and round after a job like a bloomin' squirrel in a cage. "Give us a job, sir"—"Take a man on"— "Got a wife and three children." Sick of it I am! I'd sooner lie here and rot. "Jones, you come and join the demonstration; come and 'old a flag, and listen to the ruddy orators, and go 'ome as empty as you came." There's some that seems to like *that*— the sheep! When I go seekin' for a job now, and see the brutes lookin' me up an' down, it's like a thousand serpents in me. I'm

not arskin' for any treat. A man wants to sweat hisself silly and not allowed—that's a rum start, ain't it? A man wants to sweat his soul out to keep the breath in him and ain't allowed—that's justice—that's freedom and all the rest of it! [*He turns his face towards the wall.*] You're so milky mild; you don't know what goes on inside o' me. I'm done with the silly game. If they want me, let 'em come for me! [MRS. JONES *stops cooking and stands unmoving at the table.*] I've tried and done with it, I tell you. I've never been afraid of what's before *me*. You mark my words—if you think they've broke my spirit, you're mistook. I'll lie and rot sooner than arsk 'em again. What makes you stand like that — you long-sufferin', Gawd-forsaken image — that's why I can't keep my hands off you. So now you know. Work! You can work but you haven't the spirit of a louse!

MRS. JONES [*quietly*]: You talk more wild sometimes when you're yourself, James, than when you're not. If you don't get work, how are we to go on? They won't let us stay here; they're looking to their money today, I know.

JONES: I see this Barthwick o' yours every day goin' down to Pawlyment snug and comfortable to talk his silly soul out; an' I see that young calf, his son, swellin' it about, and goin' on the razzle-dazzle. Wot 'ave they done that makes 'em any better than wot I am? They never did a day's work in their lives. I see 'em day after day—

MRS. JONES: And I wish you wouldn't come after me like that, and hang about the house. You don't seem able to keep away at all, and whatever you do it for I can't think, because of course they notice it.

JONES: I suppose I may go where I like. Where *may* I go? The other day I went to a place in the Edgware Road. "Gov'nor," I says to the boss, "take me on," I says. "I 'aven't done a stroke o' work not these two months; it takes the heart out of a man," I says; "I'm one to work; I'm not afraid of anything you can give me!" "My good man," 'e says, "I've had thirty of you here this morning. I took the first two," he says, "and that's all I want." "Thank you, then rot the world!" I says. "Blasphemin'," he says, "is not the way to get a job. Out you go, my lad!" [*He laughs sardonically.*] Don't you raise your voice because you're starvin'; don't yer even think of it; take it lyin' down! Take it like a sensible man, carn't you? And a little way down the street a lady says to me: [*Pinching his voice.*] "D' you want to earn a few pence, my man?" and gives me her dog to 'old outside a shop—fat as a butler 'e was—tons o' meat had gone to the makin' of *him.* It did 'er good, it did, made 'er feel 'erself that *charitable,* but I see 'er lookin' at the copper standin' alongside o' me, for fear I should make off with 'er bloomin' fat dog. [*He sits on the edge of the bed and puts a boot on. Then looking up.*] What's in that head o' yours? [*Almost pathetically.*] Carn't you speak for once?

[*There is a knock, and* MRS. SEDDON, *the landlady, appears, an anxious, harassed, shabby woman in working clothes.*]

MRS. SEDDON: I thought I 'eard you come in, Mrs. Jones. I've spoke to my 'usband, but he says he really can't afford to wait another day.

JONES [*with scowling jocularity*]: Never you mind what your 'usband says, you go your own way like a proper independent woman. Here, Jenny, chuck her that.

[*Producing a sovereign from his trousers pocket, he throws it to his wife, who catches it in her apron with a gasp.* JONES *resumes the lacing of his boots.*]

MRS. JONES [*rubbing the sovereign stealthily*]: I'm very sorry we're so late with it, and of course it's fourteen shillings, so if you've got six that will be right.

[MRS. SEDDON *takes the sovereign and fumbles for the change.*]

JONES [*with his eyes fixed on his boots*]: Bit of a surprise for yer, ain't it?

MRS. SEDDON: Thank you, and I'm sure I'm very much obliged. [*She does indeed appear surprised.*] I'll bring you the change.

JONES [*mockingly*]: Don't mention it.

MRS. SEDDON: Thank you, and I'm sure I'm very much obliged. [*She slides away.*]

[MRS. JONES *gazes at* JONES *who is still lacing up his boots.*]

JONES: I've had a bit of luck. [*Pulling out the crimson purse and some loose coins.*] Picked up a purse—seven pound and more.

MRS. JONES: Oh, James!

JONES: Oh, James! What about Oh, James! I picked it up I tell you. This is lost property, this is!

MRS. JONES: But isn't there a name in it, or something?

JONES: Name? No, there ain't no name. This don't belong to such as 'ave visitin' cards. This belongs to a perfec' lidy. Tike an' smell it. [*He pitches her the purse, which she puts gently to her nose.*] Now, you tell me what I ought to have done. You tell me that. You can always tell me what I ought to ha' done, can't yer?

MRS. JONES [*laying down the purse*]: I can't say what you ought to have done, James. Of course the money wasn't yours; you've taken somebody else's money.

JONES: Finding's keeping. I'll take it as wages for the time I've gone about the streets asking for what's my rights. I'll take it for what's *overdue*, d'ye hear? [*With strange triumph.*] I've got money in my pocket, my girl. [MRS. JONES *goes on again with the preparation of the meal,* JONES *looking at her furtively.*] Money in my pocket! And I'm not goin' to waste it. With this 'ere money I'm goin' to Canada. I'll let you have a pound. [*A silence.*] You've often talked of leavin' me. You've often told me I treat you badly—well I 'ope you'll be glad when I'm gone.

MRS. JONES [*impassively*]: You *have* treated me very badly, James, and of course I can't prevent your going; but I can't tell whether I shall be glad when you're gone.

JONES: It'll change my luck. I've 'ad nothing but bad luck since I first took up with you. [*More softly.*] And you've 'ad no bloomin' picnic.

MRS. JONES: Of course it would have been better for us if we had never met. We weren't meant for each other. But you're set against me, that's what you are, and you *have* been for a long time. And you treat me so badly, James, going after that Rosie and all. You don't ever seem to think of the children that I've had to bring into the world, and of all the trouble I've had to keep them, and what'll become of them when you're gone.

JONES [*crossing the room gloomily*]: If you think I want to leave the little beggars you're bloomin' well mistaken.

MRS. JONES: Of course I know you're fond of them.

JONES [*fingering the purse, half angrily*]: Well, then, you stow it, old girl. The kids'll get along better with you than when I'm here. If I'd ha' known as much as I do now, I'd never ha' had one o' them. What's the use o' bringin' 'em into a state o' things like this? It's a crime, that's what it is; but you find it out too late; that's what's the matter with this 'ere world. [*He puts the purse back in his pocket.*]

MRS. JONES: Of course it would have been better for them, poor little things; but they're your own children, and I wonder at you talkin' like that. I should miss them dreadfully if I was to lose them.

JONES [*sullenly*]: An' you ain't the only one. If I make money out there— [*Looking up, he sees her shaking out his coat—in a changed voice.*] Leave that coat alone!

[*The silver box drops from the pocket, scattering the cigarettes upon the bed. Taking up the box she stares at it; he rushes at her and snatches the box away.*]

MRS. JONES [*cowering back against the bed*]: Oh, Jem! oh, Jem!

JONES [*dropping the box on to the table*]: You mind what you're sayin'! When I go out I'll take and chuck it in the water along with that there purse. I 'ad it when I was in liquor, and for what you do when you're in liquor you're not responsible— and that's Gawd's truth as you ought to know. I don't want the thing—I won't have it. I took it out o' spite. I'm no thief, I tell you; and don't you call me one, or it'll be the worse for you.

MRS. JONES [*twisting her apron strings*]: It's Mr. Barthwick's! You've taken away my reputation. Oh, Jem, whatever made you?

JONES: What d' you mean?

MRS. JONES: It's been missed; they think it's me. Oh! whatever made you do it, Jem?

JONES: I tell you I was in liquor. I don't want it; what's the good of it to me? If I were to pawn it they'd only nab me. I'm no thief. I'm no worse than wot that young Barthwick is; he brought 'ome that purse that I picked up—a lady's purse—'ad it

off 'er in a row, kept sayin' 'e 'd scored 'er off. Well, I scored 'im off. Tight as an owl 'e was! And d' you think anything 'll happen to him?

MRS. JONES [*as though speaking to herself*]: Oh, Jem! it's the bread out of our mouths!

JONES: Is it then? I'll make it hot for 'em yet. What about that purse? What about young Barthwick? [MRS. JONES *comes forward to the table and tries to take the box;* JONES *prevents her.*] What do you want with that? You drop it, I say!

MRS. JONES: I'll take it back and tell them all about it. [*She attempts to wrest the box from him.*]

JONES: Ah, would yer?

[*He drops the box, and rushes on her with a snarl. She slips back past the bed. He follows; a chair is overturned. The door is opened;* SNOW *comes in, a detective in plain clothes and bowler hat, with clipped moustaches.* JONES *drops his arms,* MRS. JONES *stands by the window gasping;* SNOW, *advancing swiftly to the table, puts his hand on the silver box.*]

SNOW: Doin' a bit o' skylarkin'? Fancy this is what I'm after. J. B., the very same. [*He gets back to the door, scrutinizing the crest and cypher on the box. To* MRS. JONES.] I'm a police officer. Are you Mrs. Jones?

MRS. JONES: Yes, sir.

SNOW: My instructions are to take you on a charge of stealing this box from J. Barthwick, Esquire, M.P., of 6, Rockingham Gate. Anything you say may be used against you. Well, Missis?

MRS. JONES [*in her quiet voice, still out of breath, her hand upon her breast*]: Of course I did *not* take it, sir. I never have taken anything that didn't belong to me; and of course I know nothing about it.

SNOW: You were at the house this morning; you did the room in which the box was left; you were alone in the room. I find the box 'ere. You say you didn't take it?

MRS. JONES: Yes, sir, of course I say I did not take it, because I did *not*.

SNOW: Then how does the box come to be here?

MRS. JONES: I would rather not say anything about it.

SNOW: Is this your husband?

MRS. JONES: Yes, sir, this is my husband, sir.

SNOW: Do you wish to say anything before I take her? [*JONES remains silent, with his head bent down.*] Well then, Missis. I'll just trouble you to come along with me quietly.

MRS. JONES [*twisting her hands*]: Of course I wouldn't say I hadn't taken it if I had—and I *didn't* take it, indeed I didn't. Of course I know appearances are against me, and I can't tell you what really happened. But my children are at school, and they'll be coming home—and I don't know what they'll do without me!

SNOW: Your 'usband 'll see to them, don't you worry. [*He takes the woman gently by the arm.*]

JONES: You drop it—she's all right! [*Sullenly.*] I took the thing myself.

SNOW [*eying him*]: There, there, it does you credit. Come along, Missis.

JONES [*passionately*]: Drop it, I say, you blooming teck. She's my wife; she's a respectable woman. Take her if you dare!

SNOW: Now, now. What's the good of this? Keep a civil tongue, and it'll be the better for all of us. [*He puts his whistle in his mouth and draws the woman to the door.*]

JONES [*with a rush*]: Drop her, and put up your 'ands, or I'll soon make yer. You leave her alone, will yer! Don't I tell yer, I took the thing myself!

SNOW [*blowing his whistle*]: Drop your hands, or I'll take you too. Ah, would you?

[JONES, *closing, deals him a blow. A* POLICEMAN *in uniform appears; there is a short struggle and* JONES *is overpowered.* MRS. JONES *raises her hands and drops her face on them.*]

[*The curtain falls.*]

SCENE SECOND: *The* BARTHWICKS' *dining-room the same evening. The* BARTHWICKS *are seated at dessert.*

MRS. BARTHWICK: John! [*A silence broken by the cracking of nuts.*] John!

BARTHWICK: I wish you'd speak about the nuts—they're uneatable. [*He puts one in his mouth.*]

MRS. BARTHWICK: It's not the season for them. I called on the Holyroods.

[BARTHWICK *fills his glass with port.*]

JACK: Crackers, please, Dad.

[BARTHWICK *passes the crackers.
His demeanour is reflective.*]

MRS. BARTHWICK: Lady Holyrood
has got very stout. I've noticed
it coming for a long time.

BARTHWICK [*gloomily*]: Stout? [*He
takes up the crackers—with transparent airiness.*] The Holyroods
had some trouble with their
servants, hadn't they?

JACK: Crackers, please, Dad.

BARTHWICK [*passing the crackers*]:
It got into the papers. The cook,
wasn't it?

MRS. BARTHWICK: No, the lady's
maid. I was talking it over with
Lady Holyrood. The girl used
to have her young man to see
her.

BARTHWICK [*uneasily*]: I'm not
sure they were wise—

MRS. BARTHWICK: My dear John,
what are you talking about?
How could there be an alternative? Think of the effect on the
other servants!

BARTHWICK: Of course in principle—I wasn't thinking of that.

JACK [*maliciously*]: Crackers,
please, Dad.

[BARTHWICK *is compelled to pass
the crackers.*]

MRS. BARTHWICK: Lady Holyrood
told me: "I had her up," she
said; "I said to her, 'You'll leave
my house at once; I think your
conduct disgraceful. I can't tell,
I don't know, and I don't wish
to know, what you were doing.
I send you away on principle;
you need not come to me for a
character.' And the girl said:
'If you don't give me my notice,
my lady, I want a month's wages.
I'm perfectly respectable. I've

done nothing.' "—Done nothing!

BARTHWICK: H'm!

MRS. BARTHWICK: Servants have
too much license. They hang
together so terribly you never
can tell what they're really thinking; it's as if they were all in a
conspiracy to keep you in the
dark. Even with Marlow, you feel
that he never lets you know
what's really in his mind. I hate
that secretiveness; it destroys all
confidence. I feel sometimes I
should like to shake him.

JACK: Marlow's a most decent
chap. It's simply beastly every
one knowing your affairs.

BARTHWICK: The less you say
about that the better!

MRS. BARTHWICK: It goes all
through the lower classes. You
can *not* tell when they are speaking the truth. Today when I was
shopping after leaving the Holyroods, one of these unemployed
came up and spoke to me. I suppose I only had twenty yards
or so to walk to the carriage,
but he seemed to spring up in
the street.

BARTHWICK: Ah! You must be
very careful whom you speak to in
these days.

MRS. BARTHWICK: I didn't answer
him, of course. But I could see
at once that he wasn't telling
the truth.

BARTHWICK [*cracking a nut*]:
There's one very good rule—
look at their eyes.

JACK: Crackers, please, Dad.

BARTHWICK [*passing the crackers*]:
If their eyes are straightforward
I sometimes give them sixpence.
It's against my principles, but
it's most difficult to refuse. If
you see that they're desperate,

and dull, and shifty-looking, as so many of them are, it's certain to mean drink, or crime, or something unsatisfactory.

MRS. BARTHWICK: This man had dreadful eyes. He looked as if he could commit a murder. "I've 'ad nothing to eat today," he said. Just like that.

BARTHWICK: What was William about? He ought to have been waiting.

JACK [*raising his wine-glass to his nose*]: Is this the '63, Dad?

[BARTHWICK, *holding his wine-glass to his eye, lowers it and passes it before his nose.*]

MRS. BARTHWICK: I hate people that can't speak the truth. [*Father and son exchange a look behind their port.*] It's just as easy to speak the truth as not. *I've* always found it easy enough. It makes it impossible to tell what is genuine; one feels as if one were continually being taken in.

BARTHWICK [*sententiously*]: The lower classes are their own enemies. If they would only trust us, they would get on so much better.

MRS. BARTHWICK: But even then it's so often their own fault. Look at that Mrs. Jones this morning.

BARTHWICK: I only want to do what's right in that matter. I had occasion to see Roper this afternoon. I mentioned it to him. He's coming in this evening. It all depends on what the detective says. I've had my doubts. I've been thinking it over.

MRS. BARTHWICK: The woman impressed me most unfavourably.

She seemed to have no shame. That affair she was talking about —she and the man when they were young, so immoral! And before you and Jack! I could have put her out of the room!

BARTHWICK: Oh! I don't want to excuse them, but in looking at these matters one must consider—

MRS. BARTHWICK: Perhaps you'll say the man's employer was wrong in dismissing him?

BARTHWICK: Of course not. It's not there that I feel doubt. What I ask myself is—

JACK: Port, please, Dad.

BARTHWICK [*circulating the decanter in religious imitation of the rising and setting of the sun*]: I ask myself whether we are sufficiently careful in making inquiries about people before we engage them, especially as regards moral conduct.

JACK: Pass the port, please, Mother!

MRS. BARTHWICK [*passing it*]: My dear boy, aren't you drinking too much?

[JACK *fills his glass.*]

MARLOW [*entering*]: Detective Snow to see you, sir.

BARTHWICK [*uneasily*]: Ah! say I'll be with him in a minute.

MRS. BARTHWICK [*without turning*]: Let him come in here, Marlow.

[SNOW *enters in an overcoat, his bowler hat in hand.*]

BARTHWICK [*half-rising*]: Oh! Good evening!

SNOW: Good evening, sir; good evening, ma'am. I've called round to report what I've done, rather late, I'm afraid—another case took me away. [*He takes the silver box out of his pocket, causing a sensation in the* BARTHWICK *family.*] This is the identical article, I believe.

BARTHWICK: Certainly, certainly.

SNOW: Havin' your crest and cypher, as you described to me, sir, I'd no hesitation in the matter.

BARTHWICK: Excellent. Will you have a glass of [*he glances at the waning port*]—er—sherry— [*pours out sherry*]. Jack, just give Mr. Snow this.

[JACK *rises and gives the glass to* SNOW; *then, lolling in his chair, regards him indolently.*]

SNOW [*drinking off wine and putting down the glass*]: After seeing you I went round to this woman's lodgings, sir. It's a low neighbourhood, and I thought it as well to place a constable below—and not without 'e was wanted, as things turned out.

BARTHWICK: Indeed!

SNOW: Yes, sir, I 'ad some trouble. I asked her to account for the presence of the article. She could give me no answer, except to deny the theft; so I took her into custody; then her husband came for me, so I was obliged to take him, too, for assault. He was very violent on the way to the station—very violent—threatened you and your son, and altogether he was a handful, I can tell you.

MRS. BARTHWICK: What a ruffian he must be.!

SNOW: Yes, ma'am, a rough customer.

JACK [*sipping his wine, bemused*]: Punch the beggar's head.

SNOW: Given to drink, as I understand, sir.

MRS. BARTHWICK: It's to be hoped he will get a severe punishment.

SNOW: The odd thing is, sir, that he persists in sayin' he took the box himself.

BARTHWICK: Took the box himself! [*He smiles.*] What does he think to gain by that?

SNOW: He says the young gentleman was intoxicated last night— [JACK *stops the cracking of a nut, and looks at* SNOW. BARTHWICK, *losing his smile, has put his wineglass down; there is a silence.* SNOW, *looking from face to face, remarks.*]—took him into the house and gave him whisky; and under the influence of an empty stomach the man says he took the box.

MRS. BARTHWICK: The impudent wretch!

BARTHWICK: D' you mean that he—er—intends to put this forward tomorrow—

SNOW: That'll be his line, sir; but whether he's endeavouring to shield his wife, or whether [*he looks at* JACK] there's something in it, will be for the magistrate to say.

MRS. BARTHWICK [*haughtily*]: Something in what? I don't understand you. As if my son would bring a man like that into the house!

BARTHWICK [*from the fireplace, with an effort to be calm*]: My son can speak for himself, no doubt.—Well, Jack, what do you say?

MRS. BARTHWICK [*sharply*]: What does he say? Why, of course, he says the whole story's stuff!

JACK [*embarrassed*]: Well, of course, I—of course, I don't know anything about it.

MRS. BARTHWICK: I should think not, indeed! [*To* SNOW.] The man is an audacious ruffian!

BARTHWICK [*suppressing jumps*]: But in view of my son's saying there's nothing in this—this fable—will it be necessary to proceed against the man under the circumstances?

SNOW: We shall have to charge him with the assault, sir. It would be as well for your son to come down to the Court. There'll be a remand, no doubt. The queer thing is there was quite a sum of money found on him, and a crimson silk purse. [BARTHWICK *starts;* JACK *rises and sits down again.*] I suppose the lady hasn't missed her purse?

BARTHWICK [*hastily*]: Oh, no! Oh! No!

JACK: No!

MRS. BARTHWICK [*dreamily*]: No! [*To* SNOW.] I've been inquiring of the servants. This man *does* hang about the house. I shall feel much safer if he gets a good long sentence; I do think we ought to be protected against such ruffians.

BARTHWICK: Yes, yes, of course, on principle—but in this case we have a number of things to think of. [*To* SNOW.] I suppose, as you say, the man *must* be charged, eh?

SNOW: No question about that, sir.

BARTHWICK [*staring gloomily at* JACK]: This prosecution goes very much against the grain

with me. I have great sympathy with the poor. In my position I'm bound to recognise the distress there is amongst them. The condition of the people leaves much to be desired. D' you follow me? I wish I could see my way to drop it.

MRS. BARTHWICK [*sharply*]: John! it's simply not fair to other people. It's putting property at the mercy of any one who likes to take it.

BARTHWICK [*trying to make signs to her aside*]: I'm not defending him, not at all. I'm trying to look at the matter broadly.

MRS. BARTHWICK: Nonsense, John, there's a time for everything.

SNOW [*rather sardonically*]: I might point out, sir, that to withdraw the charge of stealing would not make much difference, because the facts must come out [*he looks significantly at* JACK] in reference to the assault; and as I said that charge will have to go forward.

BARTHWICK [*hastily*]: Yes, oh! exactly! It's entirely on the woman's account—entirely a matter of my own private feelings.

SNOW: If I were you, sir, I should let things take their course. It's not likely there'll be much difficulty. These things are very quick settled.

BARTHWICK [*doubtfully*]: You think so—you think so?

JACK [*rousing himself*]: I say, what shall I have to swear to?

SNOW: That's best known to yourself, sir. [*Retreating to the door.*] Better employ a solicitor, sir, in case anything should arise. We shall have the butler to prove the loss of the article. You'll excuse me going, I'm rather pressed tonight. The case may come on any time after eleven. Good evening, sir; good evening, ma'am. I shall have to produce the box in court tomorrow, so if you'll excuse me, sir, I may as well take it with me.

[*He takes the silver box and leaves them with a little bow.* BARTHWICK *makes a move to follow him, then dashing his hands beneath his coat tails, speaks with desperation.*]

BARTHWICK: I do wish you'd leave me to manage things myself. You *will* put your nose into matters you know nothing of. A pretty mess you've made of this!

MRS. BARTHWICK [*coldly*]: I don't in the least know what you're talking about. If you can't stand up for your rights, I can. I've no patience with your principles, it's such nonsense.

BARTHWICK: Principles! Good Heavens! What have principles to do with it for goodness sake? Don't you know that Jack was drunk last night!

JACK: Dad!

MRS. BARTHWICK [*in horror, rising*]: Jack!

JACK: Look here, Mother—I had supper. Everybody does. I mean to say—you know what I mean— it's absurd to call it being drunk. At Oxford everybody gets a bit "on" sometimes—

MRS. BARTHWICK: Well, I think it's most dreadful! If that is really what you do at Oxford—

JACK [*angrily*]: Well, why did you send me there? One must do as other fellows do. It's such nonsense, I mean, to call it being

drunk. Of course I'm awfully sorry. I've had such a beastly headache all day.

BARTHWICK: Tcha! If you'd only had the common decency to remember what happened when you came in. Then we should know what truth there was in what this fellow says—as it is, it's all the most confounded darkness.

JACK [*staring as though at half-formed visions*]: I just get a— and then—it's gone—

MRS. BARTHWICK: Oh, Jack! do you mean to say you were so tipsy you can't even remember—

JACK: Look here, Mother! Of course I remember I came—I must have come—

BARTHWICK [*unguardedly, and walking up and down*]: Tcha!— and that infernal purse! Good Heavens! It'll get into the papers. Who on earth could have foreseen a thing like this? Better to have lost a dozen cigarette-boxes, and said nothing about it. [*To his wife.*] It's all your doing. I told you so from the first. I wish to goodness Roper would come!

MRS. BARTHWICK [*sharply*]: I don't know what you're talking about, John.

BARTHWICK [*turning on her*]: No, you—you—you don't know anything! [*Sharply.*] Where the devil is Roper? If he can see a way out of this he's a better man than I take him for. I defy *any one* to see a way out of it. *I* can't.

JACK: Look here, don't excite Dad—I can simply say I was too beastly tired, and don't remember anything except that I came in and [*in a dying voice*] went to bed the same as usual.

BARTHWICK: Went to bed? Who knows where you went—I've lost all confidence. For all I know you slept on the floor.

JACK [*indignantly*]: I didn't, I slept on the—

BARTHWICK [*sitting on the sofa*]: Who cares where you slept; what does it matter if he mentions the—the—a perfect disgrace?

MRS. BARTHWICK: *What?* [*A silence.*] I *insist* on knowing.

JACK: Oh! nothing—

MRS. BARTHWICK: Nothing? What do you mean by nothing, Jack? There's your father in such a state about it—

JACK: It's only my purse.

MRS. BARTHWICK: Your purse! You know perfectly well you haven't got one.

JACK: Well, it was somebody else's—it was all a joke—I didn't want the beastly thing—

MRS. BARTHWICK: Do you mean that you had another person's purse, and that this man took it too?

BARTHWICK: Tcha! Of course he took it too! A man like that Jones will make the most of it. It'll get into the papers.

MRS. BARTHWICK: I don't understand. What on earth is all the fuss about? [*Bending over* JACK, *and softly.*] Jack now, tell me dear! Don't be afraid. What is it? Come!

JACK: Oh, don't, Mother!

MRS. BARTHWICK: But don't what, dear?

JACK: It was pure sport. I don't know how I got the thing. Of course I'd had a bit of a row—

I didn't know what I was doing —I was—I was—well, you know —I suppose I must have pulled the bag out of her hand.

MRS. BARTHWICK: Out of her hand? Whose hand? What bag— whose bag?

JACK: Oh! I don't know—*her* bag —it belonged to—[*in a desperate and rising voice*] a woman.

MRS. BARTHWICK: A woman? *Oh! Jack! No!*

JACK [*jumping up*]: You *would* have it. I didn't want to tell you. It's not my fault.

[*The door opens and* MARLOW *ushers in a man of middle age, inclined to corpulence, in evening dress. He has a ruddy, thin moustache, and dark, quick-moving little eyes. His eyebrows are Chinese.*]

MARLOW: Mr. Roper, sir. [*He leaves the room.*]

ROPER [*with a quick look round*]: How do you do?

[*But neither* JACK *nor* MRS. BARTHWICK *make a sign.*]

BARTHWICK [*hurrying*]: Thank goodness you've come, Roper. You remember what I told you this afternoon; we've just had the detective here.

ROPER: Got the box?

BARTHWICK: Yes, yes, but look here—it wasn't the charwoman at all; her drunken loafer of a husband took the things—he says that fellow there [*he waves his hand at* JACK, *who, with his shoulder raised, seems trying to ward off a blow*] let him into the house last night. Can you imagine such a thing!

[ROPER *laughs.*]

BARTHWICK [*with excited emphasis*]: It's no laughing matter, Roper. I told you about that business of Jack's too—don't you see—the brute took both the things—took that infernal purse. It'll get into the papers.

ROPER [*raising his eyebrows*]: H'm! The purse! Depravity in high life! What does your son say?

BARTHWICK: He remembers nothing. D—n! Did you ever see such a mess? It'll get into the papers.

MRS. BARTHWICK [*with her hand across her eyes*]: Oh! it's not that—

[BARTHWICK *and* ROPER *turn and look at her.*]

BARTHWICK: It's the idea of that woman—she's just heard—[ROPER *nods. And* MRS. BARTHWICK, *setting her lips, gives a slow look at* JACK, *and sits down at the table.*] What on earth's to be done, Roper? A ruffian like this Jones will make all the capital he can out of that purse.

MRS. BARTHWICK: I don't believe that Jack took that purse.

BARTHWICK: What—when the woman came here for it this morning?

MRS. BARTHWICK: Here? She had the impudence? Why wasn't I told?

[*She looks round from face to face —no one answers her, there is a pause.*]

BARTHWICK [*suddenly*]: What's to be done, Roper?

ROPER [*quietly to* JACK]: I suppose you didn't leave your latch-key in the door?

JACK [*sullenly*]: Yes, I did.

BARTHWICK: Good heavens! What next?

MRS. BARTHWICK: I'm certain you never let that man into the house, Jack, it's a wild invention. I'm sure there's not a word of truth in it, Mr. Roper.

ROPER [*very suddenly*]: Where did you sleep last night?

JACK [*promptly*]: On the sofa, there—[*hesitating*] that is—I—

BARTHWICK: On the sofa? D' you mean to say you didn't go to bed?

JACK [*sullenly*]: No.

BARTHWICK: If you don't remember anything, how can you remember that?

JACK: Because I woke up there in the morning.

MRS. BARTHWICK: Oh, Jack!

BARTHWICK: Good Gracious!

JACK: And Mrs. Jones saw me. I wish you wouldn't bait me so.

ROPER: Do you remember giving any one a drink?

JACK: By Jove, I do seem to remember a fellow with—a fellow with— [*He looks at* ROPER.] I say, d' you want me—?

ROPER [*quick as lightning*]: With a dirty face?

JACK [*with illumination*]: I do— I distinctly remember his—

[BARTHWICK *moves abruptly;* MRS. BARTHWICK *looks at* ROPER *angrily, and touches her son's arm.*]

MRS. BARTHWICK: You don't remember, it's ridiculous! I don't believe the man was ever here at all.

BARTHWICK: You must speak the truth, if it *is* the truth. But if you *do* remember such a dirty business, I shall wash my hands of you altogether.

JACK [*glaring at them*]: Well, what the devil—

MRS. BARTHWICK: Jack!

JACK: Well, Mother, I—I don't know what you *do* want.

MRS. BARTHWICK: We want you to speak the truth and say you never let this low man into the house.

BARTHWICK: Of course if you think that you really gave this man whisky in that disgraceful way, and let him see what you'd been doing, and were in such a disgusting condition that you don't remember a word of it—

ROPER [*quick*]: I've no memory myself—never had.

BARTHWICK [*desperately*]: I don't know what you're to say.

ROPER [*to* JACK]: Say nothing at all! Don't put yourself in a false position. The man stole the things or the woman stole the things, you had nothing to do with it. You were asleep on the sofa.

MRS. BARTHWICK: Your leaving the latch-key in the door was quite bad enough, there's no need to mention anything else. [*Touching his forehead softly.*] My dear, how hot your head is!

JACK: But I want to know what I'm to do. [*Passionately.*] I won't be badgered like this.

[MRS. BARTHWICK *recoils from him.*]

ROPER [*very quickly*]: You forget all about it. You were asleep.

JACK: Must I go down to the Court tomorrow?

ROPER [*shaking his head*]: No.

BARTHWICK [*in a relieved voice*]: Is that so?

ROPER: Yes.

BARTHWICK: But *you'll* go, Roper.

ROPER: Yes.

JACK [*with wan cheerfulness*]: Thanks, awfully! So long as I don't have to go. [*Putting his hand up to his head.*] I think if you'll excuse me—I've had a most beastly day. [*He looks from his father to his mother.*]

MRS. BARTHWICK [*turning quickly*]: Good-night, my boy.

JACK: Good-night, Mother.

[*He goes out.* MRS. BARTHWICK *heaves a sigh. There is a silence.*]

BARTHWICK: He gets off too easily. But for my money that woman would have prosecuted him.

ROPER: You find money useful.

BARTHWICK: I've my doubts whether we ought to hide the truth—

ROPER: There'll be a remand.

BARTHWICK: What! D' you mean he'll have to *appear* on the remand.

ROPER: Yes.

BARTHWICK: H'm, I thought you'd be able to— Look here, Roper, you *must* keep that purse out of the papers.

[ROPER *fixes his little eyes on him and nods.*]

MRS. BARTHWICK: Mr. Roper, don't you think the magistrate ought to be told what sort of people these Jones's are; I mean about their immorality before they were married. I don't know if John told you.

ROPER: Afraid it's not material.

MRS. BARTHWICK: Not material?

ROPER: Purely private life! May

have happened to the magistrate.

BARTHWICK [*with a movement as if to shift a burden*]: Then you'll take the thing into your hands?

ROPER: If the gods are kind. [*He holds his hand out.*]

BARTHWICK [*shaking it dubiously*]: Kind—eh? What? You going?

ROPER: Yes. I've another case, something like yours—most unexpected.

[*He bows to* MRS. BARTHWICK, *and goes out, followed by* BARTHWICK, *talking to the last.* MRS. BARTHWICK *at the table bursts into smothered sobs.* BARTHWICK *returns.*]

BARTHWICK [*to himself*]: There'll be a scandal!

MRS. BARTHWICK [*disguising her grief at once*]: I simply can't imagine what Roper means by making a joke of a thing like that!

BARTHWICK [*staring strangely*]: You! You can't imagine anything! You've no more imagination than a fly!

MRS. BARTHWICK [*angrily*]: You dare to tell me that I have no imagination.

BARTHWICK [*flustered*]: I—I'm upset. From beginning to end, the whole thing has been utterly against my principles.

MRS. BARTHWICK: Rubbish! You haven't any! Your principles are nothing in the world but sheer —fright!

BARTHWICK [*walking to the window*]: I've never been frightened in my life. You heard what Roper said. It's enough to upset one when a thing like this happens. Everything one says and does

seems to turn in one's mouth—it's—it's uncanny. It's not the sort of thing I've been accustomed to. [*As though stifling, he throws the window open. The faint sobbing of a child comes in.*] What's that? [*They listen.*]

MRS. BARTHWICK [*sharply*]: I can't stand that crying. I must send Marlow to stop it. My nerves are all on edge. [*She rings the bell.*]

BARTHWICK: I'll shut the window; you'll hear nothing.

[*He shuts the window. There is silence.*]

MRS. BARTHWICK [*sharply*]: That's no good! It's on my nerves. Nothing upsets me like a child's crying. [MARLOW *comes in.*] What's that noise of crying, Marlow? It sounds like a child.

BARTHWICK: It is a child. I can see it against the railings.

MARLOW [*opening the window, and looking out—quietly*]: It's Mrs. Jones's little boy, ma'am; he came here after his mother.

MRS. BARTHWICK [*moving quickly to the window*]: Poor little chap! John, we oughtn't to go on with this!

BARTHWICK [*sitting heavily in a chair*]: Ah! but it's out of our hands!

[MRS. BARTHWICK *turns her back to the window. There is an expression of distress on her face. She stands motionless, compressing her lips. The crying begins again.* BARTHWICK *covers his ears with his hands, and* MARLOW *shuts the window. The crying ceases.*]

[*The curtain falls.*]

ACT THREE

Eight days have passed, and the scene is a London Police Court at one o'clock. A canopied seat of Justice is surmounted by the lion and unicorn. Before the fire a worn-looking MAGISTRATE *is warming his coat-tails, and staring at two little girls in faded blue and orange rags, who are placed before the dock. Close to the witness-box is a* RELIEVING OFFICER *in an overcoat, and a short brown beard. Beside the little girls stands a bald* POLICE CONSTABLE. *On the front bench are sitting* BARTHWICK *and* ROPER, *and behind them* JACK. *In the railed enclosure are seedy-looking men and women. Some prosperous constables sit or stand about.*]

MAGISTRATE [*in his paternal and ferocious voice, hissing his s's*]: Now let us dispose of these young ladies.

USHER: Theresa Livens, Maud Livens. [*The bald* CONSTABLE *indicates the little girls, who remain silent, disillusioned, inattentive.*] Relieving officer!

[*The* RELIEVING OFFICER *steps into the witness-box.*]

USHER: The evidence you give to the Court shall be the truth, the whole truth, and nothing but the truth, so help you God! Kiss the book! [*The book is kissed.*]

RELIEVING OFFICER [*in a monotone, pausing slightly at each sentence end, that his evidence may be inscribed*]: About ten o'clock this morning, your Worship, I found these two little girls in Blue Street, Pulham, crying outside a public-house. Asked where their home was,

they said they had no home. Mother had gone away. Asked about their father. Their father had no work. Asked where they slept last night. At their aunt's. I've made inquiries, your Worship. The wife has broken up the home and gone on the streets. The husband is out of work and living in common lodging-houses. The husband's sister has eight children of her own, and says she can't afford to keep these little girls any longer.

MAGISTRATE [*returning to his seat beneath the canopy of Justice*]: Now, let me see. You say the mother is on the streets; what evidence have you of that?

RELIEVING OFFICER: I have the husband here, your Worship.

MAGISTRATE: Very well; then let us see him. [*There are cries of* "LIVENS." *The* MAGISTRATE *leans forward, and stares with hard compassion at the little girls.* LIVENS *comes in. He is quiet, with grizzled hair, and a muffler for a collar. He stands beside the witness-box.*] And you are their father? Now, why don't you keep your little girls at home? How is it you leave them to wander about the streets like this?

LIVENS: I've got no home, your Worship. I'm living from 'and to mouth. I've got no work; and nothin' to keep them on.

MAGISTRATE: How is that?

LIVENS [*ashamedly*]: My wife, she broke my 'ome up, and pawned the things.

MAGISTRATE: But what made you let her?

LIVENS: Your Worship, I'd no chance to stop 'er; she did it when I was out lookin' for work.

MAGISTRATE: Did you ill-treat her?

LIVENS [*emphatically*]: I never raised my 'and to her in my life, your Worship.

MAGISTRATE: Then what was it—did she drink?

LIVENS: Yes, your Worship.

MAGISTRATE: Was she loose in her behaviour?

LIVENS [*in a low voice*]: Yes, your Worship.

MAGISTRATE: And where is she now?

LIVENS: I don't know, your Worship. She went off with a man, and after that I—

MAGISTRATE: Yes, yes. Who knows anything of her? [*To the bald* CONSTABLE.] Is she known here?

RELIEVING OFFICER: Not in this district, your Worship; but I have ascertained that she is well known—

MAGISTRATE: Yes—yes; we'll stop at that. Now [*to the father*] you

say that she has broken up your home, and left these little girls. What provision can you make for them? You look a strong man.

LIVENS: So I am, your Worship. I'm willin' enough to work, but for the life of me I can't get anything to do.

MAGISTRATE: But have you tried?

LIVENS: I've tried everything, your Worship—I've tried my 'ardest.

MAGISTRATE: Well, well—

[*There is a silence.*]

RELIEVING OFFICER: If your Worship thinks it's a case, my people are willing to take them.

MAGISTRATE: Yes, yes, I know; but I've no evidence that this man is not the proper guardian for his children. [*He rises and goes back to the fire.*]

RELIEVING OFFICER: The mother, your Worship, is able to get access to them.

MAGISTRATE: Yes, yes; the mother, of course, is an improper person to have anything to do with them. [*To the father.*] Well, now what do you say?

LIVENS: Your Worship, I can only say that if I could get work I should be only too willing to provide for them. But what can I do, your Worship? Here I am obliged to live from 'and to mouth in these 'ere common lodging-houses. I'm a strong man—I'm willing to work—I'm half as alive again as some of 'em—but you see, your Worship, my 'air's turned a bit, owing to the fever—[*touches his hair*]—and that's against me; and I don't seem to get a chance anyhow.

MAGISTRATE: Yes—yes. [*Slowly.*] Well, I think it's a case. [*Staring his hardest at the little girls.*] Now, are you willing that these little girls should be sent to a home?

LIVENS: Yes, your Worship, I should be very willing.

MAGISTRATE: Well, I'll remand them for a week. Bring them again today week; if I see no reason against it then, I'll make an order.

RELIEVING OFFICER: Today week, your Worship.

[*The bald* CONSTABLE *takes the little girls out by the shoulders. The father follows them. The* MAGISTRATE, *returning to his seat, bends over and talks to his* CLERK *inaudibly.*]

BARTHWICK [*speaking behind his hand*]: A painful case, Roper; very distressing state of things.

ROPER: Hundreds like this in the Police Courts.

BARTHWICK: Most distressing! The more I see of it, the more important this question of the condition of the people seems to become. I shall certainly make a point of taking up the cudgels in the House. I shall move—

[*The* MAGISTRATE *ceases talking to his* CLERK.]

CLERK: Remands!

[BARTHWICK *stops abruptly. There is a stir and* MRS. JONES *comes in by the public door;* JONES, *ushered by policemen, comes from the prisoners' door. They file into the dock.*]

CLERK: James Jones, Jane Jones.

USHER: Jane Jones!

BARTHWICK [*in a whisper*]: The purse—the purse *must* be kept out of it, Roper. Whatever happens you must keep that out of the papers. [ROPER *nods.*]

BALD CONSTABLE: Hush!

[MRS. JONES, *dressed in her thin, black, wispy dress, and black straw hat, stands motionless with hands crossed on the front rail of the dock.* JONES *leans against the back rail of the dock, and keeps half turning, glancing defiantly about him. He is haggard and unshaven.*]

CLERK [*consulting with his papers*]: This is the case remanded from last Wednesday, sir. Theft of a silver cigarette-box and assault on the police; the two charges were taken together. Jane Jones! James Jones!

MAGISTRATE [*staring*]: Yes, yes; I remember.

CLERK: Jane Jones.

MRS. JONES: Yes, sir.

CLERK: Do you admit stealing a silver cigarette-box valued at five pounds, ten shillings, from the house of John Barthwick, M.P., between the hours of 11 P.M. on Easter Monday and 8:45 A.M. on Easter Tuesday last? Yes, or no?

MRS. JONES [*in a low voice*]: No, sir, I do not, sir.

CLERK: James Jones? Do you admit stealing a silver cigarette-box valued at five pounds, ten shillings, from the house of John Barthwick, M.P., between the hours of 11 P.M. on Easter Monday and 8:45 A.M. on Easter Tuesday last? And further making an assault on the police when in the execution of their duty at 3 P.M. on Easter Tuesday? Yes or no?

JONES [*sullenly*]: Yes, but I've got a lot to say about it.

MAGISTRATE [*to the* CLERK]: Yes—yes. But how comes it that these two people are charged with the same offence? Are they husband and wife?

CLERK: Yes, sir. You remember your ordered a remand for further evidence as to the story of the male prisoner.

MAGISTRATE: Have they been in custody since?

CLERK: You released the woman on her own recognisances, sir.

MAGISTRATE: Yes, yes, this is the case of the silver box; I remember now. Well?

CLERK: Thomas Marlow.

[*The cry of "Thomas Marlow" is repeated.* MARLOW *comes in, and steps into the witness-box.*]

USHER: The evidence you give to the court shall be the truth, the whole truth, and nothing but the truth, so help you God. Kiss the book.

[*The book is kissed. The silver box is handed up, and placed on the rail.*]

CLERK [*reading from his papers*]: Your name is Thomas Marlow? Are you butler to John Barthwick, M.P., of 6, Rockingham Gate?

MARLOW: Yes, sir.

CLERK: Is that the box?

MARLOW: Yes, sir.

CLERK: And did you miss the same at 8:45 on the following morning, on going to remove the tray?

MARLOW: Yes, sir.

CLERK: Is the female prisoner known to you? [MARLOW *nods.*] Is she the charwoman employed at 6, Rockingham Gate? [*Again* MARLOW *nods.*] Did you at the time of your missing the box find her in the room alone?

MARLOW: Yes, sir.

CLERK: Did you afterwards communicate the loss to your employer, and did he send you to the police station?

MARLOW: Yes, sir.

CLERK [*to* MRS. JONES]: Have you anything to ask him?

MRS. JONES: No, sir, nothing, thank you, sir.

CLERK [*to* JONES]: James Jones, have you anything to ask this witness?

JONES: I don't know 'im.

MAGISTRATE: Are you sure you put the box in the place you say at the time you say?

MARLOW: Yes, your Worship.

MAGISTRATE: Very well; then now let us have the officer.

[MARLOW *leaves the box, and* SNOW *goes into it.*]

USHER: The evidence you give to the court shall be the truth, the whole truth, and nothing but the truth, so help you God. [*The book is kissed.*]

CLERK [*reading from his papers*]: Your name is Robert Snow? You are a detective in the X. B. division of the Metropolitan police force? According to instructions received did you on Easter Tuesday last proceed to the prisoner's lodgings at 34, Merthyr Street, St. Soames's? And did you on entering see the box produced, lying on the table?

SNOW: Yes, sir.

CLERK: Is that the box?

SNOW [*fingering the box*]: Yes, sir.

CLERK: And did you thereupon take possession of it, and charge the female prisoner with theft of the box from 6, Rockingham Gate? And did she deny the same?

SNOW: Yes, sir.

CLERK: Did you take her into custody?

SNOW: Yes, sir.

MAGISTRATE: What was her behaviour?

SNOW: Perfectly quiet, your Worship. She persisted in the denial. That's all.

MAGISTRATE: Do you know her?

SNOW: No, your Worship.

MAGISTRATE: Is she known here?

BALD CONSTABLE: No, your Worship, they're neither of them known, we've nothing against them at all.

CLERK [*to* MRS. JONES]: Have you anything to ask the officer?

MRS. JONES: No, sir, thank you, I've nothing to ask him.

MAGISTRATE: Very well then—go on.

CLERK [*reading from his paper*]: And while you were taking the female prisoner did the male prisoner interpose, and endeavour to hinder you in the execution of your duty, and did he strike you a blow?

SNOW: Yes, sir.

CLERK: And did he say, "You let her go, I took the box myself"?

SNOW: He did.

CLERK: And did you blow your whistle and obtain the assistance of another constable, and take him into custody?

SNOW: I did.

CLERK: Was he violent on the way to the station, and did he use bad language, and did he several times repeat that he had taken the box himself? [SNOW *nods.*] Did you thereupon ask him in what manner he had stolen the box? And did you understand him to say he had entered the house at the invitation of young Mr. Barthwick [BARTHWICK, *turning in his seat, frowns at* ROPER] after midnight on Easter Monday, and partaken of whisky, and that under the influence of the whisky he had taken the box?

SNOW: I did, sir.

CLERK: And was his demeanour throughout very violent?

SNOW: It *was* very violent.

JONES [*breaking in*]: Violent—of course it was! You put your 'ands on my wife when I kept tellin' you I took the thing myself.

MAGISTRATE [*hissing, with protruded neck*]: Now—you will have your chance of saying what you want to say presently. Have you anything to ask the officer?

JONES [*sullenly*]: No.

MAGISTRATE: Very well then. Now let us hear what the female prisoner has to say first.

MRS. JONES: Well, your Worship, of course I can only say what I've said all along, that I didn't take the box.

MAGISTRATE: Yes, but did you know that it was taken?

MRS. JONES: No, your Worship. And, of course, to what my husband says, your Worship, I can't speak of my own knowledge. Of course, I know that he came home very late on the Monday night. It was past one o'clock when he came in, and he was not himself at all.

MAGISTRATE: Had he been drinking?

MRS. JONES: Yes, your Worship.

MAGISTRATE: And was he drunk?

MRS. JONES: Yes, your Worship, he was almost quite drunk.

MAGISTRATE: And did he say anything to you?

MRS. JONES: No, your Worship, only to call me names. And of course in the morning when I got up and went to work he was asleep. And I don't know anything more about it until I came home again. Except that Mr. Barthwick—that's my employer, your Worship—told me the box was missing.

MAGISTRATE: Yes, yes.

MRS. JONES: But of course when I was shaking out my husband's coat the cigarette-box fell out and all the cigarettes were scattered on the bed.

MAGISTRATE: You say all the cigarettes were scattered on the bed? [*To* SNOW.] Did you see the cigarettes scattered on the bed?

SNOW: No, your Worship, I did not.

MAGISTRATE: You see he says he didn't see them.

JONES: Well, they were there for all that.

SNOW: I can't say, your Worship, that I had the opportunity of going round the room; I had all my work cut out with the male prisoner.

MAGISTRATE [*to* MRS. JONES]: Well, what more have you to say?

MRS. JONES: Of course when I saw the box, your Worship, I was dreadfully upset, and I couldn't think why he had done such a thing; when the officer came we were having words about it, because it is ruin to me, your Worship, in my profession, and I have three little children dependent on me.

MAGISTRATE [*protruding his neck*]: Yes—yes—but what did he say to you?

MRS. JONES: I asked him whatever came over him to do such a thing—and he said it was the drink. He said he had had too much to drink, and something came over him. And of course, your Worship, he had had very little to eat all day, and the drink does go to the head when you have not had enough to eat. Your Worship may not know, but it is the truth. And I would like to say that all through his married life, I have never known him to do such a thing before, though we have passed through great hardships and [*speaking with soft emphasis*] I am quite sure he would not have done it if he had been himself at the time.

MAGISTRATE: Yes, yes. But don't you know that that is no excuse?

MRS. JONES: Yes, your Worship. I know that it is no excuse.

[*The* MAGISTRATE *leans over and parleys with his* CLERK.]

JACK [*leaning over from his seat behind*]: I say, Dad—

BARTHWICK: Tsst! [*Sheltering his mouth he speaks to* ROPER.] Roper, you had better get up now and say that considering the circumstances and the poverty of the prisoners, we have no wish to proceed any further, and if the magistrate would deal with the case as one of disorder only on the part of—

BALD CONSTABLE: Hssshh!

[ROPER *shakes his head.*]

MAGISTRATE: Now, supposing what you say and what your husband says is true, what I have to consider is—how did he obtain access to this house, and were you in any way a party to his obtaining access? You are the charwoman employed at the house?

MRS. JONES: Yes, your Worship, and of course if I had let him into the house it would have been very wrong of me; and I have never done such a thing in any of the houses where I have been employed.

MAGISTRATE: Well—so you say. Now let us hear what story the male prisoner makes of it.

JONES [*who leans with his arms on the dock behind, speaks in a slow, sullen voice*]: Wot I say is wot my wife says. I've never been 'ad up in a police court before, an' I can prove I took it when in liquor. I told her, and she can tell you the same, that I was goin' to throw the thing into the water sooner then 'ave it on my mind.

MAGISTRATE: But how did you get into the *house?*

JONES: I was passin'. I was goin' 'ome from the "Goat and Bells."

MAGISTRATE: The "Goat and Bells,"—what is that? A public-house?

JONES: Yes, at the corner. It was Bank 'oliday, an' I'd 'ad a drop to drink. I see this young Mr. Barthwick tryin' to find the key-hole on the wrong side of the door.

MAGISTRATE: Well?

JONES [*slowly and with many pauses*]: Well—I 'elped 'im to find it—drunk as a lord 'e was. He goes on, an' comes back again, and says, "I've got nothin' for you," 'e says, "but come in an' 'ave a drink." So I went in just as you might 'ave done yourself. We 'ad a drink o' whisky just as you might have 'ad, 'nd young Mr. Barthwick says to me, "Take a drink 'nd a smoke. Take anything you like," 'e says. And then he went to sleep on the sofa. I 'ad some more whisky—an' I 'ad a smoke—and I 'ad some more whisky—an' I carn't tell yer what 'appened after that.

MAGISTRATE: Do you mean to say that you were so drunk that you can remember nothing?

JACK [*softly to his father*]: I say, that's exactly what—

BARTHWICK: Tssh!

JONES: That's what I do mean.

MAGISTRATE: And yet you say you stole the box?

JONES: I never stole the box. I took it.

MAGISTRATE [*hissing with protruded neck*]: You did not steal it—you took it. Did it belong to you—what is that but stealing?

JONES: I took it.

MAGISTRATE: You took it—you took it away from their house and you took it to your house—

JONES [*sullenly breaking in*]: I ain't got a house.

MAGISTRATE: Very well, let us hear what this young man Mr. —Mr. Barthwick—has to say to your story.

[SNOW *leaves the witness-box. The* BALD CONSTABLE *beckons* JACK, *who, clutching his hat, goes into the witness-box.* ROPER *moves to the table set apart for his profession.*]

SWEARING CLERK: The evidence you give to the court shall be the truth, the whole truth, and nothing but the truth, so help you God. Kiss the book. [*The book is kissed.*]

ROPER [*examining*]: What is your name?

JACK [*in a low voice*]: John Barthwick, Junior.

[*The* CLERK *writes it down.*]

ROPER: Where do you live?

JACK: At 6, Rockingham Gate.

[*All his answers are recorded by the* CLERK.]

ROPER: You are the son of the owner?

JACK [*in a very low voice*]: Yes.

ROPER: Speak up, please. Do you know the prisoners?

JACK [*looking at the* JONESES, *in a low voice*]: I've seen Mrs. Jones. I—[*in a loud voice*] don't know the man.

JONES: Well, I know you!

BALD CONSTABLE: Hssh!

ROPER: Now, did you come in late on the night of Easter Monday?

JACK: Yes.

ROPER: And did you by mistake leave your latch-key in the door?

JACK: Yes.

MAGISTRATE: Oh! You left your latch-key in the door?

ROPER: And is that all you can remember about your coming in?

JACK [*in a loud voice*]: Yes, it is.

MAGISTRATE: Now, you have heard the male prisoner's story, what do you say to that?

JACK [*turning to the* MAGISTRATE, *speaks suddenly in a confident, straightforward voice*]: The fact of the matter is, sir, that I'd been out to the theatre that night, and had supper afterwards, and I came in late.

MAGISTRATE: Do you remember this man being outside when you came in?

JACK: No, sir. [*He hesitates.*] I don't think I do.

MAGISTRATE [*somewhat puzzled*]: Well, did he help you to open the door, as he says? Did *any* one help you to open the door?

JACK: No, sir—I don't think so, sir—I don't know.

MAGISTRATE: You don't know? But you must know. It isn't a usual thing for you to have the door opened for you, is it?

JACK [*with a shamefaced smile*]: No.

MAGISTRATE: Very well, then—

JACK [*desperately*]: The fact of the matter is, sir, I'm afraid I'd had too much champagne that night.

MAGISTRATE [*smiling*]: Oh! you'd had too much champagne?

JONES: May I ask the gentleman a question?

MAGISTRATE: Yes—yes—you may ask him what questions you like.

JONES: Don't you remember you said you was a Liberal, same as your father, and you asked me wot I was?

JACK [*with his hand against his brow*]: I seem to remember—

JONES: And I said to you, "I'm a bloomin' Conservative," I said; an' you said to me, "You look more like one of these 'ere Socialists. Take wotever you like," you said.

JACK [*with sudden resolution*]: No, I don't. I don't remember anything of the sort.

JONES: Well, I do, an' my word's as good as yours. I've never been had up in a police court before. Look 'ere, don't you remember you had a sky-blue bag in your 'and—

[BARTHWICK *jumps.*]

ROPER: I submit to your Worship that these questions are hardly to the point, the prisoner having admitted that he himself does not remember anything. [*There is a smile on the face of Justice.*] It is a case of the blind leading the blind.

JONES [*violently*]: I've done no more than wot he 'as. I'm a poor man; I've got no money an' no friends—he's a toff—he can do wot I can't.

MAGISTRATE: Now, now! All this won't help you—you must be quiet. You say you took this box? Now, what made you take it? Were you pressed for money?

JONES: I'm always pressed for money.

MAGISTRATE: Was that the reason you took it?

JONES: No.

MAGISTRATE [*to* SNOW]: Was anything found on him?

SNOW: Yes, your Worship. There was six pounds twelve shillin's found on him, and this purse.

[*The red silk purse is handed to the* MAGISTRATE. BARTHWICK *rises in his seat, but hastily sits down again.*]

MAGISTRATE [*staring at the purse*]: Yes, yes—let me see— [*There is a silence.*] No, no, I've nothing before me as to the purse. How did you come by all that money?

JONES [*after a long pause, suddenly*]: I declines to say.

MAGISTRATE: But if you had all that money, what made you take this box?

JONES: I took it out of spite.

MAGISTRATE [*hissing, with protruded neck*]: You took it out of spite? Well now, that's something! But do you imagine you can go about the town taking things out of spite?

JONES: If you had my life, if you'd been out of work—

MAGISTRATE: Yes, yes; I know—because you're out of work you think it's an excuse for everything.

JONES [*pointing at* JACK]: You ask 'im wot made 'im take the—

ROPER [*quietly*]: Does your Worship require this witness in the box any longer?

MAGISTRATE [*ironically*]: I think not; he is hardly profitable.

[JACK *leaves the witness-box, and, hanging his head, resumes his seat.*]

JONES: You ask 'im wot made 'im take the lady's—

[*But the* BALD CONSTABLE *catches him by the sleeve.*]

BALD CONSTABLE: Sssh!

MAGISTRATE [*emphatically*]: Now listen to me. I've nothing to do with what he may or may not have taken. Why did you resist the police in the execution of their duty?

JONES: It war n't their duty to take my wife, a respectable woman, that 'adn't done nothing.

MAGISTRATE: But I say it was. What made you strike the officer a blow?

JONES: Any man would a struck 'im a blow. I'd strike 'im again, I would.

MAGISTRATE: You are not making your case any better by violence. How do you suppose we could get on if everybody behaved like you?

JONES [*leaning forward, earnestly*]: Well, wot about 'er; who's to make up to 'er for this? Who's to give 'er back 'er good name?

MRS. JONES: Your Worship, it's the children that's preying on his mind, because of course I've lost my work. And I've had to find another room owing to the scandal.

MAGISTRATE: Yes, yes, I know—but if he hadn't acted like this nobody would have suffered.

JONES [*glaring round at* JACK]: I've done no worse than wot 'e 'as. Wot I want to know is wot's goin' to be done to 'im.

[*The* BALD CONSTABLE *again says* "Hssh!"]

ROPER: Mr. Barthwick wishes it known, your Worship, that considering the poverty of the prisoners he does not press the charge as to the box. Perhaps your Worship would deal with the case as one of disorder.

JONES: I don't want it smothered up, I want it all dealt with fair —I want my rights—

MAGISTRATE [*rapping his desk*]:

Now you have said all you have to say, and you will be quiet. [*There is a silence; the* MAGISTRATE *bends over and parleys with his* CLERK.] Yes, I think I may discharge the woman. [*In a kindly voice he addresses* MRS. JONES, *who stands unmoving with her hands crossed on the rail.*] It is very unfortunate for you that this man has behaved as he has. It is not the consequences to him but the consequences to you. You have been brought here twice, you have lost your work—[*He glares at* JONES.] and this is what always happens. Now you may go away, and I am very sorry it was necessary to bring you here at all.

MRS. JONES [*softly*]: Thank you very much, your Worship. [*She leaves the dock, and looking back at* JONES, *twists her fingers and is still.*]

MAGISTRATE: Yes, yes, but I can't pass it over. Go away, there's a good woman. [MRS. JONES *stands back. The* MAGISTRATE *leans his head on his hand: then raising it he speaks to* JONES.] Now, listen to me. Do you wish the case to be settled here, or do you wish it to go before a jury?

JONES [*muttering*]: I don't want no jury.

MAGISTRATE: Very well then, I will deal with it here. [*After a pause.*] You have pleaded guilty to stealing this box—

JONES: Not to stealin'—

BALD CONSTABLE: Hssshh!

MAGISTRATE: And to assaulting the police—

JONES: Any man as was a man—

MAGISTRATE: Your conduct here

has been most improper. You give the excuse that you were drunk when you stole the box. I tell you that is no excuse. If you choose to get drunk and break the law afterwards you must take the consequences. And let me tell you that men like you, who get drunk and give way to your spite or whatever it is that's in you, are—are—a *nuisance to the community.*

JACK [*leaning from his seat*]: Dad! that's what you said to me!

BARTHWICK: Tsst!

[*There is a silence, while the* MAGISTRATE *consults his* CLERK; JONES *leans forward waiting.*]

MAGISTRATE: This is your first offence, and I am going to give you a light sentence. [*Speaking sharply, but without expression.*] One month with hard labour.

[*He bends, and parleys with his* CLERK. *The* BALD CONSTABLE *and another help* JONES *from the dock.*]

JONES [*stopping and twisting round*]: Call this justice? What about 'im? 'E got drunk! 'E took the purse—'e took the purse but [*in a muffled shout*] it's *'is money* got 'im off—*Justice!*

[*The prisoner's door is shut on* JONES, *and from the seedy-looking men and women comes a hoarse and whispering groan.*]

MAGISTRATE: We will now adjourn for lunch! [*He rises from his seat.*]

[*The Court is in a stir.* ROPER *gets up and speaks to the reporter.* JACK, *throwing up his head, walks with a swagger to the corridor;* BARTHWICK *follows.*]

MRS. JONES [*turning to him with a humble gesture*]: Oh! sir!—

[BARTHWICK *hesitates, then yielding to his nerves, he makes a shame-faced gesture of refusal, and hurries out of court.* MRS. JONES *stands looking after him.*]

[*The curtain falls.*]

William Butler Yeats
[1865-1939]

W. B. YEATS, Irish poet and dramatist, was born on June 13, 1865, in Dublin, the eldest son of an Irish Protestant painter. His family was a curious blend of an old respected family who cared for name, the arts, and the cultivated pleasures of this world but knew nothing of practical matters and a family of no particular refinement but who knew very well how "to get on" in this world. William spent his vacations with his maternal grandparents in Sligo and was greatly impressed, as was everyone, with his grandfather, a strong, silent, powerful, and brave man, who thought nothing of jumping into the bay after an old hat. William was a shy boy who found his own ideas so vastly engrossing that he could scarcely bring himself to attend to any lessons. He was clever at school, but no scholar, and was often at the bottom of his class. However, he was a keen observer and had a retentive memory which enabled him to draw vividly on all his background for his later writing. He began writing verse at sixteen and believed that poetry was a means of lessening one's solitude without destroying peace.

He traveled between London and Dublin and met many famous men in his father's house. He became a friend of Oscar Wilde, who, believing Yeats to be alone in London, invited him for Christmas dinner. Yeats said of Wilde that he was the first man he ever heard speak in perfect sentences. Later, during Wilde's trial, Yeats defended him. At twenty-two he was still adolescent, romantic, and undirected. He was involved with revolutionary Irish politics, became a member of the Irish Republican Brotherhood, worked hard to preserve national Irish literature and language, and dabbled in mysticism, theology, and magic. Maintaining that he was only half-educated, he deplored the educational system and always wished for two things he never possessed: scholarship and self-assurance.

In 1891 he proposed to Maude Gonne, an actress involved in politics. She refused him and married a younger man, MacBride, with whom she had a daughter, Iseult. Years later Maude gave her permission for Yeats to propose to Iseult, but the daughter also refused him. When he was fifty-two he married a young English girl, Georgie Lees, with whom he had a most happy marriage. They had one son and one daughter.

His first works to gain recognition were Celtic fairy and folk tales, *The Celtic Twilight* (1893) and *Poems* (1895). He became interested in organizing a theatre of poetry in Dublin and worked to this end with Lady Gregory, with the result that the Abbey Theatre was founded, of which he was a director. The aims of Yeats's Irish dramatic movement were to present plays by Irish dramatists, on Irish subjects, history and legend, and to develop a company of Irish players. His verse play, *The Countess Kathleen,* was produced there in 1899. In 1902 Maude Gonne did *Cathleen ni Houlihan,* which was his most popular play. In 1896 he met John M. Synge, who so influenced him that Yeats modified his style. Synge taught Yeats to appreciate hard virtues and harsh facts, gave him an appetite for the "savage imagination," and persuaded him to use the syntax of common life and to reject archaisms and inversions for the common idiom. Yeats came to believe that all vigorous life contains the seeds of all good and evil, and that his style had been too long filled with "sweetness and serenity." *Deirdre,* which he began writing in 1904–5, and which was produced at the Abbey in 1906, was a transitional piece between his older and newer styles. It is written in English blank verse but lacks comic relief and peasant dialect, both of which Yeats believed essential, especially a sense of heroic "gaiety." Although he gave the legend his personal interpretation and wrote it in a dramatic, sensuous, and emotional style, it did not appear to the Abbey audience. Nor was Yeats himself entirely satisfied for he continued to rewrite *Deirdre* for years. However, he believed that a desire that could be satisfied could not be very great, whereas an unsatisfied desire was a spur to the artist—his unfulfilled passion becomes vision. Yeats insisted on passion. He felt that passion, not thought, makes tragedy. About 1915 he came under the influence of the Noh drama of Japan and his later plays strongly reflect that influence.

In 1922 he was elected to the Irish Senate and in 1928 and 1929 *The Tower* and *The Winding Stair* were published, books representing his highest poetic achievement. In 1932 his health began to fail, but he worked when he could summon the energy and began supervising radio broadcasts of modern verse. On January 28, 1939, he died of myocarditis in a little town near Monaco, Roquebrune. In 1948 his remains were brought to his great-grandfather's parish in Sligo.

Deirdre was produced by the Abbey Theatre in the autumn of 1906. The production was not a great success. Yeats rewrote the opening scenes, and the new version was played in 1907. Mrs. Patrick Campbell offered to play the role of Deirdre and her offer inspired him to rewrite still another scene. She played Deirdre successfully in Dublin and London with the Abbey Company in 1907 and 1908. Yeats was especially moved by Mrs. Campbell's passionate and solitary playing of the role.

The play is based on one of the most famous of Irish legends. The best version, according to Yeats, is in Lady Gregory's *Cuchulain of Muirthemne*. Yeats saw Deirdre as the Irish Helen, Naoise as Paris, and Conchubar as Menelaus. The events were supposed to have taken place about the time of Christ. The tale also suggests the legendary story of Tristan and Isolde.

Though *Deirdre* was written before Yeats came directly under the influence of Noh drama, the play contains a striking Noh feature which Yeats admired—the playing upon a single metaphor, such as the bird cage, the eagle, and hunting and animal images. These make up the emotional imagery of the play: the wild birds, the lovers, caught in a treacherous trap. The image is visually evoked when Naoise is brought in caught in the net by Naoise's men. The chess game serves as a kind of structural metaphor: it relates the tragic situation of the lovers to that of the ancient lovers, Lugaidh Redstripe and his wife, who also sat at chess waiting for death. The game defines the design of the tragedy: the lovers have been checkmated by the king because the king cheated in the game. All of the lovers' moves to escape the trap are futile. They can only die being true to themselves and their passion for each other.

The play has been criticized for being essentially static and undramatic, but its design is such that the action is restricted by the situation—the lovers are trapped and the dramatic life of the play is the inner life of the characters. All the characters act and speak from a fixed point and remain virtually unchanged within that fixed point: Fergus insists upon the good faith of Conchubar until it is too late; Naoise trusts in his warrior's code until it is too late; Conchubar firmly believes he is doing the just and necessary thing in betraying and trapping the lovers and killing Naoise. Only Deirdre seems to change in her efforts to avoid the catastrophe; she appeals to Naoise and Conchubar by turns; but she never really moves from her fixed position of being, her passion for Naoise. The static quality of the play is further suggested by the chorus of musicians who, as the play opens, are singing a legendary tale of tragic love and betrayal while it is unfolding before them. Life seems to be passing immediately into legend. The musicians perceive the secrets hidden within the people of the play and the design which emerges.

Deirdre is a fine example of Yeats's dramatic work because in its handling of imagery, its evocation of the inner lives of the characters, and its use of myth and legend it successfully synthesizes much of what Yeats was trying to achieve in the drama.

DRAMATIC WORKS

The Countess Kathleen, 1892
The Land of Heart's Desire, 1894
The Shadowy Waters, 1900
Cathleen ni Houlihan, 1902
Where There Is Nothing, 1902
The Hour-Glass, 1903
The Pot of Broth, 1904
The King's Threshold, 1904
On Baile's Strand, 1904
Deirdre, 1907
The Unicorn from the Stars, 1908
The Green Helmet, 1910
At the Hawk's Well, 1917
The Dreaming of the Bones, 1917
The Only Jealousy of Emer, 1919

Calvary, 1920
The Player Queen, 1922
The Cat and the Moon, 1926
Sophocles' King Oedipus, 1928
The Resurrection, 1931
Sophocles' Oedipus at Colonus, 1934
The Words upon the Window-Pane, 1934
The King of the Great Clock Tower, 1935
A Full Moon in March, 1935
The Herne's Egg, 1938
Purgatory, 1939
The Death of Cuchulain, 1939

Deirdre

★

Persons in the Play

MUSICIANS
FERGUS, *an old man*
NAOISE *(pronounced* Neesh-e),
a young king
DEIRDRE, *his queen*
A DARK-FACED MESSENGER
CONCHUBAR (*pronounced* Conohar),
*the old King of Uladh, who is still
strong and vigorous*
A DARK-FACED EXECUTIONER

A Guest-house in a wood. It is a rough house of timber;
through the doors and some of the windows one can see the
great spaces of the wood, the sky dimming, night closing
in. But a window to the left shows the thick leaves of a cop-
pice; the landscape suggests silence and loneliness. There
is a door to right and left, and through the side windows
one can see anybody who approaches either door, a moment
before he enters. In the centre, a part of the house is cur-
tained off; the curtains are drawn. There are unlighted
torches in brackets on the walls. There is, at one side, a
small table with a chessboard and chessmen upon it. At
the other side of the room there is a brazier with a fire;
two women, with musical instruments beside them, crouch
about the brazier: they are comely women of about forty.
Another woman, who carries a stringed instrument, enters
hurriedly; she speaks, at first standing in the doorway.

FIRST MUSICIAN: I have a story right, my wanderers,
That has so mixed with fable in our songs
That all seemed fabulous. We are come, by chance,
Into King Conchubar's country, and this house
Is an old guest-house built for travellers
From the seashore to Conchubar's royal house,
And there are certain hills among these woods
And there Queen Deirdre grew.
SECOND MUSICIAN: That famous queen
Who has been wandering with her lover Naoise
Somewhere beyond the edges of the world?
FIRST MUSICIAN [*going nearer to the brazier*]: Some dozen years ago,
     King Conchubar found
A house upon a hillside in this wood,
And there a child with an old witch to nurse her,
And nobody to say if she were human,
Or of the gods, or anything at all
Of who she was or why she was hidden there,
But that she'd too much beauty for good luck.
He went up thither daily, till at last
She put on womanhood, and he lost peace,

394

And Deirdre's tale began. The King was old.
A month or so before the marriage-day,
A young man, in the laughing scorn of his youth,
Naoise, the son of Usna, climbed up there,
And having wooed, or, as some say, been wooed,
Carried her off.

SECOND MUSICIAN: The tale were well enough
Had it a finish.

FIRST MUSICIAN: Hush! I have more to tell;
But gather close about that I may whisper
The secrets of a king.

SECOND MUSICIAN: There's none to hear!

FIRST MUSICIAN: I have been to Conchubar's house and followed up
A crowd of servants going out and in
With loads upon their heads: embroideries
To hang upon the walls, or new-mown rushes
To strew upon the floors, and came at length
To a great room.

SECOND MUSICIAN: Be silent; there are steps!

[*Enter Fergus, an old man, who moves about from door to window
excitedly through what follows.*]

FERGUS: I thought to find a message from the King.
You are musicians by these instruments,
And if as seems—for you are comely women—
You can praise love, you'll have the best of luck,
For there'll be two, before the night is in,
That bargained for their love, and paid for it
All that men value. You have but the time
To weigh a happy music with a sad,
To find what is most pleasing to a lover,
Before the son of Usna and his queen
Have passed this threshold.

FIRST MUSICIAN: Deirdre and her man!

FERGUS: I was to have found a message in this house,
And ran to meet it. Is there no messenger
From Conchubar to Fergus, son of Rogh?

FIRST MUSICIAN: Are Deirdre and her lover tired of life?

FERGUS: You are not of this country, or you'd know
That they are in my charge and all forgiven.

FIRST MUSICIAN: We have no country but the roads of the world.

FERGUS: Then you should know that all things change in the world,
And hatred turns to love and love to hate,
And even kings forgive.

FIRST MUSICIAN: An old man's love
Who casts no second line is hard to cure;
His jealousy is like his love.

FERGUS: And that's but true.

You have learned something in your wanderings.
He was so hard to cure that the whole court,
But I alone, thought it impossible;
Yet after I had urged it at all seasons,
I had my way, and all's forgiven now;
And you shall speak the welcome and the joy
That I lack tongue for.

FIRST MUSICIAN: Yet old men are jealous.

FERGUS [*going to door*]: I am Conchubar's near friend, and that weighed
    somewhat,
And it was policy to pardon them.
The need of some young, famous, popular man
To lead the troops, the murmur of the crowd,
And his own natural impulse, urged him to it.
They have been wandering half a dozen years.

FIRST MUSICIAN: And yet old men are jealous.

FERGUS [*coming from door*]:   Sing the more sweetly
    Because, though age is arid as a bone,
This man has flowered. I've need of music, too;
If this grey head would suffer no reproach,
I'd dance and sing—
    [*Dark-faced men with strange, barbaric dress and arms begin to
    pass by the doors and windows. They pass one by one and in
    silence.*]
                    and dance till the hour ran out,
Because I have accomplished this good deed.

FIRST MUSICIAN: Look there—there at the window, those dark men,
    With murderous and outlandish-looking arms—
They've been about the house all day.

FERGUS [*looking after them*]:   What are you?
    Where do you come from, who is it sent you here?

FIRST MUSICIAN: They will not answer you.

FERGUS: They do not hear.

FIRST MUSICIAN: Forgive my open speech, but to these eyes
    That have seen many lands they are such men
As kings will gather for a murderous task
That neither bribes, commands, nor promises
Can bring their people to.

FERGUS: And that is why
    You harped upon an old man's jealousy.
A trifle sets you quaking. Conchubar's fame
Brings merchandise on every wind that blows.
They may have brought him Libyan dragon-skin,
Or the ivory of the fierce unicorn.

FIRST MUSICIAN: If these be merchants, I have seen the goods
    They have brought to Conchubar, and understood
His murderous purpose.

FERGUS: Murderous, you say?
Why, what new gossip of the roads is this?
But I'll not hear.
FIRST MUSICIAN: It may be life or death.
There is a room in Conchubar's house, and there—
FERGUS: Be silent, or I'll drive you from the door.
There's many a one that would do more than that,
And make it prison, or death, or banishment
To slander the High King.
[*Suddenly restraining himself and speaking gently.*]
He is my friend;
I have his oath, and I am well content.
I have known his mind as if it were my own
These many years, and there is none alive
Shall buzz against him, and I there to stop it.
I know myself, and him, and your wild thought
Fed on extravagant poetry, and lit
By such a dazzle of old fabulous tales
That common things are lost, and all that's strange
Is true because 'twere pity if it were not. [*Going to the door again.*]
Quick! quick! your instruments! they are coming now.
I hear the hoofs a-clatter. Begin that song!
But what is it to be? I'd have them hear
A music foaming up out of the house
Like wine out of a cup. Come now, a verse
Of some old time not worth remembering,
And all the lovelier because a bubble.
Begin, begin, of some old king and queen,
Of Lugaidh Redstripe or another; no, not him,
He and his lady perished wretchedly.

FIRST MUSICIAN [*singing*]:
"Why is it," Queen Edain said,
"If I do but climb the stair . . .

FERGUS: Ah! that is better. . . . They are alighted now.
Shake all your cockscombs, children; these are lovers.
[*Fergus goes out.*]

FIRST MUSICIAN:
"Why is it," Queen Edain said,
"If I do but climb the stair
To the tower overhead,
When the winds are calling there,
Or the gannets calling out
In waste places of the sky,
There's so much to think about
That I cry, that I cry?"

SECOND MUSICIAN:
But her goodman answered her:
  "Love would be a thing of naught
Had not all his limbs a stir
  Born out of immoderate thought;
Were he anything by half,
  Were his measure running dry.
Lovers, if they may not laugh,
  Have to cry, have to cry."

[*Deirdre, Naoise, and Fergus have been seen for a moment through the windows, but now they have entered.*]

THE THREE MUSICIANS [*together*]:
But is Edain worth a song
  Now the hunt begins anew?
Praise the beautiful and strong;
  Praise the redness of the yew;
Praise the blossoming apple-stem.
  But our silence had been wise.
What is all our praise to them
  That have one another's eyes?

DEIRDRE: Silence your music, though I thank you for it;
  But the wind's blown upon my hair, and I
  Must set the jewels on my neck and head
  For one that's coming.
NAOISE: Your colour has all gone
  As 'twere with fear, and there's no cause for that.
DEIRDRE: These women have the raddle that they use
  To make them brave and confident, although
  Dread, toil, or cold may chill the blood o' their cheeks.
  You'll help me, women. It is my husband's will
  I show my trust in one that may be here
  Before the mind can call the colour up.
  My husband took these rubies from a king
  Of Surracha that was so murderous
  He seemed all glittering dragon. Now wearing them
  Myself wars on myself, for I myself—
  That do my husband's will, yet fear to do it—
  Grow dragonish to myself.
      [*The women have gathered about her. Naoise has stood looking
      at her, but Fergus brings him to the chess-table.*]
NAOISE: No messenger!
  It's strange that there is none to welcome us.
FERGUS: King Conchubar has sent no messenger
  That he may come himself.
NAOISE: And being himself,

Being High King, he cannot break his faith.
I have his word and I must take that word,
Or prove myself unworthy of my nurture
Under a great man's roof.
FERGUS: We'll play at chess
  Till the King comes. It is but natural
  That she should doubt him, for her house has been
  The hole of the badger and the den of the fox.
NAOISE: If I had not King Conchubar's word I'd think
  That chess-board ominous.
FERGUS: How can a board
  That has been lying there these many years
  Be lucky or unlucky?
NAOISE: It is the board
  Where Lugaidh Redstripe and that wife of his,
  Who had a seamew's body half the year,
  Played at the chess upon the night they died.
FERGUS: I can remember now, a tale of treachery,
  A broken promise and a journey's end—
  But it were best forgot.
    [*Deirdre has been standing with the women about her. They have
    been helping her to put on her jewels and to put the pigment on
    her cheeks and arrange her hair. She has gradually grown atten-
    tive to what Fergus is saying.*]
NAOISE: If the tale's true,
  When it was plain that they had been betrayed,
  They moved the men and waited for the end
  As it were bedtime, and had so quiet minds
  They hardly winked their eyes when the sword flashed.
FERGUS: She never could have played so, being a woman,
  If she had not the cold sea's blood in her.
DEIRDRE: The gods turn clouds and casual accidents
  Into omens.
NAOISE: It would but ill become us,
  Now that King Conchubar has pledged his word,
  Should we be startled by a cloud or a shadow.
DEIRDRE: There's none to welcome us.
NAOISE: Being his guest,
  Words that would wrong him can but wrong ourselves.
DEIRDRE: An empty house upon the journey's end!
  Is that the way a king that means no mischief
  Honours a guest?
FERGUS: He is but making ready
  A welcome in his house, arranging where
  The moorhen and the mallard go, and where
  The speckled heathcock on a golden dish.
DEIRDRE: Had he no messenger?

NAOISE: Such words and fears
  Wrong this old man who's pledged his word to us.
  We must not speak or think as women do,
  That when the house is all abed sit up
  Marking among the ashes with a stick
  Till they are terrified.—Being what we are
  We must meet all things with an equal mind.
  [To Fergus.] Come, let us look if there's a messenger
  From Conchubar. We cannot see from this
  Because we are blinded by the leaves and twigs,
  But it may be the wood will thin again.
  It is but kind that when the lips we love
  Speak words that are unfitting for kings' ears
  Our ears be deaf.
FERGUS: But now I had to threaten
  These wanderers because they would have weighed
  Some crazy fantasy of their own brain
  Or gossip of the road with Conchubar's word.
  If I had thought so little of mankind
  I never could have moved him to this pardon.
  I have believed the best of every man,
  And find that to believe it is enough
  To make a bad man show him at his best,
  Or even a good man swing his lantern higher.

      [Naoise and Fergus go out. The last words are spoken as they go
      through the door. One can see them through part of what follows,
      either through door or window. They move about, talking or look-
      ing along the road towards Conchubar's house.]

FIRST MUSICIAN: If anything lies heavy on your heart,
  Speak freely of it, knowing it is certain
  That you will never see my face again.
DEIRDRE: You've been in love?
FIRST MUSICIAN: If you would speak of love,
  Speak freely. There is nothing in the world
  That has been friendly to us but the kisses
  That were upon our lips, and when we are old
  Their memory will be all the life we have.
DEIRDRE: There was a man that loved me. He was old;
  I could not love him. Now I can but fear.
  He has made promises, and brought me home;
  But though I turn it over in my thoughts,
  I cannot tell if they are sound and wholesome,
  Or hackles on the hook.
FIRST MUSICIAN: I have heard he loved you
  As some old miser loves the dragon-stone
  He hides among the cobwebs near the roof.

DEIRDRE: You mean that when a man who has loved like that
   Is after crossed, love drowns in its own flood,
   And that love drowned and floating is but hate;
   And that a king who hates sleeps ill at night
   Till he has killed; and that, though the day laughs,
   We shall be dead at cock-crow.

FIRST MUSICIAN: You've not my thought.
   When I lost one I loved distractedly,
   I blamed my crafty rival and not him,
   And fancied, till my passion had run out,
   That could I carry him away with me,
   And tell him all my love, I'd keep him yet.

DEIRDRE: Ah! now I catch your meaning, that this king
   Will murder Naoise, and keep me alive.

FIRST MUSICIAN: 'Tis you that put that meaning upon words
   Spoken at random.

DEIRDRE: Wanderers like you,
   Who have their wit alone to keep their lives,
   Speak nothing that is bitter to the ear
   At random; if they hint at it at all
   Their eyes and ears have gathered it so lately
   That it is crying out in them for speech.

FIRST MUSICIAN: We have little that is certain.

DEIRDRE: Certain or not,
   Speak it out quickly, I beseech you to it;
   I never have met any of your kind
   But that I gave them money, food, and fire.

FIRST MUSICIAN: There are strange, miracle-working, wicked stones,
   Men tear out of the heart and the hot brain
   Of Libyan dragons.

DEIRDRE: The hot Istain stone,
   And the cold stone of Fanes, that have power
   To stir even those at enmity to love.

FIRST MUSICIAN: They have so great an influence, if but sewn
   In the embroideries that curtain in
   The bridal bed.

DEIRDRE: O Mover of the stars
   That made this delicate house of ivory,
   And made my soul its mistress, keep it safe!

FIRST MUSICIAN: I have seen a bridal bed, so curtained in,
   So decked for miracle in Conchubar's house,
   And learned that a bride's coming.

DEIRDRE: And I the bride?
   Here is worse treachery than the seamew suffered,
   For she but died and mixed into the dust
   Of her dear comrade, but I am to live

And lie in the one bed with him I hate.
Where is Naoise? I was not alone like this
When Conchubar first chose me for his wife;
I cried in sleeping or waking and he came,
But now there is worse need.

NAOISE [*entering with Fergus*]:   Why have you called?
I was but standing there, without the door.

DEIRDRE: I have heard terrible mysterious things,
Magical horrors and the spells of wizards.

FERGUS: Why, that's no wonder. You have been listening
To singers of the roads that gather up
The stories of the world.

DEIRDRE: But I have one
To make the stories of the world but nothing.

NAOISE: Be silent if it is against the King
Whose guest you are.

FERGUS: No, let her speak it out.
I know the High King's heart as it were my own,
And can refute a slander, but already
I have warned these women that it may be death.

NAOISE: I will not weigh the gossip of the roads
With the King's word. I ask your pardon for her:
She has the heart of the wild birds that fear
The net of the fowler or the wicker cage.

DEIRDRE: Am I to see the fowler and the cage
And speak no word at all?

NAOISE: You would have known,
Had they not bred you in that mountainous place,
That when we give a word and take a word
Sorrow is put away, past wrong forgotten.

DEIRDRE: Though death may come of it?

NAOISE: Though death may come.

DEIRDRE: When first we came into this empty house
You had foreknowledge of our death, and even
When speaking of the paleness of my cheek
Your own cheek blanched.

NAOISE: Listen to this old man.
He can remember all the promises
We trusted to.

DEIRDRE: You speak from the lips out,
And I am pleading for your life and mine.

NAOISE: Listen to this old man, for many think
He has a golden tongue.

DEIRDRE: Then I will say
What it were best to carry to the grave.
Look at my face where the leaf raddled it

And at these rubies on my hair and breast.
It was for him, to stir him to desire,
I put on beauty; yes, for Conchubar.
NAOISE: What frenzy put these words into your mouth?
DEIRDRE: No frenzy, for what need is there for frenzy
  To change what shifts with every change of the wind,
  Or else there is no truth in men's old sayings?
  Was I not born a woman?
NAOISE: You're mocking me.
DEIRDRE: And is there mockery in this face and eyes,
  Or in this body, in these limbs that brought
  So many mischiefs? Look at me and say
  If that that shakes my limbs be mockery.
NAOISE: What woman is there that a man can trust
  But at the moment when he kisses her
  At the first midnight?
DEIRDRE: Were it not most strange
  That women should put evil in men's hearts
  And lack it in themselves? And yet I think
  That being half good I might change round again
  Were we aboard our ship and on the sea.
NAOISE: We'll to the horses and take ship again.
FERGUS: Fool, she but seeks to rouse your jealousy
  With crafty words.
DEIRDRE: Were we not born to wander?
  These jewels have been reaped by the innocent sword
  Upon a mountain, and a mountain bred me;
  But who can tell what change can come to love
  Among the valleys? I speak no falsehood now.
  Away to windy summits, and there mock
  The night-jar and the valley-keeping bird!
FERGUS: Men blamed you that you stirred a quarrel up
  That has brought death to many. I have made peace,
  Poured water on the fire, but if you fly
  King Conchubar may think that he is mocked
  And the house blaze again: and in what quarter,
  If Conchubar were the treacherous man you think,
  Would you find safety now that you have come
  Into the very middle of his power,
  Under his very eyes?
DEIRDRE: Under his eyes
  And in the very middle of his power!
  Then there is but one way to make all safe:
  I'll spoil this beauty that brought misery
  And houseless wandering on the man I loved.
  These wanderers will show me how to do it;

To clip this hair to baldness, blacken my skin
With walnut juice, and tear my face with briars.
O that the creatures of the woods had torn
My body with their claws!

FERGUS: What, wilder yet!

DEIRDRE [to Naoise]: Whatever were to happen to my face
I'd be myself, and there's not any way
But this to bring all trouble to an end.

NAOISE: Leave the gods' handiwork unblotched, and wait
For their decision, our decision is past.

                    [A Dark-faced Messenger comes to the threshold.]

FERGUS: Peace, peace; the messenger is at the door;
He stands upon the threshold; he stands there;
He stands, King Conchubar's purpose on his lips.

MESSENGER: Supper is on the table. Conchubar
Is waiting for his guests.

FERGUS: All's well again?
All's well! All's well! You cried your doubts so loud
That I had almost doubted.

NAOISE: We doubted him,
And he the while but busy in his house
For the more welcome.

DEIRDRE: The message is not finished.

FERGUS: Come quickly. Conchubar will laugh, that I—
Although I held out boldly in my speech—
That I, even I—

DEIRDRE: Wait, wait! He is not done.

MESSENGER: Deirdre and Fergus, son of Rogh, are summoned;
But not the traitor that bore off the Queen.
It is enough that the King pardon her,
And call her to his table and his bed.

NAOISE: So, then, it's treachery.

FERGUS: I'll not believe it.

NAOISE: Lead on and I will follow at your heels
That I may challenge him before his court
To match me there, or match me in some place
Where none can come between us but our swords,
For I have found no truth on any tongue
That's not of iron.

MESSENGER: I am Conchubar's man,
I am content to serve an iron tongue:
That Tongue commands that Fergus, son of Rogh,
And Deirdre come this night into his house,
And none but they.   [He goes, followed by Naoise.]

FERGUS: Some rogue, some enemy,
Has bribed him to embroil us with the King;
I know that he has lied because I know

King Conchubar's mind as if it were my own,
But I'll find out the truth.

[*He is about to follow Naoise, but Deirdre stops him.*]

DEIRDRE: No, no, old man.
You thought the best, and the worst came of it;
We listened to the counsel of the wise,
And so turned fools. But ride and bring your friends.
Go, and go quickly. Conchubar has not seen me;
It may be that his passion is asleep,
And that we may escape.

FERGUS: But I'll go first,
And follow up that Libyan heel, and send
Such words to Conchubar that he may know
At how great peril he lays hands upon you.

[*Naoise enters.*]

NAOISE: The Libyan, knowing that a servant's life
Is safe from hands like mine, but turned and mocked.

FERGUS: I'll call my friends, and call the reaping-hooks,
And carry you in safety to the ships.
My name has still some power. I will protect,
Or, if that is impossible, revenge. [*Goes out by other door.*]

NAOISE [*who is calm, like a man who has passed beyond life*]:
The crib has fallen and the birds are in it;
There is not one of the great oaks about us
But shades a hundred men.

DEIRDRE: Let's out and die,
Or break away, if the chance favour us.

NAOISE: They would but drag you from me, stained with blood.
Their barbarous weapons would but mar that beauty,
And I would have you die as a queen should—
In a death-chamber. You are in my charge.
We will wait here, and when they come upon us,
I'll hold them from the doors, and when that's over,
Give you a cleanly death with this grey edge.

DEIRDRE: I will stay here; but you go out and fight.
Our way of life has brought no friends to us,
And if we do not buy them leaving it,
We shall be ever friendless.

NAOISE: What do they say?
That Lugaidh Redstripe and that wife of his
Sat at this chess-board, waiting for their end.
They knew that there was nothing that could save them,
And so played chess as they had any night
For years, and waited for the stroke of sword.
I never heard a death so out of reach
Of common hearts, a high and comely end.
What need have I, that gave up all for love,

To die like an old king out of a fable,
Fighting and passionate? What need is there
For all that ostentation at my setting?
I have loved truly and betrayed no man.
I need no lightning at the end, no beating
In a vain fury at the cage's door.
[*To Musicians.*] Had you been here when that man and his queen
Played at so high a game, could you have found
An ancient poem for the praise of it?
It should have set out plainly that those two,
Because no man and woman have loved better,
Might sit on there contentedly, and weigh
The joy comes after. I have heard the seamew
Sat there, with all the colour in her cheeks,
As though she'd say: "There's nothing happening
But that a king and queen are playing chess."
DEIRDRE: He's in the right, though I have not been born
Of the cold, heighty waves, my veins being hot,
And though I have loved better than that queen,
I'll have as quiet fingers on the board.
O, singing women, set it down in a book,
That love is all we need, even though it is
But the last drops we gather up like this;
And though the drops are all we have known of life,
For we have been most friendless—praise us for it,
And praise the double sunset, for naught's lacking
But a good end to the long, cloudy day.
NAOISE: Light torches there and drive the shadows out,
For day's grey end comes up.
[*A Musician lights a torch in the fire and then crosses before the chess-players, and slowly lights the torches in the sconces. The light is almost gone from the wood, but there is a clear evening light in the sky, increasing the sense of solitude and loneliness.*]
DEIRDRE: Make no sad music.
What is it but a king and queen at chess?
They need a music that can mix itself
Into imagination, but not break
The steady thinking that the hard game needs.
[*During the chess, the Musicians sing this song*]
Love is an immoderate thing
And can never be content
Till it dip an ageing wing
Where some laughing element
Leaps and Time's old lanthorn dims.
What's the merit in love-play,
In the tumult of the limbs
That dies out before 'tis day,

> Heart on heart, or mouth on mouth,
>   All that mingling of our breath,
>   When love-longing is but drouth
>   For the things come after death?

[*During the last verses Deirdre rises from the board and kneels at Naoise's feet.*]

DEIRDRE: I cannot go on playing like that woman
  That had but the cold blood of the sea in her veins.
NAOISE: It is your move. Take up your man again.
DEIRDRE: Do you remember that first night in the woods
  We lay all night on leaves, and looking up,
  When the first grey of the dawn awoke the birds,
  Saw leaves above us? You thought that I still slept,
  And bending down to kiss me on the eyes,
  Found they were open. Bend and kiss me now,
  For it may be the last before our death.
  And when that's over, we'll be different;
  Imperishable things, a cloud or a fire.
  And I know nothing but this body, nothing
  But that old vehement, bewildering kiss.

                           [*Conchubar comes to the door.*]
FIRST MUSICIAN: Children beware!
NAOISE [*laughing*]:   He has taken up my challenge;
  Whether I am a ghost or living man
  When day has broken, I'll forget the rest,
  And say that there is kingly stuff in him.

   [*Turns to fetch spear and shield, and then sees that Conchubar has
   gone.*]

FIRST MUSICIAN: He came to spy upon you, not to fight.
NAOISE: A prudent hunter, therefore, but no king.
  He'd find if what has fallen in the pit
  Were worth the hunting, but has come too near,
  And I turn hunter. You're not man, but beast.
  Go scurry in the bushes, now, beast, beast,
  For now it's topsy-turvy, I upon you.

                           [*He rushes out after Conchubar.*]
DEIRDRE: You have a knife there, thrust into your girdle.
  I'd have you give it me.
FIRST MUSICIAN: No, but I dare not.
DEIRDRE: No, but you must.
FIRST MUSICIAN: If harm should come to you,
  They'd know I gave it.
DEIRDRE [*snatching knife*]: There is no mark on this
  To make it different from any other
  Out of a common forge.   [*Goes to the door and looks out.*]
FIRST MUSICIAN: You have taken it,
  I did not give it you; but there are times

When such a thing is all the friend one has.

DEIRDRE: The leaves hide all, and there's no way to find
What path to follow. Why is there no sound?

　　　　　　　　　　　　　　　　[She goes from door to window.]

FIRST MUSICIAN: Where would you go?

DEIRDRE: 　　　　　　　　　　　To strike a blow for Naoise,
If Conchubar call the Libyans to his aid.
But why is there no clash? They have met by this!

FIRST MUSICIAN: Listen. I am called wise. If Conchubar win,
You have a woman's wile that can do much,
Even with men in pride of victory.
He is in love and old. What were one knife
Among a hundred?

DEIRDRE *[going towards them]*: Women, if I die,
If Naoise die this night, how will you praise?
What words seek out? for that will stand to you;
For being but dead we shall have many friends.
All through your wanderings, the doors of kings
Shall be thrown wider open, the poor man's hearth
Heaped with new turf, because you are wearing this

　　　　　　　　　　　　　　　　[Gives Musician a bracelet.]

To show that you have Deirdre's story right.

FIRST MUSICIAN: Have you not been paid servants in love's house
To sweep the ashes out and keep the doors?
And though you have suffered all for love's sake
You'd live your lives again.

DEIRDRE: 　　　　　　　　Even this last hour.

　　　　　　　[Conchubar enters with dark-faced men.]

CONCHUBAR: One woman and two men; that is the quarrel
That knows no mending. Bring in the man she chose
Because of his beauty and the strength of his youth.

　　　　　[The dark-faced men drag in Naoise entangled in a net.]

NAOISE: I have been taken like a bird or a fish.

CONCHUBAR: He cried "Beast, beast!" and in a blind-beast rage
He ran at me and fell into the nets,
But we were careful for your sake, and took him
With all the comeliness that woke desire
Unbroken in him. I being old and lenient,
I would not hurt a hair upon his head.

DEIRDRE: What do you say? Have you forgiven him?

NAOISE: He is but mocking us. What's left to say
Now that the seven years' hunt is at an end?

DEIRDRE: He never doubted you until I made him,
And therefore all the blame for what he says
Should fall on me.

CONCHUBAR: 　　　　　But his young blood is hot,
And if we're of one mind, he shall go free,

And I ask nothing for it, or, if something,
Nothing I could not take. There is no king
In the wide world that, being so greatly wronged,
Could copy me, and give all vengeance up.
Although her marriage-day had all but come,
You carried her away; but I'll show mercy.
Because you had the insolent strength of youth
You carried her away; but I've had time
To think it out through all these seven years.
I will show mercy.

NAOISE: You have many words.

CONCHUBAR: I will not make a bargain; I but ask
What is already mine.

> [*Deirdre moves slowly towards Conchubar while he is speaking,
> her eyes fixed upon him.*]

                              You may go free
If Deirdre will but walk into my house
Before the people's eyes, that they may know,
When I have put the crown upon her head,
I have not taken her by force and guile.
The doors are open, and the floors are strewed
And in the bridal chamber curtains sewn
With all enchantments that give happiness
By races that are germane to the sun,
And nearest him, and have no blood in their veins—
For when they're wounded the wound drips with wine—
Nor speech but singing. At the bridal door
Two fair king's daughters carry in their hands
The crown and robe.

DEIRDRE: O no! Not that, not that!
Ask any other thing but that one thing,
Leave me with Naoise. We will go away
Into some country at the ends of the earth.
We'll trouble you no more; and there is no one
That will not praise you if you pardon us.
"He is good, he is good," they'll say to one another;
"There's nobody like him, for he forgave
Deirdre and Naoise."

CONCHUBAR: Do you think that I
Shall let you go again, after seven years
Of longing, and of planning here and there,
And trafficking with merchants for the stones
That make all sure, and watching my own face
That none might read it?

DEIRDRE [*to Naoise*]:   It's better to go with him.
Why should you die when one can bear it all?
My life is over; it's better to obey.

Why should you die? I will not live long, Naoise.
I'd not have you believe I'd long stay living;
O no, no, no! You will go far away.
You will forget me. Speak, speak, Naoise, speak,
And say that it is better that I go.
I will not ask it. Do not speak a word,
For I will take it all upon myself.
Conchubar, I will go.

NAOISE: And do you think
That, were I given life at such a price,
I would not cast it from me? O my eagle!
Why do you beat vain wings upon the rock
When hollow night's above?

DEIRDRE: It's better, Naoise.
It may be hard for you, but you'll forget.
For what am I, to be remembered always?
And there are other women. There was one,
The daughter of the King of Leodas;
I could not sleep because of her. Speak to him;
Tell it out plain, and make him understand.
And if it be he thinks I shall stay living,
Say that I will not.

NAOISE: Would I had lost life
Among those Scottish kings that sought it of me
Because you were my wife, or that the worst
Had taken you before this bargaining!
O eagle! If you were to do this thing,
And buy my life of Conchubar with your body,
Love's law being broken, I would stand alone
Upon the eternal summits, and call out,
And you could never come there, being banished.

DEIRDRE [*kneeling to Conchubar*]: I would obey, but cannot. Pardon us.
I know that you are good. I have heard you praised
For giving gifts; and you will pardon us,
Although I cannot go into your house.
It was my fault. I only should be punished.

                    [*Unseen by Deirdre, Naoise is gagged.*]
The very moment these eyes fell on him,
I told him; I held out my hands to him;
How could he refuse? At first he would not—
I am not lying—he remembered you.
What do I say? My hands?—No, no, my lips—
For I had pressed my lips upon his lips—
I swear it is not false—my breast to his;

    [*Conchubar motions; Naoise, unseen by Deirdre, is taken behind
    the curtain.*]
Until I woke the passion that's in all,

And how could he resist? I had my beauty.
You may have need of him, a brave, strong man,
Who is not foolish at the council-board,
Nor does he quarrel by the candle-light
And give hard blows to dogs. A cup of wine
Moves him to mirth, not madness.   [*She stands up.*]
                                  What am I saying?
You may have need of him, for you have none
Who is so good a sword, or so well loved
Among the common people. You may need him,
And what king knows when the hour of need may come?
You dream that you have men enough. You laugh.
Yes; you are laughing to yourself. You say,
"I am Conchubar—I have no need of him."
You will cry out for him some day and say,
"If Naoise were but living"—[*she misses Naoise*]. Where is he?
Where have you sent him? Where is the son of Usna?
Where is he, O, where is he?
   [*She staggers over to the Musicians. The Executioner has come out
   with a sword on which there is blood; Conchubar points to it. The
   Musicians give a wail.*]
CONCHUBAR: The traitor who has carried off my wife
   No longer lives. Come to my house now, Deirdre,
   For he that called himself your husband's dead.
DEIRDRE: O, do not touch me. Let me go to him.   [*Pause.*]
   King Conchubar is right. My husband's dead.
   A single woman is of no account,
   Lacking array of servants, linen cupboards,
   The bacon hanging—and King Conchubar's house
   All ready, too—I'll to King Conchubar's house.
   It is but wisdom to do willingly
   What has to be.
CONCHUBAR: But why are you so calm?
   I thought that you would curse me and cry out,
   And fall upon the ground and tear your hair.
DEIRDRE [*laughing*]: You know too much of women to think so;
   Though, if I were less worthy of desire,
   I would pretend as much; but, being myself,
   It is enough that you were master here.
   Although we are so delicately made,
   There's something brutal in us, and we are won
   By those who can shed blood. It was some woman
   That taught you how to woo: but do not touch me:
   I shall do all you bid me, but not yet,
   Because I have to do what's customary.
   We lay the dead out, folding up the hands,
   Closing the eyes, and stretching out the feet,

> And push a pillow underneath the head,
> Till all's in order; and all this I'll do
> For Naoise, son of Usna.

CONCHUBAR: It is not fitting.
> You are not now a wanderer, but a queen,
> And there are plenty that can do these things.

DEIRDRE [*motioning Conchubar away*]: No, no. Not yet. I cannot be
>   your queen.
> Till the past's finished, and its debts are paid.
> When a man dies, and there are debts unpaid,
> He wanders by the debtor's bed and cries,
> "There's so much owing."

CONCHUBAR: You are deceiving me.
> You long to look upon his face again.
> Why should I give you now to a dead man
> That took you from a living?   [*He makes a step towards her.*]

DEIRDRE: In good time.
> You'll stir me to more passion than he could,
> And yet, if you are wise, you'll grant me this:
> That I go look upon him that was once
> So strong and comely and held his head so high
> That women envied me. For I will see him
> All blood-bedabbled and his beauty gone.
> It's better, when you're beside me in your strength,
> That the mind's eye should call up the soiled body,
> And not the shape I loved. Look at him, women.
> He heard me pleading to be given up,
> Although my lover was still living, and yet
> He doubts my purpose. I will have you tell him
> How changeable all women are; how soon
> Even the best of lovers is forgot
> When his day's finished.

CONCHUBAR: No; but I will trust
> The strength that you have praised, and not your purpose.

DEIRDRE [*almost with a caress*]: It is so small a gift and you will grant it
> Because it is the first that I have asked.
> He has refused. There is no sap in him;
> Nothing but empty veins. I thought as much.
> He has refused me the first thing I have asked—
> Me, me, his wife. I understand him now;
> I know the sort of life I'll have with him;
> But he must drag me to his house by force.
> If he refuses [*she laughs*], he shall be mocked of all.
> They'll say to one another, "Look at him
> That is so jealous that he lured a man
> From over sea, and murdered him, and yet

He trembled at the thought of a dead face!"
                              [*She has her hand upon the curtain.*]
CONCHUBAR: How do I know that you have not some knife,
  And go to die upon his body?
DEIRDRE: Have me searched,
  If you would make so little of your queen.
  It may be that I have a knife hid here
  Under my dress. Bid one of these dark slaves
  To search me for it.   [*Pause.*]
CONCHUBAR: Go to your farewells, Queen.
DEIRDRE: Now strike the wire, and sing to it a while,
  Knowing that all is happy, and that you know
  Within what bride-bed I shall lie this night,
  And by what man, and lie close up to him,
  For the bed's narrow, and there outsleep the cockcrow.
                              [*She goes behind the curtain.*]
FIRST MUSICIAN: They are gone, they are gone. The proud may lie by
    the proud.
SECOND MUSICIAN: Though we were bidden to sing, cry nothing loud.
FIRST MUSICIAN: They are gone, they are gone.
SECOND MUSICIAN: Whispering were enough.
FIRST MUSICIAN: Into the secret wilderness of their love.
SECOND MUSICIAN: A high, grey cairn. What more is to be said?
FIRST MUSICIAN: Eagles have gone into their cloudy bed.
    [*Shouting outside. Fergus enters. Many men with scythes and sickles
    and torches gather about the doors. The house is lit with the glare
    of their torches.*]
FERGUS: Where's Naoise, son of Usna, and his queen?
  I and a thousand reaping-hooks and scythes
  Demand him of you.
CONCHUBAR: You have come too late.
  I have accomplished all. Deirdre is mine;
  She is my queen, and no man can rob me.
  I had to climb the topmost bough, and pull
  This apple among the winds. Open the curtain
  That Fergus learn my triumph from her lips.
    [*The curtain is drawn back. The Musicians begin to keen with low
    voices.*]
  No, no; I'll not believe it. She is not dead—
  She cannot have escaped a second time!
FERGUS: King, she is dead; but lay no hand upon her.
  What's this but empty cage and tangled wire,
  Now the bird's gone? But I'll not have you touch it.
CONCHUBAR: You are all traitors, all against me—all.
  And she has deceived me for a second time;
  And every common man can keep his wife,

But not the King.

> [*Loud shouting outside:* "Death to Conchubar!" "Where is Naoise?"
> etc. *The dark-faced men gather round Conchubar and draw their
> swords; but he motions them away.*]

     I have no need of weapons,
There's not a traitor that dare stop my way.
Howl, if you will; but I, being King, did right
In choosing her most fitting to be Queen,
And letting no boy lover take the sway.

THE END

John Millington Synge
[1871-1909]

IN NEWTOWN LITTLE, a village near Dublin, John M. Synge was born on April 16, 1871. He was the youngest of five children and his father died when he was a year old. Until fourteen he attended private schools in Dublin and then studied with a tutor for several years. As a boy his main interest was nature, especially birds; he knew the habitat of every bird and could identify their songs. He developed an interest and considerable proficiency in music, playing very well the piano, the flute, and the violin. In '1888 he entered Trinity College in Dublin. He took prizes in Hebrew and Irish and graduated with a B.A. in 1892. He pursued his interest in music, obtained a scholarship at the Royal Irish Academy of Music in harmony and counterpoint, and then went to Germany to study music and the German language.

By 1894 he had changed his interest from music to literature, and wandered, mostly on foot, all over Germany, playing his fiddle for the poor people he met on the road or for those who gave him hospitality. He reached Paris in 1895 and lived in a garret, half-starving, lonely, and proud. In 1896 Yeats also visited Paris and was told of an Irishman living in the garret above him. Yeats advised Synge to go to the Aran Islands off the Galway coast and study the life there because it had never been expressed in literature. Synge went and was happy, he said, for the first time in his life, escaping "from the nullity of the rich and the squalor of the poor." However, Synge's health was poor and he could not remain on the island but had to travel back and forth from Dublin. He took his fiddle, conjuring tricks, and penny whistle with him when he went in order to entertain the islanders.

The Shadow of the Glen and *Riders to the Sea,* both finished in 1902–3, were based on stories which he heard on the islands, as was *The Playboy of the Western World,* written in 1905–6.

When the Abbey Theatre opened in 1904 he became, along with Yeats, one of its literary advisers. *Playboy* was produced there in 1907 and caused a riot. Yeats said they had seventy police-men inside the theatre and the newspapers said there were five hundred outside. It was strange that a man who so loved the people and their language, who took no political issue, who was simply amused and touched by reality should arouse such ani-mosity. Yeats attributed it to the people's anxiety to preserve old ways and old standards and their fear of new ones. Later, after Synge's death, his plays were both accepted and appreciated.

His last years were spent in Dublin, translating Villon and Petrarch and rewriting *Deirdre of the Sorrows,* an unfinished three-act play. He entered a nursing home, from which, he told a friend, he would never return. He was cheerful, however, even joking with the few friends who came to see him. He died there on March 24, 1909.

Synge was the first to raise the common Irish idiom to a high dramatic medium. He believed that all art is a collaboration between the writer and the people in that the playwright should use phrases which he has just heard. Thus it is necessary that the people's language be rich and full-flavored so that the writer's may also be rich and at the same time convey a sense of reality. On stage, Synge said, there must be not only reality but joy and that is why intellectual modern drama has failed, because the people have "grown sick of the false joy of the musical comedy that has been given them in place of the rich joy found only in what is superb and wild in reality."

Synge was not popular with the Dublin audience. His first production at the Abbey, *The Shadow of the Glen,* aroused hos-tility because the Irish felt it was an unfair picture of Irish mar-riage. Synge had found the raw material for the play in the Aran Islands, as he had found much of his material for his other work, including *Riders to the Sea* and *Playboy of the Western World. Playboy of the Western World* opened at the Abbey Theatre on January 26, 1907, to a full house, and the audience applauded the first act. After the first two acts of *Playboy,* the uncertain audience waited expectantly. But in the middle of the third act, at the mention of the word "shift," the audience began hissing and booing. Synge was again slandering the Irish character, particularly Irish women. General riot ensued, but the play continued and went on the following week. There was shouting and rioting in and out of the theatre, but the houses were full. Yeats returned from a trip to Scotland and called in the police. The play was roundly condemned in the theatre, in the street, and in the press as a slander on Ireland, but despite the riots and the bad response, the play was a financial success.

The germ for the play is to be found in Synge's *The Aran Islands.* An old man told him the story of a Connaught man who killed his father with a spade and fled to the island. The inhabitants hid him in a hole and kept him safe for weeks, though the police searched all over for him. Despite the reward offered for his capture, the people of the island refused to give him up. Their impulse was to protect criminals, according to Synge, because they felt a man would do no wrong unless driven by a passion which they considered as irresistible as the sea. The man was finally shipped safely to America.

Of this material, Synge created a dramatic masterpiece. Reading *The Aran Islands,* one finds it rather easy to accept Synge's statement that much of the flavor and beauty of his language comes from listening to the people themselves speak. Synge does with rural Irish folk language what later his successor at the Abbey, Sean O'Casey, does with the speech of the poor urban Irish—captures a rhythm and a flavor and a comic beauty which are unique and give life to the characters and the plays. But Synge's material was better for his purposes—the creation of a kind of folk poetry. There is more music in the language of Synge's peasants than in the speech of O'Casey's Dublin Irish.

The comedy of *Playboy* comes from its language, its characterizations, and its thematic development. The language of Pegeen and the peasants who visit her public house is comic

and creative, richly suited to the myth-making that begins with
the arrival of Christy and his strange tale of violence. The myth-
making, begun by Pegeen, creates a romantic story and a romantic hero out of Christy's deed. These people seem starved
for romantic heroes. Given weaklings like Shawn Keogh as the
only men left for women like Pegeen to marry, one can easily
understand the need. Christy's romantic image begins to take
shape in his own eyes, as well as in those of Pegeen and the
others. The cringing, father-dreading weakling begins to assume
the aspect of a real hero. Christy and his deed begin to appear
and sound like a parody of Sophocles' *Oedipus Rex*—a masterpiece of mythical and tragic beauty worked out of a remote
and primitive "dirty deed." Having begun to see himself through
the eyes of Pegeen's myth-making, Christy begins to feel himself a hero in earnest. With the coming of the races, Christy
proves himself worthy of the image. But the turnabout comes
when Christy's "da" appears, cut and bleeding, but alive. Christy
begins to fall in the eyes of his worshipers and as he suffers
downfall in their eyes, he gains stature as a true hero in his
own. His second attempt to dispatch his father is called a dirty
deed, for murder and violence are admirable only when given
the eyes and the voice of remote and romantic myth-making.
But Christy has found his strength and his true stature. His
once-tyrannical father now under control, Christy is ready for
adventure in earnest; he rejects the false myth-makers and
doubters and goes off with his da. Pegeen's belated lament is
her recognition of this loss: "I've lost the only Playboy of the
Western World."

The play seems, among other things, a satire on the Irish
themselves: their hero-worshiping, their blarney, is reduced to
empty lies and self-deception; they seem unable to distinguish
between the mythical romantic hero and the real hero. Perhaps
much of this truth, as well as the concern for Irish womanhood,
incited the Irish to riot. On a larger scale, the play might be
viewed as exploring the role of myth in history and the human
psyche—that all acts of violence are dirty deeds and all such
heroes merely killers. But the human being must romanticize
them with his myth-making, for all ordinary mortals leading

ordinary lives are starved for these romantic heroes. Of these pitiful Pegeens, Synge might say, as does Brecht's Galileo: "Pity the nation that needs heroes!" To top that, Synge also seems to be saying, "Pity the people who do not recognize their true heroes!"

Thus comedy, in *Playboy,* begins to explore depths of meaning and feeling usually attributed to tragedy. As in the work of his Russian contemporary, Anton Chekhov, Synge perceives human beings through a double focus—the comic and tragic, the ridiculous and the pathetic. Both bring drama to the point where comedy and tragedy meet and overlap. There is a sense in both that life, as in comedy, is not simply an amusing game, a ritual of the ridiculous, but that underneath that ritual men play with disaster. In this sense, the Playboy of the title is ironic and the Western refers not only to the Aran Islands but to the entire civilization that we now call the West.

DRAMATIC WORKS

In the Shadow of the Glen, 1903
Riders to the Sea, 1904
The Well of the Saints, 1905
The Playboy of the Western World, 1907
The Tinker's Wedding, 1908
Deirdre of the Sorrows, 1910

The
Playboy of
the Western World

A PLAY IN THREE ACTS

Persons in the Play

CHRISTOPHER MAHON
OLD MAHON *(his father, a squatter)*
MICHAEL JAMES FLAHERTY, called MICHAEL JAMES
(a publican)
MARGARET FLAHERTY, called PEGEEN MIKE
(his daughter)
WIDOW QUIN *(a woman of about thirty)*
SHAWN KEOGH *(her cousin, a young farmer)*
PHILLY CULLEN and JIMMY FARRELL
(small farmers)
SARA TANSEY, SUSAN BRADY, and HONOR BLAKE
(village girls)
A BELLMAN
SOME PEASANTS

The action takes place near a village, on a wild coast of Mayo. The first Act passes on an evening of autumn, the other two Acts on the following day.

ACT ONE

SCENE. *Country public-house or shebeen, very rough and untidy. There is a sort of counter on the right with shelves, holding many bottles and jugs, just seen above it. Empty barrels stand near the counter. At back, a little to left of counter, there is a door into the open air, then, more to the left, there is a settle with shelves above it, with more jugs, and a table beneath a window. At the left there is a large open fire-place, with turf fire, and a small door into inner room.* PEGEEN, *a wild-looking but fine girl, of about twenty, is writing at table. She is dressed in the usual peasant dress.*

PEGEEN [*slowly as she writes*]: Six yards of stuff for to make a yellow gown. A pair of lace boots with lengthy heels on them and brassy eyes. A hat is suited for a wedding-day. A fine tooth comb. To be sent with three barrels of porter in Jimmy Farrell's creel cart on the evening of the coming Fair to Mister Michael James Flaherty. With the best compliments of this season. Margaret Flaherty.

SHAWN KEOGH [*a fat and fair young man comes in as she signs, looks round awkwardly, when he sees she is alone*]: Where's himself?

PEGEEN [*without looking at him*]: He's coming. [*She directs the letter.*] To Mister Sheamus Mulroy, Wine and Spirit Dealer, Castlebar.

SHAWN [*uneasily*]: I didn't see him on the road.

PEGEEN: How would you see him [*licks stamp and puts it on letter*] and it dark night this half hour gone by?

SHAWN [*turning towards the door again*]: I stood a while outside wondering would I have a right to pass on or to walk in and see you, Pegeen Mike [*comes to fire*], and I could hear the cows breathing, and sighing in the stillness of the air, and not a step moving any place from this gate to the bridge.

PEGEEN [*putting letter in envelope*]: It's above at the cross-roads he is, meeting Philly Cullen; and a couple more are going along with him to Kate Cassidy's wake.

SHAWN [*looking at her blankly*]: And he's going that length in the dark night?

PEGEEN [*impatiently*]: He is surely, and leaving me lonesome on the scruff of the hill. [*She gets up and puts envelope on dresser, then winds clock.*] Isn't it long the nights are now, Shawn Keogh, to be leaving a poor girl with her own self counting the hours to the dawn of day?

SHAWN [*with awkward humour*]: If it is, when we're wedded in a short while you'll have no call to complain, for I've little will to be walking off to wakes or weddings in the darkness of the night.

PEGEEN [*with rather scornful good humour*]: You're making mighty certain, Shaneen, that I'll wed you now.

SHAWN: Aren't we after making a good bargain, the way we're only waiting these days on Father Reilly's dispensation from the bishops, or the Court of Rome.

PEGEEN [*looking at him teasingly, washing up at dresser*]: It's a wonder, Shaneen, the Holy Father'd be taking notice of the likes of you; for if I was him I wouldn't bother with this place where you'll meet none but Red Linahan, has a squint in his eye, and Patcheen is lame in his heel, or the mad Mulrannies were driven from California and they lost in their wits. We're a queer lot these times to go troubling the Holy Father on his sacred seat.

SHAWN [*scandalized*]: If we are, we're as good this place as another, maybe, and as good these times as we were for ever.

PEGEEN [*with scorn*]: As good, is it? Where now will you meet the like of Daneen Sullivan knocked the eye from a peeler, or Marcus Quin, God rest him, got six months for maiming ewes, and he a great warrant to tell stories of holy Ireland till he'd have the old women shedding down tears about their feet. Where will you find the like of them, I'm saying?

SHAWN [*timidly*]: If you don't, it's a good job, maybe; for [*with peculiar emphasis on the words*] Father Reilly has small conceit to have that kind walking around and talking to the girls.

PEGEEN [*impatiently, throwing water from basin out of the door*]: Stop tormenting me with Father Reilly [*imitating his voice*] when I'm asking only what way I'll pass these twelve hours of dark, and not take my death with the fear. [*Looking out of door.*]

SHAWN [*timidly*]: Would I fetch you the Widow Quin, maybe?

PEGEEN: Is it the like of that murderer? You'll not, surely.

SHAWN [*going to her, soothingly*]: Then I'm thinking himself will stop along with you when he sees you taking on, for it'll be a long night-time with great darkness, and I'm after feeling a kind of fellow above in the furzy ditch, groaning wicked like a maddening dog, the way it's good cause you have, maybe, to be fearing now.

PEGEEN [*turning on him sharply*]: What's that? Is it a man you seen?

SHAWN [*retreating*]: I couldn't see him at all; but I heard him groaning out, and breaking his heart. It should have been a young man from his words speaking.

PEGEEN [*going after him*]: And you never went near to see was he hurted or what ailed him at all?

SHAWN: I did not, Pegeen Mike.

It was a dark, lonesome place to be hearing the like of him.

PEGEEN: Well, you're a daring fellow, and if they find his corpse stretched above in the dews of dawn, what'll you say then to the peelers, or the Justice of the Peace?

SHAWN [*thunderstruck*]: I wasn't thinking of that. For the love of God, Pegeen Mike, don't let on I was speaking of him. Don't tell your father and the men is coming above; for if they heard that story, they'd have great blabbing this night at the wake.

PEGEEN: I'll maybe tell them, and I'll maybe not.

SHAWN: They are coming at the door. Will you whisht, I'm saying?

PEGEEN: Whisht yourself.

[*She goes behind counter.* MICHAEL JAMES, *fat jovial publican, comes in followed by* PHILLY CULLEN, *who is thin and mistrusting, and* JIMMY FARRELL, *who is fat and amorous, about forty-five.*]

MEN [*together*]: God bless you. The blessing of God on this place.

PEGEEN: God bless you kindly.

MICHAEL [*to men who go to the counter*]: Sit down now, and take your rest. [*Crosses to* SHAWN *at the fire.*] And how is it you are, Shawn Keogh? Are you coming over the sands to Kate Cassidy's wake?

SHAWN: I am not, Michael James. I'm going home the short cut to my bed.

PEGEEN [*speaking across the counter*]: He's right too, and have you no shame, Michael James, to be quitting off for the whole

night, and leaving myself lonesome in the shop?

MICHAEL [*good-humouredly*]: Isn't it the same whether I go for the whole night or a part only? and I'm thinking it's a queer daughter you are if you'd have me crossing backward through the Stooks of the Dead Women, with a drop taken.

PEGEEN: If I am a queer daughter, it's a queer father'd be leaving me lonesome these twelve hours of dark, and I piling the turf with the dogs barking, and the calves mooing, and my own teeth rattling with the fear.

JIMMY [*flatteringly*]: What is there to hurt you, and you a fine, hardy girl would knock the head of any two men in the place?

PEGEEN [*working herself up*]: Isn't there the harvest boys with their tongues red for drink, and the ten tinkers is camped in the east glen, and the thousand militia—bad cess to them!—walking idle through the land. There's lots surely to hurt me, and I won't stop alone in it, let himself do what he will.

MICHAEL: If you're that afeard, let Shawn Keogh stop along with you. It's the will of God, I'm thinking, himself should be seeing to you now. [*They all turn on* SHAWN.]

SHAWN [*in horrified confusion*]: I would and welcome, Michael James, but I'm afeard of Father Reilly; and what at all would the Holy Father and the Cardinals of Rome be saying if they heard I did the like of that?

MICHAEL [*with contempt*]: God help you! Can't you sit in by the hearth with the light lit and herself beyond in the room? You'll do that surely, for I've heard tell there's a queer fellow above, going mad or getting his death, maybe, in the gripe of the ditch, so she'd be safer this night with a person here.

SHAWN [*with plaintive despair*]: I'm afeard of Father Reilly, I'm saying. Let you not be tempting me, and we near married itself.

PHILLY [*with cold contempt*]: Lock him in the west room. He'll stay then and have no sin to be telling to the priest.

MICHAEL [*to* SHAWN, *getting between him and the door*]: Go up now.

SHAWN [*at the top of his voice*]: Don't stop me, Michael James. Let me out of the door, I'm saying, for the love of the Almighty God. Let me out [*trying to dodge past him*]. Let me out of it, and may God grant you His indulgence in the hour of need.

MICHAEL [*loudly*]: Stop your noising, and sit down by the hearth. [*Gives him a push and goes to counter laughing.*]

SHAWN [*turning back, wringing his hands*]: Oh, Father Reilly and the saints of God, where will I hide myself today? Oh, St. Joseph and St. Patrick and St. Brigid, and St. James, have mercy on me now! [SHAWN *turns round, sees door clear, and makes a rush for it.*]

MICHAEL [*catching him by the coat-tail*]: You'd be going, is it?

SHAWN [*screaming*]: Leave me go, Michael James, leave me go, you old Pagan, leave me go, or I'll get the curse of the priests on you, and of the scarlet-coated bishops of the courts of Rome.

[*With a sudden movement he pulls himself out of his coat, and disappears out of the door, leaving his coat in* MICHAEL'S *hands.*]

MICHAEL [*turning round, and holding up coat*]: Well, there's the coat of a Christian man. Oh, there's sainted glory this day in the lonesome west; and by the will of God I've got you a decent man, Pegeen, you'll have no call to be spying after if you've a score of young girls, maybe, weeding in your fields.

PEGEEN [*taking up the defence of her property*]: What right have you to be making game of a poor fellow for minding the priest, when it's your own the fault is, not paying a penny pot-boy to stand along with me and give me courage in the doing of my work? [*She snaps the coat away from him, and goes behind counter with it.*]

MICHAEL [*taken aback*]: Where would I get a pot-boy? Would you have me send the bellman screaming in the streets of Castlebar?

SHAWN [*opening the door a chink and putting in his head, in a small voice*]: Michael James!

MICHAEL [*imitating him*]: What ails you?

SHAWN: The queer dying fellow's beyond looking over the ditch. He's come up, I'm thinking, stealing your hens. [*Looks over his shoulder.*] God help me, he's following me now [*he runs into room*], and if he's heard what I said, he'll be having my life, and I going home lonesome in the darkness of the night.

[*For a perceptible moment they*

watch the door with curiosity. Some one coughs outside. Then CHRISTY MAHON, *a slight young man, comes in very tired and frightened and dirty.*]

CHRISTY [*in a small voice*]: God save all here!

MEN: God save you kindly.

CHRISTY [*going to the counter*]: I'd trouble you for a glass of porter, woman of the house. [*He puts down coin.*]

PEGEEN [*serving him*]: You're one of the tinkers, young fellow, is beyond camped in the glen?

CHRISTY: I am not; but I'm destroyed walking.

MICHAEL [*patronizingly*]: Let you come up then to the fire. You're looking famished with the cold.

CHRISTY: God reward you. [*He takes up his glass and goes a little way across to the left, then stops and looks about him.*] Is it often the police do be coming into this place, master of the house?

MICHAEL: If you'd come in in better hours, you'd have seen "Licensed for the sale of Beer and Spirits, to be consumed on the premises," written in white letters above the door, and what would the polis want spying on me, and not a decent house within four miles, the way every living Christian is a bona fide, saving one widow alone?

CHRISTY [*with relief*]: It's a safe house, so.

[*He goes over to the fire, sighing and moaning. Then he sits down, putting his glass beside him and begins gnawing a turnip, too miserable to feel the others staring at him with curiosity.*]

MICHAEL [*going after him*]: Is it yourself is fearing the polis? You're wanting, maybe?

CHRISTY: There's many wanting.

MICHAEL: Many surely, with the broken harvest and the ended wars. [*He picks up some stockings, etc., that are near the fire, and carries them away furtively.*] It should be larceny, I'm thinking?

CHRISTY [*dolefully*]: I had it in my mind it was a different word and a bigger.

PEGEEN: There's a queer lad. Were you never slapped in school, young fellow, that you don't know the name of your deed?

CHRISTY [*bashfully*]: I'm slow at learning, a middling scholar only.

MICHAEL: If you're a dunce itself, you'd have a right to know that larceny's robbing and stealing. Is it for the like of that you're wanting?

CHRISTY [*with a flash of family pride*]: And I the son of a strong farmer [*with a sudden qualm*], God rest his soul, could have bought up the whole of your old house a while since, from the butt of his tailpocket, and not have missed the weight of it gone.

MICHAEL [*impressed*]: If it's not stealing, it's maybe something big.

CHRISTY [*flattered*]: Aye; it's maybe something big.

JIMMY: He's a wicked-looking young fellow. Maybe he followed after a young woman on a lonesome night.

CHRISTY [*shocked*]: Oh, the saints forbid, mister; I was all times a decent lad.

PHILLY [*turning on* JIMMY]: You're

a silly man, Jimmy Farrell. He said his father was a farmer a while since, and there's himself now in a poor state. Maybe the land was grabbed from him, and he did what any decent man would do.

MICHAEL [*to* CHRISTY, *mysteriously*]: Was it bailiffs?

CHRISTY: The divil a one.

MICHAEL: Agents?

CHRISTY: The divil a one.

MICHAEL: Landlords?

CHRISTY [*peevishly*]: Ah, not at all, I'm saying. You'd see the like of them stories on any little paper of a Munster town. But I'm not calling to mind any person, gentle, simple, judge or jury, did the like of me.

[*They all draw nearer with delighted curiosity.*]

PHILLY: Well, that lad's a puzzle-the-world.

JIMMY: He'd beat Dan Davies' circus, or the holy missioners making sermons on the villainy of man. Try him again, Philly.

PHILLY: Did you strike golden guineas out of solder, young fellow, or shilling coins itself?

CHRISTY: I did not, mister, not sixpence nor a farthing coin.

JIMMY: Did you marry three wives maybe? I'm told there's a sprinkling have done that among the holy Luthers of the preaching north.

CHRISTY [*shyly*]: I never married with one, let alone with a couple or three.

PHILLY: Maybe he went fighting for the Boers, the like of the man beyond, was judged to be hanged, quartered and drawn. Were you off east, young fellow, fighting bloody wars for Kruger and the freedom of the Boers?

CHRISTY: I never left my own parish till Tuesday was a week.

PEGEEN [*coming from counter*]: He's done nothing, so. [*To* CHRISTY.] If you didn't commit murder or a bad, nasty thing, or false coining, or robbery, or butchery, or the like of them, there isn't anything that would be worth your troubling for to run from now. You did nothing at all.

CHRISTY [*his feelings hurt*]: That's an unkindly thing to be saying to a poor orphaned traveller, has a prison behind him, and hanging before, and hell's gap gaping below.

PEGEEN [*with a sign to the men to be quiet*]: You're only saying it. You did nothing at all. A soft lad the like of you wouldn't slit the windpipe of a screeching sow.

CHRISTY [*offended*]: You're not speaking the truth.

PEGEEN [*in mock rage*]: Not speaking the truth, is it? Would you have me knock the head of you with the butt of the broom?

CHRISTY [*twisting round on her with a sharp cry of horror*]: Don't strike me. I killed my poor father, Tuesday was a week, for doing the like of that.

PEGEEN [*with blank amazement*]: Is it killed your father?

CHRISTY [*subsiding*]: With the help of God I did surely, and that the Holy Immaculate Mother may intercede for his soul.

PHILLY [*retreating with* JIMMY]: There's a daring fellow.

JIMMY: Oh, glory be to God!

MICHAEL [*with great respect*]: That was a hanging crime, mister honey. You should have had good reason for doing the like of that.

CHRISTY [*in a very reasonable tone*]: He was a dirty man, God forgive him, and he getting old and crusty, the way I couldn't put up with him at all.

PEGEEN: And you shot him dead?

CHRISTY [*shaking his head*]: I never used weapons. I've no license, and I'm a law-fearing man.

MICHAEL: It was with a hilted knife maybe? I'm told, in the big world it's bloody knives they use.

CHRISTY [*loudly, scandalized*]: Do you take me for a slaughter-boy?

PEGEEN: You never hanged him, the way Jimmy Farrell hanged his dog from the license, and had it screeching and wriggling three hours at the butt of a string, and himself swearing it was a dead dog, and the peelers swearing it had life?

CHRISTY: I did not then. I just riz the loy and let fall the edge of it on the ridge of his skull, and he went down at my feet like an empty sack, and never let a grunt or groan from him at all.

MICHAEL [*making a sign to* PEGEEN *to fill* CHRISTY'S *glass*]: And what way weren't you hanged, mister? Did you bury him then?

CHRISTY [*considering*]: Aye. I buried him then. Wasn't I digging spuds in the field?

MICHAEL: And the peelers never followed after you the eleven days that you're out?

CHRISTY [*shaking his head*]: Never a one of them, and I walking forward facing hog, dog, or divil on the highway of the road.

PHILLY [*nodding wisely*]: It's only with a common week-day kind of a murderer them lads would be trusting their carcase, and that man should be a great terror when his temper's roused.

MICHAEL: He should then. [*To* CHRISTY.] And where was it, mister honey, that you did the deed?

CHRISTY [*looking at him with suspicion*]: Oh, a distant place, master of the house, a windy corner of high, distant hills.

PHILLY [*nodding with approval*]: He's a close man, and he's right, surely.

PEGEEN: That'd be a lad with the sense of Solomon to have for a pot-boy, Michael James, if it's the truth you're seeking one at all.

PHILLY: The peelers is fearing him, and if you'd that lad in the house there isn't one of them would come smelling around if the dogs itself were lapping poteen from the dung-pit of the yard.

JIMMY: Bravery's a treasure in a lonesome place, and a lad would kill his father, I'm thinking, would face a foxy divil with a pitchpike on the flags of hell.

PEGEEN: It's the truth they're saying, and if I'd that lad in the house, I wouldn't be fearing the looséd kharki cut-throats, or the walking dead.

CHRISTY [*swelling with surprise and triumph*]: Well, glory be to God!

MICHAEL [*with deference*]: Would

you think well to stop here and be pot-boy, mister honey, if we gave you good wages, and didn't destroy you with the weight of work?

SHAWN [*coming forward uneasily*]: That'd be a queer kind to bring into a decent quiet household with the like of Pegeen Mike.

PEGEEN [*very sharply*]: Will you whisht? Who's speaking to you?

SHAWN [*retreating*]: A bloody-handed murderer the like of . . .

PEGEEN [*snapping at him*]: Whisht I am saying; we'll take no fooling from your like at all. [*To* CHRISTY *with a honeyed voice.*] And you, young fellow, you'd have a right to stop, I'm thinking, for we'd do our all and utmost to content your needs.

CHRISTY [*overcome with wonder*]: And I'd be safe in this place from the searching law?

MICHAEL: You would, surely. If they're not fearing you, itself, the peelers in this place is decent droughty poor fellows, wouldn't touch a cur dog and not give warning in the dead of night.

PEGEEN [*very kindly and persuasively*]: Let you stop a short while anyhow. Aren't you destroyed walking with your feet in bleeding blisters, and your whole skin needing washing like a Wicklow sheep.

CHRISTY [*looking round with satisfaction*]: It's a nice room, and if it's not humbugging me you are, I'm thinking that I'll surely stay.

JIMMY [*jumps up*]: Now, by the grace of God, herself will be safe this night, with a man killed his father holding danger from the door, and let you come on, Michael James, or they'll have

the best stuff drunk at the wake.

MICHAEL [*going to the door with men*]: And begging your pardon, mister, what name will we call you, for we'd like to know?

CHRISTY: Christopher Mahon.

MICHAEL: Well, God bless you, Christy, and a good rest till we meet again when the sun'll be rising to the noon of day.

CHRISTY: God bless you all.

MEN: God bless you.

[*They go out except* SHAWN, *who lingers at door.*]

SHAWN [*to* PEGEEN]: Are you wanting me to stop along with you and keep you from harm?

PEGEEN [*gruffly*]: Didn't you say you were fearing Father Reilly?

SHAWN: There'd be no harm staying now, I'm thinking, and himself in it too.

PEGEEN: You wouldn't stay when there was need for you, and let you step off nimble this time when there's none.

SHAWN: Didn't I say it was Father Reilly . . .

PEGEEN: Go on, then, to Father Reilly [*in a jeering tone*], and let him put you in the holy brotherhoods, and leave that lad to me.

SHAWN: If I meet the Widow Quin . . .

PEGEEN: Go on, I'm saying, and don't be waking this place with your noise. [*She hustles him out and bolts the door.*] That lad would wear the spirits from the saints of peace. [*Bustles about, then takes off her apron and pins it up in the window as a blind,* CHRISTY *watching her timidly. Then she comes to him and speaks with bland good-humour.*] Let you stretch out now by the fire, young fellow. You should be destroyed travelling.

CHRISTY [*shyly again, drawing off his boots*]: I'm tired, surely, walking wild eleven days, and waking fearful in the night. [*He holds up one of his feet, feeling his blisters, and looking at them with compassion.*]

PEGEEN [*standing beside him, watching him with delight*]: You should have had great people in your family, I'm thinking, with the little, small feet you have, and you with a kind of a quality name, the like of what you'd find on the great powers and potentates of France and Spain.

CHRISTY [*with pride*]: We were great surely, with wide and windy acres of rich Munster land.

PEGEEN: Wasn't I telling you, and you a fine, handsome young fellow with a noble brow?

CHRISTY [*with a flash of delighted surprise*]: Is it me?

PEGEEN: Aye. Did you never hear that from the young girls where you come from in the west or south?

CHRISTY [*with venom*]: I did not then. Oh, they're bloody liars in the parish where I grew a man.

PEGEEN: If they are itself, you've heard it these days, I'm thinking, and you walking the world telling out your story to young girls or old.

CHRISTY: I've told my story no place till this night, Pegeen Mike, and it's foolish I was here, maybe, to be talking free, but you're decent people, I'm thinking, and yourself a kindly woman, the way I wasn't fearing you at all.

PEGEEN [*filling a sack with straw*]: You've said the like of that, maybe, in every cot and cabin where you've met a young girl on your way.

CHRISTY [*going over to her, gradually raising his voice*]: I've said it nowhere till this night, I'm telling you, for I've seen none the like of you the eleven long days I am walking the world, looking over a low ditch or a high ditch on my north or my south, into stony scattered fields, or scribes of bog, where you'd see young, limber girls, and fine prancing women making laughter with the men.

PEGEEN: If you weren't destroyed travelling, you'd have as much talk and streeleen, I'm thinking, as Owen Roe O'Sullivan or the poets of the Dingle Bay, and I've heard all times it's the poets are your like, fine fiery fellows with great rages when their temper's roused.

CHRISTY [*drawing a little nearer to her*]: You've a power of rings, God bless you, and would there be any offence if I was asking are you single now?

PEGEEN: What would I want wedding so young?

CHRISTY [*with relief*]: We're alike, so.

PEGEEN [*she puts sack on settle and beats it up*]: I never killed my father. I'd be afeard to do that, except I was the like of yourself with blind rages tearing me within, for I'm thinking you should have had great tussling when the end was come.

CHRISTY [*expanding with delight at the first confidential talk he has ever had with a woman*]: We had not then. It was a hard woman was come over the hill, and if he was always a crusty kind when he'd a hard woman setting him on, not the divil himself or his four fathers could put up with him at all.

PEGEEN [*with curiosity*]: And isn't it a great wonder that one wasn't fearing you?

CHRISTY [*very confidentially*]: Up to the day I killed my father, there wasn't a person in Ireland knew the kind I was, and I there drinking, waking, eating, sleeping, a quiet, simple poor fellow with no man giving me heed.

PEGEEN [*getting a quilt out of the cupboard and putting it on the sack*]: It was the girls were giving you heed maybe, and I'm thinking it's most conceit you'd have to be gaming with their like.

CHRISTY [*shaking his head, with simplicity*]: Not the girls itself, and I won't tell you a lie. There wasn't anyone heeding me in that place saving only the dumb beasts of the field. [*He sits down at fire.*]

PEGEEN [*with disappointment*]: And I thinking you should have been living the like of a king of Norway or the Eastern world. [*She comes and sits beside him after placing bread and mug of milk on the table.*]

CHRISTY [*laughing piteously*]: The like of a king, is it? And I after toiling, moiling, digging, dodging from the dawn till dusk with never a sight of joy or sport saving only when I'd be abroad in the dark night poaching rabbits on hills, for I was a devil to poach, God forgive me, [*very naïvely*] and I near got six months

for going with a dung fork and stabbing a fish.

PEGEEN: And it's that you'd call sport, is it, to be abroad in the darkness with yourself alone?

CHRISTY: I did, God help me, and there I'd be as happy as the sunshine of St. Martin's Day, watching the light passing the north or the patches of fog, till I'd hear a rabbit starting to screech and I'd go running in the furze. Then when I'd my full share I'd come walking down where you'd see the ducks and geese stretched sleeping on the highway of the road, and before I'd pass the dunghill, I'd hear himself snoring out, a loud lonesome snore he'd be making all times, the while he was sleeping, and he a man'd be raging all times, the while he was waking, like a gaudy officer you'd hear cursing and damning and swearing oaths.

PEGEEN: Providence and Mercy, spare us all!

CHRISTY: It's that you'd say surely if you seen him and he after drinking for weeks, rising up in the red dawn, or before it maybe, and going out into the yard as naked as an ash tree in the moon of May, and shying clods against the visage of the stars till he'd put the fear of death into the banbhs and the screeching sows.

PEGEEN: I'd be well-nigh afeard of that lad myself, I'm thinking. And there was no one in it but the two of you alone?

CHRISTY: The divil a one, though he'd sons and daughters walking all great states and territories of the world, and not a one of them, to this day, but would say their seven curses on him, and they rousing up to let a cough or sneeze, maybe, in the deadness of the night.

PEGEEN [*nodding her head*]: Well, you should have been a queer lot. I never cursed my father the like of that, though I'm twenty and more years of age.

CHRISTY: Then you'd have cursed mine, I'm telling you, and he a man never gave peace to any, saving when he'd get two months or three, or be locked in the asylums for battering peelers or assaulting men [*with depression*] the way it was a bitter life he led me till I did up a Tuesday and halve his skull.

PEGEEN [*putting her hand on his shoulder*]: Well, you'll have peace in this place, Christy Mahon, and none to trouble you, and it's near time a fine lad like you should have your good share of the earth.

CHRISTY: It's time surely, and I a seemly fellow with great strength in me and bravery of . . .

[*Someone knocks.*]

CHRISTY [*clinging to* PEGEEN]: Oh, glory! it's late for knocking, and this last while I'm in terror of the peelers, and the walking dead.

[*Knocking again.*]

PEGEEN: Who's there?
VOICE [*outside*]: Me.
PEGEEN: Who's me?
VOICE: The Widow Quin.
PEGEEN [*jumping up and giving him the bread and milk*]: Go on now with your supper, and let on to be sleepy, for if she found you were such a warrant to talk, she'd be stringing gabble till the dawn of day.

[*He takes bread and sits shyly with his back to the door.*]

PEGEEN [*opening door, with temper*]: What ails you, or what is it you're wanting at this hour of the night?

WIDOW QUIN [*coming in a step and peering at* CHRISTY]: I'm after meeting Shawn Keogh and Father Reilly below, who told me of your curiosity man, and they fearing by this time he was maybe roaring, romping on your hands with drink.

PEGEEN [*pointing to* CHRISTY]: Look now is he roaring, and he stretched away drowsy with his supper and his mug of milk. Walk down and tell that to Father Reilly and to Shaneen Keogh.

WIDOW QUIN [*coming forward*]: I'll not see them again, for I've their word to lead that lad forward for to lodge with me.

PEGEEN [*in blank amazement*]: This night, is it?

WIDOW QUIN [*going over*]: This night. "It isn't fitting," says the priesteen, "to have his likeness lodging with an orphaned girl." [*To* CHRISTY.] God save you, mister!

CHRISTY [*shyly*]: God save you kindly.

WIDOW QUIN [*looking at him with half-amazed curiosity*]: Well, aren't you a little smiling fellow? It should have been great and bitter torments did rouse your spirits to a deed of blood.

CHRISTY [*doubtfully*]: It should, maybe.

WIDOW QUIN: It's more than "maybe" I'm saying, and it'd soften my heart to see you sitting so simple with your cup and cake, and you fitter to be saying your catechism than slaying your da.

PEGEEN [*at counter, washing glasses*]: There's talking when any'd see he's fit to be holding his head high with the wonders of the world. Walk on from this, for I'll not have him tormented and he destroyed travelling since Tuesday was a week.

WIDOW QUIN [*peaceably*]: We'll be walking surely when his supper's done, and you'll find we're great company, young fellow, when it's of the like of you and me you'd hear the penny poets singing in an August Fair.

CHRISTY [*innocently*]: Did you kill your father?

PEGEEN [*contemptuously*]: She did not. She hit himself with a worn pick, and the rusted poison did corrode his blood the way he never overed it, and died after. That was a sneaky kind of murder did win small glory with the boys itself. [*She crosses to* CHRISTY's *left.*]

WIDOW QUIN [*with good-humour*]: If it didn't, maybe all knows a widow woman has buried her children and destroyed her man is a wiser comrade for a young lad than a girl, the like of you, who'd go helter-skeltering after any man would let you a wink upon the road.

PEGEEN [*breaking out into wild rage*]: And you'll say that, Widow Quin, and you gasping with the rage you had racing the hill beyond to look on his face.

WIDOW QUIN [*laughing derisively*]: Me, is it? Well, Father Reilly has cuteness to divide you now. [*She pulls* CHRISTY *up.*] There's great temptation in a man did slay his da, and we'd best be going, young fellow; so rise up and come with me.

PEGEEN [*seizing his arm*]: He'll not stir. He's pot-boy in this place, and I'll not have him stolen off and kidnabbed while himself's abroad.

WIDOW QUIN: It'd be a crazy pot-boy'd lodge him in the shebeen where he works by day, so you'd have a right to come on, young fellow, till you see my little houseen, a perch off on the rising hill.

PEGEEN: Wait till morning, Christy Mahon. Wait till you lay eyes on her leaky thatch is growing more pasture for her buck goat than her square of fields, and she without a tramp itself to keep in order her place at all.

WIDOW QUIN: When you see me contriving in my little gardens, Christy Mahon, you'll swear the Lord God formed me to be living lone, and that there isn't my match in Mayo for thatching, or mowing, or shearing a sheep.

PEGEEN [*with noisy scorn*]: It's true the Lord God formed you to contrive indeed. Doesn't the world know you reared a black lamb at your own breast, so that the Lord Bishop of Connaught felt the elements of a Christian, and he eating it after in a kidney stew? Doesn't the world know you've been seen shaving the foxy skipper from France for a threepenny bit and a sop of grass tobacco would wring the liver from a mountain goat you'd meet leaping the hills?

WIDOW QUIN [*with amazement*]: Do you hear her now, young fellow? Do you hear the way she'll be rating at your own self when a week is by?

PEGEEN [*to* CHRISTY]: Don't heed her. Tell her to go into her pigsty and not plague us here.

WIDOW QUIN: I'm going; but he'll come with me.

PEGEEN [*shaking him*]: Are you dumb, young fellow?

CHRISTY [*timidly, to* WIDOW QUIN]: God increase you; but I'm potboy in this place, and it's here I'd liefer stay.

PEGEEN [*triumphantly*]: Now you have heard him, and go on from this.

WIDOW QUIN [*looking round the room*]: It's lonesome this hour crossing the hill, and if he won't come along with me, I'd have a right maybe to stop this night with yourselves. Let me stretch out on the settle, Pegeen Mike; and himself can lie by the hearth.

PEGEEN [*short and fiercely*]: Faith, I won't. Quit off or I will send you now.

WIDOW QUIN [*gathering her shawl up*]: Well, it's a terror to be aged a score. [*To* CHRISTY.] God bless you now, young fellow, and let you be wary, or there's right torment will await you here if you go romancing with her like, and she waiting only, as they bade me say, on a sheepskin parchment to be wed with Shawn Keogh of Killakeen.

CHRISTY [*going to* PEGEEN *as she bolts the door*]: What's that she's after saying?

PEGEEN: Lies and blather, you've no call to mind. Well, isn't Shawn Keoghan an impudent fellow to send up spying on me? Wait till I lay hands on him. Let him wait, I'm saying.

CHRISTY: And you're not wedding him at all?

PEGEEN: I wouldn't wed him if a bishop came walking for to join us here.

CHRISTY: That God in glory may be thanked for that.

PEGEEN: There's your bed now. I've put a quilt upon you I'm after quilting a while since with my own two hands, and you'd best stretch out now for your sleep, and may God give you a good rest till I call you in the morning when the cocks will crow.

CHRISTY [*as she goes to inner room*]: May God bless you and Mary and St. Patrick bless you and reward .you, for your kindly talk. [*She shuts the door behind her. He settles his bed slowly, feeling the quilt with immense satisfaction.*] Well, it's a clean bed and soft with it, and it's great luck and company I've won me in the end of time—two fine women fighting for the likes of me—till I'm thinking this night wasn't I a foolish fellow not to kill my father in the years gone by.

CURTAIN

ACT TWO

SCENE, *as before. Brilliant morning light.* CHRISTY, *looking bright and cheerful, is cleaning a girl's boots.*

CHRISTY [*to himself, counting jugs on dresser*]: Half a hundred beyond. Ten there. A score that's above. Eighty jugs. Six cups and a broken one. Two plates. A power of glasses. Bottles, a school-master'd be hard set to count, and enough in them, I'm thinking, to drunken all the wealth and wisdom of the County Clare. [*He puts down the boot carefully.*] There's her boots now, nice and decent for her evening use, and isn't it grand brushes she has? [*He puts them down and goes by degrees to the looking-glass.*] Well, this'd be a fine place to be my whole life talking out with swearing Christians, in place of my old dogs and cat, and I stalking around, smoking my pipe and drinking my fill, and never a day's work but drawing a cork an odd time, or wiping a glass, or rinsing out a shiny tumbler for a decent man. [*He takes the looking-glass from the wall and puts it on the back of a chair; then sits down in front of it and begins washing his face.*] Didn't I know rightly I was handsome, though it was the divil's own mirror we had beyond, would twist a squint across an angel's brow; and I'll be growing fine from this day, the way I'll have a soft lovely skin on me and won't be the like of the clumsy young fellows do be ploughing all times in the earth and dung. [*He starts.*] Is she coming again? [*He looks out.*] Stranger girls. God help me, where'll I hide myself away and my long neck naked to the world? [*He looks out.*] I'd best go to the room maybe till I'm dressed again.

[*He gathers up his coat and the looking-glass, and runs into the inner room. The door is pushed open, and* SUSAN BRADY *looks in, and knocks on door.*]

SUSAN: There's nobody in it. [*Knocks again.*]

NELLY [*pushing her in and following her, with* HONOR BLAKE *and* SARA TANSEY]: It'd be early for them both to be out walking the hill.

SUSAN: I'm thinking Shawn Keogh was making game of us and there's no such man in it at all.

HONOR [*pointing to straw and quilt*]: Look at that. He's been sleeping there in the night. Well, it'll be a hard case if he's gone off now, the way we'll never set our eyes on a man killed his father, and we after rising early and destroying ourselves running fast on the hill.

435

NELLY: Are you thinking them's his boots?

SARA [*taking them up*]: If they are, there should be his father's track on them. Did you never read in the papers the way murdered men do bleed and drip?

SUSAN: Is that blood there, Sara Tansey?

SARA [*smelling it*]: That's bog water, I'm thinking, but it's his own they are surely, for I never seen the like of them for whity mud, and red mud, and turf on them, and the fine sands of the sea. That man's been walking, I'm telling you. [*She goes down right, putting on one of his boots.*]

SUSAN [*going to window*]: Maybe he's stolen off to Belmullet with the boots of Michael James, and you'd have a right so to follow after him, Sara Tansey, and you the one yoked the ass cart and drove ten miles to set your eyes on the man bit the yellow lady's nostril on the northern shore. [*She looks out.*]

SARA [*running to window with one boot on*]: Don't be talking, and we fooled today. [*Putting on other boot.*] There's a pair do fit me well, and I'll be keeping them for walking to the priest, when you'd be ashamed this place, going up winter and summer with nothing worth while to confess at all.

HONOR [*who has been listening at the door*]: Whisht! there's someone inside the room. [*She pushes door a chink open.*] It's a man.

[SARA *kicks off boots and puts them* where they were. They all stand in a line looking through chink.]

SARA: I'll call him. Mister! Mister! [*He puts in his head.*] Is Pegeen within?

CHRISTY [*coming in as meek as a mouse, with the looking-glass held behind his back*]: She's above on the cnuceen, seeking the nanny goats, the way she'd have a sup of goat's milk for to colour my tea.

SARA: And asking your pardon, is it you's the man killed his father?

CHRISTY [*sidling toward the nail where the glass was hanging*]: I am, God help me!

SARA [*taking eggs she has brought*]: Then my thousand welcomes to you, and I've run up with a brace of duck's eggs for your food today. Pegeen's ducks is no use, but these are the real rich sort. Hold out your hand and you'll see it's no lie I'm telling you.

CHRISTY [*coming forward shyly, and holding out his left hand*]: They're a great and weighty size.

SUSAN: And I run up with a pat of butter, for it'd be a poor thing to have you eating your spuds dry, and you after running a great way since you did destroy your da.

CHRISTY: Thank you kindly.

HONOR: And I brought you a little cut of cake, for you should have a thin stomach on you, and you that length walking the world.

NELLY: And I brought you a little laying pullet—boiled and all she is—was crushed at the fall o night by the curate's car. Feel the fat of that breast, mister.

CHRISTY: It's bursting, surely. [*He feels it with the back of his hand, in which he holds the presents.*]

SARA: Will you pinch it? Is your right hand too sacred for to use at all? [*She slips round behind him.*] It's a glass he has. Well, I never seen to this day a man with a looking-glass held to his back. Them that kills their fathers is a vain lot surely.

[*Girls giggle.*]

CHRISTY [*smiling innocently and piling presents on glass*]: I'm very thankful to you all today . . .

WIDOW QUIN [*coming in quickly, at door*]: Sara Tansey, Susan Brady, Honor Blake! What in glory has you here at this hour of day?

GIRLS [*giggling*]: That's the man killed his father.

WIDOW QUIN [*coming to them*]: I know well it's the man; and I'm after putting him down in the sports below for racing, leaping, pitching, and the Lord knows what.

SARA [*exuberantly*]: That's right, Widow Quin. I'll bet my dowry that he'll lick the world.

WIDOW QUIN: If you will, you'd have a right to have him fresh and nourished in place of nursing a feast. [*Taking presents.*] Are you fasting or fed, young fellow?

CHRISTY: Fasting, if you please.

WIDOW QUIN [*loudly*]: Well, you're the lot. Stir up now and give him his breakfast. [*To* CHRISTY.] Come here to me [*she puts him on bench beside her while the girls make tea and get his breakfast*] and let you tell us your story before Pegeen will come, in place of grinning your ears off like the moon of May.

CHRISTY [*beginning to be pleased*]: It's a long story; you'd be destroyed listening.

WIDOW QUIN: Don't be letting on to be shy, a fine, gamey, treacherous lad the like of you. Was it in your house beyond you cracked his skull?

CHRISTY [*shy but flattered*]: It was not. We were digging spuds in his cold, sloping, stony, divil's patch of a field.

WIDOW QUIN: And you went asking money of him, or making talk of getting a wife would drive him from his farm?

CHRISTY: I did not, then; but there I was, digging and digging, and "You squinting idiot," says he, "let you walk down now and tell the priest you'll wed the Widow Casey in a score of days."

WIDOW QUIN: And what kind was she?

CHRISTY [*with horror*]: A walking terror from beyond the hills, and she two score and five years, and two hundredweights and five pounds in the weighing scales, with a limping leg on her, and a blinded eye, and she a woman of noted misbehaviour with the old and young.

GIRLS [*clustering round him, serving him*]: Glory be.

WIDOW QUIN: And what did he want driving you to wed with her? [*She takes a bit of the chicken.*]

CHRISTY [*eating with growing satisfaction*]: He was letting on I was wanting a protector from the harshness of the world, and he without a thought the whole while but how he'd have her hut to live in and her gold to drink.

WIDOW QUIN: There's maybe worse than a dry hearth and a widow woman and your glass at night. So you hit him then?

CHRISTY [*getting almost excited*]: I did not. "I won't wed her," says I, "when all know she did suckle me for six weeks when I came into the world, and she a hag this day with a tongue on her has the crows and seabirds scattered, the way they wouldn't cast a shadow on her garden with the dread of her curse."

WIDOW QUIN [*teasingly*]: That one should be right company.

SARA [*eagerly*]: Don't mind her. Did you kill him then?

CHRISTY: "She's too good for the like of you," says he, "and go on now or I'll flatten you out like a crawling beast has passed under a dray." "You will not if I can help it," says I. "Go on," says he, "or I'll have the divil making garters of your limbs tonight." "You will not if I can help it," says I. [*He sits up, brandishing his mug.*]

SARA: You were right surely.

CHRISTY [*impressively*]: With that the sun came out between the cloud and the hill, and it shining green in my face. "God have mercy on your soul," says he, lifting a scythe; "or on your own," says I, raising the loy.

SUSAN: That's a grand story.

HONOR: He tells it lovely.

CHRISTY [*flattered and confident, waving bone*]: He gave a drive with the scythe, and I gave a lep to the east. Then I turned around with my back to the north, and I hit a blow on the ridge of his skull, laid him stretched out, and he split to the knob of his gullet. [*He raises the chicken bone to his Adam's apple.*]

GIRLS [*together*]: Well, you're a marvel! Oh, God bless you! You're the lad surely!

SUSAN: I'm thinking the Lord God sent him this road to make a second husband to the Widow Quin, and she with a great yearning to be wedded, though all dread her here. Lift him on her knee, Sara Tansey.

WIDOW QUIN: Don't tease him.

SARA [*going over to dresser and counter very quickly, and getting two glasses and porter*]: You're heroes surely, and let you drink a supeen with your arms linked like the outlandish lovers in the sailor's song. [*She links their arms and gives them the glasses.*] There now. Drink a health to the wonders of the western world, the pirates, preachers, poteenmakers, with the jobbing jockies; parching peelers, and the juries fill their stomachs selling judgments of the English law. [*Brandishing the bottle.*]

WIDOW QUIN: That's a right toast, Sara Tansey. Now Christy.

[*They drink with their arms linked, he drinking with his left hand, she with her right. As they are drinking, PEGEEN MIKE comes in with a milk can and stands aghast. They all spring away from CHRISTY. He goes down left. WIDOW QUIN remains seated.*]

PEGEEN [*angrily, to* SARA]: What is it you're wanting?

SARA [*twisting her apron*]: An ounce of tobacco.

PEGEEN: Have you tuppence?

SARA: I've forgotten my purse.

PEGEEN: Then you'd best be getting it and not fooling us here. [*To the* WIDOW QUIN, *with more elaborate scorn.*] And what is it you're wanting, Widow Quin?

WIDOW QUIN [*insolently*]: A penn'orth of starch.

PEGEEN [*breaking out*]: And you without a white shift or a shirt in your whole family since the drying of the flood. I've no starch for the like of you, and let you walk on now to Killamuck.

WIDOW QUIN [*turning to* CHRISTY, *as she goes out with the girls*]: Well, you're mighty huffy this day, Pegeen Mike, and, you young fellow, let you not forget the sports and racing when the noon is by.

[*They go out.*]

PEGEEN [*imperiously*]: Fling out that rubbish and put them cups away. [CHRISTY *tidies away in great haste.*] Shove in the bench by the wall. [*He does so.*] And hang that glass on the nail. What disturbed it at all?

CHRISTY [*very meekly*]: I was making myself decent only, and this a fine country for young lovely girls.

PEGEEN [*sharply*]: Whisht your talking of girls. [*Goes to counter —right.*]

CHRISTY: Wouldn't any wish to be decent in a place . . .

PEGEEN: Whisht I'm saying.

CHRISTY [*looks at her face for a moment with great misgivings,* then as a last effort, takes up a loy, and goes towards her, with feigned assurance*]: It was with a loy the like of that I killed my father.

PEGEEN [*still sharply*]: You've told me that story six times since the dawn of day.

CHRISTY [*reproachfully*]: It's a queer thing you wouldn't care to be hearing it and them girls after walking four miles to be listening to me now.

PEGEEN [*turning round astonished*]: Four miles.

CHRISTY [*apologetically*]: Didn't himself say there were only four bona fides living in the place?

PEGEEN: It's bona fides by the road they are, but that lot came over the river lepping the stones. It's not three perches when you go like that, and I was down this morning looking on the papers the post-boy does have in his bag. [*With meaning and emphasis.*] For there was great news this day, Christopher Mahon. [*She goes into room left.*]

CHRISTY [*suspiciously*]: Is it news of my murder?

PEGEEN [*inside*]: Murder, indeed.

CHRISTY [*loudly*]: A murdered da?

PEGEEN [*coming in again and crossing right*]: There was not, but a story filled half a page of the hanging of a man. Ah, that should be a fearful end, young fellow, and it worst of all for a man who destroyed his da, for the like of him would get small mercies, and when it's dead he is, they'd put him in a narrow grave, with cheap sacking wrapping him round, and pour down quicklime on his head, the way you'd see a woman pouring any frish-frash from a cup.

CHRISTY [*very miserably*]: Oh, God help me. Are you thinking I'm safe? You were saying at the fall of night, I was shut of jeopardy and I here with yourselves.

PEGEEN [*severely*]: You'll be shut of jeopardy no place if you go talking with a pack of wild girls the like of them do be walking abroad with the peelers, talking whispers at the fall of night.

CHRISTY [*with terror*]: And you're thinking they'd tell?

PEGEEN [*with mock sympathy*]: Who knows, God help you.

CHRISTY [*loudly*]: What joy would they have to bring hanging to the likes of me?

PEGEEN: It's queer joys they have, and who knows the thing they'd do, if it'd make the green stones cry itself to think of you swaying and swiggling at the butt of a rope, and you with a fine, stout neck, God bless you! the way you'd be a half an hour, in great anguish, getting your death.

CHRISTY [*getting his boots and putting them on*]: If there's that terror of them, it'd be best, maybe, I went on wandering like Esau or Cain and Abel on the sides of Neifin or the Erris plain.

PEGEEN [*beginning to play with him*]: It would, maybe, for I've heard the Circuit Judges this place is a heartless crew.

CHRISTY [*bitterly*]: It's more than Judges this place is a heartless crew. [*Looking up at her.*] And isn't it a poor thing to be starting again and I a lonesome fellow will be looking out on women and girls the way the needy fallen spirits do be looking on the Lord?

PEGEEN: What call have you to be that lonesome when there's poor girls walking Mayo in their thousands now?

CHRISTY [*grimly*]: It's well you know what call I have. It's well you know it's a lonesome thing to be passing small towns with the lights shining sideways when the night is down, or going in strange places with a dog noising before you and a dog noising behind, or drawn to the cities where you'd hear a voice kissing and talking deep love in every shadow of the ditch, and you passing on with an empty, hungry stomach failing from your heart.

PEGEEN: I'm thinking you're an odd man, Christy Mahon. The oddest walking fellow I ever set my eyes on to this hour today.

CHRISTY: What would any be but odd men and they living lonesome in the world?

PEGEEN: I'm not odd, and I'm my whole life with my father only.

CHRISTY [*with infinite admiration*]: How would a lovely handsome woman the like of you be lonesome when all men should be thronging around to hear the sweetness of your voice, and the little infant children should be pestering your steps I'm thinking, and you walking the roads.

PEGEEN: I'm hard set to know what way a coaxing fellow the like of yourself should be lonesome either.

CHRISTY: Coaxing?

PEGEEN: Would you have me think

a man never talked with the girls would have the words you've spoken today? It's only letting on you are to be lonesome, the way you'd get around me now.

CHRISTY: I wish to God I was letting on; but I was lonesome all times, and born lonesome, I'm thinking, as the moon of dawn. [*Going to door.*]

PEGEEN [*puzzled by his talk*]: Well, it's a story I'm not understanding at all why you'd be worse than another, Christy Mahon, and you a fine lad with the great savagery to destroy your da.

CHRISTY: It's little I'm understanding myself, saving only that my heart's scalded this day, and I going off stretching out the earth between us, the way I'll not be waking near you another dawn of the year till the two of us do arise to hope or judgment with the saints of God, and now I'd best be going with my wattle in my hand, for hanging is a poor thing [*turning to go*], and it's little welcome only is left me in this house today.

PEGEEN [*sharply*]: Christy! [*He turns round.*] Come here to me. [*He goes towards her.*] Lay down that switch and throw some sods on the fire. You're pot-boy in this place, and I'll not have you mitch off from us now.

CHRISTY: You were saying I'd be hanged if I stay.

PEGEEN [*quite kindly at last*]: I'm after going down and reading the fearful crimes of Ireland for two weeks or three, and there wasn't a word of your murder. [*Getting up and going over to the counter.*] They've

likely not found the body. You're safe so with ourselves.

CHRISTY [*astonished, slowly*]: It's making game of me you were [*following her with fearful joy*], and I can stay so, working at your side, and I not lonesome from this mortal day.

PEGEEN: What's to hinder you from staying, except the widow woman or the young girls would inveigle you off?

CHRISTY [*with rapture*]: And I'll have your words from this day filling my ears, and that look is come upon you meeting my two eyes, and I watching you loafing around in the warm sun, or rinsing your ankles when the night is come.

PEGEEN [*kindly, but a little embarrassed*]: I'm thinking you'll be a loyal young lad to have working around, and if you vexed me a while since with your leaguing with the girls, I wouldn't give a thraneen for a lad hadn't a mighty spirit in him and a gamey heart.

[SHAWN KEOGH *runs in carrying a cleeve on his back, followed by the* WIDOW QUIN.]

SHAWN [*to* PEGEEN]: I was passing below, and I seen your mountainy sheep eating cabbages in Jimmy's field. Run up or they'll be bursting surely.

PEGEEN: Oh, God mend them! [*She puts a shawl over her head and runs out.*]

CHRISTY [*looking from one to the other. Still in high spirits*]: I'd best go to her aid maybe. I'm handy with ewes.

WIDOW QUIN [*closing the door*]: She can do that much, and there is Shaneen has long speeches for to tell you now. [*She sits down with an amused smile.*]

SHAWN [*taking something from his pocket and offering it to* CHRISTY]: Do you see that, mister?

CHRISTY [*looking at it*]: The half of a ticket to the Western States!

SHAWN [*trembling with anxiety*]: I'll give it to you and my new hat [*pulling it out of hamper*]; and my breeches with the double seat [*pulling it off*]; and my new coat is woven from the blackest shearings for three miles around [*giving him the coat*]; I'll give you the whole of them, and my blessing, and the blessing of Father Reilly itself, maybe, if you'll quit from this and leave us in the peace we had till last night at the fall of dark.

CHRISTY [*with a new arrogance*]: And for what is it you're wanting to get shut of me?

SHAWN [*looking to the* WIDOW *for help*]: I'm a poor scholar with middling faculties to coin a lie, so I'll tell you the truth, Christy Mahon. I'm wedding with Pegeen beyond, and I don't think well of having a clever fearless man the like of you dwelling in her house.

CHRISTY [*almost pugnaciously*]: And you'd be using bribery for to banish me?

SHAWN [*in an imploring voice*]: Let you not take it badly, mister honey, isn't beyond the best place for you where you'll have golden chains and shiny coats and you riding upon hunters with the ladies of the land. [*He makes an eager sign to the* WIDOW QUIN *to come to help him.*]

WIDOW QUIN [*coming over*]: It's true for him, and you'd best quit off and not have that poor girl setting her mind on you, for there's Shaneen thinks she wouldn't suit you though all is saying that she'll wed you now.

[CHRISTY *beams with delight.*]

SHAWN [*in terrified earnest*]: She wouldn't suit you, and she with the divil's own temper the way you'd be strangling one another in a score of days. [*He makes the movement of strangling with his hands.*] It's the like of me only that she's fit for, a quiet simple fellow wouldn't raise a hand upon her if she scratched itself.

WIDOW QUIN [*putting* SHAWN's *hat on* CHRISTY]: Fit them clothes on you anyhow, young fellow, and he'd maybe loan them to you for the sports. [*Pushing him towards inner door.*] Fit them on and you can give your answer when you have them tried.

CHRISTY [*beaming, delighted with the clothes*]: I will then. I'd like herself to see me in them tweeds and hat. [*He goes into room and shuts the door.*]

SHAWN [*in great anxiety*]: He'd like herself to see them. He'll not leave us, Widow Quin. He's a score of divils in him the way it's well nigh certain he will wed Pegeen.

WIDOW QUIN [*jeeringly*]: It's true all girls are fond of courage and do hate the like of you.

SHAWN [*walking about in desperation*]: Oh, Widow Quin, what'll I be doing now? I'd inform again him, but he'd burst from Kilmainham and he'd be sure and certain to destroy me. If I wasn't so God-fearing, I'd near have courage to come behind him and run a pike into his side. Oh, it's a hard case to be an orphan and not to have your father that you're used to, and you'd easy kill and make yourself a hero in the sight of all. [*Coming up to her.*] Oh, Widow Quin, will you find me some contrivance when I've promised you a ewe?

WIDOW QUIN: A ewe's a small thing, but what would you give me if I did wed him and did save you so?

SHAWN [*with astonishment*]: You?

WIDOW QUIN: Aye. Would you give me the red cow you have and the mountainy ram, and the right of way across your rye path, and a load of dung at Michaelmas, and turbary upon the western hill?

SHAWN [*radiant with hope*]: I would surely, and I'd give you the wedding-ring I have, and the loan of a new suit, the way you'd have him decent on the wedding-day. I'd give you two kids for your dinner, and a gallon of poteen, and I'd call the piper on the long car to your wedding from Crossmolina or from Ballina. I'd give you . . .

WIDOW QUIN: That'll do so, and let you whisht, for he's coming now again.

[CHRISTY *comes in very natty in the new clothes.* WIDOW QUIN *goes to him admiringly.*]

WIDOW QUIN: If you seen yourself now, I'm thinking you'd be too proud to speak to us at all, and it'd be a pity surely to have your like sailing from Mayo to the Western World.

CHRISTY [*as proud as a peacock*]: I'm not going. If this is a poor place itself, I'll make myself contented to be lodging here.

[WIDOW QUIN *makes a sign to* SHAWN *to leave them.*]

SHAWN: Well, I'm going measuring the race-course while the tide is low, so I'll leave you the garments and my blessing for the sports today. God bless you! [*He wriggles out.*]

WIDOW QUIN [*admiring* CHRISTY]: Well, you're mighty spruce, young fellow. Sit down now while you're quiet till you talk with me.

CHRISTY [*swaggering*]: I'm going abroad on the hillside for to seek Pegeen.

WIDOW QUIN: You'll have time and plenty for to seek Pegeen, and you heard me saying at the fall of night the two of us should be great company.

CHRISTY: From this out I'll have not want of company when all sorts is bringing me their food and clothing [*he swaggers to the door, tightening his belt*], the way they'd set their eyes upon a gallant orphan cleft his father with one blow to the breeches belt. [*He opens door, then staggers back.*] Saints of glory! Holy angels from the throne of light!

WIDOW QUIN [*going over*]: What ails you!

CHRISTY: It's the walking spirit of my murdered da!

WIDOW QUIN [*looking out*]: Is it that tramper?

CHRISTY [*wildly*]: Where'll I hide

my poor body from that ghost of hell?

[*The door is pushed open, and old* MAHON *appears on threshold.* CHRISTY *darts in behind door.*]

WIDOW QUIN [*in great amusement*]: God save you, my poor man.

MAHON [*gruffly*]: Did you see a young lad passing this way in the early morning or the fall of night?

WIDOW QUIN: You're a queer kind to walk in not saluting at all.

MAHON: Did you see the young lad?

WIDOW QUIN [*stiffly*]: What kind was he?

MAHON: An ugly young streeler with a murderous gob on him, and a little switch in his hand. I met a tramper seen him coming this way at the fall of night.

WIDOW QUIN: There's harvest hundreds do be passing these days for the Sligo boat. For what is it you're wanting him, my poor man?

MAHON: I want to destroy him for breaking the head on me with the clout of a loy. [*He takes off a big hat, and shows his head in a mass of bandages and plaster, with some pride.*] It was he did that, and amn't I a great wonder to think I've traced him ten days with that rent in my crown?

WIDOW QUIN [*taking his head in both hands and examining it with extreme delight*]: That was a great blow. And who hit you? A robber maybe?

MAHON: It was my own son hit me, and he the divil a robber, or anything else, but a dirty, stuttering lout.

WIDOW QUIN [*letting go his skull and wiping her hands in her apron*]: You'd best be wary of a mortified scalp, I think they call it, lepping around with that wound in the splendour of the sun. It was a bad blow surely, and you should have vexed him fearful to make him strike that gash in his da.

MAHON: Is it me?

WIDOW QUIN [*amusing herself*]: Aye. And isn't it a great shame when the old and hardened do torment the young?

MAHON [*raging*]; Torment him, is it? And I after holding out with the patience of a martyred saint till there's nothing but destruction on, and I'm driven out in my old age with none to aid me.

WIDOW QUIN [*greatly amused*]: It's a sacred wonder the way that wickedness will spoil a man.

MAHON: My wickedness, is it? Amn't I after saying it is himself has me destroyed, and he a liar on walls, a talker of folly, a man you'd see stretched the half of the day in the brown ferns with his belly to the sun.

WIDOW QUIN: Not working at all?

MAHON: The divil a work, or if he did itself, you'd see him raising up a haystack like the stalk of a rush, or driving our last cow till he broke her leg at the hip, and when he wasn't at that he'd be fooling over little birds he had—finches and felts—or making mugs at his own self in the bit of a glass we had hung on the wall.

WIDOW QUIN [*looking at* CHRISTY]: What way was he so foolish?

It was running wild after the girls may be?

MAHON [*with a shout of derision*]: Running wild, is it? If he seen a red petticoat coming swinging over the hill, he'd be off to hide in the sticks, and you'd see him shooting out his sheep's eyes between the little twigs and the leaves, and his two ears rising like a hare looking out through a gap. Girls, indeed!

WIDOW QUIN: It was drink maybe?

MAHON: And he a poor fellow would get drunk on the smell of a pint. He'd a queer rotten stomach, I'm telling you, and when I gave him three pulls from my pipe a while since, he was taken with contortions till I had to send him in the ass cart to the females' nurse.

WIDOW QUIN [*clasping her hands*]: Well, I never till this day heard tell of a man the like of that!

MAHON: I'd take a mighty oath you didn't surely, and wasn't he the laughing joke of every female woman where four baronies meet, the way the girls would stop their weeding if they seen him coming the road to let a roar at him, and call him the looney of Mahon's.

WIDOW QUIN: I'd give the world and all to see the like of him. What kind was he?

MAHON: A small low fellow.

WIDOW QUIN: And dark?

MAHON: Dark and dirty.

WIDOW QUIN [*considering*]: I'm thinking I seen him.

MAHON [*eagerly*]: An ugly young blackguard.

WIDOW QUIN: A hideous, fearful villain, and the spit of you.

MAHON: What way is he fled?

WIDOW QUIN: Gone over the hills to catch a coasting steamer to the north or south.

MAHON: Could I pull up on him now?

WIDOW QUIN: If you'll cross the sands below where the tide is out, you'll be in it as soon as himself, for he had to go round ten miles by the top of the bay. [*She points to the door.*] Strike down by the head beyond and then follow on the roadway to the north and east.

[MAHON *goes abruptly.*]

WIDOW QUIN [*shouting after him*]: Let you give him a good vengeance when you come up with him, but don't put yourself in the power of the law, for it'd be a poor thing to see a judge in his black cap reading out his sentence on a civil warrior the like of you.

[*She swings the door to and looks at* CHRISTY, *who is cowering in terror, for a moment, then she bursts into a laugh.*]

WIDOW QUIN: Well, you're the walking Playboy of the Western World, and that's the poor man you had divided to his breeches belt.

CHRISTY [*looking out: then, to her*]: What'll Pegeen say when she hears that story? What'll she be saying to me now?

WIDOW QUIN: She'll knock the head of you, I'm thinking, and drive you from the door. God help her to be taking you for a wonder, and you a little schemer making up the story you destroyed your da.

CHRISTY [*turning to the door,*

nearly speechless with rage, half to himself]: To be letting on he was dead, and coming back to his life, and following after me like an old weazel tracing a rat, and coming in here laying desolation between my own self and the fine women of Ireland, and he a kind of carcase that you'd fling upon the sea . . .

WIDOW QUIN [*more soberly*]: There's talking for a man's one only son.

CHRISTY [*breaking out*]: His one son, is it? May I meet him with one tooth and it aching, and one eye to be seeing seven and seventy divils in the twists of the road, and one old timber leg on him to limp into the scalding grave. [*Looking out.*] There he is now crossing the strands, and that the Lord God would send a high wave to wash him from the world.

WIDOW QUIN [*scandalized*]: Have you no shame? [*Putting her hand on his shoulder and turning him round.*] What ails you? Near crying, is it?

CHRISTY [*in despair and grief*]: Amn't I after seeing the lovelight of the star of knowledge shining from her brow, and hearing words would put you thinking on the holy Brigid speaking to the infant saints, and now she'll be turning again, and speaking hard words to me, like an old woman with a spavindy ass she'd have, urging on a hill.

WIDOW QUIN: There's poetry talk for a girl you'd see itching and scratching, and she with a stale stink of poteen on her from selling in the shop.

CHRISTY [*impatiently*]: It's her like is fitted to be handling merchandise in the heavens above, and what'll I be doing now, I ask you, and I a kind of wonder was jilted by the heavens when a day was by.

[*There is a distant noise of girls' voices.* WIDOW QUIN *looks from window and comes to him, hurriedly.*]

WIDOW QUIN: You'll be doing like myself, I'm thinking, when I did destroy my man, for I'm above many's the day, odd times in great spirits, abroad in the sunshine, darning a stocking or stitching a shift; and odd times again looking out on the schooners, hookers, trawlers is sailing the sea, and I thinking on the gallant hairy fellows are drifting beyond, and myself long years living alone.

CHRISTY [*interested*]: You're like me, so.

WIDOW QUIN: I am your like, and it's for that I'm taking a fancy to you, and I with my little houseen above where there'd be myself to tend you, and none to ask were you a murderer or what at all.

CHRISTY: And what would I be doing if I left Pegeen?

WIDOW QUIN: I've nice jobs you could be doing, gathering shells to make a whitewash for our hut within, building up a little goose-house, or stretching a new skin on an old curragh I have, and if my hut is far from all sides, it's there you'll meet the wisest old men, I tell you, at the corner of my wheel, and it's there yourself and me will have great times whispering and hugging. . . .

VOICES [*outside, calling far away*]: Christy! Christy Mahon! Christy!

CHRISTY: Is it Pegeen Mike?

WIDOW QUIN: It's the young girls, I'm thinking, coming to bring you to the sports below, and what is it you'll have me to tell them now?

CHRISTY: Aid me for to win Pegeen. It's herself only that I'm seeking now. [WIDOW QUIN *gets up and goes to window.*] Aid me for to win her, and I'll be asking God to stretch a hand to you in the hour of death, and lead you short cuts through the Meadows of Ease, and up the floor of Heaven to the Footstool of the Virgin's Son.

WIDOW QUIN: There's praying.

VOICES [*nearer*]: Christy! Christy Mahon!

CHRISTY [*with agitation*]: They're coming. Will you swear to aid and save me for the love of Christ?

WIDOW QUIN [*looks at him for a moment*]: If I aid you, will you swear to give me a right of way I want, and a mountainy ram, and a load of dung at Michaelmas, the time that you'll be master here?

CHRISTY: I will, by the elements and stars of night.

WIDOW QUIN: Then we'll not say a word of the old fellow, the way Pegeen won't know your story till the end of time.

CHRISTY: And if he chances to return again?

WIDOW QUIN: We'll swear he's a maniac and not your da. I could take an oath I seen him raving on the sands today.

[*Girls run in.*]

SUSAN: Come on to the sports below. Pegeen says you're to come.

SARA TANSEY: The lepping's beginning, and we've a jockey's suit to fit upon you for the mule race on the sands below.

HONOR: Come on, will you?

CHRISTY: I will then if Pegeen's beyond.

SARA TANSEY: She's in the boreen making game of Shaneen Keogh.

CHRISTY: Then I'll be going to her now.

[*He runs out followed by the girls.*]

WIDOW QUIN: Well, if the worst comes in the end of all, it'll be a great game to see there's none to pity him but a widow woman, the like of me, has buried her children and destroyed her man. [*She goes out.*]

CURTAIN

ACT THREE

SCENE, *as before. Later in the day.* JIMMY *comes in, slightly drunk.*

JIMMY [*calls*]: Pegeen! [*Crosses to inner door.*] Pegeen Mike! [*Comes back again into the room.*] Pegeen! [PHILLY *comes in in the same state. To* PHILLY.] Did you see herself?

PHILLY: I did not; but I sent Shawn Keogh with the ass cart for to bear him home. [*Trying cupboards which are locked.*] Well, isn't he a nasty man to get into such staggers at a morning wake? and isn't herself the divil's daughter for locking, and she so fussy after that young gaffer, you might take your death with drought and none to heed you?

JIMMY: It's little wonder she'd be fussy, and he after bringing bankrupt ruin on the roulette man, and the trick-o'-the-loop man, and breaking the nose of the cockshot-man, and winning all in the sports below, racing, lepping, dancing, and the Lord knows what! He's right luck, I'm telling you.

PHILLY: If he has, he'll be rightly hobbled yet, and he not able to say ten words without making a brag of the way he killed his father, and the great blow he hit with the loy.

JIMMY: A man can't hang by his own informing, and his father should be rotten by now.

[*Old* MAHON *passes window slowly.*

PHILLY: Supposing a man's digging spuds in that field with a long spade, and supposing he flings up the two halves of that skull, what'll be said then in the papers and the courts of law?

JIMMY: They'd say it was an old Dane, maybe, was drowned in the flood. [*Old* MAHON *comes in and sits down near door listening.*] Did you never hear tell of the skulls they have in the city of Dublin, ranged out like blue jugs in a cabin of Connaught?

PHILLY: And you believe that?

JIMMY [*pugnaciously*]: Didn't a lad see them and he after coming from harvesting in the Liverpool boat? "They have them there," says he, "making a show of the great people there was one time walking the world. White skulls and black skulls and yellow skulls, and some with full teeth, and some haven't only but one."

PHILLY: It was no lie, maybe, for when I was a young lad there was a graveyard beyond the house with the remnants of a man who had thighs as long as your arm. He was a horrid man, I'm telling you, and there was many a fine Sunday I'd put him together for fun, and he with

448

shiny bones, you wouldn't meet the like of these days in the cities of the world.

MAHON [*getting up*]: You wouldn't, is it? Lay your eyes on that skull, and tell me where and when there was another the like of it, is splintered only from the blow of a loy.

PHILLY: Glory be to God! And who hit you at all?

MAHON [*triumphantly*]: It was my own son hit me. Would you believe that?

JIMMY: Well, there's wonders hidden in the heart of man!

PHILLY [*suspiciously*]: And what way was it done?

MAHON [*wandering about the room*]: I'm after walking hundreds and long scores of miles, winning clean beds and the fill of my belly four times in the day, and I doing nothing but telling stories of that naked truth. [*He comes to them a little aggressively.*] Give me a supeen and I'll tell you now.

[WIDOW QUIN *comes in and stands aghast behind him. He is facing* JIMMY *and* PHILLY, *who are on the left.*]

JIMMY: Ask herself beyond. She's the stuff hidden in her shawl.

WIDOW QUIN [*coming to* MAHON *quickly*]: You here, is it? You didn't go far at all?

MAHON: I seen the coasting steamer passing, and I got a drought upon me and a cramping leg, so I said, "The divil go along with him," and turned again. [*Looking under her shawl.*] And let you give me a supeen, for I'm destroyed travelling since Tuesday was a week.

WIDOW QUIN [*getting a glass, in a cajoling tone*]: Sit down then by the fire and take your ease for a space. You've a right to be destroyed indeed, with your walking, and fighting, and facing the sun [*giving him poteen from a stone jar she has brought in*]. There now is a drink for you, and may it be to your happiness and length of life.

MAHON [*taking glass greedily and sitting down by fire*]: God increase you!

WIDOW QUIN [*taking men to the right stealthily*]: Do you know what? That man's raving from his wound today, for I met him a while since telling a rambling tale of a tinker had him destroyed. Then he heard of Christy's deed, and he up and says it was his son had cracked his skull. O isn't madness a fright, for he'll go killing someone yet, and he thinking it's the man has struck him so?

JIMMY [*entirely convinced*]: It's a fright, surely. I knew a party was kicked in the head by a red mare, and he went killing horses a great while, till he eat the insides of a clock and died after.

PHILLY [*with suspicion*]: Did he see Christy?

WIDOW QUIN: He didn't. [*With a warning gesture.*] Let you not be putting him in mind of him, or you'll be likely summoned if there's murder done. [*Looking round at* MAHON.] Whisht! He's listening. Wait now till you hear me taking him easy and unravelling all. [*She goes to* MAHON.] And what way are you feeling, mister? Are you in contentment now?

MAHON [*slightly emotional from his drink*]: I'm poorly only, for it's a hard story the way I'm left today, when it was I did tend him from his hour of birth, and he a dunce never reached his second book, the way he'd come from school, many's the day, with his legs lamed under him, and he blackened with his beatings like a tinker's ass. It's a hard story, I'm saying, the way some do have their next and nighest raising up a hand of murder on them, and some is lonesome getting their death with lamentation in the dead of night.

WIDOW QUIN [*not knowing what to say*]: To hear you talking so quiet, who'd know you were the same fellow we seen pass today?

MAHON: I'm the same surely. The wrack and ruin of three score years; and it's a terror to live that length, I tell you, and to have your sons going to the dogs against you, and you wore out scolding them, and skelping them, and God knows what.

PHILLY [*to* JIMMY]: He's not raving. [*To* WIDOW QUIN.] Will you ask him what kind was his son?

WIDOW QUIN [*to* MAHON, *with a peculiar look*]: Was your son that hit you a lad of one year and a score maybe, a great hand at racing and lepping and licking the world?

MAHON [*turning on her with a roar of rage*]: Didn't you hear me say he was the fool of men, the way from this out he'll know the orphan's lot with old and young making game of him and they swearing, raging, kicking at him like a mangy cur.

[*A great burst of cheering outside, some way off.*]

MAHON [*putting his hands to his ears*]: What in the name of God do they want roaring below?

WIDOW QUIN [*with the shade of a smile*]: They're cheering a young lad, the champion Playboy of the Western World.

[*More cheering.*]

MAHON [*going to window*]: It'd split my heart to hear them, and I with pulses in my brain-pan for a week gone by. Is it racing they are?

JIMMY [*looking from door*]: It is then. They are mounting him for the mule race will be run upon the sands. That's the playboy on the winkered mule.

MAHON [*puzzled*]: That lad, is it? If you said it was a fool he was, I'd have laid a mighty oath he was the likeness of my wandering son [*uneasily, putting his hand to his head*]. Faith, I'm thinking I'll go walking for to view the race.

WIDOW QUIN [*stopping him, sharply*]: You will not. You'd best take the road to Belmullet and not be dilly-dallying in this place where there isn't a spot you could sleep.

PHILLY [*coming forward*]: Don't mind her. Mount there on the bench and you'll have a view of the whole. They're hurrying before the tide will rise, and it'd be near over if you went down the pathway through the crags below.

MAHON [*mounts on bench,* WIDOW QUIN *beside him*]: That's a right view again the edge of the sea

They're coming now from that point. He's leading. Who is he at all?

WIDOW QUIN: He's the champion of the world, I tell you, and there isn't a hop'orth isn't falling lucky to his hands today.

PHILLY [*looking out, interested in the race*]: Look at that. They're pressing him now.

JIMMY: He'll win it yet.

PHILLY: Take your time, Jimmy Farrell. It's too soon to say.

WIDOW QUIN [*shouting*]: Watch him taking the gate. There's riding.

JIMMY [*cheering*]: More power to the young lad!

MAHON: He's passing the third.

JIMMY: He'll lick them yet!

WIDOW QUIN: He'd lick them if he was running races with a score itself.

MAHON: Look at the mule he has, kicking the stars.

WIDOW QUIN: There was a lep! [*Catching hold of* MAHON *in her excitement.*] He's fallen! He's mounted again! Faith, he's passing them all!

JIMMY: Look at him skelping her!

PHILLY: And the mountain girls hooshing him on!

JIMMY: It's the last turn! The post's cleared for them now!

MAHON: Look at the narrow place. He'll be into the bogs! [*With a yell.*] Good rider! He's through it again!

JIMMY: He's neck and neck!

MAHON: Good boy to him! Flames, but he's in!

[*Great cheering, in which all join.*]

MAHON [*with hesitation*]: What's that? They're raising him up. They're coming this way. [*With a roar of rage and astonishment.*] It's Christy! by the stars of God! I'd know his way of spitting and he astride the moon.

[*He jumps down and makes for the door, but* WIDOW QUIN *catches him and pulls him back.*]

WIDOW QUIN: Stay quiet, will you. That's not your son. [*To* JIMMY.] Stop him, or you'll get a month for the abetting of manslaughter and be fined as well.

JIMMY: I'll hold him.

MAHON [*struggling*]: Let me out! Let me out, the lot of you! till I have my vengeance on his head today.

WIDOW QUIN [*shaking him, vehemently*]: That's not your son. That's a man is going to make a marriage with the daughter of this house, a place with fine trade, with a license, and with poteen too.

MAHON [*amazed*]: That man marrying a decent and a moneyed girl! Is it mad yous are? Is it in a crazy-house for females that I'm landed now?

WIDOW QUIN: It's mad yourself is with the blow upon your head. That lad is the wonder of the Western World.

MAHON: I seen it's my son.

WIDOW QUIN: You seen that you're mad. [*Cheering outside.*] Do you hear them cheering him in the zig-zags of the road? Aren't you after saying that your son's a fool, and how would they be cheering a true idiot born?

MAHON [*getting distressed*]: It's maybe out of reason that that man's himself. [*Cheering again.*] There's none surely will go cheering him. Oh, I'm raving with a madness that would fright the world! [*He sits down with his hand to his head.*] There was one time I seen ten scarlet divils letting on they'd cork my spirit in a gallon can; and one time I seen rats as big as badgers sucking the life blood from the butt of my lug; but I never till this day confused that dribbling idiot with a likely man. I'm destroyed surely.

WIDOW QUIN: And who'd wonder when it's your brain-pan that is gaping now?

MAHON: Then the blight of the sacred drought upon myself and him, for I never went mad to this day, and I not three weeks with the Limerick girls drinking myself silly, and parlatic from the dusk to dawn. [*To* WIDOW QUIN, *suddenly.*] Is my visage astray?

WIDOW QUIN: It is then. You're a sniggering maniac, a child could see.

MAHON [*getting up more cheerfully*]: Then I'd best be going to the union beyond, and there'll be a welcome before me, I tell you [*with great pride*], and I a terrible and fearful case, the way that there I was one time, screeching in a straitened waistcoat, with seven doctors writing out my sayings in a printed book. Would you believe that?

WIDOW QUIN: If you're a wonder itself, you'd best be hasty, for them lads caught a maniac one time and pelted the poor creature till he ran out, raving and foaming, and was drowned in the sea.

MAHON [*with philosophy*]: It's true mankind is the divil when your head's astray. Let me out now and I'll slip down the boreen, and not see them so.

WIDOW QUIN [*showing him out*]: That's it. Run to the right, and not a one will see. [*He runs off.*]

PHILLY [*wisely*]: You're at some gaming, Widow Quin; but I'll walk after him and give him his dinner and a time to rest, and I'll see then if he's raving or as sane as you.

WIDOW QUIN [*annoyed*]: If you go near that lad, let you be wary of your head, I'm saying. Didn't you hear him telling he was crazed at times?

PHILLY: I heard him telling a power; and I'm thinking we'll have right sport, before night will fall. [*He goes out.*]

JIMMY: Well, Philly's a conceited and foolish man. How could that madman have his senses and his brain-pan slit? I'll go after them and see him turn on Philly now.

[*He goes;* WIDOW QUIN *hides poteen behind counter. Then hubbub outside.*]

VOICES: There you are! Good jumper! Grand lepper! Darlint boy! He's the racer! Bear him on, will you!

[CHRISTY *comes in, in jockey's dress, with* PEGEEN MIKE, SARA, *and other girls, and men.*]

PEGEEN [*to crowd*]: Go on now and don't destroy him and he drenching with sweat. Go along, I'm saying, and have your tug-of-warring till he's dried his skin.

CROWD: Here's his prizes! A bagpipes! A fiddle was played by a poet in the years gone by! A flat and three-thorned black-thorn would lick the scholars out of Dublin town!

CHRISTY [*taking prizes from the men*]: Thank you kindly, the lot of you. But you'd say it was little only I did this day if you'd seen me a while since striking my one single blow.

TOWN CRIER [*outside, ringing a bell*]: Take notice, last event of this day! Tug-of-warring on the green below! Come on, the lot of you! Great achievements for all Mayo men!

PEGEEN: Go on, and leave him for to rest and dry. Go on, I tell you, for he'll do no more. [*She hustles crowd out;* WIDOW QUIN *following them.*]

MEN [*going*]: Come on then. Good luck for the while!

PEGEEN [*radiantly, wiping his face with her shawl*]: Well, you're the lad, and you'll have great times from this out when you could win that wealth of prizes, and you sweating in the heat of noon!

CHRISTY [*looking at her with delight*]: I'll have great times if I win the crowning prize I'm seeking now, and that's your promise that you'll wed me in a fortnight, when our banns is called.

PEGEEN [*backing away from him*]: You've right daring to go ask me that, when all knows you'll be starting to some girl in your own townland, when your father's rotten in four months, or five.

CHRISTY [*indignantly*]: Starting from you, is it? [*He follows her.*] I will not, then, and when the airs is warming in four months, or five, it's then yourself and

me should be pacing Neifin in the dews of night, the times sweet smells do be rising, and you'd see a little shiny new moon, maybe, sinking on the hills.

PEGEEN [*looking at him playfully*]: And it's that kind of a poacher's love you'd make, Christy Mahon, on the sides of Neifin, when the night is down?

CHRISTY: It's little you'll think if my love's a poacher's, or an earl's itself, when you'll feel my two hands stretched around you, and I squeezing kisses on your puckered lips, till I'd feel a kind of pity for the Lord God in all ages sitting lonesome in his golden chair.

PEGEEN: That'll be right fun, Christy Mahon, and any girl would walk her heart out before she'd meet a young man was your like for eloquence, or talk, at all.

CHRISTY [*encouraged*]: Let you wait, to hear me talking, till we're astray in Erris, when Good Friday's by, drinking a sup from a well, and making mighty kisses with our wetted mouths, or gaming in a gap of sunshine, with yourself stretched back unto your necklace, in the flowers of the earth.

PEGEEN [*in a lower voice, moved by his tone*]: I'd be nice so, is it?

CHRISTY [*with rapture*]: If the mitred bishops seen you that time, they'd be the like of the holy prophets, I'm thinking, do be straining the bars of Paradise to lay eyes on the Lady Helen of Troy, and she abroad, pacing back and forward, with a nosegay in her golden shawl.

PEGEEN [*with real tenderness*]:

And what is it I have, Christy Mahon, to make me fitting entertainment for the like of you, that has such poet's talking, and such bravery of heart?

CHRISTY [in a low voice]: Isn't there the light of seven heavens in your heart alone, the way you'll be an angel's lamp to me from this out, and I abroad in the darkness, spearing salmons in the Owen, or the Carrowmore?

PEGEEN: If I was your wife, I'd be along with you those nights, Christy Mahon, the way you'd see I was a great hand at coaxing bailiffs, or coining funny nicknames for the stars of night.

CHRISTY: You, is it? Taking your death in the hailstones, or in the fogs of dawn.

PEGEEN: Yourself and me would shelter easy in a narrow bush, [with a qualm of dread] but we're only talking, maybe, for this would be a poor, thatched place to hold a fine lad is the like of you.

CHRISTY [putting his arm round her]: If I wasn't a good Christian, it's on my naked knees I'd be saying my prayers and paters to every jackstraw you have roofing your head, and every stony pebble is paving the laneway to your door.

PEGEEN [radiantly]: If that's the truth, I'll be burning candles from this out to the miracles of God that have brought you from the south today, and I, with my gowns bought ready, the way that I can wed you, and not wait at all.

CHRISTY: It's miracles, and that's the truth. Me there toiling a long while, and walking a long while, not knowing at all I was drawing all times nearer to this holy day.

PEGEEN: And myself, a girl, was tempted often to go sailing the seas till I'd marry a Jew-man, with ten kegs of gold, and I not knowing at all there was the like of you drawing nearer, like the stars of God.

CHRISTY: And to think I'm long years hearing women talking that talk, to all bloody fools, and this the first time I've heard the like of your voice talking sweetly for my own delight.

PEGEEN: And to think it's me is talking sweetly, Christy Mahon, and I the fright of seven townlands for my biting tongue. Well, the heart's a wonder; and, I'm thinking, there won't be our like in Mayo, for gallant lovers, from this hour, today. [Drunken singing is heard outside.] There's my father coming from the wake, and when he's had his sleep we'll tell him, for he's peaceful then. [They separate.]

MICHAEL [singing outside]:
The jailor and the turnkey
  They quickly ran us down,
And brought us back as prisoners
  Once more to Cavan town.

[He comes in supported by SHAWN.]

There we lay bewailing
  All in a prison bound. . . .

[He sees CHRISTY. Goes and shakes him drunkenly by the hand, while PEGEEN and SHAWN talk on the left.]

MICHAEL [to CHRISTY]: The blessing of God and the holy angels on your head, young fellow. I hear tell you're after winning all in the sports below; and wasn't it a shame I didn't bear you along with me to Kate Cassidy's wake, a fine, stout lad, the like of you, for you'd never see the match of it for flows of drink, the way when we sunk her bones at noonday in her narrow grave, there were five men, aye, and six men, stretched out retching speechless on the holy stones.

CHRISTY [*uneasily, watching* PEGEEN]: Is that the truth?

MICHAEL: It is then, and aren't you a louty schemer to go burying your poor father unbeknownst when you'd a right to throw him on the crupper of a Kerry mule and drive him westwards, like holy Joseph in the days gone by, the way we could have given him a decent burial, and not have him rotting beyond, and not a Christian drinking a smart drop to the glory of his soul?

CHRISTY [*gruffly*]: It's well enough he's lying, for the likes of him.

MICHAEL [*slapping him on the back*]: Well, aren't you a hardened slayer? It'll be a poor thing for the household man where you go sniffing for a female wife; and [*pointing to* SHAWN] look beyond at that shy and decent Christian I have chosen for my daughter's hand, and I after getting the gilded dispensation this day for to wed them now.

CHRISTY: And you'll be wedding them this day, is it?

MICHAEL [*drawing himself up*]: Aye. Are you thinking, if I'm drunk itself, I'd leave my daughter living single with a little frisky rascal is the like of you?

PEGEEN [*breaking away from* SHAWN]: Is it the truth the dispensation's come?

MICHAEL [*triumphantly*]: Father Reilly's after reading it in gallous Latin, and "It's come in the nick of time," says he; "so I'll wed them in a hurry, dreading that young gaffer who'd capsize the stars."

PEGEEN [*fiercely*]: He's missed his nick of time, for it's that lad, Christy Mahon, that I'm wedding now.

MICHAEL [*loudly with horror*]: You'd be making him a son to me, and he wet and crusted with his father's blood?

PEGEEN: Aye. Wouldn't it be a bitter thing for a girl to go marrying the like of Shaneen, and he a middling kind of a scarecrow, with no savagery or fine words in him at all?

MICHAEL [*gasping and sinking on a chair*]: Oh, aren't you a heathen daughter to go shaking the fat of my heart, and I swamped and drownded with the weight of drink? Would you have them turning on me the way that I'd be roaring to the dawn of day with the wind upon my heart? Have you not a word to aid me, Shaneen? Are you not jealous at all?

SHANEEN [*in great misery*]: I'd be afeard to be jealous of a man did slay his da.

PEGEEN: Well, it'd be a poor thing to go marrying your like. I'm seeing there's a world of peril for an orphan girl, and isn't it a great blessing I didn't wed you, before himself came walking from the west or south?

SHAWN: It's a queer story you'd go

picking a dirty tramp up from the highways of the world.

PEGEEN [*playfully*]: And you think you're a likely beau to go straying along with, the shiny Sundays of the opening year, when it's sooner on a bullock's liver you'd put a poor girl thinking than on the lily or the rose?

SHAWN: And have you no mind of my weight of passion, and the holy dispensation, and the drift of heifers I am giving, and the golden ring?

PEGEEN: I'm thinking you're too fine for the like of me, Shawn Keogh of Killakeen, and let you go off till you'd find a radiant lady with droves of bullocks on the plains of Meath, and herself bedizened in the diamond jewelleries of Pharaoh's ma. That'd be your match, Shaneen. So God save you now! [*She retreats behind* CHRISTY.]

SHAWN: Won't you hear me telling you . . . ?

CHRISTY [*with ferocity*]: Take yourself from this, young fellow, or I'll maybe add a murder to my deeds today.

MICHAEL [*springing up with a shriek*]: Murder is it? Is it mad yous are? Would you go making murder in this place, and it piled with poteen for our drink tonight? Go on to the foreshore if it's fighting you want, where the rising tide will wash all traces from the memory of man. [*Pushing* SHAWN *towards* CHRISTY.]

SHAWN [*shaking himself free, and getting behind* MICHAEL]: I'll not fight him, Michael James. I'd liefer live a bachelor, simmering in passions to the end of time, than face a lepping savage the like of him has descended from the Lord knows where. Strike him yourself, Michael James, or you'll lose my drift of heifers and my blue bull from Sneem.

MICHAEL: Is it me fight him, when it's father-slaying he's bred to now? [*Pushing* SHAWN.] Go on you fool and fight him now.

SHAWN [*coming forward a little*]: Will I strike him with my hand?

MICHAEL: Take the loy is on your western side.

SHAWN: I'd be afeard of the gallows if I struck him with that.

CHRISTY [*taking up the loy*]: Then I'll make you face the gallows or quit off from this.

[SHAWN *flies out of the door.*]

CHRISTY: Well, fine weather be after him, [*going to* MICHAEL, *coaxingly*] and I'm thinking you wouldn't wish to have that quaking blackguard in your house at all. Let you give us your blessing and hear her swear her faith to me, for I'm mounted on the springtide of the stars of luck, the way it'll be good for any to have me in the house.

PEGEEN [*at the other side of* MICHAEL]: Bless us now, for I swear to God I'll wed him, and I'll not renege.

MICHAEL [*standing up in the centre, holding on to both of them*]: It's the will of God, I'm thinking, that all should win an easy or a cruel end, and it's the will of God that all should rear up lengthy families for the nurture of the earth. What's a single man, I ask you, eating a bit in one house and drinking a sup in another, and he with no place of his own, like an old braying jackass strayed upon the rocks? [*To* CHRISTY.] It's many would be in dread to bring your like into their house for to end them, maybe, with a sudden end; but I'm a decent man of Ireland, and I liefer face the grave untimely and I seeing a score of grandsons growing up little gallant swearers by the name of God, than go peopling my bedside with puny weeds the like of what you'd breed, I'm thinking, out of Shaneen Keogh. [*He joins their hands.*] A daring fellow is the jewel of the world, and a man did split his father's middle with a single clout, should have the bravery of ten, so may God and Mary and St. Patrick bless you, and increase you from this mortal day.

CHRISTY AND PEGEEN: Amen, O Lord!

[*Hubbub outside.*]

[*Old* MAHON *rushes in, followed by all the crowd, and* WIDOW QUIN. *He makes a rush at* CHRISTY, *knocks him down, and begins to beat him.*]

PEGEEN [*dragging back his arm*]: Stop that, will you. Who are you at all?

MAHON: His father, God forgive me!

PEGEEN [*drawing back*]: Is it rose from the dead?

MAHON: Do you think I look so easy quenched with the tap of a loy? [*Beats* CHRISTY *again.*]

PEGEEN [*glaring at* CHRISTY]: And it's lies you told, letting on you had him slitted, and you nothing at all.

CHRISTY [*catching* MAHON'S *stick*]: He's not my father. He's a raving maniac would scare the world. [*Pointing to* WIDOW QUIN.] Herself knows it is true.

CROWD: You're fooling Pegeen! The Widow Quin seen him this day, and you likely knew! You're a liar!

CHRISTY [*dumbfounded*]: It's himself was a liar, lying stretched out with an open head on him, letting on he was dead.

MAHON: Weren't you off racing the hills before I got my breath with the start I had seeing you turn on me at all?

PEGEEN: And to think of the coaxing glory we had given him, and he after doing nothing but hitting a soft blow and chasing northward in a sweat of fear. Quit off from this.

CHRISTY [*piteously*]: You've seen my doings this day, and let you save me from the old man; for why would you be in such a scorch of haste to spur me to destruction now?

PEGEEN: It's there your treachery is spurring me, till I'm hard set to think you're the one I'm after lacing in my heart-strings half-an-hour gone by. [*To* MAHON.] Take him on from this, for I think bad the world should see me raging for a Munster liar, and the fool of men.

MAHON: Rise up now to retribution, and come on with me.

CROWD [*jeeringly*]: There's the playboy! There's the lad thought he'd rule the roost in Mayo. Slate him now, mister.

CHRISTY [*getting up in shy terror*]: What is it drives you to torment me here, when I'd asked the thunders of the might of God to blast me if I ever did hurt to any saving only that one single blow.

MAHON [*loudly*]: If you didn't, you're a poor good-for-nothing, and isn't it by the like of you the sins of the whole world are committed?

CHRISTY [*raising his hands*]: In the name of the Almighty God. . . .

MAHON: Leave troubling the Lord God. Would you have him sending down droughts, and fevers, and the old hen and the cholera morbus?

CHRISTY [*to* WIDOW QUIN]: Will you come between us and protect me now?

WIDOW QUIN: I've tried a lot, God help me, and my share is done.

CHRISTY [*looking round in desperation*]: And I must go back into my torment is it, or run off like a vagabond straying through the Unions with the dusts of August making mudstains in the gullet of my throat, or the winds of March blowing on me till I'd take an oath I felt them making whistles of my ribs within?

SARA: Ask Pegeen to aid you. Her like does often change.

CHRISTY: I will not then, for there's torment in the splendour of her like, and she a girl any moon of midnight would take pride to meet, facing southwards on the heaths of Keel. But what did I want crawling forward to scorch my understanding at her flaming brow?

PEGEEN [*to* MAHON, *vehemently, fearing she will break into tears*]: Take him on from this or I'll set the young lads to destroy him here.

MAHON [*going to him, shaking his stick*]: Come on now if you wouldn't have the company to see you skelped.

PEGEEN [*half laughing, through her tears*]: That's it, now the world will see him pandied, and he an ugly liar was playing off the hero, and the fright of men.

CHRISTY [*to* MAHON, *very sharply*]: Leave me go!

CROWD: That's it. Now Christy. If them two set fighting, it will lick the world.

MAHON [*making a grab at* CHRISTY]: Come here to me.

CHRISTY [*more threateningly*]: Leave me go, I'm saying.

MAHON: I will maybe, when your legs is limping, and your back is blue.

CROWD: Keep it up, the two of you. I'll back the old one. Now the playboy.

CHRISTY [*in low and intense voice*]: Shut your yelling, for if you're after making a mighty man of me this day by the power of a lie, you're setting me now to think if it's a poor thing to be lonesome, it's worse maybe to go mixing with the fools of earth.

[MAHON *makes a movement towards him.*]

CHRISTY [*almost shouting*]: Keep off . . . lest I do show a blow unto the lot of you would set the guardian angels winking in the clouds above. [*He swings round with a sudden rapid movement and picks up a loy.*]

CROWD [*half frightened, half amused*]: He's going mad! Mind yourselves! Run from the idiot!

CHRISTY: If I am an idiot, I'm after hearing my voice this day saying words would raise the topknot on a poet in a merchant's town. I've won your racing, and your lepping, and . . .

MAHON: Shut your gullet and come on with me.

CHRISTY: I'm going, but I'll stretch you first.

[*He runs at old* MAHON *with the loy, chases him out of the door, followed by crowd and* WIDOW QUIN. *There is a great noise outside, then a yell, and dead silence for a moment.* CHRISTY *comes in, half dazed, and goes to fire.*]

WIDOW QUIN [*coming in, hurriedly, and going to him*]: They're turning again you. Come on, or you'll be hanged, indeed.

CHRISTY: I'm thinking, from this out, Pegeen'll be giving me praises the same as in the hours gone by.

WIDOW QUIN [*impatiently*]: Come by the back-door. I'd think bad to have you stifled on the gallows tree.

CHRISTY [*indignantly*]: I will not, then. What good'd be my lifetime, if I left Pegeen?

WIDOW QUIN: Come on, and you'll be no worse than you were last night; and you with a double murder this time to be telling to the girls.

CHRISTY: I'll not leave Pegeen Mike.

WIDOW QUIN [*impatiently*]: Isn't there the match of her in every parish public, from Binghamstown unto the plain of Meath? Come on, I tell you, and I'll find you finer sweethearts at each waning moon.

CHRISTY: It's Pegeen I'm seeking only, and what'd I care if you brought me a drift of chosen females, standing in their shifts itself, maybe, from this place to the Eastern World?

SARA [*runs in, pulling off one of her petticoats*]: They're going to hang him. [*Holding out petticoat and shawl.*] Fit these upon him, and let him run off to the east.

WIDOW QUIN: He's raving now; but we'll fit them on him, and I'll take him, in the ferry, to the Achill boat.

CHRISTY [*struggling feebly*]: Leave me go, will you? when I'm thinking of my luck today, for she will wed me surely, and I a proven hero in the end of all.

[*They try to fasten petticoat round him.*]

WIDOW QUIN: Take his left hand, and we'll pull him now. Come on, young fellow.

CHRISTY [*suddenly starting up*]: You'll be taking me from her? You're jealous, is it, of her wedding me? Go on from this.

[*He snatches up a stool, and threatens them with it.*]

WIDOW QUIN [*going*]: It's in the mad-house they should put him, not in jail, at all. We'll go by the back-door, to call the doctor, and we'll save him so.

[*She goes out, with* SARA, *through inner room. Men crowd in the doorway.* CHRISTY *sits down again by the fire.*]

MICHAEL [*in a terrified whisper*]: Is the old lad killed surely?

PHILLY: I'm after feeling the last gasps quitting his heart.

[*They peer in at* CHRISTY.]

MICHAEL [*with a rope*]: Look at the way he is. Twist a hangman's knot on it, and slip it over his head, while he's not minding at all.

PHILLY: Let you take it, Shaneen. You're the soberest of all that's here.

SHAWN: Is it me to go near him, and he the wickedest and worst with me? Let you take it, Pegeen Mike.

PEGEEN: Come on, so.

[*She goes forward with the others, and they drop the double hitch over his head.*]

CHRISTY: What ails you?

SHAWN [*triumphantly, as they pull the rope tight on his arms*]: Come on to the peelers, till they stretch you now.

CHRISTY: Me!

MICHAEL: If we took pity on you, the Lord God would, maybe, bring us ruin from the law today, so you'd best come easy, for hanging is an easy and a speedy end.

CHRISTY: I'll not stir. [*To* PEGEEN.] And what is it you'll say to me, and I after doing it this time in the face of all?

PEGEEN: I'll say, a strange man is a marvel, with his mighty talk; but what's a squabble in your back-yard, and the blow of a loy, have taught me that there's a great gap between a gallous story and a dirty deed. [*To* MEN.]

Take him on from this, or the lot of us will be likely put on trial for his deed today.

CHRISTY [*with horror in his voice*]: And it's yourself will send me off, to have a horny-fingered hangman hitching his bloody slip-knots at the butt of my ear.

MEN [*pulling rope*]: Come on, will you?

[*He is pulled down on the floor.*]

CHRISTY [*twisting his legs round the table*]: Cut the rope, Pegeen, and I'll quit the lot of you, and live from this out, like the madmen of Keel, eating muck and green weeds, on the faces of cliffs.

PEGEEN: And leave us to hang, is it, for a saucy liar, the like of you? [*To* MEN.] Take him on, out from this.

SHAWN: Pull a twist on his neck, and squeeze him so.

PHILLY: Twist yourself. Sure he cannot hurt you, if you keep your distance from his teeth alone.

SHAWN: I'm afeard of him. [*To* PEGEEN.] Lift a lighted sod, will you, and scorch his leg.

PEGEEN [*blowing the fire, with a bellows*]: Leave go now, young fellow, or I'll scorch your shins.

CHRISTY: You're blowing for to torture me. [*His voice rising and growing stronger.*] That's your kind, is it? Then let the lot of you be wary, for, if I've to face the gallows, I'll have a gay march down, I tell you, and shed the blood of some of you before I die.

SHAWN [*in terror*]: Keep a good hold, Philly. Be wary, for the love of God. For I'm thinking he would liefest wreak his pains on me.

CHRISTY [*almost gaily*]: If I do lay my hands on you, it's the way you'll be at the fall of night, hanging as a scarecrow for the fowls of hell. Ah, you'll have a gallous jaunt I'm saying, coaching out through Limbo with my father's ghost.

SHAWN [*to* PEGEEN]: Make haste, will you? Oh, isn't he a holy terror, and isn't it true for Father Reilly, that all drink's a curse that has the lot of you so shaky and uncertain now?

CHRISTY: If I can wring a neck among you, I'll have a royal judgment looking on the trembling jury in the courts of law. And won't there be crying out in Mayo the day I'm stretched upon the rope with ladies in their silks and satins snivelling in their lacy kerchiefs, and they rhyming songs and ballads on the terror of my fate?

[*He squirms round on the floor and bites* SHAWN'S *leg.*]

SHAWN [*shrieking*]: My leg's bit on me. He's the like of a mad dog, I'm thinking, the way that I will surely die.

CHRISTY [*delighted with himself*]: You will then, the way you can shake out hell's flags of welcome for my coming in two weeks or three, for I'm thinking Satan hasn't many have killed their da in Kerry, and in Mayo too.

[*Old* MAHON *comes in behind on all fours and looks on unnoticed.*]

MEN [*to* PEGEEN]: Bring the sod, will you?

PEGEEN [*coming over*]: God help him so. [*Burns his leg.*]

CHRISTY [*kicking and screaming*]: O, glory be to God!

[*He kicks loose from the table, and they all drag him towards the door.*]

JIMMY [*seeing old* MAHON]: Will you look what's come in?

[*They all drop* CHRISTY *and run left.*]

CHRISTY [*scrambling on his knees face to face with old* MAHON]: Are you coming to be killed a third time, or what ails you now?

MAHON: For what is it they have you tied?

CHRISTY: They're taking me to the peelers to have me hanged for slaying you.

MICHAEL [*apologetically*]: It is the will of God that all should guard their little cabins from the treachery of law, and what would my daughter be doing if I was ruined or was hanged itself?

MAHON [*grimly, loosening* CHRISTY]: It's little I care if you put a bag on her back, and went picking cockles till the hour of death; but my son and myself will be going our own way, and we'll have great times from this out telling stories of the villainy of Mayo, and the fools is here. [*To* CHRISTY, *who is freed.*] Come on now.

CHRISTY: Go with you, is it? I will then, like a gallant captain with his heathen slave. Go on now and I'll see you from this day stewing my oatmeal and washing my spuds, for I'm master of all fights from now. [*Pushing* MAHON.] Go on, I'm saying.

MAHON: Is it me?

CHRISTY: Not a word out of you. Go on from this.

MAHON [*walking out and looking back at* CHRISTY *over his shoulder*]: Glory be to God! [*With a broad smile.*] I am crazy again! [*Goes.*]

CHRISTY: Ten thousand blessings upon all that's here, for you've turned me a likely gaffer in the end of all, the way I'll go romancing through a romping lifetime from this hour to the dawning of the judgment day. [*He goes out.*]

MICHAEL: By the will of God, we'll have peace now for our drinks. Will you draw the porter, Pegeen?

SHAWN [*going up to her*]: It's a miracle Father Reilly can wed us in the end of all, and we'll have none to trouble us when his vicious bite is healed.

PEGEEN [*hitting him a box on the ear*]: Quit my sight. [*Putting her shawl over her head and breaking out into wild lamentations.*] Oh my grief, I've lost him surely. I've lost the only Playboy of the Western World.

CURTAIN

William Somerset
Maugham
[1874-1965]

I WAS NEVER STAGE-STRUCK," said Somerset Maugham. He preferred the theatre when the auditorium was dark and the stage
unset, with the flats against the back wall. He very much enjoyed rehearsals, particularly the dress rehearsal, but he took
no pleasure in seeing his plays done with an audience present.
He put so much of himself into even his slightest pieces that
he was embarrassed to hear the lines spoken aloud to a crowd
of people. This keeping of himself to himself had long been a
characteristic of Maugham's. He was born in Paris on January
24, 1874, the youngest of six sons, and he counted the first eight
years of his life happy ones. Then his mother died and two years
later his father. The transition at the age of ten from a happy,
congenial environment to a bleak, joyless one with his uncle,
an English vicar, was painful for a boy who was shy, sickly, and
plagued with a stammer. At eighteen, after a year on the continent, he had acquired a love of literature and of travel. At a loss
for a career, he became a half-hearted medical student and qualified in 1897; however, after working in the out-patient ward, he
developed a real interest in the patients rather than in medicine
and as a result wrote his first novel, *Liza of Lambeth*, 1897,
which, despite its being a case study, was modestly successful

and encouraged him to write. His interest in and curiosity about people were very strong. He never cared to enter into conversations but was an attentive listener and found even bores interesting from his writer's viewpoint. He was an inveterate notebook keeper and constantly jotted down remarks that he heard and descriptive details of people he encountered.

After traveling in Italy and Spain he wrote some short stories and several sketch books and, returning to England, wrote seven novels between 1898 and 1908. He first gained fame and money through the theatre. He said, "I began to write plays, as do most young writers, I expect, because it seemed less difficult to set down on paper the things people said than to construct a narrative." However, after several plays had been turned down, he deliberately began to write plays to please because he was poor and had no intention of starving in a garret if he could help it. He had discovered that money was like a sixth sense without which he could not properly enjoy the other five. Also he recognized his facility for amusing dialogue and for constructing a comic situation. He believed that he had other, more serious qualities, but he reserved those and used only what he needed to turn out successful comedies—and successful they were. His *Lady Frederick,* produced in 1907, an epigrammatic comedy of manners, was a great hit. In 1909, after several more such hits, he began to write as he pleased and turned out comedies that satirized conventions. In all he did three adaptations, several one-act plays, and twenty-seven full-length plays. "The secret of playwriting," he said, "can be given in two maxims: stick to the point and whenever you can, cut."

During World War I he served with the Red Cross and the British Intelligence. His constitution was never strong, and he spent the winter of 1917 in a tuberculosis sanatorium in Scotland. In the 1920's he traveled all over the world and wrote many short stories and several travel books. In 1928 he bought the Villa Mauresque at Cap Ferrat on the French Riviera, which was his home until he died, December 16, 1965.

Our Betters was written in 1915 in Rome and was first presented in Atlantic City in 1917, then in New York in the same year. It did not appear in London until 1923. In that London production the censor found the climactic scene too shocking and had Lord Bleane go to the summer house instead of Bessie. Maugham said, "In the drama I have found myself at home in the traditional moulds." *Our Betters* is in the Restoration tradition. The interest lies not in action but in conversation, which is urbane, a trifle sentimental, and does not preach. "The playwright's aim," said Maugham, "is not now to represent life as it is (a tragic business) but to comment on it satirically and amusingly." *Our Betters* is a devastating satire on the snobbery of American expatriates and the English leisure class. Some critics have thought it the best comedy of manners since the Restoration. The satirical tone is somewhat sharper and more bitter than that found in Wycherley or Congreve. The treatment of social intrigue and hypocrisy is more cynical and less joyous. The characters in Wycherley and Congreve seem to be having a good time at the game of dissembling; Maugham's characters seem, by contrast, a little more desperate and perverse. The language is the life of the play; it is often sharp and brilliant. Occasionally, as in the speeches of the plain dealers Fleming and Bessie, there is straightforward talk. The effect is to heighten the cynicism and sense of corruption in the other characters and to diminish the laughter and fun. There is a middle-class decency about Fleming and Bessie and they stand outside the society of dissemblers. In Restoration drama the sympathetic characters are usually the wittiest and cleverest within the society of maskers and manipulators. In Maugham's play, the wittiest and cleverest is Pearl, the arch-manipulator. She manages to manipulate successfully to the end. The sympathetic characters, Fleming and Bessie, have no recourse but to remain outsiders and to leave. Their happy ending is simply to avoid becoming part of Pearl's hypocritical set.

There are some realistic touches—such as the Princess' speech about her tragic-pathetic part—which are foreign to the Restoration comedies but suggest the influence of the realistic drama of the transition period. Also the play treats a number of current social manifestations and interests: the snobbery of Americans seeking aristocratic marriages, the decline of the English aristocracy which is putting itself up for sale to the highest bidder, the increasing expatriation of rich Americans, seeking cultured and sophisticated society abroad, and the mores and manners of the international set.

Although Maugham called the prose drama one of the lesser arts, he wrote plays that were well made in the best professional sense. His dialogue was always entertaining and polished, often epigrammatic. His language was written to be spoken and listened to. As in his fiction, he told a good story on the stage and told it well. Most of his thirty-odd plays achieved popular success. *The Circle* has been one of the most anthologized and produced of his plays, though Maugham himself found some fault with its motivation. Among his other successes are *The Land of Promise* (1914), *Caroline* (1916), *Home and Beauty* (1919), *East of Suez* (1922), *The Letter* (1927), *The Constant Wife* (1927), *The Breadwinner* (1930), and *Sheppey* (1933). In 1908 Maugham set a record for the number of new plays in production at the same time—four in the same season. No year passes without one or more of Maugham's plays in production somewhere in the American or English theatre.

DRAMATIC WORKS

Dates of production and publication of Maugham's plays vary more widely than with other dramatists discussed in this book. Dates given here are those for the production of the plays; publication dates, where different, appear in parentheses.

A Man of Honour, 1903
Lady Frederick, 1907 (1912)
Jack Straw, 1908 (1911)
Mrs. Dot, 1908 (1912)
The Explorer, 1908 (1912)
Penelope, 1909 (1912)
Smith, 1909 (1913)
The Tenth Man, 1910 (1913)
Landed Gentry, 1910 (1913)
Loaves and Fishes, 1911 (1924)
The Land of Promise, 1914 (1913)
The Unattainable (Caroline),
    1916 (1923)

Our Betters, 1917 (1923)
Caesar's Wife, 1919 (1922)
Home and Beauty (Too Many Husbands), 1919 (1923)
The Unknown, 1920
The Circle, 1921
East of Suez, 1922
The Constant Wife, 1926 (1927)
The Letter, 1927
The Sacred Flame, 1928 (1929)
The Breadwinner, 1930
For Services Rendered, 1932
Sheppey, 1933

Our Betters

A COMEDY IN THREE ACTS

CHARACTERS

LADY GRAYSTON
DUCHESSE DE SURENNES
PRINCIPESSA DELLA CERCOLA
ELIZABETH SAUNDERS
ARTHUR FENWICK
THORNTON CLAY
FLEMING HARVEY
ANTHONY PAXTON
LORD BLEANE
POLE
ERNEST

The action of the play takes place at Lady Grayston's house in Grosvenor Street, Mayfair, and at her husband's place in Suffolk, Abbots Kenton.

ACT ONE

SCENE: *The drawing-room at* LADY GRAYSTON'S *house in Grosvenor Street, Mayfair. It is a sumptuous double room, of the period of George II, decorated in green and gold, with a coromandel screen and lacquer cabinets; but the coverings of the chairs, the sofas and cushions, show the influence of Bakst and the Russian Ballet; they offer an agreeable mixture of rich plum, emerald green, canary and ultramarine. On the floor is a Chinese carpet, and here and there are pieces of Ming pottery.*

It is about half-past four, early in the season, and a fine day.

[*When the curtain rises, from the street below is heard the melancholy chant of the lavender man.*]

Won't you buy my sweet
    lavender?
Sixteen blue branches for a
    penny.
If you buy it once,
You'll buy it twice,
For it makes your clothes
Smell very nice—
Sweet-scented lavender.

[BESSIE SAUNDERS *comes in. She is a very pretty American girl, of twenty-two, with fair hair and blue eyes. She is dressed in the latest 'mode. She wears a hat and gloves, and carries a bag. She has just come in from the street. She has in her hand a telephone message, and going over to the telephone she takes up the receiver.*]

BESSIE: Gerrard 4321. Is that the Berkeley? Put me through to Mr. Harvey, please. Fleming Harvey, that's right. [*She listens and smiles.*] Yes. Who d'you think it is? [*She laughs.*] I've just got your telephone message. Where have you sprung from? That's fine. How long are you staying in London? I see. I want to see you at once. Nonsense. This very minute. Now just jump into a taxi and come right away. Pearl will be in presently. Ring off, Fleming. No, I will not ring off first. [*A pause.*] Are you there? How tiresome you are. You might be half-way here by now. Well, hustle.

[*She puts down the receiver and begins to take off her gloves.* POLE, *the butler, comes in with a bunch of roses.*]

POLE: These flowers have just come for you, miss.
BESSIE: Oh! Thank you. Aren't

they lovely? You must give me something to put them in, Pole.

POLE: I'll bring a vase, miss.

[*He goes out. She buries her face in the flowers and inhales their fragrance. The* BUTLER *enters with a bowl filled with water.*]

BESSIE: Thank you. You're sure they *are* for me? There's no label.

POLE: Yes, miss. The person who brought them said they was for you, miss. I asked if there wasn't a card, and he said no, miss.

BESSIE [*with a faint smile*]: I think I know who they're from. [*She begins to arrange the flowers.*] Her ladyship hasn't come in yet, has she?

POLE: Not yet, miss.

BESSIE: D'you know if anyone is coming in to tea?

POLE: Her ladyship didn't say, miss.

BESSIE: You'd better prepare for fifteen, then.

POLE: Very good, miss.

BESSIE: I was being funny, Pole.

POLE: Yes, miss? Shall I take the paper away, miss?

BESSIE [*with a slight sigh of resignation*]: Yes, do, will you? [*The telephone bell rings.*] Oh, I forgot, I switched the telephone on here. See who it is.

[POLE *takes up the receiver and listens, then puts his hand over its mouth.*]

POLE: Will you speak to Lord Bleane, miss?

BESSIE: Say I'm not at home.

POLE: Miss Saunders hasn't come in yet. I beg pardon, my lord. I didn't recognise your lordship's voice. [*A pause.*] Well, my lord, I did hear them say there was a private view they thought of going to at the Grosvenor. You might find Miss Saunders there.

BESSIE: You needn't elaborate, Pole.

POLE: I was only making it more convincing, miss. [*Listening.*] I think so, my lord. Of course, I couldn't say for certain, my lord; they might have gone out to Ranelagh.

BESSIE: Really, Pole!

POLE: Very good, my lord. [*He puts down the receiver.*] His lordship asked if you was expected in to tea, miss.

BESSIE: I see.

POLE: Is there anything else, miss?

BESSIE: No, Pole, thank you.

[*He goes out. She finishes arranging the flowers. The door is flung open and* LADY GRAYSTON *comes in, followed by* FLEMING HARVEY. PEARL — LADY GRAYSTON — *is a handsome, dashing creature, a woman of thirty-four, with red hair, and a face outrageously painted. She is dressed in a Paris frock, but of greater daring both in colour and cut than a Frenchwoman would wear.* FLEMING *is a nice-looking young American in clothes that were obviously made in New York.*]

PEARL: My dear Bessie, I've found an entirely strange young man on the doorstep who says he is a cousin.

BESSIE [*giving him her hands enthusiastically*]: Fleming.

FLEMING: I introduced myself to Lady Grayston. She drove up just as they were opening the door. Please reassure your sister, Bessie. She looks upon me with suspicion.

BESSIE: You must remember Fleming Harvey, Pearl.

PEARL: I've never set eyes on him in my life. But he looks quite nice.

BESSIE: He is.

PEARL: He's apparently come to see you.

FLEMING: I rang up five minutes ago and Bessie ordered me to come round right away.

PEARL: Well, make him stop to tea. I've got to telephone. I've suddenly remembered that I've asked twelve people to dinner.

BESSIE: Does George know?

PEARL: Who is George?

BESSIE: Don't be absurd, Pearl. George—your husband.

PEARL: Oh! I couldn't make out who you meant. No, he doesn't know. But what's much more important, the cook doesn't know either. I'd forgotten George was in London. [*She goes out.*]

BESSIE: George generally dines out when Pearl is giving a party, because he doesn't like people he doesn't know, and he seldom dines at home when we're alone, because it bores him.

FLEMING: It doesn't sound as if Sir George enjoyed many of the benefits of home life.

BESSIE: Now let's sit down and make ourselves comfortable. You are going to stay to tea, aren't you?

FLEMING: It's not a beverage that I'm in the habit of imbibing.

BESSIE: When you've been in England a month you won't be able to do without it. When did you land?

FLEMING: This morning. You see,

I've lost no time in coming to see you.

BESSIE: I should think not. It *is* good to see someone straight from home.

FLEMING: Have you been having a good time, Bessie?

BESSIE: Wonderful! Since the beginning of the season, except when Pearl has had people here, I've been out to lunch and dinner every day, and I've been to a ball every night, generally two and sometimes three.

FLEMING: Gee!

BESSIE: If I stopped now I'd drop down dead.

FLEMING: D'you like England?

BESSIE: I adore it. I think it's too bad of dad never to have let me come over to London before. Rome and Paris are nothing. We're just trippers there, but here we're at home.

FLEMING: Don't get too much at home, Bessie.

BESSIE: Oh, Fleming, I never thanked you for sending me the roses. It was perfectly sweet of you.

FLEMING [*with a smile*]: I didn't send you any roses.

BESSIE: Didn't you! Well, why didn't you?

FLEMING: I hadn't time. But I will.

BESSIE: It's too late now. I naturally thought they were from you, because Englishmen don't send flowers in the same way as American boys do.

FLEMING: Is that so?

[*There is a slight pause.* BESSIE *gives him a quick look.*]

BESSIE: Fleming, I want to thank

you for that charming letter you wrote me.

FLEMING: There's no occasion to do that, Bessie.

BESSIE: I was afraid you might feel badly about it. But we'll always be the greatest friends, won't we?

FLEMING: Always.

BESSIE: After all, you were eighteen when you asked me to marry you, and I was sixteen. It wasn't a very serious engagement. I don't know why we didn't break if off before.

FLEMING: I suppose it never occurred to us.

BESSIE: I'd almost forgotten it, but when I came over here I thought I'd better make everything quite clear.

FLEMING [*with a smile*]: Bessie, I believe you're in love.

BESSIE: No, I'm not. I tell you I'm having a wonderful time.

FLEMING: Well, who sent you the roses?

BESSIE: I don't know. Lord Bleane.

FLEMING: You're not going to marry a lord, Bessie?

BESSIE: Have you any objection?

FLEMING: Well, on first principles, I think American girls had better marry American men, but then I happen to be an American man.

BESSIE *looks at him for a moment.*]

BESSIE: Pearl gave a dinner party last night. I was taken in by a cabinet minister, and on the other side of me I had an ambassador. Just opposite was a man who'd been Viceroy in India. Madame Angelotti dined with us, and she sang afterwards, and a lot of people came on from an official dinner in their stars and ribands. Pearl looked superb. She's a wonderful hostess, you know. Several people told me they would rather come here than to any house in London. Before Pearl married George Grayston she was engaged to a boy who was in business in Portland, Oregon.

FLEMING [*smiling*]: I see you're quite determined to marry a lord.

BESSIE: No, I'm not. I'm keeping an open mind on the subject.

FLEMING: What d'you mean by that?

BESSIE: Well, Fleming, it hasn't escaped my notice that a certain noble lord is not unwilling to lay his beautiful coronet at my feet.

FLEMING: Don't talk like a novelette, Bessie.

BESSIE: But it feels just like a novelette. The poor dear is trying to propose to me every time he sees me, and I'm doing all I can to prevent him.

FLEMING: Why?

BESSIE: I don't want to refuse him, and then wish I hadn't.

FLEMING: You could easily make him ask you again. Women find that so simple.

BESSIE: Ah, but supposing he went right away to shoot big game in Africa. It's what they do, you know, in novelettes.

FLEMING: I'm reassured about one thing. You're not in the least in love with him.

BESSIE: I told you I wasn't. You don't mind my saying all this to you, Fleming?

FLEMING: Gracious, no; why should I?

BESSIE: You're sure you don't feel sore at my throwing you over?

FLEMING [*cheerfully*]: Not a bit.

BESSIE: I am glad, because then I can tell you all about the noble lord.

FLEMING: Has it occurred to you that he wants to marry you for your money?

BESSIE: You can put it more prettily. You can say that he wants to marry me with my money.

FLEMING: And is that a prospect that allures you?

BESSIE: Poor dear, what else can he do? He's got a large place to keep up, and he simply hasn't a cent.

FLEMING: Really, Bessie, you amaze me.

BESSIE: I shan't when you've been here a month.

[PEARL *comes in.*]

PEARL: Now, Bessie, tell me all about this strange young man.

BESSIE: He's quite capable of telling you about himself.

PEARL [*to* FLEMING]: How long are you staying?

FLEMING: A couple of months. I want to see something of English life.

PEARL: I see. D'you want to improve your mind or d'you want to go into society?

FLEMING: I suppose I couldn't ' combine the two.

PEARL: Are you rich?

FLEMING: Not at all.

PEARL: It doesn't matter, you're good-looking. If one wants to be a success in London one must either have looks, wit, or a bank-balance. You know Arthur Fenwick, don't you?

FLEMING: Only by reputation.

PEARL: How superciliously you say that!

FLEMING: He provides bad food to the working classes of the United States at an exorbitant price. I have no doubt he makes a lot of money.

BESSIE: He's a great friend of Pearl's.

PEARL: When he first came over because they turned up their noses at him in New York, I said to him: My dear Mr. Fenwick, you're not good-looking, you're not amusing, you're not well-bred, you're only rich. If you want to get into society you must spend money.

FLEMING: It was evidently in the nature of a straight talk.

BESSIE: We must do what we can for Fleming, Pearl.

PEARL [*with a chuckle*]: We'll introduce him to Minnie Surennes.

FLEMING: Who in the world is she?

PEARL: The Duchesse de Surennes. Don't you remember? She was a Miss Hodgson. Chicago people. Of course, they're nobody in America, but that doesn't matter over here. She adores good-looking boys, and I daresay she's getting rather tired of Tony. [*To* BESSIE.] By the way, they're coming in this afternoon.

BESSIE: I don't like Tony.

PEARL: Why not? I think he's charming. He's the most unprincipled ruffian I ever met.

FLEMING: Is Tony the duke?

PEARL: What duke? Her husband? Oh no, she divorced him years ago.

BESSIE: I think Fleming would like the Princess much better

PEARL: Oh, well, he'll meet her here today, too.

BESSIE: She was a Miss van Hoog, Fleming.

FLEMING: Is she divorced too?

PEARL: Oh no, her husband's an Italian. It's very difficult to get a divorce in Italy. She's only separated. She's quite nice. She's one of my greatest friends. She bores me a little.

[POLE *comes in to announce* THORNTON CLAY *and then goes out.* THORNTON CLAY *is a stout American with a bald head and an effusive manner. He is somewhat overdressed. He speaks with a marked American accent.*]

POLE: Mr. Thornton Clay.

CLAY: How d'you do?

PEARL: You're the very person we want, Thornton. An entirely strange young man has suddenly appeared on my doorstep, and says he's my cousin.

CLAY: My dear Pearl, that is a calamity which we Americans must always be prepared for.

BESSIE: I won't have you say such things, Mr. Clay. Fleming is not only our cousin, but he's my very oldest friend. Aren't you, Fleming?

PEARL: Bessie has a charming nature. She really thinks that friendship puts one under an obligation.

FLEMING: Since you're talking of me, won't you introduce me to Mr. Clay?

PEARL: How American you are!

FLEMING [*smiling*]: It's not unnatural, is it?

PEARL: Over here we haven't the passion that you have in America for introducing people. My dear Thornton, allow me to present to you my long-lost cousin, Mr. Fleming Harvey.

CLAY: It's so long since I was in America that I almost forget, but I believe the proper answer to that is: Mr. Fleming Harvey, I'm pleased to make your acquaintance.

FLEMING: Aren't you an American, Mr. Clay.

CLAY: I won't deny that I was born in Virginia.

FLEMING: I beg your pardon, I thought from the way you spoke . . .

CLAY [*interrupting*]: But, of course, my home is London.

PEARL: Nonsense, Thornton, your home is wherever there's a first-class hotel.

CLAY: I went to America seven years ago. My father died and I had to go and settle up his affairs. Everyone took me for an Englishman.

FLEMING: That must have gratified you very much, Mr. Clay.

CLAY: Of course, I haven't a trace of an American accent. I suppose that was the reason. And then my clothes. [*He looks down at them with satisfaction.*]

PEARL: Fleming wants to see life in London, Thornton. He can't do better than put himself under your wing.

CLAY: I know everyone who's worth knowing. I can't deny that.

PEARL: Thornton calls more countesses by their Christian names than any man in town.

CLAY: I'll get him cards for some good balls, and I'll see that he's asked to one or two of the right parties.

PEARL: He's good-looking, and I'm sure he dances well. He'll be a credit to you, Thornton.

CLAY [*to* FLEMING]: But, of course, there's really nothing I *can* do for you. At Lady Grayston's you are in the very hub of society. I don't mean the stuffy, old-fashioned society, that goes about in barouches and bores itself stiff, but the society that counts, the society that figures in the newspapers. Pearl is the most wonderful hostess in London.

PEARL: What *do* you want, Thornton?

CLAY: In this house, sooner or later, you'll meet every re-markable man in England except one. That is George Grayston. And he's only remarkable because he's her husband.

PEARL [*with a chuckle*]: I might have known you were only saying a pleasant thing in order to make the next one more disagreeable.

CLAY: Of course, I can't make out why you never ask George to your parties. Personally I like him.

PEARL: That's all the nicer of you, Thornton, since he always speaks of you as that damned snob.

CLAY [*with a shrug of the shoulders*]: Poor George, he has such a limited vocabulary. I met Flora della Cercola at luncheon today. She told me she was coming to tea with you.

PEARL: She's getting up a concert in aid of something or other, and she wants me to help her.

CLAY: Poor Flora, with her good works! She takes philanthropy as a drug to allay the pangs of unrequited love.

PEARL: I always tell her she'd do much better to take a lover.

CLAY: You'll shock Mr. Harvey.

PEARL: It won't hurt him. It'll do him good.

CLAY: Did you ever know her husband?

PEARL: Oh yes, I met him. Just the ordinary little Dago. I cannot imagine why she should ever have been in love with him. She's an extraordinary creature. D'you know, I'm convinced that she's never had an affair.

CLAY: Some of these American women are strangely sexless.

FLEMING: I have an idea that some of them are even virtuous.

PEARL [*with a smile*]: It takes all sorts to make a world.

[POLE *enters to announce the* DUCHESSE DE SURRENNES, *and then goes out.*]

POLE: The Duchesse de Surennes.

[*The* DUCHESSE *is a large, dark woman of forty-five with scarlet lips and painted cheeks, a woman of opulent form, bold, self-assured and outrageously sensual. She suggests a drawing of a Roman Emperor by Aubrey Beardsley. She is gowned with a certain dashing magnificence, and wears a long string of large pearls round her neck. During the conversation* POLE *and two footmen bring in tea, and place it in the back drawing-room.*]

PEARL: My dear, how nice of you to come.

DUCHESSE: Isn't Tony here?

PEARL: No.

DUCHESSE: He said he was coming straight here.

PEARL: I daresay he's been delayed.

DUCHESSE: I can't understand it. He telephoned a quarter of an hour ago that he was starting at once.

PEARL [*reassuringly*]: He'll be here presently.

DUCHESSE [*with an effort over herself*]: How pretty you're looking, Bessie. No wonder all the men I meet rave about you.

BESSIE: Englishmen are so shy. Why don't they rave *to* me?

DUCHESSE: They'll never let you go back to America.

PEARL: Of course she's never going back. I'm determined that she shall marry an Englishman.

CLAY: She'll make a charming addition to our American peeresses.

PEARL: And there'll be another that you can call by her Christian name, Thornton.

BESSIE: I wish you wouldn't talk as if I hadn't a word to say in the matter.

CLAY: Of course you've got a word to say, Bessie—a very important one.

BESSIE: Yes, I suppose?

CLAY: Exactly.

PEARL: Pour out the tea, darling, will you?

BESSIE: Surely. [*To* CLAY.] I know you don't share Fleming's contempt for tea, Mr. Clay.

CLAY: I couldn't live a day without it. Why, I never travel without a tea basket.

FLEMING [*ironically*]: Is that so?

CLAY: You Americans who live in America . . .

FLEMING [*under his breath*]: So queer of us.

CLAY: Despise the delectable habit of drinking tea because you are still partly barbarous.

The hour that we spend over it is the most delightful of the day. We do not make a business of eating as at luncheon or dinner. We are at ease with ourselves. We toy with pretty cakes as an excuse for conversation. We discuss the abstract, our souls, our morals; we play delicately with the concrete, our neighbour's new bonnet or her latest lover. We drink tea because we are a highly civilised nation.

FLEMING: I must be very stupid, but I don't follow.

CLAY: My dear fellow, the degree of a nation's civilisation is marked by its disregard for the necessities of existence. You have gone so far as to waste money, but we have gone farther; we waste what is infinitely more precious, more transitory, more irreparable—we waste time.

DUCHESSE: My dear Thornton, you fill me with despair. Compton Edwardes has cut me off my tea. I thought he was only depriving me of a luxury, now I see he's depriving me also of a religious rite.

FLEMING: Who in heaven's name is Compton Edwardes, that he should have such influence?

PEARL: My dear Fleming, he's the most powerful man in London. He's the great reducer.

FLEMING: Gracious! What does he reduce?

PEARL: Fat.

DUCHESSE: He's a perfect marvel, that man. Do you know, the Duchess of Arlington told me he'd taken nine pounds off her.

PEARL: My dear, that's nothing. Why, Clara Hollington gave me her word of honour she'd lost over a stone.

BESSIE [*from the tea-table*]: Anyone who wants tea must come and fetch it.

[*The men saunter over to the next room, while* PEARL *and the* DUCHESSE *go on with their conversation.*]

DUCHESSE: Who is that nice-looking young man, Pearl?

PEARL: Oh, he's a young American. He pretends to be a cousin of mine. He's come to see Bessie.

DUCHESSE: Does he want to marry her?

PEARL: Good heavens, I hope not. He's only an old friend. You know the funny ways they have in America.

DUCHESSE: I suppose nothing is really settled about Harry Bleane?

PEARL: No. But I shouldn't be surprised if you saw an announcement in the Morning Post one day.

DUCHESSE: Has she enough money for him?

PEARL: She has a million.

DUCHESSE: Not pounds?

PEARL: Oh no, dollars.

DUCHESSE: That's only eight thousand a year. I shouldn't have thought he'd be satisfied with that.

PEARL: People can't expect so much nowadays. There won't be any more enormous heiresses as there were in your time. Besides, Harry Bleane isn't such a catch as all that. Of course, it's better to be an English baron than an Italian count, but that's about all you can say for it.

DUCHESSE: Of course she'll accept him?

PEARL: Oh yes, she's crazy to live in England. And as I tell her, it's quite pleasant to be a peeress even now.

DUCHESSE: What on earth can have happened to Tony?

PEARL: My dear, he's not likely to have been run over by a motor-bus.

DUCHESSE: I'm not afraid of motor-buses running over him; I'm afraid of him running after Gaiety girls.

PEARL [*drily*]: I should have thought you kept a very sharp eye on him.

DUCHESSE: You see, he hasn't got anything to do from morning till night.

PEARL: Why doesn't he get a job?

DUCHESSE: I've been trying to get him something, but it's so difficult. You've got such a lot of influence, Pearl. Can't you do something? I should be so grateful.

PEARL: What can he do?

DUCHESSE: Anything. And as you know he's very good-looking.

PEARL: Does he know French and German?

DUCHESSE: No, he has no gift for languages.

PEARL: Can he type and write shorthand?

DUCHESSE: Oh, no. Poor dear, you can hardly expect that.

PEARL: Can he do accounts?

DUCHESSE: No, he has no head for figures.

PEARL [*reflectively*]: Well, the only thing I can see that he'd do for is a government office.

DUCHESSE: Oh, my dear, if you only could manage that. You

can't think what a comfort it would be for me to know that he couldn't get into mischief at least from ten to four every day.

[POLE *announces* TONY PAXTON. TONY *is a handsome youth of twenty-five, in beautiful clothes, with engaging manners and a charming smile.*]

POLE: Mr. Paxton.

PEARL: Well, Tony, how is life?

TONY: Rotten. I haven't backed a winner or won a rubber this week.

PEARL: Ah well, that's the advantage of not having money, you can afford to lose it.

DUCHESSE [*bursting in*]: Where have you been, Tony?

TONY: I? Nowhere.

DUCHESSE: You said you were coming straight here. It doesn't take twenty-five minutes to get here from Dover Street.

TONY: I thought there wasn't any hurry. I was just hanging about the club.

DUCHESSE: I rang up the club again, and they said you'd gone.

TONY [*after a very slight pause*]: I was downstairs having a shave, and I suppose they never thought of looking for me in the barber's shop.

DUCHESSE: What on earth did you want to be shaved for at half-past four in the afternoon?

TONY: I thought you'd like me to look nice and clean.

PEARL: Go and get Bessie to give you some tea, Tony; I'm sure you want it after the strenuous day you've had. [*He nods and walks into the inner room.*] Minnie, how can you be so silly? You can't expect to keep a man if you treat him like that.

DUCHESSE: I know he's lying to me, there's not a word of truth in anything he says: but he's so slim I can never catch him out. Oh, I'm so jealous.

PEARL: Are you really in love with him?

DUCHESSE: He's everything in the world to me.

PEARL: You shouldn't let yourself be carried away like this.

DUCHESSE: I'm not cold-blooded like you.

PEARL: You seem to have a passion for rotters, and they always treat you badly.

DUCHESSE: Oh, I don't care about the others. Tony is the only one I've ever really loved.

PEARL: Nonsense! You were just as much in love with Jack Harris. You did everything in the world for him. You taught him to wear his clothes. You got him into society. And the moment he could do without you he chucked you. Tony will do just the same.

DUCHESSE: I'm not going to be such a fool this time. I'm going to take care he can't do without me.

PEARL: I can't imagine what you see in him. You must know that . . .

DUCHESSE [*interrupting*]: There's very little I don't know. He's a liar, a gambler, an idler, a spendthrift, but in his way he is fond of me. [*Appealingly.*] You can see he's fond of me, can't you?

PEARL: He's so much younger than you, Minnie.

DUCHESSE: I can't help it. I love him.

PEARL: Oh, well, I suppose it's no

good talking. As long as he makes you happy.

DUCHESSE: He doesn't. He makes me miserable. But I love him. . . . He wants me to marry him, Pearl.

PEARL: You're not going to?

DUCHESSE: No, I won't be such a fool as that. If I married him I'd have no hold over him at all.

[*Enter* POLE *to announce the* PRINCESS DELLA CERCOLA. *She is a tall, thin woman of thirty-five, with a pale, haggard face and great dark eyes. She is a gentle, kind creature, but there is something pathetic, almost tragic, in her appearance. She is dressed, though very well, and obviously by a Paris dressmaker, more quietly than the* DUCHESSE *or* PEARL. *She has not only wealth, but distinction.*]

POLE: Princess della Cercola.

[*Exit.* PEARL *gets up to receive her. They kiss.*]

PEARL: Darling!

PRINCESS: D'you hate me for coming to bother you? I ran up because I know how difficult you are to catch. [*Kissing the* DUCHESSE.] How are you, Minnie?

DUCHESSE: Don't ask me for a subscription, Flora. I'm so poor.

PRINCESS [*smiling*]: Wait till I tell you what it's for, and then you'll remember that you had a father called Spencer Hodgson.

DUCHESSE [*with a little groan*]: As if I wanted to be reminded of it!

PEARL: You're so absurd, Minnie. You should make a joke of the pork. I always tell people about father's hardware store, and

when I haven't got a funny story to tell about it, I invent one.

PRINCESS: You've made your father quite a character in London.

PEARL: That's why I never let him come over. He couldn't possibly live up to his reputation.

[FLEMING HARVEY *comes forward from the inner room.*]

FLEMING: I'm going to say good-bye to you.

PEARL: You mustn't go before I've introduced you to Flora. Flora, this is Mr. Fleming Harvey. He's just come from America. He probably carries a six-shooter in his hip-pocket.

FLEMING: I'm told I mayn't say I'm pleased to make your acquaintance, Princess.

PRINCESS: When did you land?

FLEMING: This morning.

PRINCESS: I envy you.

FLEMING: Because I landed this morning?

PRINCESS: No, because a week ago you were in America.

DUCHESSE: Flora!

FLEMING: I was beginning to think it was something to be rather ashamed of.

PRINCESS: Oh, you mustn't pay any attention to Pearl and the Duchesse. They're so much more English than the English.

PEARL: I notice you show your devotion to the country of your birth by staying away from it, Flora.

PRINCESS: Last time I was in America it made me so unhappy that I vowed I'd never go there again.

DUCHESSE: I was there ten years

ago, when I was divorcing Gaston. I hadn't been in America since my marriage, and I'd forgotten what it was like. Oh, it was so crude. Oh, it was so provincial. You don't mind my saying so, Mr. Harvey?

FLEMING: Not at all. You're just as American as I am, and there's no reason why among ourselves we shouldn't abuse the mother that bore us.

DUCHESSE: Oh, but I don't look upon myself as American. I'm French. After all, I haven't a trace of an American accent. To show you how it got on my nerves, I almost didn't divorce Gaston because I thought I couldn't bring myself to stay in America long enough.

PRINCESS: It's not because it was crude and provincial that I was unhappy in America. I was unhappy because after all it was home, the only real home I've ever had, and I was a stranger.

PEARL: My dear Flora, you're being very sentimental.

PRINCESS [*smiling*]: I'm sorry; I apologise. You're a New Yorker, Mr. Harvey?

FLEMING: I'm proud of it, madam.

PRINCESS: New York's wonderful, isn't it? It has something that no other city in the world has got. I like to think of Fifth Avenue on a spring day. The pretty girls in their smart frocks and neat shoes, who trip along so gaily, and all the good-looking boys.

DUCHESSE: I grant you that; some of the boys are too lovely for words.

PRINCESS: Everyone is so strong and confident. There's such an exaltation in the air. You feel in the passers-by a serene and unshakable belief in the future. Oh, it's very good to be alive in Fifth Avenue on a sunny day in April.

FLEMING: It's good for an American to hear another American say such pleasant things about his country.

PRINCESS: You must come and see me, and you shall tell me all the news of home.

PEARL: How high the newest building is, and how much money the latest millionaire has got.

FLEMING: Good-bye.

PEARL: Have you made friends with Thornton Clay?

FLEMING: I hope so.

PEARL: You must get him to give you the address of his tailor.

FLEMING: Aren't you pleased with my clothes?

PEARL: They're very American, you know.

FLEMING: So am I.

[THORNTON CLAY *comes forward. The* DUCHESSE *strolls over to the inner room and is seen talking with* BESSIE *and* TONY PAXTON.]

PEARL: Thornton, I was just telling Mr. Harvey that you'd take him to your tailor.

CLAY: I was going to suggest it.

FLEMING: My clothes are not at all a success.

PEARL: Who d'you go to? Stultz?

CLAY: Of course. He's the only tailor in London. [*To* FLEMING.] Of course he's a German, but art has no nationality.

FLEMING: I'm pleased at all events to think that it's a German tailor who's going to make me look like an Englishman.

[*He goes out.* THORNTON *makes his farewells.*]

CLAY: Good-bye, Pearl.

PEARL: Are you going? Don't forget you're coming down to Kenton on Saturday.

CLAY: I won't, indeed. I adore your week-end parties, Pearl. I'm so exhausted by Monday morning that I'm fit for nothing for the rest of the week. Good-bye.

[*He shakes hands and goes out. As he is going,* POLE *opens the door to announce* LORD BLEANE. *He is a young man, very English in appearance, pleasant, clean and well-groomed.*]

POLE: Lord Bleane. [*Exit.*]

PEARL: Dear Harry, how nice of you to come.

BLEANE: I'm in absolute despair.

PEARL: Good heavens, why?

BLEANE: They're sending a mission to Rumania to hand the Garter to some bigwig and I've got to go with it.

PEARL: Oh, but that'll be very interesting.

BLEANE: Yes, but we start tomorrow, and I shan't be able to come down to Kenton on Saturday.

PEARL: When do you come back?

BLEANE: In four weeks.

PEARL: Then come down to Kenton the Saturday after that.

BLEANE: May I?

PEARL: You must go and break the news to Bessie. She was so looking forward to your visit.

BLEANE: D'you think she'll give me some tea?

PEARL: I have no doubt, if you ask her nicely.

[*He goes over to the inner room.*]

PRINCESS: Now I've got you to myself for two minutes. You will help me with my concert, won't you?

PEARL: Of course. What do you want me to do? I'll make Arthur Fenwick take any number of tickets. You know how charitable he is.

PRINCESS: It's for a very good cause.

PEARL: I'm sure it is. But don't harrow me with revolting stories of starving children. I'm not interested in the poor.

PRINCESS [*smiling*]: How can you say that?

PEARL: Are you? I often wonder if your philanthropy isn't an elaborate pose. You don't mind my saying that, do you?

PRINCESS [*good-humouredly*]: Not at all. You have no heart, and you can't imagine that anyone else should have.

PEARL: I have plenty of heart, but it beats for people of my own class.

PRINCESS: I've only found one thing really worth doing with all this money I have, and that is to help a little those who need help.

PEARL [*with a shrug*]: So long as it makes you happy.

PRINCESS: It doesn't, but it prevents me from being utterly miserable.

PEARL: You make me so impatient, Flora. You've got more money than you know what to do with. You're a princess. You've practically got rid of your husband. I cannot imagine what more you want. I wish I could get rid of mine.

PRINCESS [*smiling*]: I don't know what you've got to complain of in George.

PEARL: That's just it. I shouldn't mind if he beat me or made love to chorus girls. I could divorce him then. Oh, my dear, thank your stars that you had a husband who was grossly unfaithful to you. Mine wants me to live nine months of the year in the country and have a baby every five minutes. I didn't marry an Englishman for that.

PRINCESS: Why *did* you marry him?

PEARL: I made a mistake. I'd lived all my life in New York. I was very ignorant. I thought if you were a baronet you must be in society.

PRINCESS: I often wonder if you're happy, Pearl.

PEARL: Do you? Of course I'm happy.

PRINCESS: An ambassador told me the other day that you were the most powerful woman in London. It's very wonderful how you've made your way. You had nothing very much to help you.

PEARL: Shall I tell you how it was done? By force of character, wit, unscrupulousness, and push.

PRINCESS [*smiling*]: You're very frank.

PEARL: That has always been my pose.

PRINCESS: I sometimes think there's positive genius in the way you've ignored the snubs of the great.

PEARL [*with a chuckle*]: You're

being very unpleasant, Flora.

PRINCESS: And there's something very like heroism in the callousness with which you've dropped people when they've served your turn.

PEARL: You're driving me to the conclusion that you don't altogether approve of me.

PRINCESS: On the other hand I can't help admiring you. You've brought all the determination, insight, vigour, strength, which have made our countrymen turn America into what it is, to get what you wanted. In a way your life has been a work of art. And what makes it more complete is that what you've aimed at is trivial, transitory, and worthless.

PEARL: My dear Flora, people don't hunt in order to catch a fox.

PRINCESS: Sometimes, doesn't it make you rather nervous, when you're sitting on the top of your ladder, in case anyone should give it a kick as he passes?

PEARL: It'll want more than a kick to topple my ladder over. D'you remember when that silly woman made such a fuss because her husband was in love with me? It wasn't till I only just escaped the divorce court that the duchesses really took me up.

[*The* DUCHESSE *comes forward with* TONY PAXTON.]

DUCHESSE: We really must be going, Pearl. I expect my masseur at six. Compton Edwardes told me about him. He's wonderful, but he's so run after, if you keep him waiting a moment he goes away.

PEARL: My dear, do be careful. Fanny Hallam got herself down to a mere nothing but it made her look a hundred.

DUCHESSE: Oh, I know, but Compton Edwardes has recommended to me a wonderful woman who comes every morning to do my face.

PEARL: You are coming to my ball, aren't you?

DUCHESSE: Of course we're coming. Yours are almost the only parties in London where one amuses oneself as much as at a night club.

PEARL: I'm having Ernest to come in and dance.

DUCHESSE: I thought of having him one evening. How much does he charge for coming in socially?

PEARL: Twenty guineas.

DUCHESSE: Good heavens, I could never afford that.

PEARL: What nonsense! You're far richer than I am.

DUCHESSE: I'm not so clever, darling. I can't think how you do so much on your income.

PEARL [amused]: I'm a very good manager.

DUCHESSE: One would never think it. Good-bye, dear. Are you coming, Tony?

TONY: Yes. [She goes out. Shaking hands with PEARL.] I've not had a word with you today.

PEARL [chaffing him]: What are we to do about it?

PRINCESS: I must get Minnie to go to my concert. Minnie.

[She goes out. TONY is left face to face with PEARL.]

TONY: You're looking perfectly divine today. I don't know what there is about you.

PEARL [amused, but not disconcerted]: It is nice of you to say so.

TONY: I simply haven't been able to take my eyes off you.

PEARL: Are you making love to me?

TONY: That's nothing new, is it?

PEARL: You'll get into trouble.

TONY: Don't be disagreeable, Pearl.

PEARL: I don't remember that I ever told you you might call me Pearl.

TONY: It's how I think of you. You can't prevent me from doing that.

PEARL: Well, I think it's very familiar.

TONY: I don't know what you've done to me. I think of you all day long.

PEARL: I don't believe it for a minute. You're an unprincipled ruffian, Tony.

TONY: Do you mind?

PEARL [with a chuckle]: Shameless creature. I wonder what it is that Minnie sees in you.

TONY: I have all sorts of merits.

PEARL: I'm glad you think so. I can only discover one.

TONY: What is that?

PEARL: You're somebody else's property.

TONY: Oh!

PEARL [holding out her hand]: Good-bye. [He kisses her wrist. His lips linger. She looks at him from under her eyelashes.] It doesn't make you irresistible, you know.

TONY: There's always the future.

PEARL: The future's everybody's property.

TONY [*in an undertone*]: Pearl.

PEARL: Be quick and go. Minnie will be wondering why you don't come.

[*He goes out.* PEARL *turns away with a smile.* BESSIE *and* LORD BLEANE *advance into the room.*]

PEARL: Has Harry broken the news to you that he can't come down to us on Saturday?

[*The* PRINCESS *comes in.*]

PRINCESS: I've got my subscription.

PEARL: I kept Tony up here as long as I could so as to give you a chance.

PRINCESS [*with a laugh*]: That was really tactful.

PEARL: Poor Minnie, she's as mean as cat's meat. [*With a glance at* BESSIE *and* LORD BLEANE.] If you'd like to come down to the morning-room we can go through my visitors' book and see who'll be useful to you.

PRINCESS: Oh, that would be kind of you.

PEARL [*to* BLEANE]: Don't go till I come back, will you? I haven't had a word with you yet.

BLEANE: All right.

[PEARL *and the* PRINCESS *go out.*]

BESSIE: I wonder if you sent me these flowers, Lord Bleane?

BLEANE: I did. I thought you wouldn't mind.

BESSIE: It was very kind of you.

[*She takes two of the roses and puts them in her dress.* BLEANE *is overcome with shyness. He does not know how to begin.*]

BLEANE: D'you mind if I light a cigarette?

BESSIE: Not at all.

BLEANE [*as he lights it*]: D'you know, this is the first time I've ever been alone with you. It was very tactful of Lady Grayston to leave us.

BESSIE: I'm not sure if it wasn't a trifle too tactful.

BLEANE: I was hoping most awfully to have the chance of getting a talk with you.

[*The song of the lavender is heard again in the street.* BESSIE *welcomes the diversion.*]

BESSIE: Oh, listen, there's the lavender man come back again. [*She goes to the window and listens.*] Throw him down a shilling, will you?

BLEANE: All right. [*He takes a coin from his pocket and throws it into the street.*]

BESSIE: I seem to feel all the charm of England in that funny little tune. It suggests cottage gardens, and hedges, and winding roads.

BLEANE: My mother grows lavender at home. When we were kids we were made to pick it, and my mother used to put it in little muslin bags and tie them up with pink ribbon. And she used to put them under the pillows of one's bed and in all the drawers. Shall I ask her to send you some?

BESSIE: Oh, that would be such a bother for her.

BLEANE: It wouldn't. She'd like to. And you know, it's not like the lavender you buy. It knocks spots off anything you can get in shops.

BESSIE: You must hate leaving London at this time of year.

BLEANE: Oh, I'm not very keen on London. [*Making a dash for it.*] I hate leaving you.

BESSIE [*with comic desperation*]: Let's not talk about me, Lord Bleane.

BLEANE: But that's the only topic that occurs to me.

BESSIE: There's always the weather in England.

BLEANE: You see, I'm off tomorrow.

BESSIE: I never saw anyone so obstinate.

BLEANE: I shan't see you again for nearly a month. We haven't known one another very long, and if I hadn't been going away I expect I'd have thought it better to wait a bit.

BESSIE [*clasping her hands*]: Lord Bleane, don't propose to me.

BLEANE: Why not?

BESSIE: Because I shall refuse you.

BLEANE: Oh!

BESSIE: Tell me about the part of the country you live in. I don't know Kent at all. Is it pretty?

BLEANE: I don't know. It's home.

BESSIE: I love those old Elizabethan houses that you have in England with all their chimneys.

BLEANE: Oh, ours isn't a show place, you know. It's just a rather ugly yellow brick house that looks like a box, and it's got a great big stucco portico in front of it. I think the garden's rather jolly.

BESSIE: Pearl hates Abbots Kenton. She'd sell it if George would. She's only really happy in London.

BLEANE: I don't know that I was so particularly struck on Bleane till I was over in France. When I was in hospital at Boulogne there didn't seem much to do but to think about things. . . . It didn't seem as if I *could* get well. I knew I should if they'd only let me come home, but they wouldn't; they said I couldn't be moved. . . . It's rather bleak in our part of the country. We've got an east wind that people find a bit trying, but if you've been used to it all your life it bucks you up wonderful. In summer it can be awfully hot down there, but there's always something fresh and salt in the air. You see, we're so near the marshes. . . . It was only just across the water, and it seemed such an awful long way off. I ain't boring you, am I?

BESSIE: No. I want you to tell me.

BLEANE: It's a funny sort of country. There are a lot of green fields and elm trees, and the roads wind about—it's rotten for motoring; and then you have the marshes, with dykes in them— we used to jump them when we were boys, and fall in mostly; and then there's the sea. It doesn't sound much, but I felt it was the most ripping thing I knew. And then there are hop-fields—I forgot them—and the oast-houses. They're rather picturesque, I suppose. I expect it's like the lavender to you. To me it's just England.

[BESSIE *gets up and walks towards the window. In the distance is heard the melancholy cry of the lavender man.*]

BLEANE: What are you thinking about?

BESSIE: It must be very wonderful to feel like that about one's home. I've never known anything but a red stone house in Nineteenth Street. As soon as dad can get a decent offer for it we're going to move further up town. Mother has a fancy for Seventy-Second Street, I don't know why.

BLEANE: Of course, I know it couldn't mean the same to a girl that it means to me. I shouldn't expect anyone to live there always. I can be quite happy in London.

BESSIE [*with a smile*]: You're determined to do it?

BLEANE: If you *could* bring yourself to marry me, I'd try and give you a good time.

BESSIE: Well, I suppose that's a proposal.

BLEANE: I've never made one before, and it makes me a bit nervous.

BESSIE: You haven't said anything that I can answer yes or no to.

BLEANE: I don't want to say anything that you *can* answer no to.

BESSIE [*with a chuckle*]: Let me say that I'll think it over, may I?

BLEANE: I'm going away tomorrow.

BESSIE: I'll give you an answer when you come back.

BLEANE: But that won't be for four weeks.

BESSIE: It'll give us both a chance to make up our minds. After all, it *is* rather a serious step. You may come to the conclusion that you don't really want to marry me.

BLEANE: There's no fear of that.

BESSIE: You're coming down to Kenton for the week-end after you get back. If you change your mind send Pearl a wire putting yourself off. I shall understand, and I shan't be in the least hurt or offended.

BLEANE: Then it's good-bye till then.

BESSIE: Yes. And . . . thank you very much for wishing to marry me.

BLEANE: Thank you very much for not refusing me outright.

[*They shake hands and he goes out. She walks over to the window to look at him, glances at the watch on her wrist, and then leaves the room. In a moment* POLE *shows in* ARTHUR FENWICK. *He is a tall, elderly man with a red face and grey hair.*]

POLE: I'll tell her ladyship you're here, sir.

FENWICK: That'll be very good of you.

[POLE *goes out.* FENWICK *takes a cigar from his case, and the evening paper from a table, and settles himself down comfortably to read and smoke. He makes himself very much at home.* PEARL *comes in.*]

PEARL: Aren't Bessie and Harry Bleane here?

FENWICK: No.

PEARL: That's very strange. I wonder what can have happened.

FENWICK: Never mind about Bessie and Harry Bleane. Give me your attention now.

PEARL: You're very late.

FENWICK: I like to come when I stand a chance of finding you alone, girlie.

PEARL: I wish you wouldn't call me girlie, Arthur. I do hate it.

FENWICK: That's how I think of you. When I'm present at one of your big set-outs, and watch you like a queen among all those lords and ambassadors and bigwigs, I just say to myself, She's my girlie, and I feel warm all over. I'm so proud of you then. You've got there, girlie, you've got there.

PEARL [*smiling*]: You've been very kind to me, Arthur.

FENWICK: You've got brains, girlie, that's how you've done it. It's brains. Underneath your flighty ways and that casual air of yours, so that one might think you were just enjoying yourself and nothing more, I see you thinking it all out, pulling a string here and a string there; you've got them in the hollow of your hand all the time. You leave nothing to chance, Pearl, you're a great woman.

PEARL: Not great enough to make you obey your doctor's orders.

FENWICK [*taking the cigar out of his mouth*]: You're not going to ask me to throw away the first cigar I've had today?

PEARL: To please me, Arthur. They're so bad for you.

FENWICK: If you put it like that I must give in.

PEARL: I don't want you to be ill.

FENWICK: You've got a great heart, girlie. The world just thinks you're a smart, fashionable woman, clever, brilliant, beautiful, a leader of fashion, but I know different. I know you've got a heart of gold.

PEARL: You're a romantic old thing, Arthur.

FENWICK: My love for you is the most precious thing I have in the world. You're my guiding star, you're my ideal. You stand to me for all that's pure and noble and clean in womanhood. God bless you, girlie. I don't know what I should do if you failed me. I don't believe I could live if I ever found out that you weren't what I think you.

PEARL [*with her tongue in her cheek*]: You shan't, if I can help it.

FENWICK: You do care for me a little, girlie?

PEARL: Of course I do.

FENWICK: I'm an old man, girlie.

PEARL: What nonsense! I look upon you as a mere boy.

FENWICK [*flattered*]: Well, I expect a good many young men would be glad to have my physique. I can work fourteen hours on end and feel as fresh as a daisy at the end of it.

PEARL: Your vitality is wonderful.

FENWICK: I sometimes wonder what it is that first drew you to me, girlie.

PEARL: I don't know. I suppose it was the impression of strength you give.

FENWICK: Yes, I've often been told that. It's very difficult for people to be with me long without realising that—well, that I'm not just the man in the street.

PEARL: I always feel I can rely on you.

FENWICK: You couldn't have said anything to please me better. I want you to rely on me. I know you. I'm the only man who's ever understood you. I know that, deep down in that big, beating, human heart of yours, you're a timid, helpless little thing, with the innocence of a child, and you want a man like me to stand between you and the world. My God, how I love you, girlie!

PEARL: Take care, there's the butler.

FENWICK: Oh, damn it, there's always the butler.

[POLE *comes in with a telegram and a parcel of books.*]

PEARL [*taking the telegram and glancing at the parcel*]: What's that, Pole?

POLE: They're books, my lady. They've just come from Hatchard's.

PEARL: Oh, I know. Undo them, will you? [POLE *cuts open the parcel and takes out a bundle of four or five books.* PEARL *opens the telegram.*] Oh, bother! There's no answer, Pole.

POLE: Very good, my lady. [*Exit.*]

FENWICK: Is anything the matter?

PEARL: That fool Sturrey was dining here tonight, and he's just wired to say he can't come. I do hate having my parties upset. I'd asked ten people to meet him.

FENWICK: That's too bad.

PEARL: Pompous owl. He's refused invitation after invitation. I asked him six weeks ago this time, and he hadn't the face to say he was engaged.

FENWICK: Well, I'm afraid you must give him up. I daresay you can do without him.

PEARL: Don't be a fool, Arthur. I'll get hold of him somehow. He may be Prime Minister one of these days. [*She reflects a moment.*] I wonder what his

telephone number is. [*She gets up and looks in a book, then sits down at the telephone.*] Gerrard 7035. If he comes once because I force him to he'll come again because he likes it. This house is like the kingdom of heaven: I have to compel them to come in. . . . Is Lord Sturrey in? Lady Grayston. I'll hold the line. [*Making her voice sweet and charming.*] Is that you, Lord Sturrey? It's Pearl Grayston speaking. I just rang up to say it doesn't matter a bit about tonight. Of course, I'm disappointed you can't come. But you must come another day, will you? That's very nice of you. How about this day week? Oh, I'm sorry. Would Thursday suit you? Oh! Well, how about Friday? You're engaged every evening next week? You are in demand. Well, I'll tell you what, get your book and tell me what day you are free.

FENWICK: You're the goods, girlie. You'll get there.

PEARL: Tuesday fortnight. Yes, that'll suit me beautifully. 8:30. I'm so glad you chose that day, because I'm having Kreisler in to play. I shall look forward to seeing you. Good-bye. [*She puts down the receiver.*] This time I've got him. The ape thinks he understands music.

FENWICK: Have you got Kreisler for Tuesday fortnight?

PEARL: No.

FENWICK: Are you sure you can get him?

PEARL: No, but I'm sure you can.

FENWICK: You shall have him, girlie. [*She takes the books that* POLE *brought in and puts them about the room. One she places face downwards, open.*] What are you doing that for?

PEARL: They're Richard Twining's books. He's coming to dinner tonight.

FENWICK: Why d'you trouble about authors, girlie?

PEARL: London isn't like New York, you know. People like to meet them over here.

FENWICK: I should have thought your position was quite strong enough to do without them.

PEARL: We live in a democratic age. They take the place in society of the fools whom kings kept about their courts in the middle ages. They have the advantage that they don't presume on their position to tell one home truths. They're cheap. A dinner and a little flattery is all they want. And they provide their own clothes.

FENWICK: You litter up your house with their rotten books.

PEARL: Oh, but I don't keep them. These are on approval. I shall send them all back to the bookseller tomorrow morning.

FENWICK: Pearl, you're a little wonder. When you want to go into business you come to me and I'll take you into partnership.

PEARL: How is business?

FENWICK: Fine! I'm opening two new branches next week. They 'laughed at me when I first came over here. They said I'd go bankrupt. I've turned their silly old methods upside down. He laughs longest who laughs last.

PEARL [*reflectively*]: Ah, I can't help thinking that's what my dressmaker said when she sent me in my bill.

[*He gives a slight start and looks at her shrewdly. He sees her blandly smiling.*]

FENWICK: Girlie, you promised me you wouldn't run up any more bills.

PEARL: That's like promising to love, honour, and obey one's husband, the kind of undertaking no one is really expected to carry out.

FENWICK: You naughty little thing.

PEARL: It's Suzanne—you know, the dressmaker in the Place Vendôme. The war has dislocated her business and she wants to get her money in. It isn't very convenient for me to pay just at present. It's rather a large sum. [*She gives him a sheaf of typewritten documents.*]

FENWICK: This looks more like a five-act play than a bill.

PEARL: Clothes are expensive, aren't they? I wish I could dress in fig-leaves. It would be cheap, and I believe it would suit me.

FENWICK [*putting the bill in his pocket*]: Well, I'll see what I can do about it.

PEARL: You are a duck, Arthur. . . . Would you like me to come and lunch with you tomorrow?

FENWICK: Why, sure.

PEARL: All right. Now you must go, as I want to lie down before I dress for dinner.

FENWICK: That's right. Take care of yourself, girlie, you're very precious to me.

PEARL: Good-bye, dear old thing.

FENWICK: Good-bye, girlie.

[*He goes out. As he goes to the door the telephone rings.* PEARL *takes up the receiver.*]

PEARL: You're speaking to Lady Grayston. Tony! Of course I knew your voice. Well, what is it? I'm not at all stern. I'm making my voice as pleasant as I can. I'm sorry you find it disagreeable. [*She gives a chuckle.*] No, I'm afraid I couldn't come to tea tomorrow. I shall be engaged all the afternoon. What is the day after tomorrow? [*Smiling.*] Well, I must ask Bessie. I don't know if she's free. Of course I'm not coming alone. It would be most compromising.

A nice-looking young man like you. What would Minnie say? Oh, I know all about that. . . . I didn't promise anything. I merely said the future was everybody's property. A sleepless night. Fancy! Well, good-bye. . . . Tony, do you know the most enchanting word in the English language? Perhaps.

[*She puts down the telephone quickly, and the curtain falls.*]

END OF THE FIRST ACT

ACT TWO

The Scene is a morning-room at Abbots Kenton, the GRAY-STONS' place in the country. It has an old-fashioned, comfortable look; nothing is very new; the chintzes are faded. Three long french windows lead on to a terrace. It is after dinner, a fine night, and the windows are open.

[*The women of the party are sitting down, waiting for the men; they are* PEARL *and* BESSIE, *the* DUCHESSE DE SURENNES *and the* PRINCESS DELLA CERCOLA.]

PRINCESS: You must be exhausted after all the tennis you played this afternoon, Minnie.
DUCHESSE: Not a bit. I only played four sets.
PRINCESS: You played so vigorously. It made me quite hot to look at you.
DUCHESSE: If I didn't take exercise I should be enormous. Oh, Flora, how I envy you! You can eat anything you choose and it

has no effect on you. And what makes it so unfair is that you don't care about food. I am a lazy and a greedy woman. I never eat any of the things I like, and I never miss a day without taking at least an hour's exercise.
PRINCESS [*smiling*]: If mortification is the first step in sanctity, I'm sure you must be on the high road to it.
PEARL: One of these days you'll give up the struggle, Minnie, and, like Flora, take to good works.
DUCHESSE [*with immense decision*]: Never! I shall lie on my death-bed with my hair waved

and a little rouge on my cheeks, and with my last breath murmur: Not gruel, it's so fattening.

PEARL: Well, you'll have more serious tennis tomorrow. Harry Bleane plays much better than Thornton.

DUCHESSE: It was very tiresome of him not to come till it was just time to dress.

PEARL: He only got back from Rumania yesterday, and he had to go down to see his mother. [*With an amused glance at her sister.*] Bessie asked me not to put him next her at dinner.

BESSIE: Pearl, you are a cat! I do think it's hateful the way you discuss my private affairs with all and sundry.

DUCHESSE: My dear Bessie, they've long ceased to be your private affairs.

PEARL: I'm afraid Bessie misses her opportunities. Just before he went to Rumania I left them alone together, and nothing happened. All my tact was wasted.

BESSIE: Your tact was too obvious, Pearl.

DUCHESSE: Well, do be quick and bring him to the scratch, my dear. I'm growing tired of people asking me, Is he going to propose or is he not?

BESSIE: Don't they ever ask, Is she going to accept him or is she not?

DUCHESSE: Of course you'll accept him.

BESSIE: I'm not so sure.

PRINCESS [*smiling*]: Perhaps it depends on the way he asks.

PEARL: For heaven's sake, don't expect too much romance. Englishmen aren't romantic. It makes them feel absurd. George proposed to me when he was in New York for the Horse Show. I wasn't very well that day, and I was lying down. I was looking a perfect fright. He told me all about a mare he had, and he told me all about her father and her mother and her uncles and her aunts, and then he said: [*Imitating him.*] Look here, you'd better marry me.

PRINCESS: How very sudden.

PEARL: Oh, I said, why didn't you tell me you were going to propose? I'd have had my hair waved. Poor George, he asked, *Why?*

DUCHESSE: The French are the only nation who know how to make love. When Gaston proposed to me he went down on his knees, and he took my hand, and he said he couldn't live without me. Of course I knew that, because he hadn't a cent, but still it thrilled me. He said I was his guiding star and his guardian angel—oh, I don't know what! It was beautiful! I knew he'd been haggling with papa for a fortnight about having his debts paid; but it was beautiful.

PRINCESS: Were you quite indifferent to him?

DUCHESSE: Oh, quite. I'd made up my mind to marry a foreigner. People weren't very nice to us in Chicago. My cousin Mary had married the Count de Moret, and mother couldn't bear Aunt Alice. She said, If Alice has got hold of a Count for Mary, I'm determined that you shall have a Duke.

PEARL: And you did.

DUCHESSE: I wish you could have seen the fuss those Chicago

people made of me when I went over last. It was hard to realise that I used to cry my eyes out because I wasn't asked to the balls I wanted to go to.

PRINCESS: Still, I hope Bessie won't marry any man she doesn't care for.

PEARL: My dear, don't put ideas in the child's head. The French are a much more civilised nation than we are, and they've come to the conclusion long ago that marriage is an affair of convenience rather than of sentiment. Think of the people you know who've married for love. After five years do they care for one another any more than the people who've married for money?

PRINCESS: They have the recollection.

PEARL: Nonsense! As if anyone remembered an emotion when he no longer felt it!

DUCHESSE: It's true. I've been in love a dozen times, desperately, and when I've got over it and look back, though I remember I was in love, I can't for the life of me remember my love. It always seems to me so odd.

PEARL: Believe me, Bessie, the flourishing" state of father's hardware store is a much sounder basis for matrimonial happiness than any amount of passion.

BESSIE: Oh, Pearl, what is this you've been telling people about dad selling bananas?

PEARL: Bananas? Oh, I remember. They were saying that Mrs. Hanley used to wash the miners' clothes in California. That and her pearls are taking her everywhere. I wasn't going to be

outdone, so I said father used to sell bananas in the streets of New York.

BESSIE: He never did anything of the kind.

PEARL: I know he didn't, but I thought people were getting rather tired of the hardware store, and I made a perfectly killing story out of it. I had a new Callot frock on and I thought I could manage the bananas.

DUCHESSE: A most unpleasant vegetable. So fattening.

[*The men come in.* THORNTON CLAY, ARTHUR FENWICK, *and* FLEMING. PEARL *and* BESSIE *get up.*]

BESSIE: You've been a long time.

DUCHESSE: Where is Tony?

CLAY: He and Bleane are finishing their cigars.

DUCHESSE: Well, Mr. Harvey, are you still enjoying life in London?

CLAY: He should be. I've got him invitations to all the nicest parties. But he will waste his time in sight-seeing. The other day—Thursday, wasn't it?—I wanted to take him to Hurlingham, and he insisted on going to the National Gallery instead.

PEARL [*smiling*]: What an outrageous proceeding!

FLEMING: I don't see that it was any more outrageous for me than for you. I saw you coming in just as I was going out.

PEARL: I had a reason to go. Arthur Fenwick has just bought a Bronzino, and I wanted to see those in the National Gallery.

DUCHESSE: I think it's much more likely that you had an assignation. I've always heard it's a wonderful place for that. You never meet any of your friends, and if you do they're there for the same purpose, and pretend not to see you.

FLEMING: I certainly only went to see the pictures.

CLAY: But, good heavens, if you want to do that there's Christie's, and there you *will* meet your friends.

FLEMING: I'm afraid you'll never make a man of fashion out of me, Thornton.

CLAY: I'm beginning to despair. You have a natural instinct for doing the wrong thing. D'you know, the other day I caught him in the act of delivering half a bagful of letters of introduction? I implored him to put them in the waste-paper basket.

FLEMING: I thought as people had taken the trouble to give them to me, it was only polite to make use of them.

CLAY: Americans give letters so carelessly. Before you know where you are you'll know all the wrong people. And, believe me, the wrong people are very difficult to shake off.

FLEMING [amused]: Perhaps some of my letters are to the right people.

CLAY: Then they'll take no notice of them.

FLEMING: It looks as though the wrong people had better manners than the right ones.

CLAY: The right people *are* rude. They can afford to be. I was a very young man when I first came to London, and I made mistakes. All of us Americans make mistakes. It wanted a good deal of character to cut people who'd taken me about, asked me to dine, stay with them in the country, and heaven knows what, when I found they weren't the sort of people one ought to know.

PEARL: Of course, one has to do it.

DUCHESSE: Of course. It shows that you have a nice nature, Thornton, to worry yourself about it.

CLAY: I'm curiously sentimental. Another of our American faults. I remember when I'd been in London two or three years, I knew pretty well everyone that was worth knowing, but I'd never been asked to Hereford House. The duchess doesn't like Americans anyway, and she'd been very disagreeable about me in particular. But I was determined to go to her ball. I felt it wasn't the sort of function I could afford to be left out of.

PEARL: They're very dull balls.

CLAY: I know, but they're almost the only ones you can't go to without an invitation. Well, I found out that the duchess had a widowed sister who lived in the country with her two daughters. Lady Helen Blair. My dear, she was a very stuffy, dowdy woman of fifty-five, and her two daughters were stuffier and dowdier still, and if possible, older. They were in the habit of coming up to London for the season. I got introduced to them, and I laid myself out. I took them to the play, I showed them round the Academy, I stood them luncheons, I gave them cards for private views, for a month I worked like a

Trojan. Then the duchess sent out her invitations, and the Blair girls had half a dozen cards for their young men. I received one, and, by George, I'd earned it. Of course, as soon as I got my invitation I dropped them, but you know I felt quite badly about it.

DUCHESSE: I expect they're used to that.

CLAY: A strangely tactless woman, Lady Helen Blair. She wrote and asked me if I was offended about anything because I never went near them.

PEARL: I wish those men would come, and then we could dance.

DUCHESSE: Oh, that'll be charming! It's such good exercise, isn't it? I'm told that you dance divinely, Mr. Harvey.

FLEMING: I don't know about that. I dance.

DUCHESSE [*to the* PRINCESS]: Oh, my dear, who d'you think I danced with the other night? [*Impressively.*] Ernest.

PRINCESS: Oh!

DUCHESSE: My dear, don't say, Oh! like that. Don't you know who Ernest is?

PEARL: Ernest is the most sought after man in London.

PRINCESS: You don't mean the dancing-master?

DUCHESSE: Oh, my dear, you mustn't call him that. He'd be furious. He isn't a professional. He gives lessons at ten guineas an hour, but only to oblige. He's invited to all the best dances.

FLEMING: One of the things that rather surprised me at balls was to see all these dancing-masters. Do English girls like to be pawed about by Greeks, Dagos and Bowery toughs?

CLAY: You Americans who live in America, you're so prudish.

DUCHESSE: Believe me, I would go to *any* dance where there was the remotest chance of meeting Ernest. It's a perfect dream to dance with him. He showed me a new step, and I can't get it quite right. I don't know what I shall do if I don't run across him again very soon.

PRINCESS: But why don't you let him give you a lesson?

DUCHESSE: My dear, ten guineas an hour! I couldn't possibly afford that. I'm sure to meet him at a dance in a day or two, and I shall get a lesson for nothing.

PEARL: You ought to make him fall in love with you.

DUCHESSE: Oh, my dear, if he only would! But he's so run after.

[BLEANE *and* TONY PAXTON *come in from the terrace.*]

DUCHESSE: At last!

TONY: We've been taking a stroll in the garden.

PEARL: I hope you showed him my tea-house.

BESSIE: It's Pearl's new toy. You must be sure to admire it.

PEARL: I'm very proud of it. You know, George won't let me do anything here. He says it's his house, and he isn't going to have any of my muck. He won't even have new chintzes. Well, there was an old summer-house just over there, and it was all worm-eaten and horrid and tumble-down, what they call picturesque, but it was rather a nice place to go and have tea in as it had a really charming view; I wanted to pull it down and put up a smart Japanese tea-house instead, but George wouldn't hear of it, because, if you please, his mother—a peculiarly plain woman—used to sit and sew there. Well, I bided my time, and the other day, when George was in London, I pulled down the old summer-house, got my Japanese tea-house down from town, put it up, and everything finished by the time George came back twenty-four hours later. He very nearly had an apoplectic stroke. If he had I should have killed two birds with one stone.

BESSIE: Pearl!

PRINCESS: I don't know why you've furnished it so elaborately.

PEARL: Well, I thought in the hot weather I'd sleep there sometimes. It'll be just like sleeping in the open air.

FENWICK: These young people want to start dancing, Pearl.

PEARL: Where would you like to dance, in here with the gramophone, or in the drawing-room with the pianola?

BESSIE: Oh, in the drawing-room.

PEARL: Let's go there then.

BESSIE [*to* CLAY]: Come and help me get the rolls out.

CLAY: Right you are.

[*They go out, followed by the* DUCHESSE *and* PEARL, TONY, FENWICK, *and* BLEANE.]

FLEMING [*to the* PRINCESS]: Aren't you coming?

PRINCESS: No, I think I'll stay here for the present. But don't bother about me. You must go and dance.

FLEMING: There are enough men

without me. I'm sure Thornton Clay is a host in himself.

PRINCESS: You don't like Thornton?

FLEMING: He's been very kind to me since I came to London.

PRINCESS: I was watching your face when he told that story about the Hereford ball. You must learn to conceal your feelings better.

FLEMING: Didn't you think it was horrible?

PRINCESS: I've known Thornton for ten years. I'm used to him. And as you say yourself, he's very kind.

FLEMING: That's what makes life so difficult. People don't seem to be good or bad as the squares on a chessboard are black or white. Even the worthless ones have got good traits, and it makes it so hard to know how to deal with them.

PRINCESS [*smiling a little*]: You don't approve of poor Thornton?

FLEMING: What do you expect me to think of a man who's proud of having forced his way into a house where he knew he wasn't wanted? He reckons success by the number of invitations he receives. He holds himself up to me as an example. He tells me that if I want to get into society, I must work for it. What do they think of a man like Thornton Clay in England? Don't they despise him?

PRINCESS: Everywhere, in New York just as much as in London, there are masses of people struggling to get into society. It's so common a sight that one loses the sense of there being anything disgraceful in it. Pearl would tell you that English society is a little pompous; they welcome a man who can make them laugh. Thornton is very useful. He has high spirits, he's amusing, he makes a party go.

FLEMING: I should have thought a man could find some better use for his life than that.

PRINCESS: Thornton has plenty of money. Do you think there is any point in his spending his life making more? I sometimes think there's too much money in America already.

FLEMING: There are things a man can do beside making money.

PRINCESS: You know, American wealth has reached a pitch when it was bound to give rise to a leisured class. Thornton is one of the first members of it. Perhaps he doesn't play the part very well, but remember he hasn't had the time to learn it that they've had in Europe.

FLEMING [*smiling*]: I'm afraid you don't think me very charitable.

PRINCESS: You're young. It's a real pleasure to me to know a nice clean American boy. And I'm so glad that you're not going to be dazzled by this English life that dazzles so many of our countrymen. Amuse yourself, learn what you can from it, take all the good it offers you and go back to America.

FLEMING: I shall be glad to go back. Perhaps I ought never to have come.

PRINCESS: I'm afraid you're not very happy.

FLEMING: I don't know what makes you think that.

PRINCESS: It's not very hard to

see that you're in love with Bessie.

FLEMING: Did you know that I was engaged to her?

PRINCESS [*surprised*]: No.

FLEMING: I was engaged to her before I went to Harvard. I was eighteen then, and she was sixteen.

PRINCESS: How very early in life you young people settle things in America!

FLEMING: Perhaps it was rather silly and childish. But when she wrote and told me that she thought we'd better break it off, I discovered I cared more than I thought.

PRINCESS: What did you say to her?

FLEMING: I couldn't try to hold her to a promise she gave when she was a schoolgirl. I answered that I sympathised and understood.

PRINCESS: When did this happen?

FLEMING: A couple of months ago. Then I got the chance to go over to Europe and I thought I'd come to see what was going on. It didn't take me long to tumble.

PRINCESS: You're bearing it very well.

FLEMING: Oh, the only thing I could do was to be pleasant. I should only have bored her if I'd made love to her. She took our engagement as an amusing joke, and there wasn't anything for me to do but accept her view of it. She was having the time of her life. At first I thought perhaps she'd grow tired of all these balls and parties, and then if I was on the spot I might persuade her to come back to America with me.

PRINCESS: You may still.

FLEMING: No, I haven't a chance. The first day I arrived she told me how wonderful she thought this English life. She thinks it full and varied. She thinks it has beauty.

PRINCESS: That sounds rather satirical.

FLEMING: Pearl has been very nice to me. She's taken me about, I've driven with her constantly, I've sat in her box at the opera, I'm her guest at the moment. If I had any decency I'd hold my tongue.

PRINCESS: Well?

FLEMING [bursting out impetuously]: There's something in these surroundings that makes me feel terribly uncomfortable. Under the brilliant surface I suspect all kinds of ugly and shameful secrets that everyone knows and pretends not to. This is a strange house in which the husband is never seen and Arthur Fenwick, a vulgar sensualist, acts as host; and it's an attractive spectacle, this painted duchess devouring with her eyes a boy young enough to be her son. And the conversation—I don't want to seem a prude, I daresay people over here talk more freely than the people I've known; but surely there are women who don't have lovers, there are such things as honour and decency and self-restraint. If Bessie is going to remain over here I wish to God she'd marry her lord at once and get out of it quickly.

PRINCESS: D'you think she'll be happy?

FLEMING: Are they any of them happy? How can they expect to be happy when they marry for . . . [The PRINCESS gives a sudden start, and FLEMING stops short.] I beg your pardon. I was forgetting. Please forgive me. You see, you're so different.

PRINCESS: I'm sorry I interrupted you. What were you going to say?

FLEMING: It wasn't of any importance. You see, I've been thinking it over so much that it's rather got on my nerves. And I haven't been able to tell anyone what I was thinking about. I'm dreadfully sorry.

PRINCESS: You were going to say, how can they expect to be happy when they marry for a trumpery title? You thought, they're snobs, vulgar snobs, and the misery of their lives is the proper punishment for their ignoble desires.

FLEMING [very apologetically]: Princess.

PRINCESS [ironically]: Princess.

FLEMING: Believe me, I hadn't the smallest intention of saying anything to wound you.

PRINCESS: You haven't. It's too true. Most of us who marry foreigners are merely snobs. But I wonder if it's all our fault. We're not shown a better way of life. No one has even hinted to us that we have any duty towards our own country. We're blamed because we marry foreigners, but columns are written about us in the papers, and our photographs are in all the magazines. Our friends are excited and envious. After all, we are human. At first, when people addressed me as Princess, I couldn't help feeling thrilled.

Of course it was snobbishness.

FLEMING: You make me feel a terrible cad.

PRINCESS: But sometimes there've been other motives, too. Has it ever occurred to you that snobbishness is the spirit of romance in a reach-me-down? I was only twenty when I married Marino. I didn't see him as a fortune-hunting Dago, but as the successor of a long line of statesmen and warriors. There'd been a pope in his family, and a dozen cardinals, one of his ancestors had been painted by Titian; for centuries they'd been men of war, with power of life and death; I'd seen the great feudal castle, with its hundred rooms, where they had ruled as independent sovereigns. When Marino came and asked me to marry him it was romance that stood in his shoes and beckoned to me. I thought of the palace in Rome, which I had visited as a tripper, and where I might reign as mistress. I thought it was splendid to take my place after all those great ladies, Orsinis, Colonnas, Gaetanis, Aldobrandinis. I loved him.

FLEMING: But there's no need to tell me that you could never do anything from an unworthy motive.

PRINCESS: My husband's family had been ruined by speculation. He was obliged to sell himself. He sold himself for five million dollars. And I loved him. You can imagine the rest. First he was indifferent to me, then I bored him, and at last he hated me. Oh, the humiliation I endured. When my child died I couldn't bear it any longer; I left him. I went back to America. I found myself a stranger. I was out of place, the life had become foreign to me; I couldn't live at home. I settled in England; and here we're strangers too. I've paid very heavily for being a romantic girl.

[BESSIE *comes in.*]

BESSIE: Really, Fleming, it's too bad of you to sit in here and flirt with the Princess. We want you to come and dance.

[*The* PRINCESS, *agitated, gets up and goes out into the garden.*]

BESSIE [*looking after her*]: Is anything the matter?

FLEMING: No.

BESSIE: Are you coming to dance, or are you not?

FLEMING: I had quite a talk with Lord Bleane after dinner, Bessie.

BESSIE [*smiling*]: Well?

FLEMING: Are you going to accept the coronet that he's dangling before your eyes?

BESSIE: It would be more to the point if you asked whether I'm going to accept the coronet that he's laying at my feet.

FLEMING: He's a very nice fellow, Bessie.

BESSIE: I know that.

FLEMING: I wanted to dislike him.

BESSIE: Why?

FLEMING: Well, I don't think much of these English lords who run after American girls for their money. I expected him to be a brainless loafer, with just enough cunning to know his market value, but he's a modest, unassuming fellow. To tell you the truth, I'm puzzled.

BESSIE [*chaffing him*]: Fancy that!

FLEMING: I think it's a low-down thing that he's doing, and yet he doesn't seem a low-down fellow.

BESSIE: He might be in love with me, you know.

FLEMING: Is he?

BESSIE: No.

FLEMING: Are you going to marry him?

BESSIE: I don't know.

FLEMING: I suppose he's come here to ask you?

BESSIE [*after a short pause*]: He asked me a month ago. I promised to give him an answer when he came back from Rumania. . . . I'm in a panic. He's waiting to get me alone. I was able to be quite flippant about it when I had a month before me, but now, when I've got to say yes or no, I'm so jumpy I don't know what to do with myself.

FLEMING: Don't marry him, Bessie.

BESSIE: Why not?

FLEMING: Well, first, you're no more in love with him than he is with you.

BESSIE: And then?

FLEMING: Isn't that enough?

BESSIE: I wonder if you realise what he offers me. Do you know what the position of an English peeress is?

FLEMING: Does it mean so much to be called Your Ladyship by tradesmen?

BESSIE: You donkey, Fleming. If I marry an American boy my life will be over; if I marry Harry Bleane it will be only just beginning. Look at Pearl. I could do what she's done; I could do more, because George Grayston isn't ambitious. I could make Harry do anything I liked. He would go into politics, and I should have a salon. Why, I could do anything.

FLEMING [*dryly*]: I don't know why you should be in a panic. You've evidently made up your mind. You'll have a brilliant marriage with crowds outside the church, your photograph will be in all the papers, you'll go away for your honeymoon, and you'll come back. What will you do then?

BESSIE: Why, settle down.

FLEMING: Will you break your heart like the Princess because your husband has taken a mistress, or will you take lovers like the Duchesse de Surennes, or will you bore yourself to death like Pearl because your husband is virtuous, and wants you to do your duty?

BESSIE: Fleming, you've got no right to say things like that to me.

FLEMING: I'm sorry if I've made you angry. I had to say it.

BESSIE: Are you quite sure that it's for my sake you don't want me to marry Lord Bleane?

FLEMING: Yes, I think it is. When you broke off our engagement I didn't blame you. You wouldn't have done it if you'd cared for me, and it wasn't your fault if you didn't. When I came over I saw that I could expect nothing but friendship from you. You must do me the justice to acknowledge that during this month I haven't given the smallest sign that I wanted anything else.

BESSIE: Oh, you've been charming. You always were the best friend I've had.

FLEMING: If in a corner of my heart I kept my love for you, that is entirely my affair. I don't know that it puts you to any inconvenience, and it pleases me. I'm quite sure that I'm only thinking now of your happiness. Go back to America, and fall in love with some nice fellow, and marry him. You'll have all my best wishes. Perhaps your life won't be so brilliant or so exciting, but it will be simpler and wholesomer, and more becoming.

BESSIE: You're a dear, Fleming, and if I said anything disagreeable just now, forgive me. I didn't mean it. I shall always want you to be my dearest friend.

[LORD BLEANE *enters from the terrace.*]

BLEANE: I was looking for you everywhere. I wondered where you'd got to.

[*There is a moment's pause.* FLEMING HARVEY *looks from* BESSIE *to* BLEANE.]

FLEMING: I really must go and dance with the Duchesse or she'll never forgive me.

BLEANE: I've just been dancing with her. My dear fellow, it's the most violent form of exercise I've ever taken.

FLEMING: I'm in very good condition. [*He goes out.*]

BLEANE: Blessings on him.

BESSIE: Why?

BLEANE: Because he's left us alone. Ask me another.

BESSIE: I don't think I will.

BLEANE: Then I'll ask you one.

BESSIE: Please don't. Tell me all about Rumania.

BLEANE: Rumania is a Balkan State. Its capital is Bucharest. It has long been known for its mineral springs.

BESSIE: You're in very high spirits tonight.

BLEANE: You may well wonder. Everything has conspired to depress them.

BESSIE: Oh, what nonsense!

BLEANE: First I was in England thirty-six hours before I had a chance of seeing you; secondly, when I arrived you'd already gone up to dress; then, when I was expecting to sit next you at dinner, I was put between Lady Grayston and the Princess; and, lastly, you made me pound away at that beastly pianola when I wanted to dance with you.

BESSIE: Well, you've survived it all.

BLEANE: What I want to point out to you is that if notwithstanding I'm in high spirits, I must have a most engaging nature.

BESSIE: I never dreamt of denying it.

BLEANE: So much to the good.

BESSIE: The man's going to propose to me.

BLEANE: No, I'm not.

BESSIE: I beg your pardon. My mistake.

BLEANE: I did that a month ago.

BESSIE: There's been a change of moon since then, and no proposal holds good after the new moon.

BLEANE: I never knew that.

BESSIE: You've been down to see your mother.

BLEANE: She sends you her love.

BESSIE: Have you told her?

BLEANE: I told her a month ago.

[BESSIE *does not speak for a moment; when she answers it is more gravely.*]

BESSIE: You know, I want to be frank with you. You won't think it disagreeable of me, will you? I'm not in love with you.

BLEANE: I know. But you don't positively dislike me?

BESSIE: No. I like you very much.

BLEANE: Won't you risk it then?

BESSIE [*almost tragically*]: I can't make up my mind.

BLEANE: I'll do all I can to make you happy. I'll try not to make a nuisance of myself.

BESSIE: I know quite well that I wouldn't marry you if you weren't who you are, and I'm afraid I know that you wouldn't marry me if I hadn't a certain amount of money.

BLEANE: Oh, yes, I would.

BESSIE: It's nice of you to say so.

BLEANE: Don't you believe it?

BESSIE: I suppose I'm a perfect fool. I ought to play the game prettily. You see, I know that you can't afford to marry a girl who isn't well-to-do. Everyone knows what I have. Pearl has taken good care that they should. You wouldn't ever have thought of me otherwise. We're arranging a deal. You give your title and your position, and I give my money. It's a commonplace thing enough, but somehow it sticks in my throat.

[BLEANE *hesitates a moment, and walks up and down thinking.*]

BLEANE: You make me feel an awful swine. The worst of it is that some part of what you say is true. I'm not such a fool that I didn't see your sister was throwing us together. I don't want to seem a conceited ass, but a fellow in my sort of position can't help knowing that many people think him rather a catch. Mothers of marriageable daughters are very transparent sometimes, you know, and if they don't marry their daughters they're determined it shan't be for want of trying.

BESSIE: Oh, I can quite believe that. I have noticed it in American mothers, too.

BLEANE: I knew it would be a good thing if I married you. I don't suppose I should have thought about you if I hadn't been told you were pretty well off. It's beastly now, saying all that.

BESSIE: I don't see why.

BLEANE: Because after a bit I found out I'd fallen in love with you. And then I didn't care if you hadn't got a bob. I wanted to marry you because—because I didn't know what to do without you.

BESSIE: Harry!

BLEANE: Do believe me. I swear it's true. I don't care a hang about the money. After all, we could get along without it. And I love you.

BESSIE: It's very good to hear you say that. I'm so absurdly pleased and flattered.

BLEANE: You do believe it, don't you?

BESSIE: Yes.

BLEANE: And will you marry me?

BESSIE: If you like.

BLEANE: Of course I like. [*He takes her in his arms and kisses her.*]

BESSIE: Take care, someone might come in.

BLEANE [*smiling and happy*]: Come into the garden with me.

[*He stretches out his hand, she hesitates a moment, smiles, takes it, and together they go out on to the terrace. For a moment the music of a one-step is heard more loudly, and then the* DUCHESSE *and* TONY PAXTON *come in. She sinks into a chair fanning herself, and he goes over to a table, takes a cigarette, and lights it.*]

DUCHESSE: Did you see? That was Harry Bleane and Bessie. I wondered where they were.

TONY: You've got eyes like a lynx.

DUCHESSE: I'm positive they were hand in hand.

TONY: It looks as if she'd worked it at last.

DUCHESSE: I don't know about that. It looks as if he'd worked it.

TONY: She's not such a catch as all that. If I were a peer I'd sell myself for a damned sight more than eight thousand a year.

DUCHESSE: Don't stand so far away, Tony. Come and sit on the sofa by me.

TONY [*going over to her*]: I say, I've been talking to Bleane about two-seaters.

DUCHESSE [*very coldly*]: Oh!

TONY [*giving her a look out of the corner of his eye*]: He says I can't do better than get a Talbot.

DUCHESSE: I don't see why you want a car of your own. You can always use one of mine.

TONY: That's not the same thing. After all, it won't cost much. I can get a ripper for just over twelve hundred pounds, with a really smart body.

DUCHESSE: You talk as though twelve hundred pounds were nothing at all.

TONY: Hang it all, it isn't anything to you.

DUCHESSE: What with the income tax and one thing and another, I'm not so terribly flush just now. No one knows the claims I have on me. Because one has a certain amount of money one's supposed to be made of it. They don't realise that if one spends it in one way one can't spend it in another. It cost me seven thousand pounds to have my house redecorated.

TONY [*sulkily*]: You said I could buy myself a car.

DUCHESSE: I said I'd think about it. I wasn't under the impression that you'd go and order one right away.

TONY: I've practically committed myself now.

DUCHESSE: You only want a car so that you can be independent of me.

TONY: Well, hang it all, you can't expect me to be tied to your apron-strings always. It's a bit thick if whenever I want to take a man down to play golf I have to ring up and ask if I can have one of your cars. It makes me look such an ass.

DUCHESSE: If it's only to play golf you want it, I'm sure anyone would rather go down to the links in a comfortable Rolls-Royce than in a two-seater.

[*A silence.*]

TONY: If you don't want to give me a car, why on earth did you say you would?

DUCHESSE [*putting her hand on him*]: Tony.

TONY: For goodness' sake don't touch me.

DUCHESSE [*hurt and mortified*]: Tony!

TONY: I don't want to force you to make me presents. I can quite well do without a two-seater. I can go about in omnibuses if it comes to that.

DUCHESSE: Don't you love me?

TONY: I wish you wouldn't constantly ask me if I love you. It is maddening.

DUCHESSE: Oh, how can you be so cruel to me!

TONY [*exasperated*]: D'you think this is quite the best place to choose to make a scene?

DUCHESSE: I love you with all my heart. I've never loved anybody as much as I love you.

TONY: No man could stand being loved so much. D'you think it's jolly for me to feel that your eyes are glued on me whatever I'm doing? I can never put my hand out without finding yours there ready to press it.

DUCHESSE: I can't help it if I love you. That's my temperament.

TONY: Yes, but you needn't show it so much. Why don't you leave me to do the love-making?

DUCHESSE: If I did that there wouldn't be any love-making.

TONY: You make me look such a fool.

DUCHESSE: Don't you know there's nothing in the world I wouldn't do for you?

TONY [*quickly*]: Well, why don't you marry me?

DUCHESSE [*with a gasp*]: I can't do that. You know that I can't do that.

TONY: Why not? You could still call yourself Duchesse de Surennes.

DUCHESSE: No; I've always told you nothing would induce me to marry.

TONY: That shows how much you love me.

DUCHESSE: Marriage is so middle-class. It takes away all the romance of love.

TONY: You simply want to have your freedom and keep me bound hand and foot. D'you think it's jolly for me to know what people say about me? After all, I have got some pride.

DUCHESSE: I'm sure we shall be able to get you a job soon, and then no one will be able to say anything.

TONY: I'm getting fed up with the whole business; I tell you that straight. I'd just as soon chuck it.

DUCHESSE: Tony, you don't mean to say you want to leave me. I'll kill myself if you do. I couldn't bear it, I couldn't bear it. I'll kill myself.

TONY: For God's sake, don't make such a row.

DUCHESSE: Say you don't mean it, Tony. I shall scream.

TONY: After all, I've got my self-respect to think of. It seems to me the best thing would be if we put a stop to the whole thing now.

DUCHESSE: Oh, I can't lose you. I can't.

TONY: No one can say I'm mercenary, but hang it all, one has to think of one's future. I shan't be twenty-five for ever. I ought to be settling down.

DUCHESSE: Don't you care for me any more?

TONY: Of course I care for you. If I didn't, d'you think I'd have let you do all you have for me?

DUCHESSE: Then why d'you make me so unhappy?

TONY: I don't want to make you unhappy, but really sometimes you are unreasonable.

DUCHESSE: You mean about the car?

TONY: I wasn't thinking about the car then.

DUCHESSE: You can have it if you like.

TONY: I don't want it now.

DUCHESSE: Tony, don't be unkind.

TONY: I'm not going to take any more presents from you.

DUCHESSE: I didn't mean to be unreasonable. I'd like you to have the car, Tony. I'll give you a cheque for it tomorrow. [*Coaxingly.*] Tell me what the body's like.

TONY [*sulkily*]: Oh, it's a torpedo body.

DUCHESSE: You'll take me for drives in it sometimes?

[*He turns round and looks at her, she puts out her hand, he thaws, and smiles engagingly.*]

TONY: I say, you are awfully kind to me.

DUCHESSE: You do like me a little, don't you?

TONY: Of course I do.

DUCHESSE: You have a good heart, Tony. Kiss me.

TONY [*kissing her, pleased and excited*]: I saw an awfully jolly body in a shop in Trafalgar Square the day before yesterday. I've got half a mind to get the people who made your body to copy it.

DUCHESSE: Why don't you get it at the shop you saw it at? My people are terribly expensive, and they aren't any better than anybody else.

TONY: Well, you see, I don't know anything about the firm. I just happened to catch sight of it as I was passing.

DUCHESSE: What on earth were you doing in Trafalgar Square on Thursday? I thought you were going to Ranelagh.

TONY: I was put off. I hadn't got anything to do, so I thought I'd just slope round the National Gallery for half an hour.

DUCHESSE: That's the last place I should have expected you to go to.

TONY: I don't mind having a look at pictures now and then.

[*A sudden suspicion comes to the* DUCHESSE *that he was there with* PEARL, *but she makes no sign that he can see.*]

DUCHESSE [*blandly*]: Did you look at the Bronzinos?

TONY [*falling into the trap*]: Yes. Arthur Fenwick bought one the other day at Christie's. He paid a devil of a price for it too.

DUCHESSE [*clenching her hands in the effort to hide her agitation*]: Oh?

TONY: I do think it's rot, the prices people pay for old masters. I'm blowed if I'd give ten thousand pounds for a picture.

DUCHESSE: We'll go to the National Gallery together one of these days, shall we?

TONY: I don't know that I want to make a habit of it, you know.

[PEARL *and* THORNTON CLAY *come in. During the conversation the* DUCHESSE *surreptitiously watches* PEARL *and* TONY *for signs of an intelligence between them.*]

PEARL: I've got great news for you. Bessie and Harry Bleane are engaged.

DUCHESSE: Oh, my dear, I'm so glad. How gratified you must be!

PEARL: Yes, I'm delighted. You must come and congratulate them.

CLAY: Above all we must congratulate one another. We've all worked for it, Pearl.

TONY: He hadn't much chance, poor blighter, had he?

PEARL: We're going to have one more dance, and then Arthur wants to play poker. You must come.

CLAY [*to the* DUCHESSE]: Will you dance this with me, Minnie?

DUCHESSE: I'd like to.

[CLAY *gives her his arm. She throws* TONY *and* PEARL *a glance, and purses her lips. She goes out with* CLAY.]

PEARL: You haven't danced with me yet, Tony. You should really pay some attention to your hostess.

TONY: I say, don't go.

PEARL: Why not?

TONY: Because I want to talk to you.

PEARL [*flippantly*]: If you want to whisper soft nothings in my ear, you'll find the one-step exceedingly convenient.

TONY: You're a little beast, Pearl.

PEARL: You've been having a long talk with Minnie.

TONY: Oh, she's been making me a hell of a scene.

PEARL: Poor thing, she can't help it. She adores you.

TONY: I wish she didn't, and you did.

PEARL [*with a chuckle*]: My dear, it's your only attraction for me that she adores you. Come and dance with me.

TONY: You've got a piece of hair out of place.

PEARL: Have I? [*She takes a small glass out of her bag and looks at herself. As she does so* TONY *steps behind her and kisses her neck.*] You fool, don't do that. Anyone might see us.

TONY: I don't care.

PEARL: I do. Arthur's as jealous as cats' meat.

TONY: Arthur's playing the pianola.

PEARL: There's nothing wrong with my hair.

TONY: Of course there isn't. You're perfectly divine tonight. I don't know what there is about you.

PEARL: You're a foolish creature, Tony.

TONY: Let's go in the garden.

PEARL: No, they'll be wondering where we are.

TONY: Hang it all, it's not so extraordinary to take a stroll instead of dancing.

PEARL: I don't want to take a stroll.

TONY: Pearl.

PEARL: Yes?

[*She looks at him. For a moment they stare at one another in silence. A hot flame of passion leaps up suddenly between them, and en-*

velops them, so that they forget everything but that they are man and woman. The air seems all at once heavy to breathe. PEARL, *like a bird in a net, struggles to escape; their voices sink, and unconsciously they speak in whispers.*]

PEARL: Don't be a fool, Tony.

TONY [*hoarsely*]: Let's go down to the tea-house.

PEARL: No, I won't.

TONY: We shall be quite safe there.

PEARL: I daren't. It's too risky.

TONY: Oh, damn the risk!

PEARL [*agitated*]: I can't!

TONY: I'll go down there and wait.

PEARL [*breathlessly*]: But—if they wonder where I am.

TONY: They'll think you've gone up to your room.

PEARL: I won't come, Tony.

TONY: I'll wait for you.

[*As he goes out,* ARTHUR FENWICK *comes in.* PEARL *gives a slight start, but quickly recovers herself.*]

FENWICK: Look here, I'm not going on pounding away at that wretched pianola unless you come and dance, Pearl.

PEARL [*exhausted*]: I'm tired, I don't want to dance any more.

FENWICK: Poor child, you look quite pale.

PEARL: Do I? I thought I'd put plenty of rouge on. Am I looking revolting?

FENWICK: You always look adorable. You're wonderful. I can't think what you see in an old fellow like me.

PEARL: You're the youngest man I've ever known.

FENWICK: How well you know the thing to say to please me!

[*He is just going to take her in his arms, but instinctively she draws back.*]

FENWICK: Let's play poker now, shall we?

FENWICK: Not if you're tired, darling.

PEARL: I'm never too tired for that.

FENWICK: You don't know how I adore you. It's a privilege to be allowed to love you.

PEARL [*sure of herself again*]: Oh, what nonsense! You'll make me vain if you say things like that.

FENWICK: You do love me a little, don't you? I want your love so badly.

PEARL: Why, I dote on you, you silly old thing.

[*She takes his face in her hands and kisses him, avoids his arms that seek to encircle her, and goes towards the door.*]

FENWICK: Where are you going?

PEARL: I'm just going to my room to arrange my face.

FENWICK: My God, how I love you, girlie! There's nothing in the world I wouldn't do for you.

PEARL: Really?

FENWICK: Nothing.

PEARL: Then ring for Pole and tell him to set out the card-table and bring the counters.

FENWICK: And I was prepared to give you a sable coat or a diamond tiara.

PEARL: I much prefer chinchilla and emeralds.

FENWICK [*taking her hand*]: Must you really go and arrange your face?

PEARL: Really!

FENWICK: Be quick then. I can hardly bear you out of my sight. [*He kisses her hand.*]

PEARL [*looking at him tenderly*]: Dear Arthur.

[*She goes out.* FENWICK *rings the bell. Then he goes on the terrace and calls out.*]

FENWICK: Thornton, we're going to play poker. Get them to come along, will you?

CLAY [*outside*]: Right-ho!

[POLE *comes in.*]

FENWICK: Oh, Pole, get the card-table ready.

POLE: Very good, sir.

FENWICK: And we shall want the counters. Let's have those mother-o'-pearl ones that I brought down last time I was here.

POLE: Very good, sir.

[*The* PRINCESS *comes in.* POLE *proceeds to bring a card-table into the centre of the room and unfolds it. He gets a box of counters out of a drawer, and puts them on the table.*]

FENWICK: Pearl has just gone to her room. She'll be here in one minute.

PRINCESS [*looking at the preparations*]: This looks like more dissipation.

FENWICK: We were going to have a little game of poker. I don't think we ought to play very long, Pearl is looking terribly tired.

PRINCESS: I don't wonder. She's so energetic.

FENWICK: She does too much. Just now when I came in she was quite white. I'm really very uneasy about her. You see, she never spares herself.

PRINCESS: Fortunately she's extremely strong.

FENWICK: She has a constitution of iron. She's a very wonderful woman. It's very seldom you meet a woman like Pearl. She's got a remarkable brain. I've frequently discussed business with her, and I've been amazed at her clear grasp of complicated matters. I owe a great deal to her. And she's good, Princess, she's good. She's got a heart of gold.

PRINCESS: I'm sure she has.

FENWICK: She'll always do a good turn to anybody. She's the most generous, the most open-handed woman I've ever met.

[*The* DUCHESSE *comes in as he says these words.*]

DUCHESSE: Who is this?

FENWICK: We were talking of our hostess.

DUCHESSE: I see.

[*She has her bag in her hand; when the others are not looking she hides it behind a sofa.*]

FENWICK: I have no hesitation in saying that Pearl is the most remarkable woman in England. Why, she's got half the Cabinet in her pocket. She's very powerful.

DUCHESSE: I have often thought that if she'd lived in the reign of Charles II she would have been a duchess in her own right.

FENWICK [*innocently*]: Maybe. She would adorn any sphere. She's got everything—tact, brains, energy, beauty.

DUCHESSE: Virtue.

FENWICK: If I were the British people, I'd make her Prime Minister.

PRINCESS [*smiling*]: You're an excellent friend, Mr. Fenwick.

FENWICK: Of course, you've heard of her hostel for young women alone in London?

DUCHESSE [*sweetly*]: Yes, there was a great deal about it in the papers, wasn't there?

FENWICK: That's a thing I've always admired in Pearl. She has a thoroughly modern understanding of the value of advertisement.

DUCHESSE: Yes, she has, hasn't she?

FENWICK: Well, believe me, she conceived the idea of that hostel, built it, endowed it, organised it, all on her own. It cost twenty thousand pounds.

DUCHESSE: But surely, Mr. Fenwick, you paid the twenty thousand pounds. Pearl hasn't got sums like that to throw away on charity.

FENWICK: I gave the money, but the money isn't the important thing. The idea, the organisation, the success, are all due to Pearl.

DUCHESSE: It has certainly been one of the best advertised of recent philanthropic schemes.

[THORNTON CLAY, BESSIE, BLEANE, *and* FLEMING *come in.*]

CLAY: We're all dying to play poker.

FENWICK: The table is ready.

BESSIE: Where is Pearl?

FENWICK: She's gone to her room. She'll be back in a minute.

[*The gather round the table and sit down.*]

BESSIE: You're going to play, Princess?

PRINCESS: Oh, I don't think so, I'll look on. I'm going to bed in a minute.

BESSIE: Oh, you must play.

[*The* PRINCESS *smiles, shrugs her shoulders, and approaches the table.*]

FENWICK: Leave a place for Pearl.

DUCHESSE: You must leave one for Tony, too.

CLAY: What's he doing?

DUCHESSE: He'll be here presently.

FENWICK: Shall I give out the counters? What would you like to play for?

PRINCESS: Don't let it be too high.

DUCHESSE: How tiresome of you, Flora! I think I'm in luck tonight.

FENWICK: We don't want to ruin anyone. Shilling antes. Will that suit you?

PRINCESS: Very well.

FENWICK [*to* CLAY]: The whites are a shilling, Thornton, reds two, and blues five bob. Mr. Harvey, you might count some out, will you?

FLEMING: Sure.

[*The three of them start counting out the counters.*]

DUCHESSE: Oh, how stupid of me, I haven't got my bag.

FENWICK: Never mind, we'll trust you.

DUCHESSE: Oh, I'd rather pay at once. It saves so much bother. Besides, I hate not having my bag.

PRINCESS: One always wants to powder one's nose if one hasn't got it.

DUCHESSE: Bessie dear, I left it in Pearl's new tea-house. Do run and fetch it for me.

BESSIE: Certainly.

BLEANE: No, I'll go.

BESSIE: You don't know the way. I can go through the bushes. It's only twenty yards. You stop and count out the counters. [*She goes out.*]

FENWICK: There's five pounds here. Will you take them, Princess?

PRINCESS: Thank you. Here's my money.

DUCHESSE: I'll give you my fiver as soon as Bessie brings my bag.

CLAY: How on earth came you to leave it in the tea-house?

DUCHESSE: I'm so careless. I'm always leaving my bag about.

FLEMING: Here's another five pounds.

PRINCESS: What beautiful counters they are!

FENWICK: I'm glad you like them. I gave them to Pearl. They've got her initials on them.

CLAY: Let's have a hand before Pearl comes. Lowest deals.

[*They all cut.*]

FLEMING: Table stakes, I suppose?

FENWICK: Oh yes, it makes it a much better game.

CLAY: Your deal, Fenwick.

FENWICK: Ante up, Princess.

PRINCESS: I beg your pardon.

[*She pushes forward a counter.* FENWICK *deals. The others take up their cards.*]

FENWICK: Two shillings to come in.

FLEMING: I'm coming in.

BLEANE: I always come in.

FENWICK: I oughtn't to, but I shall all the same. Are you going to make good your ante, Princess?

PRINCESS: I may just as well, mayn't I?

FENWICK: That's how I've made a fortune. By throwing good money after bad. Would you like a card?

PRINCESS: I'll have three.

[FENWICK *gives them to her.*]

CLAY: The Princess has got a pair of deuces.

FLEMING: I'll have one.

[FENWICK *gives it to him.*]

BLEANE: One never gets that straight, Harvey. I'll take five.

FENWICK: That's what I call a real sport.

CLAY: Nonsense. It just means he can't play.

BLEANE: It would be rather a sell for you if I got a flush.

CLAY: It would, but you haven't.

[FENWICK *has given him cards and* BLEANE *looks at them.*]

BLEANE: You're quite right, I haven't.

[*He flings them down. Through the next speeches the business with the cards follows the dialogue.*]

FENWICK: Don't you want any cards, Duchesse?

DUCHESSE: No, I'm out of it.

CLAY: I'll have three. I thought you were in luck.

DUCHESSE: Wait a minute. You'll be surprised.

FENWICK: Dealer takes two.

CLAY: Who bets?

PRINCESS: I'm out of it.

CLAY: I said it was a pair of deuces.

FLEMING: I'll bet five shillings.

CLAY: I'll take it and raise five shillings.

FENWICK: I suppose I must risk my money. What have I got to put down? Ten shillings?

FLEMING: There's five shillings, and I'll raise you five shillings more.

CLAY: No, I've had enough.

FENWICK: I'll take you and raise you again.

FLEMING: Very well. And once more.

FENWICK: I'll see you.

[BESSIE *comes in. The* DUCHESSE *has been watching for her.* BESSIE *is excessively disturbed.*]

DUCHESSE: Ah, there's Bessie.

FENWICK [*to* FLEMING]: What have you got?

DUCHESSE: Did you find my bag?

BESSIE [*with a gasp*]: No, it wasn't there.

DUCHESSE: Oh, but I remember distinctly leaving it there. I'll go and look for it myself. Mr. Fenwick, will you come with me?

BESSIE: No, don't—you can't go into the tea-house.

PRINCESS [*surprised*]: Bessie, is anything the matter?

BESSIE [*in a strained voice*]: The door of the tea-house is locked.

DUCHESSE: Oh, it can't be. I saw Pearl and Tony go in there just now.

[BESSIE *suddenly hides her face and bursts into a flood of tears.*]

PRINCESS [*starting to her feet*]: Minnie, you devil! What have you been doing?

DUCHESSE: Don't ask what I've been doing.

FENWICK: You must be mistaken. Pearl went up to her room.

DUCHESSE: Go and look for her. . . .

[FENWICK *is about to start from his chair. The* PRINCESS *puts her hand on his shoulder.*]

PRINCESS: Where are you going?

DUCHESSE: I saw her.

[*For a moment there is a pause.*]

CLAY [*in an embarrassed way*]: Well, we'd better go on with our game, hadn't we?

[*The* PRINCESS *and* BLEANE *are bending over* BESSIE, *trying to get her to control herself.*]

FLEMING: That was your money, Mr. Fenwick.

FENWICK [*staring in front of him, with a red face and blood-shot eyes, under his breath*]: The slut. The slut.

[*The* DUCHESSE *takes her bag from behind the cushion, gets out the stick for her lips, and her mirror, and begins to paint them.*]

CLAY: You'd better deal, Fleming. The Princess won't play, I expect.

DUCHESSE: Deal me cards. I want to play.

CLAY: Bleane, come on. We'd better go on with our game. Take Bessie's chips.

[BLEANE *comes forward.* FLEMING *deals the cards. A stormy silence hangs over the party, broken only by the short speeches referring to the game; they play trying to relieve the tension. They are all anxiously awaiting* PEARL, *afraid she will come, knowing she must, and dreading the moment; they are nervous and constrained.*]

CLAY: Your ante, Bleane.

[BLEANE *puts forward a counter. The cards are dealt in silence.*]

CLAY: I'm coming in.

[FENWICK *looks at his cards, puts forward a couple of counters, but does not speak.* FLEMING *puts forward counters.*]

FLEMING: D'you want a card?
BLEANE: Three, please.
CLAY: Two.
FENWICK [*with an effort over himself*]: I'll have three.

[FLEMING *deals them as they ask. Just as he has given* FENWICK *his,* PEARL *comes in, followed by* TONY. TONY *is smoking a cigarette.*]

PEARL: Oh, have you started already?
FENWICK [*violently*]: Where have you been?
PEARL: I? My head was aching a little and I went for a turn in the garden. I found Tony composing a sonnet to the moon.
FENWICK: You said you were going to your room.
PEARL: What are you talking about?

[*She looks round, sees the* DUCHESSE'S *look of angry triumph, and gives a slight start.*]

DUCHESSE: Once too often, my dear, once too often.

[PEARL *takes no notice. She sees* BESSIE. BESSIE *has been staring at her with miserable eyes, and now she hides her face.* PEARL *realises that everything is discovered. She turns coolly to* TONY.]

PEARL: You damned fool, I told you it was too risky.

END OF THE SECOND ACT

ACT THREE

The Scene is the same as in the last act, the morning-room at Kenton. It is next day, Sunday, about three in the afternoon, and the sun is shining brightly.

[*The* PRINCESS, THORNTON CLAY, *and* FLEMING *are sitting down.* FLEMING *lights another cigarette.*]

PRINCESS: Is it good for you to smoke so many cigarettes?
FLEMING: I shouldn't think so.
CLAY: He must do something.
PRINCESS: Perhaps you can get up a game of tennis later on.
FLEMING: It's very hot for tennis.
CLAY: Besides, who will play?
PRINCESS: You two could have a single.
CLAY: If we only had the Sunday papers it would be something.
PRINCESS: You can hardly expect them in a place like this. I don't suppose there are many trains on Sunday.
CLAY: I wonder if dinner is going

to be as cheerful as luncheon was.

FLEMING: Did Pearl send any explanation for not appearing at luncheon?

PRINCESS: I haven't an idea.

CLAY: I asked the butler where she was. He said she was lunching in bed. I wish I'd thought of that.

PRINCESS: I'm afraid we were rather silent.

CLAY: Silent! I shall never forget that luncheon. Minnie subdued —and silent. Tony sulky—and silent. Bessie frightened—and silent. Bleane embarrassed—and silent. Fenwick furious—and silent. I tried to be pleasant and chatty. It was like engaging the pyramids in small-talk. Both of you behaved very badly. You might have given me a little encouragement.

FLEMING: I was afraid of saying the wrong thing. The Duchesse and Bessie looked as if they'd burst into tears on the smallest provocation.

PRINCESS: I was thinking of Pearl. What a humiliation! What a horrible humiliation!

FLEMING: What d'you think she'll do now?

CLAY: That's what I'm asking myself. I have an idea that she won't appear again till we're all gone.

PRINCESS: I hope she won't. She's always so sure of herself, I couldn't bear to see her pale and mortified.

CLAY: She's got plenty of courage.

PRINCESS: I know. She may force herself to face us. It would be a dreadful ordeal for all of us.

FLEMING: D'you think she's feeling it very much?

PRINCESS: She wouldn't be human if she weren't. I don't suppose she slept any better last night than the rest of us. Poor thing, she must be a wreck.

FLEMING: It was a terrible scene.

PRINCESS: I shall never forget it. The things that Minnie said. I couldn't have believed such language could issue from a woman's throat. Oh, it was horrible.

CLAY: It was startling. I've never seen a woman so beside herself. And there was no stopping her.

FLEMING: And with Bessie there.

PRINCESS: She was crying so much, I doubt if she heard.

CLAY: I was thankful when Minnie had the hysterics and we were able to fuss over her and dab her face and slap her hands. It was a very welcome diversion.

FLEMING: Does she have attacks like that often?

CLAY: I know she did when the young man before Tony married an heiress. I think she has one whenever there's a crisis in the affairs of her heart.

FLEMING: For goodness' sake, Thornton, don't talk about it as if it were a joke.

CLAY [*surprised*]: What's the matter, Fleming?

FLEMING: I think it's abominable to treat the whole thing so flippantly.

CLAY: Why, I was very sympathetic. I wasn't flippant. Who got the sal volatile? I got the sal volatile.

FLEMING [*with a shrug of the shoulders*]: I daresay my nerves are a bit on edge. You see, before,

I only thought things were rather queer. It's come as, well, as a shock to discover exactly what the relations are between all these people. And what I can't very easily get over is to realise that I'm the only member of the party who doesn't take it as a matter of course.

CLAY: We shall never make a man of the world of you, Fleming.

FLEMING: I'm afraid that didn't sound very polite, Princess. I beg your pardon.

PRINCESS: I should have few friends if I demanded the standard that you do. I've learned not to judge my neighbours.

FLEMING: Is it necessary to condone their vices?

PRINCESS: You don't understand. It's not entirely their fault. It's the life they lead. They've got too much money and too few responsibilities. English women in our station have duties that are part of their birthright, but we, strangers in a strange land, have nothing to do but enjoy ourselves.

FLEMING: Well, I thank God Bleane is a decent man, and he'll take Bessie out of all this.

[*The* DUCHESSE *comes in. Unlike the* PRINCESS, *who is in a summer frock, suitable for the country, the* DUCHESSE *wears a town dress and a hat.*]

PRINCESS: You've been changing your frock, Minnie.

DUCHESSE: Yes. I'm leaving this house in half an hour. I'd have gone this morning, if I'd been able to get away. I always thought it a detestable hole, but now that I've discovered there are only two trains on Sunday, one at nine, and the other at half-past four, I have no words to express my opinion of it.

CLAY: Yet you have an extensive vocabulary, Minnie.

DUCHESSE: I've been just as much a prisoner as if I'd been shut up with lock and key. I've been forced to eat that woman's food. I thought every mouthful would choke me.

PRINCESS: Do keep calm, Minnie. You know how bad it is for you to upset yourself.

DUCHESSE: As soon as I found there wasn't a train I sent over to the garage and said I wanted to be taken to London at once. Would you believe it, I couldn't get a car.

CLAY: Why not?

DUCHESSE: One of the cars went up to town early this morning, and the other is being overhauled. There's nothing but a luggage cart. I couldn't go to London in a luggage cart. As it is I shall have to go to the station in it. I shall look ridiculous.

CLAY: Have you ordered it?

DUCHESSE: Yes. It's to be round at the door in a few minutes.

CLAY: What on earth can Pearl have sent the car up to London for?

DUCHESSE: To show her spite.

PRINCESS: That's not like her.

DUCHESSE: My dear, she's been my greatest friend for fifteen years. I know her through and through, and I tell you that she hasn't got a single redeeming quality. And why does she want to have the car overhauled today? When you're giving a party the least you can do is to see

that your cars are in running
order.

PRINCESS: Oh, well, that was an
accident. You can't blame her
for that.

DUCHESSE: I only have one thing
to be thankful for, and that is
that she has had the decency to
keep to her room. I will be just.
It shows at least that she has
some sense of shame.

CLAY: You know, Minnie, Pearl
has a good heart. She didn't
mean to cause you pain.

DUCHESSE: Are you trying to excuse her, Thornton?

CLAY: No, I think her conduct
is inexcusable.

DUCHESSE: So do I. I mean to
have nothing more to do with
her. It's a judgment on me. I
disliked her the first time I
saw her. One should always
trust one's first impressions. Now
my eyes are opened. I will never
speak to her again. I will cut her
dead. I hope you'll tell her that,
Thornton.

CLAY: If that's a commission
you're giving me, it's not a very
pleasant one.

PRINCESS: Will you let me have
a word or two with Minnie?

CLAY: Why, of course. Come
along, Fleming.

[CLAY *and* FLEMING HARVEY *go
into the garden.*]

DUCHESSE: My dear, if you're going to ask me to turn the other
cheek, don't. Because I'm not
going to. I'm going to do all I
can to revenge myself on that
woman. I'm going to expose
her. I'm going to tell everyone
how she's treated me. When I
was her guest.

PRINCESS: You must take care
what you say for your own sake,
Minnie.

DUCHESSE: I know quite enough
about her to make her position
in London impossible. I'm going
to ruin her.

PRINCESS: What about Tony?

DUCHESSE: Oh, I've finished with
him. Ah! I'm not the kind of
woman to stand that sort of
treatment. I hope he'll end in
the gutter.

PRINCESS: Don't you care for him
any more?

DUCHESSE: My dear, if he was
starving, and went down on his
bended knees to me for a piece
of bread, I wouldn't give it to
him. He revolts me.

PRINCESS: Well, I'm very glad.
It distressed me to see you on
those terms with a boy like that.
You're well rid of him.

DUCHESSE: My dear, you needn't
tell me that. He's a thorough
wrong 'un, and that's all there
is about it. He hasn't even had
the decency to try and excuse
himself. He hasn't even made
an attempt to see me.

PRINCESS [*gives her a quick look*]:
After all, he never really cared
for you. Anyone could see that.

DUCHESSE [*her voice breaking*]:
Oh, don't say that, Flora. I
couldn't bear it. He loved me.
Until that woman came between
us I know he loved me. He
couldn't help loving me. I did
everything in the world for him.
[*She bursts into tears.*]

PRINCESS: Minnie. My dear, don't
give way. You know what a
worthless creature he is. Haven't
you any self-respect?

DUCHESSE: He's the only man I've

ever loved. I could hardly bear him out of my sight. What shall I do without him?

PRINCESS: Take care, here he is.

[TONY *comes in. He is startled at seeing the* DUCHESSE. *She turns away and hurriedly dries her tears.*]

TONY: Oh, I beg your pardon. I didn't know anyone was here. I was looking for some cigarettes.

[*He stands there awkwardly, not knowing whether to go or stay. The* PRINCESS *looks at him reflectively. There is a moment's silence. Then she shrugs her shoulders and goes out. He looks at the* DUCHESSE, *who stands with her back to him. He hesitates a moment, then, almost on the tips of his toes, walks over to the cigarettes, fills his case, takes another look at the* DUCHESSE, *and is in the act of tip-toeing out of the room when she stops him with her question.*]

DUCHESSE: Where are you going?

TONY: Nowhere in particular.

DUCHESSE: Then you'd better stay here.

TONY: I thought you wished to be alone.

DUCHESSE: Is that why you've kept away from me all day?

[*He sinks sulkily into an armchair. The* DUCHESSE *finally turns round and faces him.*]

DUCHESSE: Haven't you got anything to say for yourself at all?

TONY: What's the good of talking?

DUCHESSE: You might at least say you're sorry for the pain you've caused me. If you'd had any affection for me you wouldn't have done all you could to avoid me.

TONY: I knew you'd only make a scene.

DUCHESSE: Good heavens, you surely don't expect me not to make a scene.

TONY: The whole thing's very unfortunate.

DUCHESSE: Ha! Unfortunate. You break my heart and then you say it's unfortunate.

TONY: I didn't mean that. I meant it was unfortunate that you caught us out.

DUCHESSE: Oh, hold your stupid tongue. Every word you say is more unfortunate than the last.

TONY: It's because I knew you'd take offence at everything I said that I thought the best thing I could do was to keep out of the way.

DUCHESSE: You're heartless, heartless. If you'd had any decent feeling you couldn't have eaten the lunch you did. But you munched away, munched, munched, munched, till I could have killed you.

TONY: Well, I was hungry.

DUCHESSE: You oughtn't to have been hungry.

TONY: What are you going to do about it?

DUCHESSE: About your appetite? Pray to God your next mouthful chokes you.

TONY: No, about the other.

DUCHESSE: I'm going to leave this house this afternoon.

TONY: D'you want me to come, too?

DUCHESSE: What d'you suppose it matters to me whether you go or stay?

TONY: If you go I shall have to go, too.

DUCHESSE: You ought to start

soon then. It's four miles to the station. I shall be obliged if you will not get in the same carriage as me.

TONY: I'm not going to walk. They can run me down in a car.

DUCHESSE: There's nothing but a luggage cart, and I'm going in that.

TONY: Isn't there room for me?

DUCHESSE: No.

TONY: When d'you want me to move out of my flat?

DUCHESSE: What has that got to do with me?

TONY: You know very well that *I* can't pay the rent.

DUCHESSE: That's your look-out.

TONY: I shall go to the colonies.

DUCHESSE: That's the very best thing you can do. I hope you'll have to break stones, and dig, and paint—with lead paint. I hope you're miserable.

TONY: Oh, well, it'll have its compensations.

DUCHESSE: Such as?

TONY: I shall be my own master. I was about fed up with this, I can tell you.

DUCHESSE: Yes, you can say that now.

TONY: D'you think it was all jam, never being able to call my soul my own? I was sick to death of it.

DUCHESSE: You cad!

TONY: Well, you may just as well know the truth.

DUCHESSE: D'you mean to say you never cared for me? Not even at the beginning?

[*He shrugs his shoulders, but does not answer. She speaks the next phrases in little gasps gradually weakening as her emotion overcomes her. He stands before her in sulky silence.*]

DUCHESSE: Tony, I've done everything in the world for you. I've been like a mother to you. How *can* you be so ungrateful. You haven't got any heart. If you had you'd have asked me to forgive you. You'd have made some attempt to . . . Don't you *want* me to forgive you?

TONY: What d'you mean by that?

DUCHESSE: If you'd only asked me, if you'd only shown you were sorry, I'd have been angry with you, I wouldn't have spoken to you for a week, but I'd have forgiven you—I'd have forgiven you, Tony. But you never gave me a chance. It's cruel of you, cruel!

TONY: Well, anyhow, it's too late now.

DUCHESSE: Do you want it to be too late?

TONY: It's no good grousing about the past. The thing's over now.

DUCHESSE: Aren't you sorry?

TONY: I don't know. I suppose I am in a way. I don't want to make you unhappy.

DUCHESSE: If you wanted to be unfaithful to me, why didn't you prevent me from finding out? You didn't even trouble to take a little precaution.

TONY: I was a damned fool, I know that.

DUCHESSE: Are you in love with that woman?

TONY: No.

DUCHESSE: Then why did you? Oh, Tony, how could you?

TONY: If one felt about things at night as one does next morning, life would be a dashed sight easier.

DUCHESSE: If I said to you, Let's let bygones be bygones and start afresh, what would you say, Tony?

[She looks away. He rests his eyes on her reflectively.]

TONY: We've made a break now. We'd better leave it at that. I shall go out to the colonies.

DUCHESSE: Tony, you don't mean that seriously. You could never stand it. You know, you're not strong. You'll only die.

TONY: Oh, well, one can only die once.

DUCHESSE: I'm sorry for all I said just now, Tony. I didn't mean it.

TONY: It doesn't matter.

DUCHESSE: I can't live without you, Tony.

TONY: I've made up my mind. It's no good talking.

DUCHESSE: I'm sorry I was horrid to you, Tony. I'll never be again. Won't you forget it? Oh, Tony, won't you forgive me? I'll do anything in the world for you if only you won't leave me.

TONY: It's a rotten position I'm in. I must think of the future.

DUCHESSE: Oh, but Tony, I'll make it all right for you.

TONY: It's very kind of you, but it's not good enough. Let's part good friends, Minnie. If I've got to walk to the station, it's about time I was starting. [He holds out his hand to her.]

DUCHESSE: D'you mean to say it's good-bye? Good-bye for ever? Oh, how can you be so cruel!

TONY: When one's made up one's

mind to do a thing, it's best to do it at once.

DUCHESSE: Oh, I can't bear it. I can't bear it. [She begins to cry.] Oh, what a fool I was! I ought to have pretended not to see anything. I wish I'd never known. Then you wouldn't have thought of leaving me.

TONY: Come, my dear, pull yourself together. You'll get over it.

DUCHESSE [desperately]: Tony, if you want to marry me—I'm willing to marry you.

[A pause.]

TONY: I should be just as dependent on you. D'you think it would be jolly for me having to come to you for every five pounds I wanted?

DUCHESSE: I'll settle something on you so that you'll be independent. A thousand a year. Will that do?

TONY: You are a good sort, Minnie. [He goes over and sits down beside her.]

DUCHESSE: You will be kind to me, won't you?

TONY: Rather! And look here, you needn't give me that two-seater. I shall be able to drive the Rolls-Royce.

DUCHESSE: You didn't want to go to the colonies, did you?

TONY: Not much.

DUCHESSE: Oh, Tony, I do love you so.

TONY: That's right.

DUCHESSE: We won't stay another minute in this house. Ring the bell, will you? You'll come with me in the luggage cart?

TONY [touching the bell]: I much prefer that to walking.

DUCHESSE: It's monstrous that

there shouldn't be a motor to take luggage to the station. It's a most uncomfortable house to stay in.

TONY: Oh, beastly. D'you know that I didn't have a bathroom attached to my bedroom?

[POLE *comes in.*]

DUCHESSE: Is the luggage cart ready, Pole?

POLE: I'll enquire, your grace.

DUCHESSE: My maid is to follow in the morning with the luggage. Mr. Paxton will come with me. [*To* TONY.] What about your things?

TONY: Oh, they'll be all right. I brought my man with me.

POLE: Her ladyship is just coming downstairs, your grace.

DUCHESSE: Oh, is she? Thank you, that'll do, Pole.

POLE: Very good, your grace.

[*He goes out. As soon as he closes the door behind him the* DUCHESSE *springs to her feet.*]

DUCHESSE: I won't see her. Tony, see if Thornton is on the terrace.

TONY: All right. [*He goes to the french window.*] Yes. I'll call him, shall I? Clay, come here a minute, will you?

[*He goes out.* THORNTON CLAY *comes in, followed immediately by the* PRINCESS *and* FLEMING.]

DUCHESSE: Thornton, I'm told Pearl is coming downstairs.

CLAY: At last.

DUCHESSE: I won't see her. Nothing will induce me to see her.

PRINCESS: My dear, what is to be done? We can't make her remain upstairs in her own house.

DUCHESSE: No, but Thornton can

speak to her. She's evidently ashamed of herself. I only ask one thing, that she should keep out of the way till I'm gone.

CLAY: I'll do my best.

DUCHESSE: I'm going to walk up and down till the luggage cart is ready. I haven't taken my exercise today. [*She goes out.*]

CLAY: If Pearl is in a temper that's not a very pleasant message to give her.

PRINCESS: You won't find her in a temper. If she's dreadfully upset, tell her what Minnie says gently.

FLEMING: Here is Bessie. [*She comes in.*] It appears that Pearl is just coming downstairs.

BESSIE: Is she?

PRINCESS: Have you seen her this morning, Bessie?

BESSIE: No. She sent her maid to ask me to go to her, but I had a headache and couldn't.

[*They look at her curiously. She is inclined to be abrupt and silent. It may be imagined that she has made up her mind to some course, but what that is the others cannot tell.* FLEMING *goes over and sits beside her.*]

FLEMING: I'm thinking of going back to America next Saturday, Bessie.

BESSIE: Dear Fleming, I shall be sorry to lose you.

FLEMING: I expect you'll be too busy to think about me. You'll have to see all kinds of people, and then there's your trousseau to get.

BESSIE: I wish you could come over to Paris with me, Princess, and help me with it.

PRINCESS: I? [*She gets an inkling*

of what BESSIE *means.*] Of course, if I could be of any help to you, dear child. . . . [*She takes* BESSIE'S *hand and gives her a fond smile.* BESSIE *turns away to hide a tear that for a moment obscures her eyes.*] Perhaps it's a very good idea. We must talk about it.

[PEARL *comes in. She is perfectly cool and collected, radiant in a wonderful, audacious gown; she is looking her best and knows it. There is nothing in her manner to indicate the smallest recollection of the episode that took place on the preceding evening.*]

PEARL [*brightly*]: Good-morning.

CLAY: Good-afternoon.

PEARL: I knew everyone would abuse me for coming down so late. It was such a lovely day I thought it was a pity to get up.

CLAY: Don't be paradoxical, Pearl, it's too hot.

PEARL: The sun streamed into my room, and I said, It's a sin not to get up on a morning like this. And the more I said I ought to get up, the more delightful I found it to lie in bed. How is your head, Bessie?

BESSIE: Oh, it's better, thank you.

PEARL: I was sorry to hear you weren't feeling up to the mark.

BESSIE: I didn't sleep very well.

PEARL: What have you done with your young man?

BESSIE: Harry? He's writing letters.

PEARL: Spreading the glad tidings, I suppose. You ought to write to his mother, Bessie. It would be a graceful attention. A charming, frank little letter, the sort of thing one would expect an *ingénue* to write. Straight from the heart.

CLAY: I'm sure you'd love to write it yourself, Pearl.

PEARL: And we must think about sending an announcement to the *Morning Post.*

FLEMING: You think of everything, Pearl.

PEARL: I take my duties as Bessie's chaperon very seriously. I've already got a brilliant idea for the gown I'm going to wear at the wedding.

FLEMING: Gee!

PEARL: My dear Fleming, don't say Gee, it's so American. Say By Jove.

FLEMING: I couldn't without laughing.

PEARL: Laffing. Why can't you say laughing?

FLEMING: I don't want to.

PEARL: How obstinate you are. Of course, now that Bessie is going to marry an Englishman she'll have to take lessons. I know an excellent woman. She's taught all the American peeresses.

FLEMING: You surprise me.

PEARL: She's got a wonderful method. She makes you read aloud. And she has long lists of words that you have to repeat twenty times a day—half instead of haf, and barth instead of bath, and carnt instead of can't.

FLEMING: By Jove instead of Gee?

PEARL: Peeresses don't say By Jove, Fleming. She teaches them to say Good heavens instead of Mercy.

FLEMING: Does she make money by it?

PEARL: Pots. She's a lovely woman. Eleo Dorset had an accent that you could cut with a knife when she first came over, and in three months she hadn't got any more than I have.

BESSIE [*getting up. To* FLEMING]: D'you think it's too hot for a turn in the garden?

FLEMING: Why, no.

BESSIE: Shall we go then? [*They go out together.*]

PEARL: What's the matter with Bessie? She must have swallowed a poker last night. No wonder she couldn't sleep. It's enough to give anyone indigestion.

CLAY: You know that Minnie is going this afternoon, Pearl?

PEARL: Yes, so I heard. It's such a bore there are no cars to take her to the station. She'll have to go in the luggage cart.

CLAY: She doesn't wish to see you.

PEARL: Oh, but I wish to see her.

CLAY: I daresay.

PEARL: I must see her.

CLAY: She asked me to tell you that she only wished you to do one thing, and that is to keep out of the way till she's gone.

PEARL: Then you can go and tell her that unless she sees me she shan't have the luggage cart.

CLAY: Pearl!

PEARL: That's my ultimatum.

CLAY: Can you see me taking a message like that to the Duchesse?

PEARL: It's four miles to the station, and there's not a scrap of shade all the way.

CLAY: After all, it's not a very unreasonable request she's making.

PEARL: If she wants the luggage cart she must come and say good-bye to me like a lady.

CLAY [*to the* PRINCESS]: What am I to do? We used up all the sal volatile last night.

PRINCESS: I'll tell her if you like.

D'you really insist on seeing her, Pearl?

PEARL: Yes, it's very important. [*The* PRINCESS *goes out.* PEARL *watches her go with a smile.*] I'm afraid Flora is shocked. She shouldn't know such people.

CLAY: Really, Pearl, your behaviour is monstrous.

PEARL: Never mind about my behaviour. Tell me how luncheon went off.

CLAY: My dear, it was like a gathering of relations who hate one another, after the funeral of a rich aunt who's left all her money to charity.

PEARL: It must have been priceless. I'd have given anything to be there.

CLAY: Why weren't you?

PEARL: Oh, I knew there'd be scenes, and I'm never at my best in a scene before luncheon. One of the things I've learnt from the war is that a general should choose his own time for a battle.

CLAY: Minnie moved heaven and earth to get away this morning.

PEARL: I knew she couldn't. I knew none of them could go till the afternoon.

CLAY: The train service is atrocious.

PEARL: George says that is one of the advantages of the place. It keeps it rural. There's one at nine and another at half-past four. I knew that not even the most violent disturbances would get people up at eight who never by any chance have breakfast till ten. As soon as I awoke I took the necessary steps.

CLAY [*interrupting*]: You slept?

PEARL: Oh yes, I slept beautifully.

There's nothing like a little excitement to give me a good night.

CLAY: Well, you certainly had some excitement. I've rarely witnessed such a terrific scene.

PEARL: I sent out to the garage and gave instructions that the old Rolls-Royce was to be taken down at once and the other was to go to London.

CLAY: What for?

PEARL: Never mind. You'll know presently. Then I did a little telephoning.

CLAY: Why were you so anxious to prevent anybody from leaving the house?

PEARL: I couldn't have persuaded myself that my party was a success if half my guests had left me on Sunday morning. I thought they might change their minds by the afternoon.

CLAY: If that's your only reason, I don't think it's a very good one.

PEARL: It isn't. I will be frank with you, Thornton. I can imagine that a very amusing story might be made out of this episode. I never mind scandal, but I don't expose myself to ridicule if I can help it.

CLAY: My dear Pearl, surely you can trust the discretion of your guests. Who do you think will give it away?

PEARL: You.

CLAY: I? My dear Pearl, I give you my word of honour . . .

PEARL [calmly]: My dear Thornton, I don't care twopence about your word of honour. You're a professional entertainer, and you'll sacrifice everything to a good story. Why, don't you remember that killing story about your father's death? You dined out a whole season on it.

CLAY: Well, it was a perfectly killing story. No one would have enjoyed it more than my poor old father.

PEARL: I'm not going to risk anything, Thornton. I think it's much better there should be no story to tell.

CLAY: No one can move the clock backwards, Pearl. I couldn't help thinking at luncheon that there were the elements of a very good story indeed.

PEARL: And you'll tell it, Thornton. Then I shall say: My dear, does it sound probable? They all stayed quite happily till Monday morning; Sturrey and the Arlingtons dined on the Sunday night, and we had a very merry evening. Besides, I was lunching with Minnie only two days afterwards. And I shall say: Poor Thornton, he *is* such a liar, isn't he?

CLAY: I confess that if you are reconciled with Minnie it will take a great deal of the point away from my story. What about Arthur Fenwick?

PEARL: He's a sensualist, and the sensual are always sentimental.

CLAY: He scared me dreadfully at luncheon. He was eating a dressed crab, and his face grew every minute more purple. I was expecting him to have an apoplectic fit.

PEARL: It's not an unpleasant death, you know, Thornton, to have a stroke while you're eating your favourite dish.

CLAY: You know, there are no excuses for you, Pearl.

PEARL: Human nature excuses so much, Thornton.

CLAY: You really might have left Tony alone. This habit you have of snitching has got you into trouble before.

PEARL: People are so selfish. It just happens that I find no man so desirable as one that a friend of mine is in love with. I make allowances for the idiosyncrasies of my friends. Why shouldn't they make allowances for mine?

[*The* DUCHESSE *comes in, erect and haughty, with the air of Boadicea facing the Roman legions.* PEARL *turns to her with an ingratiating smile.*]

PEARL: Ah, Minnie.

DUCHESSE: I'm told the only way I can leave this house is by submitting to the odious necessity of seeing you.

PEARL: I wish you wouldn't go, Minnie. Lord Sturrey is coming over to dinner tonight, and so are the Arlingtons. I always take a lot of trouble to get the right people together, and I hate it when anybody fails me at the last minute.

DUCHESSE: D'you think anything would have induced me to stay so long if there'd been any possibility of getting away?

PEARL: It wouldn't have been nice to go without saying good-bye to me.

DUCHESSE: Don't talk nonsense, Pearl.

PEARL: D'you know that you behaved very badly last night, and I ought to be extremely angry with you?

DUCHESSE: I? Thornton, the woman's as mad as a hatter.

PEARL: You really oughtn't to have made a scene before Harry Bleane. And, you know, to tell Arthur wasn't playing the game. If you wanted to tell anyone, why didn't you tell George?

DUCHESSE: In the first place, he wasn't here. He never is.

PEARL: I know. He says that now society has taken to coming down to the country for week-ends he prefers London.

DUCHESSE: I'll never forgive you. Never. Never. Never. You'd got Arthur Fenwick. Why weren't you satisfied with him? If you wanted to have an affair with anyone, why didn't you take Thornton? He's almost the only one of your friends with whom you haven't. The omission is becoming almost marked.

PEARL: Thornton never makes love to me except when other people are looking. He can be very passionate in the front seat of my box at the opera.

CLAY: This conversation is growing excessively personal. I'll leave you. [*He goes out.*]

PEARL: I'm sorry I had to insist on your seeing me, but I had something quite important to say to you.

DUCHESSE: Before you go any further, Pearl, I wish to tell you that I'm going to marry Tony.

PEARL [*aghast*]: Minnie! Oh, my dear, you're not doing it to spite me? You know, honestly, he doesn't interest me in the slightest. Oh, Minnie, do think carefully.

DUCHESSE: It's the only way I can keep him.

PEARL: D'you think you'll be happy?

DUCHESSE: What should you care if I'm happy?

PEARL: Of course I care. D'you think it's wise? You're giving yourself into his hands. Oh, my dear, how can you risk it?

DUCHESSE: He said he was going out to the colonies. I love him. . . . I believe you're really distressed. How strange you are, Pearl! Perhaps it's the best thing for me. He may settle down. I was very lonely sometimes, you know. Sometimes, when I had the blues, I almost wished I'd never left home.

PEARL: And I've been moving heaven and earth to get him a job. I've been on the telephone this morning to all the Cabinet Ministers I know, and at last I've done it. That's what I wanted to tell you. I thought you'd be so pleased. I suppose now he won't want it.

DUCHESSE: Oh, I'm sure he will. He's very proud, you know. That's one of the things I liked in him. He had to be dependent on me, and that's partly why he always wanted to marry me.

PEARL: Of course, you'll keep your title.

DUCHESSE: Oh yes, I shall do that.

PEARL [going towards her as if to kiss her]: Well, darling, you have my very, very best wishes.

DUCHESSE [drawing back]: I'm not going to forgive you, Pearl.

PEARL: But you've forgiven Tony.

DUCHESSE: I don't blame him. He was led away.

PEARL: Come, Minnie, don't be spiteful. You might let bygones be bygones.

DUCHESSE: Nothing will induce me to stay in this house another night.

PEARL: It's a very slow train, and you'll have to go without your tea.

DUCHESSE: I don't care.

PEARL: You won't arrive in London till half-past eight, and you'll have to dine in a restaurant.

DUCHESSE: I don't care.

PEARL: You'll be grubby and hot. Tony will be hungry and out of temper. And you'll look your age.

DUCHESSE: You promised me the luggage cart.

PEARL [with a sigh]: You shall have it; but you'll have to sit on the floor, because it hasn't got any seats.

DUCHESSE: Pearl, it's not going to break down on the way to the station?

PEARL: Oh, no. How can you suspect me of playing a trick like that on you? . . . [With a tinge of regret.] It never occurred to me.

[THORNTON CLAY comes in.]

CLAY: Pearl, I thought you'd like to know that Fenwick is coming to say good-bye to you.

DUCHESSE: I'll go and tell Tony about the job you've got him. By the way, what is it?

PEARL: Oh, it's something in the Education Office.

DUCHESSE: How very nice. What do they do there?

PEARL: Nothing. But it'll keep him busy from ten to four.

[The DUCHESSE goes out.]

PEARL: She's going to marry him.

CLAY: I know.

PEARL: I'm a wonderful matchmaker. First Bessie and Harry Bleane, and now Minnie and Tony Paxton. I shall have to find someone for you, Thornton.

CLAY: How on earth did you manage to appease her?

PEARL: I reasoned with her. After all, she should be glad the boy has sown his wild oats before he marries. And besides, if he were her husband, of course she wouldn't expect fidelity from him; it seems unnatural to expect it when he isn't.

CLAY: But she's going all the same.

PEARL: I've got a quarter of an hour yet. Give me your handkerchief, will you?

CLAY [*handing it to her*]: You're not going to burst into tears?

PEARL [*she rubs her cheeks violently*]: I thought I ought to look a little wan and pale when Arthur comes in.

CLAY: You'll never love me, Pearl. You tell me all your secrets.

PEARL: Shall I tell you what to do about it? Take the advice I give to Americans who come over to London and want to see the Tower: say you've been, and don't go.

CLAY: D'you think you can bring Arthur round?

PEARL: I'm sure I could if he loved me.

CLAY: My dear, he dotes on you.

PEARL: Don't be a fool, Thornton. He loves his love for me. That's quite a different thing. I've only got one chance. He sees himself as the man of iron. I'm going to play the dear little thing racket.

CLAY: You're a most unscrupulous woman, Pearl.

PEARL: Not more than most. Please go. I think he ought to find me alone.

[CLAY *goes out.* PEARL *seats herself in a pensive attitude and looks down at the carpet; in her hand she holds dejectedly an open volume of poetry. Presently* ARTHUR FENWICK *comes in. She pretends not to see him. He is the strong man, battered but not beaten, struggling with the emotion which he tries to master.*]

FENWICK: Pearl!

PEARL [*with a jump*]: Oh, how you startled me. I didn't hear you come in.

FENWICK: I daresay you're surprised to see me. I thought it was necessary that we should have a short conversation before I left this house.

PEARL [*looking away*]: I'm glad to see you once more.

FENWICK: You understand that everything is over between us.

PEARL: If you've made up your mind, there's nothing for me to say. I know that nothing can move you when you've once done that.

FENWICK [*drawing himself up a little*]: No. That has always been part of my power.

PEARL: I wouldn't have you otherwise.

FENWICK: I don't want to part from you in anger, Pearl. Last night I could have thrashed you within an inch of your life.

PEARL: Why didn't you? D'you think I'd have minded that from the man I loved?

FENWICK: You know I could never hit a woman.

PEARL: I thought of you all through

the long hours of the night, Arthur.

FENWICK: I never slept a wink.

PEARL: One would never think it. You must be made of iron.

FENWICK: I think I am sometimes.

PEARL: Am I very pale!

FENWICK: A little.

PEARL: I feel a perfect wreck.

FENWICK: You must go and lie down. It's no good making yourself ill.

PEARL: Oh, don't bother about me, Arthur.

FENWICK: I've bothered about you so long. It's difficult for me to get out of the habit all at once.

PEARL: Every word you say stabs me to the heart.

FENWICK: I'll get done quickly with what I had to tell you and then go. It's merely this. Of course, I shall continue the allowance I've always made you.

PEARL: Oh, I couldn't take it. I couldn't take it.

FENWICK: You must be reasonable, Pearl. This is a matter of business.

PEARL: It's a question I refuse to discuss. Nothing would have induced me to accept your help if I hadn't loved you. Now that there can be nothing more between us—no, no, the thought outrages me.

FENWICK: I was afraid that you'd take up that attitude. Remember that you've only got eight thousand a year of your own. You can't live on that.

PEARL: I can starve.

FENWICK: I must insist, Pearl, for my own sake. You've adopted a style of living which you would never have done if you hadn't had me at the back of you. I'm morally responsible, and I must meet my obligations.

PEARL: We can only be friends in future, Arthur.

FENWICK: I haven't often asked you to do anything for me, Pearl.

PEARL: I shall return your presents. Let me give you my pearl necklace at once.

FENWICK: Girlie, you wouldn't do that.

PEARL [pretending to try and take the necklace off]: I can't undo the clasp. Please help me. [She goes up to him and turns her back so that he may get at it.]

FENWICK: I won't. I won't.

PEARL: I'll tear it off my neck.

FENWICK: Pearl, you break my heart. Do you care for me so little that you can't bear to wear the trifling presents I gave you?

PEARL: If you talk to me like that I shall cry. Don't you see that I'm trying to keep my self-control?

FENWICK: This is dreadful. This is even more painful than I anticipated.

PEARL: You see, strength is easy to you. I'm weak. That's why I put myself in your hands. I felt your power instinctively.

FENWICK: I know, I know, and it was because I felt you needed me that I loved you. I wanted to shelter you from the storms and buffets of the world.

PEARL: Why didn't you save me from myself, Arthur?

FENWICK: When I look at your poor, pale little face I wonder what you'll do without me, girlie.

PEARL [her voice breaking]: It'll

be very hard. I've grown so used to depending on you. Whenever anything has gone wrong, I've come to you and you've put it right. I was beginning to think there was nothing you couldn't do.

FENWICK: I've always welcomed obstacles. I like something to surmount. It excites me.

PEARL: You seemed to take all my strength from me. I felt strangely weak beside you.

FENWICK: It wasn't necessary that we should both be strong. I loved you because you were weak. I liked you to come to me in all your troubles. It made me feel so good to be able to put everything right for you.

PEARL: You've always been able to do the impossible.

FENWICK [*impressively*]: I have never found anything impossible.

PEARL [*deeply moved*]: Except to forgive.

FENWICK: Ah, I see you know me. I never forget. I never forgive.

PEARL: I suppose that's why people feel there's something strangely Napoleonic about you.

FENWICK: Maybe. And yet—though you're only a woman, you've broken me, Pearl, you've broken me.

PEARL: Oh no, don't say that. I couldn't bear that. I want you to go on being strong and ruthless.

FENWICK: Something has gone out of my life for ever. I almost think you've broken my heart. I was so proud of you. I took so much pleasure in your success. Why, whenever I saw your name in the society columns of the papers it used to give me a thrill of satisfaction. What's going to become of you now, girlie? What's going to become of you now?

PEARL: I don't know; I don't care.

FENWICK: This fellow, does he care for you? Will he make you happy?

PEARL: Tony? He's going to marry the Duchesse. [FENWICK *represses a start.*] I shall never see him again.

FENWICK: Then if I leave you, you'll have nobody but your husband.

PEARL: Nobody.

FENWICK: You'll be terribly lonely, girlie.

PEARL: You will think of me sometimes, Arthur, won't you?

FENWICK: I shall never forget you, girlie. I shall never forget how you used to leave your fine house in Mayfair and come and lunch with me down town.

PEARL: You used to give me such delicious things to eat.

FENWICK: It was a treat to see you in your beautiful clothes sharing a steak with me and a bottle of beer. I can order a steak, Pearl, can't I?

PEARL: And d'you remember those delicious little onions that we used to have? [*She seems to taste them.*] M . . . M . . . M . . . It makes my mouth water to think of them.

FENWICK: There are few women who enjoy food as much as you do, Pearl.

PEARL: D'you know, next time you dined with me, I'd made up my mind to give you an entirely English dinner. Scotch broth, herrings, mixed grill, saddle of lamb and then enormous marrow bones.

[FENWICK *can hardly bear the thought, his face grows red, his eyes bulge, and he gasps.*]

FENWICK: Oh, girlie! [*With utter abandonment.*] Let's have that dinner. [*He seizes her in his arms and kisses her.*] I can't leave you. You need me too much.

PEARL: Arthur, Arthur, can you forgive me?

FENWICK: To err is human, to forgive divine.

PEARL: Oh, how like you that is!

FENWICK: If you must deceive me, don't let me ever find out. I love you too much.

PEARL: I won't, Arthur, I promise you I won't.

FENWICK: Come and sit on the sofa and let me look at you. I seem to see you for the first time.

PEARL: You know, you wouldn't have liked the walk to the station. It's four miles in the sun. You're a vain old thing, and your boots are always a little too small for you.

[BESSIE *comes in. She stops as she sees* PEARL *and* FENWICK *sitting hand in hand.*]

PEARL: Are you going out, Bessie?

BESSIE: As soon as Harry has finished his letters, we're going for a walk.

PEARL [*to* FENWICK]: You mustn't squeeze my hand in Bessie's presence, Arthur.

FENWICK: You're a very lucky girl, Bessie, to have a sister like Pearl. She's the most wonderful woman in the world.

PEARL: You're talking nonsense, Arthur. Go and put some flannels on. It makes me quite hot to look at you in that suit. We'll try and get up a little tennis after tea.

FENWICK: Now, you mustn't tire yourself, Pearl. Remember those white cheeks of yours.

PEARL [*with a charming look at him*]: Oh, I shall soon get my colour back now.

[*She gives him her hand to kiss and he goes out.* PEARL *takes a little mirror out of her bag and looks at herself reflectively.*]

PEARL: Men are very trivial, foolish creatures. They have kind hearts. But their heads. Oh dear, oh dear, it's lamentable. And they're so vain, poor dears, they're so vain.

BESSIE: Pearl, tomorrow, when we go back to London, I'm going away.

PEARL: Are you? Where?

BESSIE: The Princess is going to take me over to Paris for a few days.

PEARL: Oh, is that all? Don't stay away too long. You ought to be in London just at present.

BESSIE: On my return I'm proposing to stay with the Princess.

PEARL [*calmly*]: Nonsense.

BESSIE: I wasn't asking your permission, Pearl. I was telling you my plans.

PEARL [*looks at her for a moment reflectively*]: Are you going to make me a scene, too? I've already gone through two this afternoon. I'm rather tired of them.

BESSIE: Please don't be alarmed. I've got nothing more to say.

[*She makes as though to leave the room.*]

PEARL: Don't be a little fool, Bessie. You've been staying with me all the season. I can't allow you to leave my house and go and live with Flora. We don't want to go out of our way to make people gossip.

BESSIE: Please don't argue with me, Pearl. It's not my business to reproach you for anything you do. But it isn't my business, either, to stand by and watch.

PEARL: You're no longer a child, Bessie.

BESSIE: I've been blind and foolish. Because I was happy and having a good time, I never stopped to ask for explanations of this, that and the other. I never thought. . . . The life was so gay and brilliant—it never struck me that underneath it all— Oh, Pearl, don't make me say what I have in my heart, but let me go quietly.

PEARL: Bessie, dear, you must be reasonable. Think what people would say if you suddenly left my house. They'd ask all sorts of questions, and heaven knows what explanations they'd invent. People aren't charitable, you know. I don't want to be hard on you, but I can't afford to let you do a thing like that.

BESSIE: Now that I know what I do, I should never respect myself again if I stayed.

PEARL: I don't know how you can be so unkind.

BESSIE: I don't want to be that, Pearl. But it's stronger than I am. I must go.

PEARL [*with emotion*]: I'm so fond of you, Bessie. You don't know how much I want you with me. After all, I've seen so little of you these last few years. It's been such a comfort to me to have you. You were so pretty and young and sweet, it was like a ray of April sunshine in the house.

BESSIE: I'm afraid you think women are as trivial, foolish creatures as men, Pearl.

[PEARL *looks up and sees that* BESSIE *is not in the least taken in by the pathetic attitude.*]

PEARL [*icily*]: Take care you don't go too far, Bessie.

BESSIE: There's no need for us to quarrel. I've made up my mind, and there's the end of it.

PEARL: Flora's a fool. I shall tell her that I won't have her take you away from me. You'll stay with me until you're married.

BESSIE: D'you want me to tell you that I can hardly bear to speak to you? You fill me with shame and disgust. I want never to see you again.

PEARL: Really, you drive me beyond endurance. I think I must be the most patient woman in the world to put up with all I've had to put up with today. After all, what have I done? I was a little silly and incautious. By the fuss you all make one would think no one had ever been incautious and silly before. Besides, it hasn't got anything to do with you. Why don't you mind your own business?

BESSIE [*bitterly*]: You talk as though your relations with Arthur Fenwick were perfectly natural.

PEARL: Good heavens, you're not

going to pretend you didn't know about Arthur. After all, I'm no worse than anybody else. Why, one of the reasons we Americans like London is that we can live our own lives and people accept things philosophically. Eleo Gloster, Sadie Twickenham, Maimie Hartlepool—you don't imagine they're faithful to their husbands? They didn't marry them for that.

BESSIE: Oh, Pearl, how can you? How can you? Haven't you any sense of decency at all? When I came in just now and saw you sitting on the sofa with that gross, vulgar, sensual old man—oh! [*She makes a gesture of disgust.*] You can't love him. I could have understood if . . . but—oh, it's so disgraceful, it's so hideous. What can you see in him? He's nothing but rich. . . . [*She pauses, and her face changes as a thought comes to her, and coming horrifies her.*] It's not because he's rich? Pearl! Oh!

PEARL: Really, Bessie, you're very silly, and I'm tired of talking to you.

BESSIE: Pearl, it's not that? Answer me. Answer me.

PEARL [*roughly*]: Mind your own business.

BESSIE: He was right, then, last night, when he called you that. He was so right that you didn't even notice it. A few hours later you're sitting hand in hand with him. A slut. That's what he called you. A slut. A slut.

PEARL: How dare you! Hold your tongue. How dare you!

BESSIE: A kept woman. That's what you are.

PEARL [*recovering herself*]: I'm a fool to lose my temper with you.

BESSIE: Why should you? I'm saying nothing but the truth.

PEARL: You're a silly little person, Bessie. If Arthur helps me a little, that's his affair, and mine. He's got more money than he knows what to do with, and it amuses him to see me spend it. I could have twenty thousand a year from him if I chose.

BESSIE: Haven't you got money of your own?

PEARL: You know exactly what I've got. Eight thousand a year. D'you think I could have got the position I have on that? You're not under the impression all the world comes to my house because of my charm, are you? I'm not. You don't think the English want us here? You don't think they like us marrying their men? Good heavens, when you've known England as long as I have you'll realise that in their hearts they still look upon us as savages and Red Indians. We have to force ourselves upon them. They come to me because I amuse them. Very early in my career I discovered that the English can never resist getting something for nothing. If a dancer is the rage, they'll see her at my house. If a fiddler is in vogue, they'll hear him at my concert. I give them balls. I give them dinners. I've made myself the fashion, I've got power, I've got influence. But everything I've got—my success, my reputation, my notoriety—I've bought it, bought it, bought it.

BESSIE: How humiliating!

PEARL: And, finally, I've bought you a husband.

BESSIE: That's not true. He loves me.

PEARL: D'you think he'd have loved you if I hadn't shown you to him in these surroundings, if I hadn't dazzled him by the brilliant people among whom he found you. You don't know what love is made of. D'you think it's nothing that he should hear a Prime Minister pay you compliments. Of course I bought him.

BESSIE [*aghast*]: It's horrible.

PEARL: You know the truth now. It'll be very useful to you in your married life. Run away and take your little walk with Harry Bleane. I'm going to arrange my face.

[*She goes out.* BESSIE *is left ashamed and stunned.* BLEANE *comes in.*]

BLEANE: I'm afraid I've kept you waiting. I'm so sorry.

BESSIE [*dully*]: It doesn't matter at all.

BLEANE: Where shall we go? You know the way about these parts, and I don't.

BESSIE: Harry, I want you to release me. I can't marry you.

BLEANE [*aghast*]: Why?

BESSIE: I want to go back to America. I'm frightened.

BLEANE: Of me?

BESSIE: Oh no, I know that you're a dear, good creature; I'm frightened of what I may become.

BLEANE: But I love you, Bessie.

BESSIE: Then that's all the more reason for me to go. I must tell you frankly. I'm not in love with you, I only like you. I would never have dreamt of marrying

you, if you hadn't been who you are. I wanted to have a title. That's why Pearl married her husband, and that's why the Duchess married. Let me go, Harry.

BLEANE: I knew you didn't love me, but I thought you might come to in time. I thought if I tried I could make you love me.

BESSIE: You didn't know that I was nothing but a self-seeking, heartless snob.

BLEANE: I don't care what you say of yourself, I know that you can be nothing but what is true and charming.

BESSIE: After what you've seen last night? After what you know of this house? Aren't you disgusted with all of us?

BLEANE: You can't think I could class you with the Duchesse and . . . [*He stops.*]

BESSIE: Pearl at my age was no different from what I am. It's the life.

BLEANE: But perhaps you won't want to lead it. The set you've been living in here isn't the only set in England. It makes a stir because it's in the public eye. Its doings are announced in the papers. But it isn't a very good set, and there are plenty of people who don't very much admire it.

BESSIE: You must let me try and say what I have in my heart. And be patient with me. You think I can make myself at home in your life. I've had a hint of it now and then. I've seen a glimpse of it through Pearl's laughter and the Duchesse's sneers. It's a life of dignity, of responsibilities, and of public duty.

BLEANE [*with a rueful smile*]: You make it very strenuous.

BESSIE: It comes naturally to the English girls of your class. They've known it all their lives, and they've been brought up to lead it. But we haven't. To us it's just tedious, and its dignity is irksome. We're bored, and we fall back on the only thing that offers, pleasure. You've spoken to me about your house. It means everything to you because it's associated with your childhood and all your people before you. It could only mean something to me if I loved you. And I don't.

BLEANE: You've made me so wretched. I don't know what to say to you.

BESSIE: If I make you wretched now, it's so that we may both be saved a great deal of unhappiness later on. I'm glad I don't care for you, for it would make it so much harder for me to go. And I've got to go. I can't marry you. I want to go home. If I marry ever I want to marry in my own country. That is my place.

BLEANE: Don't you think you could wait a little before you decide finally?

BESSIE: Don't put difficulties in my way. Don't you see that we're not strong enough for the life over here? It goes to our head; we lose our bearings; we put away our own code, and we can't adopt the code of the country we come to. We drift. There's nothing for us to do but amuse ourselves, and we fall to pieces. But in America we're safe. And

perhaps America wants us. When we come over here we're like soldiers deserting our country in time of war. Oh, I'm homesick for America. I didn't know how much it meant to me till now. Let me go back, Harry.

BLEANE: If you don't want to marry me, of course, I'm not going to try and make you.

BESSIE: Don't be angry, and be my friend always.

BLEANE: Always.

BESSIE: After all, three months ago you didn't know me. In three months more you will have forgotten me. Then marry some English girl, who can live your life and share your thoughts. And be happy.

[PEARL *comes in. She has rouged her cheeks, and has once more the healthy colour which is usual with her. She is evidently jubilant.*]

PEARL: The car has just come back from London. [*She goes to the french window and calls.*] Minnie!

BESSIE: I shall tell Pearl tomorrow.

BLEANE: I won't post my letters then. I'll go and get them out of the box.

BESSIE: Forgive me.

[*He goes out. The* DUCHESSE *and* CLAY *appear at the window.*]

DUCHESSE: Did you call me?

PEARL: The car has just come back from London, so it can take you to the station.

DUCHESSE: That's a mercy. I didn't at all like the idea of going to the station in the luggage cart. Where is Flora? I must say good-bye to her.

PEARL: Oh, there's plenty of time now. The car will run you down in ten minutes.

[TONY *comes in, then the* PRINCESS *and* FLEMING.]

DUCHESSE: Tony, the car has returned, and is going to take us to the station.

TONY: Thank God for that! I should have looked a perfect fool in that luggage cart.

CLAY: But what on earth did you send the car to London for, anyway?

PEARL: In one minute you'll see.

[ARTHUR FENWICK *comes in. He has changed into flannels.*]

FENWICK: Who is that gentleman that's just arrived, Pearl?

PEARL: The man of mystery.

[*The* BUTLER *comes in, followed by* ERNEST, *and after announcing him goes out.*]

POLE: Mr. Ernest.

DUCHESSE: Ernest!

CLAY: Ernest?

[*He is a little dark man, with large eyes, and long hair neatly plastered down. He is dressed like a tailor's dummy, in black coat, white gloves, silk hat, patent leather boots. He is a dancing master, and overwhelmingly gentlemanly. He speaks in mincing tones.*]

ERNEST: Dear Lady Grayston.

PEARL [*shaking hands with him*]: I'm so glad you were able to come. [*To the others.*] You were talking about Ernest last night, and I thought we would have nothing to do this evening and he would cheer and comfort us. I sent the car up to London

with orders to bring him back dead or alive.

ERNEST: My dear Lady Grayston, I'm sure I'll get into no end of trouble. I had all sorts of calls to pay this afternoon, and I was dining out, and I'd promised to go to a little hop that the dear Duchess of Gloster was giving. But I felt I couldn't refuse *you.* You've always been such a good friend to me, dear Lady Grayston. You must excuse me coming in my town clothes, but your chauffeur said there wasn't a moment to lose, so I came just as I am.

PEARL: But you look a perfect picture.

ERNEST: Oh, don't say that, dear Lady Grayston; I know this isn't the sort of thing one ought to wear in the country.

PEARL: You remember the Duchesse de Surennes?

ERNEST: Oh, of course I remember the Duchesse.

DUCHESSE: Dear Ernest!

ERNEST: Dear Duchesse!

DUCHESSE: I thought I was never going to see you again, Ernest.

ERNEST: Oh, don't say that, it sounds too sad.

PEARL: It's such a pity you must go, Minnie. Ernest could have shown you all sorts of new steps.

ERNEST: Oh, dear Duchesse, you're not going the very moment I come down? That is unkind of you.

DUCHESSE [*with an effort*]: I must go. I must go.

ERNEST: Have you been practising that little step I showed you the other day? My dear friend, the Marchioness of Twickenham—not the *old* one, you know, the *new* one—is beginning to do it so well.

DUCHESSE [*struggling with herself*]: Have we time, Pearl? I should like Ernest to dance just one two-step with me.

PEARL: Of course there's time. Thornton, set the gramophone.

[THORNTON CLAY *at once starts it, and the notes of the two-step tinkle out.*]

DUCHESSE: You don't mind, Ernest, do you?

ERNEST: I love dancing with you, Duchesse.

[*They take up their positions.*]

DUCHESSE: Just one moment. It always makes me so nervous to dance with you, Ernest.

ERNEST: Oh, now, don't be silly, dear Duchesse.

[*They begin to dance.*]

ERNEST: Now hold your shoulders like a lady. Arch your back, my dear, arch your back. Don't look like a sack of potatoes. If you put your foot there, I shall kick it.

DUCHESSE: Oh, Ernest, don't be cross with me.

ERNEST: I shall be cross with you, Duchesse. You don't pay any attention to what I say. You must give your mind to it.

DUCHESSE: I do! I do!

ERNEST: And don't dance like an old fish-wife. Put some vim into it. That's what I always say about these modern dances: you want two things, vim and nous.

DUCHESSE [*plaintively*]: Ernest!

ERNEST: Now don't cry. I'm saying all this for your good, you know. What's wrong with you

is that you've got no passion.

DUCHESSE: Oh, Ernest, how can you say such a thing. I've always looked upon myself as a very passionate woman.

ERNEST: I don't know anything about that, dear Duchesse, but you don't get it into your dancing. That's what I said the other day to the dear Marchioness of Twickenham—not the *new* one, you know, the *old* one—You must put passion into it, I said. That's what these modern dances want—passion, passion.

DUCHESSE: I see exactly what you mean, Ernest.

ERNEST: And you must dance with your eyes as well, you know. You must look as if you had a knife in your garter, and as if you'd kill me if I looked at another woman. Don't you see how I'm looking, I'm looking as though I meant, Curse her! how I love her. There!

[*The music stops and they separate.*]

DUCHESSE: I have improved, Ernest, haven't I?

ERNEST: Yes, you've improved, dear Duchesse, but you want more practice.

PEARL: Minnie, why on earth don't you stay, and Ernest will give you a real lesson this evening.

ERNEST: That's what you want, Duchesse.

[*The* DUCHESSE *wrestles with her soul.*]

DUCHESSE: Tony, d'you think we can stop?

TONY: I didn't want to go away. It's rotten going up to town this evening. What on earth are we going to do with ourselves when we get there?

DUCHESSE: Very well, Pearl, if it'll please you, we'll stop.

PEARL: This is nice of you, Minnie.

DUCHESSE: You're very naughty sometimes, Pearl, but you have a good heart, and I can't help being fond of you.

PEARL [*with outstretched arms*]: Minnie!

DUCHESSE: Pearl!

[*They clasp one another and affectionately embrace.*]

ERNEST: What an exquisite spectacle—two ladies of title kissing one another.

BESSIE [*to* FLEMING]: They're not worth making a fuss about. I'm sailing for America next Saturday!

THE END

Selected Bibliographies

HENRY ARTHUR JONES

Collected Editions and Other Works

Jones, Henry Arthur, *The Foundations of a National Drama*. London: Chapman & Hall, Ltd., 1913.

————, *The Renascence of the English Drama*. London: Macmillan, 1895.

————, *The Representative Plays of Henry Arthur Jones*, edited, with historical, biographical, and critical commentary by Clayton Hamilton. Boston: Little Brown, 1925.

Biographical and Critical Studies

Allen, Percy, "Henry Arthur Jones," in *Fortnightly Review*, new series, vol. cxxv, 1929.

Cordell, Richard, *Henry Arthur Jones and the Modern Drama*. New York: R. Long & R. R. Smith, 1932.

Jones, Doris A., *Taking the Curtain Call:* The Life and Letters of Henry Arthur Jones. New York: Macmillan, 1930.

ARTHUR WING PINERO

Dunkel, Wilbur Dwight, *Sir Arthur Pinero*. Chicago: University of Chicago Press, 1941.

Fyfe, H. H., *Sir Arthur Wing Pinero's Plays and Players*. London: E. Benn, 1930.

Pinero, Arthur Wing, *Robert Louis Stevenson as a Dramatist,* Dramatic Museum of Columbia University *Papers on Play-Making*, First Series, Vol. IV, New York, 1914.

The Social Plays of Arthur Wing Pinero, ed. Clayton Hamilton, 4 vols. New York: E. P. Dutton & Company, 1917–1922.

OSCAR WILDE

Collected Editions

Wilde, Oscar, *Plays*. New York: Modern Library, n.d.

————, *Works,* ed. with an introduction by G. F. Martin. London: Collins, 1963.

————, *Writings of Oscar Wilde.* London: A. R. Keller & Co., 1907, 15 Vols.

Biographical and Critical Studies

Brasol, Boris, L., *Oscar Wilde, the Man, the Artist, the Martyr.* New York: Scribner's, 1938.

Broad, Lewis, *The Friendships and Follies of Oscar Wilde.* London: Hutchinson, 1954.

Douglas, Lord Alfred Bruce, *Oscar Wilde and Myself.* New York: Duffield & Co., 1914.

————, *Oscar Wilde: a Summing Up.* London: Richards, 1950.

Ervine, St. John G., *Oscar Wilde: a Present Time Appraisal.* London: G. Allen & Unwin, 1951.

Harris, Frank, *Oscar Wilde: His Life and Confessions.* New York: the author, 1916. Also published by Covici, Friede, 1930.

————, *Oscar Wilde,* with a preface by Bernard Shaw. London: Constable, 1938.

Henderson, Archibald, *Interpreters of Life and Modern Spirit.* New York: M. Kennerly, 1911.

————, *European Dramatists.* Cincinnati: Stewart & Kidd, 1918.

Housman, Laurence, *Echo de Paris.* New York: Appleton, 1924.

Hyde, Harford M., *Oscar Wilde: the Aftermath.* London: Methuen, 1963.

Laver, James, *Oscar Wilde.* London: Published for British Council by Longmans, Green, 1954.

Lewis, Lloyd and H. J. Smith, *Oscar Wilde Discovers America.* New York: Harcourt, Brace & Company, 1936.

Millard, Christopher S., *Bibliography of Oscar Wilde.* London: Laurie, 1914.

Ojala, Aatos, *Aestheticism and Wilde.* Helsinki, 1954.

O'Sullivan, Vincent, *Aspects of Wilde.* New York: H. Holt & Company, 1936.

Pearson, Hesketh, *Oscar Wilde, His Life and Wit.* New York: Harper & Brothers, 1946.

————, *The Life of Oscar Wilde.* London: Methuen, 1954.

Ransome, Arthur, *Oscar Wilde, a Critical Study.* London: M. Secker, 1912.

Renier, G. J., *Oscar Wilde.* London: Peter Davies, Ltd., 1933.

Roditi, Edouard, *Oscar Wilde.* Norfolk, Connecticut: New Directions, 1947.

Sherard, R. H., *The Story of an Unhappy Friendship.* London: Greening & Company, Ltd., 1905.

————, *Life of Wilde.* London: T. W. Laurie, 1906.

————, *Bernard Shaw, Frank Harris and Oscar Wilde.* London: T. W. Laurie, Ltd., 1937.

Snider, Rose, *Satire in the Comedies of Congreve, Sheridan, Wilde and Coward.* Orono, Maine, 1937.

Symons, Arthur, *A Study of Oscar Wilde.* London: C. J. Symons, 1930.

Winwar, Frances, *Oscar Wilde and the Yellow 'Nineties.* New York: Harper & Brothers, 1940.

Woodcock, George, *The Paradox of Oscar Wilde.* New York: Macmillan, 1950.

Yü, Margaret Man Sang, *Two Masters of Irony.* Hong Kong: Hong Kong University Press, 1957.

GEORGE BERNARD SHAW

Collected Editions and Other Works

Shaw, George Bernard, *Bernard Shaw and Mrs. Patrick Campbell,* their correspondence, ed. by Alan Dent. New York: Knopf, 1952.

―――, *Collected Letters, 1874–1897,* ed. by Dan H. Laurence. New York: Dodd, Mead & Co., 1965.

―――, *The Complete Plays of Bernard Shaw.* London: Odhams Press, Ltd., 1937.

―――, *Complete Plays,* with prefaces. New York: Dodd, Mead, 1962. 6 vols.

―――, *The Crime of Imprisonment,* illustrated by William Gropper. New Yord: Philosophical Library, 1946.

―――, *Ellen Terry and Bernard Shaw;* a correspondence edited by Christopher St. John. New York: Putnam, 1931.

―――, *Everybody's Political What's What.* New York: Dodd, Mead and Co., 1944.

―――, *Fabian Essays in Socialism,* ed. by G. B. Shaw, introd. by Sidney Webb. London: Fabian Society & G. Allen & Unwin, 1920.

―――, *Florence Farr, Bernard Shaw & W. B. Yeats;* letters ed. by Clifford Bax. Dublin, Ireland: Cuala Press, 1941.

―――, *Letters to Granville Barker,* ed. by C. B. Purdom. New York: Theatre Arts Books, 1957.

―――, *Major Critical Essays.* London: Constable & Co., 1955.

―――, *Our Theatres in the Nineties.* London: Constable & Co., 1932.

―――, *Platform and Pulpit,* ed. with an introd. by Dan H. Laurence. New York: Hill and Wang, 1961.

―――, *Plays and Players; Essays on the Theatre.* London: Oxford University Press, 1952.

―――, *The Quintessence of Ibsenism.* New York: Brentano, 1905.

―――, *Shaw on Music.* Garden City, New York: Doubleday, 1955.

―――, *Shaw on Theatre,* ed. by E. J. West. New York: Hill and Wang, 1958.

Biographical and Critical Studies

Bentley, Eric, *Bernard Shaw*. New York: New Directions, 1957.

Brustein, Robert, *The Theatre of Revolt*. Boston: Little Brown & Co. 1964.

Burton, Richard, *Bernard Shaw: The Man and the Mask*. New York: Henry Holt & Co., Inc., 1916.

Chesterton, G. K., *George Bernard Shaw*. New York: Dodd and Lane, 1910.

Colbourne, Maurice, *The Real Bernard Shaw*. New York: Dodd, Mead & Co., Inc., 1940.

Collis, John S., *Shaw*. New York: Alfred A. Knopf, 1925.

D'Angelo, Evelyn, "George Bernard Shaw's Theory of Stage Representation." *Quarterly Journal of Speech,* June, 1929, 15: 330–349.

Ellehauge, Martin, *The Position of Bernard Shaw in European Drama and Philosophy*. New York: G. E. Stechert & Co., 1931.

Ervine, St. John, *Bernard Shaw: His Life, Work and Friends*. London, 1956.

Gassner, John, *Masters of the Drama*. New York: Dover Publications, 1945.

Harris, Frank, *Bernard Shaw*. New York: Simon and Schuster, Inc., 1931.

Henderson, Archibald, *Bernard Shaw: Playboy and Prophet*. New York, 1932.

————, *George Bernard Shaw: His Life and Works*. London, 1911.

————, *George Bernard Shaw: Man of the Century*. New York, 1956.

————, "George Bernard Shaw Self-Revealed." *Fortnightly Review,* 125 (1926), 433–42, 610–18.

————, *Table-Talk of G.B.S.* London, 1925.

Huneker, James, *Iconoclasts.* New York: Charles Scribner's Sons, 1905.

————, "The Quintessence of Shaw," in *George Bernard Shaw: A Critical Survey,* ed. Louis Kronenberger. New York, 1957.

Irvine, William, *The Universe of G.B.S.* New York: Whittlesey House, 1949.

Joad, C. E. M., *Shaw*. London: Victor Gollancz, Ltd., 1949.

Kaye, Julian B., *Bernard Shaw and the Nineteenth Century Tradition*. Norman, Okla.: University of Oklahoma Press, 1958.

Kozelka, Paul, *A Glossary to the Plays of Bernard Shaw*. New York, 1959.

Kronenberger, Louis, ed., *George Bernard Shaw: A Critical Survey*. New York: The World Publishing Company, 1953.

Lowenstein, F. E., *The Rehearsal Copies of Bernard Shaw's Plays: A Bibliographical Study*. London, 1950.

MacCarthy, Sir Desmond, *The Court Theatre, 1904–1907; a Commentary and Criticism*. London, 1907.

————, *Shaw*. London, 1951.

Mander, Raymond, and Mitchenson, Joe, *Theatrical Companion to*

Shaw; A Pictorial Record of the First Performances of the Plays of George Bernard Shaw. London, 1954.

Meisel, Martin, *Shaw and the Nineteenth-Century Theater.* Princeton, N.J.: Princeton University Press, 1963.

Nethercot, Arthur H., *Men and Supermen: The Shavian Portrait Gallery.* New York: Benjamin Blom, 1966.

Norwood, Gilbert, *Euripides and Shaw, with Other Essays.* Boston: John W. Luce & Co., 1921.

Pearson, Hesketh, *G.B.S.: A Full-Length Portrait.* New York: Harper & Brothers, 1942.

Perry, Henry Ten Eyck, *Masters of Dramatic Comedy and Their Social Themes.* Cambridge: Harvard University Press, 1939.

Rattray, Robert Fleming, *Bernard Shaw: A Chronicle.* London, 1951.

Shaw, Charles, *Bernard's Brethren. With Comments by Bernard Shaw.* London: Constable, 1939.

Spencer, Terrence J., *The Dramatic Principles of George Bernard Shaw,* diss. Stanford, 1957. University Microfilms.

Wilson, Edmund: *The Triple Thinkers.* New York: Harcourt, Brace & Co., 1938. See the chapter "Bernard Shaw at Eighty," a brilliant study.

Winsten, S., Editor, *G.B.S. 90.* New York: Dodd, Mead & Co., Inc., 1946.

SIR JAMES MATTHEW BARRIE

Collected Editions

Barrie, Sir James Matthew, *Plays.* New York: Charles Scribner's Sons, 1929.

————, *Representative Plays.* New York: Charles Scribner's Sons, 1926.

Biographical and Critical Studies

Asquith, Lady Cynthia Mary Evelyn, *Portrait of Barrie.* London: J Barrie, 1954.

Blake, George, *Barrie and the Kailyard School.* New York: Roy Publishers, 1951.

Braybrooke, Patrick, *J. M. Barrie: A Study in Fairies and Mortals* Philadelphia: J. B. Lippincott Company, 1925.

Chalmers, Patrick R., *Barrie Inspiration.* London: Peter Davies, Ltd 1938.

Darlington, William A., *J. M. Barrie.* Glasgow and London: Blacki & Son, Ltd., 1938.

Darton, F. J. Harvey, *J. M. Barrie.* London: James Nisbet & Co. 1929.

Ellehauge, Martin, *Striking Figures among Modern English Dramatists* (with an introductory essay by Maurice Maeterlinck). London: Williams and Norgate, 1931.

Green, Roger L., *J. M. Barrie.* New York: H. Z. Walck, 1961.

Hammerton, Sir John A., *Barrie: The Story of a Genius.* New York: Dodd, Mead & Co., Inc., 1929.

Mackail, Denis G., *Barrie: The Story of J.M.B.* New York: Charles Scribner's Sons, 1941.

Morgan, Arthur E., *Tendencies of Modern English Drama.* New York: Charles Scribner's Sons, 1923.

Moult, Thomas, *Barrie.* New York: Charles Scribner's Sons, 1928.

Parker, W. M., *Modern Scottish Writers.* Edinburgh: Hodge, 1917.

Pellizzi, Camillo, *English Drama: The Last Great Phase* (translated by Rowan Williams). New York: The Macmillan Co., 1935.

Phelps, William Lyon, *Essays on Modern Dramatists.* New York: The Macmillan Co., 1921.

Roy, James A., *James Matthew Barrie: An Appreciation.* New York: Charles Scribner's Sons, 1938.

Scott, Dixon, *Men of Letters* (with an introduction by Max Beerbohm). Garden City: Doubleday, Doran & Co., Inc., 1923.

Short, Ernest H., *Theatrical Cavalcade.* London: Eyre and Spottiswoode Publishers, Ltd., 1942.

Skinner, Richard D., *Our Changing Theatre.* New York: Dial Press, 1931.

Walbrook, Henry M., *J. M. Barrie and the Theatre.* London: F. V. White and Co., Ltd., 1922.

Walkley, Arthur B., *Drama and Life.* London: Methuen & Co., 1907.

JOHN GALSWORTHY

Collected Editions

Galsworthy, John, *Plays.* London: Duckworth, 1932.

———, *Plays.* New York: Charles Scribner's Sons, 1948.

———, *Representative Plays of John Galsworthy.* New York: Charles Scribner's Sons, 1924.

Biographical and Critical Studies

Baker, George Pierce, Introduction to *Representative Plays of John Galsworthy.* New York: Charles Scribner's Sons, 1924.

Clark, Barrett H., *A Study of the Modern Drama,* rev. ed. New York: D. Appleton-Century Co., Inc., 1938.

Coats, Robert H., *John Galsworthy as a Dramatic Artist.* New York: Charles Scribner's Sons, 1926.

Croman, Natalie, *John Galsworthy: A Study in Continuity and Contrast.* Cambridge: Harvard University Press, 1933.

Cunliffe, John W., *Modern English Playwrights*. New York: Harper & Brothers, 1927.

Dupont, V., *John Galsworthy: The Dramatic Artist*. Paris: M. Didier, 1942.

Ervine, St. John, *The Theatre in My Time*. New York: Barrows Mussey, Inc., 1934.

Galsworthy, John, "Anglo-American Drama and Its Future" in *Another Sheaf*. New York: Charles Scribner's Sons, 1919.

———, "Some Platitudes Concerning Drama" in *The Inn of Tranquillity*. New York: Charles Scribner's Sons, 1912.

Guedalla, Philip, *A Gallery*. New York: G. P. Putnam's Sons, 1924.

Marrot, H. V., *Life and Letters of John Galsworthy*. New York: Charles Scribner's Sons, 1936.

Morgan, Arthur E., *Tendencies of Modern English Drama*. New York: Charles Scribner's Sons, 1923.

Ould, Hermon, *John Galsworthy*. London: Chapman and Hall, Ltd., 1934.

Schalit, Leon, *John Galsworthy: A Survey* (translated by Ethel E. Coe and Therese Harbury). Charles Scribner's Sons, 1929.

WILLIAM BUTLER YEATS

Selected Editions and Other Works

Autobiographies. London: Macmillan, 1956.

Collected Plays. London: Macmillan, 1934.

Collected Plays. London: Macmillan, 1953.

The Collected Works in Verse and Prose, vols. i–viii. Stratford on Avon: Shakespeare Head Press, 1908.

Essays and Introductions. London: Macmillan, 1961.

Florence Farr, Bernard Shaw, W. B. Yeats: Letters, edited by C. Bax. London: Home and Van Thal, 1946.

Four Plays for Dancers. London: Macmillan, 1921.

The Letters of W. B. Yeats, edited by A. Wade, London: R. Hart-Davis, 1954.

Plays in Prose and Verse, Written for an Irish Theatre and generally with the help of a Friend. London: Macmillan, 1922.

Plays and Controversies. London: Macmillan, 1923.

Pl. for an I.T., vol. iii: *"The King's Threshold" and "On Baile's Strand" Being Volume Three of Plays for an Irish Theatre*. London: Bullen, 1904.

Pl. for an I.T., vol. v: *"Deirdre": Being Volume Five of Plays for an Irish Theatre*. Dublin: Manusel, 1907.

Pl. for an I.T., Coll. Ed.: *Plays for an Irish Theatre, with Designs by Gordon Craig*. London and Stratford on Avon: Bullen, 1911.

The Variorum Edition of the Plays of W. B. Yeats, edited by Russell K.

Alspach, assisted by Catharine C. Alspach. London: Macmillan, 1966.

Biographical and Critical Studies

Bjersby, B., *The Interpretation of the Cuchulain Legend in the Works of W. B. Yeats.* Upsala Irish Studies i, Upsala, 1950.

Bowra, C. M., *The Heritage of Symbolism.* London: Macmillan, 1943.

Boyd, E. A., *Ireland's Literary Renaissance.* Dublin and London: Maunsel, 1916.

———, *The Contemporary Drama of Ireland.* Dublin: The Talbot Press; London: T. Fisher Unwin, 1918.

Ellis-Fermor, U., *The Irish Dramatic Movement.* London: Methuen, 1954.

Ellmann, R., *The Identity of Yeats.* London: Macmillan, 1954.

———, *Yeats: The Man and The Masks.* London: Macmillan, 1949.

Fay, Gerard, *The Abbey Theatre: Cradle of Genius.* London: Hollis and Carter, 1958.

Gregory, Lady Augusta, *Cuchulain of Muirthemne,* with a Preface by W. B. Yeats. London: John Murray, 1902.

———, *Gods and Fighting Men,* with a Preface by W. B. Yeats. London: John Murray, 1904.

———, *Lady Gregory's Journals,* edited by Lennox Robinson. Dublin: Putnam and Co. Ltd., 1946.

———, *Our Irish Theatre.* New York and London: G. P. Putnam's Sons, 1914.

Gwynn, S. (editor), *Scattering Branches: Tributes to the Memory of W. B. Yeats.* London: Macmillan, 1940.

Hall, J., and Steinmann, M. (editors), *The Permanence of Yeats: Select Criticism.* New York: Macmillan, 1950.

Henn, T. R., *The Lonely Tower.* London: Methuen, 1950.

Hoare, D. M., *The Works of Morris and of Yeats in Relation to Early Saga Literature.* Cambridge University Press, 1937.

Hone, J. M., *W. B. Yeats, 1865-1939.* London: Macmillan, 1942.

Howarth, H., *The Irish Writers: 1880-1940.* New York: Hill and Wang, 1959.

Jeffares, A. N., *W. B. Yeats: Man and Poet.* London: Routledge and Kegan Paul, 1949.

Kavanagh, Peter, *The Irish Theatre; Being a History of the Drama in Ireland from the Earliest Period up to the Present Day.* Tralee, 1946.

Krans, H. S., *William Butler Yeats and the Irish Literary Revival.* London: Heinemann, 1905 (Contemporary Men of Letters Series).

MacNeice, L., *The Poetry of W. B. Yeats.* Oxford University Press, 1941.

Malone, A. E., *The Irish Drama.* London: Constable, 1929.

Menon, V. K. N., *The Development of W. B. Yeats.* Edinburgh: Oliver and Boyd, 1942.

Moore, George, *Hail and Farewell!* (3 vols.). London: Heinemann, 1919–20.

Parkinson, T., *W. B. Yeats, Self-Critic: A Study of His Early Verse.* Berkeley: University of California Press, 1951.

Reid, F., *W. B. Yeats: A Critical Study.* London: Martin Secker, 1915.

Robinson, L. (compiler), *Ireland's Abbey Theatre: A History, 1899–1951.* London: Sidgwick and Jackson, 1951.

Robinson, L. (editor), *The Irish Theatre* (Lectures delivered during the Abbey Theatre Festival held in Dublin in August 1938). London: Macmillan, 1939.

Saul, G. B., *Prolegomena to the Study of Yeats's Plays.* Philadelphia: University of Pennsylvania Press, 1958.

Ure, P., *Towards a Mythology: Studies in the Poetry of W. B. Yeats.* Liverpool University Press, 1946.

————, *W. B. Yeats.* Edinburgh: Oliver & Boyd Ltd., 1963.

Ussher, A., *Three Great Irishmen: Shaw, Yeats, Joyce.* London: Gollancz, 1952.

Weygandt, C., *Irish Plays and Playwrights.* London: Constable, 1913.

Wilson, F. A. C., *W. B. Yeats and Tradition.* London: Gollancz, 1958.

JOHN MILLINGTON SYNGE

Collected Editions

Synge, John M., *The Works of John M. Synge,* 4 vols. Dublin: Maunsel & Co., 1910.

————, *The Works of John M. Synge,* 4 vols. Boston: John W. Luce & Co., 1912.

————, *The Dramatic Works of John M. Synge.* Dublin: Maunsel & Co., 1915.

————, *Plays.* London: George Allen & Unwin, 1924.

————, *Plays,* revised collected edition. London: George Allen & Unwin, 1932.

————, *The Complete Works of John M. Synge.* New York: Random House, *c.* 1935.

————, *John M. Synge: Collected Plays.* Harmondsworth, Middlesex: Penguin Books, 1952.

————, *John M. Synge: Plays, Poems and Prose.* London: J. M. Dent & Sons, 1941.

Biographical and Critical Works

Bickley, Francis, *J. M. Synge and the Irish Dramatic Movement.* London: Constable, 1912.

Bourgeois, Maurice, *John Millington Synge and the Irish Dramatic Movement.* London: Constable, 1913.

Boyd, Ernest A., *Ireland's Literary Renaissance.* New York: J. Lane Co., 1916.

———, *The Contemporary Drama of Ireland.* Boston: Little, Brown & Co., 1928.

Byrne, Dawson, *The Story of Ireland's National Theatre.* Dublin: The Talbot Press, 1929.

Corkery, Daniel, *Synge and Anglo-Irish Literature.* New York: Longmans, Green & Co., 1931.

Coxhead, Elizabeth, *J. M. Synge and Lady Gregory.* Writers and Their Work, No. 149. London: Longmans, Green, 1962.

———, *Lady Gregory: A Literary Portrait.* London: Macmillan, 1961.

Ellis-Fermor, Una, *The Irish Dramatic Movement,* 2nd. ed., rev. London: Methuen, 1954.

Fay, Gerard, *The Abbey Theatre: Cradle of Genius.* Dublin: Clonmore and Reynolds, 1958.

Greene, David H. and Edward M. Stephens, *J. M. Synge, 1871–1909.* New York: Macmillan, 1959.

Gregory, Lady Isabella A., *Our Irish Theatre.* New York: G. P. Putnam's Sons, 1913.

Howarth, Herbert, *The Irish Writers: Literature and Nationalism, 1880–1940.* New York: Hill and Wang, 1959.

Howe, Percival Presland, *J. M. Synge: A Critical Study.* London: Martin Secker, 1912.

Kavanagh, Peter, *The Story of the Abbey Theatre.* New York: Devin-Adair, 1950.

Malone, Andrew E., *The Irish Drama.* London: Constable, 1929.

Masefield, John, *John M. Synge: A Few Personal Recollections with Biographical Notes.* Churchtown, Dundrum: Cuala Press, 1915.

Modern Drama, IV (December 1961). This issue is devoted to Synge and O'Casey.

Moore, George, *Hail and Farewell:* Vol. III. London: Heinemann, 1920.

O'Connor, Frank, "Synge." In Lennox Robinson, ed., *The Irish Theatre: Lectures Delivered During the Abbey Theatre Festival Held in Dublin in August 1938.* London: Macmillan, 1939.

O Síocháin, P. A., *Aran: Islands of Legend.* Dublin: Foilsiúcháin Eireann, 1962.

Peacock, Ronald, *The Poet in the Theatre.* New York: Hill and Wang, 1946.

Price, Alan, *Synge and Anglo-Irish Drama.* London: Methuen, 1961.

Robinson, Lennox, *Ireland's Abbey Theatre: A History, 1899–1951.* London: Sidgwick and Jackson, 1951.

Setterquist, Jan, *Ibsen and the Beginnings of Anglo-Irish Drama. I: John Millington Synge.* Upsala Irish Studies, No. 2. Upsala: Upsala University, 1951.

Synge, the Reverend Samuel, *Letters to My Daughter: Memories of John Millington Synge.* Dublin and Cork: Talbot Press, 1931.

Taylor, Estella Ruth, *The Modern Irish Writers: Cross Currents of Criticism.* Lawrence: University of Kansas Press, 1954.

Weygandt, Cornelius, *Irish Plays and Playwrights.* Boston: Houghton Mifflin & Co., 1913.

WILLIAM SOMERSET MAUGHAM

Collected Editions and Other Works

Maugham, W. Somerset, *The Plays of W. S. Maugham.* London: William Heinemann, 1912, 15 vols.

————, *Plays,* London: William Heinemann, 1931–34, 6 vols.

————, *The Collected Plays.* London: William Heinemann, 1952, 3 vols.

————, *The Summing Up.* London: William Heinemann, 1938.

————, *A Writer's Notebook.* London: William Heinemann, 1949.

Biographical and Critical Studies

Brander, Laurence, *Somerset Maugham, a Guide.* Edinburgh: Oliver & Boyd, 1963.

Brophy, John, *Somerset Maugham.* London: Published for the British Council by Longmans, Green, 1952.

Cordell, Richard A., *W. Somerset Maugham.* New York: T. Nelson & Sons, 1937.

————, *Somerset Maugham; a Biographical and Critical Study.* Bloomington: Indiana University Press, 1960.

Jonas, Klaus W., ed., *The Maugham Enigma; an Anthology.* New York: Citadel Press, 1954.

————, *The World of Somerset Maugham; an Anthology.* New York: British Book Centre, 1959.

Mander, Raymond, *Theatrical Companion to Maugham;* a pictorial record of the first performances of the plays of W. Somerset Maugham. London: Rockcliff, 1955.

Pfeiffer, Karl G., *W. Somerset Maugham; a Candid Portrait.* New York: W. W. Norton, 1959.

Stott, Raymond T., *Maughamiana, the Writings of W. Somerset Maugham;* being a handlist of works by William Somerset Maugham and of his contributions to certain selected periodicals. London: Heinemann, 1950.